Ada

AN INTRODUCTION TO THE ART AND SCIENCE OF PROGRAMMING

Selected Titles From
The Benjamin/Cummings Series in Computer Science

G. Andrews
Concurrent Programming: Principles and Practices (1991)

C. Batini, S. Ceri and S. Navathe
Database Design: An Entity-Relationship Approach (1991)

G. Booch
Object Oriented Design with Applications (1991)

G. Brookshear
Computer Science: An Overview, Third Edition (1991)

R. Elmasri and S. B. Navathe
Fundamentals of Database Systems (1989)

C. N. Fischer and R. J. LeBlanc
Crafting a Compiler with C (1991)

P. Helman, R. Veroff, and F. Carrano
Intermediate Problem Solving and Data Structure: Walls and Mirrors, Second Edition (1991)

D. W. Gonzalez
Ada Programmer's Handbook with LRM (1991)

A. Kelley and I. Pohl
A Book on C: Programming in C, Second Edition (1990)

A. Kelley and I. Pohl
C by Dissection: Essentials of C Programming, Second Edition (1992)

G. F. Luger and W. A. Stubblefield
Artificial Intelligence and the Design of Expert Systems (1989)

N. Miller
File Structures Using Pascal

N. Miller and C. G. Petersen
File Structures with Ada (1990)

I. Pohl
C++ for C Programmers (1990)

I. Pohl
C++ for Pascal Programmers (1990)

I. Pohl
Turbo C++ (1991)

W. J. Savitch
Pascal: An Introduction to the Art and Science of Programming, Third Edition (1990)

R. Sebesta
VAX: Assembly Language Programming, Second Edition (1991)

R. Sebesta
Concepts of Programming Languages (1989)

M. Sobell
A Practical Guide to UNIX System V, Release 4 (1991)

M. Weiss
Data Structures and Algorithm Analysis (1991)

I.N.

Ada

AN INTRODUCTION TO THE ART AND SCIENCE OF PROGRAMMING

Walter J. Savitch
University of California, San Diego

Charles G. Petersen
Mississippi State University

The Benjamin/Cummings Publishing Company, Inc.
Redwood City, California • Menlo Park, California
Reading, Massachusetts • New York • Don Mills, Ontario
Wokingham, U.K. • Amsterdam • Bonn • Sydney
Singaporc • Tokyo • Madrid • San Juan

Executive Editor: Dan Joraanstad
Sponsoring Editor: John Thompson
Production Coordinator: Megan Rundel
Copyeditor: Barbara Conway
Interior Design Modification: Victoria Philp
Chapter Opening Illustrations: Joe MacGown
Cover Design: The Belmont Studio
Composition: ExecuStaff

Library of Congress Cataloging-in-Publication Data

Savitch, Walter J., 1943–
Ada : an introduction to the art and science of programming / Walter J. Savitch, Charles G. Petersen.
p. cm.
Includes bibliographical references and index.
ISBN 0-8053-7070-6
1. Ada (Computer program language) I. Petersen, Charles G. II. Title.
QA76.73.A35S27 1992
005.13'3—dc20 91-36659
CIP

OpenAda is a registered trademark of Meridian Software Systems, Inc.

ISBN 0-8053-7070-6
1 2 3 4 5 6 7 8 9 10-DO-95 94 93 92 91

The Benjamin/Cummings Publishing Company, Inc.
390 Bridge Parkway
Redwood City, CA 94065

ABOUT THE AUTHORS

Savitch received his B.S. in Mathematics from the University of New Hampshire and his Ph.D. in Mathematics from the University of California, Berkeley. After receiving his Ph.D. in 1969, he joined the Computer Science faculty at the University of California, San Diego, where he is currently Professor of Computer Science. He is the author of three other computer science textbooks, as well as numerous articles on complexity of computation, computational linguistics, and computer science education.

Walter J. Savitch

Petersen holds a bachelor's degree in Electrical Engineering and is a registered professional engineer. He worked for 10 years in industry before returning to graduate school to complete a master's degree in Computer Science. He received his Ph.D. from Iowa State University in Higher Education and has been teaching computer science at the university level since 1972. He is the author of three other computer science textbooks and several articles dealing with computer science topics and curriculum issues.

Charles G. Petersen

PREFACE

Introduction

This book is designed for introductory programming courses that use the Ada programming language. Courses may be as short as one quarter or as long as one academic year. The book includes a thorough introduction to programming techniques and covers most aspects of the Ada programming language. The material in the book assumes no previous knowledge of computers and no mathematics beyond high school algebra.

While this book is based on the very successful third edition of *Pascal: An Introduction to the Art and Science of Programming* by Walter J. Savitch, it was not written by simply replacing all occurrences of Pascal code with Ada code. It is a different textbook based on a distinctly different programming language. However, most of the same well-tested examples and exercises are used, and the general writing style and level are similar.

One of the reasons that Pascal has enjoyed such success in recent years is that it allows professors to teach the things they feel are necessary, but without all the trappings of a large, complex language. Compared to Pascal, Ada is a large complex language. However, by starting small and building upward, it is possible to use the same pedagogy that is used to teach Pascal to teach programming in Ada.

There are a number of approaches that can be used to teach Ada to beginning students. The approach in this book might be called ''The bottom-up approach.'' Bottom-up means that we start with the subjects such as variable declarations, simple arithmetic expressions, and simplified input/output and build upward to subprograms and packages.

Features

Early Introduction of Subprograms. It has been the authors' experience in teaching introductory programming that the early introduction of subprograms is sound pedagogy. This approach is now widely accepted.

The early introduction of subprograms and parameters allows exercise programs to be written using completely modular subprograms. Programming without parameters invariably violates the generally accepted principles of software engineering and forces students to practice techniques that must later be unlearned. Introducing parameters early eliminates the need to teach programming techniques that will later be rejected. Some instructors want subprograms before control structures and others insist on subprograms after control structures. After much consultation, we have taken the approach that the simplest of control structures, If-Then-Else and Loop-Exit-When, will be introduced before subprograms because it allows more substantial examples to motivate the use of subprograms.

Packages as Soon as Possible. How early should packages be introduced? Our philosophy concerning the early introduction to subprograms carries over into packages. In order to make the use of packages meaningful, it is necessary to have something meaningful to put into them. This means that packages must be introduced after subprograms have been studied to allow for more substantial examples to motivate the use of packages.

Object-Oriented Design and Abstract Data Types. Two chapters are dedicated to arrays, covering both one- and multi-dimensional arrays. Heavy emphasis is placed on programming techniques such as reading data into arrays, manipulating partially filled arrays, and the design of data structures using arrays. Array coverage is followed by a chapter with complete coverage of records. Object-oriented design and the use of abstract data types (ADTs) are introduced along with the material on arrays and records. These topics are a natural part of good program design and Ada is a language that encourages the use of software engineering principles.

Generic Packages. The next logical step is to introduce generics. The concept of generic packages is introduced during the discussion of the package TEXT__IO. The major thrust in the case studies in the later chapters is using generic packages in the implentation of our abstract data types.

Designed for Interactive Programming. All programs are designed for use in an interactive environment, following the modern approach to the development of programs. However, batch processing and related topics are not ignored. The book contains sections on techniques for batch processing and two chapters on programs using both text and nontext files.

Case Studies. Every chapter has at least one Case Study that begins with a discussion of the problem, moves on to the development of pseudocode algorithms, then to the writing of actual code segments, and finally to a complete, fully tested program. The Ada code in all of the complete programs has been copied directly from the text files which have been compiled and run using several different Ada compilers, under several different operating systems on machines from PCs to large mainframes.

Programming Style. There is no officially mandated standard Ada style for the writing of programs. Various schemes have been proposed and some professors have developed their own style guide for student use. After much debate, we have decided to use the style that is used in the Reference Manual for the Ada Programming Language (ANSI/ML-STD-1815A). It is a very simplistic style which is probably best for beginning students.

TEXT__IO. Many professors now feel that there are subjects in programming that should be taught but that are not available in Pascal. For example, run-time error processing, information hiding, encapsulation, reuse, input and output for enumeration, and generics are features that are available in Ada, which makes Ada a natural choice for updating a traditional Pascal course. The difficult part in getting started in Ada from the bottom up, is explaining the TEXT__IO package and its enclosed generic packages. Specific details of four approaches are provided as a trailing section to the preface. These four approaches are:

1. Use TEXT__IO as described in the language reference manual. This requires the student to include instantiations of necessary packages.
2. Compile instantiations of INTEGER__IO and FLOAT__IO into a student library. This is simpler and requires that the student **with** and **use** necessary packages.
3. Compile a package which is a subset of TEXT__IO into a student library. This is the approach used in this book; we call our package simple I__O. This is even simpler in that the student only has to **with** and **use** package I__O.
4. Compile a procedure into a student library and make all student programs a separate unit of this procedure. This is the simplest from the beginner's point of view because the student only states that this is a separate compilation unit.

   Approach 2, 3, or 4 is only used until packages are introduced, for then they are not required.

Self-Test and Summary Sections. Self-Test Exercises, with answers in the back of the book, are provided throughout each chapter. Each chapter contains a complete Summary of Problem Solving and Programming Techniques, as well as a complete Summary of Ada Constructs. The Ada summary includes templates and typical examples for quick and easy reference.

Flexibility. The order in which topics can be covered is extremely flexible. The more advanced topics—such as recursion, some software engineering topics, some numeric programming techniques, and a substantial amount of data structures including records, files, and access types—are packaged into chapters that can be covered in almost any desired order. Alternately, a subset of the chapters can be chosen to form a shorter course. The chapter on text files is divided into two parts to allow for two possibilities: either postponing the topic entirely until later in a course, or briefly introducing it early and giving more detail later on. To add even more flexibility, sections with optional topics are included throughout the book. The dependency chart at the front of this book shows the possible orders in which the chapters can be covered without losing continuity.

Support Material

A chapter-by-chapter *Instructor's Guide* is available. All of the complete programs in this text are included with the *Instructor's Guide* in machine-readable form on a program disk. Thus it is possible, through the instructor, to have all the programs available for students to run without having to type them in. The program disk also contains all of the necessary code for the implementation of any of the approaches for handling input-output as discussed earlier.

Solutions to many of the programming assignments in the back of each chapter will be made available in machine-readable form to instructors and computer professionals directly from the authors for a nominal fee of $35. Send your request on school or business letterhead along with $35 to:

Charles G. Petersen
Drawer CS
Mississippi State, MS 39762

Please specify 3.5″ or 5.25″ disk, and HD or DD format.

Acknowledgments

A special thanks goes to Alan Apt, the original editor on the project, whose idea it was to combine the talents of the authors to make this book possible. Also, thanks to John Thompson who picked up the ball after Alan moved up the corporate ladder.

As authors and professors, we are blessed with institutions (Mississippi State University and University of California, San Diego) that provided a conducive environment and ample facilities for this project. (Without e-mail it would have taken much longer for authors at these two distant institutions to complete this project.) Thanks also goes to Tuskegee University and Don Fuhr, the Computer Center Director for providing facilities and computer time so that programs could be tested on a VAX computer using VAX-ADA. Eric W. Olsen at Meridian Software Systems helped us by providing a copy of their Open Ada compiling environment.

Students in two different classes at different institutions class tested much of the material in this book. Thanks goes to those students at Mississippi State University and California State University, Long Beach.

The reviewers made numerous suggestions that helped improve the book. Thanks to Susan Richman at Pennsylvania State University, Harrisburg for her intuitive insight; to Major John J. (Jay) Spegele at the United States Naval Academy for his practical approach to teaching; to Charles (Chuck) Engle at the Florida Institute of Technology who kept reminding us when our Pascal was showing; to Joel

Carissimo at California State University, Long Beach for class testing the material while working from a draft manuscript; to Bob Kitzberger of TeleSoft for his real-world perspective; to Frances Van Scoy at West Virginia University; and to Joseph Lang at the University of Dayton.

Specific Information of Different Input-Output Approaches

1. The first of these approaches is to simply tell the student to put the following few lines at the beginning of every program.

```
with TEXT_IO;
procedure MAIN is
    package INTEGER_IO is new TEXT_IO.INTEGER_IO ( INTEGER );
    package FLOAT_IO is new TEXT_IO.FLOAT_IO ( FLOAT );
    package BOOLEAN_IO is new TEXT_IO.ENUMERATION_IO ( BOOLEAN );
    use INTEGER_IO;
    use FLOAT_IO;
    use BOOLEAN_IO;
```

   a. You can try to explain what is going on but in the authors' opinion, this just complicates what may be an already complicated and confusing situation for beginning students,
   b. or you can simply tell them to just do it and that they will learn what is going on in due time.

   The remaining three approaches require that something be compiled into an Ada library to which the student has access.

   All Ada compilers must maintain a library system of previously compiled programs. The way that this is accomplished depends on the compiler. Some compilers have a special program that must be run before any program units can be compiled in a directory. For instance, an Ada library is created on the Meridian AdaVantage system by doing a Newlib. This Newlib is used once and only once in any given directory in which the user wishes to compile. On the PC's the Newlib is a BAT or command file, the code from any of the three schemes that follow can be compiled as part of the stream of commands in the command file. All of this helps students get started with as little encumbering as possible. When packages are introduced in the text, Text_IO is discussed and then these approaches can be and should be abandoned. Programs beyond the chapter on packages use Text_IO as intended in the design of the language.

2. The second approach requires that the following lines be compiled into the student library.

```
with TEXT_IO;
package INTEGER_IO is new TEXT_IO.INTEGER_IO ( INTEGER );
package FLOAT_IO is new TEXT_IO.FLOAT_IO ( FLOAT );
package BOOLEAN_IO is new TEXT_IO.ENUMERATION_IO ( BOOLEAN );
```

Once this is done, the student need add only the following two lines to the beginning of every program.

```
with TEXT_IO, INTEGER_IO, FLOAT_IO, BOOLEAN_IO;
use TEXT_IO, INTEGER_IO, FLOAT_IO, BOOLEAN_IO;
```

3. The third approach is the one that we have chosen to present in this text. It requires that the following package be compiled into the student library or a system library to which the student has access. This package is included as part of the program disk that will accompany the instructor's guide.

```
with IO_EXCEPTIONS;
with TEXT_IO;;
use TEXT_IO;
package I_O is

    package INTEGER_IO is new TEXT_IO.INTEGER_IO ( INTEGER );
    use INTEGER_IO;
    package FLOAT_IO is new TEXT_IO.FLOAT_IO ( FLOAT );
    use FLOAT_IO;
    package BOOLEAN_IO is new TEXT_IO.ENUMERATION_IO ( BOOLEAN );
    use BOOLEAN_IO;

    procedure GET ( ITEM : out INTEGER; WIDTH : in FIELD := 0 )
        renames INTEGER_IO.GET;
    procedure GET ( ITEM : out FLOAT; WIDTH : in FIELD := 0 )
        renames FLOAT IO.GET;
    procedure GET ( ITEM : out BOOLEAN )
        renames BOOLEAN_IO.GET;
    procedure GET ( ITEM : out CHARACTER )
        renames TEXT_IO.GET;
    procedure GET ( ITEM : out STRING )
        renames TEXT_IO.GET;
    procedure GET_LINE ( ITEM : out STRING; LAST : out NATURAL )
        renames TEXT_IO.GET_LINE;
    procedure SKIP_LINE ( SPACING : in POSITIVE_COUNT := 1 )
        renames TEXT_IO.SKIP_LINE;
```

```
    procedure PUT ( ITEM  : in INTEGER;
                    WIDTH : in FIELD :=
                    INTEGER_IO.DEFAULT_WIDTH;
                    BASE  : in NUMBER_BASE := DEFAULT_BASE )
        renames INTEGER_IO.PUT;
    procedure PUT ( ITEM : in FLOAT;
                    FORE : in FIELD := DEFAULT_FORE;
                    AFT  : in FIELD := DEFAULT_AFT;
                    EXP  : in FIELD := DEFAULT_EXP )
        renames FLOAT_IO.PUT;
    procedure PUT ( ITEM  : in BOOLEAN;
                    WIDTH : in FIELD    :=
                    BOOLEAN_IO.DEFAULT_WIDTH;
                    SET   : in TYPE_SET := DEFAULT_SETTING )
        renames BOOLEAN_IO.PUT;
procedure PUT ( ITEM : in CHARACTER )
        renames TEXT_IO.PUT;
    procedure PUT ( ITEM : in STRING)
        renames TEXT_IO.PUT;
    procedure PUT_LINE ( ITEM : STRING)
        renames TEXT_IO.PUT_LINE;
    procedure NEW_LINE ( SPACING : in POSITIVE_COUNT := 1 )
        renames TEXT_IO.NEW_LINE;

    function END_OF_LINE return BOOLEAN
        renames TEXT_IO.END_OF_LINE;
    function END_OF_FILE return BOOLEAN
        renames TEXT_IO.END_OF_FILE;

    procedure SET_COL ( TO : in POSITIVE_COUNT )
        renames TEXT_IO.SET_COL;
    procedure SET_LINE ( TO : in POSITIVE_COUNT )
        renames TEXT_IO.SET_LINE;

    function COL return POSITIVE_COUNT
        renames TEXT_IO.COL;
    function LINE return POSITIVE_COUNT
        renames TEXT_IO.LINE;

    DATA_ERROR : exception
        renames IO_EXCEPTIONS.DATA_ERROR;
    END_ERROR : exception
        renames IO_EXCEPTIONS.END_ERROR;

end I_O;
```

Once this has been done, all programs begin with the following line:

```
with I_O; use I_O;
```

4. The fourth approach is the one that is favored by the authors for a number of pedagogical reasons. Unfortunately, the feedback on this approach has not been overwhelming, but it is included as part of the program disk in the case that like minded instructors might want to use it.

   This approach requires that the following code be compiled into the student's library or into the system library.

```
with TEXT_IO;
procedure RUN is
    package INTEGER_IO is new TEXT_IO.INTEGER_IO ( INTEGER );
    package FLOAT_IO is new TEXT_IO.FLOAT_IO ( FLOAT );
    package BOOLEAN_IO is new TEXT_IO.ENUMERATION_IO ( BOOLEAN );
    use TEXT_IO;
    use INTEGER_IO;
    use FLOAT_IO;
    use BOOLEAN_IO;
    procedure MAIN is separate;
begin
    MAIN;
end RUN;
```

As part of the Newlib (or whatever it is called), compile this program unit into the newly established library. Once it is done the user never sees it and doesn't even know it exists; the user just begins writing Ada programs. The following are two examples:

Example 1

```
separate ( RUN )
procedure MAIN is
begin
    PUT ( ''Congratulations, Alan, '' );
    PUT ( ''on your first Ada program.'' );
    NEW_LINE;
end MAIN;
```

Assume the above program is in file 'prog1.ada'. To compile simply type:

ada (or whatever the copiler is called) **prog1.ada**

then to prepare the program for execution, type:

bamp (or whatever the linker is called) **run**

to link the program and then to execute the program type:

```
run
```

Example 2

```
separate ( RUN )
procedure MAIN is
    MONTHS,
    PAYMENT : INTEGER;
begin
    PUT ( ''Congratulations, Alan, '' );
    PUT ( ''on your $10,000 win!'' );
    NEW_LINE;
    PUT_LINE ( ''Spread payments over how many month?'' );
    GET ( MONTHS );
    PAYMENT := 10_000 / MONTHS;
    PUT ( ''Your monthly payment will be $'' );
    PUT ( PAYMENT, 1 );
    NEW_LINE;
end MAIN;
```

Note that the only overhead necessary to make this work is the one line '**separate** (RUN)' and the fact that the main procedure must be called 'MAIN'.

A very similar thing can be done using the Janus Ada compiler by compiling the same Ada program unit given above directly into the JanusAda directory; the directory where the compiler resides. The VAX Ada compiler and the Verdix and Sun UNIX compiler require the creation of a library in a manner very similar to the Meridian AdaVantage system. The point here is that these three methods are easy to accomplish regardless of what Ada system is used.

Dependency Chart of Chapters and Location of Key Ada Constructs

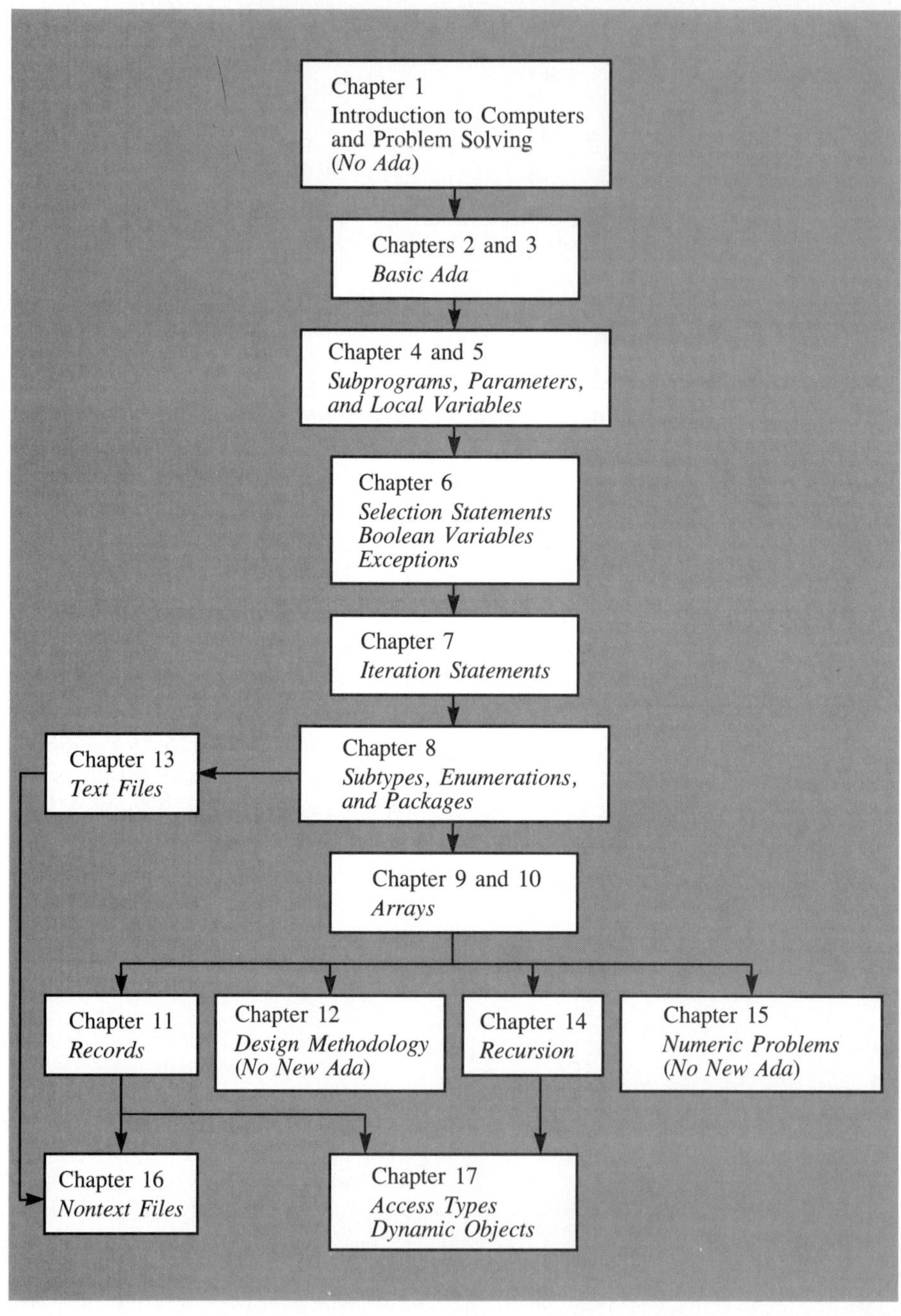

TABLE OF CONTENTS

CHAPTER 7

Problem Solving Using Loops 261

CHAPTER 8

More Data Types and an Introduction to Packages 315

CHAPTER 9

Arrays for Problem Solving 371

CHAPTER 17

Dynamic Data Structures 703

C H A P T E R

1

INTRODUCTION TO COMPUTERS AND PROBLEM SOLVING

John V. Atanasoff

Atanasoff, along with his assistant Clifford Berry, invented the first electronic digital computer, the ABC (Atanasoff-Berry Computer), in 1939. Atanasoff was a physicist at Iowa State University and needed faster ways to perform computations for physics problems.

Chapter Contents

In this chapter we outline some of the basic concepts common to all computer systems and all programming languages. The theme here, and throughout this book, is that there is a methodology of effective programming that is relatively independent of the particular programming language used or the particular computer used. In fact, this chapter presents no details of the Ada programming language.

What a Computer Is

In less than one human lifetime, computers have rapidly evolved from a scientific curiosity to an indispensible tool used in virtually all areas of our lives. They handle financial transactions, control manufacturing processes, keep track of airline reservations, forecast weather, control spacecraft—the list goes on seemingly without end. But just what are these things called *computers?*

The basic nature of computers is surprisingly simple. Computers are machines that perform very simple tasks according to specified instructions. Their ability to perform so many of these simple tasks with such great speed and with a high degree of accuracy is what makes computers so useful. One can think of a computer as a clerk who does nothing all day but sit and perform trivial, routine tasks according to a given set of instructions, and who does so with perfect accuracy, infinite patience, a flawless memory, and unimaginable speed.

The Modern Digital Computer

software/hardware

A set of instructions for a computer to follow is called a *program.* The collection of programs used by a computer is referred to as the *software* for that computer. The actual physical machines that make up a computer installation are referred to as *hardware.* In this book we are concerned almost exclusively with software, but a brief overview of how hardware is organized will be useful.

Most computers are organized as shown in Figure 1.1. They can be thought of as having four main components: the input device(s), the output device(s), the central processing unit (CPU), and the memory.

input keyboard

An *input device* is any device that allows a person to communicate information to the computer. For readers of this book, the input device is likely to be a keyboard rather like a typewriter keyboard, but it could be some other type of device or could consist of a variety of devices.

output display screen

An *output device* performs the opposite task. It allows the computer to communicate information to the user. One of the most common output devices is a display screen that resembles a television screen. This display screen is often referred to as a *CRT screen* or *monitor.* (The initials CRT stand for *Cathode Ray Tube.*) The keyboard and display screen are frequently thought of as a single unit called a *video display terminal (VDT),* or simply a *terminal.* Quite often there is more than one output device. For example, in addition to the display screen there may be a typewriter or typewriterlike device to produce printed output. These devices for producing printed output are called, appropriately enough, *printers.*

memory

To store input and have the equivalent of scratch paper for performing calculations, computers are provided with *memory.* The memory is very simple. It consists of a long list of numbered locations called *words* or, more descriptively, *memory locations.* The number of memory locations varies from one computer to another, ranging from a few thousand to many millions. In fact, memory may be added to a computer

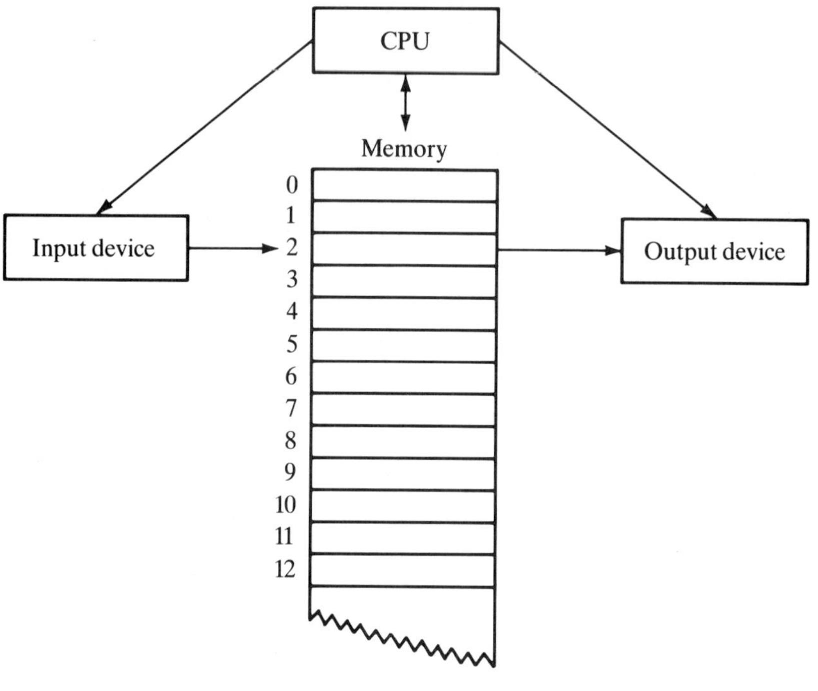

Figure 1.1 Main components of a computer.

almost without limit, although once the memory size exceeds certain thresholds, the computer system must be made a bit more sophisticated. Each memory location or word contains a string of zeros and ones. The contents of these locations can change. Hence, you can think of each memory location as a tiny blackboard on which the computer may write and erase. In most computers all locations contain the same number of zero/one digits; some typical sizes are 16, 32, and 64 digits. A digit that assumes only the value zero or one is called a *bit.* (The word BIT is an acronym that stands for BInary digiT.) If somebody tells you that you are working on a 32 bit machine, they mean that each memory location in your computer can hold 32 bits, that is, 32 digits, each either zero or one.

The fact that the information in a computer's memory is represented as zeros and ones need not be of great concern to a person programming in Ada. The reasons for using only zeros and ones have to do with the physics of hardware design. Computers using larger repertoires of digits can and have been designed. The use of zeros and ones does, however, have a few implications that you should be aware of. First, the computer has to do its arithmetic in something called *binary notation.* We will discuss binary arithmetic further in Chapter 15. A more important point is that the computer needs to interpret these strings of zeros and ones as numbers, letters, instructions, or other types of information. The computer performs these interpretations automatically according to certain codes. A different code is used for each different type of item that can be stored in a location: one code for letters, another for whole numbers, another for fractions, another for instructions, and so on. For example, in one commonly used set of codes, 1000001 is the code for the letter A and also for the number 65. In order to know what the string 1000001 in a particular location stands for, the computer must keep track of which code is currently being used for that location. Fortunately for us, the programmer today seldom needs to be concerned with such codes and can safely reason as though the locations actually contain letters, numbers, or whatever is desired.

secondary memory
disks

The memory we just described is called *main memory*. Most computers have additional memory called *secondary memory,* also frequently called *secondary storage* or *auxiliary storage.* Main memory serves as a temporary memory that is used only while the computer is actually following the instructions in a program. Secondary memory is used by the computer to keep a permanent record of information for processing at a later time. On small computers secondary memory is likely to consist of something called a *floppy disk* or *diskette,* and on larger computers it is likely to be something called a *hard disk.* Magnetic tape units are also commonly used for secondary memory. A typical computer installation with different kinds of memory is diagrammed in Figure 1.2. We will not be concerned with secondary memory until we reach the topics in Chapters 13 and 16.

The *central processing unit,* or *CPU* for short, is the controlling unit of the computer, the brain of the computer to use a human analogy. It is the CPU that follows the instructions in a program and performs the calculations specified by the program. The CPU is, however, a very simple brain. It can only follow a set of simple instructions provided by the programmer. It also directs (controls) the operations of the other units of the computer according to the instructions provided.

Typical CPU instructions say things like ''interpret the zeros and ones as numbers, add the number in memory location 37 to the number in memory location 59, and then put the answer in location 83'' or ''read a letter of input, convert it to its code as a string of zeros and ones, and place it in memory location 1298.'' The CPU can do subtraction, multiplication, and division as well as addition. It can move things from one memory location to another. It can interpret strings of zeros and ones as letters and send the letters to an output device. The CPU also has some primitive ability to rearrange the order of instructions. Needless to say, CPU instructions vary somewhat from computer to computer. The CPU of a modern computer can have as many as several hundred available instructions. However, all these instructions are typically about as simple as those we have just described.

At this point you may be wondering where in the computer the program is kept. The answer is, in the memory. Thus, the memory serves as a place to store both the program and data values; and also as a kind of ''scratch paper'' for doing calculations. Usually we conceptualize the program as something outside of memory, but occasionally we will need to be aware of the fact that it actually resides in memory.

That is it. That is all there is to a computer. Conceptually it is a simple machine. Its power comes from the size of its memory, its speed, its accuracy, and the sophistication of its programs. Your computer may not be configured exactly as we have portrayed it, but it will be similar and, more importantly, will behave exactly as if it were the very machine we have just described.

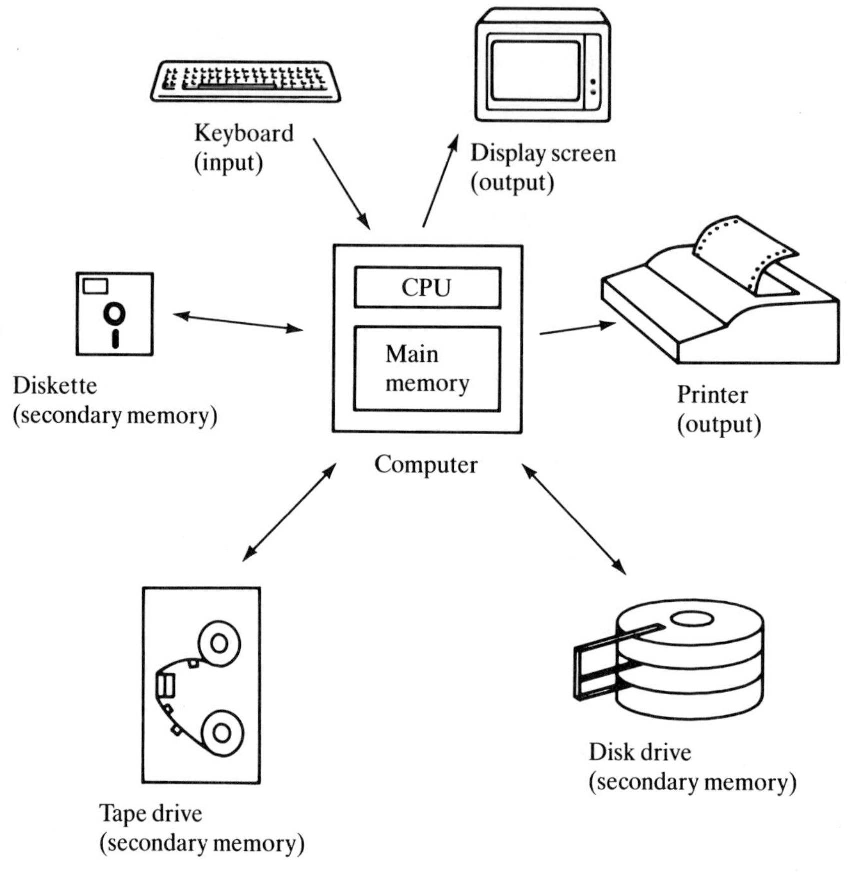

Figure 1.2 A typical computer installation.

The Notion of an Algorithm

When learning your first programming language, it is easy to get the impression that the hard part of solving a problem on a computer is translating your ideas into the specific language that will be fed into the computer. This definitely is not the case. The most difficult part of solving a problem on a computer is coming up with the method of solution. After you come up with a method of solution, it is routine to translate your method into the required language, be it Ada or some other programming language. When solving a problem with a computer, it is therefore helpful to ignore temporarily the computer programming language and to concentrate instead on formulating the steps of the solution and writing them down in plain English, as if the instructions were to be given to a human being. A set of instructions expressed in this way is frequently referred to as an *algorithm.*

algorithm

program

A set of instructions that leads to a solution is called an algorithm. Some approximately equivalent words are "recipe," "method," "directions," and "routine." The instructions may be expressed in a programming language or a human language. Our algorithms will be expressed in English and in the programming language Ada. An algorithm expressed in a language that a computer interprets as instructions is called a *program,* which explains why computer languages are called *programming languages.*

The word *algorithm* has a long history, but its meaning has recently taken on a new character. The word itself derives from the name of the ninth-century Arabic mathematician and astronomer Al-Khowarizmi, who wrote an early and famous textbook on the manipulation of numbers and equations entitled *Kitab al-jabr w'al-muqabala.* The similar-sounding word *algebra* was derived from the Arabic word *al-jabr* which appears in the title of this text, and is often translated as *reuniting* or *restoring.* The entire title can be translated as "Rules for reuniting and reducing." The meanings of the words *algebra* and *algorithm* used to be much more intimately related than they are now. Indeed, until very recently the word *algorithm* usually referred to algebraic rules for solving numeric equations.

Today the word *algorithm* refers to a wide variety of instructions for manipulating symbolic as well as numeric entities. The properties that qualify a set of instructions as an algorithm now are determined by the nature of the instructions and not by the things to which they apply. To qualify as an algorithm, a set of instructions must completely and unambiguously specify the steps to be taken and the order in which they are to be performed. The instructions cannot rely on any intelligence on the part of the person or machine that will follow the instructions. The follower of an algorithm does exactly what the algorithm says, neither more nor less.

sample algorithm

An example may help to clarify the concept. Figure 1.3 contains an algorithm expressed in rather stylized English. The algorithm determines the number of times a specified name occurs on a list of names. If the list contains the winners of each of last season's football games and the name is that of your favorite team, then the algorithm determines how many games your team won. The algorithm is short and simple but is otherwise very typical of the algorithms we will be dealing with.

The instructions numbered 1 through 5 in our sample algorithm are meant to be carried out in that order. Unless otherwise specified, we will always assume that the instructions of an algorithm are carried out in the order in which they are written. Most interesting algorithms do, however, specify some change of order, usually a repeating of some instruction again and again, as in instruction 4 of our sample algorithm.

input or data
output

This simple example illustrates a number of important points about algorithms. Algorithms are usually given some information. In our example the algorithm was given a name and a list of names. The information that is given to an algorithm is called *input* or *data.* Algorithms usually give an answer, or answers, back. In the example the answer was a number. The answers given by an algorithm are called *output.* In addition to being able to remember input and output, algorithms typically need to remember some other information. In the example a single number was remembered; the number changed as the algorithm proceeded and only the last value of the number was output.

```
begin
        1. Request the list of names and call it NAME_LIST;
        2. Request the name being sought and call it KEY_NAME;
        3. On a blackboard called COUNT write the number zero;
        4. Repeat the following for each name on NAME_LIST;
             If the name is the same as KEY_NAME then add one to the
               number written on COUNT;
               the old number is erased,
               leaving only one number on COUNT
        5. Announce the number written on COUNT as the answer;
end
```

Figure 1.3 An algorithm.

One final observation about our sample algorithm: It always ends. No matter how long the list is, the algorithm always gets to the end of the list and announces an answer. Some algorithms never terminate. For example, the algorithms used by computerized airline reservation systems. They never terminate; they just keep adding and deleting reservations forever, or until the airline goes bankrupt or changes its computer system. An algorithm that might not end is called a *partial algorithm.* An algorithm that is guaranteed to end is called a *total algorithm.* Some authors, especially in more advanced texts, reserve the word *algorithm* for what we call a total algorithm. However, we will use the word to mean any algorithm, whether or not it is guaranteed to terminate.

Programs and Data

running a program

As we already noted, a program is just an algorithm written in a language that can be fed into a computer. As shown in Figure 1.4, the input to a computer can be thought of as consisting of two parts: a program and some data. The data is what we conceptualize as the input to the algorithm that the computer will follow. In other words, the data is the input to the program, and both the program and the data are input to the computer. The word *input* is thus being used in two slightly different ways. This does require you to exercise some care to keep from getting confused, but this is standard usage and you may as well get used to it. For the sample algorithm of the previous section, the data was the name sought and the list of names to be searched. To get a computer to carry out the algorithm, both the algorithm (translated into some programming language) and the data are given as input to the computer. Whenever we give both a program and some data to a computer, we are said to be *running a program* on the data, and the computer is said to be *executing a program* on the data.

The word *data* also has a much more general meaning than the one we have just given. In its most general sense, it means any information available to the computer

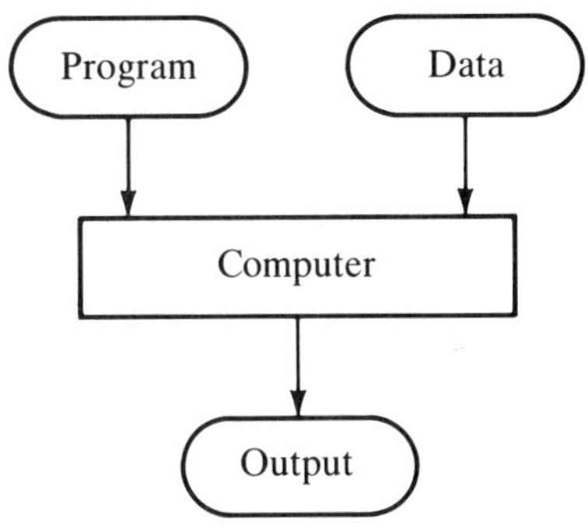

Figure 1.4 Simple view of running a program.

or to some part of the computer. The word is commonly used in both the narrow sense and the more general sense; you must rely on context to decide which meaning is intended.

High-Level Languages

high-level language

The Ada programming language is a high-level language, as are most of the other programming languages you are likely to have heard of, such as FORTRAN, BASIC, COBOL, Pascal, C, and Modula. High-level languages resemble human languages in many ways. They are designed to be easy for human beings to write programs in and easy for human beings to read. As a typical example of a high-level language, Ada uses English words combined in ways that resemble English sentences. For example, the following is a line or statement from an Ada program:

```
if X = Y and Z = W then PUT ( "answer is 42" ); end if
```

With the knowledge that to PUT means to display on the screen, you can read and understand this instruction almost without any explanation.

low-level language

A high-level language, like Ada, contains instructions that are much more complicated than the simple instructions a computer's CPU is capable of following. The kind of language a computer can understand is called a *low-level language.* A typical low-level instruction might be the following:

```
ADD X Y Z
```

This instruction might mean ''add the number in the memory location called X to the number in the memory location called Y and place the result in the memory location called Z.''

assembly language

The above sample instruction is written in what is called *assembly language.* Although assembly language is almost the same as the language understood by the computer it must undergo one simple translation before the computer can use it. To get a computer to follow an assembly language instruction, the words need to be translated into strings of zeros and ones. For example, the word ADD might translate to 0110, the X might translate to 1001, the Y to 1010, and the Z to 1011. The version of the above instruction that the computer ultimately follows would then be

```
0110100110101011
```

machine language

Programs written in the form of zeros and ones are said to be written in *machine language,* because that is the version of the program that the computer (the machine) actually reads and follows. Assembly language and machine language are almost the same thing, and the distinction between them will not be important to us. The important distinction is that between machine language and a high-level language such as Ada.

Do not bother to memorize our assembly language instruction to add two numbers, nor its translation into a string of zeros and ones. The exact assembly language instructions and their translation into zeros and ones will differ from machine to machine. The only point to remember is that any high-level language must be translated into machine language before the computer can understand and follow the program.

compiler

A program that translates a high-level language, like Ada, to a machine language is called a *compiler.* A compiler is thus a somewhat peculiar sort of program in that its input or data is some other program and its output is yet another program. To avoid confusion, the input program is usually called the *source program,* and the translated version is called the *object program* or *object code.* The word *code* is frequently used to mean a program or a part of a program, and this usage is particularly common when referring to object programs. You can think of a compiler as a translator: It translates programs in one language into programs in another language. A human analogy might be the translation of an English sentence into a Greek sentence.

Now suppose you want to run an Ada program. To get the computer to follow your Ada instructions, you proceed as follows. First, run the compiler using your Ada program as data. Notice that in this case the Ada program is not being treated as a set of instructions. To the compiler your Ada program is just a long string of characters. The output will be another long string of characters, which is the machine language equivalent of the Ada program. Before the machine language program can be run, it must first be *linked.* Linking a program is a process required by the operating system to incorporate the code produced by the compiler with the necessary system routines that allow the program to run on this particular computer. As a beginning programmer it is not necessary for you to understand the details of this linking process, but you should realize it is a necessary step in the overall process of getting a program to run. After the program is linked, you run this machine language program (object code) with what you normally think of as the data for the Ada program. The output will be what you normally conceptualize as the output of the Ada program. The process is easier to visualize if you have three computers available, as diagrammed in Figure 1.5.

In reality the entire process just described is facilitated on one computer by special programs called *systems programs.* Although there is but one computer, the systems programs make it appear as though a big box, represented by the dotted line in Figure 1.5, were built around three computers. You simply place your Ada program

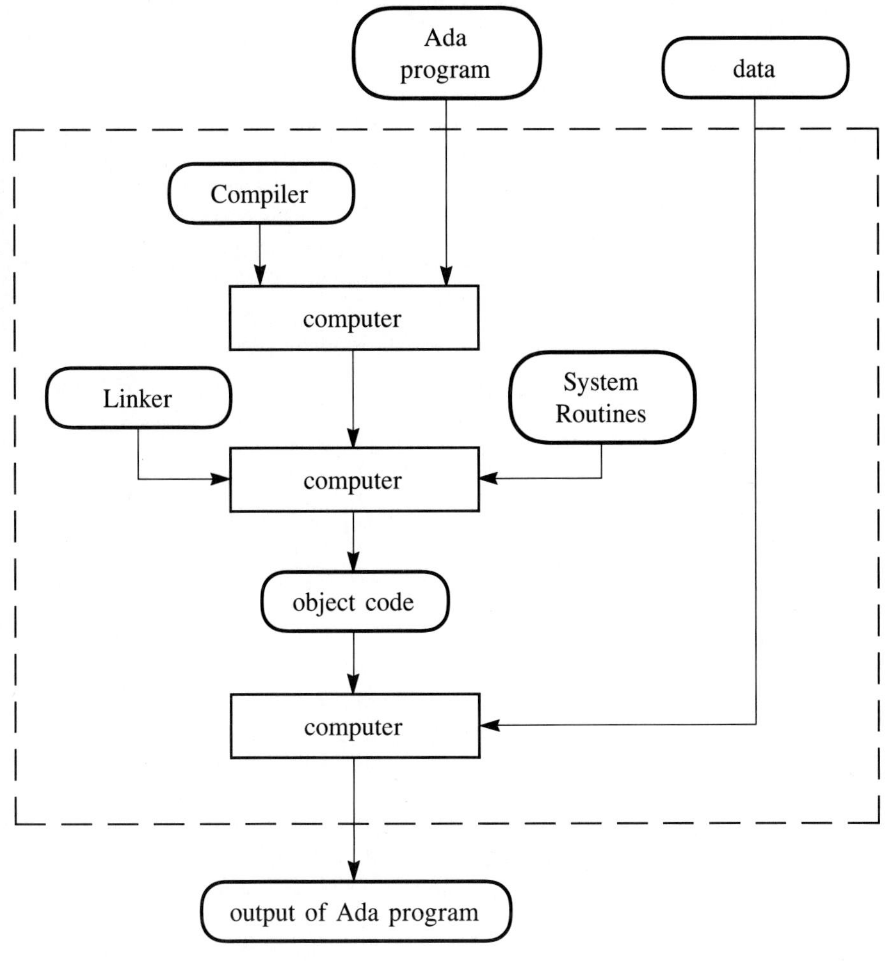

Figure 1.5 Compiling and running an Ada program.

and data in the box and the rest is taken care of automatically. You can think of the computer as actually running the Ada program. None of this is peculiar to Ada. The translation process is the same with any high-level programming language.

The Ada Programming Language

In this book we will use a programming language called Ada. Ada is a high-level, general-purpose programming language. When we say Ada is a general-purpose language, we mean that it is suitable for a diverse range of applications. Indeed, it is commonly used to write programs for a wide variety of applications, including numeric scientific calculations, business data processing, text editing, as well as writing various systems programs, including compilers.

The Ada language was developed for the United States Department of Defense (DoD) by an international team led by Jean Ichbiah at CII Honeywell Bull in France during the late 1970s. This ended a long process that began in about 1974, when the DoD decided it needed a common language for many of its applications. Existing languages then in use were rejected for various reasons. A document was prepared that described the requirements for this new language. This document was reviewed and refined a number of times by experts in programming language design, and it was reported in a series of documents with interesting names that reflect the increasing rigidity of the requirements for the language. The original document was called "Strawman," followed by "Woodenman," "Tinman," and "Ironman."

Seventeen companies submitted proposals for the new language based on the "Ironman" document. Four companies were chosen to independently develop the new language. Since the names of the companies were known to the final reviewers, the language designs were color-coded to help provide anonymity. The companies were CII Honeywell Bull (Green), Intermetrics (Red), Softech (Blue), and SRI International (Yellow). The Green and Red language designs were chosen for a final round of reviews that led to the "Steelman" document. On May 2, 1979, the Green language was chosen as the new DoD standard.

The language, known as "the Green language" and later simply called "the DoD language," was officially named Ada in honor of Augusta Ada Byron (1815–52), daughter of the poet Lord Byron. She is also known as Ada Lovelace, since she was Countess of Lovelace. Lovelace had a technically helpful association with Charles Babbage, who at that time was working on a mechanical computer he called the *analytical engine.* Many authorities consider Babbage's analytical engine to be the first programmable computer and consider Ada to be the first computer programmer.

After some final revisions the Ada language was submitted to the American National Standards Institute (ANSI) as a standard. The ANSI standard *Reference Manual for the Ada Programming Language* was published in 1983. (Common terminology for this manual is *Language Reference Manual,* or LRM for short.) Many consider the LRM to be a complex document and not intended for beginners. It serves, however, as the standard reference manual upon which the design of all Ada compilers is based.

The Ada language has a design that facilitates the writing of programs in a style that is now generally accepted as good standard programming practice. It is a big, powerful language, but when used properly it can be a good language to use when learning to program computers. Moreover, it does not lose its usefulness after you learn the rudiments of programming. It is widely available and is frequently used by professional programmers inside and outside the defense industry. Also, a number of other popular programming languages are similar to Ada and are thus easy to learn once you have mastered Ada.

Programming Environments

operating system

Our description of compiling and running an Ada program is a correct but oversimplified picture of what actually happens when you run an Ada program. Systems programs on modern computers include many other programs besides the compiler. The main systems program is called the *operating system.* It is the program in charge of other programs—the manager, so to speak. It keeps track of which program is run on which piece of data; it brings out the editor program, which allows you to use the computer as a typewriter for writing your programs; it puts the editor program away and brings out the appropriate compiler when needed; it also runs the machine language program that the compiler produces. On a computer with many simultaneous users, the operating system also keeps the various users from interfering with one another. It does this by moving resources from one user to another at such high speeds that, unless the number of users is very high, each user is given the illusion of being the only one using the computer. The operating system also does whatever accounting and security checking is needed. While all this is going on, the programs that are running usually produce various pieces of information as output. For example, the compiler will look for mistakes in your program and will give one or more output messages should it find any errors.

Computer facilities are now configured in a wide variety of ways. Small computers, called *microcomputers* or *personal computers,* are dedicated to a single user. Large computers, called *main frames,* can serve numerous simultaneous users by means of special operating systems called *time-sharing systems.* Often, the computer facility will consist of a *network,* connecting a number of different computers together so they can share certain resources, such as printers and secondary storage devices. The particular configuration you are working on will matter little to our study of programming techniques. For our purposes they all serve the same function and behave similarly.

editor
files

We have outlined the basic tasks involved in running a program. They are common to all systems. However, the details will vary from system to system, and you must find out many of these details before you can run a program. Your system will have a program, called an *editor,* that lets you use the computer as a typewriter. The system will also allow you to store programs and to retrieve them at a later time. The program that controls this storing and retrieving is usually called a *file manager,* or some similar term such as *file system* or *filer.* You will need to learn how to use both the editor and the file manager. Finally, you will have to learn how to get the compiler program to translate your program into machine code and how to run the machine language program. (On many systems the processes of compiling and then running the program are combined into a single process.)

Although you will need to find out these details about your computer system, at this point you do not need to know anything about how to write a program in Ada or in any other programming language. The rest of this book is devoted to teaching you how to go from a problem to an Ada program to solve that problem.

Designing Programs

Designing a program is frequently a difficult task. There is no complete set of rules, no algorithm to tell you how to write programs. Program design is a creative process. Still, there is the outline of a plan to follow. The outline is given in diagrammatic form in Figure 1.6. As indicated there, the entire program design process can be divided into two phases: the problem solving phase and the implementation phase. The result of the *problem solving phase* is an algorithm for solving the problem. The algorithm is expressed in English. To produce a program in a programming language such as Ada, the algorithm is translated into the programming language. Producing the final program from the algorithm is called the *implementation phase.*

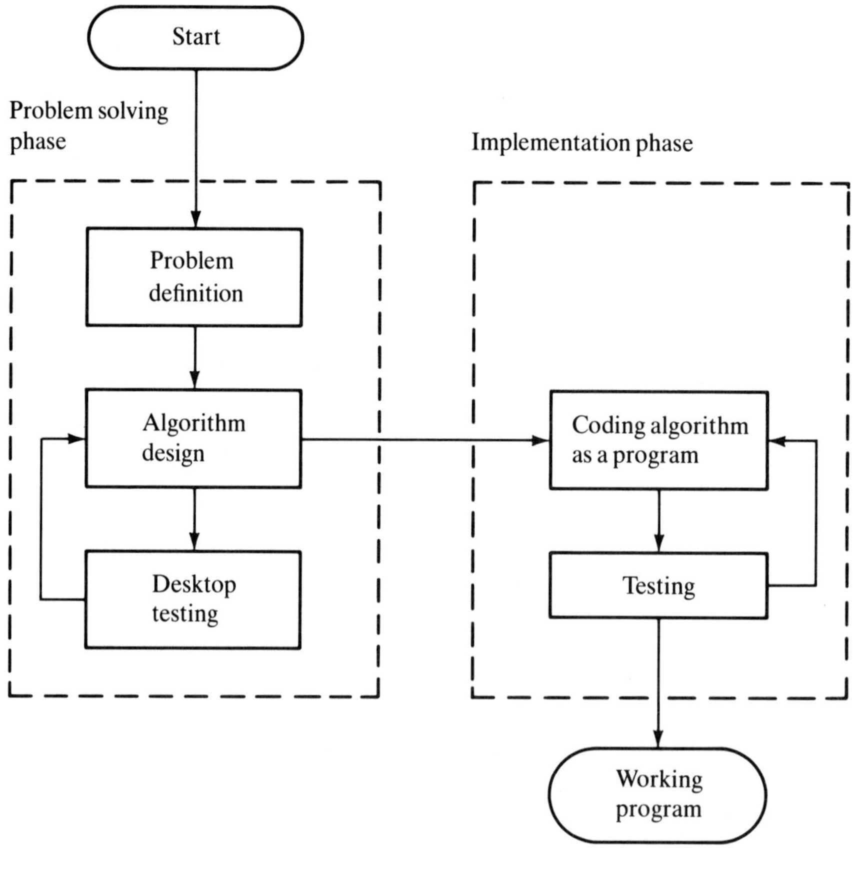

Figure 1.6 Idealized program design process.

problem definition

The first step in the problem solving phase, and the first step in the entire design process, is to be certain that the task is completely and precisely specified. Do not take this step lightly. If you do not know exactly what you want as the output of your program, you may be surprised at what your program produces. Be certain that you know what the input to the program will be and exactly what information should be in the output, as well as what form that information should be in. For example, if the program is a bank accounting program, you must know not only the interest rate but also whether it is to be compounded annually, monthly, daily, or whatever. If the program is supposed to write poetry, you need to determine whether the poems can be in free verse or must be in iambic pentameter or some other meter.

problem solving phase

Many novice programmers do not understand the need to design an algorithm before writing a program in Ada and so try to short-circuit the process by omitting the problem solving phase entirely or else reducing it to just the problem definition part. This seems reasonable. Why not ''go for the mark'' and save time? The answer is that it does not save time! Experience has shown that the two-phase process produces a correctly working program faster. The two-phase process simplifies the algorithm-design phase by isolating it from the detailed rules of a programming language such as Ada. The result is that the algorithm-design process becomes much less intricate and much less prone to error. For a modest-sized program it can represent the difference between a half day of careful work and several frustrating days of looking for mistakes in a poorly understood program.

implementation phase

The implementation phase is not trivial. There are details to worry about, details that occasionally can be quite subtle, but it is much simpler than you might think at first. Once you become familiar with Ada, or any other programming language, the translation of an algorithm from English into the programming language becomes a routine task.

testing

As indicated in Figure 1.6, testing takes place in both phases. The algorithm is tested, and if it is found to be deficient, it is redesigned. That testing is performed by mentally going through the algorithm and executing the steps yourself. On large algorithms this will require the aid of pencil and paper. The Ada program is tested by compiling it and running it on some sample input data. The compiler will give error messages for certain kinds of errors. To find other types of errors, you must somehow check to see if the output is correct.

The diagram in Figure 1.6 is an idealized picture of the process. It is the basic picture you should have in mind, but reality is sometimes more complicated. In reality you can discover mistakes and deficiencies at unexpected times, and you may have to back up, as shown in Figure 1.7. For example, testing the algorithm may reveal that the problem definition was incomplete. In those cases you must back up and reformulate the definition. Occasionally, deficiencies in the definition or algorithm may not be observed until a program is tested. In that case you must back up and modify the definition or algorithm and all that follows it in the design process.

Chapter 2 contains an introduction to the Ada language and some complete examples of this design process.

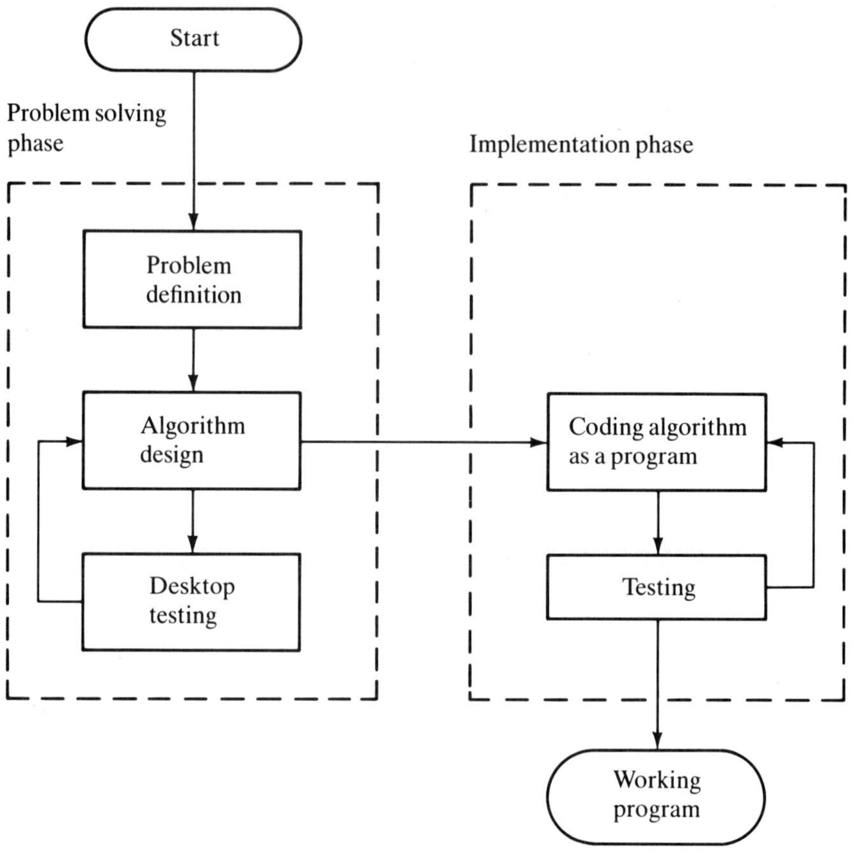

Figure 1.7 Realistic program-design process.

Summary of Terms

algorithm Detailed, unambiguous, step-by-step instructions for carrying out a task.

assembly language Almost the same thing as machine language. The only difference is that assembly language instructions are expressed in a slightly more readable form, instead of being coded as strings of zeros and ones. See *machine language.*

auxiliary storage Another name for secondary memory.

code Sometimes used to mean a program or part of a program.

compiler A program that translates programs from a high-level language to machine language.

CPU The Central Processing Unit of a computer. It performs the actual calculations and the manipulation of memory according to the instructions in a machine language program.

data The word has two meanings: (1) the input to an algorithm or program; (2) any information that is available to an algorithm or to a computer.

editor A program that allows the computer to be used as a typewriter. An editor also has a number of commands that are more powerful than those of a typewriter, such as moving an entire piece of text from one place to another.

execute When an instruction is carried out by a computer, either directly or in some translated form, the computer is said to execute the instruction. When a computer follows the instructions in a complete program, it is said to execute the program.

file manager Also called a filer or file system. A program that allows the user to store and retrieve objects called files. Among other things, a file can contain an Ada program. Hence, a file manager is the program used to store and retrieve Ada programs.

hardware The actual physical parts of a computer or computer system.

high-level language A programming language that includes larger, more powerful instructions and typically a grammar that is somewhat like English. Programs in a high-level language usually cannot be directly executed by computers. See *machine language.*

machine language A language that can be directly executed by a computer. Programs in machine language consist of very simple instructions, such as adding two numbers. These simple instructions are coded as strings of zeros and ones. See *assembly language.*

main memory The memory that the computer uses as temporary "scratch paper" when carrying out a computation. Main memory is sometimes called RAM (Random Access Memory). See *secondary memory.*

object program The translated version of a program produced by a compiler. See *source program.*

operating system The program that controls and manages all other programs. You communicate with the computer through the operating system.

program A sequence of instructions to be executed by the computer. The instructions may be followed directly or translated and then followed.

running a program When a program and some data are given to a computer in such a way that the computer is instructed to carry out the program using the data, that is called running the program (on the data).

secondary memory The memory a computer uses to store information in a permanent or semipermanent state. (When the computer does not have sufficient main memory for a computation, then it is also used as an addition to main memory.) See *main memory.*

software Another term for programs.

source program The input program to be translated by a compiler. See *object program.*

Exercises

This book contains three kinds of exercises: Self-Test Exercises, Interactive Exercises, and Programming Exercises. The Self-Test Exercises are designed to provide you with a quick test of your understanding. The answers are relatively short and can be checked by comparing them to the answers provided in the back of the book. The Interactive Exercises are designed to be done at the terminal. They are typically short programming exercises and are designed to give you a hands-on feel for the material. They may be done quickly; you need not worry too much about style details when doing them. The Programming Exercises are suitable exercises to be assigned as homework in a course. In this chapter the Programming Exercises ask you to produce algorithms in English; in subsequent chapters they ask you to go through the entire design process and produce a working Ada program.

Self-Test Exercises

1. Write an algorithm to add two whole numbers. The input to the algorithm is to be two strings of digits representing the two numbers. For example, the number 1066 is thought of as the four symbols 1-0-6-6. The algorithm should be capable of being followed by a child who has not yet learned to do addition.

2. Write an algorithm to tell if an input word is a palindrome. (A palindrome is a word that is the same spelled backwards and forwards, such as "`radar.`")

3. Write an algorithm to count the number of occurrences of each letter in an input word. For example, the input word `pop` contains two `p`'s and one `o`.

Interactive Exercises

4. A good illustration of an algorithm is the instruction set for the U.S. Internal Revenue Service's long form 1040. If you have a copy readily available, read it through and notice how very explicit the instructions are.

Programming Exercises

5. Write an algorithm to multiply two whole numbers. The rules are the same as in Exercise 1.

6. Write an algorithm to subtract one whole number from another. The rules are the same as in Exercise 1. (This is harder than it sounds.)

7. Write an algorithm to divide one whole number by another whole number. The rules are the same as in Exercise 1.

8. Write an algorithm that takes a page of text as data (input) and corrects the spacing according to the following rules: There should be exactly one space between two adjacent words, except that there are two spaces between adjacent sentences and paragraphs are indented by exactly three spaces. Define the start of a paragraph as one or more

spaces (indentation) at the start of a line. The data may contain any number of spaces, except that you may assume that there are no spaces inside of words, and that there is at least one space between any two words on the same line. The output is to be written onto a second sheet of paper.

9. Many banks and savings and loan institutions compute interest on a daily basis. On a balance of $1000 with an interest rate of 6%, the interest earned in one day is 0.06 times $1000 divided by 365 (because it is only for one day of a 365-day year). This yields $0.16 in interest, so the balance is then $1000.16. The interest for the second day will be 0.06 times $1000.16 divided by 365. Design an algorithm that takes three inputs—the amount of a deposit, the interest rate, and a duration in weeks—and then calculates the account balance at the end of the duration specified.

10. Negotiating a consumer loan is not always straightforward. One form of loan is the discount installment loan, which works as follows. Suppose the face value of a loan is $1000, the interest rate is 15%, and the duration is 18 months. The interest is computed by multiplying the face value of $1000 by 0.15 to yield $150. That figure is then multiplied by the loan period of 1.5 years to yield $225 as the total interest owed. That amount is immediately deducted from the face value, leaving the consumer with only $775. Repayment is made in equal monthly installments based on the face value. So the monthly loan payment will be $1000 divided by 18, or $55.56. This method of calculation may not be too bad if the consumer needs $775, but the calculation is a bit more complicated if the consumer needs $1000. Design an algorithm that takes three inputs—the amount the consumer needs to receive, the interest rate, and the duration of the loan in months—and then calculates the face value required for the consumer to receive the amount needed and also calculates the monthly payment.

References for Further Reading

R. E. Pattis, *Karel the Robot: a Gentle Introduction to the Art of Programming* (New York: Wiley, 1981). An introduction to algorithms and programming in a very simple setting.

H. L. Capron and B. K. Williams, *Computers and Data Processing* (Redwood City, CA: The Benjamin/Cummings Publishing Co., 1982). A simple introduction to programming systems and modern uses of computers. This book would be good if you are completely bewildered by Chapter 1.

L. Goldschlager and A. Lister, *Computer Science—A Modern Introduction,* from the Prentice-Hall International Series in Computer Science (Englewood Cliffs, NJ: Prentice-Hall, 1982). Discusses in more detail many of the issues presented in this chapter. Written at the introductory level.

T. Kidder, *The Soul of a New Machine* (New York: Avon Books, 1981). A popular description of the engineering effort that went into designing a specific computer. It is entertaining, and you do pick up a few technical facts as well.

CHAPTER

2

INTRODUCTION TO PROBLEM SOLVING WITH ADA

Augusta Ada Lovelace

Augusta Ada Byron (1815–1852) was Lord Byron's daughter and the Countess of Lovelace. Lovelace was a mathematician, an unusual avocation for women of that era. Her major claim to fame is through her association with Charles Babbage and his ''Analytical Engine,'' a mechanical computer, where the essential ideas of programming were developed. The programming language we study in this textbook was named in honor of Lovelace. Some consider her to be the world's first computer programmer.

Chapter Contents

In this chapter we give an introduction to the Ada programming language. We explain some sample programs and present enough details of the Ada language to allow you to write some simple programs. We continue the discussion of problem solving, which we began in Chapter 1, by presenting some fundamental techniques for designing algorithms. Finally, we illustrate these design techniques by developing two additional Ada programs from the problem definition stage to final working programs.

The Notion of a Program Variable

Programs manipulate data such as numbers and letters. To store data produced by computations and to give the data a name, Ada and many other common programming languages use *objects*. An object is an entity that has a name and contains a data value. Names in Ada and other programming languages are called *identifiers*. Ada has two kinds of objects: *variables* and *constants*. The word *variable,* meaning changeable, describes an object whose value can be changed during the execution of a program, and the word *constant,* meaning unchanging, describes an object whose value cannot be changed. Variables are the very heart of a programming language like Ada. They have some similarities to the variables used in algebra and related branches of mathematics, but they definitely are not the same thing. They traditionally have longer names than the variables used in algebra. In an Ada program an identifier (object name) is written as a string or sequence of letters and digits that begins with a letter. An identifier also may have embedded underlines between any of its letters or digits. Although an identifier may have more than one underline embedded in it, those underlines may not be adjacent to one another (e.g., `one__two` is illegal). Here are some sample names (think of name and identifier as meaning the same thing) for Ada variables:

```
sum first_number two_by_2 on_3 SALLY Joe rate Time
```

variables and values

Ada variables can hold numbers or other types of data, but for the moment we will confine our attention to variables that hold only numbers. These variables are rather like small blackboards on which numbers can be written. Just as a number written on a blackboard can be changed, so too can a number held by an Ada variable be changed. Like blackboards, a variable might contain no number at all, or it might contain the number left there by the last operation performed on that variable. The words *hold* and *contain,* when applied to variables, are synonymous and, if you think in terms of the blackboard analogy, refer to the item written on the figurative blackboard. The number, or other type of data held in a variable, is called its *value.*

memory locations and variables

Most compilers translate variables into memory locations. A memory location is assigned to each variable, and the value of the variable, in a coded form consisting of zeros and ones, is kept in that location. For example, Figure 2.1 contains an Ada program that uses the three variables `FIRST_NUMBER`, `SECOND_NUMBER`, and `SUM`. When that program is compiled, the compiler might assign the locations 1001, 1002, and 1003 to the variables `FIRST_NUMBER`, `SECOND_NUMBER`, and `SUM`, respectively. When the value of a variable is changed, the coded number in its assigned memory location also changes. Whether or not your particular compiler actually assigns memory locations to variables is irrelevant; the compiler makes the program act as if just such an assignment was made.

Program

```
with I_O; use I_O;
procedure MAIN is
    FIRST_NUMBER  : INTEGER;
    SECOND_NUMBER : INTEGER;
    SUM           : INTEGER;
begin -- Main
    PUT ( "Enter two numbers, separated by a space" );
    NEW_LINE;
    PUT ( "then press the return/enter key." );
    NEW_LINE;
    GET ( FIRST_NUMBER );
    GET ( SECOND_NUMBER );
    SKIP_LINE;
    SUM := FIRST_NUMBER + SECOND_NUMBER;
    PUT ( FIRST_NUMBER );
    PUT ( " Plus " );
    PUT ( SECOND_NUMBER );
    PUT ( " Equals " );
    PUT ( SUM );
    NEW_LINE;
    PUT ( "Enter another two numbers" ); NEW_LINE;
    GET ( FIRST_NUMBER );
    GET ( SECOND_NUMBER );
    SKIP_LINE;
    SUM := FIRST_NUMBER + SECOND_NUMBER;
    PUT ( FIRST_NUMBER );
    PUT ( " Plus " );
    PUT ( SECOND_NUMBER );
    PUT ( " Equals " );
    PUT ( SUM );
    NEW_LINE;
end MAIN;
```

Sample Dialogue

```
Enter two numbers, separated by a space
then press the return/enter key.
4 5
     4 Plus      5 Equals       9
Enter another two numbers
8 9
     8 Plus      9 Equals      17
```

Figure 2.1 An Ada program.

To illustrate how program variables can change value, we will give a step-by-step explanation of the program displayed in Figure 2.1. Unless otherwise noted, we will always assume that you use a keyboard to input data and a screen is used to display the output. That is the form of input and output used in Figure 2.1.

Stepping Through a Program

statements

In Figure 2.1 the lines between **begin** and **end** contain instructions to be carried out by the computer. Such instructions are called *statements*. A semicolon at the end of each statement is used to terminate the statement, but a minor point of punctuation like this need not be a serious concern for you yet. The first four statements do not affect any variables. They simply cause the following phrase to appear on the display screen and then move the cursor to the next line:

```
Enter two numbers, separated by a space
then press the return/enter key.
```

Suppose that, in response to this, you type **4**, press the spacebar, type **5**, and press the return key. (Pressing the return key starts a new line, much like using the carriage return on a typewriter. On some keyboards the return key is marked *Enter*, on others it simply has the symbol ↵.)

The next three statements tell the computer what to do with these numbers.

```
GET ( FIRST_NUMBER );
GET ( SECOND_NUMBER );
SKIP_LINE;
```

The GET statements are instructions to the computer to "get" the two numbers from the keyboard and place them into the variables FIRST_NUMBER and SECOND_NUMBER. It causes the value of the variable FIRST_NUMBER to become equal to the first number you typed in, namely **4**, and the value of SECOND_NUMBER to become equal to the second number you typed in, namely 5. The SKIP_LINE statement instructs the computer to skip over any other values on the input line (i.e., skip to the beginning of the next line).

Recall that our hypothetical compiled translation of the Ada program assigned memory location 1001 to FIRST_NUMBER and 1002 to SECOND_NUMBER. This means that location 1001 in the computer's memory now contains a coded version of the number **4**, and location 1002 contains the code for **5**. Prior to this time, the variables FIRST_NUMBER and SECOND_NUMBER had no known value.

The next statement in our sample program is

```
SUM := FIRST_NUMBER + SECOND_NUMBER;
```

The meaning of FIRST_NUMBER + SECOND_NUMBER is as you might guess. It instructs the computer to add the value of FIRST_NUMBER to the value of SECOND_NUMBER; in other words, to add **4** to **5** and get **9**. When the translated version of this statement is executed, the computer (the CPU to be precise) retrieves the **4** from location 1001 and the **5** from location 1002 and adds them together to obtain **9**. This statement also says that the resultant number **9** becomes the value of the variable SUM and so goes into the location assigned to SUM, namely 1003.

assignment operator

The symbol **:=** is called the *assignment operator,* and statements such as the one under discussion are called *assignment statements.* The assignment operator is composed of two symbols, a colon and an equal sign, but it is considered to be one item and is always treated as a single unit. There can be no spaces between the colon and the equal sign in the assignment operator. Many people pronounce the assignment operator as "gets the value," which describes the action; others simply say "assignment operator." Some people even read it literally as "colon equals," but the meaning of the assignment operator is not derived from the usual meaning of the colon and equal symbols. The symbol **:=** means change the value of the variable on the left-hand side to whatever value is given on the right-hand side. We will say more about the assignment operator shortly, but first let us explain the rest of our sample program.

The next group of statements in our sample program is

```
PUT ( FIRST_NUMBER );
PUT ( " Plus " );
PUT ( SECOND_NUMBER );
PUT ( " Equals " );
PUT ( SUM );
NEW_LINE;
```

The result of these assignment statements appears on the screen as follows:

```
4 Plus 5 Equals 9
```

For the moment do not worry about why words like **" Plus "** are written with quotation marks and blanks before and after them; we will come back to those details shortly. For now, simply note that the values of the variables and the words in quotes are output to the screen in the order in which they occur in the PUT statements.

changing the value of a variable

The rest of the program is almost a repetition of what we have just discussed. The program requests another two numbers with the following statements:

```
PUT ( "Enter another two numbers" ); NEW_LINE;
```

This time suppose that you type **8** and **9**, again separate the numbers by a blank and terminate the line by pressing the return key. The two numbers are input when the program executes the following statements in the program:

```
GET ( FIRST_NUMBER );
GET ( SECOND_NUMBER );
SKIP_LINE;
```

This second group of input statements sets the value of FIRST_NUMBER equal to **8** and the value of SECOND_NUMBER equal to **9**. The old values of **4** and **5** are lost.

The second assignment statement,

```
SUM := FIRST_NUMBER + SECOND_NUMBER;
```

changes the value of SUM to the value of FIRST_NUMBER plus the value of SECOND_NUMBER. In other words, the value of SUM is changed to **8** plus **9**, or **17**. The old value of SUM is lost. The final group of output statements displays these new values of FIRST_NUMBER, SECOND_NUMBER, and SUM.

Figure 2.1 also shows the complete dialogue between you and the computer as it would appear on the screen. The material you typed in and the output produced by the program are shown in different typefaces, which helps to clarify where the different lines come from. In reality, they would appear in the same typeface.

Assignment Statements

expression

An *assignment statement* always consists of a variable on the left-hand side of the assignment operator and an *expression* on the right-hand side. The expression may be a variable, a number, or a more complicated expression such as one made up of variables, numbers, and arithmetic operators (e.g., addition and subtraction). This statement instructs the computer to evaluate the expression on the right-hand side and to set the value of the variable on the left-hand side equal to that value of the expression. A few more examples may help to clarify the way these statements work.

In Ada the multiplication sign is not the traditional symbol used in mathematics but is represented by an asterisk, as shown in the following assignment statement:

```
SUM := FIRST_NUMBER * SECOND_NUMBER;
```

This statement is just like the assignment statements in our sample program, except it performs multiplication rather than addition. The statement changes the value of SUM to the product of the values of FIRST_NUMBER and SECOND_NUMBER. Of course, that makes SUM a poor choice for the name of our variable, but the program will still run. When the computer sees the identifier SUM, it knows it is a variable capable of storing integers, but it does not know or care that it spells an English word indicating addition. In all cases, however, you should try to name variables in a way that describes what they are.

The expression on the right-hand side of an assignment statement can simply be another variable. The statement

```
FIRST_NUMBER := SECOND_NUMBER;
```

changes the value of the variable FIRST_NUMBER so it is the same as the value of SECOND_NUMBER. The value of SECOND_NUMBER is not affected. This example is illustrated in Figure 2.2.

numeric literal

As yet another example, the following statement changes the value of SECOND_NUMBER to **3**:

```
SECOND_NUMBER := 3;
```

The number **3** on the right-hand side of the assignment operator is what you have usually called a *constant* in your mathematics classes. It was called a constant because, unlike a variable, its value cannot change. Unfortunately, in Ada the LRM has a technical

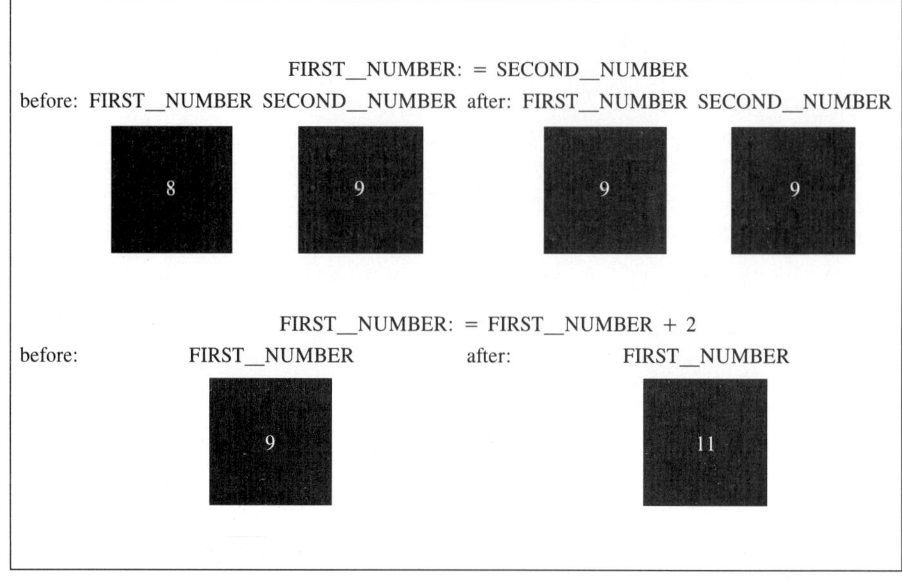

Figure 2.2 The assignment operator.

term for a constant of this kind; it is called a *numeric literal.* Thus, all numeric values are called numeric literals. There is a reason for this, as we will see as we go along. We may from time to time simply call them numbers, but we will not call them constants any more.

Since the value of a variable can change over time, and since the assignment operator is one vehicle for changing that value, there is an element of time involved in the meaning of an assignment statement. First, the expression on the right-hand side of the assignment operator is evaluated. After that, the value of the variable on the left side of the operator is changed to the value that was obtained from that expression. This means that a variable can meaningfully occur on both sides of an assignment operator. As an example, consider this statement:

```
FIRST_NUMBER := FIRST_NUMBER + 2;
```

This statement increases the value of `FIRST_NUMBER` by `2`.

Data Types—An Introduction

A *data type* is what the words say it is, a type or category of data. Each variable can hold only one type of data. In our sample Ada program, all variables are of type `INTEGER`, which means that their values are integers. An integer is any whole number, such as the following:

```
38    0    1    89    3987    -12    -5
```

The value of a variable of type INTEGER cannot be a fraction. The variables FIRST_NUMBER, SECOND_NUMBER, and SUM in the program in Figure 2.1 can never contain numbers with fractional parts like 1/2 or 3.1416. Numbers with fractions are of another data type called FLOAT, which we will discuss later in this section.

variable declarations

Every variable in an Ada program must be *declared*; that is, the type of the variable must be stated. This is done at the beginning of the program, before the word **begin**. In our first sample program the variables were declared by the following line:

```
FIRST_NUMBER  : INTEGER;
SECOND_NUMBER : INTEGER;
SUM           : INTEGER;
```

The declaration consists of a list of variables separated by commas, followed by a colon, followed by a type name, and finally ended with a semicolon. Extra blanks may be added so long as you do not insert blanks in the middle of the word INTEGER or the variable names.

There are two reasons for requiring these declarations: to clarify your thinking by reminding you what type of data the variable will be used for and to provide information to the compiler. Recall that the computer has in its memory only strings of zeros and ones. It uses a special scheme to encode each integer into a string of zeros and ones that it can use. It uses a different encoding scheme to produce strings of zeros and ones for letters. The declaration tells the compiler and ultimately the computer which code to use.

floats

Numbers that include a fractional part, such as the ones below, are of type FLOAT:

```
2.71828    0.098    -15.8    100053.98
```

numeric literals

In an Ada program, such numbers are called *numeric literals*. Each numeric literal has a type, such as INTEGER or FLOAT. The computer makes a distinction between whole numbers considered to be of type INTEGER and whole numbers considered to be of type FLOAT when it processes numeric literals. In particular, the numeric literal for INTEGER 3 is written **3** whereas the numeric literal for the FLOAT number 3 is written **3.0**. We will have more to say about this distinction in the next section.

Just as with numbers, a numeric variable has a type such as INTEGER or FLOAT. A variable PAY_RATE is declared to be of type FLOAT in the following way:

```
PAY_RATE : FLOAT;
```

This declaration could be read, "PAY_RATE is of type FLOAT."

characters

The data type for letters or, more generally, any single symbol is CHARACTER. Two variables, F and LETTER, of type CHARACTER are declared as follows:

```
F, LETTER : CHARACTER;
```

An object of type CHARACTER can hold any character on the input keyboard. CHARACTER objects hold only one character; they cannot hold strings containing more than one character. For example, F could hold an 'A' or a '+' or a '9' or an 'a'. The upper- and lowercase letters are considered to be different characters.

quotes

The apostrophes or single quotes, or simply quotes as they are usually called in computer programming, indicate that we literally mean a letter, a digit, or a special character. Therefore, F is used for a variable named F, whereas 'f' is used for the lowercase version of the sixth letter of the alphabet. This is an important distinction. For example, the statement

```
LETTER := F;
```

changes the value of the variable LETTER to the value of the variable F. So, if F contains the letter 'A', this statement changes the value of LETTER to 'A'. On the other hand, the statement

```
LETTER := 'f';
```

changes the value of the variable LETTER to the letter 'f', which is quite another thing. The program in Figure 2.3 illustrates this important distinction.

Program

```
with I_O; use I_O;
procedure MAIN is
    F      : CHARACTER;
    LETTER : CHARACTER;
begin
    F := 'A';
    LETTER := F;
    PUT ( "The first value of LETTER is:" ); NEW_LINE;
    PUT ( LETTER ); NEW_LINE;
    LETTER := 'f';
    PUT ( "The second value of LETTER is:" ); NEW_LINE;
    PUT ( LETTER ); NEW_LINE;
    PUT ( "I hope this has helped to explain quotes." );
    NEW_LINE;
end MAIN;
```

Sample Dialogue

```
The first value of LETTER is:
A
The second value of LETTER is:
f
I hope this has helped to explain quotes.
```

Figure 2.3 Using apostrophes and quotation marks.

character literal
string literal

In Ada there is a distinction between the way a single character and a string of characters is represented. Single quotes are used to enclose a single character. A single character thus enclosed is referred to in the LRM as a *character literal.* Character literals are of the type CHARACTER. Quotation marks, or double quotes as they are often called in computer programming, enclose a string of one or more characters. A string of characters enclosed in quotation marks is referred to in the LRM as a *string literal.* You have already seen string literals used in some of the output statements in the programs in Figures 2.1 and 2.3. We will discuss string literals in more depth later.

Unlike some printed text, Ada has only one kind of single quote; opening and closing quotes are the same symbol. Similarly, Ada has only one kind of double quote; the opening and closing double quotes are the same symbol.

An expression consisting of a character literal, such as **'X'**, has the same sort of value as a numeric literal, such as **3** or **5.98**. They are, however, different data types: **'x'** is of type CHARACTER, **3** is of type INTEGER, and **5.98** is of type FLOAT. Be sure to note that while **'3'** and **3** are both literals, they are very different values. The first is a character, a mere symbol. It is of type CHARACTER and may be used on the right-hand side of an assignment statement to give a value to a variable of type CHARACTER. The value 3 is a number. It is of type INTEGER and may be used to give a value to a variable of type INTEGER.

sample declarations

It is perfectly acceptable to have variables of more than one type in a program. In such cases they all are declared at once, following this format:

```
with I_O; use I_O;
procedure MAIN is
     FIRST_NUMBER, SECOND_NUMBER: INTEGER;
     TIME: FLOAT;
     INITIAL: CHARACTER;
begin
     instructions go here
end MAIN;
```

The variables need not be declared in any particular order. The following declaration is equivalent to the previous one:

```
FIRST_NUMBER  : INTEGER;
INITIAL       : CHARACTER;
SECOND_NUMBER : INTEGER;
TIME          : FLOAT;
```

This declaration puts the variables in alphabetical order, but you also can order variables according to how they are used in the program. The alphabetized method is consistent and can be important in large programs with many variables. You may wish to "pretty up" the appearance of the declaration by aligning the colons, which also tends to enhance readability.

Pitfall

Uninitialized Variables

Until a program gives a value to a variable, that variable has no known value. For example, if the variable X has not been given a value either as the left-hand side of an assignment statement or by being used in a GET statement (or by any of the methods still to be discussed), then the following statement will not produce the intended result:

```
Y := X + 1;
```

Since the value of X is not known, the entire expression **X + 1** has an unpredictable value. A variable like X that has not been given a value is said to be *uninitialized.*

What happens in this situation depends on your particular system. You may get an error message warning you that **X** has been used without being initialized. In other less ideal situations, the value of **X** may be set to some random quantity determined by whatever was left in the computer's memory by the previously run program. Therefore, it is possible that when the program is run twice with the same input data it may display two different outputs. Whenever a program gives different output on the same data and without any change in the program itself, you should suspect an uninitialized variable.

Some programming languages automatically initialize all numeric variables to zero. In general this is not true of Ada. It may be true on some Ada systems, but you cannot and should not count on it.

One way to ensure that a variable has an appropriate initial value is to give it a value when you declare it. With a minor addition to the declaration of a variable, you also can initialize it. The following three examples show variables being given initial values when they are declared:

```
NUMBER  : INTEGER := 0;
INITIAL : CHARACTER := 'a';
TIME    : FLOAT := 10.9;
```

The initialization part of each of these declarations is exactly like the right-hand side of an assignment statement. The INTEGER variable, NUMBER, is assigned the value of zero prior to the execution of any statement. Similarly, INITIAL is assigned the initial value of the lowercase letter **'a'**, and TIME is initialized to **10.9**. Giving a variable a value when it is declared ensures that it has a known value when the program begins.

More about FLOAT Values

floats versus integers

Conceptually a whole number is a special kind of FLOAT number, namely, one that happens to have all zeros after the decimal point. If that were the only difference between the two types, we would never have need to use the type INTEGER. However, there is another important difference. Numbers of type INTEGER are stored as exact values, while numbers of type FLOAT are stored only as approximate values. Thus, if you know that some value will always be a whole number in the range allowed by your computer, it is best to make it of type INTEGER. The precision with which FLOAT values are stored varies from one computer to another, but on most computer systems the extra digits in the following assignment statement are pointless:

```
PI := 3.14159265358979323846
```

The program is likely to give exactly the same output when the FLOAT value is changed to

```
PI := 3.14159
```

Numeric literals of type FLOAT are written differently from those of type INTEGER. Numeric literals of type INTEGER must not contain a decimal point. Numbers of type FLOAT may be written in two different forms. The simple form for FLOAT literals is like the everyday way of writing decimal fractions. When written in this form a FLOAT literal must contain a decimal point and must contain at least one digit before and one digit after the decimal point. No number in Ada may contain a comma. Hence, of the following, none are allowed as numbers of type FLOAT (nor as numbers of type INTEGER):

```
1,000.009    -.05    72.
```

However, numeric literals in Ada may contain embedded, but not adjacent, underlines, as in identifiers. Hence, the number 1,000.009 could be written as **1_000.009**.

In addition to the simple notation that we have been using for FLOAT numbers, there is another more complicated notation for expressing literals of type FLOAT. This notation is frequently called *scientific notation* or *floating point notation,* from which the type name FLOAT is derived. It is particularly handy for writing very large numbers and very small fractions. For example, the numbers

3.67 times 10^{17} = 367000000000000000.0
and 5.89 times 10^{-6} = 0.00000589

are best expressed in Ada by the numeric literals **3.67E17** and **5.89E-6**, respectively. **E** stands for *exponent* and means that the number before **E** is multiplied by **10** to the power designated by the number that follows. This *E notation* is used because keyboards normally do not have any way to write exponents as superscripts.

Another way to interpret **E** notation is to think of the number after **E** as telling you to move the decimal point that many places left or right. The sign of the number after **E** indicates the direction in which to move the decimal point: positive is right and negative is left. For example, to change **3.49E4** to a number without **E**, you move the decimal point **4** places to the right and obtain **34900.0**, which is another way of writing the same number. If the number after **E** is negative, you move the decimal point the indicated number of spaces to the left. So **3.49E-2** and **0.0349** are two ways of writing the same number. Notice that in both cases, extra zeros were inserted as needed.

E notation syntax

There are rigid rules for writing numbers in **E** notation. The number before **E** can be any decimal number, with or without a plus or minus sign. It need not contain a decimal point at all, but if it does there must be at least one digit before and at least one digit after the decimal point. The number after **E** is called the *exponent* and must be a whole number, either positive, negative, or zero. It cannot contain a decimal point. The following are all correctly formed numbers of type FLOAT:

```
9.34E13   5.0E7   0.5E-27   -8.62713E21
1.234E-15   -6.783E-12   1.0E+13   +34.7556
```

By contrast, none of the following are acceptable numeric literals:

```
.5E12   -.7E13   3.5E22.5
```

The first two are incorrect because they have no digit before the decimal point. The last one is incorrect because it has a decimal point in the exponent.

If there is no decimal point in the **E** notation number, it is of type INTEGER. Thus **1E4** is an example of an integer literal using **E** notation and it has the same numeric value as **10000**.

Mixing Types

integers in place of floats

In Ada programs **2** and **2.0** are different kinds of numbers: the first is of type INTEGER and is an exact value; the second is of type FLOAT and represents an approximate value. You cannot use an INTEGER value where the computer expects a FLOAT value, nor can you use a FLOAT where the computer expects an INTEGER. If your program contains **2** where it should contain **2.0**, the computer will not know what you mean. Hence, if FLOAT_VARIABLE is a variable of type FLOAT, the following is not allowed:

```
FLOAT_VARIABLE := 2;
```

Likewise, if INTEGER_VARIABLE is of type INTEGER, the following is illegal in Ada:

```
INTEGER_VARIABLE := 2.0;
```

This sort of type conflict is not likely to arise in such a simplistic manner. However, the same principle applies in more subtle situations. The following example is a more likely mistake and is illegal whenever FLOAT_VARIABLE is of type FLOAT and INTEGER_VARIABLE is of type INTEGER:

```
INTEGER_VARIABLE := FLOAT_VARIABLE;
```

A variable may contain only values of its declared type.

Arithmetic Expressions

Numbers and variables of the types INTEGER and FLOAT may be combined in arithmetic expressions, but only if the programmer explicitly converts the INTEGER value to FLOAT or the FLOAT value to INTEGER. This explicit type conversion is accomplished in the following manner: To convert an INTEGER value to FLOAT use

FLOAT (*integer_value* **)**

For example:

```
FLOAT_VARIABLE := FLOAT ( 2 );
FLOAT_VARIABLE := FLOAT ( INTEGER_VARIABLE );
FLOAT_VARIABLE := FLOAT ( INTEGER_VARIABLE + 2 );
FLOAT_VARIABLE := FLOAT ( INTEGER_VARIABLE ) + 2.5;
```

To convert a FLOAT value to INTEGER, use

INTEGER (*float_value* **)**

For example:

```
INTEGER_VARIABLE := INTEGER ( 2.0 );
INTEGER_VARIABLE := INTEGER ( FLOAT_VARIABLE );
INTEGER_VARIABLE := INTEGER ( FLOAT_VARIABLE + 2.0 );
```

In the conversion process the FLOAT value is rounded up to the next larger integer if the value after the decimal point is greater than 0.5. Floating point values are approximate values, so if the number after the decimal is equal to 0.5 you have a more difficult case. Within the accuracy of the system, values that are halfway between may round up or down.

You can use parentheses to build more complicated expressions from these simpler ones, but the same basic rule applies: *no mixed mode arithmetic.* In other words, you cannot mix FLOAT values and INTEGER values in arithmetic operations without applying explicit type conversions. The old adage applies: you cannot mix apples and oranges.

The arithmetic operators **+ - * /** (add, subtract, multiply, and divide, respectively) are available for both INTEGER and FLOAT values, but only if both operands are of the same type. For example, the following statements use the variables X, N, M, and Y, and each variable is either a FLOAT or an INTEGER. The first assignment statement is a well-formed arithmetic expression only if all variables are of type INTEGER. The second assignment statement is a well-formed arithmetic expression only if they are all FLOAT variables.

```
1. X := 2 * ( N + ( M - 3 ) + 4 * Y );
2. X := 2.0 * ( N + ( M - 3.0 ) + 4.0 * Y );
```

mixing floats and integers

Suppose, however, the variables are declared as follows:

```
N, M : INTEGER;
X, Y : FLOAT;
```

Then neither assignment statement 1 nor 2 is legal in Ada. In assignment statement 3, the INTEGER value that results from the operations of **+** and – on N, M, and **3** is converted to a FLOAT value which is then compatible with the operations of **+** and ***** on X, Y, **2.0**, and **4.0**.

```
3. X := 2.0 * FLOAT ( N + M - 3 ) + 4.0 * Y;
```

Notice that the type of an arithmetic expression is determined by the types of its subexpressions and is not determined by the particular value of the expression. Whether or not an arithmetic expression evaluates to a ''whole number'' is irrelevant to the type of the expression. The quantity **4 - 2** is always an INTEGER value. Similarly, the quantity **4.0 - 2.0** is always a FLOAT value.

Any reasonable spacing will do in arithmetic expressions. You can insert spaces before and after operations, and you can insert parentheses, as in the previous examples, or you can omit them. The spaces are used only because it produces a result that is easy to read. The following two assignment statements produce exactly the same resultant value for X. (Spacing in expressions is a matter of style and readability; it has no effect on the result.)

```
X := 2.0 * FLOAT ( N + M - 3 ) + 4.0 * Y;
X:=2.0*FLOAT(N+M-3)+4.0*Y;
```

parentheses

The order of operations can always be determined by parentheses, as illustrated in the following expressions:

```
(X + Y) * Z
X + (Y * Z)
```

To evaluate the first expression, you add X and Y and then multiply the result by Z. To evaluate the second expression, you multiply Y and Z and then add the result to X.

precedence rules

If you omit parentheses, the computer follows precedence rules similar to those used in everyday arithmetic. For example,

```
X + Y * Z
```

is evaluated by first doing the multiplication and then doing the addition. Except for some standard cases, such as a string of additions or a simple multiplication embedded inside an addition, it is best to use parentheses, even if the intended order of operations is the one dictated by the precedence rules. The parentheses make the expression easier to read and less prone to programmer error. Unlike some written and printed mathematical formulas that contain square brackets and various other enclosure symbols, Ada arithmetic expressions can contain only one kind, namely parentheses.

While we are on the subject of arithmetic operations, we should point out that Ada has an operator for exponentiation. There is an Ada equivalent of *exponents*

F^I and I^J

where I and J are of type INTEGER, and F is of type FLOAT. However, there is no Ada equivalent for a floating point value raised to a floating point power. The exponentiation operator in Ada is two asterisks (**) with no space between them. Thus, F^I and I^J are written F ** I and I ** J, respectively.

The exact precedence rules for the operations we have seen so far are given in Figure 2.4. For reference purposes, a complete set of Ada precedence rules are given in Appendix D.

Order of Evaluation of Arithmetic Expressions

1. If parentheses are present, they determine the order of evaluation.
2. If the order is not determined by parentheses, then exponentiation operations are done first, then multiplication and division, followed by any addition and subtraction operations.
3. If there is still a question as to which operation to perform first, the competing operations are performed from left to right.

Figure 2.4 Precedence rules of arithmetic expressions.

The following is an example using rule 1 from Figure 2.4:

```
( 2 + 3 ) * ( 6 - 1 ) becomes
    5     *     5     which is equal to
          25
```

Rule 2 applies here:

```
2 + 3 ** 2 * 6 becomes
2 +   9    * 6 because exponentiation comes
                       before multiplication
2 +       54 because multiplication comes before addition
  56   is the final result
```

Here is an example using rule 3:

```
10 / 2 * 6 becomes
   5   * 6 because those operations at the same level are
                     done left to right
       30 is the final result
```

All three rules apply here:

```
( 2 + 4 ) * 2 ** 2 / 8 becomes
( 2 + 4 ) *   4    / 8 because of rule 2
    6     *   4    / 8 because of rule 1
         24        / 8 because of rule 3
               3 is the final result
```

Figure 2.5 shows some examples of common kinds of arithmetic expressions and how they would be expressed in Ada. All variables used in Figure 2.5 are of type FLOAT.

Mathematical Formula	Ada Expression
$b^2 - 4ac$	`B ** 2 - 4.0 * A * C`
$x(y + z)$	`X * ( Y + Z )`
$\frac{1}{x^2 + x + 1}$	`1.0 / ( X ** 2 + X + 1.0 )`
$\frac{a + b}{c - d}$	`( A + B ) / ( C - D )`

Figure 2.5 Ada arithmetic expressions.

Simple Output

put You can use PUT statements (such as those used in our sample program in Figure 2.1) to display the values of variables as well as strings of text on the screen. Each PUT statement displays only one value on the screen. The PUT statement can display any of the different types of variables as well as strings, but each must be in a separate PUT. The strings of characters are enclosed in double quotes (quotation marks). The items to be output are listed in separate PUT statements in the order in which they are to appear on the screen.

new_line The NEW_LINE statement causes the cursor on the screen to move to the next line. When the output goes to a printer, NEW_LINE causes the equivalent of a carriage return and a line feed, i.e., one new line on the printer.

blanks No extra space is inserted before or after strings or the values of variables of type CHARACTER, which is why a quoted string in the samples usually starts and ends with a blank. The blanks keep the various strings and numbers from running together.

Values of type FLOAT are often output in E notation. For example, if X is a variable of type FLOAT, the statements

outputting floats

```
X := 1234.56;
PUT ( X );
```

produce an output that looks something like

```
1.2345600000000E03
```

which means

1.2345600000000 times 10^3

and is another expression for the number 1234.56.

You must observe some details about quoted strings when you include them in PUT statements, or anyplace else for that matter. Remember that double quotes are used, and both the opening and the closing quotation marks are the same single character symbol ("). If you want to include a double quote symbol within a quoted string, you must use two double quotes; otherwise the computer interprets the double quote as marking the end of a quoted string. Single quotes appear in a quoted string as just one single quote. For example, the output of

quotes inside of quotes

```
PUT ( "He said, ""Surf's Up""" );
```

is the following:

```
He said, "Surf's Up"
```

Consider the following statements:

put and new_line

```
PUT ( "First line" );
NEW_LINE;
PUT ( "Second line" );
NEW_LINE;
```

They cause the following to appear on the screen:

```
First line
Second line
```

On the other hand, these statements

```
PUT ( "First line" );
PUT ( "Second line" );
NEW_LINE;
```

cause the following to appear on the screen:

```
First lineSecond line
```

The last output statement in a program should always be a NEW_LINE rather than a PUT, because some systems require that the end of all lines, including the last line of output, be explicitly indicated. Always ending with a NEW_LINE always works well regardless of the system you use.

You should note two useful forms of NEW_LINE. First, you can use NEW_LINE without previous output; it simply causes the computer to move to the next line. Second, you can use NEW_LINE (n) to move the cursor down **n** lines on the screen, which is handy for moving down more than one line. The value of **n** must be of type INTEGER. The statements

```
PUT ( "Line one" );
NEW_LINE ( 2 );
PUT ( "Line three" );
NEW_LINE;
```

cause the following to appear on the screen:

```
Line one

Line three
```

An additional property of the PUT statement is that you can place an expression inside parentheses. The expression is evaluated, and its value is output. So the following is permitted and has the obvious meaning:

```
PUT ( FIRST_NUMBER );
PUT ( " Plus " );
PUT ( SECOND_NUMBER );
PUT ( " Equals " );
PUT ( FIRST_NUMBER + SECOND_NUMBER );
NEW_LINE;
```

Input

get and skip__line

GET and SKIP_LINE statements are for input and are analogous to PUT and NEW_LINE. You write a GET statement the same way as PUT, with a single item enclosed in parentheses. The item in a GET must always be a variable. GET instructs the computer to read an input value and set the value of the variable equal to the value read. For this discussion we will assume that you type the input from a keyboard, but the details are similar for data you input from other sources.

Variables of the types INTEGER, FLOAT, and CHARACTER may be given values with a GET statement. Later we will introduce other data types besides these three. For now assume that only values of type INTEGER, FLOAT, and CHARACTER may be read in from the keyboard.

The SKIP_LINE statement forces the computer to ignore any other values on the present input line that have not been read with GET statements. For example, consider the following statements and input values:

```
GET ( ONE_VALUE );
SKIP_LINE;
GET ( A_SECOND_VALUE );
GET ( AND_A_THIRD_VALUE );
SKIP_LINE;

23 45   667 2
8 12 155
```

The value 23 is assigned to ONE_VALUE. The values 45, 667, and 2 are skipped over. The value 8 is assigned to A_SECOND_VALUE, and AND_A_THIRD_VALUE gets 12. The value 155 is skipped.

Different GET statements may call for different types of variables, and the types of the values input for each GET statement should match the type of the variable in parentheses. If a variable in a GET statement is of type FLOAT, the number you type in for that variable must be a floating point number such as **12.5**. If the variable is of type FLOAT and the number is **12.0**, you should not enter it as the integer number **12**; using **12** produces a serious problem. In a similar manner, if a variable is of type INTEGER, the number you type in for that variable should also be of type INTEGER. Of course, you should never try to fill a variable of type INTEGER or FLOAT with a character, such as a letter of the alphabet.

blanks in input

When entering numbers, you must insert one or more blanks between numbers on the same line so that the computer knows where one number ends and the next begins. The situation with characters is different. Anything you type, including a blank, is a value of type CHARACTER. You therefore enter no space before an input character that is intended for a variable of type CHARACTER.

Designing Input and Output

prompt lines

When the computer executes a GET statement, it expects data to be entered at the keyboard. If none is typed in, it simply waits for it. The program must tell you when to type in data. The computer will not automatically ask you to enter data. That is why the sample programs contain statements like the following:

```
PUT ( "Enter two numbers" ); NEW_LINE;
```

These output statements *prompt* the user to enter data.

echoing input

When you enter data from a terminal, the input appears on the screen as you type it. Nonetheless, the program should always write out the input values sometime before the program ends. This is called *echoing* the input and serves as a check to see that the computer reads the input correctly. Just because the input looks good on the screen does not mean that it was read correctly. There could be an unnoticed typing mistake, or the input could be read incorrectly because the line breaks are not where the program expected them to be. Echoing input serves as a test of the integrity of the input data.

Pitfall

Input in Wrong Order

A human being given two numbers that represent height and weight can figure which number is which no matter in what order the numbers appear. There is nobody who is 180 feet tall and weighs 6 pounds. However, a computer makes no such test for reasonableness and would happily accept such numbers for height and weight. You must always be careful that your programs instruct the user to input values in the correct order, or the program is likely either to terminate abnormally or to produce incorrect results.

Names: Identifiers

A name used in an Ada program is called an *identifier*. The form of an identifier was defined earlier in this chapter. With the exception of one special class of identifiers that we will discuss later in this section, any Ada identifier can be used as the name of an object in an Ada program.

long identifiers

The Ada standard sets no limit on the length of an Ada identifier. All letters, digits, and underlines are significant, but there is no difference between upper- and lowercase letters when used in an identifier. (Upper- and lowercase letters are considered different when they appear in quoted strings or as the values of variables of type CHARACTER.)

reserved words

A special class of identifiers, called *reserved words*, have a predefined meaning in the Ada language and cannot be used as names for anything else, such as variables. The following is a list of the reserved words we have seen so far:

```
with use procedure is begin end
```

A complete list of reserved words is given in Appendix A.

There is no capitalization "standard" prescribed in the LRM, although various people have recommended some guidelines. This book uses the convention on upper- and lowercase letters established by the LRM. It is a very simplistic style with only three rules:

- All reserved words in the Ada language are written using all lowercase letters.
- All other identifiers that the programmer must make up are written using all uppercase letters, such as in SUM.
- If an identifier is made up of two words, such as THE_ANSWER, the words will be separated by an underline to enhance readability.

You never use two spellings that differ only in the case of some or all of their letters.

You may wonder why other words we defined as part of the Ada language are not on the list of reserved words. What about INTEGER, CHARACTER, and GET? Although these words do have predefined meanings, you are allowed to change their meanings. Such identifiers are called *standard identifiers*. Needless to say, using a standard identifier as a name for something other than its standard meaning can be confusing and dangerous and, thus, should be avoided. The safest and easiest practice is to treat standard identifiers as if they were reserved words.

standard identifiers

Putting the Pieces Together

You now know enough details about Ada to write a program. All you need to do is put the pieces together in the right order and with the correct punctuation.

Ada programs start with a line called the *procedure specification,* which consists of the reserved word **procedure**, followed by an identifier to serve as the name of the program, followed by the reserved word **is**. For simplicity we have chosen the procedure name to be MAIN, as in "this is the main procedure in the program." As for the first line in our previous examples, **with** I_O; **use** I_O;, for now always include it. Using it helps you get started in the simplest way and avoids some of the input-output complexity that is possible in the language.

procedure specification

After the procedure specification come the variable declarations. Next comes what we will call the *block* of the program, which consists of a list of statements that serve as the instructions to be followed. This is the algorithm part and is set off by the reserved words **begin** and **end**. All statements are terminated by semicolons. Ada programs end with the name of the procedure, in our simple case MAIN, followed by a semicolon.

block

In Ada any two identifiers or numbers must be separated by either one or more spaces, a line break, or a punctuation symbol (such as a comma, semicolon, or colon), or by a combination of two or more of these separators. Hence the sample program specification cannot be **procedure**MAIN. However, the Ada compiler accepts any number of extra blanks between identifiers.

spacing

Ada allows you wide latitude in deciding when to start a new line. Two or more statements may be placed on the same line. (Placing more than one statement on a line is considered by many as a bad practice and, in general, should be avoided.) With one exception, a line may be broken anyplace that a blank is allowed. The one exception is that you cannot break a quoted string across two lines. For example, the following is not allowed:

line breaks

```
PUT ( "You may NOT break a quote
        across two lines like this." );
```

Almost any pattern of spacing and line breaks is acceptable to the compiler. However, as we point out in the next section, programs should always be arranged so they are easy to read.

Introduction to Programming Style

All the sample programs in this chapter were laid out in a particular format. For example, the statements were all indented the same amount, and the declarations were aligned. This and other matters of style are of more than aesthetic interest. A program that is written with careful attention to style is easier to read, easier to correct if it contains a mistake, and easier to change should that prove desirable at some later time.

indenting blank lines

A program should be laid out so elements that are naturally thought of as a group are made to look like a unit. The standard way of doing this is to indent everything in that group by the same amount. Another way to make a program more readable is to skip a line between pieces that are logically thought of as separate. The important point is to make separations on the basis of indentations and line breaks. The exact number of spaces in an indentation is a matter of personal style. Sometimes there are also natural break indicators, such as the words **begin** and **end**, which can be made to stand out and frame a group.

choosing names

Variables, constants, and even program names should at least hint at their meaning or use. It is easy to just use X, Y, and Z again and again as variables for numbers. You can do this and still produce working programs, but it is much easier to understand a program if the variables have meaningful names. Contrast the statement

```
X := Y * Z;
```

with the more suggestive statement:

```
PAY := RATE * HOURS;
```

The two statements accomplish the same thing, but the second is easier to understand.

Exercises

Self-Test Exercises

1. What is the output produced by the following program?

```
with I_O; use I_O;
procedure MAIN is
    X, Y : INTEGER;
  begin
    X := 2;
    Y := 3;
    Y := X;
    PUT ( X ); PUT ( Y ); NEW_LINE;
  end MAIN;
```

2. What is the output produced by the following program?

```
with I_O; use I_O;
procedure MAIN is
    X : INTEGER;
begin
    X := 2;
    X := X + 1;
    PUT ( X );
    NEW_LINE;
end MAIN;
```

3. What is the output produced by the following program?

```
with I_O; use I_O;
procedure MAIN is
    A, B, C : CHARACTER;
begin
    A := 'b'; B := 'c'; C := A;
    PUT ( A ); PUT ( B ); PUT ( C ); PUT ( 'c' );
    NEW_LINE;
end MAIN;
```

4. Which of the following are correctly formed numeric literals of type INTEGER?

`3.5   4.0   4.   4   1,295   9/3   8/5   '7'`

5. Which of the following are correctly formed numeric literals of type FLOAT?

`98.6 -33.4 .89 -.89 3,987.85 4. 4 4.0 -0.89`

6. Which of the following are correctly formed numeric literals of type FLOAT?

`.57E12 57E12 0.75E-12 57E3.7 57.9E3.7 -9.8E2`

7. Convert each of the following (non-Ada) arithmetic expressions into Ada arithmetic expressions. (Assume all variables are of type FLOAT.)

$3x \qquad 3x + y \qquad \frac{x + y}{7} \qquad \frac{3x + y}{z + 2}$

8. What (if anything) is wrong with the following declarations?

(a)
```
count : Integer        ;
Answer : Character; AMOUNT:    integer;
```

(b)
```
Time: Integer;
  Rate: Floating;
```

(c)
```
Count1; Count2: integer;
     Rate: float;
```

(d)
```
first_number, second_number: integer;
      AVE: float
```

9. What are the types of the values of the following expressions? (You need not evaluate them.)

```
2 * 3    5 * (7 + 4 / 2)    '3'    2.0000    2E9
```

10. The following program contains errors. What are they?

```
with I_O; use I_O;
procedure MAIN is
begin
     PUT ("Hello"); NEW_LINE;
     PUT ("This program was written in a hurry);
     PUT( 'It contains a few mistakes');
     PUT ( "CAN YOU FIND THEM?")
     PUT ("The compiler can");
end MAIN;
```

11. What is the value of each of the following expressions?

```
2 + 3 - 4 * 5
( 2 ** 3 + 4 ) / 3
2 + 3 ** 4 - 1
( 10 / 5 + 3 ) ** 3 + 1
( 2 + 3 ) * ( 4 - 6 ) / ( 10 / 2 )
```

Interactive Exercises

12. Type and run the following program:

```
with I_O; use I_O;
procedure MAIN is
begin
     PUT ( "Hello. " ); NEW_LINE;
     PUT ( "End of program" ); NEW_LINE;
end MAIN;
```

13. Write a program that reads in one integer, multiplies it by 2, and then displays the product on the screen.

Problem Solving and Program Design

To keep from getting confused when designing a program and to produce a readable, easy-to-change program requires patience and a systematic approach to the design process. In Chapter 1 we outlined one systematic approach that required you to carefully analyze the problem, design an algorithm for a hypothetical person to follow, and then translate the algorithm into an Ada program for the computer to follow. One very basic design technique for producing the algorithm is called *top-down design*. The next section introduces this technique and illustrates it with a design example.

Top-Down Design

stepwise refinement

A good plan of attack for designing an algorithm is to break down the task to be accomplished into a few big subtasks, and then decompose each big subtask into smaller subtasks, replace the smaller subtasks by even smaller subtasks, and so forth. Eventually the subtasks become so small that they are trivial to implement in Ada or whatever language you are using. This method is called either *top-down design, stepwise refinement,* or, more graphically, *divide and conquer.*

Not only is stepwise refinement an efficient design method, it also produces an algorithm that is easy to understand and relatively easy to modify. This is very important as most programs are changed at some time, and some of them are being changed constantly. For example, a simple computerized airline reservation system might be expanded to keep track of seat as well as flight reservations. The top-down design method is illustrated in the two Case Studies included in this chapter.

Case Study

A Guessing Game

Problem Definition

We want to design a program to play a simple game with the user. The rules of the game are as follows: The user chooses two numbers and then tries to guess the average of these two numbers. The user could calculate the average with pencil and paper, but the idea is to choose relatively big, complicated numbers and to really guess rather than compute the average. The program is supposed to let the user know whether or not the guess was correct. This is not much of a game; nonetheless, it can be used to illustrate the program design process.

Discussion

subcomponents

The steps of this program can be broken into three main subcomponents:

`begin`

1. Get the user to input two numbers and a guess of their average;
2. Calculate the average;
3. Output enough information to permit the user to easily check if the guess is correct

`end`

Algorithm

An algorithm for the first subcomponent is the following:

1a. Ask the user to type in two numbers;
1b. GET (FIRST_NUMBER); GET (SECOND_NUMBER); SKIP_LINE;
1c. Ask the user to guess their average and enter the guess;
1d. GET (GUESS); SKIP_LINE;

pseudocode

The algorithm for subcomponent 1 contains a mixture of Ada and English. This is quite common. When the Ada way to express a step is obvious, there is little point in writing it in English. When the steps are large or complicated, they usually are expressed first in English. This combination of English and Ada is sometimes called *pseudocode*.

implementation phase

The algorithm for subcomponent 1 translates into the following Ada code:

```
PUT ( "Enter TWO INTEGERS, separated by a SPACE" ); NEW_LINE;
PUT ( "Then press RETURN" ); NEW_LINE;
GET ( FIRST_NUMBER ); GET ( SECOND_NUMBER ); SKIP_LINE;
PUT ( "Now GUESS their AVERAGE." ); NEW_LINE;
PUT ( "Enter your GUESS, then press RETURN" ); NEW_LINE;
GET ( GUESS ); SKIP_LINE;
```

The second component is to compute the average of the numbers held in the variables FIRST_NUMBER and SECOND_NUMBER. The definition of average yields this algorithm:

Algorithm

2a. Compute the sum of FIRST_NUMBER and SECOND_NUMBER;
2b. Divide the sum by 2 to get the average;

To translate this, use another variable of type FLOAT to hold the average. If you call the variable AVERAGE, you get the following Ada code for subcomponent 2:

```
AVERAGE := FLOAT ( FIRST_NUMBER + SECOND_NUMBER ) / 2.0;
```

Designing step 3 requires some thinking. Since you are not yet an experienced programmer, you can settle for a very simpleminded solution. The computer will announce the user's guess and the correct average. The user can then see if the guess matches the true average. This solution is simple enough to translate directly into Ada as follows:

```
PUT ( "You guessed" ); PUT ( GUESS ); NEW_LINE;
PUT ( "The right answer is " ); PUT ( AVERAGE ); NEW_LINE;
```

The complete program is shown in Figure 2.6. A blank line separates the code for each of the three major subcomponents.

Program

```
with I_O; use I_O;
procedure MAIN is
    AVERAGE : FLOAT;
    FIRST_NUMBER : INTEGER;
    GUESS : FLOAT;
    SECOND_NUMBER : INTEGER;
begin
    PUT ( "Enter TWO INTEGERS, separated by a SPACE" ); NEW_LINE;
    PUT ( "Then press RETURN" ); NEW_LINE;
    GET ( FIRST_NUMBER ); GET ( SECOND_NUMBER ); SKIP_LINE;
    PUT ( "Now GUESS their AVERAGE" ); NEW_LINE;
    PUT ( "Enter your GUESS, then press RETURN" ); NEW_LINE;
    GET ( GUESS ); SKIP_LINE;

    AVERAGE := FLOAT ( FIRST_NUMBER + SECOND_NUMBER ) / 2.0;

    PUT ( "You guessed " ); PUT ( GUESS ); NEW_LINE;
    PUT ( "The right answer is " ); PUT ( AVERAGE ); NEW_LINE;
end MAIN;
```

Sample Dialogue

```
Enter TWO INTEGERS, separated by a SPACE
Then press RETURN
56 99
Now GUESS their AVERAGE
Enter your GUESS, then press RETURN
76.5
You guessed 7.65000E+01
The right answer is 7.75000E+01
```

Figure 2.6 Game-playing program.

Integer Division

There is a version of division that applies only to values of type `INTEGER` and that returns values of type `INTEGER`. It is essentially the ''long division'' you learned in grade school. For example, 17 divided by 5 yields 3 with a remainder of 2. The two numbers obtained from integer division in this way can be produced with the operators / and **rem**. The / operation yields the number of times one number ''goes into'' another. The **rem** operation gives the remainder. In both cases the divisor goes second. For example, the statements

```
PUT ( "17 Divided by 5 is " ); PUT ( 17 / 5 ); NEW_LINE;
PUT ( "with a Remainder of " ); PUT ( 17 rem 5); NEW_LINE;
```

yield the following output:

```
17 Divided by 5 is 3
with a Remainder of 2
```

Figure 2.7 shows the relationship of these operations to grade school long division. Figure 2.8 illustrates the differences between the two kinds of division in Ada.

```
     4      ← 12 / 3              4      ← 14 / 3
 3 ) 12                       3 ) 14
     12                           12
     ---                          ---
     0      ← 12 rem 3            2      ← 14 rem 3
```

Figure 2.7 The operators rem and /.

Expression	INTEGER Value	Expression	FLOAT Value
102 / 10	10	102.0 / 10.0	10.2
102 rem 10	2		
5 / 2	2	5.0 / 2.0	2.5
5 rem 2	1		

Figure 2.8 The different kinds of division.

Desktop Testing

You may tend to assume that the person or machine following your instructions will not do anything ''stupid'' and will fill in any ''obvious'' detail. Both of these assumptions are incorrect when applied to computers. The computer does exactly what the program instructions say, and in your design strategy these instructions are simply translations of the instructions in an algorithm expressed in English or pseudocode. Hence the algorithm should be tested before you attempt to translate it into an Ada program. The testing can be performed by mentally stepping through the algorithm and carrying out the instructions. By stepping through an algorithm you can see it in operation and can detect many mistakes in detail as well as finding any missing details. When doing this, you will want to use a pencil and paper to write down the values of the variables and to keep track of how the values change.

Case Study

Making Change

In this section you will design a sample program to make change. Given an amount of money, the program will tell how many of each coin, such as quarters, dimes, and so forth, it takes to equal the given amount.

Problem Definition

The statement of the task to be accomplished by the program seems pretty clear, but before we go on let us make sure that as few details as possible are left unspecified. For example, what is the range of input for which the program must work? Does it need to give out dollars as change or not? If yes, what denominations of bills should it use? What should it do with an input of zero? The answers depend on how the program will be used.

For this example, assume the program will be used by a cashier who has no trouble with dollars but needs to be told what coins to hand out. This cashier is at least smart enough to know that zero cents means no coins, so you can assume that the change is some amount of change from one to ninety-nine cents. Are there any other points left unspecified? What if the cashier runs out of some particular coin? After all, this cashier is not too smart; that is why you were asked to write the program. You inquire and discover that the cashier usually has very few if any half-dollar coins, occasionally runs out of nickels, but never runs out of any other coin. After consulting with the cashier's boss, you decide to ignore half-dollar coins and nickels. These coins will just be brought to the bank at the end of the day.

Algorithm

Now that you understand the problem, you can start to design an algorithm. Your first attempt is the following: *outline*

begin
1. Input the amount;
2. Compute a combination of quarters, dimes, and pennies whose value equals the amount;
3. Output the coins;

end

This algorithm breaks the problem into three subproblems. Now you must solve these subproblems and produce some Ada code for the solutions. (In this context the word *code* means a part of a program.)

The first subproblem is easy: simply read the amount into some variable. To make the program easy to read, choose the name AMOUNT for this variable. You accomplish subproblem 1 by the following:

```
PUT ( "Enter an amount of change" ); NEW_LINE;
PUT ( "from 1 to 99 cents:" ); NEW_LINE;
GET ( AMOUNT ); SKIP_LINE;
```

The second subproblem is still quite large, and it will help to break it down into still smaller components. One sensible breakdown is the following:

Algorithm

refinement

2a. Compute the number of quarters to give out;
2b. Compute the number of dimes to give out;
2c. Compute the number of pennies to give out;

data flow

These subproblems are not completely independent. For example, the number of dimes given out will depend on the number of quarters given out. The number of dimes to give out will be computed on the basis of the original amount minus the total value of the quarters given out. When you analyze the information being passed between subproblems, you will see that there are two different notions of amount. There is the original amount input; you decided to save this amount in the variable called AMOUNT. You also need a variable to store the amount left to be given out as we calculate the number of quarters, dimes, and pennies. You might be tempted to use the variable AMOUNT for this purpose by decreasing it successively by the values of quarters and dimes. However, you want to output the original amount when you output the numbers of coins, so you want to preserve the value of AMOUNT unchanged. You therefore introduce a new variable called AMOUNT_LEFT, which at various points in the computation will hold the amount still left to be given as coins. At the start of the computation to calculate coins, the entire amount is the amount left. Therefore, you insert the following assignment before you calculate the number of coins:

```
AMOUNT_LEFT := AMOUNT;
```

After the number of quarters to be given out is calculated, AMOUNT_LEFT will be decreased by the value of the quarters given out. After the number of dimes is computed, AMOUNT_LEFT will be further decreased by the value of the dimes. The movement of information such as the value of AMOUNT_LEFT from one subtask to another is often called *data flow.* This interaction of subtasks is diagrammed in Figure 2.9. Diagrams like this are called *data flow diagrams.*

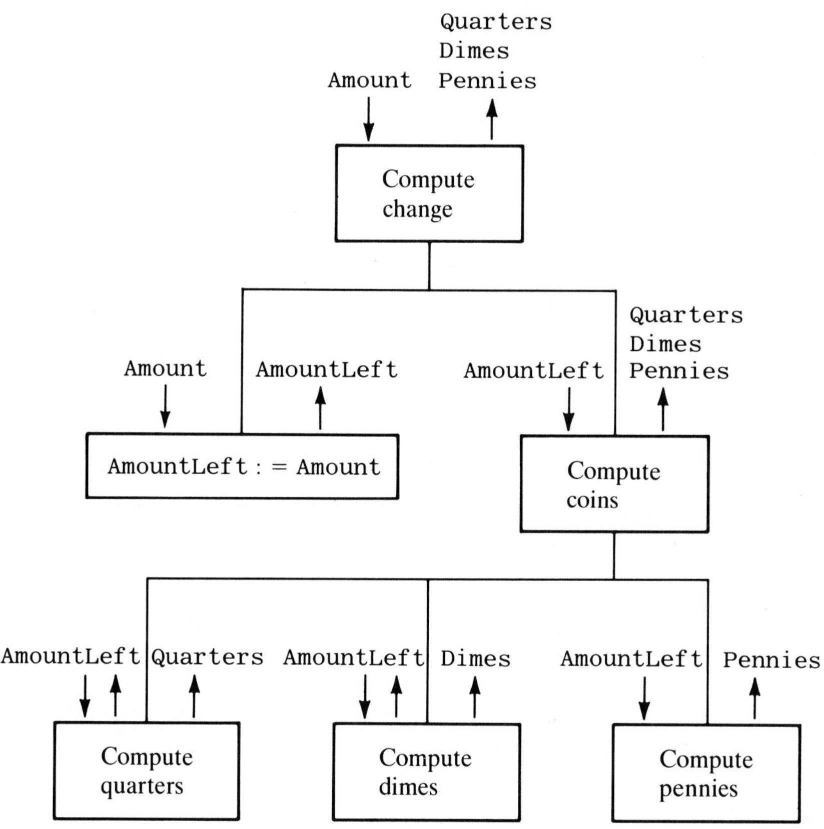

Data Summary

`Amount`: the amount to be given as change.
`AmountLeft`: used to keep track of the amount not yet calculated as some type of coins.
`Quarters, Dimes, Pennies`: the numbers of coins to be given out.

Figure 2.9 Data flow diagram for change program.

second refinement

The smaller components into which subproblem 2 is subdivided can now be rewritten into the following more detailed decomposition of subproblem 2:

Algorithm

2a. Compute the maximum number of quarters in AMOUNT_LEFT and decrease AMOUNT_LEFT by the total value of the quarters;
2b. Compute the maximum number of dimes in AMOUNT_LEFT and decrease AMOUNT_LEFT by the total value of the dimes;
2c. Compute the number of pennies in AMOUNT_LEFT;

analysis of possible solutions

Subproblem 2a is already expressed as two smaller components. First, you must compute the maximum number of quarters in AMOUNT_LEFT. You could subtract 25 from AMOUNT_LEFT as many times as possible (without going negative) and count the number of times you do that. That would work, but before you jump to the keyboard and type it up, think about whether there is a simpler solution. There is.

The number of times you can subtract 25 from AMOUNT_LEFT is the number of times 25 "goes into" AMOUNT_LEFT, and you have a standard Ada operator for that. The following equation calculates the number of times 25 goes into AMOUNT_LEFT:

```
AMOUNT_LEFT / 25
```

This gives you the number of quarters to give out, and this amount is stored in a variable called QUARTERS. Therefore, the first part of subproblem 2a can be accomplished by the following Ada statement:

```
QUARTERS := AMOUNT_LEFT / 25;
```

The decrease in the amount left after giving out the quarters can be computed by the following statement:

```
AMOUNT_LEFT := AMOUNT_LEFT - 25 * QUARTERS;
```

That formula will work, but again there is a simpler expression for the new amount left. The amount left after giving out as many quarters as possible is just the remainder from dividing the old value of AMOUNT_LEFT by 25. In Ada, that is expressed by

```
AMOUNT_LEFT := AMOUNT_LEFT rem 25;
```

You can accomplish the complete subtask 2a with the following Ada code:

```
QUARTERS := AMOUNT_LEFT / 25;
AMOUNT_LEFT := AMOUNT_LEFT rem 25;
```

You can accomplish subproblem 2b by a similar piece of Ada code:

```
DIMES := AMOUNT_LEFT / 10;
AMOUNT_LEFT := AMOUNT_LEFT rem 10;
```

Subproblem 2c is very simple, since the remaining amount is given out as pennies. You can use the following statement:

```
PENNIES := AMOUNT_LEFT;
```

You can accomplish subproblem 3 by a series of PUT and NEW_LINE statements that output the values of the variables QUARTERS, DIMES, and PENNIES. As a check to make sure that the original amount was entered correctly, the value of AMOUNT is also output. The complete program is shown in Figure 2.10.

echoing input

Program

```
with I_O; use I_O;
procedure MAIN is
    AMOUNT      : INTEGER;
    AMOUNT_LEFT : INTEGER;
    DIMES       : INTEGER;
    PENNIES     : INTEGER;
    QUARTERS    : INTEGER;
begin
    PUT ( "Enter an amount of change" ); NEW_LINE;
    PUT ( "from 1 to 99 cents." ); NEW_LINE;
    GET ( AMOUNT ); SKIP_LINE;
    AMOUNT_LEFT := AMOUNT;
    QUARTERS := AMOUNT_LEFT / 25;
    AMOUNT_LEFT := AMOUNT_LEFT rem 25;
    DIMES := AMOUNT_LEFT / 10;
    AMOUNT_LEFT := AMOUNT_LEFT rem 10;
    PENNIES := AMOUNT_LEFT;
    PUT ( AMOUNT ); PUT ( " cents can be given as:" ); NEW_LINE;
    PUT ( QUARTERS ); PUT ( " quarters" ); NEW_LINE;
    PUT ( DIMES ); PUT ( " dimes and" ); NEW_LINE;
    PUT ( PENNIES ); PUT ( " pennies" ); NEW_LINE;
end MAIN;
```

Sample Dialogue

```
Enter an amount of change
from 1 to 99 cents.
67
    67 cents can be given as:
    2 quarters
    1 dime and
    7 pennies
```

Figure 2.10 A program to make change.

Exploring the Solution Space

The previous discussion about computing the number of quarters illustrates an important lesson about algorithms and their design. There is always more than one algorithm for

alternative solutions

a given task. Just because you have found one algorithm do not assume you have found the best algorithm. It always pays to look for an alternative possibly simpler or more efficient algorithm. (However, the emphasis should always be on having a *correct* algorithm.)

solution by analogy

The last case study illustrates another technique to help in your search for algorithms. An existing algorithm can often be adapted to fit a new problem. In the case study you used the following statements to compute the number of quarters and the amount left after giving out that many quarters:

```
QUARTERS := AMOUNT_LEFT / 25;
AMOUNT_LEFT := AMOUNT_LEFT rem 25;
```

To obtain a similar solution for dimes, all you needed to do was replace `25` by `10`.

We will present other techniques for algorithm design in later chapters, but first we will summarize the tools we have developed thus far for designing algorithms and Ada programs.

Summary of Problem Solving Techniques

- Before writing an Ada program, design the algorithm (method of solution) that the program will use. The algorithm can be expressed in a combination of Ada and English known as *pseudocode*.
- Algorithms should be designed using the top-down (also called stepwise refinement or divide and conquer) method described in this chapter.
- When designing programs by the top-down method you should explicitly analyze the flow of information between subtasks.
- Algorithms can sometimes be produced by adapting some known algorithm to fit the new problem.
- Always look for alternative solutions. Just because you have found one solution to a problem does not mean that you have found the best solution.
- An algorithm should be given desktop testing before it is translated into an Ada program.

Summary of Programming Techniques

Both pseudocode and the final Ada program should use meaningful names for variables.

- Use a pattern of indenting, spacing, and line breaks similar to the sample programs.
- All data has a data type. Be sure to check that variables and constants are of the correct data type.
- Use enough parentheses in arithmetic expressions to make the order of operations clear.
- Be sure that all variables are initialized before your program attempts to use their values.

- When programming interactively, always include prompt lines in a program whenever the user is expected to enter data.
- Programs should always echo input.

Summary of Ada Constructs

A summary similar in form to the following one will appear in each subsequent chapter of this book. The entries in the summary consist of three parts:

- An outline of the syntax (form) of the construct
- One or more typical examples of the construct
- An explanation of the construct

Occasionally, one or two of the parts are omitted.

identifier

Syntax:
Any sequence of letters, digits, and embedded underlines that begins with a letter. Consecutive underlines are not allowed.

Example:

```
SUM_2
```

Identifiers are used as names for variables and other items in programs.

variable declarations

Syntax: The item enclosed in square brackets [ ] is optional.

variable_list_1 : *type_1* [:= *expression*];
variable_list_2 : *type_2* [:= *expression*];
.
.
.
variable_list_n : *type_n* [:= *expression*];

Examples:

```
FIRST_NUMBER, SECOND_NUMBER : INTEGER;
RATE : FLOAT := 4.59;
```

Each variable list is composed of identifiers separated by commas. All identifiers on *variable_list_1* are declared to name variables of type *type_1,* all the identifiers on *variable_list_2* are declared to name variables of type *type_2,* and so forth. The types may be any type names. They may appear in any order and may be repeated. The types we have seen so far are `INTEGER`, for a whole number value; `FLOAT`, for a number value with a fractional part; and `CHARACTER`, for a value that is a single character. The optional expression must evaluate to the same type as the type name. If the optional assignment is used in the declaration, the value of the expression will be the initial value of the items in the variable list.

the type integer

Syntax:

```
INTEGER
```

The value of a variable of this data type is any whole number (positive, negative, or zero) that the computer system can handle. A numeric literal of this type is written as a string of digits optionally prefixed with a plus or a minus sign. The value is stored exactly.

the type float

Syntax:

```
FLOAT
```

The value of a variable of this data type is any number that, when written in the usual decimal notation, has at least one digit before and after the decimal point. The value is stored as an approximate value. A numeric literal of this type may be in either of the following forms, optionally preceded by a plus or a minus sign:

- A sequence of digits containing a decimal point that has at least one digit before the decimal point and at least one digit after the decimal point.
- A floating point number followed by the letter **E**, followed by an integer number. The number before the **E** must be a floating point number as in form 1.

the type characters

Syntax:

```
CHARACTER
```

This data type consists of single characters. A literal is formed by placing the character in single quotes. For example, `'A'`, `'$'`, and `'3'`.

assignment statement

Syntax:

variable **:=** *expression* **;**

Example:

```
SUM := FIRST_NUMBER + SECOND_NUMBER;
```

The *expression* is evaluated and the value of the *variable* is set to that value. The *variable* and the value of the *expression* must be of the same type.

integer division

Syntax:

integer__expression__1 / *integer__expression__2*
integer__expression__1 **rem** *integer__expression__2*

Examples:

```
QUOTIENT := 14 / 3;
REMAINDER := 14 rem 3;
```

The / operator returns the quotient obtained from dividing the value of the first expression by the value of the second; the **rem** operator returns the remainder. In the examples, the value of QUOTIENT is changed to **4** and that of REMAINDER to **2**.

float division

Syntax:

float__expression__1 / *float__expression__2*

Example:

```
FLOAT_QUOTIENT := 14.0 / 3.0;
```

The / operator is also used to obtain the quotient from dividing the values of two floating point expressions. The result of floating point division is always another floating point value that represents an approximate value. In the example, FLOAT_QUOTIENT is assigned the value of 4.666. . .6. The exact number of digits in a floating point value is system dependent, but it is typically 6 to 7 digits.

output statements

Syntax:

PUT (*expression*);

Examples:

```
PUT ( " Answer is " );
PUT ( SUM );
```

The PUT statement outputs the value of *expression* to the primary output device, usually a display screen. Each PUT statement will output one and only one value.

Syntax:

NEW_LINE;
NEW_LINE (*number__of__lines*);

Examples:

```
NEW_LINE;
NEW_LINE ( 3 );
```

NEW_LINE causes the cursor on the screen to move down one line and over to the left margin. The NEW_LINE statement has an optional form that causes the cursor to move down an integer *number_of_lines* and over to the left margin.

quoted strings

Example:

```
"He said, ""Surf's up"" "
```

When used in a PUT, the string inside the double quotes is output to the screen. Both the opening and closing quotes are the same symbol. To include a double quote inside of a quoted string, you must use two consecutive double quotes. Quoted strings may include single quotes but may not be broken across two lines.

input statements

Syntax:

```
GET ( variable );
```

Examples:

```
GET ( FIRST_NUMBER );
GET ( SECOND_NUMBER );
```

This statement causes the computer to read a value from the primary input device, usually the keyboard, and to set the value of *variable* to this value. The value input must correspond in type to the variable's type.

Syntax:

```
SKIP_LINE
```

The SKIP_LINE statement causes the computer to ignore the rest of the input on the present input line. A succeeding GET will input values starting at the beginning of the succeeding input line.

Exercises

Self-Test Exercises

14. Determine the value of each of the following Ada arithmetic expressions:

```
15 / 12        15 rem 12        15.0 / 12.0
24 / 12        24 rem 12        24.0 / 12.0
123 / 100      123 rem 100      123.0 / 100.0
200 / 100      200 rem 100      200.0 / 100.0
99 / 2         99 rem 2         99.0 / 2.0
2 / 3          2 rem 3          2.0 / 3.0
```

Interactive Exercises

15. Write a program that reads two integers into the variables `I` and `J` and then outputs `I / J` and `I rem J`. Run the program several times with different pairs of integers as input.

16. Write a program that converts a number of seconds to the equivalent number of minutes and seconds. Use the `rem` and `/` operators.

17. Type and run the program given in Figure 2.1. Then modify the program to do subtraction instead of addition. Do not forget to change the string `" Plus "` to something appropriate. Run the modified program. Next modify the program to do multiplication instead of addition or subtraction. Run that program.

18. Modify your program from the previous exercise to use data and variables of type `FLOAT` instead of type `INTEGER`. Run the program. Modify the program again to do division instead of multiplication.

19. Modify your program from the previous exercise to output the equal sign symbol instead of the word `"Equals"`.

20. Write an Ada program that reads in a character typed on the keyboard and then writes it to the screen twice.

21. Write an Ada program that reads in two characters and then writes them both out twice. Remember that the blank is a perfectly good character to the computer, so things will go wrong if you separate the characters by a blank.

22. Type and run the program shown in Figure 2.6.

23. Modify the program from the previous exercise to output one additional line that gives the amount by which the user's guess missed the true average. For this exercise it is acceptable to output zero or a negative number as the amount by which the guess missed the true average.

Programming Exercises

24. Write an Ada program that reads in two integers and then outputs their sum, difference, and product.

25. Write an Ada program that reads in two integers, divides one by the other, places the result in a variable of type `FLOAT`, and then outputs the two numbers and their quotient. Be sure to include an output statement that warns the user not to give input that would cause the computer to try to divide by zero.

26. A class has four exams in one term. Write a program that reads in a student's four exam scores, as integers, and outputs the student's average.

27. A metric ton is 35,273.92 ounces. Write a program that reads in the weight of a package of breakfast cereal in ounces and then outputs the weight in metric tons as well as the number of boxes of cereal needed to yield one metric ton of cereal.

28. A government research lab has concluded that certain chemicals commonly used in foods cause death in laboratory mice. A friend of yours is desperate to lose weight

but cannot give up soda pop. Your friend wants to know how much diet soda pop it is possible to drink without dying as a result. Write a program to supply the answer. The input to the program is the amount of artificial sweetener needed to kill a mouse, the weight of the mouse, and the weight of the dieter. To ensure the safety of your friend, be sure the program requests the weight at which the dieter will stop dieting, rather than the dieter's current weight. Assume that diet soda contains 1/10 of 1% artificial sweetener.

29. A Celsius (centigrade) temperature C can be converted to an equivalent Fahrenheit temperature F according to the following formula:

$$F = (9.0 / 5.0)\ C + 32.0$$

Write an Ada program that reads in a Celsius temperature as a decimal number and then outputs the equivalent Fahrenheit temperature.

30. The straight-line method for computing the yearly depreciation in value D for an item is given by the following formula:

$$D = \frac{(P - S)}{Y}$$

where P is the purchase price, S is the salvage value, and Y is the number of years the item is used. Write a program that takes as input the purchase price of an item, its expected number of years of service, and its expected salvage value and then outputs the yearly depreciation for the item.

31. An automobile is used for commuting purposes. Write a program that takes as input the distance of the commute, the automobile's fuel efficiency in miles per gallon, and the price of gasoline and then outputs the cost of gasoline for the commute.

32. Workers at a particular company have won a 7.6% pay increase. Moreover, the increase is retroactive for six months. Write a program that takes an employee's previous annual salary as input and outputs the amount of retroactive pay due the employee, the new annual salary, and the new monthly salary.

33. The public utilities commission has decided that the electric company overcharged its customers for two months last year. To make up the difference to the customers, the commission orders the company to decrease each of next month's bills by 10%. The city also levies a 3% utility tax, which will be applied to the bill before it is discounted. Also, the 10% discount does not apply to the utility tax. Assume electricity costs $0.16 per kilowatt-hour. Write a program to compute next month's electricity bill given the number of kilowatt-hours consumed as input.

34. Write an Ada program for the algorithm about discount installment loans that was given as Exercise 10 in Chapter 1.

CHAPTER

3

MORE ADA AND PROGRAMMING TECHNIQUES

Jean Ichbiah

Ichbiah, a Frenchman, headed the team at CII-Honeywell Bull that developed the Ada programming language for the United States Department of Defense. The language was defined and redefined in a series of documents (Strawman, Woodenman, Tinman, Ironman, Steelman). Ichbiah's team was included in a group of four companies that vied for this government contract. The language from each team was color coded (Red, Green, Yellow, Blue) for anonymity during the review process. Ichbiah's Green language was the eventual winner.

Chapter Contents

In this chapter we present some more features of the Ada language, including a mechanism that allows Ada programs to choose between alternative actions. We develop two more sample programs, from the problem formulation stage to an Ada program. In the process we illustrate some new problem solving techniques. We also present some key programming techniques, including techniques for testing programs and correcting programming errors. Since programming style is of more than just aesthetic importance, this chapter both opens and closes with remarks on style. The first topic is an Ada construct that is used to make programs more readable and easier to modify.

Naming Literals

There are two problems with literals in a computer program. The first is that they carry no mnemonic value. For example, when the number **10** is encountered in a program, the number gives no hint of its significance. If the program is a banking program, it might be the number of branch offices or the number of teller windows at the main office. To understand the program, you need to know the significance of each literal. The second problem is that when a program needs to be changed, the process of changing literals tends to introduce errors. Suppose that **10** occurs twelve times in a banking program; four times it represents the number of branch offices, and eight times it represents the number of teller windows at the main office. When the bank opens a new branch and the program needs to be updated, there is a good chance that some **10**'s that should be changed to **11** will not be, or some that should not be changed to **11** will be changed. Ada provides a simple mechanism to deal with all of these problems.

constant declaration

In Ada you can assign a name to a constant and then use the name in place of the constant. This is done with a *constant declaration.* In Ada a constant declaration is very similar to a variable declaration, but with two significant additions: 1) the reserved word **constant** and 2) a required assigned value.

A constant declaration begins with an identifier, which is the constant object and thus the name to be associated with a single value. The identifier is followed by a colon, followed by the reserved word **constant**, followed by the type of the identifier, followed by the assignment operator (**:=**), and then a value. The declaration also includes sufficient blanks to separate the various pieces and is ended with a semicolon. In this case an example is clearer than the definition. The following gives the name BRANCH_COUNT to the number **10**:

```
BRANCH_COUNT : constant INTEGER := 10;
```

To declare more than one constant, simply list them all as separate declarations, like so:

```
BRANCH_COUNT : constant INTEGER := 10;
WINDOW_COUNT : constant INTEGER := 10;
INTEREST_RATE : constant FLOAT := 0.06;
ACCOUNT_CODE : constant CHARACTER := 'S';
```

Any identifier that is not a reserved word may be used as a name. Any type of constant can be named in this way.

Once a literal has been given a name by a constant declaration, the identifier naming the literal can then be used anyplace the literal is allowed, and it will have exactly the same meaning as the literal it names.

To change a named constant, you need only change the constant declaration. The meaning of all occurrences of BRANCH_COUNT can be changed from **10** to **11** by simply changing the first **10** in the above declaration.

string constants

You can also assign a name to a quoted string of characters with a constant declaration. (A quoted string of characters is called a *string literal.*) For example, the following assigns the name NAME to a long string:

```
NAME : constant STRING := "Mr. E. Z. Victim";
```

The identifier NAME can be used anyplace the string literal can be used and will have the same meaning as the constant. In particular, if the program contains this constant declaration, then the statements

```
PUT ( "Program designed exclusively for " );
PUT ( NAME );
NEW_LINE;
```

will cause the following to appear on the screen:

```
Program designed exclusively for Mr. E. Z. Victim
```

Remember that you do not enclose string constant identifiers like NAME in quotes. That will not produce the result you want.

Although unnamed numeric literals are allowed in a program, you should seldom use them. It often makes sense to use unnamed literals for well-known, easily recognizable, and unchangeable quantities, such as **100** for the number of centimeters in a meter. However, all other numeric literals should be given names with a constant declaration, and then you should use the name rather than the literal. This will make your programs easier to read and easier to change.

Comments

To make a program understandable, you should include some explanatory notes at key places in the program. Such notes are called *comments.* In Ada, and most other programming languages, there are provisions for including such comments within the text of a program.

In Ada a comment may be inserted almost anyplace, as long as it is preceded by the symbol `--`, sometimes called a double hyphen. Note, there are no spaces between the two hyphens. The compiler simply ignores anything between the double hyphen and the end of that line. Ada requires a double hyphen on each line of a comment. The only time that a double hyphen does not signify the beginning of a comment is when it appears inside a string literal.

when to comment

Each program unit of any substantial size or complexity should be explained by a comment. In particular, each program should open with a comment that explains what the program does, as in the following sample heading:

```
procedure MAIN is
--                  Accepts property assessed value,
--                  property tax rate, mortgage rate, and
--                  loan balance as input.
--                  Computes the annual after tax cost of the property.

--                  Assumes a 28% marginal income tax rate and
--                  full depreciation write-off as a business expense.
--                  Uses 30-year straight line depreciation.
```

In this book, comments usually are written on a line by themselves, with the -- in the first two columns and the comment prose beginning in column 20. This makes them stand out from the program text.

It is difficult to say just how many comments a program should contain. The only correct answer is, ''just enough,'' and this answer does not convey a lot to the novice programmer. It will take some experience to get a feel for how and when it is best to generate comments. Whenever something is important and not obvious, it merits a comment. However, too many comments are as bad as too few. A program that has a comment on each line can be so buried in comments that it hides the structure of the program and it hides the critical comments in a sea of obvious observations. Comments like the following contribute nothing to understanding and should not appear in a program:

```
DISTANCE := SPEED * TIME; --Computes the distance traveled
```

Formatted Output

field width

When using PUT for integer output, you can specify the exact number of spaces used to display each value that is output. To do so simply add a comma and a number after the expression, variable, or constant that is to be output. The number following the comma is called a *field width* and specifies the total number of spaces allocated for outputting the number or other type of value. For example,

```
NUMBER := 123;
PUT ( "Start-field" );
PUT ( NUMBER, 5 );
PUT ( "End-field" );
NEW_LINE;
```

produces the following output (there are two spaces between the d and the 1):

```
Start-field  123End-field
```

Any extra spaces are always in front of the value being output. If you allow too few spaces, it is not a disaster; the computer will allocate more space, but the format may not be what you desired.

output as a subprogram

In your first few programs, it may be best to omit field width specifications and just settle for the spacing that the system decides on. It makes sense to omit such detail on your first version of a program. First get your program to work. Then go back and add the field widths if you want neater output. This is a good example of the divide-and-conquer program design strategy. The task of designing a program can frequently be subdivided into two main subprograms: computing some quantities and displaying them in a neat and clear manner. When solving the problem of how to compute the quantities, there is no need to confuse the issue with questions about the number of spaces needed to output the quantities. That is a separate problem.

In this book we will frequently omit field width specifications from the PUT statements in our sample programs. In many cases the program presented is only a solution to the task of computing quantities. To get a program with neat-looking output, it may be necessary to add some field width specifications.

field specifications for floats

At least one case definitely demands a field width and other related output *field specifications* to avoid looking ridiculous. When the output is an amount of dollars and cents, an output without a field specification usually looks absurd, as in

```
Total cost including tax is $ 1.56347690000000E01
```

This screen display is a poor way to say the cost is $15.63. Adding the field width specification **3,2,0** converts the output into a reasonable format. The first number, **3**, says to allow a total of three spaces before the decimal point in the output. The second number, **2**, says to allow exactly two digits after the decimal point. This second number is also preceded by a comma. The third number, if it is **0**, tells the computer not to use the **E** notation. (For now don't worry about other values for the third number.) As an example, consider the following lines from an Ada program:

```
COST := 15.63;
PUT ( "Total cost including tax is $" );
PUT ( COST, 3, 2, 0 );
NEW_LINE;
```

These lines produce the following output (there is one space between the $ and the 1.):

```
Total cost including tax is $ 15.63
```

Example Using Constants and Formatted Output

The program in Figure 3.1 was designed for a new, not yet federally or state chartered, savings institution. This institution is installing an automated 24-hour teller and has a limited amount of capital to spend on hardware and software. The program in Figure 3.1 was designed to handle deposits.

Program

```
with I_O; use I_O;
procedure MAIN is
--                    Accepts deposit amounts as input and writes out the
--                    value of the deposit plus interest after one year.
    BRANCH_COUNT : constant INTEGER := 2;
    COUNT_WIDTH  : constant INTEGER := 2;
    MONEY_WIDTH  : constant INTEGER := 4;
    MOTTO        : constant STRING
                            := "We'll take your money any time.";
    NAME         : constant STRING := "FLY BY NIGHT THRIFT";
    RATE         : constant FLOAT := 7.25;
    RATE_WIDTH   : constant INTEGER := 2;
    AMOUNT       : FLOAT;
    DEPOSIT      : FLOAT;
    INTEREST     : FLOAT;
begin
    PUT ( "WELCOME TO " ); PUT ( NAME ); NEW_LINE;
    PUT ( MOTTO ); NEW_LINE;
    PUT ( "We currently pay: " ); NEW_LINE;
    PUT ( RATE, RATE_WIDTH, 2, 0 ); PUT ( "% on deposits." ); NEW_LINE;
    PUT ( "AND have" ); NEW_LINE;
    PUT ( BRANCH_COUNT, COUNT_WIDTH ); PUT ( " offices to serve YOU!" );
    NEW_LINE ( 2 );
    PUT ( "ENTER the amount of your DEPOSIT at " ); NEW_LINE;
    PUT ( "the keyboard and press the RETURN KEY." ); NEW_LINE;
    PUT ( "PLEASE, do NOT type in a $ sign." ); NEW_LINE;
    GET ( DEPOSIT ); SKIP_LINE;
    PUT ( "Next, put your money in an ENVELOPE," ); NEW_LINE;
    PUT ( "WRITE your NAME on the envelope," ); NEW_LINE;
    PUT ( "and slip it UNDER THE DOOR." ); NEW_LINE;
    PUT ( "Thank you for your deposit of:" ); NEW_LINE;
    PUT ( '$' ); PUT ( DEPOSIT, MONEY_WIDTH, 2, 0 ); NEW_LINE;
    INTEREST := RATE / 100.00 * DEPOSIT;
--                      The division by 100.00
--                      changes the percent figure to a fraction.
    AMOUNT := DEPOSIT + INTEREST;
    PUT ( "In just one short year" ); NEW_LINE;
    PUT ( "your deposit will grow to" ); NEW_LINE;
    PUT ( '$' ); PUT ( AMOUNT, MONEY_WIDTH, 2, 0 ); NEW_LINE;
    PUT ( "Thank you for choosing " ); PUT ( NAME ); PUT ( '!' );
    NEW_LINE;
end MAIN;
```

Sample Dialogue

```
WELCOME TO FLY BY NIGHT THRIFT
We'll take your money any time.
We currently pay:
 7.25% on deposits.
AND have
 2 offices to serve YOU!

ENTER the amount of your DEPOSIT at
the keyboard and press the RETURN KEY.
PLEASE, do NOT type in a $ sign.
100.00
Next, put your money in an ENVELOPE,
WRITE your NAME on the envelope,
and slip it UNDER THE DOOR.
Thank you for your deposit of:
$ 100.00
In just one short year
your deposit will grow to
$ 107.25
Thank you for choosing FLY BY NIGHT THRIFT!
```

Figure 3.1 Comments and named constants.

Since the board of directors is not sure that their current name represents sound marketing practice, the name has been placed in a constant declaration. This makes it easier to change the name if they later decide that they prefer something more dignified, such as "Nocturnal Aviators Savings and Thrift Association, Inc." The motto also is named in a constant declaration, as are almost all constants in the program. Even the field widths for formatted output are given names. For example, the fifth PUT is equivalent to

```
PUT ( RATE, 3, 2, 0 );
```

Allowable Range for Numbers

large and small

For each implementation of Ada, there is a largest allowable positive number of type INTEGER and a smallest allowable negative number of type INTEGER. The language Ada has predefined attributes called FIRST and LAST. INTEGER'LAST is a constant equal to the largest value of type INTEGER that can be used on the computer. This number will vary from one installation to another. You do not need to include it in a constant declaration. It is already defined for you.

The symbol between the word INTEGER and LAST is a single quote. The phrase is pronounced ''integer's attribute last'' (some simply say ''integer tick last,'' where *tick* is slang for *single quote*).

The smallest value of type INTEGER is INTEGER'FIRST. It is not necessarily the minus of INTEGER'LAST, but it will be close to that value. The terms FIRST and LAST represent a range of numbers from the first one in the range (the smallest value) to the last one in the range (the largest value).

Like the numbers of type INTEGER, there is a largest positive number and a smallest negative number of type FLOAT that the computer can handle. The largest allowable number of type FLOAT, FLOAT'LAST, is always much larger than the largest allowable number of type INTEGER, and the smallest allowable negative number of type FLOAT, FLOAT'FIRST, is always much smaller than the smallest negative number of type INTEGER.

It is easy to discover these limits. To discover the smallest and largest possible integer and float values for your machine, simply compile and run the following program:

```
with I_O; use I_O;
procedure MAIN is
begin
    PUT ( "Largest Integer = " ); PUT ( INTEGER'LAST ); NEW_LINE;
    PUT ( "Smallest Integer = " ); PUT ( INTEGER'FIRST ); NEW_LINE;
    PUT ( "Largest Float = " ); PUT ( FLOAT'LAST ); NEW_LINE;
    PUT ( "Smallest Float = " ); PUT ( FLOAT'FIRST ); NEW_LINE;
end MAIN;
```

When the above program was run on the authors' PC (Personal Computer) the following results appeared on the screen.

```
Largest Integer = 32767
Smallest Integer = -32768
Largest Float = 3.40282E+38
Smallest Float = -3.40282E+38
```

More about Commenting

One way to comment a program is to insert comment statements saying what the programmer expects to be true when the program execution reaches that statement. Such comments are often called *assertions* because they *assert* something that you hope is true. For example, Figure 3.2 shows the change-making program from Figure 2.10 with comment assertions added.

```
with I_O; use I_O;
procedure MAIN is
--                Input  : The amount of change.
--                Output : The coins used.
--                Description : Determines the exact number of coins used
--                              to give an amount between 1 and 99
--                              cents.
    AMOUNT,
    AMOUNT_LEFT,
    DIMES,
    PENNIES,
    QUARTERS : INTEGER;
begin
    PUT ( "Enter an amount of change" ); NEW_LINE;
    PUT ( "from 1 to 99 cents" ); NEW_LINE;
    GET ( AMOUNT ); SKIP_LINE;
    AMOUNT_LEFT := AMOUNT;
    QUARTERS := AMOUNT_LEFT / 25;
--                quarters is the maximum number of quarters in
--                amount_left.
   AMOUNT_LEFT := AMOUNT_LEFT rem 25;
--                amount_left has been decreased by the value of the
--                number of quarters specified by the variable
--                quarters.
   DIMES := AMOUNT_LEFT / 10;
--                dimes is the maximum number of dimes in amount_left.
   AMOUNT_LEFT := AMOUNT_LEFT rem 10;
--                amount_left has been decreased by the value of
--                the number of dimes specified by the variable dimes.
   PENNIES := AMOUNT_LEFT;
   PUT ( AMOUNT ); PUT ( " cents can be given as:" ); NEW_LINE;
   PUT ( QUARTERS ); PUT ( " quarters" ); NEW_LINE;
   PUT ( DIMES ); PUT ( " dimes and" ); NEW_LINE;
   PUT ( PENNIES ); PUT ( " pennies" ); NEW_LINE;
end MAIN;
```

Figure 3.2 Program with simple comment assertions.

As we proceed with our study of programming techniques, we will introduce some powerful and more sophisticated ways of using assertions.

Testing and Debugging

A mistake in a program is usually called a *bug,* and the process of eliminating bugs is called *debugging.* In this section we will describe the three main kinds of programming mistakes and give some hints on how to correct them.

syntax errors

The compiler will catch certain kinds of mistakes and will write out an error message when it does find a mistake. The compiler will detect what are called *syntax errors.* The *syntax* of a language consists of the grammar and punctuation rules for the language. These rules determine whether or not your program follows the rules for the form of an Ada program. If your program violates some syntax rule, such as omitting a semicolon or failing to declare a variable, the compiler will issue an error statement.

interpreting error messages

If the compiler discovers that your program contains a syntax error, it will tell you where the error probably is and what kind of error it is likely to be. If the compiler says your program contains a syntax error, you can be confident that it does. However, the compiler may be incorrect about either the location or the nature of the error. It does a better job of determining the location of an error, to within a line or two, than it does of determining the source of the error. As a general rule, the compiler is likely to be right about the location of the first syntax error in your program, but it may not know what the nature of the error is. The reason for this is the compiler must guess at what you meant to write down and can easily guess wrong. After all, it cannot read your mind.

Error messages after the first one are more likely to be incorrect with respect to either the location or the nature of the error. Again, this is because the compiler must guess your meaning. If the compiler's first guess was incorrect, this affects its analysis of any future mistake, since the analysis is based on a false assumption.

Programs tend to contain numerous matching pairs, such as quotes, parentheses, and other delimiters to be discussed later. A common syntax error is to miss one end of some matching pair. The compiler always detects such an omission, but the error message may be a little confusing.

As an illustration, consider the following PUT statements:

```
PUT ( "Answer is ); PUT ( X 2 ); PUT ( " in miles." );
```

The first PUT statement has a double quote missing in the string literal, yet the compiler will not find a mistake until it reaches the string literal in the third PUT statement. The error message will probably say the error is in the neighborhood of the word **in** and may or may not mention a missing quote. The reason for this is that the compiler perceives the string literal

```
"Answer is ); PUT ( X 2 ); PUT ( "
```

as the first item to be written out. After all, it is a perfectly legitimate string literal. If you realize that the mistake is in the string in the first PUT and you add the quote, you will get:

```
PUT ( "Answer is "); PUT ( X 2 ); PUT ( " in miles." );
```

This will, of course, still produce a compiler error message pointing out the missing comma between the **X** and the 2. In many cases, of which this is just one example, one mistake can hide another. In this case the missing quote caused the compiler to ignore the missing comma.

Sooner or later you will find yourself in a situation in which you are absolutely certain your program is correct, yet the compiler will not accept it and insists that there is a mistake in a particular line. The natural assumption is that there is a mistake in the compiler and that your program is correct. Occasionally there are mistakes in compilers, but they are rare, and it is extremely unlikely that the fault is in the compiler. Frequently it is a mistake that you cannot see for either physical or psychological reasons. You may have typed the alphabetic letter `'O'` when you meant to type the digit zero. There may be a real and visible mistake that you unconsciously correct in your mind, and so you always miss the mistake. When you cannot find anything wrong with the line, try retyping it. Amazingly enough, this will sometimes cure the problem.

run-time errors

There are certain kinds of errors that the computer system can detect only when a program is run. Appropriately enough these are called *run-time errors.* Ada programs detect run-time errors and output an appropriate error message in the form of "Exception not handled". In Ada an *exception* is an exception to the normal operation, and it must be taken care of, or *handled.* The distinction between syntax errors and run-time errors is illustrated in Figure 3.3.

numeric_error

Many typical run-time errors have to do with numeric calculations. If an integer expression tries to evaluate to some value greater than `INTEGER'LAST`, the system should detect this fact when the program is run and output an error message stating that the exception was a `NUMERIC_ERROR`. A similar message is output when `FLOAT` valued expressions get too large or too small. The system also provides a run-time error message if the program attempts to divide by zero. Other run-time errors have to do with features of Ada that we have not yet introduced. These errors will be discussed as the relevant Ada features are introduced.

logical errors

If the compiler approved of your program and the program ran once with no run-time error messages, this does not guarantee that it is correct. Remember, the compiler only tells you if you wrote a syntactically correct Ada program. It does not tell you whether the program does what you want it to do. Mistakes in the underlying algorithm or in translating the algorithm into Ada are called *logical errors.* If the compiler approves of your program and there are no run-time errors, but the program does not perform properly, then undoubtedly your program contains a logical error. Logical errors are the hardest kind to diagnose because the computer gives you no error messages to help find the error. It cannot reasonably be expected to give any error messages. For all the computer knows, you may have meant what you wrote. As an example of a simple logical error, suppose that when we wrote the change making program in Figure 3.2, we were confused about the distinction between `/` and **rem**, so we mistakenly wrote

```
AMOUNT_LEFT := AMOUNT_LEFT / 25;
```

instead of

```
AMOUNT_LEFT := AMOUNT_LEFT rem 25;
```

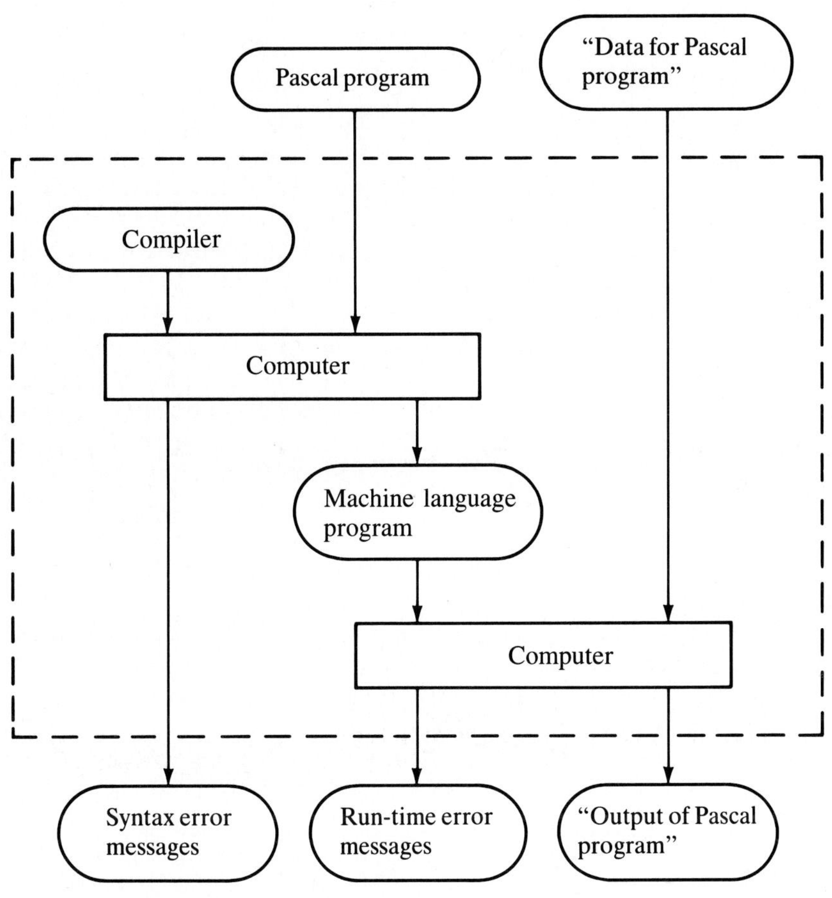

Figure 3.3 Syntax and run-time errors.

There would be no way for the computer to tell we made a mistake. As far as the computer is concerned we did not make a mistake; we wrote a completely legitimate program. Unfortunately, it was not exactly the program we wanted. If you insert this logical error into the program in Figure 3.2, it will compile and run without precipitating an error message. It will give output in the desired format. However, it usually will give an incorrect output for the numbers of dimes and pennies. This would be an example of a logical error. There are no syntax errors and no run-time errors, but the program is incorrect nonetheless.

Other logical errors are more complicated. As another example using the same change making example, suppose we forgot to decrease the amount left as we gave out coins. In other words, suppose we calculated quarters, dimes, and pennies in the following incorrect way.

```
QUARTERS := AMOUNT / 25;
DIMES := AMOUNT / 10;
PENNIES := AMOUNT / 1;
```

This also would be a logical error. The program would still run, but it would give incorrect output.

These sample errors may seem ridiculously naive. It may seem that they are unlikely to occur and, moreover, that they would be easy to find if you did make one of them. This is not so at all. Remember, all errors are obvious once they are discovered. But at the time that you make an error it is always an undiscovered, hidden error. Otherwise, why would you make it?

make a listing

A *listing* of a program is a copy of the program written on paper and is produced by a printer. When debugging a program, it may help to have a listing of the program. This allows you to have a view of the entire program and also makes it easy to write notes on the program.

testing

To test a new program for logical errors, you should run the program on several sets of representative data and check the program's performance on those inputs. If the program passes those tests, you can have more confidence in it, but this is still not an absolute guarantee that the program is correct. It still may not do what you want it to do when it is run on other data.

The only way to justify confidence in a program is to program carefully and so avoid most errors. This approach is far better than trying to fix a program that is riddled with errors. The errors may go undetected, and even if you do detect the presence of an error, it may not be easy to locate its source.

Tracing

Sometimes simply looking at the output of a program does not give enough information to locate a logical or other type of error. If the program gives incorrect output, you know it is wrong, but you may not know where the mistake is. One way to find out more about a program is to write out values of variables as they change. For example, again consider the program in Figure 3.2 The value of the variable AMOUNT_LEFT is never written out. Yet if we had mistakenly written / instead of **rem** in the following statement

```
AMOUNT_LEFT := AMOUNT_LEFT rem 25;
```

then the quickest way to notice the error is to notice how the value of AMOUNT_LEFT changes. To help locate mistakes such as this when testing the program, it is a good idea to insert some temporary output statements for variables that are changed but otherwise are not output to show this change. For example, in the program in Figure 3.2, we might insert

```
PUT ( "amount_left = " ); PUT ( AMOUNT_LEFT ); NEW_LINE;
```

This step is called *tracing.*

These trace statements are temporary statements that do not appear in the final program, so we want them to be easy to find and delete. One way to accomplish this is by labeling each one with a suitable comment such as

```
--                  TEMPORARY DEBUG OUTPUT
    PUT ( "amount_left = " ); PUT ( AMOUNT_LEFT ); NEW_LINE;
```

Use of Assertions in Testing
(Optional)

If your program contains assertions, you can use them as a guide in deciding what variables to trace and where to place the PUT statements. For example, consider the following code from Figure 3.2.

```
--                  Quarters is the maximum number of quarters
--                  in amount_left cents.
    AMOUNT_LEFT := AMOUNT_LEFT rem 25;
--                  amount_left has been decreased by the value of
--                  the number of quarters specified by Quarters.
```

It suggests that the variable QUARTERS as well as both the old and the new value of AMOUNT_LEFT should be output at this point. To help you interpret the output, you also can write out the assertion. So the following would be a sensible collection of temporary output statements to insert at the location of these assertions.

```
--                  TEMPORARY DEBUG OUTPUT
    PUT ( "Quarters is the maximum number" ); NEW_LINE;
    PUT ( "of quarters in amount_left cents." ); NEW_LINE;
    PUT ( "quarter = " ); PUT ( Quarters );
    PUT ( "amount_left = ); PUT ( AMOUNT_LEFT ); NEW_LINE;
          AMOUNT_LEFT := AMOUNT_LEFT rem 25;
--                  TEMPORARY DEBUG OUTPUT
    PUT ( "amount_left has been decreased by the value of " );
    NEW_LINE;
    PUT ( "the number of quarters specified by Quarters." );
    NEW_LINE;
    PUT ( "amount_left = " ); PUT ( AMOUNT_LEFT ); NEW_LINE;
```

It is possible to place quotes around the actual assertion and then insert it in a PUT. However, if you do that, there is a high probability that you will leave one of the quotes in the program when you finish your debugging and attempt to restore the assertion to its former state. For this reason it is probably better to just repeat the assertion. Then you can delete entire lines rather than parts of lines when you clean up the final program. Since most editors make it easy to copy and edit lines, this need not be an onerous typing chore.

Exercises

Self-Test Exercises

1. What is the output produced by the following program?

```
with I_O; use I_O;
procedure MAIN is
        NUMBER : INTEGER;
begin
        NUMBER := -1234;
        PUT ( "START" );
        PUT ( NUMBER, 8 );
        PUT ( "END" );
        NEW_LINE;
end MAIN;
```

2. What is the output produced by the following program?

```
with I_O; use I_O;
procedure MAIN is
        NUMBER : FLOAT;
begin
        NUMBER := -12.3456;
        PUT ( "START" );
        PUT ( NUMBER, 5, 2, 0 );
        PUT ( "END" );
        NEW_LINE;
end MAIN;
```

Interactive Exercises

3. Write a program that outputs the smallest and largest INTEGER and FLOAT values to the screen.
4. Type in and run the program given in Figure 3.1. Change the name of the institution, its motto, and the interest rate, and then run it again.
5. Write a program that reads a value of type FLOAT and then writes it to the screen using the following PUT statements:

```
PUT ( "START" ); PUT ( R, 2, 2, 0 ); PUT ( "END" );
```

(Don't forget the NEW_LINE.) Run the program several times trying different numbers. Try some negative as well as positive numbers. Try a number that does not fit into the format specified, such as **1234.56**.

Syntax Diagrams

syntax

The rules of grammar for a programming language are called the *syntax* rules of the language. The syntax rules determine whether or not a string of characters forms a program that the compiler can translate into machine code. There is a standard diagrammatic way to represent the syntax of programming languages. These diagrams are called, appropriately enough, *syntax diagrams.* Figure 3.4 contains simplified syntax diagrams for many of the Ada constructs we have presented so far.

using syntax diagrams

The procedure for using syntax diagrams is quite intuitive. Each diagram is labeled to indicate what it describes. To test whether a string of symbols (what we call the *candidate string*) satisfies the description, start at the inward-pointing arrow on the left end of the diagram, and at the same time place a marker at the beginning of the questionable string you wish to test; a mental marker usually works, but you can use a real marker such as your finger or a pencil point. Every time you encounter something in italics (*something*) or in bold face (**another thing**) in the syntax diagram, check that your marker is at an object of the form described, and then move your pointer to the next element in the string. Objects in **bold face** are meant literally. For example, the **constant** can only match the word with the letters **c**-**o**-**n**-**s**-**t**-**a**-**n**-**t**. Objects enclosed in angle brackets correspond to defined objects. For example, any Ada identifier matches the italicized *identifier.* If in this way you can get completely through the syntax diagram and completely through the candidate string, then the candidate string satisfies the syntax diagram. For example, if the diagram is labeled *constant_declarations,* the string satisfies the description of a constant declaration.

Since the diagrams can have branches, there is usually more than one path through a syntax diagram. A candidate string satisfies the diagram provided it matches one such path. To check the candidate, you must find the path. It is somewhat like a maze puzzle. If there is some way through the diagram, then the string passes the test. However, the diagram does not tell you how to find a path through the maze of the syntax diagram.

Syntax diagrams do not tell you about spacing, but it is intended that the objects be separated in some appropriate way, usually by one or more blanks. Syntax diagrams give an almost but not quite complete description of the programming language syntax. Anything that fails the syntax diagram check definitely is not a correctly formed object of the kind described by the syntax diagram. A candidate that passes the syntax diagram test usually must also pass some other simple tests, such as having blanks in the right places.

We will include syntax diagrams as we develop the Ada language. A complete set of syntax diagrams can be found in Appendix B, but the simpler ones in the chapters will probably prove more useful.

object__declarations

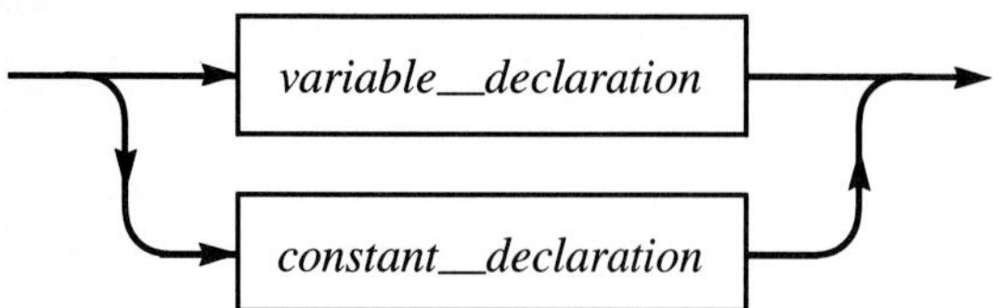

variable declaration

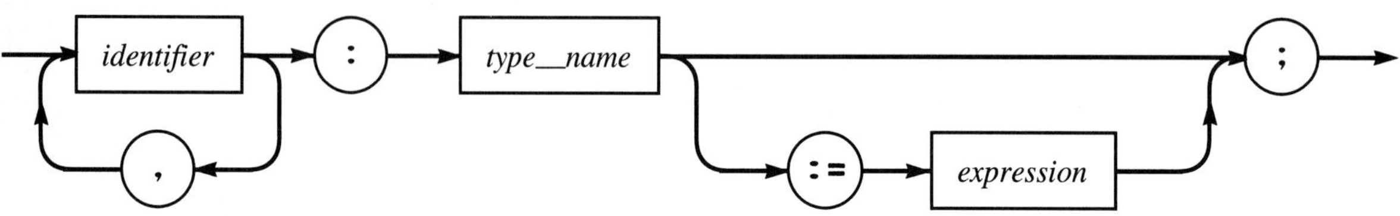

constant__declaration

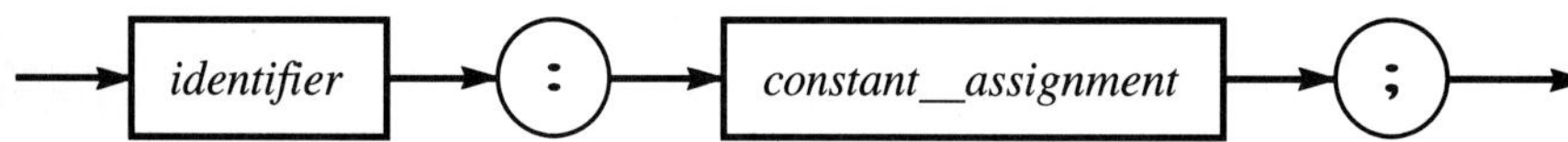

constant__assignment

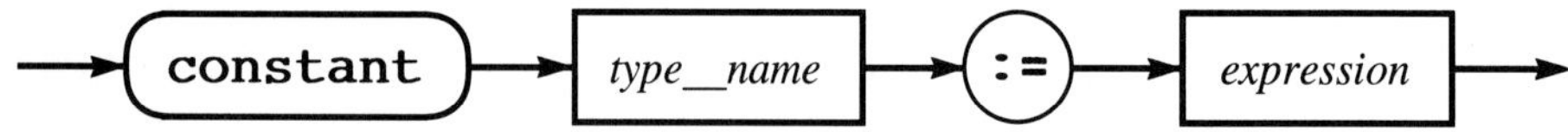

sequence of statements

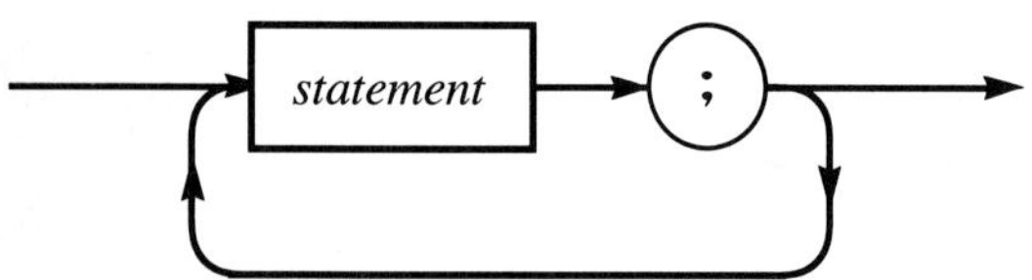

statement

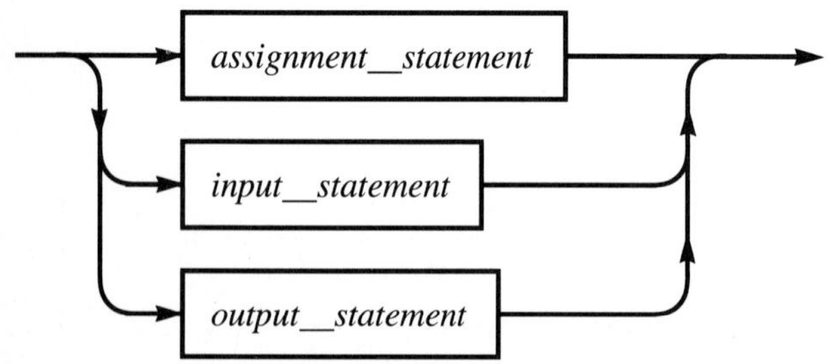

assignment__statement

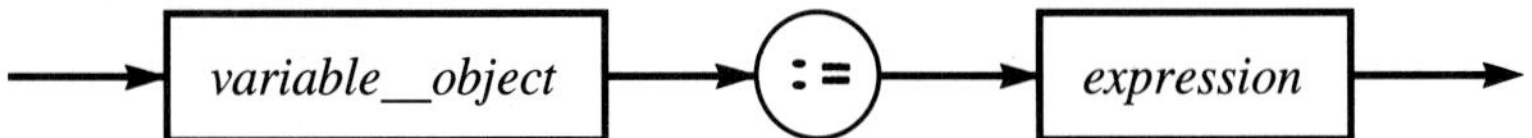

input__statement

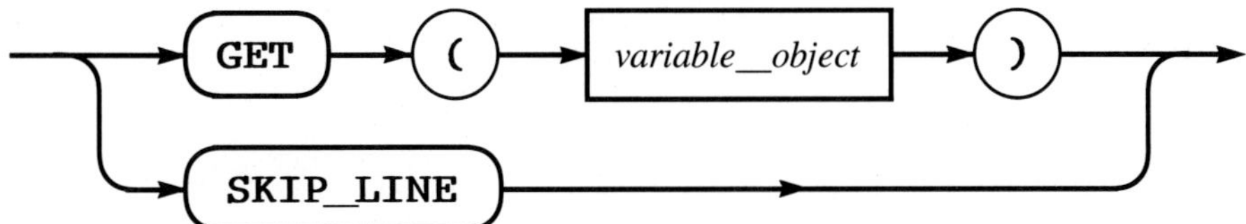

output__statement

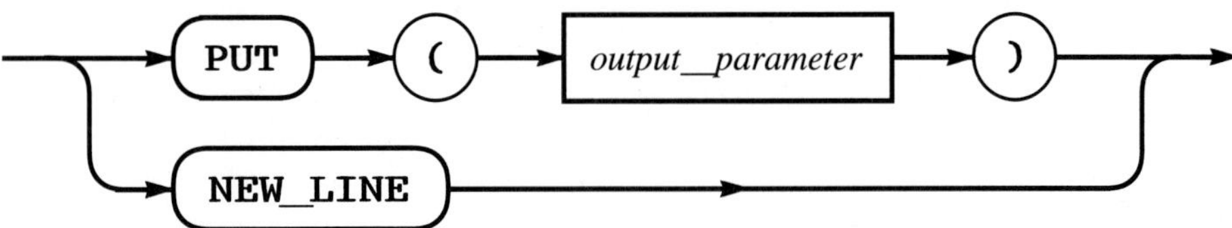

output__parameter

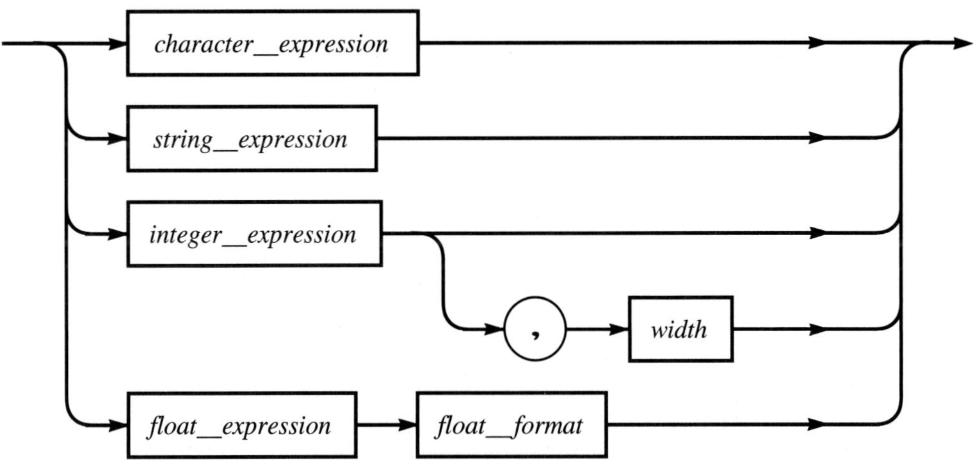

float__format

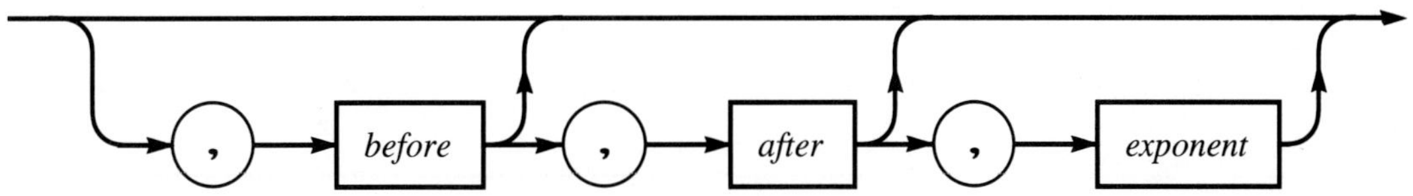

width, before, after, exponent

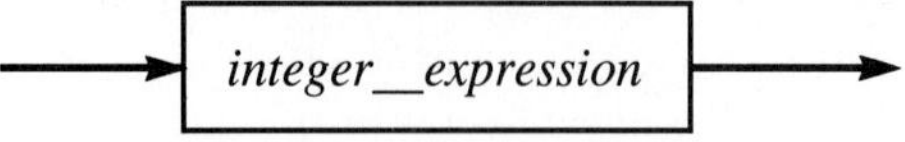

Figure 3.4 Some syntax diagrams (does not show all possibilities).

Simple Branching—If-Then-Else

Sometimes it is necessary to have a program action that chooses one of two alternatives depending on the input to the program. For example, suppose you want to design a program to compute a week's salary for an hourly employee. Assume the firm pays an overtime rate of 1½ times the regular rate for all hours after the first 40 hours worked. As long as the employee works 40 or more hours, pay can be determined by the following pseudocode expression:

```
PAY_RATE * 40 + 1.5 * PAY_RATE * ( HOURS_WORKED - 40 )
```

If, however, there is a possibility that the employee will work less than 40 hours, this formula will unfairly pay a negative amount of overtime. The correct pay formula for an employee who works less than 40 hours is simple:

```
PAY_RATE * HOUR_WORKED
```

If both more than and less than 40 hours of work are possible, then the program will need to choose between the two formulas. To compute the employee's gross (before deductions) pay, the program action should be

Decide whether or not `HOURS_WORKED > 40`.
If it is, do the following pseudocode statement:

```
GROSS_PAY := PAY_RATE * 40 + 1.5 * PAY_RATE * (HOURS_WORKED - 40)
```

Otherwise (i.e., if `HOURS <= 40`), do the following:

```
GROSS_PAY := PAY_RATE * HOUR_WORKED
```

There is an Ada statement that does exactly this kind of branching action. The *if-then-else* statement chooses between two alternative actions. For example, the desired program action can be accomplished using the following pseudocode statement:

```
if HOURS_WORKED > 40 then
    GROSS_PAY := PAY_RATE * 40 + 1.5 * PAY_RATE * (HOURS_WORKED - 40);
else
    GROSS_PAY := PAY_RATE * HOURS_WORKED;
end if;
```

A complete program that uses this statement is given in Figure 3.5. In the program we have given names to the numbers `40` and `1.5`. If the computation had been more complicated, it would have been a good idea to use named constants even in the pseudocode.

Program

```
with I_O; use I_O;
procedure MAIN is
--                    Input : Hourly pay rate
--                    Output : Weekly pay
--                    Description : Computes the weekly pay
--                                  for an hourly employee
    MAXIMUM_REGULAR_TIME : constant INTEGER := 40;
    OVERTIME_FACTOR      : constant FLOAT   := 1.5;
--                    Factor used in computing overtime pay rate
    GROSS_PAY    : FLOAT;
    HOURS_WORKED : INTEGER;
    HOURLY_RATE  : FLOAT;
begin
    PUT ( "Enter the hourly rate of pay." ); NEW_LINE;
    GET ( HOURLY_RATE ); SKIP_LINE;
    PUT ( "Enter the number of hours worked," ); NEW_LINE;
    PUT ( "rounded up to a whole number of hours." ); NEW_LINE;
    GET ( HOURS_WORKED ); SKIP_LINE;
    if HOURS_WORKED > MAXIMUM_REGULAR_TIME then
        GROSS_PAY := HOURLY_RATE * FLOAT ( MAXIMUM_REGULAR_TIME )
                   + OVERTIME_FACTOR * HOURLY_RATE
                   * FLOAT ( HOURS_WORKED - MAXIMUM_REGULAR_TIME );
    else
        GROSS_PAY := HOURLY_RATE * FLOAT ( HOURS_WORKED );
    end if;
    PUT ( "Hours worked = " ); PUT ( HOURS_WORKED, 2 ); NEW_LINE;
    PUT ( "Hourly pay rate = $" ); PUT ( HOURLY_RATE, 2, 2, 0 );
    NEW_LINE;
    PUT ( "Gross pay = $" ); PUT ( GROSS_PAY, 2, 2, 0 ); NEW_LINE;
end MAIN;
```

Sample Dialogue 1

```
Enter the hourly rate of pay.
20.00
Enter the number of hours worked,
rounded up to a whole number of hours.
30
Hours worked = 30
Hourly pay rate = $20.00
Gross pay = $600.00
```

Sample Dialogue 2

```
Enter the hourly rate of pay.
10.00
Enter the number of hours worked,
rounded up to a whole number of hours.
41
Hours worked = 41
Hourly pay rate = $10.00
Gross pay = $415.00
```

Figure 3.5 An if-then-else branch.

The form of an *if-then-else* statement is as follows:

if *expression comparison__operator another__expression* **then**
  *first__sequence__*of*__Ada__statements*
else
  *second sequence__*of*__Ada statements*
end if;

The phrase *sequence__of__Ada__statements* implies that there may be one or more Ada statements. When the program reaches the *if-then-else,* exactly one set of the two embedded sequences of statements is executed. The two expressions are evaluated and compared. If the comparison turns out to be true, then the first sequence of statements is performed. If the comparison fails, then the second sequence of statements is executed. Every *if-then-else* statement is terminated with an **end if.** The **end** and **if** are two separate reserved words separated by one or more blanks. All statements in Ada are terminated with a semicolon.

relational operators

Any two arithmetic expressions may be compared using the comparison operators: *greater-than, less-than, greater-than-or-equal, less-than-or-equal, equal,* and *not equal.* A list of these *relational operators* is given in Figure 3.6. Some of the operators have unusual spellings as two symbols, because most keyboards do not have symbols such as ≤ and ≠. For example, the Ada expression to use in place of ≠ is the symbol pair /=. These symbol pairs are considered to be single items, so you may not insert any spaces between the two symbols.

Math	Ada	English	Ada Sample	Math Equivalent
=	=	equals	`ans = 'N'`	ans = 'N'
≠	/=	not equals	`x /= y`	$x \neq y$
<	<	less than	`x < 2`	$x < 2$
≤	<=	less than or equal	`x <= 1`	$x \leq 1$
>	>	greater	`y > 0`	$y > 0$
≥	>=	greater than or equal	`y >= 1`	$y \geq 1$

Figure 3.6 List of relational operators.

These comparisons are a special case of a more general class of expressions called *boolean expressions*. We will discuss the general case in Chapter 6. For now we will use only arithmetic expressions and operators of the forms just described, plus some simple comparisons of character values.

You can use an *if-then-else* statement to compare two character values to see whether they are equal or unequal. For example, suppose that ANSWER is a variable of type CHARACTER and the program is about to execute the following *if-then-else* statement:

```
if ANSWER = 'Y' then
    PUT ( "I guess you said Yes." );
else
    PUT ( "You did not say Yes." );
end if;
```

If the value of ANSWER is 'Y', then the first PUT will be executed. If its value is anything other than 'Y', then the second PUT statement will be executed.

ordering of characters

When relational operators such as < and <= are applied to items of type CHARACTER, they check for alphabetic order. Hence, 'A' < 'B' is true and 'z' < 'h' is false. It may not be obvious how relational operators treat the interaction of uppercase and lowercase letters. In Ada, the values of all uppercase letters are less than the values of lowercase letters; hence 'Z' < 'a' evaluates to true.

Pitfall

Equality Operator

Upper- and lowercase letters are considered to be different character values. This can sometimes lead to bewildering results when comparing characters. For example, the comparison `ANSWER = 'Y'` fails if the value of `ANSWER` is `'y'`. In Chapter 6 we will discuss good ways to avoid this problem. For now you will simply have to keep this problem in mind and program around it.

The approximate nature of `FLOAT` values can cause special problems when used in some comparisons involving equality. Since values of type `FLOAT` are approximate quantities, it makes no sense to test then for *exact* equality. In particular, values of type `FLOAT` should never be used with the equality operator, since the comparison is, for all practical purposes, meaningless. This rule applies to exact inequality as well. Testing `FLOAT` values using the inequality operator `/=` is equally meaningless and equally dangerous.

Optional Else

It is sometimes the case that we want one of the two alternatives in an *if-then-else* branch to do nothing at all. In Ada this can be accomplished by omitting the *else* and its accompanying sequence of statements. For example, if the value of `SALES` is less than or equal to `MINIMUM` when the following statement is executed, then that statement causes nothing to happen. In that case the program would do nothing and then proceed to the output statements.

```
if SALES > MINIMUM then
    SALARY := SALARY + BONUS;
end if;
PUT ( "Salary = " );
PUT ( SALARY );
NEW_LINE;
```

A program using *if-then* without the `else` part is shown in Figure 3.7. Figure 3.8 gives a syntax diagram that shows the syntax for both varieties of `if` statements.

Program

```
with I_O; use I_O;
procedure MAIN is
    AGE : INTEGER;
```

```
begin
    PUT ( "Please enter your age." ); NEW_LINE;
    GET ( AGE ); SKIP_LINE;
    if AGE >= 18 then
        PUT ( "You are old enough to join the army." ); NEW_LINE;
    end if;
    if AGE >= 21 then
        PUT ( "You are old enough to drink."); NEW_LINE;
    end if;
    PUT ( "Good luck!" ); NEW_LINE;
end MAIN;
```

Sample Dialogue

```
Please enter your age.
19
You are old enough to join the army.
Good luck!
```

Figure 3.7 Program with if-then statements.

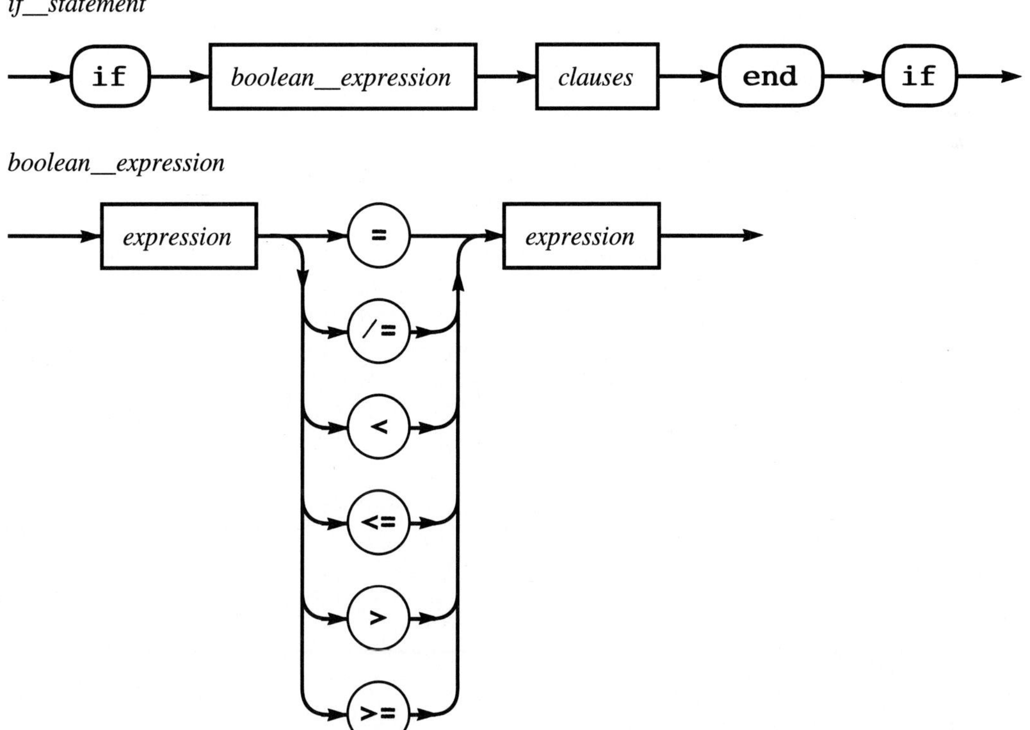

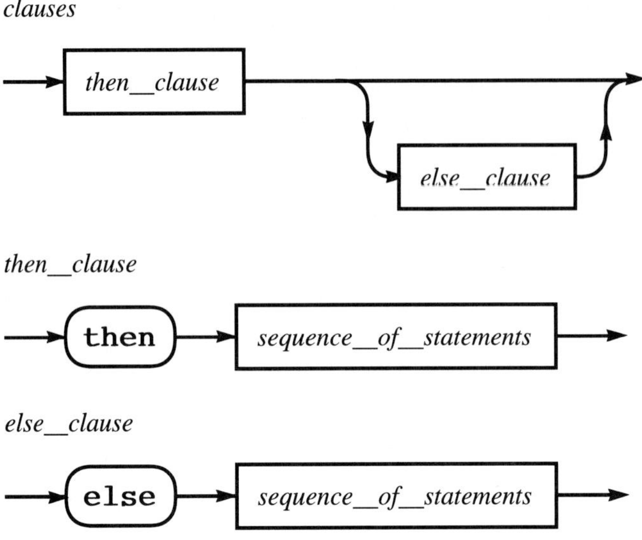

Figure 3.8 Syntax of the `if` statement.

Iterative Enhancement

One way to design a program is to simplify the design goals so as to make the programming task easier and to then design the simpler version of the program. After that, features can be added. For example, the program for making change that we designed in Chapter 2 and reproduced in Figure 3.2 worked acceptably in a variety of situations. However, we can enhance its performance by adding additional denominations of coins, such as nickels and half-dollar coins, to use in giving change.

This process of first designing a simple program and then adding features and refinements is sometimes referred to as *iterative enhancement.* Using this technique to develop a program makes each stage relatively easy to design, yet the final program is long, complicated, and powerful. It is not the same technique as top-down design, but it is another way to divide a large programming problem into smaller, more manageable size subproblems. There is another very important advantage to this approach: At each stage of the process, you have a complete working program that does something meaningful and useful. This is a great psychological boost. Moreover, if you fail to achieve the final programming goal by some deadline, you will at least have a working program and not just a collection of disconnected pieces of code.

Case Study

Payroll Calculation

Problem Definition

We wish to design a program to compute the weekly pay for an hourly employee. The program will take the number of hours worked and the hourly pay rate as input and will output the gross pay as well as the net pay after deducting for taxes. To make the problem clear, we need to specify some additional details, namely, how the overtime and tax is computed. For this problem, overtime will be computed as 1½ times the usual rate and will apply to all hours after the first 40 hours worked. The tax will be 10% of all income over $200.

Discussion

This problem lends itself to the iterative enhancement technique described in the previous section, and we will apply it here. We will first design the program to compute the gross pay. We will then enhance it to obtain a version that also computes tax and net pay, and finally we will produce a version with formatted output. We have already produced the first version of our program that computes gross pay. It is the program in Figure 3.5.

enhancements

Once we have a working program to compute gross pay, we can enhance it by adding code to compute the tax and net pay. The algorithms for computing tax and net pay follow directly from the problem definition.

Algorithm

```
if GROSS_PAY > $200 then
    TAX := 10% of ( GROSS_PAY - $200 );
else
    TAX := 0;
end if;
NET_PAY := GROSS_PAY - TAX;
```

Adding this computation to the program produces the version in Figure 3.9. The final enhancement is obtained once that program is fully debugged and working by improving the output as shown in Figure 3.10.

Program

```
with I_O; use I_O;
procedure MAIN is
--                    INPUT  : Hourly pay rate
--                    OUTPUT : Weekly pay
--                    DESCRIPTION : Computes the weekly pay
--                                  for an hourly employee
    EXEMPTION               : constant FLOAT   := 200.00;
--                    $200.0 free of tax
    MAXIMUM_REGULAR_TIME : constant INTEGER := 40;
--                    Maximum number of hours at the regular rate
    OVERTIME_FACTOR         : constant FLOAT   := 1.5;
--                    Factor used in computing overtime pay rate
    TAX_RATE                : constant FLOAT   := 0.10;
--                    10% tax bracket
    GROSS_PAY    : FLOAT;
    HOURLY_RATE  : FLOAT;
    HOURS_WORKED : INTEGER;
    NET_PAY      : FLOAT;
    TAX          : FLOAT;
begin
    PUT ( "Enter the hourly rate of pay." ); NEW_LINE;
    GET ( HOURLY_RATE ); SKIP_LINE;
    PUT ( "Enter the number of hours worked," ); NEW_LINE;
    PUT ( "rounded up to a whole number of hours." ); NEW_LINE;
    GET ( HOURS_WORKED ); SKIP_LINE;
    if HOURS_WORKED > MAXIMUM_REGULAR_TIME then
        GROSS_PAY := HOURLY_RATE * FLOAT ( MAXIMUM_REGULAR_TIME )
                     + OVERTIME_FACTOR * HOURLY_RATE
                     * FLOAT ( HOURS_WORKED - MAXIMUM_REGULAR_TIME );
    else
        GROSS_PAY := HOURLY_RATE * FLOAT ( HOURS_WORKED );
    end if;
    if GROSS_PAY > EXEMPTION then
        TAX := TAX_RATE * ( GROSS_PAY - EXEMPTION );
    else
        TAX := 0.0;
    end if;
    NET_PAY := GROSS_PAY - TAX;
    PUT ( "Hours worked = " ); PUT ( HOURS_WORKED ); NEW_LINE;
    PUT ( "Hourly pay rate = $" ); PUT ( HOURLY_RATE ); NEW_LINE;
    PUT ( "Gross pay = $" ); PUT ( GROSS_PAY ); NEW_LINE;
    PUT ( "Tax = $" ); PUT ( TAX );
    PUT ( "Net pay = $" ); PUT ( NET_PAY ); NEW_LINE;
end MAIN;
```

Sample Dialogue

```
Enter the hourly rate of pay.
20.00
Enter the number of hours worked,
rounded up to a whole number of hours.
30
Hours worked = 30
Hourly pay rate = $ 2.00000000000000E+01
Gross pay = $ 6.00000000000000E+02
Tax = $ 4.00000000000000E+01 Net pay = $ 5.60000000000000E+02
```

Figure 3.9 Enhanced version of program in Figure 3.5.

Program

```
with I_O; use I_O;
procedure MAIN is
--                          INPUT : Hourly pay rate
--                          OUTPUT : Weekly pay
--                          DESCRIPTION : Computes the weekly pay
--                                        for an hourly employee
    CENTS_WIDTH                 : constant INTEGER := 2;
    DIGITS_BEFORE_DECIMAL : constant INTEGER := 4;
    EXPONENT_WIDTH              : constant INTEGER := 0;
--                          Used to format the money amounts
    EXEMPTION                   : constant FLOAT := 200.00; -- free of tax
    MAXIMUM_REGULAR_TIME        : constant INTEGER := 40;
--                          Maximum number of hours at the regular rate
    OVERTIME_FACTOR             : constant FLOAT := 1.5;
--                          Factor used in computing overtime pay rate
    TAX_RATE            : constant FLOAT := 0.10; -- 10% tax bracket
    GROSS_PAY           : FLOAT;
    HOURLY_RATE         : FLOAT;
    HOURS_WORKED        : INTEGER;
    NET_PAY             : FLOAT;
    TAX                 : FLOAT;
begin
    PUT ( "This program computes" ); NEW_LINE;
    PUT ( "the weekly pay for an hourly employee." ); NEW_LINE;
    PUT ( "All hours after the first " );
    PUT ( MAXIMUM_REGULAR_TIME, 2 ); NEW_LINE;
    PUT ( " are paid at a rate of" ); NEW_LINE;
    PUT ( OVERTIME_FACTOR, 1, 2, 0 );
```

```
    PUT ( " times the basic rate." ); NEW_LINE;
    PUT ( "Enter the hourly rate of pay." ); NEW_LINE;
    GET ( HOURLY_RATE ); SKIP_LINE;
    PUT ( "Enter the number of hours worked," ); NEW_LINE;
    PUT ( "rounded up to a whole number of hours." ); NEW_LINE;
    GET ( HOURS_WORKED ); SKIP_LINE;
    if HOURS_WORKED > MAXIMUM_REGULAR_TIME then
        GROSS_PAY := HOURLY_RATE * FLOAT ( MAXIMUM_REGULAR_TIME )
                   + OVERTIME_FACTOR * HOURLY_RATE
                   * FLOAT ( HOURS_WORKED - MAXIMUM_REGULAR_TIME );
    else
        GROSS_PAY := HOURLY_RATE * FLOAT ( HOURS_WORKED );
    end if;
    if GROSS_PAY > EXEMPTION then
        TAX := TAX_RATE * ( GROSS_PAY - EXEMPTION );
    else
        TAX := 0.0;
    end if;
    NET_PAY := GROSS_PAY - TAX;
    PUT ( "Hours worked = " ); PUT ( HOURS_WORKED, 2 ); NEW_LINE;
    PUT ( "Hourly pay rate = $" );
    PUT ( HOURLY_RATE,
          DIGITS_BEFORE_DECIMAL,
          CENTS_WIDTH,
          EXPONENT_WIDTH );
    NEW_LINE;
    PUT ( "Gross pay = $" );
    PUT ( GROSS_PAY,
          DIGITS_BEFORE_DECIMAL,
          CENTS_WIDTH,
          EXPONENT_WIDTH );
    NEW_LINE;
    PUT ( "Tax = $" );
    PUT ( TAX,
          DIGITS_BEFORE_DECIMAL,
          CENTS_WIDTH,
          EXPONENT_WIDTH );
    PUT ( " Net pay = $" );
    PUT ( NET_PAY, DIGITS_BEFORE_DECIMAL, CENTS_WIDTH, EXPONENT_WIDTH );
    NEW_LINE;
end MAIN;
```

Sample Dialogue

```
This program computes
the weekly pay for an hourly employee.
All hours after the first 40
  are paid at a rate of
1.50 times the basic rate.
Enter the hourly rate of pay.
20.00
Enter the number of hours worked,
rounded up to a whole number of hours.
30
Hours worked = 30
Hourly pay rate = $ 20.00
Gross pay = $ 600.00
Tax = $ 40.00 Net pay = $ 560.00
```

Figure 3.10 Further enhanced version of program in Figure 3.9.

Simple Looping Statements

Most programs include some action that is repeated a number of times. For example, the program in Figure 3.10 computes the weekly pay for a single worker. If there are 10 workers employed by the company, then a more complete payroll program would repeat this calculation 10 times. A portion of a program that repeats a statement or group of statements is called a *loop*. Ada has a number of ways to create and control loops; all of these constructions are, however, based on a *simple loop statement*. We will first illustrate its use with a short toy example and then do a more realistic example.

Suppose you want your program to execute the following statements three times:

```
PUT ( " Hello " );
NEW_LINE;
```

You could, of course, repeat these output statements three times in your program, but we want an example of a loop. Hence, we will do this with a **`loop`**. Figure 3.11 contains a program with a loop statement that accomplishes our task.

Program

```
with I_O; use I_O;
procedure MAIN is
    NUMBER_COMPLETED : INTEGER := 0;
```

```
begin
    loop
        exit when NUMBER_COMPLETED = 3;
        PUT ( "Hello" );
        NEW_LINE;
        NUMBER_COMPLETED := NUMBER_COMPLETED + 1;
    end loop;
    PUT ( "End of program" );
    NEW_LINE;
end MAIN;
```

Output

```
Hello
Hello
Hello
End of program
```

Figure 3.11 Program with a loop.

body of a loop

The action that is repeated in our sample loop is the sequence of statements between the **loop** and the **end loop**.

```
exit when NUMBER_COMPLETED = 3;
PUT ( "Hello" );
NEW_LINE;
NUMBER_COMPLETED := NUMBER_COMPLETED + 1;
```

The action that is repeated in a loop is called the *body* of the loop, and so this is the body of our sample loop. The number of times that the body is repeated is controlled by the line

```
exit when NUMBER_COMPLETED = 3;
```

The meaning of the loop statement is suggested by these English words: Execute the body repeatedly; stop when the value of NUMBER_COMPLETED is equal to 3. Stated another way, the loop body is repeated until it is time to **exit**. We will give a precise definition of the loop statement syntax and action shortly. However, let us first discuss the action of our sample loop using the intuitive description suggested by the English words. That intuition is sufficient to understand our example.

In the program in Figure 3.11, the variable NUMBER_COMPLETED is initialized to 0 in the declaration. Since the value 0 is not equal to 3, we continue; the loop body is executed. The first time the loop body is executed the word Hello is written to the screen and the value of NUMBER_COMPLETED is changed to 1, the number of times the body of the loop has been executed. Hence, after executing the loop body once, the condition

```
NUMBER_COMPLETED = 3
```

is not satisfied, and so the loop body is executed again. This causes another Hello to be written out and changes the value of NUMBER_COMPLETED from 1 to 2.

Since this new number is still not equal to `3`, the loop body is executed yet one more time. This outputs a third `Hello` and changes the value of `NUMBER_COMPLETED` from `2` to `3`. After executing the loop body three times, the condition

```
NUMBER_COMPLETED = 3
```

is satisfied and the loop terminates.

The condition `NUMBER_COMPLETED = 3` in Figure 3.11 can be replaced by any other comparison and the body can be replaced by any Ada sequence of statements whatsoever. Choosing these two things correctly will produce a loop to perform any looping action that you might wish.

The syntax of the simple loop statement is as follows: *syntax*

```
loop
        sequence__of__statements
end loop;
```

The *sequence__of__statements* in the body of the loop will normally contain an exit when statement as the first statement. The part after the reserved words **exit when** is the same sort of comparison as we have been using after the **if** in an **if-then-else** statement. In our sample loop the comparison is

```
NUMBER_COMPLETED = 3
```

As we noted when we discussed the **if-then-else** statement, this kind of comparison of two expressions is a special case of a more general class of expressions called boolean expressions. In Chapter 6 we will describe other boolean expressions, all of which can be used in loop statements. Until then we will use only the simple comparisons discussed in this chapter.

The body of a loop can contain any Ada statements. The body of a loop is the part that is repeated. Every execution of the loop body is called an *iteration* of the loop. The expression, after the reserved words **exit when**, controls the number of loop iterations, that is, the number of times the body of the loop is executed.

action of a loop statement

When the loop statement with an **exit when** as its first statement is executed, the first thing that happens is that the boolean expression (i.e., the comparison) following the words **exit when** is checked. If it is satisfied, then no action is taken and the program proceeds to the next statement after the **end loop**. If the comparison turns out to be false, then the entire body of the loop is executed. At least one of the expressions being compared typically contains something that might change, such as the value of `NUMBER_COMPLETED` in our example. After the body of the loop is executed, the comparison is again checked. This process is repeated again and again until the terminating or exiting condition is satisfied. After each iteration of the loop body the comparison is again checked, and if it is not satisfied, then the entire loop body is executed again; if it is satisfied, then the loop statement ends and the program proceeds to the next statement in the program, the one following the **end loop**.

Loop Example—Charge Card Balance

Suppose you have a bank charge card with a balance owed of $50, and suppose the bank charges you 2% per month interest. How many months can you let pass without making any payments before your balance will exceed $100? One way to solve this problem is to simply read each monthly statement and count the number of months that go by until your balance reaches $100 or more. Better still, you can calculate the monthly balances with a program, rather than waiting for the statements to arrive. In this way you will obtain an answer without having to wait so long.

After one month the balance would be $50 plus 2% of $50, which happens to be a total of $51. After two months the balance will be $51 plus 2% of $51, which is $52.02. After three months the balance will be $52.02 plus 2% of $52.02, and so on. In general, each month increases the balance by 2%. A program could keep track of the balance by storing it in a variable called BALANCE. The change in the value of BALANCE for one month can be calculated as follows:

```
BALANCE := BALANCE + 0.02 * BALANCE;
```

If we repeat this action until the value of BALANCE reaches **100** and count the number of times we make this monthly change, then we will know the number of months it takes for our balance to reach 100. To do this we need another variable to count the number of times we change the balance. Let us call this new variable COUNT. What we want our program to do is given by the pseudocode in Figure 3.12.

```
    BALANCE := 50.00;
    COUNT := 0;
--                  The loop starts here.
    Do the following until the BALANCE >= 100.00, and continue to
    do it again and again until the BALANCE >= 100.00:
        BALANCE := BALANCE + 0.02 * BALANCE;
        COUNT := COUNT + 1;
--                  The loop ends here
```

Figure 3.12 Pseudocode for a loop.

The **loop** statement corresponding to the loop in Figure 3.12 is the following:

```
loop
   exit when BALANCE >= 100.00;
   BALANCE := BALANCE + 0.02 * BALANCE;
   COUNT := COUNT + 1;
end loop;
```

A complete program containing this **loop** is given in Figure 3.13.

Program

```
with I_O; use I_O;
procedure MAIN is
--          INPUT  : none
--          OUTPUT : The number of months and the dollar value.
--          DESCRIPTION : This program calculates the number of
--                        months it takes for an account balance
--                        to grow from $50 to $100, assuming a
--                        monthly interest rate of 2%.
--                        In a real program the numbers 50, 100,
--                        and 0.02 would be input.
--                        That was not done here so that the code
--                        would be very simple.
    BALANCE : FLOAT := 50.00;
    COUNT   : INTEGER := 0;
begin
    PUT ( "This program tells you how long it takes" ); NEW_LINE;
    PUT ( "to accumulate a balance of $100, starting with" ); NEW_LINE;
    PUT ( "an initial balance of $50 owed." ); NEW_LINE;
    PUT ( "The interest charge is 2% per month" );
    NEW_LINE ( 2 );
    loop -- One month's change
        exit when BALANCE >= 100.00;
        BALANCE := BALANCE + 0.02 * BALANCE;
        COUNT := COUNT + 1;
    end loop; -- One month's change
    PUT ( "After " ); PUT ( COUNT ); PUT (" months" ); NEW_LINE;
    PUT ( "Your balance due will be $" ); PUT ( BALANCE, 4, 2, 0 );
    NEW_LINE;
end MAIN;
```

Output

```
This program tells you how long it takes
to accumulate a balance of $100, starting with
an initial balance of $50 owed.
The interest charge is 2% per month

After 36 months
Your balance due will be $ 101.99
```

Figure 3.13 Charge card program.

Pitfall

Infinite Loops

A **loop** does not terminate until the condition after the words **exit when** is satisfied. This condition normally contains a variable that will change its value so the condition will eventually become true and therefore terminate the loop. However, if you make a mistake and write your program so that the condition is never satisfied, then the loop will run forever. A loop that runs forever is called an *infinite loop*. Obviously, if you forget to include an **exit when** as one of the statements in the body of a loop, you will create an infinite loop.

For example, the following will write out the positive even numbers less than 12. That is, it will output the numbers 2, 4, 6, 8, and 10, one per line, and then the loop will end.

```
NUMBER := 2; -- Initializes number
loop
      exit when NUMBER = 12;
      PUT ( NUMBER );
      NEW_LINE;
      NUMBER := NUMBER + 2;
end loop;
```

The value of NUMBER is increased by 2 on each loop iteration until it reaches the value 12. At that point the condition after the reserved words **exit when** is satisfied, and so the loop ends.

Now suppose we want to write out the odd numbers less than 12, rather than the even numbers. We might, mistakenly, think that all we need to do is change the initializing statement to

```
NUMBER := 1; -- Initialize number
```

With this mistake, the loop is an infinite loop. The value of NUMBER goes from 11 to 13. The value of NUMBER is never equal to 12, so the loop never terminates.

dangers of = and /=

This sort of problem is common when loops are terminated by checking a numeric quantity for an exact value. When dealing with numbers, it is always safer to test for passing a value. For example, the following will work fine as the **exit** statement in our **loop**:

```
exit when NUMBER >= 12;
```

With this change, NUMBER can be initialized to any positive number and the loop will still terminate.

A program that is in an infinite loop will run forever unless some external force terminates it. Since you can now write a program that contains an infinite loop, it is a good idea to learn how to force a program to terminate. The method for forcing a program to stop varies from system to system. Usually there is a special key that can be pressed to terminate a program whether or not it has reached the final `end`.

Using Known Algorithms

Before you rush off to design a program from scratch, it is a good idea to see if there is a well-known algorithm to solve the task at hand. There are clever, well-known algorithms for many tasks. Often these algorithms are the product of much research and brilliant insights. In such cases the known algorithm is likely to be better than one designed in a short time, so you should use the known algorithm and go directly to the implementation phase.

Case Study

Solving for the Square Root

Problem Definition

Many formulas require the use of the square root of a value or expression. We will design a program to solve for the square root of a floating point value. Our program will input a floating point value called the *radicand,* compute its square root, and output both the radicand and the square root.

Discussion

This is a well-known problem, and there is a standard method for computing the square root of a value. The method requires the repeated computation of the following formula until the values of `OLD_ESTIMATE` and `NEW_ESTIMATE` are very close to one another.

```
NEW_ESTIMATE := ( OLD_ESTIMATE + RADICAND / OLD_ESTIMATE ) / 2.0;
```

This iteration technique for computing the square root is called the *Newton-Raphson method.*

Algorithm

1. Input the radicand.
2. Compute a rough estimate.
3. Stop if the estimate is close.
4. Evaluate the formula.
5. Repeat steps 3 and 4.
6. Output the radicand and the root.

The final program is given in Figure 3.14. Step 2 of the algorithm calls for the computation of a rough estimate for the square root. There are any number of possibilities that could be used and still make the algorithm. In our example in Figure 3.14, we chose the rough estimate to be half of the radicand. The **exit when** checks the controlling boolean expression before the rest of the body of the loop is executed. This is true even for the very first time the **loop** might execute the body. Therefore, it is critically important that all relevant variables be initialized before the **loop** begins. We chose the ERROR value to be something small and relative to the size of the radicand. A value of **0.001** for the relative size of the ERROR ensures roughly three significant digits of accuracy in the final result.

In Figure 3.14 an additional arithmetic operator, **abs**, is introduced. **abs** is short for *absolute value* and performs that mathematical operation. **abs** ensures that the value of whatever immediately follows it is a positive value. If the value is negative, it is converted to its positive equivalent; for example, **abs** (−3) becomes 3.

Program

```
with I_O; use I_O;
procedure MAIN is
--                  INPUT   : The radicand
--                  OUTPUT  : The square root
--                  DESCRIPTION : This program computes the square root
--                                of the radicand using the
--                                Newton-Raphson iteration method.
    AFTER    : constant INTEGER := 3;
    BEFORE   : constant INTEGER := 2;
    EXPONENT : constant INTEGER := 0;
    ERROR,
    NEW_ESTIMATE,
    OLD_ESTIMATE,
    RADICAND : FLOAT;
begin
    PUT ( "Enter the value for which you wish the square root" );
    NEW_LINE;
    GET ( RADICAND ); SKIP_LINE;
    if RADICAND < 0.0 then
        PUT ( "There is no real square root for a negative number" );
```

```
  else
      OLD_ESTIMATE := RADICAND;
      NEW_ESTIMATE := RADICAND / 2.0;
      ERROR := RADICAND * 0.001;
      loop
          exit when abs ( OLD_ESTIMATE - NEW_ESTIMATE ) <= ERROR;
          OLD_ESTIMATE := NEW_ESTIMATE;
          NEW_ESTIMATE :=
                  ( OLD_ESTIMATE + RADICAND / OLD_ESTIMATE ) / 2.0;
      end loop;
      PUT ( "The square root of " );
      PUT ( RADICAND, BEFORE, AFTER, EXPONENT );
      PUT ( " is " );
      PUT ( NEW_ESTIMATE, BEFORE, AFTER, EXPONENT );
  end if;
  NEW_LINE;
end MAIN;
```

Sample Dialogue 1

```
Enter the value for which you wish the square root
385.25
The square root of 385.250 is 19.628
```

Sample Dialogue 2

```
Enter the value for which you wish the square root
-0.012
There is no real square root for a negative number
```

Sample Dialogue 3

```
Enter the value for which you wish the square root
0.012
The square root of 0.012 is 0.110
```

Figure 3.14 Square root program.

Defensive Programming

testing for the "impossible"

Notice that in the program in Figure 3.14, we tested to see if the radicand is negative, since a negative number has no real square root. However, we know that a negative number has no square root, and we "know" the program will not be used with a negative number. Therefore, it seems that the test is not needed. However, in programming it is always wise to assume that something will go wrong. It is amazing how often it does. A good idea is to test for possible mistakes such as negative square roots or division by zero. The computer is likely to give an error statement anyway, but it may not be clear, and the error will cause the program to abort. So it is best to include a test within the Ada program as we have done.

More about Indenting and Commenting

Indenting should display the structure of a program. If there is a statement within a statement, it is best to indicate this by indenting in some way. In particular an if-then-else statement and a loop statement should be indented, as we have been doing or in some similar manner. The important point is to use some type of indenting that shows the structure, and you should be consistent within any one program. The exact layout is not precisely dictated.

Since we can have more than one `if/end if` pair in a program, it is a good idea to align the `if` with its corresponding `end if`. Likewise, it is best to align any `else` clauses with their `if` and `end if`. The sequence of statements should be indented from the `if` and the `else`. Example:

```
if boolean expression then
    sequence of statements
else
    sequence of statements
end if;
```

A similar situation exists for the `loop/end loop` pair. Notice that the square root program has a `loop` inside an `if`. It is a good idea to align the `loop` with its corresponding `end loop`. The code inside a `loop` should be indented to physically show that it is indeed inside the `loop`.

Summary of Problem Solving Techniques

- Program errors can be classified into three groups: syntax errors, run-time errors, and logical errors. The computer will usually tell you about errors in the first two categories.
- To test for and locate logical errors, one technique is to trace variables.
- Problems can be solved and programs written in phases. First, a simple version is designed and tested, and then enhancements are added in a later version.
- When designing a program, first check to see if there is a well-know algorithm for the task to be solved.

Summary of Programming Techniques

- Almost all literals in a program should be given meaningful names with a constant declaration.
- Comments should be inserted to explain major subsections or any unclear part of a program. Inserting assertions is one very effective way to comment a program.
- When you use if-then-else statements, the code inside should be indented to clearly display the two alternatives. Even without the `else`, some sort of indenting should be used. Align the `if`, the `else`, and the `end if`. Each `if` has an `end if`.
- Indent the code inside a `loop` statement, and align the `loop` with its `end loop`.
- When solving problems involving numbers of type FLOAT, do not use a test for exact equality or exact inequality (= or /=). Since such numbers are only approximately represented in the computer, it makes no sense to test them for equality.
- It is often a good idea to include tests for errors such as division by zero and negative square roots within a program.

Summary of Ada Constructs

constant declarations

Syntax:

```
identifier_1 : constant type_name := literal_1;
identifier_2 : constant type_name := literal_2;
     .
     .
     .
identifier_n : constant type_name := literal_n;
```

Example:

```
RATE : constant FLOAT := 7.25;
MOTTO : constant STRING := "We aim to please";
DAYS : constant INTEGER := 90;
```

The value *literal 1* is given the name *identifier 1,* the value *literal 2* is given the name *identifier 2,* and so forth. The second example uses a STRING literal. The identifiers can be any Ada identifiers that are not reserved words. The identifiers can then be used anyplace that the literals can be used and will have the same value as the literals they name.

maximum and minimum values

Syntax:

```
type_name'LAST
```

A predefined attribute that when associated with INTEGER or FLOAT gives a value equal to the largest value of that type that the computer system can handle.

```
type_name'FIRST
```

A predefined attribute that when associated with INTEGER or FLOAT gives a value equal to the smallest negative value of that type that the computer system can handle. Examples:

```
SMALLEST_INTEGER := INTEGER'FIRST;
LARGEST_VALUE := FLOAT'LAST;
```

comments

Syntax:

```
-- text <end_of_line>
```

Example:

```
--                    This is a Comment
```

The text between the symbol -- (double hyphen) and the end of that line is ignored by the compiler and so has no effect on the program. No blanks are allowed between the two hyphens.

formatted output

Syntax (for arguments to PUT):

integer_expression_to_be_output, *width_integer_expression*
or
float_expression_to_be_output,
    before_integer_expression,
    after_integer_expression,
    exponent_integer_expression

Examples:

```
PUT ( HOURS, 6 );
PUT ( PAY_RATE, 3, 2, 0 )
```

In the first example the number 6 indicates the total number of spaces to be used to output the value. The value will appear at the right-hand end of that field, and any extra spaces will be filled with blanks. The version with one number may be used with any output value of type INTEGER.

The second example can only be used for values of type FLOAT. The *before_integer_expression* (3 in the example) indicates the width of the field for the digits **before** the decimal point. The *after_integer_expression* (2 in the example) indicates the exact number of digits that will appear **after** the decimal point. If the *exponent_integer_expression* evaluates to zero, as in the example, then the output is not in the **E** notation.

if-then-else statement

Syntax:

if *expression 1_relational_operator_expression 2* **then**
    sequence_of_statements_1
else
    sequence_of_statements_2
end if;

Example:

```
if X > 0 then
     PUT ( "Value of X is greater than zero" );
     NEW_LINE;
else
     PUT ( "Value of X is zero or negative" );
     NEW_LINE;
end if;
```

sequence__of__statements__1 and *sequence__of__statements__2* may be any number (one or more) of Ada statements. If the relation between the two expressions is true, the *sequence__of__statements__1* is executed. If the relation does not hold, then *sequence__of__statements__2* is executed.

if-then statement

Syntax:

```
if expression__1 relational__operator expression__2 then
   sequence__of__statements
end if;
```

Example:

```
if X > 0 then
     PUT ( "Value of X is greater than zero" );
     NEW_LINE;
end if;
```

sequence__of__statements may be any number (one or more) of Ada statements. If the relation between the two expressions is true, the *sequence__of__statements* is executed. If the relation does not hold, no action is taken.

loop statement

Syntax:

```
loop
     sequence__of__statements
end loop;
```

The *sequence__of__statements* inside the **loop/end loop** pair are executed over and over again, until an **exit when** (see next entry) causes it to stop. If one of those statements is not an **exit when** statement, you will have an infinite loop.

Example:

```
SUM := 0;
VALUE := 5;
loop
      exit when VALUE <= 0;
      SUM := SUM + VALUE;
      VALUE := VALUE - 1;
end loop;
```

The *sequence__of__statements* can be any Ada statements. When the **loop** is executed, the relation between the two expressions (VALUE and 0 in this case) is first checked. If it is not satisfied, then the entire *sequence__of__statements* inside the **loop/end loop** pair is executed. If the relation does hold, then nothing happens. This process is repeated again and again. First the relation between the two expressions is checked. If it is not satisfied, the entire *sequence__of__statements* inside the **loop/end loop** pair is executed. If it is satisfied, the **loop** terminates and the program goes on to the next item.

exit when statement

Syntax:

exit when *boolean__expression*;

The use of an **exit when** statement is restricted: It can only appear inside a **loop** statement. The program will exit the loop when the *boolean expression* is true. If the *boolean expression* evaluates to false, the **exit when** statement does nothing, and execution continues with the next statement in the loop.

Exercises

Self-Test Exercises

6. What is the output produced by the following program?

```
with I_O; use I_O;
procedure MAIN is
    NUMBER : INTEGER;
begin
    NUMBER := 3;
    if 2 > NUMBER then
        PUT ( "First Put" );
    else
        PUT ( "Second Put" );
    end if;
    NEW_LINE;
    if 2 > NUMBER then
        PUT ( "Third Put" );
        NEW_LINE;
    end if;
    PUT ( "Fourth Put" );
    NEW_LINE;
end MAIN;
```

7. Classify the following as true or false (when used in an Ada if-then-else statement):

```
24 rem 12 /= 0
'y' = 'Y'
'H ' <= 'J'
-12 <= INTEGER'LAST
```

8. Determine the value of each of the following Ada arithmetic expressions:

```
FLOAT ( 16 )                    FLOAT ( 4 + 5 )
INTEGER ( 6.8 )                 INTEGER ( -6.8 )
INTEGER ( 6.8 + 0.5 )           INTEGER ( -6.8 + 0.5 )
abs ( 6.8 )                     abs ( -6.8 )
INTEGER'LAST                    FLOAT'FIRST
```

9. Convert the following mathematical and English expressions into Ada boolean expressions:

$x^2 \leq y + 1$
zulu is positive
water is not zero
eggs is evenly divisible by 12

10. What is the output of the following program?

```
with I_O; use I_O;
procedure MAIN is
     VALUE : INTEGER := 12;
begin
     loop
          exit when VALUE <= 0;
          VALUE := VALUE - 5;
     end loop;
     PUT ( VALUE );
     NEW_LINE;
end MAIN;
```

Interactive Exercises

11. Write a program that reads in an integer and outputs a statement telling whether the number is positive or not.

12. Write a program that reads in a character and outputs a statement telling whether or not the character typed in is `'n'`.

13. Write a program that reads in an uppercase letter and outputs a message telling whether or not that letter follows **`'M'`** in the alphabet.

14. Write a program that reads in an integer and outputs a statement telling whether or not the number is evenly divisible by 3. If the number is not divisible by 3, then the program should also output the remainder obtained when the number is divided by 3.

15. Write a program that reads in a decimal number and applies the conversion function `INTEGER` to the number so that a rounded number is output.

16. Determine the smallest `FLOAT` value e such that your computer can distinguish between 1 and $1 + e$. Feel free to use the trial-and-error method.

17. Substitute `20` for `25` in Figure 3.2 (or do something similar), and give the program to a friend to debug. Ask your friend to do something equally perverse to you.

18. Modify the program in Figure 3.13 so it shows the balance after each month.

19. Embed the loop example from the "Summary of Ada Constructs" in a program and run the program. Input the numbers `1`, `2`, `3`, and `0`, one per line. Do not forget to initialize the variables `VALUE` and `SUM`.

Programming Exercises

20. A liter is 0.264179 gallons. Write a program that reads in the number of liters of gasoline consumed by the user's car and the number of miles traveled by the car. Produce as output the number of miles per gallon the car delivers. Use a constant declaration for the number of liters per gallon.

21. The gravitational attractive force between two bodies of mass m_1 and m_2 separated by a distance d is given by

$$F = \frac{Gm_1m_2}{d^2}$$

where G is the universal gravitational constant:

$$G = 6.673 \times 10^{-8}\ cm^3/g\ sec^2$$

Write a program that reads in the mass of two bodies and the distance between them, and then outputs the gravitational force between them. The output should be in dynes; one dyne equals a g cm/sec^2. Use a constant declaration for G.

22. According to Einstein's famous equation, the amount of energy E produced when an amount of mass m is completely converted to energy is given by the formula

$$E = mc^2$$

where c is the speed of light. Write a program that reads in a mass in grams and outputs the amount of energy produced when the mass is converted to energy. The speed of light is approximately

$$2.997925 \times 10^{10}\ cm/sec$$

If the mass is given in grams, then the formula yields the energy expressed in ergs. Use a constant declaration to name the speed of light.

23. Write a program that reads in a weight in pounds and ounces and outputs the weight expressed in kilograms and grams. One pound equals 0.453592 kilograms. Use a constant declaration. The program should contain a loop that allows the user to repeat the calculation for other values until the user says he/she wants to quit.

24. Write a program that reads in a distance expressed in kilometers and outputs the distance expressed in miles. One kilometer equals 0.62137 miles. Use a constant declaration. The program should contain a loop that allows the user to repeat the calculation for other values until the user says he/she wants to quit.

25. Write a program that calculates change for a cashier. The program requests the cost of the item. The user then types in the cost as a decimal numeral. In a similar manner the program next requests and receives the amount tendered by the customer. It then calculates the cost of the item, including sales tax. (Use 6% as the sales tax value.) It also calculates the amount of change due the customer. Finally, the program outputs the cost, including tax, echoes the amount tendered, and outputs the amount of change. Use a constant declaration for the tax rate. Be sure to use field specifications so as to produce output that looks reasonable. The program should contain a loop that allows the user to repeat the calculation for other values until the user says he/she wants to quit.

26. Write a program that gauges the amount of inflation over the past year. The program asks for the price of an item (such as a hot dog or a one-carat diamond), both one year ago and today. It estimates the inflation rate as the difference in price divided by the year-ago price.

27. Enhance your program from the previous exercise by having it also print out the estimated price of the item in one and in two years from the time of the calculation. The increase in cost in one year is estimated as the inflation rate times the price.

28. The price of stocks are normally given to the nearest eighth of a dollar; for example, $29\frac{7}{8}$ or $89\frac{1}{2}$. Write a program that computes the value of the user's holding of one stock. The program asks for the number of stocks held, the whole-dollar portion of the price, and the fraction portion. The fraction portion is to be input as two integer values, one for the numerator and one for the denominator. The program should contain a loop that allows the user to repeat the calculation for other values until the user says he/she wants to quit.

29. The relationship between the sides (*a*, *b*) of a right triangle and the hypotenuse (*h*) is given by the Pythagorean formula:

$$a^2 + b^2 = h^2$$

Write a program that reads in the two sides of a right triangle and computes the hypotenuse of the triangle.

30. The area of a triangle whose sides are *a*, *b*, and *c* can be computed by the formula:

$$A = \sqrt{x(s - a)(s - b)(s - c)}$$

where $s = (a+b+c)/2$. Write a program that reads in the three sides of a triangle and outputs the area of the triangle.

31. Rewrite the change-making program in Figure 3.2 so it takes as input any amount of dollars and cents (as a number of type `FLOAT`) and outputs the correct number of bills as well as the coins to give as change. Use bill denominations of \$1, \$5, and \$20 only. The program should contain a loop that allows the user to repeat the calculation for other values until the user says he/she wants to quit.

32. An hourly employee is paid at a rate of $9.73 per hour for regular hours worked per week. Any hours over that are paid at the overtime rate of 1½ times that. From the worker's gross pay, 6% is withheld for social security tax, 14% is withheld for federal income tax, 5% is withheld for state income tax, and $6 per week is withheld for union dues. If the worker has three or more covered dependents, then an additional $10 is withheld to cover the extra cost of health insurance beyond what the employer pays. Write a program that takes as input the number of hours worked in a week and the number of dependents, and then outputs the worker's gross pay, each withholding, and the net take-home pay for the week.

33. A bicycle salesperson is offered a choice of wage plans: (a) $3.50 per hour for 40 hours plus a 10% commission on sales; (b) a straight 15% commission on sales with no other salary. Write a program that takes as input the salesperson's expected weekly sales and outputs the expected wages paid under each plan, and also announces the best-paying plan.

34. Write a program that computes the cost of postage on a first-class letter according to the following rate scale: 30 cents for the first ounce or fraction of an ounce, 8 cents for each additional half ounce, plus a $5 service charge if the customer desires special delivery.

References for Further Reading

The following reference manuals are designed for individuals who already know some other programming language besides Ada:

Reference Manual for the Ada Programming Language, ANSI/MIL-STD-1815A-1983, United States Department of Defense.

Gonzales, Dean W. *Ada Programmers Handbook* (Redwood City, CA: Benjamin/Cummings Publishing Co., 1991).

CHAPTER 4

DESIGNING SUBPROGRAMS FOR SUBDIVIDING PROBLEMS

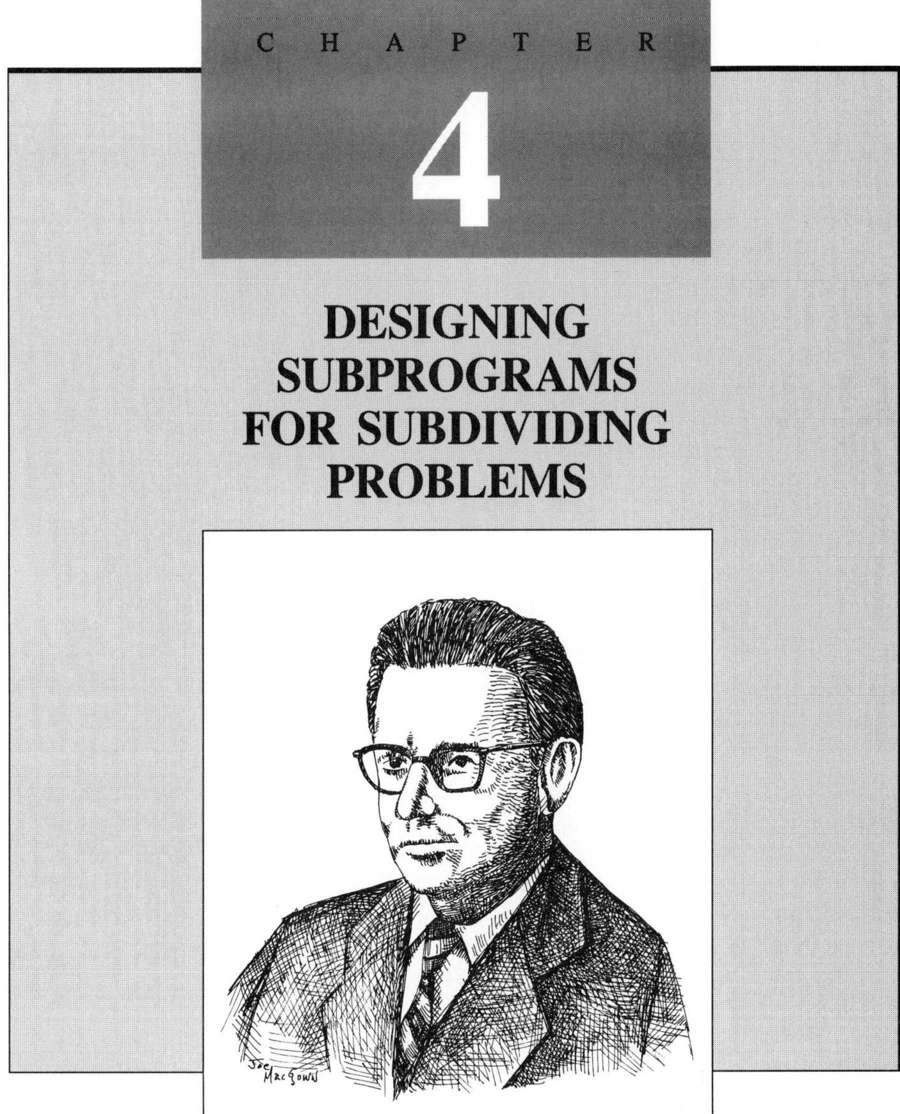

Konrad Zuse

This German pioneer developed some early sophisticated relay computers, most of which were destroyed during World War II. Zuse is also known for his work in the early development of computer programming languages. Up till this time most programming languages were very low level and were developed strictly for a particular machine. His Plankalkuls (Plancalculus) was one of the first high-level languages and was designed in general with no machine in mind.

Chapter Contents

A good way to design an algorithm to solve a problem is to break it down into subproblems and solve these subproblems by smaller, simpler algorithms. Ultimately the subalgorithms to solve these subproblems are translated into Ada code, and the entire larger algorithm containing these subalgorithms is translated into an Ada program. Since the subalgorithms are algorithms, it is natural to think of them as smaller programs within a larger program. Moreover, preserving this structure in the final Ada program makes the program easy to understand, easy to change, if need be, and, as will become apparent, easy to write, test, and debug. Ada, like most programming languages, has facilities to include program-like entities inside of programs. The Ada term for such program-like entities is *subprograms.* In this chapter we introduce the two kinds of subprograms, procedures and functions, and give some guidelines for using them effectively.

Simple Ada Procedures

In Ada you can assign a name to a sequence of statements by means of something called a *procedure body declaration.* You can then use the procedure name as a statement in the program, and this will have the same effect as executing the sequence of statements. For example, the following is a sample procedure body declaration that assigns the name COMPLIMENT to four output statements:

procedure body declaration

```
procedure COMPLIMENT is
begin
    PUT ( "A lovely letter." ); NEW_LINE;
    PUT ( "One of my favorites." ); NEW_LINE;
end COMPLIMENT;
```

In a program with this procedure body declaration, the identifier COMPLIMENT, terminated with a semicolon, can be used anyplace a statement can be used, and when it is executed it will cause the following to appear on the screen:

use of procedures

```
A lovely letter.
One of my favorites.
```

This is illustrated in Figure 4.1.

The syntax for a simple procedure body declaration is as follows. The first part of the procedure is called the *specification.* It consists of the word **procedure** followed by any (nonreserved-word) identifier to serve as the procedure name. The remainder of the procedure body declaration consists of the reserved word **is**, followed by what we will call the procedure *block.* The block of the procedure is a sequence of statements enclosed between a **begin**/**end** pair. You end a procedure body declaration with the name of the procedure, followed by a semicolon after the final **end**. In an Ada program, procedure body declarations must be placed after the variable and constant object declarations and before the main program's block. The order of declarations within a program is shown in Figure 4.2.

procedure declaration syntax

A procedure name that occurs inside the body of a program is considered to be a special kind of statement known as a *procedure call* or a *procedure invocation.* These procedure call statements are treated just like any other kind of statement when it comes to syntactic detail. In particular, it must always be terminated with a semicolon.

procedure call

Introduction to Parameters

Suppose we want to design a program to help a cashier total the cash on hand at the end of a work day. The cashier counts the number of each coin and enters the number of each coin. The program then computes the dollar value of the coins. To avoid input

Program

```
with I_O; use I_O;
procedure MAIN is
    FIRST_INITIAL,
    LAST_INITIAL : CHARACTER;

    procedure COMPLIMENT is
    begin -- Compliment
        PUT ( "A lovely letter." ); NEW_LINE;
        PUT ( "One of my favorites." ); NEW_LINE;
    end COMPLIMENT;

begin -- Main
    PUT ( "Please enter your first initial." ); NEW_LINE;
    GET ( FIRST_INITIAL ); SKIP_LINE;
    COMPLIMENT;
    PUT ( "Now enter your last initial." ); NEW_LINE;
    GET ( LAST_INITIAL ); SKIP_LINE;
    COMPLIMENT;
    PUT ( "Pleased to meet you");
    PUT ( FIRST_INITIAL ); PUT ( '.' );
    PUT ( LAST_INITIAL ); PUT ( '.' );
    NEW_LINE;
end MAIN;
```

Sample Dialogue

```
Please enter your first initial.
J
A lovely letter.
One of my favorites.
Now enter your last initial.
R
A lovely letter.
One of my favorites.
Pleased to meet you J.R.
```

Figure 4.1 Program with a procedure.

```
with I_O; use I_O;
procedure MAIN is
        object__declaration
        procedure__body__declarations
begin
        sequence__of__statements
end MAIN;
```

Figure 4.2 Order of declarations.

errors, each input statement is prefaced by a warning of exactly what to input and how to input it. The program might start out as follows:

```
PUT ( "Enter the number of half dollar coins." ); NEW_LINE;
PUT ( "Do not total the value of the coin(s)." ); NEW_LINE;
PUT ( "Just enter the number of coins." ); NEW_LINE;
GET ( HALF_DOLLARS ); SKIP_LINE;
```

The program might next request the number of quarters, as follows:

```
PUT ( "Enter the number of quarters." ); NEW_LINE;
PUT ( "Do not total the value of the coin(s)." ); NEW_LINE;
PUT ( "Just enter the number of coins." ); NEW_LINE;
GET ( QUARTERS ); SKIP_LINE;
```

Notice that the last three lines of these two pieces of code do the same thing, namely, prompt the user with input instructions and then input one number. Since this is a repeated subproblem, it makes sense to declare these three lines as a procedure. There is, however, one problem with this idea. The last line is slightly different in these two pieces of code. One time we use the variable HALF_DOLLARS and one time we use the variable QUARTERS. One solution would be to make the procedure only two lines long and omit the last line from the procedure, just as we chose to omit the first line. That will work, but it is not a very good solution. What we really want is a procedure that has an object that we can associate with the variable HALF_DOLLARS in the first procedure call, associate with the variable QUARTERS in the second call, and associate with the variables DIMES, NICKELS, and PENNIES later on. Ada allows us to do just that.

formal out parameters

The objects declared in a procedure specification are called *formal parameters,* and the declaration looks similar to a variable declaration. For example, in the following procedure specification, NUMBER_OF_COINS is a formal parameter:

```
procedure GET_NUMBER ( NUMBER_OF_COINS : out INTEGER )
```

Parameters are used to pass information into and out of a procedure. A formal parameter may be any identifier other than a reserved word. The reserved word **out** indicates a direction in which information is *passed.* A formal **out** parameter passes information out of the procedure. The procedure, GET_NUMBER, uses a formal parameter called NUMBER_OF_COINS and performs the job we desire. It is included in the program in Figure 4.3.

actual parameters

To use the procedure with the particular variable HALF_DOLLARS to receive the information from the formal **out** parameter, NUMBER_OF_COINS, you use a *procedure call* that looks like the following:

```
GET_NUMBER ( HALF_DOLLARS );
```

The variable in the procedure call, in this case HALF_DOLLARS, is called an *actual parameter.* An actual parameter that is associated with a formal **out** parameter is passed the value of the formal parameter when the procedure terminates. For example, HALF_DOLLARS (the actual parameter) is assigned the value of NUMBER_OF_COINS (the formal **out** parameter) when the procedure

Program

```
with I_O; use I_O;
procedure MAIN is
--                 INPUT  : The number of each type of coin
--                 OUTPUT : The total value of all coins
--                 DESCRIPTION : The program reads in the number
--                               of coins for each type of coin
--                               and computes the total value
--                               of all the coins.

    AFTER : constant INTEGER := 2;
    BEFORE : constant INTEGER := 4;
    EXPONENT : constant INTEGER := 0;
    DIMES,
    HALF_DOLLARS,
    NICKELS,
    PENNIES,
    QUARTERS : INTEGER;
    TOTAL : FLOAT;

    procedure GET_NUMBER ( NUMBER_OF_COINS : out INTEGER ) is
--                 INPUT  : None
--                 OUTPUT : The number of coins >= 0
--                 DESCRIPTION : The procedure prompts the user
--                               and reads in the number of coins
    begin -- Get_Number
        PUT ( "Do not total the value of the coin(s)." );
        NEW_LINE;
        PUT ( "Just enter the number of coins." );
        NEW_LINE;
        GET ( NUMBER_OF_COINS );
        SKIP_LINE;
    end GET_NUMBER;

begin -- Main
    PUT ( "Enter the number of half dollars." ); NEW_LINE;
    GET_NUMBER ( HALF_DOLLARS );
    PUT ( "Enter the number of quarters." ); NEW_LINE;
    GET_NUMBER ( QUARTERS );
    PUT ( "Enter the number of dimes." ); NEW_LINE;
    GET_NUMBER ( DIMES );
    PUT ( "Enter the number of nickels." ); NEW_LINE;
    GET_NUMBER ( NICKELS );
    PUT ( "Enter the number of pennies." ); NEW_LINE;
    GET_NUMBER ( PENNIES );
```

```
    TOTAL := 0.50 * FLOAT ( HALF_DOLLARS )
           + 0.25 * FLOAT ( QUARTERS )
           + 0.10 * FLOAT ( DIMES )
           + 0.05 * FLOAT ( NICKELS )
           + 0.01 * FLOAT ( PENNIES );
    PUT ( HALF_DOLLARS ); PUT ("half dollars,"); NEW_LINE;
    PUT ( QUARTERS ); PUT ("quarters," ); NEW_LINE;
    PUT ( DIMES ); PUT ("dimes,"); NEW_LINE;
    PUT ( NICKELS ); PUT ("nickels," ); NEW_LINE;
    PUT ( PENNIES ); PUT ("pennies" ); NEW_LINE;
    PUT ( "total to: $" ); PUT ( TOTAL, BEFORE, AFTER, EXPONENT );
    NEW_LINE;
end MAIN;
```

Sample Dialogue

```
Enter the number of half dollars.
Do not total the amount.
Just enter the number of coins.
12
Enter the number of quarters.
Do not total the amount.
Just enter the number of coins.
325
Enter the number of dimes.
Do not total the amount.
Just enter the number of coins.
103
Enter the number of nickels.
Do not total the amount.
Just enter the number of coins.
107
Enter the number of pennies.
Do not total the amount.
Just enter the number of coins.
57
    12 half dollars,
   325 quarters,
   103 dimes,
   107 nickels,
    57 pennies
total to: $ 103.47
```

Figure 4.3 Program that uses parameter passing.

GET_NUMBER terminates. As the program in Figure 4.3 illustrates, a procedure may be called more than once using different actual parameters each time.

Notice that a formal parameter has a type that must be stated in the procedure specification, and that the corresponding actual parameters must have the same type. The type specification for a formal parameter looks very much like a variable declaration and is given in the procedure specification in parentheses after the procedure name. Since the type of the parameter is given in the procedure specification, it need not be given anyplace else. In particular, it should not be declared in the variable declarations of the program.

The reserved word **out**, which is sandwiched between the colon and the type name, is called the *mode.* The mode of the formal parameter indicates the direction in which information is passed. Ada has three modes for formal parameters. The mode **out** indicates that information is to be passed out of the procedure to the actual parameter. The mode **in**, covered later in this chapter, indicates that information is to be passed into the procedure from the actual parameter. Lastly, the mode **in out** indicates that information is to be passed both into the procedure from the actual parameter to the formal parameter and out of the procedure from the formal parameter to the actual parameter. Note that **in out** is two separate words.

Parameter Lists

formal parameter list

A procedure can have any number of formal parameters. They all are simply listed in parentheses after the procedure name in the procedure specification and are separated by semicolons. For example, one procedure specification might be

```
procedure OUTPUT ( FORMAL_PARAMETER_1 : out INTEGER;
                   FORMAL_PARAMETER_2 : out FLOAT;
                   FORMAL_PARAMETER_3 : out FLOAT )
```

When two or more formal parameters are of the same mode and the same type and occur one after the other in the list of parameters, they may be combined so their mode and type need only be written once. In that case the combined parameters are separated by commas. For example, the following procedure specification is equivalent to the one just given:

```
procedure OUTPUT ( FORMAL_PARAMETER_1 : out INTEGER;
                   FORMAL_PARAMETER_2,
                   FORMAL_PARAMETER_3 : out FLOAT )
```

Notice that there is a parameter mode (in this case **out**) for each group of formal parameters.

actual parameter list

In a procedure call statement, the actual parameters are given in parentheses after the procedure name (e.g., GET_NUMBER (DIMES);). When the procedure call is executed, the actual parameters are associated with the formal parameters in the procedure specification declaration. The association follows this ordering: The first parameter listed in the procedure call is associated with the first formal parameter listed in the procedure specification, the second actual parameter is associated with the second formal parameter, and so forth. When a procedure like OUTPUT is called, there always must be the same number of actual parameters in a procedure call as there are formal parameters in the procedure specification. Moreover, the type of each actual parameter must be the same as the type of the corresponding formal parameter it replaces. Hence, in the following sample procedure call,

```
OUTPUT ( NUMBER, PRICE, BILL );
```

the actual variable parameter NUMBER must be a variable of type INTEGER; the actual variable parameters PRICE and BILL must be variables of type FLOAT. The variable NUMBER is associated with FORMAL_PARAMETER_1 in the procedure specification, PRICE is associated with FORMAL_PARAMETER_2, and BILL is associated with FORMAL_PARAMETER_3.

As indicated by this example, one minor syntactic difference between formal and actual parameters is that the actual parameters are separated by commas rather than a combination of commas and semicolons. The list of parameters, either formal in the procedure specification or actual in the call, is referred to as a *parameter list.*

The program in Figure 4.3 has the following output statements:

```
PUT ( "Enter the number of half dollars." ); NEW_LINE;
```

This line is repeated for each type of coin. The only difference is that the string literal "quarters," "dimes," "nickels," or "pennies" is substituted for "half dollars." The following code segment illustrates how these output statements can be modified and moved into the GET_NUMBER procedure. The complete program is given in Figure 4.4.

```
PUT ( "Enter the number of " );
PUT ( TYPE_OF_COIN );
NEW_LINE;
```

The GET_NUMBER procedure specification is modified to include a formal **in** parameter that receives a character string that represents the TYPE_OF_COIN. The procedure call is modified to include a string of characters as well as a variable name.

The program in Figure 4.4 is an example of a program with more than one procedure. The program has a GET_NUMBER procedure and a PUT_NUMBER procedure. The call to the PUT_NUMBER procedure replaces the following line from Figure 4.3,

```
PUT ( HALF_DOLLARS ); PUT ("half dollars," ); NEW_LINE;
```

with

```
PUT_NUMBER ( HALF_DOLLARS, "half dollars," );
```

A similar call is made for the other types of coins.

Program

```
with I_O; use I_O;
procedure MAIN is
--                  INPUT  : The count of each type of coin
--                  OUTPUT : The total value of all coins
--                  DESCRIPTION : The program reads in the number of
--                                coins for each type of coin and computes
--                                the total value of all the coins

   AFTER : constant INTEGER := 2;
   BEFORE : constant INTEGER := 4;
   EXPONENT : constant INTEGER := 0;
   DIMES,
   HALF_DOLLARS,
   NICKELS,
   PENNIES,
   QUARTERS : INTEGER;
   TOTAL : FLOAT;

   procedure GET_NUMBER ( TYPE_OF_COIN : in STRING;
                          NUMBER_OF_COINS : out INTEGER ) is
--                  INPUT  : The type of the coin
--                  OUTPUT : The number of coins
--                  DESCRIPTION : The procedure prompts the user
--                                and reads in the number of coins
   begin -- Get_Number
      PUT ( "Enter the number of" );
      PUT ( TYPE_OF_COIN );
      NEW_LINE;
      PUT ( "Do not total the amount." ); NEW_LINE;
      PUT ( "Just enter the number of coins." ); NEW_LINE;
      GET ( NUMBER_OF_COINS ); SKIP_LINE;
   end GET_NUMBER;

   procedure PUT_NUMBER ( NUMBER_OF_COINS : in INTEGER;
                          TYPE_OF_COIN : in STRING ) is
--                  INPUT  : A character string that represents the
--                           denomination of the coin and the number
--                           coins for this denomination.
--                  OUTPUT : None
--                  DESCRIPTION : The procedure displays on the screen
--                                the denomination of the coin and the
--                                number of coins in that denomination.
```

```
    begin -- Put_Number
        PUT ( TYPE_OF_COIN );
        PUT ( NUMBER_OF_COINS );
        NEW_LINE;
    end PUT_NUMBER;

begin -- Main
    GET_NUMBER ( "half dollars.", HALF_DOLLARS );
    GET_NUMBER ( "quarters.", QUARTERS );
    GET_NUMBER ( "dimes.", DIMES );
    GET_NUMBER ( "nickels.", NICKELS );
    GET_NUMBER ( "pennies.", PENNIES );
    TOTAL := 0.50 * FLOAT ( HALF_DOLLARS )
          + 0.25 * FLOAT ( QUARTERS )
          + 0.10 * FLOAT ( DIMES )
          + 0.05 * FLOAT ( NICKELS )
          + 0.01 * FLOAT ( PENNIES );
    PUT_NUMBER ( HALF_DOLLARS, "half dollars," );
    PUT_NUMBER ( QUARTERS, "quarters," );
    PUT_NUMBER ( DIMES, "dimes," );
    PUT_NUMBER ( NICKELS, "nickels," );
    PUT_NUMBER ( PENNIES, "pennies," );
    PUT ( "total to: $" ); PUT ( TOTAL, BEFORE, AFTER, EXPONENT );
    NEW_LINE;
end MAIN;
```

Figure 4.4 Program with `in` and `out` parameters.

Mixed Parameter Lists

You may use any number of parameters in a procedure, and they may have any combination of modes: **in**, **out**, or **in out**. You simply list them all in the procedure specification. For example, one procedure specification might be

```
procedure SAMPLE ( W : in FLOAT;
                   X : in out FLOAT;
                   Y, Z : out CHARACTER )
```

Each formal parameter has a type and mode associated with it. Those for sending information into the procedure are marked with the mode **in**, meaning input parameter. Those for sending information out of the procedure are output parameters and are marked with the mode **out**. If information is to be passed into the procedure and also out of the procedure via a given formal parameter, the parameter is an input-output parameter and is given the mode **in out**.

In the sample specification, X is an input-output parameter; W is an input parameter; and Y and Z are output parameters. The various formal parameters are separated by semicolons. When two or more consecutive parameters are of the same type and mode, you can combine their type specifications in the way illustrated by Y and Z in the sample specification. The details are summarized by the syntax diagram in Figure 4.5.

Notice that the section of the syntax diagram for *mode* has an alternative with nothing in it (the top line). This implies that one of the alternatives for mode is no mode at all, but this is not the case. If there is no mode specified, the compiler assumes the mode to be **in**. In general, the use of this empty mode alternative is not considered good programming practice for procedures.

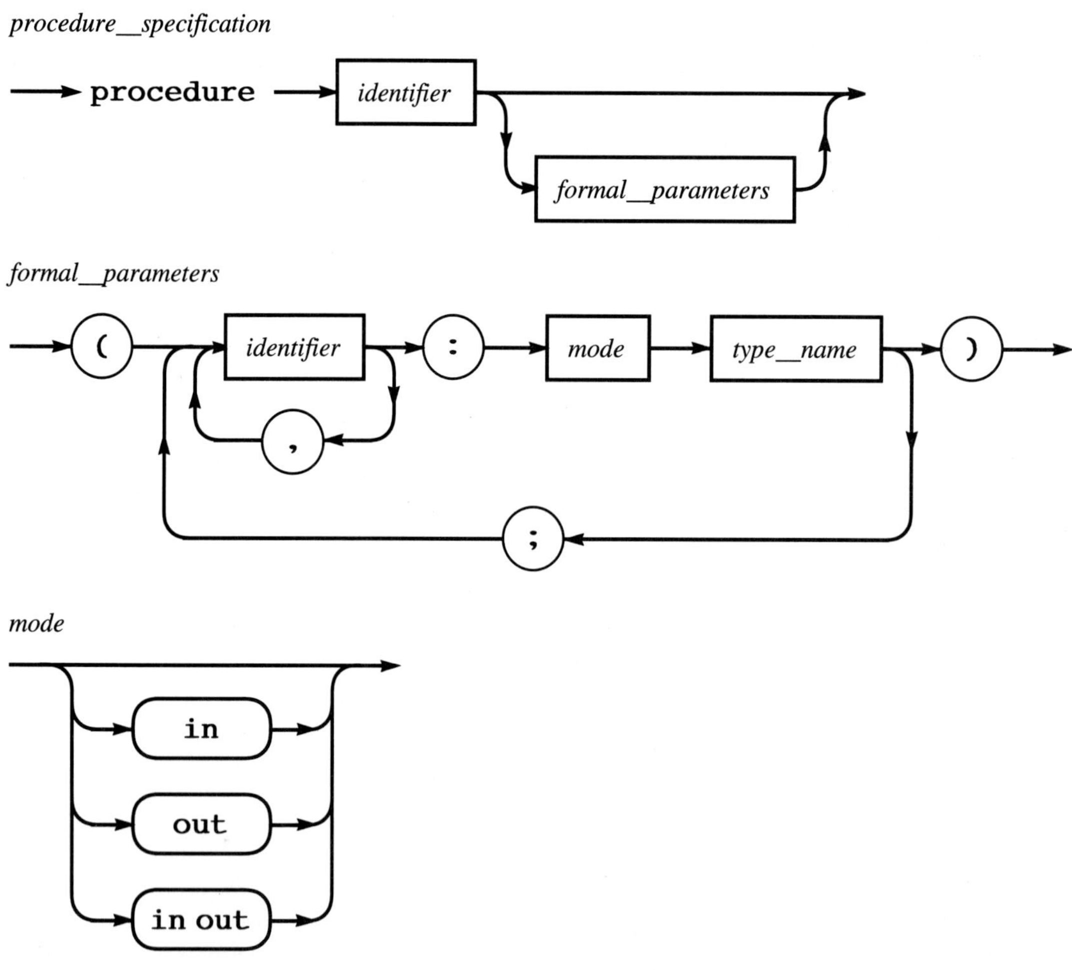

Figure 4.5 Syntax for a procedure specification.

In the procedure call the actual parameters are given in parentheses after the procedure name, and they must correspond in type to the formal parameters. For example, given the procedure specification

```
procedure SAMPLE ( W : in FLOAT;
                   X : in out FLOAT;
                   Y, Z : out CHARACTER )
```

and the procedure call

```
SAMPLE ( 2.5, A, B, C );
```

The variable A must have been declared to be of type FLOAT and the variables B and C must have been declared to be of type CHARACTER. All actual **in out** and **out** parameters must be variables, so in the above example, A must be a variable. The other parameter **2.5** is associated with an **in** parameter (W in this example). An **in** parameter may be associated with an actual parameter that is either a variable, a constant, or a more complicated expression.

Figure 4.6 has the same coin program as Figures 4.3 and 4.4, but this time the computation of the TOTAL is done in a procedure called COMPUTE_TOTAL that has TOTAL as an **in out** parameter. The value of the parameter TOTAL is passed into the procedure when the procedure is called, and the new value is passed out of the procedure when it finishes. Besides the parameter TOTAL, the COMPUTE_TOTAL procedure has two **in** parameters. The VALUE of the denomination of the coin and the NUMBER_OF_COINS of that denomination are passed into the procedure and used in the computation of the new TOTAL.

Program

```
with I_O; use I_O;
procedure MAIN is
--              INPUT  : The count of each type of coin
--              OUTPUT : The total value of all coins
--              DESCRIPTION : The program reads in the number of
--                            coins for each type of coin and computes
--                            the total value of all the coins

    AFTER : constant INTEGER := 2;
    BEFORE : constant INTEGER := 4;
    EXPONENT : constant INTEGER := 0;
    DIMES,
    HALF_DOLLARS,
    NICKELS,
    PENNIES,
    QUARTERS : INTEGER;
    TOTAL : FLOAT := 0.00;
```

```
    procedure GET_NUMBER ( TYPE_OF_COIN : in STRING;
                           NUMBER_OF_COINS : out INTEGER ) is
--                  INPUT  : The type of the coin
--                  OUTPUT : The number of coins
--                  DESCRIPTION : The procedure prompts the user
--                                and reads in the number of coins
    begin -- Get_Number
        PUT ( "Enter the number of" ); PUT ( TYPE_OF_COIN );
        NEW_LINE;
        PUT ( "Do not total the amount." ); NEW_LINE;
        PUT ( "Just enter the number of coins." ); NEW_LINE;
        GET ( NUMBER_OF_COINS ); SKIP_LINE;
    end GET_NUMBER;

    procedure COMPUTE_TOTAL ( TOTAL : in out FLOAT;
                              VALUE : in FLOAT;
                              NUMBER_OF_COINS : in INTEGER ) is
--                  INPUT  : The previous total value of coins,
--                           the value of this denomination of coin,
--                           the number of coins for this denomination.
--                  OUTPUT : A new value for total.
--                  DESCRIPTION : The procedure computes the dollar and
--                                cent value for this denomination of
--                                coin and adds it to the previous
--                                total.
    begin -- Compute_Total
        TOTAL := TOTAL + VALUE * FLOAT ( NUMBER_OF_COINS );
    end COMPUTE_TOTAL;

    procedure PUT_NUMBER ( TYPE_OF_COIN : in STRING;
                           NUMBER_OF_COINS : in INTEGER ) is
--                  INPUT  : A character string that represents the
--                           denomination of the coin and the number of
--                           coins for this denomination.
--                  OUTPUT : None
--                  DESCRIPTION : The procedure displays on the screen
--                                the denomination of the coin and the
--                                number of coins in that denomination.
    begin -- Put_Number
        PUT ( TYPE_OF_COIN );
        PUT ( NUMBER_OF_COINS );
        NEW_LINE;
    end PUT_NUMBER;
```

```
begin -- Main
    GET_NUMBER ( "half dollars," HALF_DOLLARS );
    GET_NUMBER ( "quarters," QUARTERS );
    GET_NUMBER ( "dimes," DIMES );
    GET_NUMBER ( "nickels," NICKELS );
    GET_NUMBER ( "pennies," PENNIES );
    COMPUTE_TOTAL ( TOTAL, 0.50, HALF_DOLLARS );
    COMPUTE_TOTAL ( TOTAL, 0.25, QUARTERS );
    COMPUTE_TOTAL ( TOTAL, 0.10, DIMES );
    COMPUTE_TOTAL ( TOTAL, 0.05, NICKELS );
    COMPUTE_TOTAL ( TOTAL, 0.01, PENNIES );
    PUT_NUMBER ( "half dollars," HALF_DOLLARS );
    PUT_NUMBER ( "quarters," QUARTERS );
    PUT_NUMBER ( "dimes," DIMES );
    PUT_NUMBER ( "nickels," NICKELS );
    PUT_NUMBER ( "pennies," PENNIES );
    PUT ( "total to: $" ); PUT ( TOTAL, BEFORE, AFTER, EXPONENT );
    NEW_LINE;
end MAIN;
```

Figure 4.6 Program with an `in out` parameter.

In Out Parameters

two-way data

A formal **in out** parameter declaration looks very much like a variable declaration. In fact it can be treated just like any other variable inside the body of the procedure. Conceptually the only difference between an **in out** parameter and any other variable is that the **in out** parameter is assigned the value of its associated actual parameter at the time of the procedure call. Information is thus passed into the procedure. When the procedure terminates, the value of the **in out** parameter is passed back to its associated actual parameter. Information is thus passed out of the procedure. The use of **in out** parameters provides a *two-way* passage of information. Because of this two-way passage of information, the actual parameter *must* be a variable.

Out Parameters

one-way data

Although a formal **out** parameter looks like a variable to be used inside the procedure, it is not a variable in the same sense that we have used the term *variable* before. Ada places restrictions on how an **out** parameter can be used. As stated earlier, an **out** parameter is used to pass information out of a procedure. What was not stated before is that that is all an **out** parameter can be used for inside the procedure. An **out** parameter *must* be assigned a value inside the procedure. An **out** parameter cannot be used in any expression, thus it cannot appear on the right-hand side of the **:=**. An **out** parameter is assigned a value in the procedure either via a GET statement or by appearing on the left-hand side of an assignment statement. When the procedure terminates, the value of the **out** parameter is passed out of the procedure to its associated actual parameter. There is a *one-way* passage of information out of the procedure; no information is passed into an **out** parameter.

In Parameters

one-way data

There is another mode for parameters called the **in** parameter. An **in** parameter is a ''one-way'' parameter; it can be used to supply information to a procedure, but it cannot be used to get information out of a procedure. Although an **in** parameter looks like a variable, it is not; it is a constant. At the time of the procedure call, the **in** parameter is assigned the value of its associated actual parameter. Inside the procedure body the formal **in** parameter is treated just like any other constant object, thus it cannot appear on the left-hand side of the **:=**.

Only **in** parameters allow us to use more complicated expressions as the actual parameters in a procedure call. This notion is best introduced by means of an example.

Suppose we want to write a procedure that will output the area of a rectangle to the screen. In this case the procedure will have two parameters: one for the length and one for the width of the rectangle. Our first attempt at writing the procedure might be as follows:

```
procedure OUTPUT_AREA ( LENGTH, WIDTH : in out INTEGER ) is
begin
    PUT ( "A rectangle of dimensions:" ); NEW_LINE;
    PUT ( LENGTH ); PUT ( " by " );
    PUT ( WIDTH ); PUT ( " inches" );
    NEW_LINE;
    PUT ( "Has area " );
    PUT ( LENGTH * WIDTH );
    PUT ( " square inches" );
    NEW_LINE;
end OUTPUT_AREA;
```

This will work, but in some situations it is inconvenient. If the length and width are stored in variables, say X and Y, then to output the area of the rectangle, the following procedure call will do nicely:

```
OUTPUT_AREA ( X, Y );
```

Suppose, however, that we wish to output the area of a rectangle 4 inches long by 3 inches wide. Since the actual parameters must be variables (because the formal parameters are **in out**), first we will have to set two variables equal to **4** and **3**, and then we could use the variables as the actual parameters. That is unfortunate. It would be easier and cleaner if we could write the following expression and then have the computer substitute **4** for the formal parameter LENGTH and **3** for the formal parameter WIDTH:

```
    OUTPUT_AREA ( 4, 3 );
--                  Will not work with an in out
                    parameter
```

As the comment states, this simply will not work with **in out** parameters. To make the above procedure call work, we must change LENGTH and WIDTH to **in** parameters.

To make LENGTH and WIDTH **in** parameters in our sample procedure, all we need to do is to omit the **out** to produce the following procedure specification:

```
procedure OUTPUT_AREA ( LENGTH, WIDTH : in INTEGER )
```

The rest of the procedure is unchanged.

actual in parameters

When a procedure with formal **in** parameters is called, it must be supplied with one actual **in** parameter to correspond to each formal **in** parameter. The actual **in** parameter is first evaluated and its *value* is then passed or assigned to the formal **in** parameter. For example, if the actual **in** parameter is a variable X whose value is **5**, then it is the **5** that is passed. After the values of the formal **in** parameters have been set, the statements in the procedure declaration are executed.

Another way of looking at it is to think of a formal **in** parameter as a constant declaration that looks like this:

formal_in_parameter **: constant** *type_name* **:=** *actual_in_parameter;*

The computer evaluates the actual **in** parameter to obtain a value and then passes this value into the formal **in** parameter, whose value cannot be changed by the procedure.

expressions as parameters

Since only the value of an actual **in** parameter is used, the actual **in** parameter can be any expression that evaluates to the specified type. That means the actual **in** parameter can be a variable, but it might instead be a constant or arithmetic expression or anything that evaluates to a value of the correct type. Hence, with OUTPUT_AREA, all of the following sample procedure calls are allowed (X and Y are variables of type INTEGER):

```
OUTPUT_AREA ( X, Y );
OUTPUT_AREA ( 7, 8 );
OUTPUT_AREA ( X + 7, Y rem X );
```

summary of the kinds of parameters

There are six kinds of parameters: formal **in** parameters, actual **in** parameters, formal **out** parameters, actual **out** parameters, formal **in out** parameters, and actual **in out** parameters. The long names convey meaning about how the parameters are used. The way to think of parameters is in a two-step process: first, the parameter is either *formal* or *actual*; second, it is either **in**, **out**, or **in out**. These two three-way distinctions yield the six possible kinds of parameters. A *formal parameter* appears in a procedure specification and is used to pass information into and/or out of the procedure. The *actual parameter* governs what is passed into a procedure and/or acts as a receiver of information passed out of a procedure.

A formal parameter and its corresponding actual parameter are either both called **in** parameters, **out** parameters, or **in out** parameters. The distinction among **in**, **out**, and **in out** parameters refers to the manner in which information is passed. In the case of **in out** parameters, the actual parameter is a variable whose value is passed into a procedure and in return receives a value from the procedure. In the case of **in** parameters, the actual parameter may be a more complicated expression, and it is the value of the expression that is passed to the formal parameter, which is then treated as a named constant. In the case of **out** parameters, the actual parameter is a variable whose value will be given the value that the formal parameter passes out of the procedure upon completion of that procedure.

Most programming languages have a distinction similar to **in**, **out**, and **in out** parameters. All programming languages with facilities for parameters employ the distinction between formal and actual parameters.

Procedures Calling Procedures

One procedure may include a call to another procedure. The only restriction is that a procedure call cannot appear before the procedure is declared. An example is given in Figure 4.7. The program in that figure is similar to the one in Figure 4.6, and in fact the procedures GET_NUMBER, COMPUTE_TOTAL, and PUT_NUMBER are identical to the procedures of the same name in Figure 4.6. The difference is that they are now declared and called inside a new procedure called PROCESS_COIN.

The procedure PROCESS_COIN is declared in the MAIN procedure and is called, in MAIN's block, once for each denomination of coin. A character string representing the type of the coin and a floating point constant for its value are passed into the PROCESS_COIN procedure. The value of TOTAL is also passed into the procedure. Since the third parameter in the procedure specification is of mode **in out**, a value will also be passed out of the procedure and assigned to TOTAL, giving it a new value. Notice that with this sort of arrangement, there is no need for the variables HALF_DOLLARS, QUARTERS, DIMES, NICKELS, and PENNIES.

The value of the parameter TYPE_OF_COIN in procedure PROCESS_COIN is in turn passed into the procedures GET_NUMBER and PUT_NUMBER. The values of the parameters VALUE and TOTAL are in turn passed into the procedure COMPUTE_TOTAL. A new value for the parameter TOTAL is passed out of COMPUTE_TOTAL and is in turn passed back out of PROCESS_COIN to the MAIN procedure. The procedure MAIN in turn passes TOTAL on in the succeeding calls to PROCESS_COIN. Each time PROCESS_COIN is called, it passes new values on to GET_NUMBER, COMPUTE_TOTAL, and PUT_NUMBER. Each time PROCESS_COIN is called, a new value for TOTAL is returned to the MAIN procedure.

Program

```
with I_O; use I_O;
procedure MAIN is
--                    INPUT   : The count of each type of coin
--                    DESCRIPTION : The program reads in the number of
--                                  coins for each type of coin and computes
--                                  the total value of all the coins
    AFTER : constant INTEGER := 2;
    BEFORE : constant INTEGER := 4;
    EXPONENT : constant INTEGER := 0;
    TOTAL : FLOAT := 0.00;

    procedure PROCESS_COIN ( TYPE_OF_COIN : in STRING;
                             VALUE : in FLOAT;
                             TOTAL : in out FLOAT ) is
--                    INPUT   : The type of the coin (denomination),
--                              the value of this denomination, and
--                              previous total dollar and cent value
--                              for the coins.
--                    OUTPUT : The new value for total
--                    DESCRIPTION : The procedure calls other
--                                  procedures which in turn get the
--                                  number of coins, computes a new
--                                  total, and displays information.
        NUMBER_OF_COINS : INTEGER;

        procedure GET_NUMBER ( TYPE_OF_COIN : in STRING;
                               NUMBER_OF_COINS : out INTEGER ) is
--                    INPUT   : The type of the coin
--                    OUTPUT : The number of coins
--                    DESCRIPTION : The procedure prompts the user
--                                  and reads in the number of coins
        begin -- Get_Number
            PUT ( "Enter the number of " );
            PUT ( TYPE_OF_COIN );
            PUT ( " coins." );
            NEW_LINE;
            PUT ( "Do not total the amount." );
            NEW_LINE;
            PUT ( "Just enter the number of coins." );
            NEW_LINE;
            GET ( NUMBER_OF_COINS );
            SKIP_LINE;
        end GET_NUMBER;
```

```
        procedure COMPUTE_TOTAL ( NUMBER_OF_COINS : in INTEGER;
                                  VALUE : in FLOAT;
                                  TOTAL : in out FLOAT ) is
--                 INPUT  : The previous total value of coins,
--                          the value of this denomination of coin,
--                          the number of coins for this denomination.
--                 OUTPUT : A new value for total.
--                 DESCRIPTION : The procedure computes the dollar and
--                               cent value for this denomination of
--                               coin and adds it to the previous
--                               total.
        begin -- Compute_Total
            TOTAL := TOTAL + FLOAT ( NUMBER_OF_COINS ) * VALUE;
        end COMPUTE_TOTAL;

        procedure PUT_NUMBER ( TYPE_OF_COIN : in STRING;
                               NUMBER_OF_COINS : in INTEGER ) is
--                 INPUT  : A character string that represents the
--                          denomination of the coin and the number of
--                          coins for this denomination.
--                 OUTPUT : None
--                 DESCRIPTION : The procedure displays on the screen
--                               the denomination of the coin and the
--                               number of coins in that denomination.
        begin -- Put_Number
            PUT ( TYPE_OF_COIN );
            PUT ( NUMBER_OF_COINS );
            NEW_LINE;
        end PUT_NUMBER;

    begin -- Process_Coin
        GET_NUMBER ( TYPE_OF_COIN, NUMBER_OF_COINS );
        COMPUTE_TOTAL ( NUMBER_OF_COINS, VALUE, TOTAL );
        PUT_NUMBER ( TYPE_OF_COIN, NUMBER_OF_COINS );
    end PROCESS_COIN;

begin -- Main
    PROCESS_COIN ( "Half_dollars", 0.50, TOTAL );
    PROCESS_COIN ( "Quarters" , 0.25, TOTAL );
    PROCESS_COIN ( "Dimes", 0.10, TOTAL );
    PROCESS_COIN ( "Nickels", 0.05, TOTAL );
    PROCESS_COIN ( "Pennies", 0.01, TOTAL );
    PUT ( "total to: $" ); PUT ( TOTAL, BEFORE, AFTER, EXPONENT );
    NEW_LINE;
end MAIN;
```

Sample Dialogue

```
Enter the number of Half_dollars coins.
Do not total the amount.
Just enter the number of coins.
12
Half_dollars   12
Enter the number of Quarters coins.
Do not total the amount.
Just enter the number of coins.
325
Quarters   325
Enter the number of Dimes coins.
Do not total the amount.
Just enter the number of coins.
103
Dimes   103
Enter the number of Nickels coins.
Do not total the amount.
Just enter the number of coins.
107
Nickels   107
Enter the number of Pennies coins.
Do not total the amount.
Just enter the number of coins.
57
Pennies   57
total to: $ 103.47
```

Figure 4.7 A program with procedures calling procedures.

What Kind of Parameter to Use

Deciding whether to use `in`, `out`, or `in out` parameters is fairly easy. If the procedure is only supposed to provide information to some other part of the program, then use an `out` parameter (or parameters) and have the procedure set the value of the `out` parameter(s). If the parameter is only being used to give information to the procedure, rather than get information out of the procedure, an `in` parameter should be used. If the parameter is used both to give information to the procedure and to provide information to some other part of the program, use an `in out` parameter. An `in out` parameter is the only mode of parameter that can be used like a variable. The other modes are restricted in their use. Some of the differences between the two kinds of parameters are listed in Figure 4.8.

	MODE		
	`in`	`out`	`in out`
Can be used to pass information to a procedure	YES	NO	YES
Can be used to pass information back to the calling procedure	NO	YES	YES
Can be treated like a variable and pass information to a procedure and back to the calling procedure	NO	NO	YES
Expressions allowed as actual parameters	YES	NO	NO

Figure 4.8 Differences among formal parameters.

data flow

Choosing what parameters as well as what kinds of parameters a procedure will use will be a trivial matter, provided you design your algorithm with attention to the flow of information between procedures. When you divide the problem specification for your program into subprograms, make three lists for each subprogram. One list includes all the information that will be needed to execute the subprogram; call this the *in* list. Another list should show all the information that must be provided by this subprogram to other subprograms or to the calling program; call this the *out* list. If some quantity appears on both lists, it must be a quantity that will be changed by the procedure; it really belongs on an *in out* list and so should be an **`in out`** parameter. The **`in`** parameters are easy to derive from the rest of the *in* list. The **`out`** parameters are easy to derive from the rest of the *out* list. This produces three lists as the final data description.

Procedural Abstraction

One purpose of procedures is to simplify your reasoning by *abstracting* away irrelevant properties of a program part. When using a procedure, we need only think about what the procedure does; we need not think about how it does it. When we use the procedure `COMPUTE_TOTAL`, which appears in Figures 4.6 and 4.7, we need only know that it computes the total value of the coins up to this point; we need not concern ourselves with how it computes this amount. This detail need not concern us when we use the procedure.

Once a procedure is written, the details of how it works can be ignored. What it does should be expressed in a comment at the start of the procedure body declaration. This comment should tell anybody who wants to use the procedure all that he or she needs to know in order to use it. The user of the procedure should not need even to look at the procedure's block of statements (those statements after the **begin** for the procedure).

designing procedures

Procedural abstraction is more than a way to summarize a procedure's actions. It should be the first step in designing and writing a procedure. When you design a program, you should specify what each procedure does before you start to design how the procedure will do it. In particular, the comments that describe a procedure's actions and the list of parameters that show which items may be affected by the procedure should be designed and written down before starting to design the procedure body. If you later discover that your specification cannot be realized in a reasonable way, you may need to back up and rethink what a procedure should do, but by clearly specifying what you think the procedure should do, you will minimize both design errors and wasted time writing code that does not fit the problem at hand.

Procedural abstraction is a way to keep your reasoning about your personal programs clearer. It is even more important when programming as a team. In team situations, one programmer often does not know how a procedure written by another programmer works, and need not know. In a way you have already experienced this. We wrote a procedure that calculates square roots. You can use this procedure effectively even if you know little about extracting square roots, and you certainly do not need to know the details of how this particular algorithm extracts square roots.

Exercises

Self-Test Exercises

1. What is the output of the following program?

```
with I_O; use I_O;
procedure MAIN is
    procedure FRIENDLY is
    begin -- Friendly
        PUT ( "Hello" ); NEW_LINE;
    end FRIENDLY;
    procedure SHY is
    begin -- Shy
        PUT ( "Goodbye" ); NEW_LINE;
    end SHY;
```

```
begin -- Main
    PUT ( "Begin Conversation" ); NEW_LINE;
    SHY;
    FRIENDLY;
    PUT ( "One more time: " ); NEW_LINE;
    FRIENDLY;
    SHY;
    PUT ( "End Conversation" ); NEW_LINE;
end MAIN;
```

2. What is the output of the following program?

```
with I_O; use I_O;
procedure MAIN is
    A, B : INTEGER;
    procedure ARTHUR ( X : in out INTEGER;
                       Y : out INTEGER ) is
    begin
        X := 2;
        X := X + 1;
        Y := 2 * X;
    end ARTHUR;
begin -- Main
    A := 4;
    B := 5;
    ARTHUR ( A, B );
    PUT ( A ); PUT ( B ); NEW_LINE;
    A := 4;
    B := 5;
    ARTHUR ( B, A );
    PUT ( A ); PUT ( B ); NEW_LINE;
end MAIN;
```

3. What is the output of the following program?

```
with I_O; use I_O;;
procedure MAIN is
    procedure ONE is
    begin
        PUT ( "One" );
    end ONE;
    procedure TWO is
    begin
        ONE;
        PUT ( "Two" );
    end TWO;
```

```
      procedure THREE is
      begin
         TWO;
         PUT ( "Three" );
         NEW_LINE;
      end THREE;
begin -- Main
      ONE;
      NEW_LINE;
      TWO;
      NEW_LINE;
      THREE;
      NEW_LINE;
end MAIN;
```

4. What is the output of the following program?

```
with I_O; use I_O;
procedure MAIN is
      X : INTEGER := 1;
      Y : INTEGER := 2;
      procedure TRICKY ( Y, X : in INTEGER ) is
      begin
            PUT ( X ); PUT ( Y ); NEW_LINE;
      end TRICKY;
begin -- Main
      TRICKY ( Y, X );
      TRICKY ( Y, Y );
      TRICKY ( X, Y );
end MAIN;
```

5. Write a procedure with one **in out** parameter of type INTEGER that leaves the parameter unchanged if it is positive or zero and changes it to zero if its value is negative.

6. Write a procedure with one formal **in out** parameter, ANSWER, of type CHARACTER. If the value of ANSWER is 'Y' the procedure changes it to 'y'; if the value is anything else it is not changed.

Case Study

Change-Making Program with Procedures

Problem Definition

We will redesign the change-making program from Chapter 2 so that it uses procedures for subproblems. The program will accept an amount between **1** and **99** and will output a combination of quarter, dime, and penny coins that total that many cents.

Discussion

For reference, let us summarize our previous analysis of subproblems and data flow for this problem. We needed a variable AMOUNT for holding the total amount of money, we also needed variables to hold the number of each coin as well as a variable AMOUNT_LEFT to hold the amount left as we proceeded down the list of coins from quarters to dimes to pennies, computing the number of each coin to be given out. The breakdown into subproblems is summarized in the following pseudocode.

Algorithm

begin -- Main
1. INPUT_AMOUNT : Input the amount and store it in the variable AMOUNT;
2. AMOUNT_LEFT := AMOUNT;
3. COMPUTE_CHANGE : Compute a combination of quarters, dimes and pennies whose value equals AMOUNT_LEFT;
4. OUTPUT_COINS : Output AMOUNT and the number of each coin

end MAIN;

All subproblems, except subproblem 2, will be implemented as procedures. Subproblem 3, COMPUTE_CHANGE, is further subdivided as follows. We will implement each of these smaller subproblems as a procedure.

begin -- Compute_Change

3a. COMPUTE_QUARTERS : Compute the maximum number of quarters in CHANGE, and decrease CHANGE by the total value of quarters;

3b. COMPUTE_DIMES : Compute the maximum number of dimes in CHANGE, and decrease CHANGE by the total value of dimes;

3c. COMPUTE_PENNIES: Compute the number of pennies in CHANGE;

end COMPUTE_CHANGE;

Figure 4.9 lists all of the procedures and their parameters and categorizes the parameters as **in**, **out**, or **in out**.

	in	out	in out
INPUT_AMOUNT		AMOUNT	
COMPUTE_CHANGE	CHANGE	QUARTERS DIMES PENNIES	
COMPUTE_QUARTERS		QUARTERS	CHANGE
COMPUTE_DIMES		DIMES	CHANGE
COMPUTE_PENNIES		PENNIES	CHANGE
OUTPUT_COINS	AMOUNT QUARTERS DIMES PENNIES		

Figure 4.9 Procedures and parameters for making change.

procedures for subproblems

The completed program is in Figure 4.10. That program is equivalent to the one in Figure 2.10. The two programs will carry on exactly the same dialogue with the user, but the version with procedures explicitly shows the breakdown of the program into smaller subalgorithms.

When you examine the program, you will find an apparent discrepancy in the way the parameter CHANGE for the procedure COMPUTE_CHANGE is listed in Figure 4.9 and the way it is declared in the actual program in Figure 4.10. Notice that the parameter CHANGE is listed as an **in** parameter. That is intuitively correct. However, CHANGE is used inside the procedure to pass information into and out of the other compute procedures. We expect the COMPUTE_QUARTERS procedure to reduce the value of CHANGE, thus we are using CHANGE as a variable. Any parameter that is used inside a procedure as a variable must be an **in out** parameter. An **in** parameter value can only be used, it cannot be changed. An **out** parameter can only be assigned a value, it cannot be used for any other purpose.

Program

```
with I_O; use I_O;
procedure MAIN is
--              INPUT  : Amount of change.
--              OUTPUT : The correct number of quarters, dimes,
--                       and pennies for the amount of change.
--              DESCRIPTION : Computes the coins used to give an
--                            amount between 1 and 99 cents.
```

```
    AMOUNT,
    AMOUNT_LEFT,
    NUMBER_OF_DIMES,
    NUMBER_OF_PENNIES,
    NUMBER_OF_QUARTERS : INTEGER;

    procedure INPUT_AMOUNT ( CENTS : out INTEGER ) is
--                    INPUT  : None
--                    OUTPUT : The amount of change in cents.
--                    DESCRIPTION : Prompt the user and read in the
--                                  amount of change between 1 and 99 cents.
    begin -- Input_Amount
        PUT ( "Enter an amount of change" ); NEW_LINE;
        PUT ( "from 1 to 99 cents: " ); NEW_LINE;
        GET ( CENTS ); SKIP_LINE;
    end INPUT_AMOUNT;

    procedure COMPUTE_QUARTERS ( QUARTERS : out INTEGER;
                                  CHANGE : in out INTEGER ) is
--                    INPUT  : The amount of change.
--                    OUTPUT : The number of quarters and change left.
--                    DESCRIPTION : Computes the maximum number of
--                                  quarters in the change, and decreases
--                                  change by the value of the quarters.
    begin -- Compute_Quarters
        QUARTERS := CHANGE / 25;
        CHANGE := CHANGE rem 25;
    end COMPUTE_QUARTERS;

    procedure COMPUTE_DIMES ( DIMES : out INTEGER;
                              CHANGE : in out INTEGER ) is
--                    INPUT  : The amount of change.
--                    OUTPUT : The number of dimes and change left.
--                    DESCRIPTION : Computes the maximum number of
--                                  dimes in the change, and decreases
--                                  change by the value of the dimes.
    begin -- Compute_Dimes
        DIMES := CHANGE / 10;
        CHANGE := CHANGE rem 10;
    end COMPUTE_DIMES;

    procedure COMPUTE_PENNIES ( PENNIES : out INTEGER;
                                CHANGE : in out INTEGER ) is
--                    INPUT  : The amount of change.
--                    OUTPUT : The number of pennies and change left.
--                    DESCRIPTION : Computes the maximum number of
--                                  pennies in the change, and decreases
--                                  change by the value of the pennies.
```

```
    begin -- Compute_Pennies
         PENNIES := CHANGE;
         CHANGE := 0;
    end COMPUTE_PENNIES;

    procedure COMPUTE_CHANGE ( CHANGE : in out INTEGER;
                               QUARTERS,
                               DIMES,
                               PENNIES : out INTEGER ) is
--                    INPUT  : The amount of change.
--                    OUTPUT : The number of quarters, dimes, pennies.
--                    DESCRIPTION : Computes the maximum number of each
--                                  coin in change.
    begin -- Compute_Change
         COMPUTE_QUARTERS ( QUARTERS, CHANGE );
         COMPUTE_DIMES ( DIMES, CHANGE );
         COMPUTE_PENNIES ( PENNIES, CHANGE );
    end COMPUTE_CHANGE;

    procedure OUTPUT_COINS ( CHANGE,
                             QUARTERS,
                             DIMES,
                             PENNIES : in INTEGER ) is
--                    INPUT  : The total amount of change and
--                             the number of each coin.
--                    OUTPUT : None
--                    DESCRIPTION : Displays the information on the screen
    begin -- Output_Coins
         PUT ( CHANGE );
         PUT ( " cents can be given as: " );
         NEW_LINE;
         PUT ( QUARTERS ); PUT ( " quarters" ); NEW_LINE;
         PUT ( DIMES ); PUT ( " dimes and" ); NEW_LINE;
         PUT ( PENNIES ); PUT ( " pennies" ); NEW_LINE;
    end OUTPUT_COINS;

begin -- Main
    INPUT_AMOUNT ( AMOUNT );
    AMOUNT_LEFT := AMOUNT;
    COMPUTE_CHANGE ( AMOUNT_LEFT,
                     NUMBER_OF_QUARTERS,
                     NUMBER_OF_DIMES,
                     NUMBER_OF_PENNIES );
    OUTPUT_COINS ( AMOUNT,
                   NUMBER_OF_QUARTERS,
                   NUMBER_OF_DIMES,
                   NUMBER_OF_PENNIES );
end MAIN;
```

Sample Dialogue

```
Enter an amount of change
from 1 to 99 cents:
96
       96 cents can be given as:
        3 quarters
        2 dimes and
        1 pennies
```

Figure 4.10 Change-making program using procedures.

We first wrote this change-making program without procedures and then rewrote it using procedures. We did this simply because we did not know about procedures when we first wrote the program. Normally each subproblem is translated into a subprogram, in this case a procedure, before it is used in any Ada program. The stepwise refinement of programs into subprograms and the writing of procedures go hand in hand.

Pitfall

Incorrectly Ordered Parameter Lists

In the example given, if the order of an actual parameter list did not correspond to the desired association pattern for passage of information, the program would not perform correctly. The computer associates the first actual parameter with the first formal parameter, the second actual parameter with the second formal parameter, and so forth. It does not care about any mnemonic matches, such as NUMBER_OF_QUARTERS for QUARTERS or NUMBER_OF_PENNIES for PENNIES. To see what can happen when parameter lists are ordered incorrectly, let us once again consider the change-making program in Figure 4.10. Suppose we had mistakenly ordered the actual parameters in the procedure call to OUTPUT_COINS as follows:

```
OUTPUT_COINS ( AMOUNT,
               NUMBER_OF_PENNIES,
               NUMBER_OF_DIMES,
               NUMBER_OF_QUARTERS );
```

Then the last portion of the output would change to

```
96 cents can be given as
 1 quarters
 2 dimes and
 3 pennies
```

If the formal and actual parameters do not match in type, the computer will give an error message. However, in cases such as this one where all the parameters are of the same type, a misordering of the parameter list will simply produce an incorrect result.

Generalizing Procedures

Once you have broken a problem down into subproblems, it is a good idea to look for general procedures that can solve more than one subproblem merely by varying some of their parameters. For example, if you look back at the change-making program in Figure 4.10, you will notice that the procedure for calculating the numbers of quarters and the one for computing the number of dimes are very similar. They each contain one application of / to find the number of coins and one application of **rem** to find the amount left after giving out that many coins. For quarters the calculation is

```
QUARTERS := AMOUNT_LEFT / 25;
AMOUNT_LEFT := AMOUNT_LEFT rem 25;
```

For computing dimes it is

```
DIMES := AMOUNT_LEFT / 10;
AMOUNT_LEFT := AMOUNT_LEFT rem 10;
```

These two calculations differ in just two places: in one case QUARTERS is used on the left-hand side of the assignment operator, and in the other case DIMES is used; in one case 25 is used where in the other case 10 is used. We can use two formal parameters to obtain a single procedure that can realize either of these computations. If we call these parameters NUMBER and COIN_VALUE, the more general calculation with parameters reads as follows:

```
NUMBER := AMOUNT_LEFT / COIN_VALUE;
AMOUNT_LEFT := AMOUNT_LEFT rem COIN_VALUE;
```

The complete procedure, called COMPUTE_COINS, as well as the procedure COMPUTE_CHANGE that calls it are shown in Figure 4.11. We have extended the procedure COMPUTE_CHANGE so that it also uses nickels. With the general procedure COMPUTE_COINS at our disposal, this is easy to do. We could just as easily add half-dollar coins, and such additions do not significantly complicate the program. If efficiency is a major issue, the last call to COMPUTE_COINS can be replaced by the following simpler way to set the value of PENNIES:

```
PENNIES := AMOUNT_LEFT;
```

Notice that in order to make the general procedure COMPUTE_COINS work in a variety of cases, we needed to add one additional parameter beyond those needed by the specialized procedures such as COMPUTE_QUARTERS. One often needs to add one or more parameters to a procedure design in order to fit the procedure to a particular use.

As was true in this example, it is often the case that the generalization is not apparent until after you have written a few of the more specialized procedures that it will replace. If that turns out to be true, and the generalized procedure is sensible, do not hesitate to discard the old procedures and replace them with this new procedure. The work done on the old procedures is not wasted. It helped you to find the better solution.

```
procedure COMPUTE_COINS ( COIN_VALUE : in INTEGER;
                          NUMBER     : out INTEGER;
                          CHANGE     : in out INTEGER ) is
--              INPUT  : The value of the coin and
--                       the amount of change.
--              OUTPUT : The number of coins and change left.
--              DESCRIPTION : Computes the maximum number of
--                            coins in a denomination in the change,
--                            and decreases change by the value
--                            of the denomination.
begin -- Compute_Coins
    NUMBER := CHANGE / COIN_VALUE;
    CHANGE := CHANGE rem COIN_VALUE;
end COMPUTE_COINS;

procedure COMPUTE_CHANGE ( CHANGE : in out INTEGER;
                           QUARTERS,
                           DIMES,
                           PENNIES : out INTEGER ) is
--              INPUT  : The amount of change.
--              OUTPUT : The number of quarters, dimes, pennies.
--              DESCRIPTION : Computes the maximum number of each
--                            coin in change.
begin -- Compute_Change
    COMPUTE_COINS ( 25, QUARTERS, CHANGE );
    COMPUTE_COINS ( 10, DIMES, CHANGE );
    COMPUTE_COINS (  1, PENNIES, CHANGE );
end COMPUTE_CHANGE;
```

Figure 4.11 General procedures for number of coins.

Simple Ada Functions

We have already encountered some predefined standard conversion functions, such as **INTEGER (** *float_value* **)** and **FLOAT (** *integer_value* **)**. These functions are provided as part of the Ada language. You can also define new functions within an Ada program. We will now describe how these new functions are designed and used.

call These programmer-defined functions are called in exactly the same way as the standard functions we have been using. To *call* any function in Ada, the program provides the function with zero or more parameters, and the function returns a single value. For example, in the statement

```
INTEGER_VALUE := INTEGER ( 2.9 + 0.5 );
```

the function `INTEGER` returns the value `3`. A function call is a particular kind of expression, and like all other expressions, it has a value. That value is called the value *returned* by the function.

value returned

An Ada function is used differently from a procedure. A procedure call is a statement, and like any statement, it performs some action. A function call is an expression, and like any expression, it returns a value. Although it is called in a different way, you declare a function in much the same way as you declare a procedure. Function body declarations and procedure body declarations appear in the same place in a program, that is, in the declarative part of the program before the **`begin`**. Function and procedure body declarations may be intermixed. To get the feel of these function body declarations, we will start with a simple example.

A Sample Function Body Declaration

parameter list

Figure 4.12 shows a program with a function body declaration for a function called `CUBE`. This function takes one parameter of type `INTEGER` and returns a value of type `INTEGER`; more specifically, it returns the cube of its parameter. Function specifications have formal parameter lists that have the same syntax as procedure parameter lists, with one exception: the mode of parameter passage must always be **`in`**. The sample function has one formal parameter whose value is set equal to the value of the function's actual parameter when the function is called. The purpose of restricting the mode to **`in`** only is to eliminate the side effects that would occur if a function were allowed to return values via **`in out`** or **`out`** parameters. The purpose of a function is to return a single value; if you design a subprogram to return more than one value, it must be a procedure.

function specification

Although a function specification greatly resembles a procedure specification, it does differ in some ways from a procedure specification. First, it starts with the word **`function`** rather than the word **`procedure`**. Two more significant differences are concerned with specifying the value to be returned. The first significant difference is that the function is given a **`return`** type in the function specification. In Figure 4.12 the second instance of `INTEGER` (the one at the end, after the **`return`**) tells the compiler that this function will return a value type `INTEGER`. Thus, this function can only be used in places where it is appropriate to use a value of type `INTEGER`.

The type of the value returned for a given function may be any Ada type. Thus far we have seen `INTEGER`, `FLOAT`, `CHARACTER`, and `BOOLEAN` types; later in this book we will discuss additional types. The complete syntax for a function specification is given in Figure 4.13.

Since the *only* mode allowed in a function parameter list is **`in`**, and since a blank or empty mode means the same thing, we will, as a standard practice in this book, leave the mode empty in all future function specifications.

Program

```
with I_O; use I_O;
procedure MAIN is
--                        INPUT  : An integer value between 1 and 10.
--                        OUTPUT : Displays the values that have been cubed.
--                        DESCRIPTION : A test program for the cube function.
     NUMBER : INTEGER;
     TWO_CUBED : INTEGER;
     function CUBE ( ROOT : INTEGER ) return INTEGER is
--                        INPUT : A value to be cubed.
--                        OUTPUT : The cube of the input value.
--                        DESCRIPTION : Raises the root to the 3rd power.
     begin -- Cube
          return ROOT ** 3;
     end CUBE;
begin -- Main
     TWO_CUBED := CUBE ( 2 );
     PUT ( "2 cubed is"); PUT ( TWO_CUBED ); NEW_LINE;
     PUT ( "Enter a number between 1 and 10:" ); NEW_LINE;
     GET ( NUMBER ); SKIP_LINE;
     PUT ( NUMBER, 1 ); PUT ("cubed is");
     PUT ( CUBE ( NUMBER ) );
     NEW_LINE;
end MAIN;
```

Sample Dialogue

```
2 cubed is        8
Enter a number between 1 and 10:
3
3 cubed is       27
```

Figure 4.12 A test program for a cube function.

The Return Statement

The second major difference between a function and a procedure is that, somewhere within the block of the function body declaration, there *must* be a **return** statement. This is the way the function body declaration specifies the value to be returned. A template for the **return** statement in a function takes the following form:

return *expression*;

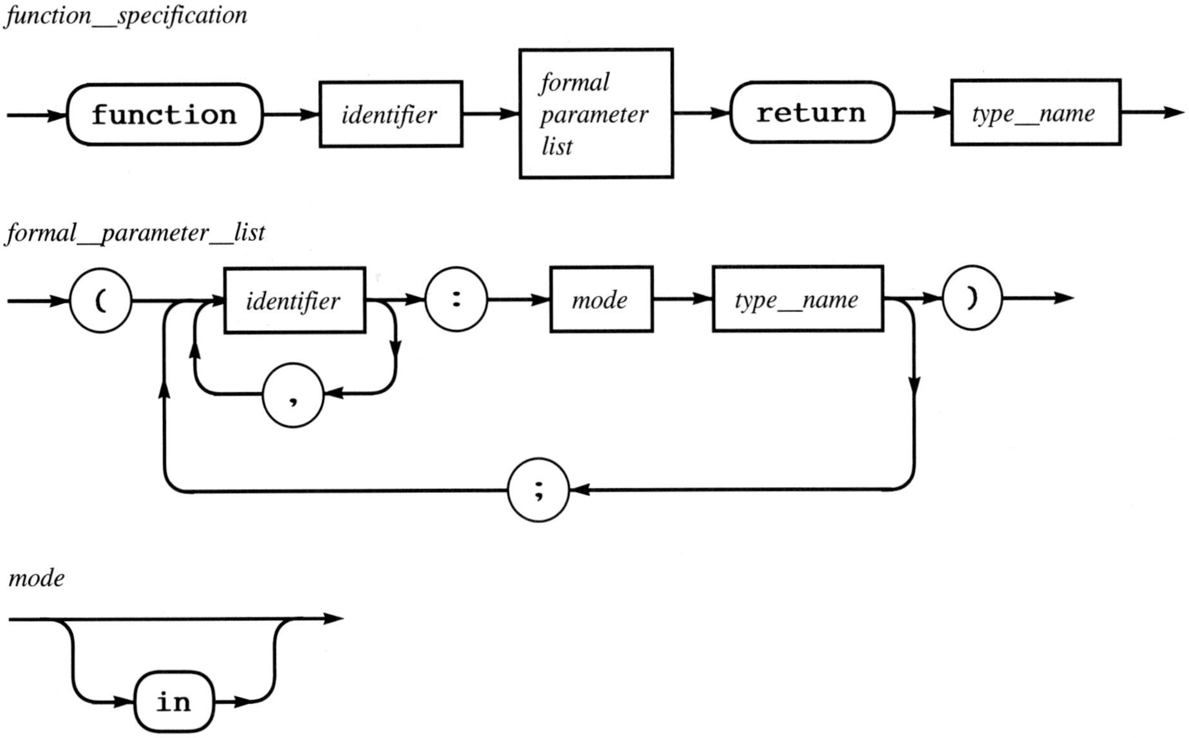

function_specification

formal_parameter_list

mode

Figure 4.13 Syntax for a function specification.

Every function must have at least one statement that consists of the reserved word **return** followed by an *expression*. The expression's resultant value must be of the same type as the type following the **return** in the function specification. Whatever value the expression evaluates to when the **return** statement is executed is the value that will be returned by the function when it is called. When the **return** statement in the function is executed, the expression is evaluated, the function execution is terminated, and the expression's value is returned.

value returned

In the sample program in Figure 4.12, the following statement appears:

```
return ROOT ** 3;
```

The statement means, return the value of the expression ROOT times ROOT times ROOT as the value for the function CUBE. When the function CUBE is called in the program statement

```
NUMBER := CUBE ( 2 );
```

the value of the parameter, in this case 2, is used to set the value of ROOT, and the expression ROOT ** 3 is evaluated. The statement

```
return ROOT ** 3;
```

says to return this value, namely 8, as the value of the function. In the sample program, the value returned for CUBE (2), and hence the new value of NUMBER, is 8.

Remember, a **return** followed by an expression *must* appear in a function. It may appear as often as is needed. The first **return** to be executed terminates the function.

A **return** statement with an expression may *never* be used in a procedure. However, a **return** without a following expression *may* appear in a procedure. It is a statement that can appear anywhere in the block of the procedure just as any other statement. It may appear as often as is needed. When a **return** statement in a procedure is executed, the procedure terminates execution. At that point any **in out** or **out** parameters return values to the calling procedure just as they normally would. The program continues execution, just as it normally would, with the statement following the procedure call. Remember, the first **return** to be executed terminates the procedure. The general form for the syntax for the **return** statement is given in Figure 4.14.

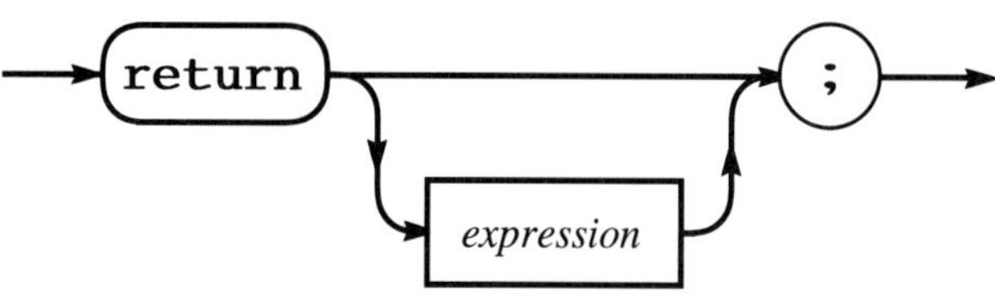

Figure 4.14 Syntax for the return statement.

Functions with Multiple Returns

Since a function must always return a value, a function block must always contain at least one statement, a **return** statement that contains an expression. Every call of the function must cause one of these **return** statements to be executed. A function can contain more than one such statement, but only one of them will be executed. When a **return** statement is executed, the function is terminated. The value of the expression in the **return** is what is returned as a value for the function.

For example, consider the function in Figure 4.15. It assumes that its parameter is one of these symbols: 'y', 'Y', 'n', or 'N'. It returns the uppercase versions of these parameters, so if the parameter is 'y' or 'Y' it returns Y'; if the parameter is 'n' or 'N' it returns N'. The function might be used to process yes/no answers. For example, to terminate the test loop, we used the boolean expression *example*

```
UPPER_CASE ( ANSWER ) = 'N'
```

instead of

```
ANSWER = 'n'
or
ANSWER = 'N'
```

The function tests the value of ANSWER. If its value is 'n' (lowercase), then 'N' (uppercase) is returned. If the value of ANSWER is 'y', 'Y' is returned. If ANSWER is neither 'y' nor 'n', then the function UPPER_CASE returns whatever ANSWER is, with no change of case.

Program

```
with I_O; use I_O;
procedure MAIN is
--              INPUT   : Upper- and lowercase characters
--                        'y', 'Y', 'n', or 'N'
--              OUTPUT : The uppercase version.
--              DESCRIPTION : This is a test program for the
--                            upper- and lowercase characters
   ANSWER : CHARACTER;
   functionUPPER_CASE ( ANSWER : CHARACTER )
           return CHARACTER is
--              INPUT   : One of the following characters
--                        'y', 'Y', 'n', or 'N'
--              OUTPUT : The uppercase version of answer.
--              DESCRIPTION : Tests for 'n' or 'y' and returns
--                            'N' or 'Y', respectively.
   begin -- Upper_Case
       if ANSWER = 'n' then
          return 'N';
       else
          if ANSWER = 'y' then
             return 'Y';
          else
             return ANSWER;
          end if;
       end if;
   end UPPER_CASE;
```

```
begin -- Main
    PUT ( "This is a test." ); NEW_LINE;
    loop
        PUT ( "Answer yes or no:" ); NEW_LINE;
        GET ( ANSWER ); SKIP_LINE;
        PUT ( "The uppercase version of" );
        NEW_LINE;
        PUT ( "the first letter you typed is:" );
        PUT ( UPPER_CASE ( ANSWER ) ); NEW_LINE;
        PUT ( "Test again! (y/n)" ); NEW_LINE;
        GET ( ANSWER ); SKIP_LINE;
        exit when UPPER_CASE ( ANSWER ) = 'N';
    end loop;
    PUT ( "End of test." ); NEW_LINE;
end MAIN;
```

Sample Dialogue

```
This is a test.
Answer yes or no:
no
The uppercase version of
the first letter you typed is: N
Test again! (y/n)
y
Answer yes or no:
No
The uppercase version of
the first letter you typed is: N
Test again! (y/n)
Yes
Answer yes or no:
yes
The uppercase version of
the first letter you typed is: Y
Test again! (y/n)
y
Answer yes or no:
YES
The uppercase version of
the first letter you typed is: Y
Test again! (y/n)
n
End of test.
```

Figure 4.15 A function that changes its mind.

Side Effects

The purpose of a function is to take the values of some parameters and return a *single* value, but an Ada function can actually do more. A function cannot do everything that a procedure can do. A function is not allowed to have **in out** nor **out** parameters. A function can, however, change the value of a variable that is outside the function, write a message to the screen, read a value from the keyboard, or do anything else like that that a procedure can do, so long as it also returns a value. However, it is usually a bad idea to use any of these other features when designing functions.

what a function can do

If a function changes the value of a variable outside of the function or causes a GET or PUT statement to be executed, that extra feature is referred to as a *side effect.* Side effects are usually a bad idea. We think of a function as simply returning a value, and if we want it to do more, it is usually clearer to write a procedure rather than a function and to return the value via an **in out** or **out** parameter. Mathematicians think of functions as taking zero or more parameters and generating a single value. If the logic of your program requires that the parameters be used to generate more than one value, use a procedure.

what a function should not do

Exercises

Self-Test Exercises

7. What is the output of the following program?

```
with I_O; use I_O;
procedure MAIN is
     function CRAZY ( NUMBER : INTEGER )
               return CHARACTER is
     begin -- Crazy
          if NUMBER = 1 then
               return 'A';
          end if;
          if NUMBER = 2 then
               return 'B';
          end if;
          return 'X';
     end CRAZY;
begin -- Main
     PUT ( CRAZY ( 1 ) ); PUT ( CRAZY ( 2 ) ); PUT ( CRAZY ( 3 ) );
     NEW_LINE;
end MAIN;
```

8. What is wrong with the following function body declaration?

```
function POWER_OF_TWO ( POWER : INTEGER )
         return INTEGER is
    INDEX : INTEGER := 1;
begin
    POWER_OF_TWO := 1;
    loop
        exit when INDEX > POWER;
        POWER_OF_TWO := POWER_OF_TWO * 2;
        INDEX := INDEX + 1;
    end loop;
end POWER_OF_TWO;
```

9. Write a function that has two parameters for the length and width of a rectangle and that returns the area of a rectangle with those dimensions.

10. Write a function body declaration for a function that has one parameter of type `INTEGER` and returns the letter `'P'` if the number is positive and the letter `'N'` if it is zero or negative.

11. For each of the following subproblems, tell whether it is best implemented as a function or as a procedure:
   a. Converting a given number of miles to an equivalent number of kilometers.
   b. Converting a given number of centimeters to feet and inches.
   c. Displaying the output of a program on the screen.
   d. Computing the net income and the tax due on an income tax return, given the gross income and the adjustments to income.
   e. Computing an automobile's miles per gallon, given the miles traveled and the number of gallons of gasoline consumed.

Case Study

Supermarket Pricing with Function and Procedures

Problem Definition

We have been commissioned by the Super-Duper supermarket chain to write a program that will determine the retail price of an item, given suitable input. Their pricing policy is that any item that is expected to sell in less than one week is marked up 5%, and any item that is expected to stay on the shelf for one week or more is marked up 10% over the wholesale price.

Discussion

Like many programming problems, this one breaks down into three subprograms: input the data, do a computation, and then output the results. For this example we will call the subprograms, respectively, GET_INPUT, COMPUTE_PRICE, and GIVE_OUTPUT. Figure 4.16 is a table that presents the subprograms and the in and out lists for the parameters.

	in	out
GET_INPUT		COST TIME
COMPUTE_PRICE	COST TIME	PRICE
GIVE_OUTPUT	COST TIME PRICE	

Figure 4.16 Parameter in and out lists.

The procedure GET_INPUT will prompt the user and read in the values for COST and TIME. These values will then be passed out of the procedure to the MAIN procedure as WHOLESALE_COST and EXPECTED_SHELF_LIFE. These two values will then be passed into the COMPUTE_PRICE function, which will compute the price and return that value to the MAIN procedure, where it is assigned to RETAIL_PRICE. The last procedure, GIVE_OUTPUT, is to be passed all of this information and displays it on the screen in a form the user can read. The subprogram specifications are as follows:

```
procedure GET_INPUT ( COST : out FLOAT;
                      TIME : out INTEGER )

function COMPUTE_PRICE ( COST : in FLOAT;
                         TIME : in INTEGER )
                         return FLOAT

procedure GIVE_OUTPUT ( COST  : in FLOAT;
                        TIME  : in INTEGER;
                        PRICE : in FLOAT )
```

Algorithm

The algorithm for the COMPUTE_PRICE function is straightforward:

```
if TIME < 7
    return cost + 5% of cost
else
    return cost + 10% of cost
```

The complete program is displayed in Figure 4.17.

Program

```
with I_O; use I_O;
procedure MAIN is
--                  INPUT  : The wholesale cost of an item and
--                           its expected shelf life.
--                  OUTPUT : The wholesale cost, the shelf life, and
--                           the retail price of an item.
--                  DESCRIPTION : Determines the retail price of an item
--                                according to the pricing policies of
--                                the Super-Duper supermarket chain.
--                                A markup of 5% for items with shelf
--                                life of less than 7 days, otherwise
--                                10%.
    AFTER          : constant INTEGER := 2;
    BEFORE         : constant INTEGER := 2;
    EXPONENT       : constant INTEGER := 0;
    HIGH_MARK_UP   : constant FLOAT := 0.10;
    LOW_MARK_UP    : constant FLOAT := 0.05;
    THRESHOLD      : constant INTEGER := 7;
    EXPECTED_SHELF_LIFE : INTEGER;
    RETAIL_PRICE,
    WHOLESALE_COST      : FLOAT;

    procedure GET_INPUT ( COST : out FLOAT; TIME : out INTEGER ) is
--                      INPUT  : None
--                      OUTPUT : The wholesale cost and
--                               the expected shelf life
    begin -- Get_Input
        PUT ( "Enter the wholesale cost of item:" ); NEW_LINE;
        GET ( COST ); SKIP_LINE;
        PUT ( "Enter expected number of days until sold:" ); NEW_LINE;
        GET ( TIME ); SKIP_LINE;
    end GET_INPUT;
```

```
    function COMPUTE_PRICE ( COST : FLOAT;
                             TIME : INTEGER )
                             return FLOAT is
--                INPUT  : The wholesale cost and
--                         the expected shelf life
--                OUTPUT : The retail price
--                DESCRIPTION : The retail price based of a markup
--                              5% for shelf life of less than 7 days
--                              otherwise 10%.
    begin -- Compute_Price
        if TIME < THRESHOLD then
            return ( 1.00 + LOW_MARK_UP ) * COST;
        else
            return ( 1.00 + HIGH_MARK_UP ) * COST;
        end if;
    end COMPUTE_PRICE;

    procedure GIVE_OUTPUT ( COST  : in FLOAT;
                            TIME  : in INTEGER;
                            PRICE : in FLOAT ) is
--                INPUT : The wholesale cost, the expected shelf
--                        life, and the retail price.
--               DESCRIPTION : Displays the information on the screen
    begin -- Give_Output
        PUT ( "Wholesale cost = $" );
        PUT ( COST, BEFORE, AFTER, EXPONENT );
        NEW_LINE;
        PUT ( "Expected time until sold = " );
        PUT ( TIME );
        PUT ("days" );
        NEW_LINE;
        PUT ( "Retail price = $" );
        PUT ( PRICE, BEFORE, AFTER, EXPONENT );
        NEW_LINE;
    end GIVE_OUTPUT;

begin -- Main
    PUT ( "This program determines" ); NEW_LINE;
    PUT ( "retail price for stock items." ); NEW_LINE;
    GET_INPUT ( WHOLESALE_COST, EXPECTED_SHELF_LIFE );
    RETAIL_PRICE := COMPUTE_PRICE
    (WHOLESALE_COST,EXPECTED_SHELF_LIFE);
    GIVE_OUTPUT ( WHOLESALE_COST, EXPECTED_SHELF_LIFE, RETAIL_PRICE );
end MAIN;
```

Sample Dialogue

```
This program determines
retail price for stock items.
Enter the wholesale cost of item:
1.21
Enter expected number of days until sold:
5
Wholesale cost = $ 1.21
Expected time until sold =        5 days
Retail price = $ 1.27
```

Figure 4.17 Supermarket pricing program.

Choosing Parameter Names

Subprograms are self-contained units that are best designed separately from the rest of the program. On large programming projects, a different programmer may be assigned to write each subprogram. The programmer should choose the most meaningful names he or she can find for formal parameters. The actual parameters that will be associated with the formal parameters should also be given meaningful names, often chosen by somebody else. Proceeding in this way, it is likely that some or all parameters may have formal and actual parameters of the same name. That is perfectly acceptable. Figure 4.18 is an example of a program in which the formal and actual parameters are given identical names. Technically speaking, the formal parameter `PRICE` and the actual parameter `PRICE` are two different objects that just happen to have the same name. The computer will still associate the actual parameter `PRICE` with the formal parameter `PRICE`. Programs with parameters of the same name are handled in the same way by the compiler as those with differently named formal and actual parameters.

This unrestricted choice for parameter names is an important part of the top-down, divide-and-conquer method of writing programs. When you are writing a subprogram, you should be concentrating on the subprogram and what it does. You should not have to be thinking about what names are used for variables in the main program.

After you become comfortable with parameters, you will naturally tend to give formal and actual parameters the same names. However, for your first few programs, it may make it easier to understand parameters if you use different names for formal and actual parameters.

Program

```
with I_O; use I_O;
procedure MAIN is
    TAXRATE : constant FLOAT := 0.06;
    BILL    : FLOAT;
    NUMBER  : INTEGER;
    PRICE   : FLOAT;
    function TOTAL ( NUMBER : INTEGER;
                     PRICE  : FLOAT )
                     return FLOAT is
    begin -- Total
        return FLOAT ( NUMBER ) * ( PRICE + TAXRATE * PRICE );
    end TOTAL;
begin -- Main
    PUT ( "Enter price and number of items:" ); NEW_LINE;
    GET ( PRICE ); GET ( NUMBER ); SKIP_LINE;
    BILL := TOTAL ( NUMBER, PRICE );
    PUT ( NUMBER ); PUT ("items at $" );
    PUT ( PRICE, 3, 2, 0 ); NEW_LINE;
    PUT ( "Total Bill $" ); PUT ( BILL, 3, 2, 0 ); NEW_LINE;
end MAIN;
```

Figure 4.18 Function call with formal and actual parameters of the same name.

Summary of Problem Solving and Programming Techniques

- When designing programs by the top-down method, subproblems are normally implemented as subprograms.
- Parameters are used to pass information between procedures.
- The first steps in designing a procedure are to decide what duty it is supposed to accomplish and what information it needs.
- Analyzing the flow of information into and out of a procedure will make it clear what parameters are needed and whether they should be **in**, **out**, or **in out** parameters.
- **in out** parameters are used to give information to a procedure and to get information out of a procedure. They are treated as variables inside the procedure.
- **in** parameters are used only to give information to a procedure, but they are treated as constants objects inside the procedure.
- **out** parameters are used only to get information out of a procedure and cannot be treated as variables but can only be assigned a value inside the procedure.

- Constants and complicated expressions, as well as variables, may be used as actual **in** parameters. Only variables may be used as actual **in out** or **out** parameters.
- When you are designing a program, it is very common for one or more subprograms to be the computation of a single value. In those cases the subprograms should be implemented as functions.
- A restatement of a problem definition can often yield an algorithm or a hint of an algorithm for the problem.
- When you are designing functions, it is usually a bad idea to allow side effects, such as changing the value of variables outside the function or performing input-output commands. If such things are needed, it is better to use a procedure.
- Once a subprogram is written and debugged, a user should not have to know how it works. The subprogram specification and accompanying comments should explain what the subprogram does, and that should suffice to use the procedure.
- Look for opportunities to combine two or more procedures into one more general procedure.

Summary of Ada Constructs

procedure body declaration

Syntax:

```
procedure procedure_name [ ( formal_parameter_list ) ] is
      declarations
begin
      sequence_of_statements
end procedure_name;
```

Example:

```
procedure CHECK ( HOURS  : in INTEGER;
                  SALARY : out FLOAT;
                  TAX    : out FLOAT ) is
   PAYRATE : constant FLOAT := 12.50;
   TAXRATE : constant FLOAT := 0.25;
begin -- Check
   SALARY := PAYRATE * FLOAT ( HOURS );
   TAX := TAXRATE * SALARY;
end CHECK;
```

The *sequence_of_statements* may be any Ada statements and may contain the formal parameters. The square brackets in the syntax mean that the parameters and their enclosing parentheses are optional. (See the next two entries in this summary.)

procedure specification

Syntax:

```
procedure procedure_name [ ( formal_parameter_list ) ]
```

Examples:

```
procedure CHECK ( HOURS   : in INTEGER;
                  SALARY  : out FLOAT
                  TAX     : out FLOAT )
procedure CHECK ( HOURS   : in INTEGER;
                  SALARY,
                  TAX     : out FLOAT )
```

The procedure specification is the first thing in a procedure declaration. The *procedure__name* can be any identifier other than a reserved word. The *formal__parameter__list* is a list of identifiers that will serve as formal parameters. Each formal parameter is followed by a colon and its mode and type. The modes are **in**, **out**, and **in out**. The parameters are separated by semicolons. Consecutive formal parameters of the same kind (i.e., same type and mode) may (optionally) be grouped together and separated by commas. The above two examples are equivalent.

formal parameter

A formal parameter appears in a subprogram specification and is associated with an actual parameter when the subprogram is called.

procedure call

Syntax:

procedure__name **(** *actual__parameter__list* **);**

Example:

```
CHECK ( 40, PAY_FOR_JOE, TAX_FROM_JOE );
```

The *actual__parameter__list* contains the actual parameters separated by commas. In this example there must be exactly as many actual parameters as there are formal parameters. The first actual parameter is associated with the first formal parameter, the second actual parameter is associated with the second formal parameter and so forth. Corresponding formal and actual parameters must agree in type. If a formal parameter is an **out** or **in out** parameter, then the corresponding actual parameter must be a variable. If a formal parameter is an **in** parameter, then the corresponding actual parameter may be anything that evaluates to the type of the formal parameter. When a procedure is called, an association is made between the actual parameters and the corresponding formal parameters. In the case of **in** and **in out** parameters, values are passed from the actual parameters to the formal parameter; then the procedure statements are executed.

actual parameter

The entity associated with a formal parameter when a subprogram is called an *actual parameter*. The actual parameters are listed in a subprogram call, as shown in the previous example.

in out parameter

Formal and actual parameters come in pairs. If the pair is a pair of **in out** parameters, then **in out** is written after the formal parameter in the formal parameter list of the procedure specification. If the pair is a pair of **in out** parameters, the actual parameter must be a variable. The formal parameter is associated with the actual parameter, and when the procedure is called, the value of actual parameter is passed or assigned to the corresponding formal parameter. When the procedure ends, the value of the formal parameter is passed out to the actual parameter.

out parameters

Formal and actual parameters come in pairs. If the formal parameter is followed by **out** in the formal parameter list of the procedure specification, then the pair is a pair of **out** parameters. If the pair is a pair of **out** parameters, the actual parameter must be a variable of the same type as the formal parameter. No value is passed to the formal parameter when the procedure is called. A formal **out** parameter cannot be treated as a variable, but must be assigned a value inside the procedure. When the procedure terminates, the value of the formal parameter is passed out to the actual parameter.

in parameters

Formal and actual parameters come in pairs. If the formal parameter is followed by **in** in the formal parameter list of a subprogram specification, then the pair is a pair of **in** parameters. If the pair is a pair of **in** parameters, the actual parameter may be anything that evaluates to the type of the corresponding formal parameter, and when the subprogram is called, the value of the formal parameter is set equal to the value of the associated actual parameter. A formal **in** parameter is treated as a named constant inside the subprogram.

function specification

Syntax:

function *function_name optional_parameters*
    return *type_returned*

optional_parameters

nothing
or
(*formal_parameter_list*)

Example:

```
function AREA ( LENGTH, WIDTH : FLOAT )
            return FLOAT
```

The *formal_parameter_list* can be anything that is allowed as a procedure formal parameter list, except that the mode of parameter passage must always be **in**. The *type returned* may be any predefined or user defined type name.

function body declaration

The syntax for a function body declaration is the same as that for a procedure body declaration except for two points: the specification of a function is as described above, and the block of the function must contain a **return** statement with an expression.

return from function

Syntax:

```
return expression;
```

Example:

```
function SMALLER ( FIRST, SECOND : INTEGER )
            return INTEGER is
begin -- Smaller
      if FIRST < SECOND then
            return FIRST;
      else
            return SECOND;
      end if;
end SMALLER;
```

The value of the expression at the time the **return** statement is executed is the value returned by the function. There *must* be a **return** statement in the block of a function. It is permissible to have more than one **return** statement in a function.

return from procedure

Syntax:

```
return;
```

It is permissible to have one or more **return** statements of this form in a procedure. It is *not required* that a procedure have a **return** statement. If a **return** statement is executed in a procedure, the procedure terminates at that point. Any **in out** or **out** parameters are copied out, and execution continues from the point just after the procedure call.

function call

Syntax:

function_name (*actual_parameter_list*)

Example:

```
X := AREA ( 3.79, 8.9 );
```

A function call can appear in exactly the same places that a constant or variable of the type returned by the function can appear. It is like an expression and evaluates to a value of the type specified in the function body declaration. This value is called the *return value.* The return value is the value of the expression in the **return** statement at the time the **return** statement is executed. The *actual parameter list* is handled in exactly the same way as an actual parameter list for a procedure. At the time that the function call is evaluated the statements in the block of the function body declaration are executed. Side effects are possible but should be avoided.

Exercises

Self-Test Exercises

12. What is the output produced by the following program?

```
with I_O; use I_O;
procedure MAIN is
     GEORGE : BOOLEAN;
     function LOVELACE ( NEWTON : INTEGER )
               return BOOLEAN is
     begin -- Lovelace
               return NEWTON < 0;
     end LOVELACE;
begin -- Main
     if LOVELACE ( 5 ) then
          PUT ( "hello" );
     else
          PUT ( "hi" );
     end if;
     NEW_LINE;
     GEORGE := LOVELACE ( -8 );
     if GEORGE then
          PUT ( "good-bye" );
     else
          PUT ( "so long" );
     end if;
     NEW_LINE;
end MAIN;
```

13. Write a boolean function of two INTEGER parameters that returns TRUE if the first argument evenly divides the second and returns FALSE otherwise.

14. Write a boolean function body declaration for a function IN_ORDER that has three integer parameters and returns TRUE if the three integer parameters are in ascending order. So, IN_ORDER (1, 2, 3) should return TRUE and IN_ORDER (1, 3, 2) should return FALSE.

15. Can an **in out** parameter be used to give information to a procedure?

16. Can an **out** parameter be used to give information to a procedure?

17. Can an **out** parameter be used to get information out of a procedure?

18. Can an **in** parameter be used to get information out of a procedure?

19. Which of the following are allowed as actual **in** parameters of type INTEGER? (X is a variable of type INTEGER.)

X   X + 1   *abs* (2 * X)   25

20. Which of the expressions in Exercise 12 are allowed as actual **in out** parameters of type INTEGER?

21. Which of the expressions in Exercise 12 are allowed as actual **in** parameters of type INTEGER?

22. Can an actual **in out** parameter be a variable?

23. Can an actual **in** parameter be a variable?

24. Can an actual **in out** parameter be a constant?

25. Can an actual **in** parameter be a constant?

Interactive Exercises

26. What is the output of the following program?

```
with I_O; use I_O;
procedure MAIN is
     X, Y : INTEGER;
     procedure SAM ( X, Y : in INTEGER ) is
     begin -- Sam
          PUT ( X ); PUT ( Y ); NEW_LINE;
     end SAM;
begin
     X := 1;
     Y := 2;
     SAM ( X, Y );
     SAM ( Y, X );
end MAIN;
```

27. Write a procedure to find the area of a rectangle and store the answer in an **out** parameter called RECTANGLE_AREA. This procedure will have two **in** parameters, as in PUT_NUMBER (Figure 4.7), plus the **out** parameter RECTANGLE_AREA, for a total of three formal parameters. Embed this in a program and run the program.

28. Write a procedure with three parameters, one **in** parameter of type FLOAT and two **out** parameters of type INTEGER. One variable parameter is set to the whole number part of the floating point value; the other is set to the value of the first digit after the decimal point.

Programming Exercises

29. Write a program that reads in a floating point number (representing that many inches) and then outputs the area of a square with sides of that length and the area of a circle with diameter that length. Use two procedures to compute the two areas.

30. Write a procedure that has two formal parameters, one for the radius of a circle and one for the circumference. The procedure computes the circumference of a circle with the given radius and stores the answer in the parameter for the circumference. Embed this in a program to compute the circumference of a circle.

31. Write a program that converts from dollars to Mexican pesos or from pesos to dollars, depending on the user's desire. The user is asked which conversion he/she wants performed. If the desired conversion is pesos to dollars, then the program reads in an amount in Mexican pesos as well as the peso-to-dollar exchange rate. After that, the program outputs the equivalent amount in dollars and cents. If the user instead requests a conversion from dollars to pesos, then the roles of dollars and pesos are interchanged. Use at least four procedures: one for input, one for output, one to convert from pesos to dollars, and one to convert from dollars to pesos. (If you wish you can write one more general procedure in place of the last two mentioned. You may find it convenient to have two output procedures, one for each type of conversion.)

32. Write a program that writes 'HELLO' to the screen one letter at a time. Use four procedures for the four letters H, E, L, and O. Each letter should be a pattern of asterisks at least five times as large as the regular letters on your screen. Each letter of the word should be indented more than the previous letter. So the output looks something like this:

```
H
  E
    L
      L
        O
```

except that it should be larger. To get the next letter, the user presses the return key. (The entire word need not fit on the screen at one time.)

33. Write a procedure that has one **in** parameter of type CHARACTER. The procedure writes 'YES' to the screen if the parameter value is 'y' and 'NO' if it is anything else. Embed it in a test program.

34. Write two parameterless procedures, one to write each of the words 'YES' and 'NO' to the screen in large letters made up of asterisks. The letters should be at least five times the normal size of letters on your screen. Use these procedures to redo the previous exercise to output larger words.

35. Write a program that asks the user to type in his/her height, weight, and age, and then computes clothes sizes according to the following formulas: hat size = weight in pounds divided by height in inches and all that multiplied by 2.9; sweater size (chest in inches) = height times weight divided by 301 and then adjusted by adding 1/8 inch for each 10 years over age 30; waist in inches = weight divided by 5.7 and then adjusted by adding 1/10 inch for each 2 years over age 28. Use procedures for each calculation.

36. You have a choice of two different auto repair mechanics with different rate structures. One charges a flat fee of $20, plus $5.00 for each quarter hour. The other charges $18 for the first quarter hour and then $5.75 for each quarter hour after that. Any fraction of a quarter hour counts as a full quarter hour, so 1.26 hours counts as six quarter hours. Write a program that accepts the number of hours as input, displays the two charges, and announces which is cheaper. Use four or more procedures.

37. Write a function body declaration for a function called GRADER that takes a numeric score and returns a letter grade. GRADER has one parameter of type INTEGER and returns a value of type CHARACTER. Use these rules to determine

the letter grade: 90 to 100 is an A, 80 to 89 is a B, 70 to 79 is a C, 60 to 69 is a D, and less than 60 is an F. Embed it in a test program.

38. Write a function body declaration for a function that computes interest on a credit card account balance. The function has parameters for the initial balance, the monthly interest rate, and the number of months for which interest must be paid. The value returned is the interest due. Do not forget to compound the interest, that is, to charge interest on the interest due. The interest due is added into the balance due, and the interest for the next month is computed using this larger balance. Embed the function in a test program.

39. Write a program that gives the user the choice of computing any of the following: the area of a circle, a square, a rectangle, or a triangle. The program should include a loop to allow the user to do as many calculations as desired. Use a different function for each of the different kinds of calculations.

40. To discourage excess consumption, an electric company charges its customers a lower rate for the first 250 kilowatt hours, namely $0.11 for each of the first 250 kilowatt hours, and a higher rate of $0.17 for each additional kilowatt hour. In addition, a 10% surtax is added to the final bill. Write a program to calculate electric bills, given the number of kilowatt hours consumed as input. Use two function body declarations, one to compute the amount due without the surtax and one to compute the total due. The block for the second function should include a call to the first function.

41. The greatest common divisor of two positive integers is the largest integer that divides them both. For example, the greatest common divisor of 9 and 6 is 3. Write a function body declaration for a function with two integer parameters that returns their greatest common divisor.

42. The game of *Nim* is played as follows. There are three piles of sticks. Two players take turn making moves. A move consists of picking up as many sticks as the player desires, subject to the following constraints: All the sticks must be picked up from the same pile, and a player must pick up at least one stick. The player who picks up the last stick loses. Write a program to play *Nim* with the user. The piles of sticks should initially contain three, five, and seven sticks each. The computer can use any strategy you wish, so long as it obeys the rules. Display the piles as three lists of a symbol of your choice, such as `'!'`, so the piles are displayed as something like this:

```
!!!
!!!!!
!!!!!!!
```

43. Write a program to compute the monthly cost of a house, based on the following four input values: the purchase price, the annual fuel costs, the tax rate expressed at tax per $1000, and the down payment. The monthly cost is 1/12 the annual cost obtained by summing the costs of tax, fuel, and mortgage. The annual tax is obtained by multiplying the tax rate by the purchase price. For example, if the rate is $20.50 per $1000 and the purchase price is $100,000, then the annual tax is $2,050. The annual mortgage cost is 10% of the balance left after deducting the down payment from the purchase price. The program should repeat the calculation for new inputs as often as the user desires.

CHAPTER

5

SUBPROGRAMS FOR MODULAR DESIGN

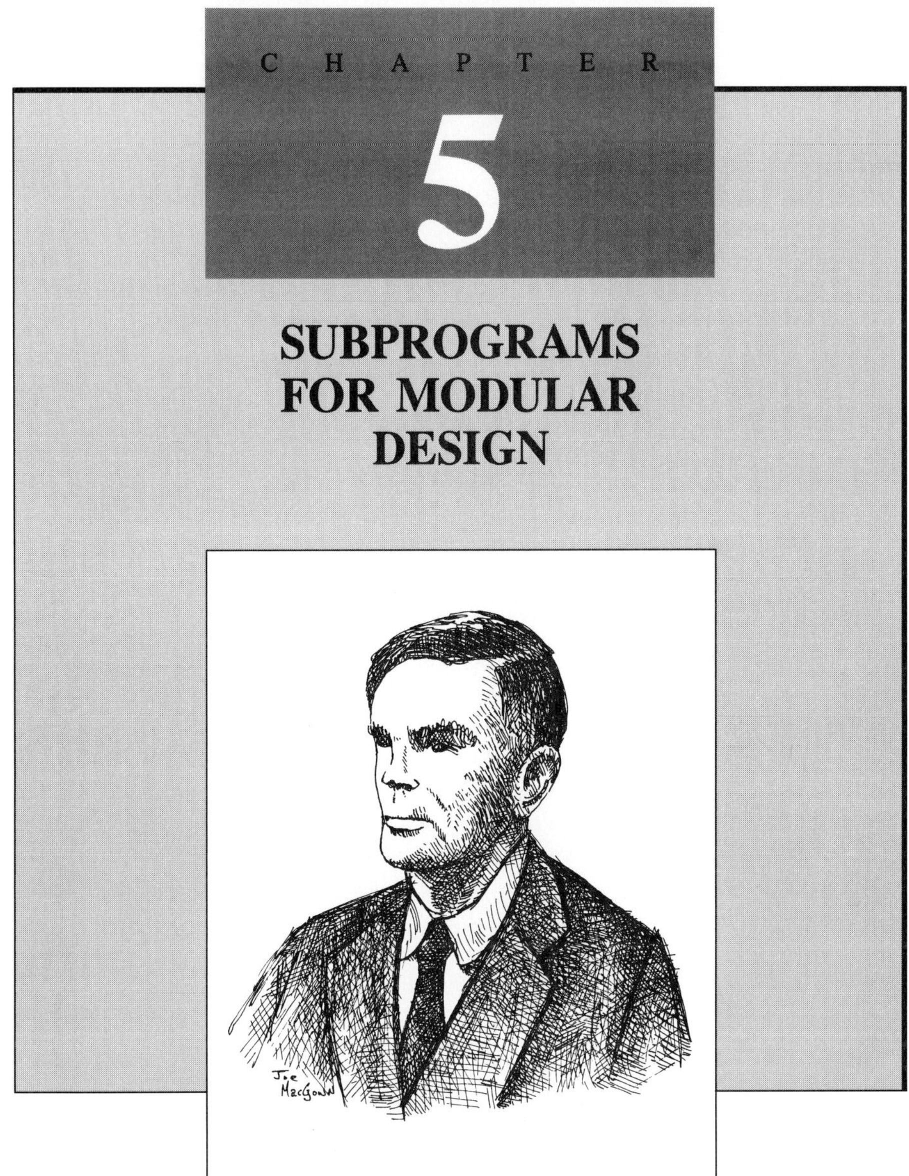

Alan M. Turing

Alan M. Turing (1912–1954) was an English mathematician and logician. He is considered by many to be the father of computer science because he was the first to study algorithms and programs in a mathematically precise way. He designed a mathematical model of a general-purpose computer known today as the ''Turing machine.'' It was a conceptual device, a toy of the mind, but very useful in theorem proving. Turing was also a key member of the British intelligence team that broke the German military code during World War II.

Chapter Contents

Subprograms separate a program into smaller, and hence more manageable, pieces. To get the full benefit of this decomposition, the subprograms must be self-contained units that are meaningful outside the context of any particular program. A program that is built out of such self-contained subprograms is often said to have a *modular* design. In this chapter we show how a subprogram may be made self-contained by having its own independent set of variables. After introducing these variables, known as *local variables,* we then use the construct to give examples of modular design.

Local Variables

exchange example

To introduce the notion of a local variable, we will consider a simple but frequently occurring problem and design a procedure to solve this problem.

Suppose we wish to write a procedure to interchange the values of two variables of type INTEGER. The procedure specification will be

```
procedure EXCHANGE ( FIRST_NUMBER, SECOND_NUMBER : in out INTEGER )
```

The block of the procedure presents more of a problem. An obvious but incorrect thing to try is

```
FIRST_NUMBER := SECOND_NUMBER;
SECOND_NUMBER := FIRST_NUMBER;
```

This sets the new value of FIRST_NUMBER to the old value of SECOND_NUMBER, as desired. But it sets the new value of SECOND_NUMBER to the *new* value of FIRST_NUMBER and so leaves SECOND_NUMBER unchanged. (If this seems unclear, plug in some values and see what happens.) What we need to do is to save the original value of FIRST_NUMBER before we change the value of FIRST_NUMBER. We can then use that saved value to set the value of SECOND_NUMBER. What we need is another variable to temporarily hold this saved value. Let us call this extra variable TEMPORARY and assume that it is declared in the MAIN procedure to be of type INTEGER. The correct procedure now reads

```
procedure EXCHANGE ( FIRST_NUMBER, SECOND_NUMBER : in out INTEGER ) is
--                    Interchanges the value of FIRST_NUMBER
--                    and SECOND_NUMBER.
--                    Assumes TEMPORARY declared in Main.
begin -- Exchange
    TEMPORARY := FIRST_NUMBER;
    FIRST_NUMBER := SECOND_NUMBER;
    SECOND_NUMBER := TEMPORARY;
end EXCHANGE;
```

procedural abstraction

That will work nicely except for one annoying detail. Since the procedure EXCHANGE changes the value of TEMPORARY, we must remember not to use the variable TEMPORARY for anything else. This is most unfortunate. The whole idea of top-down design and procedures is to break big problems into smaller problems. We make no headway in this direction if, when designing a procedure, we need to remember the details of how all the other procedures work. Once we get a procedure to work, we should only need to remember what it does and not how it does it. The principle of procedural abstraction that we advocated in Chapter 4 says that the procedure specification and one explanatory comment are all we should need to remember.

In this case the following three lines should be all we need to know to use the procedure safely and effectively:

```
procedure EXCHANGE ( FIRST_NUMBER, SECOND_NUMBER : in out INTEGER )
--                  Interchanges the value of FIRST_NUMBER
--                  and SECOND_NUMBER.
```

Clearly, these three lines are not all we need to remember. We must also remember that the variable TEMPORARY has its value changed.

local variables Ideally, we should not have to remember anything about TEMPORARY, not even that it was used. What we need is a special version of the variable TEMPORARY that exists only for the duration of the procedure call. Fortunately Ada and many other programming languages allow such variables. They are called *local variables.*

global variables A *local variable* is a variable that is declared within a procedure and is not available outside that procedure. Variables that are declared for the entire program are called *global variables.* Local variables are declared just like global variables, except that the declaration is placed inside the procedure body between the procedure specification and the **begin** that marks the start of the procedure block. A local variable is only meaningful inside the procedure. No statement outside of the procedure body may reference the local variable.

The program in Figure 5.1 includes the procedure EXCHANGE, with TEMPORARY declared as a local variable. Output statements have been added to the procedure to show the value of the local variable. Although the EXCHANGE procedure has numerous useful applications, this particular MAIN program does not have any applications. It is just an example to illustrate how global and local variables work.

Program

```
with I_O; use I_O;
procedure MAIN is
    FIRST_NUMBER,
    SECOND_NUMBER,
    TEMPORARY : INTEGER;
    procedure EXCHANGE ( FIRST_NUMBER,
                         SECOND_NUMBER : in out INTEGER ) is
        TEMPORARY : INTEGER; -- does not exist outside Exchange
    begin -- Exchange
        TEMPORARY := FIRST_NUMBER;
        FIRST_NUMBER := SECOND_NUMBER;
        SECOND_NUMBER := TEMPORARY;
        PUT ( FIRST_NUMBER );
        PUT ( SECOND_NUMBER );
        PUT ( TEMPORARY );    -- the temporary in Exchange
        NEW_LINE;
    end EXCHANGE;
```

```
begin -- Main
    FIRST_NUMBER := 1;
    SECOND_NUMBER := 2;
    TEMPORARY := 3;
    PUT ( FIRST_NUMBER );
    PUT ( SECOND_NUMBER );
    PUT ( TEMPORARY );           -- the temporary in Main
    NEW_LINE;
    EXCHANGE ( FIRST_NUMBER, SECOND_NUMBER );
    PUT ( FIRST_NUMBER );
    PUT ( SECOND_NUMBER );
    PUT ( TEMPORARY );           -- the temporary in Main
    NEW_LINE;
end MAIN;
```

Output

```
1    2    3
2    1    1
2    1    3
```

Figure 5.1 Procedure with a local variable.

interpreting local variables

The program in Figure 5.1 has two variables called TEMPORARY: one global variable declared for the entire program and one local variable declared for the procedure EXCHANGE. What is the relationship between these two different variables called TEMPORARY? They share the same name, but they are two totally different variables. The computer does manage to keep track of these two different variables, even though they have but one name between them. It is as if the computer acts in the following way. When a variable name appears in the block of a procedure (between the **begin** and the **end**) the compiler checks to see if a variable of that name is declared locally (inside the procedure); if it is, the name refers to the local variable. On the other hand, if the variable name is not declared locally, the compiler checks to see if it is declared globally; if it is, the name refers to the global variable. If the variable name is declared both locally and globally, the name refers to the local variable within the procedure. Any changes made to the local variable have no effect on the global variable of the same name. Inside the procedure, the inner TEMPORARY, in effect, masks (covers or hides) the outer TEMPORARY, so the outer TEMPORARY is not visible inside the procedure.

example

In the procedure block in Figure 5.1, the identifier TEMPORARY on the left-hand side of the assignment operator names the local variable, not the global variable. Hence, the global variable is not changed. That is why the third output line is

2 1 3

If TEMPORARY were not declared as a local variable, that is, if the following line were omitted from the procedure body,

```
TEMPORARY : INTEGER;
```

then the output would be the following instead:

```
1    2    3
2    1    1
2    1    1
```

Because the computer handles local variables in this way, we can design procedures using local variables and not even bother to remember which identifiers we used for the local variables. If, outside the procedure, we reuse those identifiers to mean something else, the computer will know we mean something else.

Case Study

Grade Warnings

Problem Definition

We want to design a program that can be used early in the school term to let students know if they are making satisfactory progress in a class. It is presumed that two tests are sufficient to obtain a meaningful early indication of progress, so the program will read two test scores and output an answer, telling whether or not the average of the two scores is passing. Since there is some danger that a student might use the program at the wrong time, the program will tell the student to see the instructor if the student has not taken exactly two tests.

Discussion and Algorithm

The program will simply ask the student how many tests he or she has taken. If the student has taken any number other than two tests, then the program tells the student to see the instructor. Hence, the main outline of the program is

```
if the student has not taken exactly two tests then
   Output ( ''See the instructor.'' )
else
   Read in the two test scores
   Compute the average
   Output a suitable message
```

The two test scores will be read in by a procedure called READ_SCORES. Since the student might make a mistake in entering test scores, the procedure will echo back the test scores and ask the student if they were entered correctly. If they are not correct, the student is given a chance to reenter the scores. A **loop** statement is used to repeat this check until the student says the scores are correct. It will read the two scores, display the scores, and then ask if the scores are correct; if they are not, the student is given a chance to reenter the scores. A second procedure called MESSAGE will test the average of the two test scores and output an appropriate message to the screen. Figure 5.2 shows the procedures and their parameters.

	in	**out**
READ_SCORES		SCORE_1 SCORE_2
MESSAGE	AVERAGE	

Figure 5.2 Parameters for grade-warning program.

The complete program is given in Figure 5.3. Notice that the complete program has both a global and a local variable named ANSWER. In both cases this is the most natural name to use. Since one of the two variables is local, this coincidence of names is not a problem. The variable ANSWER in READ_SCORES is used to hold an answer from the user that is only needed by that procedure and is never passed out of the procedure. Whenever a variable is only used within a procedure it should be made a local variable, so we will make ANSWER a local variable. Figure 5.2 lists SCORE_1 and SCORE_2 as **out** parameters from procedure READ_SCORES, but Figure 5.3 shows them as **in out**. **out** parameters can only be assigned a value, they cannot be referenced in any other way. In Figure 5.3 the scores are assigned a value through the GET statements and referenced in the PUT statements. If a parameter is to be both assigned a value and referenced in a procedure, the parameter must be **in out**.

Program

```
with I_O; use I_O;
procedure MAIN is
--                INPUT : The number of tests taken
--                        and two test scores.
--                OUTPUT : Pass-Fail message to the student.
--                DESCRIPTION : Compares the average of two tests
--                              to a passing score.
```

```
    AFTER : constant INTEGER := 2;
    BEFORE : constant INTEGER := 4;
    EXPONENT : constant INTEGER := 0;
    PASSING : constant INTEGER := 70;
    ANSWER : INTEGER;
    AVERAGE : FLOAT;
    TEST_1, TEST_2 : INTEGER;
    procedure READ_SCORES ( SCORE_1, SCORE_2 : in out INTEGER ) is
--                    INPUT  : None.
--                    OUTPUT : Two exam scores.
--                    DESCRIPTION : Input two scores from the keyboard.
--                                  Prompt the student for correctness
--                                  and allow retries if wrong.
        ANSWER : CHARACTER := 'n';
    begin -- Read_Scores
        loop
            exit when ANSWER = 'y';
            PUT ( "Enter your two test scores:" ); NEW_LINE;
            GET ( SCORE_1 ); GET ( SCORE_2 ); SKIP_LINE;
            PUT ( "The scores are " );
            PUT ( SCORE_1 ); PUT ( SCORE_2 ); NEW_LINE;
            PUT ( "Is that correct? (y/n)" ); NEW_LINE;
            GET ( ANSWER ); SKIP_LINE;
            if ANSWER /= 'y' then
                PUT ( "OK. Try again." ); NEW_LINE;
            end if;
        end loop;
    end READ_SCORES;
    procedure MESSAGE ( AVERAGE : in FLOAT ) is
--                    INPUT  : The average of two test scores.
--                    OUTPUT : None.
--                    DESCRIPTION : Displays a message on the screen
--                                  informing the student if his test
--                                  average is passing or not.
    begin
        PUT ( "Your average is " );
        PUT ( AVERAGE, BEFORE, AFTER, EXPONENT );
        NEW_LINE;
        PUT ( "To pass you need at least " );
        PUT ( PASSING );
        NEW_LINE;
        if AVERAGE >= FLOAT ( PASSING ) then
            PUT ( "You are passing so far." ); NEW_LINE;
        else
            PUT ( "Warning: you are failing!" ); NEW_LINE;
        end if;
    end MESSAGE;
```

```
begin -- Main
    PUT ( "Begin assessment of class work:" ); NEW_LINE;
    PUT ( "How many tests have you taken?" ); NEW_LINE;
    GET ( ANSWER ); SKIP_LINE;
    if ANSWER /= 2 then
        PUT ( "See the instructor." ); NEW_LINE;
    else
        READ_SCORES ( TEST_1, TEST_2 );
        AVERAGE := FLOAT ( TEST_1 + TEST_2 ) / 2.0;
        MESSAGE ( AVERAGE );
    end if;
end MAIN;
```

Sample Dialogue 1

```
Begin assessment of class work:
How many tests have you taken?
1
See the instructor.
```

Sample Dialogue 2

```
Begin assessment of class work:
How many tests have you taken?
2
Enter your two test scores:
57 90
The scores are  57  90
Is that correct? (y/n)
n
OK. Try again.
Enter your two test scores:
75 90
The scores are  75  90
Is that correct? (y/n)
y
Your average is  82.50
To pass you need at least  70
You are passing so far.
```

Figure 5.3 Grade-warning program.

Formal Parameters Are Local Also

Formal parameters are local to the subprogram in which they are declared and thus are not known outside the subprogram. Formal **in** parameters are treated as named constants inside the subprogram. There are two differences between a formal **in** parameter and other constants:

1. A formal **in** parameter is assigned the value of an associated actual parameter when the subprogram is called
2. A formal **in** parameter exists only within the subprogram in which it is declared.

Once inside the subprogram, they are treated exactly alike.

Formal **out** parameters are local to the procedure in which they are declared. They are given a value inside the procedure, and that value is passed to the associated actual parameter when the procedure terminates. The formal **out** parameter name is not known outside the procedure.

Formal **in out** parameters are treated as local variables inside the procedure in which they are declared and have all the properties of any other variable declared in a procedure. There are, however, two differences between formal **in out** parameters and local variables:

1. A formal **in out** parameter is given the value of the associated actual parameter when the procedure is called. Thus, its initial value comes from outside the procedure, where any variables declared inside the procedure can only be given values inside the procedure.
2. A formal **in out** parameter gives its value back out of the procedure to its associated actual parameter when the procedure terminates. When the procedure terminates, the values of any local variables are gone, disappear, vanish, and thus are not known outside the procedure.

Case Study

A Function to Compute n Factorial

Problem Definition

The mathematical function n factorial (written n!) returns the product of all of the values up to some value n. The general formula is

$$n! = 1 * 2 * 3 * \ldots * n$$

The value of n must be greater than or equal to 0. By convention, $0! = 1$.

We wish to write an Ada function that, when given a value NUMBER, returns the factorial of that value. The function specification for N_FACTORIAL will be the following:

```
    function N_FACTORIAL ( NUMBER : INTEGER ) return INTEGER
--              INPUT  :  A number >=0.
--              OUTPUT :  The factorial of the number.
--              DESCRIPTION : Repeatedly multiplies successive
--                            integer values up to number.
--                            For number = 0, return 1.
```

Discussion

We wish to compute the value

```
( (... (1 * 2) * 3) * ...) * next_value)
```

NUMBER times.

Many problem definitions are already algorithms, sometimes in a disguised form. To obtain an algorithm for translation into Ada often requires little more than rephrasing the definition. In this case the definition gives us an algorithm for computing the value we want: Simply multiply integer values up to NUMBER. To do this we use a **loop**, a local variable COUNT that counts up to NUMBER, and a local variable PRODUCT to hold the partial products:

algorithm from definition

```
COUNT := 1
PRODUCT := 1
loop
    exit when COUNT > NUMBER
    PRODUCT := PRODUCT * COUNT
    COUNT := COUNT + 1
return THE PRODUCT
```

Notice that the **loop** is used simply to repeat a statement execution NUMBER times. The local variable COUNT is initialized to **1** and incremented each time around the loop until it is greater than NUMBER.

initialize value

Since the variable PRODUCT appears on the right-hand side of the assignment statement inside the **loop**, it must be given a value before the loop is executed. The correct value is **1**. To see that this is true, notice that if PRODUCT is initialized with the value **1**, and the value of NUMBER is **0**, then no loop iteration takes place, but the PRODUCT is still **1**, which is the correct value for **0!**. If the value of NUMBER is **1**, then after one loop iteration, the value of PRODUCT will be **1 * 1** or **1**, which is correct for **1!**.

Algorithm

At this stage the algorithm is complete; initialize PRODUCT to **1** and execute the loop. This sets PRODUCT equal to the value we want to compute. To return this value as the value of the function, we need add only the statement

```
return PRODUCT;
```

The complete function body is exhibited in Figure 5.4.

Program

```
with I_O; use I_O;
procedure MAIN is
--                  INPUT  : A nonnegative integer.
--                  OUTPUT : The factorial of the input value.
--                  DESCRIPTION : Test the n! function.
    ANSWER : CHARACTER;
    NONNEGATIVE_INTEGER : INTEGER;
    function N_FACTORIAL ( NUMBER : INTEGER ) return INTEGER is
--                  INPUT  : A number >=0.
--                  OUTPUT : The factorial of the number.
--                  DESCRIPTION : Repeatedly multiplies successive
--                                integer values up to number.
--                                For number = 0, return 1.
        COUNT   : INTEGER := 1;
        PRODUCT : INTEGER := 1;
    begin -- N_Factorial
        loop
            exit when COUNT > NUMBER;
            PRODUCT := PRODUCT * COUNT;
            COUNT := COUNT + 1;
        end loop;
        return PRODUCT;
    end N_FACTORIAL;
begin -- Main
    loop
        PUT ( "Enter a nonnegative integer." ); NEW_LINE;
        GET ( NONNEGATIVE_INTEGER ); SKIP_LINE;
        PUT ( "The factorial of " );
        PUT ( NONNEGATIVE_INTEGER );
        NEW_LINE;
        PUT ( "is " );
        PUT ( N_FACTORIAL ( NONNEGATIVE_INTEGER ) );
        NEW_LINE ( 2 );
        PUT ( "Another test? (yes/no)" ); NEW_LINE;
        GET ( ANSWER ); SKIP_LINE;
        exit when ANSWER = 'n'
              or ANSWER = 'N';
    end loop;
end MAIN;
```

Sample Dialogue

```
Enter a nonnegative integer.
3
The factorial of 3
is 6

Another test? (yes/no)
yes
Enter a nonnegative integer.
5
The factorial of 5
is 120

Another test? (yes/no)
no
```

Figure 5.4 Function to find n!.

The local variable COUNT could have been initialized to the value of 2, and the algorithm would still perform properly. If NUMBER is 0 or 1, the loop terminates at the first test of the **exit when**, and the PRODUCT returned is its initial value of 1, which is the correct value. If NUMBER is 2 the value returned is the PRODUCT of 1 * 2 or 2 which is the correct value.

Other Local Identifiers

local declarations

Identifiers other than variable names may be local to a subprogram. Any kind of declaration allowed in an Ada program is also allowed in an Ada subprogram. A subprogram may have local named constants and local subprograms of its own, as well as local variables. The interpretation of these other locally declared identifiers is similar to that of local variables. The local named constant or local subprogram exists only while the subprogram in which it is declared is executing. Outside of the subprogram, you can reuse a local identifier to name something else. The ordering of local declarations in a subprogram is the same as the ordering of declarations within a program.

local constants

local procedures

Figure 5.5 shows a procedure that has a local constant and a local procedure, in addition to local variables. There are two string constants called OPENING_LINE, one global and one local to the procedure BREAK_ICE. The identifier COMPLIMENT is defined globally to be a string constant. However, within the procedure body BREAK_ICE, it is also declared to be the name of a local procedure. Within the procedure BREAK_ICE, the identifier COMPLIMENT names a procedure. Outside the procedure BREAK_ICE, it names a string constant. Note that the procedure COMPLIMENT, which is local to the procedure BREAK_ICE, is not visible to the procedure MAIN.

Program

```
with I_O; use I_O;
procedure MAIN is
    COMPLIMENT : constant STRING := "You're a wonderful person.";
    FAREWELL : constant STRING := "I hope we meet again.";
    OPENING_LINE : constant STRING
                 := "Hello, my name is Ronald Gollum.";

    procedure BREAK_ICE is
        OPENING_LINE : constant STRING
                     := "Haven't we met somewhere before?";
        FIRST_INITIAL,
        LAST_INITIAL : CHARACTER;
        procedure COMPLIMENT is
        begin -- COMPLIMENT
            PUT ( "A lovely name." ); NEW_LINE;
            PUT ( "I really like that name." ); NEW_LINE;
        end COMPLIMENT;
    begin -- Break_Ice
        PUT ( OPENING_LINE ); NEW_LINE;
        SKIP_LINE;
        PUT ( "What is your first name?" ); NEW_LINE;
        GET ( FIRST_INITIAL ); SKIP_LINE;
        COMPLIMENT;
        PUT ( "What is your last name?" ); NEW_LINE;
        GET ( LAST_INITIAL ); SKIP_LINE;
        COMPLIMENT;
        PUT ( "Pleased to meet you " );
        PUT ( FIRST_INITIAL ); PUT ( '.' );
        PUT ( LAST_INITIAL ); PUT ( '.' );
        NEW_LINE;
    end BREAK_ICE;
begin -- Main
    PUT ( OPENING_LINE ); NEW_LINE;
    BREAK_ICE;
    PUT ( COMPLIMENT ); NEW_LINE;
    PUT ( FAREWELL ); NEW_LINE;
end MAIN;
```

Sample Dialogue

```
Hello, my name is Ronald Gollum.
Haven't we met somewhere before?
I don't think so.
What is your first name?
Jane
A lovely name.
I really like that name.
```

```
What is your last name?
Doe
A lovely name.
I really like that name.
Pleased to meet you J.D.
You're a wonderful person.
I hope we meet again.
```

Figure 5.5 Program using local identifiers.

An advantage of local subprograms is that they make the calling subprogram a self-contained unit. Hence, if they are not used outside of the calling subprogram, it makes sense to use local subprograms.

Pitfall

Use of Global Variables

the problem with global variables

Ada allows subprograms to change global variables that are not actual parameters. If NUMBER is a global variable of type INTEGER, then the compiler will accept and translate the following procedure:

```
procedure BAD_FORM is
begin
   PUT ( "Enter a number:" ); NEW_LINE;
   GET ( NUMBER ); SKIP_LINE;
   PUT ( "Thanks, I'll give that number to the program" );
   NEW_LINE;
end BAD_FORM;
```

However, it is almost always a bad idea to use global variables in this way.

Subprograms should be self-contained units that are meaningful outside the context of the program. This means that the subprogram's interaction with the rest of the program should be entirely through parameters. Any other interaction between the subprogram and the rest of the program is referred to as a *side effect*. As indicted in Figure 5.6, side effects are considered undesirable. If a subprogram changes a global variable (other than an actual parameter), that is a side effect. Except in very rare circumstances, global variables should not appear anyplace in a subprogram body. If a temporary variable is needed in a subprogram, use a local variable, not a global variable. If you want the program to change the value of a global variable, use a formal **out** or **in out** parameter in a procedure specification, and then use the global variable as the actual parameter in a procedure call.

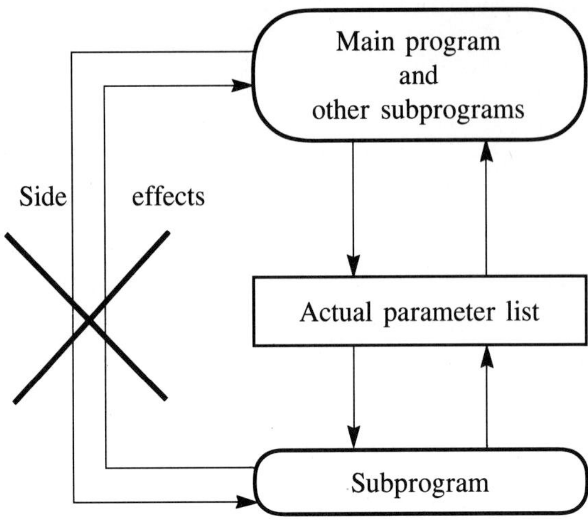

Figure 5.6 Side effects.

The prohibition against global variables is often phrased as ''no global variables in subprograms,'' which has lead to confusion on the part of some novice programmers. The prohibition does not mean that subprograms cannot manipulate global variables. In fact changing global variables is the common and accepted way for procedures to pass information from one procedure to another. However, those global variables should always be actual parameters. Global variables should not be used directly in the statements within a procedure body; instead you should use a formal parameter or local variable.

global constants

Although global variables should not appear in a subprogram body, it is perfectly acceptable to use globally defined named constants in a subprogram body (as we did in Figure 5.3). The difference is that constants cannot be changed by the subprogram, so there is no danger of their being changed inadvertently. In fact it is very convenient to have all the defined constants in a program displayed together at the top of the program so they can be changed easily should the program ever need to be revised.

Exercises

Self-Test Exercises

1. Predict the output of the following program:

```
with I_O; use I_O;
procedure MAIN is
    NUMBER : INTEGER;
```

```
        procedure SALLY is
            NUMBER : INTEGER;
        begin -- Sally
            NUMBER := 7;
            PUT ( NUMBER ); NEW_LINE;
        end SALLY;
    begin -- Main
        NUMBER := 11;
        SALLY;
        PUT ( NUMBER ); NEW_LINE;
    end MAIN;
```

2. Predict the output of the following program:

```
    with I_O; use I_O;
    procedure MAIN is
        BOZO : INTEGER;
        procedure TEST is
            BOZO : constant STRING := "Hi Folks";
        begin
            PUT ( BOZO );
            PUT ( " in procedure" );
            NEW_LINE;
        end TEST;
    begin
        BOZO := 21;
        TEST;
        PUT ( BOZO );
        PUT ( " outside of procedure" );
        NEW_LINE;
    end MAIN;
```

3. Predict the output of the following program:

```
    with I_O; use I_O;
    procedure MAIN is
        ALPHA, BRAVO, CHARLIE : INTEGER;
        procedure FUNNY ( XI, PHI : in out INTEGER );
              CHARLIE : INTEGER;
        begin -- Funny
              XI := 4;
              PHI := 5;
              CHARLIE := 6;
              PUT (XI); PUT (PHI); PUT ( CHARLIE );
              NEW_LINE;
        end FUNNY;
    begin
        ALPHA := 1;
        BRAVO := 2;
```

```
        CHARLIE := 3;
        PUT ( ALPHA ); PUT ( BRAVO ); PUT ( CHARLIE );
        NEW_LINE;
        FUNNY ( ALPHA, BRAVO );
        PUT ( ALPHA ); PUT ( BRAVO ); PUT ( CHARLIE );
        NEW_LINE;
    end MAIN;
```

4. What will be the output of the program in Exercise 3 if the procedure call is changed to

```
FUNNY ( BRAVO, ALPHA );
```

5. What will be the output of the program in Exercise 3 if the procedure call is changed to

```
FUNNY ( ALPHA, ALPHA );
```

6. What will be the output of the program in Exercise 3 if the procedure call is changed to

```
FUNNY ( ALPHA, CHARLIE );
```

(This one is tricky. If you do not understand the answer, you may wish to leave it for now and return to it after you have more practice with local variables.)

Scope of an Identifier

A variable that is declared in a subprogram is local to that subprogram. Its meaning is confined to that subprogram, and you need not even be aware of its existence at any time, other than when you write the subprogram. That is the beauty of local declarations. As long as you think of each subprogram as a self-contained unit and design each unit separately, you will never even notice that the same identifier names appear in two or more different places in a program. Life is not as easy for the computer. The computer must decide the meaning of each variable or other identifier in the program. If there is more than one declaration for a single identifier name, it must decide which declaration goes with each of the occurrences of that identifier name. How it decides is the topic of this section.

scope of declaration

A set of declarations, prefaced by an optional parameter list, together with the sequence of statements that apply to this program unit, is called the *scope of declaration.* The scope of declaration is the region of the program text over which the declaration has its effect. *Scope of declaration* is the technical term, but in most cases it is simply referred to as the *scope,* which is the word we will use. The term *scope* is used to refer to a subprogram and also to an entire program. The syntax for a scope of declaration is summarized in Figure 5.7.

The subprogram body consists of the word **procedure** or **function**, followed by the subprogram name (an identifier), followed by a scope (of declaration) that includes the remainder of the subprogram body. The formal parameter list is part

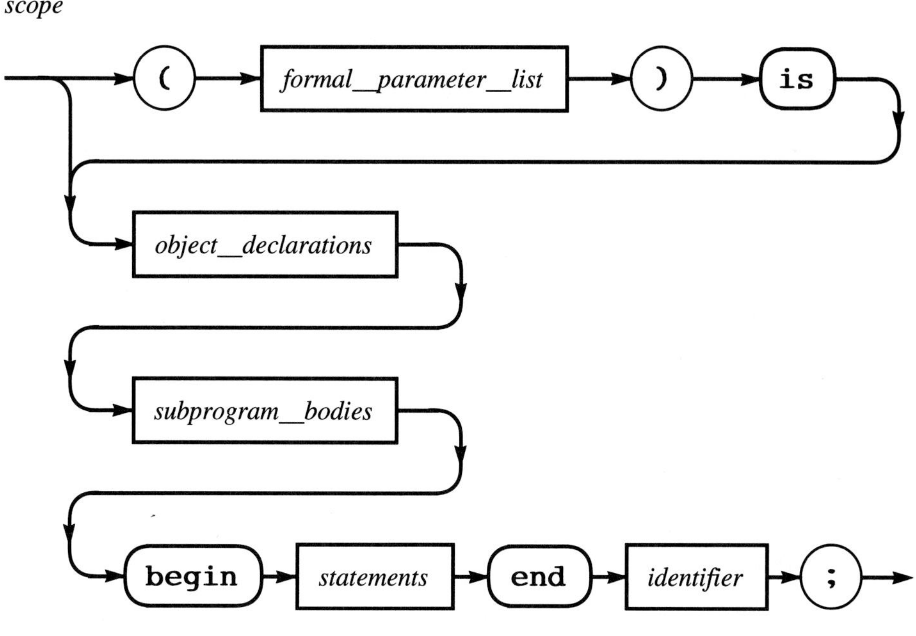

Figure 5.7 Syntax of a scope of declaration.

of the scope of declaration. All the identifiers described at the start of a scope are said to be *local to that scope* or, equivalently, *in the scope* of the subprogram. The meaning given to an identifier by the parameter list or by a declaration applies only within the scope.

If an identifier is declared or is listed as a formal parameter in each of two scopes, one within the other, then its meaning *within the inner scope* is the one *determined by the declaration or parameter list at the start of the inner scope.*

If an identifier is given a meaning within the scope of a subprogram, then when the subprogram is called, the identifier takes on that meaning, and when the subprogram call is over, it loses that identity. If an identifier with the same name had a meaning before the subprogram call, then that meaning is suspended for the duration of the subprogram call, but it returns with all its properties preserved when the subprogram call is completed. Figure 5.8 shows a possible arrangement of scopes for a program.

Figure 5.9 contains a program designed to illustrate the notion of scope. The single identifier `PIE` appears in three different scopes, so the program contains three different variables all named `PIE`. Each occurrence of the identifier `PIE` names one of these three variables. The three different boxes indicate the three areas of meaning for the identifier `PIE`.

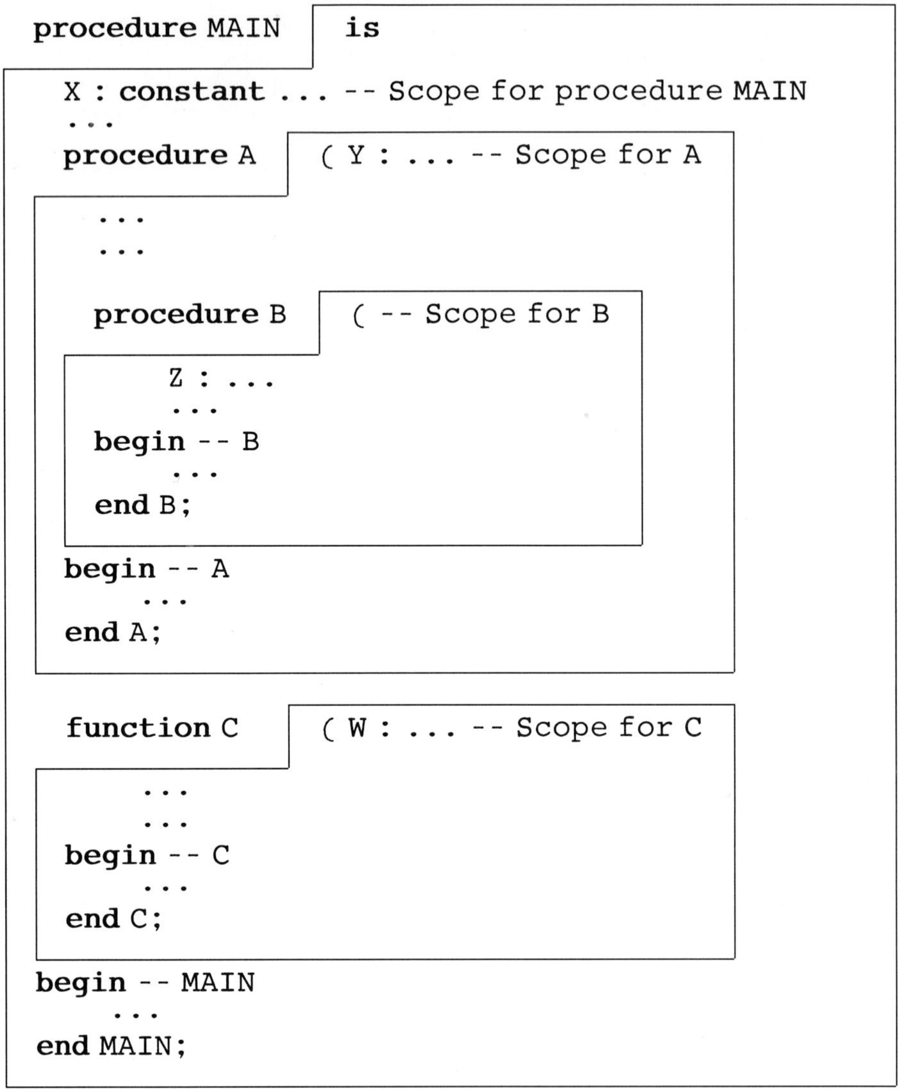

```
procedure MAIN is
   X : constant ... -- Scope for procedure MAIN
   ...
   procedure A ( Y : ... -- Scope for A
      ...
      ...
      procedure B ( -- Scope for B
            Z : ...
            ...
      begin -- B
            ...
      end B;
   begin -- A
         ...
   end A;

   function C ( W : ... -- Scope for C
         ...
         ...
   begin -- C
         ...
   end C;
begin -- MAIN
      ...
end MAIN;
```

Figure 5.8 Scope of identifiers.

Program

```
with I_O; use I_O;

procedure MAIN is
  PIE : INTEGER;

  procedure APPLE is
     PIE : INTEGER;
  begin -- Apple
     PUT ( "****Start Apple" ); NEW_LINE;
     PIE := 3;
     PUT ( "****In Apple, pie = " ); PUT ( PIE );
     NEW_LINE;
     PUT ( "****End Apple" ); NEW_LINE;
  end APPLE;

  procedure BAKER is
     PIE : INTEGER;
  begin -- Baker
     PUT ( "*Start Baker" ); NEW_LINE;
     PIE := 2;
     PUT ( "*In Baker, pie = " ); PUT ( PIE );
     NEW_LINE;
     APPLE;
     PUT ( "*In Baker, pie = " ); PUT ( PIE );
     NEW_LINE;
     PUT ( "*End Baker" ); NEW_LINE;
  end BAKER;

begin -- Main
    PUT ( "Start Program" ); NEW_LINE;
    PIE := 1;
    PUT ( "Global pie = " ); PUT ( PIE ); NEW_LINE;
    BAKER;
    PUT ( "Global pie = " ); PUT ( PIE ); NEW_LINE;
    PUT ( "End Program" ); NEW_LINE;
end MAIN;
```

Output

```
Start Program
Global pie =     1
*Start Baker
*In Baker, pie =     2
****Start Apple
****In Apple, pie =     3
****End Apple
*In Baker, pie =     2
*End Baker
Global pie =     1
End Program
```

Figure 5.9 One identifier in three scopes.

When a subprogram uses (or references) an identifier, say PIE, the computer *always* picks the local definition of that identifier. A *reference* to an identifier means that that identifier appears in the sequence of statements between the **begin** and the **end** of a subprogram.

In Figure 5.9 when the MAIN procedure references PIE in the assignment statement

```
PIE := 1;
```

the PIE that is used is the one declared in the MAIN procedure; that is, the PIE declared in the third line of the program.

When the MAIN procedure calls procedure BAKER, and procedure BAKER references the variable PIE in an assignment statement and an output statement, the PIE that is used is the one local to procedure BAKER; that is, the PIE declared in the scope associated with procedure BAKER.

Procedure BAKER in turn calls procedure APPLE. Procedure APPLE also references the identifier PIE. Again, the computer uses the occurrence of PIE that is local to the scope in which the reference is made. In procedure APPLE, the variable PIE that is used is the one declared in the scope associated with procedure APPLE.

Case Study

Automobile Bargaining

Problem Definition

A consumer service organization has commissioned you to write a program that will help people bargain for a low price when purchasing an automobile. The program will take as input the list price of the basic automobile and the list price of the desired options. It will output the lowest price that a dealer will accept. The buyer then can hold out for this price. The organization tells you that dealers will accept a price that is 10% above the dealer's cost of the automobile plus options. They also tell you that the cost of the automobile or options is one half the list price, except that on economy cars the dealer must also pay an additional delivery charge. Currently all cars with a list price of less than $15,000 are considered to be economy cars, and the delivery charge is $300.

Discussion

This problem breaks down into three main subprograms: input the data (INPUT_DATA), do a computation (COMPUTE_OFFER), and then output the results (OUTPUT_DATA). The computation subprogram further decomposes into two smaller subprograms: determine the dealer's cost (COMPUTE_COST), and calculate the lowest acceptable price (COMPUTE_PRICE). Since the dealer's cost is slightly different for the basic automobile and the options, we can subdivide this computation into these two subcomputations. At this point we decide on parameters by deciding what information is needed in the subprogram and what information is returned by the subprogram. The breakdown of the program into subprograms with parameters is shown in Figure 5.10.

Throughout the analysis above, we discover that three of the procedures (COMPUTE_OFFER, COMPUTE_COST, and COMPUTE_PRICE) have but a single output value. This seems to be an ideal situation for the use of functions. So, in the final implementation of the program (Figure 5.11), a function is used for each of these instead of a procedure.

local variable

The variable DEALER_COST, shown below in function COMPUTE_OFFER, is never used outside the function. It is used to hold an intermediate value that is calculated by the function; it is only used to temporarily hold a value before that value is passed on to function COMPUTE_PRICE. Hence, we will make it a local variable in the function COMPUTE_OFFER. The function will read as follows:

```
function COMPUTE_OFFER ( BASE_PRICE, OPTIONS : in FLOAT )
                                   return FLOAT is
      DEALER_COST : FLOAT;
begin -- Compute_Offer
    DEALER_COST := COMPUTE_COST ( BASE_PRICE, OPTIONS );
    return COMPUTE_PRICE ( DEALER_COST );
end COMPUTE_OFFER;
```

	in	out
INPUT_DATA		BASE_PRICE OPTIONS
OUTPUT_DATA	BASE_PRICE OPTIONS LOWEST_PRICE	
COMPUTE_OFFER	BASE_PRICE OPTIONS	LOWEST_PRICE
COMPUTE_COST	BASE_PRICE OPTIONS	DEALER_COST
COMPUTE_PRICE	DEALER_COST	LOWEST_COST

Figure 5.10 Subprograms and parameters for automobile pricing.

Algorithm

The algorithm for computing the dealer's cost is obtained by formalizing the description given to us in the problem definition. It uses two new variables BASE_COST and OPTIONS_COST.

```
if the car is an economy car then
   BASE_COST is 0.5 * (the base price) + (the delivery charge)
else -- it is not an economy car
   BASE_COST is 0.5 * (the base price)
OPTIONS_COST is 0.5 * (the list price of all options)
(the dealer's cost) is BASE_COST + OPTIONS_COST;
```

The algorithm is implemented as the function COMPUTE_COST. The variables BASE_COST and OPTIONS_COST are not used outside of the function COMPUTE_COST, so they will be local variables. The complete program is given in Figure 5.11.

Program

```
with I_O; use I_O;
procedure MAIN is
--                INPUT  : The sticker price of an automobile
--                         without options and the price of
--                         all desired options.
--                OUTPUT : Prompt messages, the sticker price,
--                         price of options, and the dealer's
--                         lowest price.
--                DESCRIPTION : Determines the dealer's minimum
--                              acceptable price on an automobile.
```

```
    AFTER : constant INTEGER := 2;
    BEFORE : constant INTEGER := 5;
    DELIVERY : constant FLOAT := 300.00;
    EXPONENT : constant INTEGER := 0;
    LUXURY_PRICE : constant FLOAT := 15_000.00;
    MARK_UP : constant FLOAT := 0.10;
    WHOLESALE_FACTOR : constant FLOAT := 0.50;
    BASE_PRICE,
    LOWEST_PRICE,
    OPTIONS : FLOAT;
    procedure INPUT_DATA ( BASE_PRICE, OPTIONS : out FLOAT ) is
--                     INPUT  : None
--                     OUTPUT : The base sticker price without options
--                              and the price of all options.
--                     DESCRIPTION : Prompts the user and inputs
--                                   base and options price.
    begin -- Input_Data
        PUT ( "Enter the base sticker price (without options):" );
        NEW_LINE;
        GET ( BASE_PRICE ); SKIP_LINE;
        PUT ( "Enter the total sticker price for all options:" );
        NEW_LINE;
        GET ( OPTIONS ); SKIP_LINE;
    end INPUT_DATA;
    function COMPUTE_OFFER ( BASE_PRICE, OPTIONS : in FLOAT )
                                  return FLOAT is
--                     INPUT  : The base sticker price and the price
--                              of all options.
--                     OUTPUT : The lowest dealer price.
--                     DESCRIPTION : Calls functions to compute the
--                                   dealer's cost and his lowest
--                                   possible price.
        DEALER_COST : FLOAT;
        function COMPUTE_COST ( BASE_PRICE, OPTIONS : in FLOAT )
                                     return FLOAT is
--                     INPUT  : The base sticker price and the price
--                              of all options.
--                     OUTPUT : The dealer's cost.
--                     DESCRIPTION : Determines dealer cost based on
--                                   sticker price, options, wholesale,
--                                   and delivery costs.
            BASE_COST,
            OPTIONS_COST : FLOAT;
```

```
        begin -- Compute_Cost
            if BASE_PRICE < LUXURY_PRICE then
                BASE_COST := WHOLESALE_FACTOR * BASE_PRICE + DELIVERY;
            else
                BASE_COST := WHOLESALE_FACTOR * BASE_PRICE;
            end if;
            OPTIONS_COST := WHOLESALE_FACTOR * OPTIONS;
            return BASE_COST + OPTIONS_COST;
        end COMPUTE_COST;
        function COMPUTE_PRICE ( DEALER_COST : in FLOAT )
                                 return FLOAT is
--                   INPUT  : The dealer's cost for an automobile.
--                   OUTPUT : The lowest price the dealer will take.
--                   DESCRIPTION : Determines the lowest possible
--                                 dealer price based on a given
--                                 markup.
        begin -- Compute_Price
            return ( 1.00 + MARK_UP ) * DEALER_COST;
        end COMPUTE_PRICE;
    begin -- Compute_Offer
        DEALER_COST := COMPUTE_COST ( BASE_PRICE, OPTIONS );
        return COMPUTE_PRICE ( DEALER_COST );
    end COMPUTE_OFFER;
    procedure OUTPUT_DATA ( BASE_PRICE,
                            OPTIONS,
                            LOWEST_PRICE : in FLOAT ) is
--                   INPUT  : The base sticker price plus options
--                            and the dealer's lowest price.
--                   OUTPUT : None
--                   DESCRIPTION : Displays messages advising the
--                                 user what price to offer for
--                                 the new car.
    begin -- Output_Data
        PUT ( "List price for basic model: $" );
        PUT ( BASE_PRICE, BEFORE, AFTER, EXPONENT );
        NEW_LINE;
        PUT ( "List price of options: $" );
        PUT ( OPTIONS, BEFORE, AFTER, EXPONENT );
        NEW_LINE;
        PUT ( "Dealer's lowest total price: $" );
        PUT ( LOWEST_PRICE, BEFORE, AFTER, EXPONENT );
        NEW_LINE;
        PUT ( "Go for it!" ); NEW_LINE;
    end OUTPUT_DATA;
```

```
begin -- Main
    PUT ( "I will help you get a bargain on your new car." );
    NEW_LINE;
    INPUT_DATA ( BASE_PRICE, OPTIONS );
    LOWEST_PRICE := COMPUTE_OFFER ( BASE_PRICE, OPTIONS );
    OUTPUT_DATA ( BASE_PRICE, OPTIONS, LOWEST_PRICE );
end MAIN;
```

Sample Dialogue

```
I will help you get a bargain on your new car.
Enter the base sticker price (without options):
13_000.00
Enter the total sticker price for all options:
4_000.00
List price for basic model: $13000.00
List price of options: $ 4000.00
Dealer's lowest total price: $ 9680.00
Go for it!
```

Figure 5.11 Automobile-pricing program.

Testing Subprograms

Because they divide big problems into smaller problems of more manageable size, subprograms make programs easier to write and easier to change. You can solve each subprogram separately, write it up as a subprogram, and then test it separately.

driver programs

As a sample case, consider the auto-pricing program in Figure 5.11. We can test each of the subprograms separately. We can check the procedure INPUT_DATA by using a program such as the one in Figure 5.12. Having tested this procedure, we can go on to test the other subprograms.

Program

```
with I_O; use I_O;
procedure MAIN is
--                  INPUT  : The base sticker price without options
--                           and the price of all options.
--                  OUTPUT : The base sticker price without options
--                           and the price of all options.
--                  DESCRIPTION : Tests the Input_Data procedure.
```

```
    AFTER : constant INTEGER := 2;
    BEFORE : constant INTEGER := 5;
    EXPONENT : constant INTEGER := 0;
    BASE_PRICE,
    OPTIONS : FLOAT;
    procedure INPUT_DATA ( BASE_PRICE, OPTIONS : out FLOAT ) is
--                  INPUT   : None
--                  OUTPUT : The base sticker price without options
--                           and the price of all options.
--                  DESCRIPTION : Prompts the user and inputs
--                                base and options price.
    begin -- Input_Data
        PUT ( "Enter the base sticker price (without options):" );
        NEW_LINE;
        GET ( BASE_PRICE ); SKIP_LINE;
        PUT ( "Enter the total sticker price for all options:" );
        NEW_LINE;
        GET ( OPTIONS ); SKIP_LINE;
    end INPUT_DATA;
begin -- Main
    INPUT_DATA ( BASE_PRICE, OPTIONS );
    PUT ( "Base price = " );
    PUT ( BASE_PRICE, BEFORE, AFTER, EXPONENT );
    NEW_LINE;
    PUT ( "Options price = " );
    PUT ( OPTIONS, BEFORE, AFTER, EXPONENT );
    NEW_LINE;
end MAIN;
```

Figure 5.12 Test 1.

We can test the function COMPUTE_COST with a program such as the one in Figure 5.13. The function COMPUTE_PRICE can be tested by a similar program. Once these two functions have been tested, we can test the function COMPUTE_OFFER. Testing programs, like those shown in Figures 5.12 and 5.13, are often called *driver programs*.

Program

```
with I_O; use I_O;
procedure MAIN is
--                      INPUT : The base sticker price without options
--                              and the price of all options.
--                      OUTPUT : The base sticker price without options,
--                               the price of all options, and dealer
                                 cost.
--                      DESCRIPTION : Test the Compute_Cost procedure.
     AFTER : constant INTEGER := 2;
     BEFORE : constant INTEGER := 5;
     DELIVERY : constant FLOAT := 300.00;
     EXPONENT : constant INTEGER := 0;
     LUXURY_PRICE : constant FLOAT := 15_000.00;
     WHOLESALE_FACTOR : constant FLOAT := 0.50;
     BASE_PRICE,
     DEALER_COST,
     OPTIONS : FLOAT;
     function COMPUTE_COST ( BASE_PRICE, OPTIONS : in FLOAT )
                              return FLOAT is
--                       INPUT  : The base sticker price and the price
--                                of all options.
--                       OUTPUT : The dealer's cost.
--                       DESCRIPTION : Determines dealer cost based on
--                                     sticker price, options,
                                       wholesale,
--                                     and delivery costs.
          BASE_COST,
          OPTIONS_COST : FLOAT;
     begin -- Compute_Cost
          if BASE_PRICE < LUXURY_PRICE then
              BASE_COST := WHOLESALE_FACTOR * BASE_PRICE + DELIVERY;
          else
              BASE_COST := WHOLESALE_FACTOR * BASE_PRICE;
          end if;
          OPTIONS_COST := WHOLESALE_FACTOR * OPTIONS;
          return BASE_COST + OPTIONS_COST;
     end COMPUTE_COST;
begin -- Main
     PUT ( "Enter list price for base price and options" );
     NEW_LINE;
     GET ( BASE_PRICE ); GET ( OPTIONS ); SKIP_LINE;
     DEALER_COST := COMPUTE_COST ( BASE_PRICE, OPTIONS );
     PUT ( "Base price = " );
     PUT ( BASE_PRICE, BEFORE, AFTER, EXPONENT );
     NEW_LINE;
```

```
    PUT ( "Options price = " );
    PUT ( OPTIONS, BEFORE, AFTER, EXPONENT );
    NEW_LINE;
    PUT ( "Dealer cost = " );
    PUT ( DEALER_COST, BEFORE, AFTER, EXPONENT );
    NEW_LINE;
end MAIN;
```

Sample Dialogue

```
Enter list price for base price and options
13_000.00 4_000.00
Base price = 13000.00
Options price = 4000.00
Dealer cost = 8800.00
```

Figure 5.13 Test 2.

Testing Strategies

bottom-up testing

Each subprogram in a program should receive a separate test. The method we outlined for testing the automobile-pricing program is called *bottom-up testing* and is one of two basic methods for testing a program. In the bottom-up testing strategy, each subprogram is tested and debugged before any subprogram that uses it is tested. One possible order for bottom-up testing of our automobile-pricing program is given in Figure 5.14, where test 1 means test this one first, test 2 means test this one second, and so on.

If you test each subprogram separately, you will find most of the mistakes in your program. Moreover, you will find out which subprogram contains the mistake. If instead you test the entire program, and if there is a mistake, then you will probably find out that the mistake exists, but you may have no idea where it is. Even worse, you may think you know where the mistake is but be mistaken.

Testing each subprogram separately may sound like a very time-consuming process. However, if you follow this strategy, you will find that the time saved by quickly locating bugs will allow you to write the final program faster than if you wrote and tested the program as a single undivided unit.

Top-Down and Bottom-Up Strategies

top-down testing

The bottom-up testing strategy, presented in the previous section, is a reasonable strategy for testing a small program or small portions of a larger program. However, when testing a large program, the bottom-up strategy does not always make sense. The best

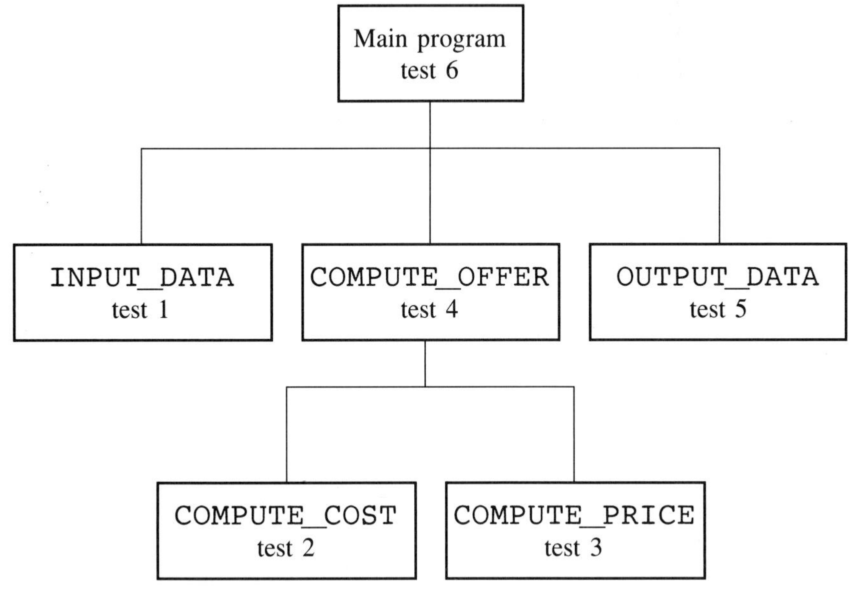

Figure 5.14 One order for bottom-up testing.

way to design a program is top-down. First, break the problem down into subproblems. Then write subprograms for the subproblems. These subprograms will contain calls to yet other subprograms to solve smaller subproblems. To test the basic design strategy, it frequently is a good idea to test each subprogram before going on to design the subprograms it uses. This method of testing is called *top-down testing*. For example, a possible top-down order for testing the subprograms in our automobile-pricing program is given in Figure 5.15. Again, the number (1, 2, . . .) represents the order of testing.

stub programs

How can you test a subprogram or program, such as the automobile pricing program, before writing the subprograms it uses? The answer is to write simple versions of the missing subprograms and to use these simplified versions to test the calling program (or subprogram). The simple version will not do what the final subprogram is supposed to do, but it will behave like the subprogram is supposed to behave on the test cases for which it is used. One such approach is to write the subprograms with parameters and comments, but with only a few minimal statements in the block. These minimal statements consist of an output statement that displays the name of the subprogram and any necessary subprogram calls. It is also a good idea to assign some reasonable value to all **out** parameters. The block of the main procedure, however, is complete. This early version of the program, with these simplified versions of subprograms, is frequently called a *stub program.* The stub program is a complete, compilable, executable program, but does not perform computations. It has all of the documentation and parameters of the completed program. The output from the program not only displays the names of all subprograms that are called but also shows the order in which they were called. An example of the stub program for automobile pricing is given in Figure 5.16.

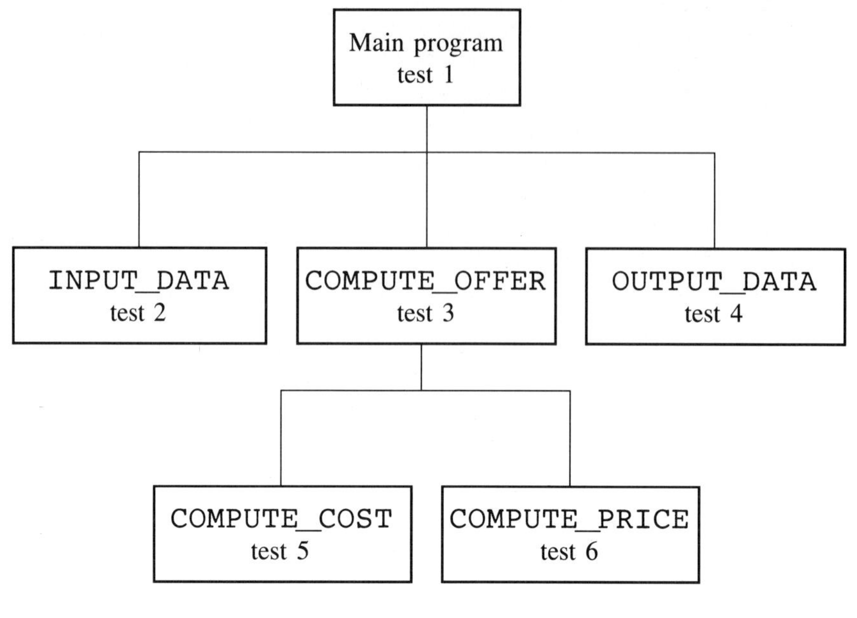

Figure 5.15 One order for top-down testing.

The next step, using this stub program approach, is to fill in the code for the procedure INPUT_DATA, and then compile and execute the program. The succeeding steps are to do the same with procedure OUTPUT_DATA, and then the functions COMPUTE_COST and COMPUTER_PRICE, and finally COMPUTE_OFFER.

Program

```
with I_O; use I_O;
procedure MAIN is
--                    INPUT  : The sticker price of an automobile
--                             without options and the price of
--                             all desired options.
--                    OUTPUT : Prompt messages, the sticker price,
--                             price of options and the dealer's
--                             lowest price.
--                    DESCRIPTION : Determines the dealer's minimum
--                                  acceptable price on an automobile.
```

```
    AFTER : constant INTEGER := 2;
    BEFORE : constant INTEGER := 5;
    DELIVERY : constant FLOAT := 300.00;
    EXPONENT : constant INTEGER := 0;
    MARK_UP : constant FLOAT := 0.10;
    WHOLESALE_FACTOR : constant FLOAT := 0.50;
    BASE_PRICE,
    LOWEST_PRICE,
    OPTIONS : FLOAT;
    procedure INPUT_DATA ( BASE_PRICE, OPTIONS : out FLOAT ) is
--                INPUT  : None
--                OUTPUT : The base sticker price without options
--                         and the price of all options.
--                DESCRIPTION : Prompts the user and inputs
--                              base and options price.
    begin -- Input_Data
        PUT ( "Input_Data" ); NEW_LINE;
        BASE_PRICE := 10_000.00;
        OPTIONS := 1_000.00;
    end INPUT_DATA;
    function COMPUTE_OFFER ( BASE_PRICE, OPTIONS : in FLOAT )
                             return FLOAT is
--                INPUT  : The base sticker price and the price
--                         of all options.
--                OUTPUT : The lowest dealer price.
--                DESCRIPTION : Calls functions to compute the
--                              dealer's cost and his lowest
--                              possible price.
        DEALER_COST : FLOAT;
        function COMPUTE_COST ( BASE_PRICE, OPTIONS : in FLOAT )
                                return FLOAT is
--                INPUT  : The base sticker price and the price
--                         of all options.
--                OUTPUT : The dealer's cost.
--                DESCRIPTION : Determines dealer cost based on
--                              sticker price, options, wholesale,
--                              and delivery costs.
            BASE_COST,
            OPTIONS_COST : FLOAT;
        begin -- Compute_Cost
            PUT ( "Compute_Cost" ); NEW_LINE;
            return 8_000.00;
        end COMPUTE_COST;
```

```
        function COMPUTE_PRICE ( DEALER_COST : in FLOAT )
                                 return FLOAT is
--                   INPUT  : The dealer's cost for an automobile.
--                   OUTPUT : The lowest price the dealer will take.
--                   DESCRIPTION : Determines the lowest possible
--                                 dealer price based on a given
--                                 markup.
        begin -- Compute_Price
            PUT ( "Compute_Price" ); NEW_LINE;
            return 7_000.00;
        end COMPUTE_PRICE;
    begin -- Compute_Offer
        PUT ( "Compute_Offer" ); NEW_LINE;
        DEALER_COST := COMPUTE_COST ( BASE_PRICE, OPTIONS );
        return COMPUTE_PRICE ( DEALER_COST );
    end COMPUTE_OFFER;
    procedure OUTPUT_DATA ( BASE_PRICE,
                            OPTIONS,
                            LOWEST_PRICE : in FLOAT ) is
--                   INPUT  : The base sticker price plus options,
--                            and the dealer's lowest price.
--                   OUTPUT : None
--                   DESCRIPTION : Displays messages advising the
--                                 user what price to offer for a
--                                 given priced automobile.
    begin -- Output_Data
        PUT ( "Output_Data" ); NEW_LINE;
        end OUTPUT_DATA;
    begin -- Main
        PUT ( "I will help you get a bargain on your new car." );
        NEW_LINE;
        INPUT_DATA ( BASE_PRICE, OPTIONS );
        LOWEST_PRICE := COMPUTE_OFFER ( BASE_PRICE, OPTIONS );
        OUTPUT_DATA ( BASE_PRICE, OPTIONS, LOWEST_PRICE );
    end MAIN;
```

Sample Output

```
I will help you get a bargain on your new car.
Input_Data
Compute
Compute_Cost
Compute_Price
Output_Data
```

Figure 5.16 Stubbed program.

The advantages of bottom-up testing are obvious. Each procedure is tested with fully debugged, final versions of the procedures it uses. Hence, any problems discovered can be attributed to the procedure being tested. The advantage of top-down testing is that it allows you to test your basic design strategy before you get too far along in the design process. It allows you to test whether or not a particular breakdown of the program into subprograms will work as desired. If it will not, there is no need to solve the subprograms. In that case you need to back up and rethink the way you divided the program into subprograms. It also lets you test the exact specification of what each procedure should do, before you go ahead and design the details of how it will do it.

mixed strategies

Sometimes it is best to test bottom-up, sometimes it is best to test top-down, and sometimes it is best to mix the two strategies, testing some procedures bottom-up and some top-down. Figure 5.17 gives a mixed strategy that we could have used to design and test our automobile-pricing program. If the procedures are designed in the order given there, you will be following the order given in the stub program approach. The stub program approach does not preclude bottom-up testing of some of the major procedures before they are inserted into the program, so you end up with a mixed strategy that combines bottom-up and top-down testing.

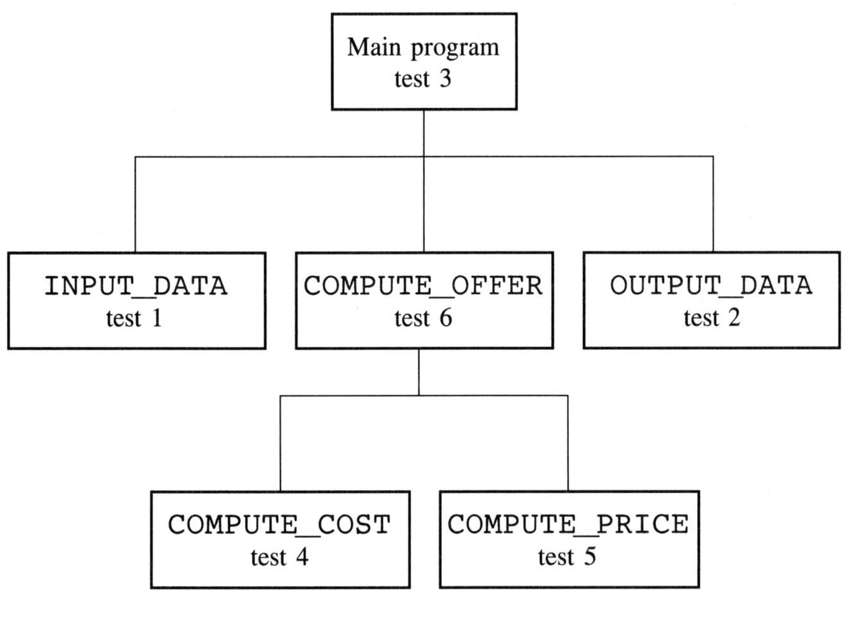

Figure 5.17 One order for a mixed strategy.

Preconditions and Postconditions

One way to document what a procedure does is by means of special purpose assertion comments known as *preconditions* and *postconditions.* A precondition is an assertion that says what is expected to be true whenever the procedure is used. The procedure should not be used and cannot be expected to perform correctly unless the precondition holds. A postcondition states the relevant facts that will be true after the procedure is executed in a situation in which all the preconditions hold. For example, the following are possible pre- and postconditions for the function COMPUTE_OFFER in Figure 5.11. The preconditions are stated in the procedure's INPUT comment section, because they reflect the input conditions to the procedure. In a similar fashion, the postconditions are stated in the procedure's OUTPUT comment section.

```
function COMPUTE_OFFER ( BASE_PRICE, OPTIONS : in FLOAT )
                              return FLOAT is
--            INPUT  : The base sticker price and the price
--                       of all options.
--            OUTPUT : The lowest dealer price.
--            DESCRIPTION : Calls functions to compute the
--                            dealer's cost and his lowest
--                            possible price.
```

You should include a comment with each procedure specification. The comment need not follow this exact format of writing preconditions and postconditions, but it should describe any conditions that must hold before the procedure is called, and it should say what effects will be produced by executing the procedure. The comment should also explain everything else that a programmer using the procedure needs to know, such as what other procedures it calls, what defined constants it uses, and what variables it changes. One popular method for displaying this comment is to block the comment in a box to make it stand out.

```
function COMPUTE_OFFER ( BASE_PRICE, OPTIONS : in FLOAT )
                              return FLOAT is
--**********************************************************
--*           INPUT  : The base sticker price and the price  *
--*                      of all options.                     *
--*           OUTPUT : The lowest dealer price.              *
--*           DESCRIPTION : Calls function to compute the    *
--*                           dealer's cost and his lowest   *
--*                           possible price.                *
--**********************************************************
```

On large programming projects that involve more than one programmer, this comment should also contain the author's name and the date written, as well as the date and nature of any modifications to the procedure. In this book we will use a somewhat shorter comment format to save space.

Summary of Problem Solving and Programming Techniques

- Use local variables to hold any temporary information that a subprogram may need for its calculations but that is not needed by any other part of the program.
- The interaction of a subprogram and the rest of the program should be via parameters. Global variables normally should not appear in a subprogram body.
- A formal **in** parameter is a local named constant that is initialized to the value of the associated actual parameter when the subprogram is called. It is possible to use it just like any other local named constant.
- Each subprogram should be tested separately in a program that contains no subprograms except itself and possibly some other subprograms that have already been fully tested and debugged.
- You can test a subprogram before all the subprograms it uses have been written. To do so, use simplified versions (stubs) of the missing subprograms.
- Stubbed programs use simplified versions of subprograms and a combination of top-down and bottom-up testing.
- Preconditions and postconditions are a type of assertion that can be used effectively to document subprograms.

Summary of Ada Constructs

subprogram_body

Syntax:

```
subprogram_specification is
        local_object_declarations
        local_subprogram_bodies
begin
        sequence_of_statements
end subprogram_name ;
```

```
procedure procedure_name ( formal_parameter_list )
or
function function_name ( formal_parameter_list )
                              return type_name
```

subprogram_specification

The *sequence_of_statements* may be any Ada statements. See the following entries for details on local declarations.

local variable

A local variable is one that is declared within a procedure body. A local variable exists only for the duration of the procedure call. The identifier used to name a local variable can also be used to name another variable (or constant or other object) outside of the procedure body.

local identifier

A local identifier is one that is declared within a procedure. The object it names exists only for the duration of the procedure call. A same identifier can also be used outside of the procedure body to name something else. Local variable names, local constant names, and local procedure names are examples of local identifiers.

global variable

A variable that is declared for the entire program; that is, one whose scope is the scope of the entire program.

scope of declaration

A scope of declaration (or simply scope) consists of a parameter list, followed by a set of declarations, followed by the statements they apply to, enclosed in a **begin**/**end** pair. (If there is no parameter list or no declarations, it is still a scope.)

scope of an identifier

The scope in which an identifier is declared is called its *scope of declaration.* If the same identifier is declared in two scopes, one inside the other, then in the inner scope its meaning is the one declared in the inner scope. The scope of declaration is the region of program text over which the declaration has its effect.

Exercises

Interactive Exercises

7. Run the program in Figure 5.1 twice, once as shown and once omitting the local variable declaration:

```
TEMPORARY : INTEGER;
```

8. Write a procedure to interchange the value of two variables of type CHARACTER.

Programming Exercises

9. Write a procedure with two variable parameters, NUMBER_1 and NUMBER_2, of type INTEGER, that will sort the two values so that after the procedure is called, NUMBER_1 is less than or equal to NUMBER_2. The procedure either leaves the values of the variables unchanged or else interchanges the two values. Your procedure will include a call to the procedure EXCHANGE from Figure 5.1. Embed the procedure in a test program.

10. Write a program that computes the annual after-tax cost of a new house for the first year of ownership. The cost is computed as the annual mortgage cost minus the tax savings. The input should be the price of the house and the down payment. The annual mortgage cost can be estimated as 3% of the initial loan balance credited

toward paying off the loan principal, plus 10% of the initial loan balance in interest. The initial loan balance is the price minus the down payment. Assume a 35% marginal tax rate, and assume that interest payments are tax deductible. So the tax savings is 35% of the interest payment. Use at least three subprograms.

11. Write a program for the discount installment loan algorithm described in Exercise 10 of Chapter 1. Implement subproblems as subprograms.

12. Write a program that reads in a length in feet and inches and then outputs the equivalent length in meters and centimeters. Use at least three subprograms: one for input, one or more for calculating, and one for output. There are 0.3048 meters in a foot, 100 centimeters in a meter, and 12 inches in a foot.

13. Write a program like that of the previous exercise that converts meters and centimeters into feet and inches.

14. Write a program that reads in a weight in pounds and ounces and then outputs the equivalent weight in kilograms and grams. Use at least three subprograms: one for input, one or more for calculating, and one for output. There are 2.2046 pounds in a kilogram, 1000 grams in a kilogram, and 16 ounces in a pound.

15. Write a program like that of the previous exercise that converts from kilograms and grams into pounds and ounces.

16. Combine, modify, and extend your programs from the previous four exercises into a single program that can perform a choice of conversions from the system of weights and measures commonly used in the U.S. to the metric system and vice versa. It first asks the user whether he or she wants to convert from metric to U.S. measurements or from U.S. to metric. It then asks the user whether he or she wishes to deal with weights or lengths. It then performs the desired calculation. For example, in one case the program asks for a weight in pounds and ounces and outputs the weight expressed in kilograms and grams. Use subprogram calls as the substatements in if-then-else statements. Some of these subprograms will in turn have if-then-else statements with other subprogram calls for their statements. Include a loop to repeat this calculation as often as the user desires.

17. Enhance the program in Figure 4.10 so that it accepts as input an amount of dollars and cents as a value of type `FLOAT` and then outputs the bills as well as the coins that equal that amount. Use bill denominations of $20, $5, and $1. Also include nickels as a possible coin in this version. Use the procedure `COMPUTE_COINS` from Figure 4.11 and one other similar procedure to compute numbers of bills. Include a loop to repeat this calculation as often as the user desires.

18. Write a program that is a major improvement on the change-making program in Figure 4.4. This improved version asks for the amount tendered by the customer as well as the price and number of the items. It responds with the price, the number of items, the total bill, the amount tendered, and the change due. It then goes on to tell the cashier exactly what combination of bills and coins will equal the amount of change. Use subprograms for subproblems. The change-making program in Figure 4.10 can be used as a model for the last part. It would pay to do the previous exercise before doing this one. Include a loop to repeat this calculation as often as the user desires.

19. Write a procedure with two **in** parameters of type INTEGER called NUMBER and WIDTH. The procedure writes NUMBER to the screen in the conventional way, with commas every three spaces. WIDTH is used as the field width specification for the total number of spaces, *including commas.* Note that you will have to use other field width specifications derived from WIDTH inside PUT statements within the procedure block. If WIDTH is too small, the procedure uses the minimum width that will hold the output.

20. Redo (or do for the first time) Exercise 20 from Chapter 3. Use three procedures: one for input, one for output, and one to perform the calculation.

21. Redo (or do for the first time) Exercise 26 from Chapter 3. Use three procedures: one for input, one for output, and one to perform the calculation.

22. Redo (or do for the first time) Exercise 27 from Chapter 3. Use three procedures: one for input, one for output, and one to perform the calculation.

23. Redo (or do for the first time) Exercise 29 from Chapter 3. Use three procedures: one for input, one for output, and one to perform the calculation.

24. Redo (or do for the first time) Exercise 30 from Chapter 3. Use three procedures: one for input, one for output, and one to perform the calculation.

25. Redo (or do for the first time) Exercise 32 from Chapter 3. Use three procedures: one for input, one for output, and one to perform the calculation.

26. Redo (or do for the first time) Exercise 34 from Chapter 3. Use three procedures: one for input, one for output, and one to perform the calculation.

DESIGNING PROGRAMS THAT MAKE CHOICES

George Boole

Boole (1815–1864) was a British logician and mathematician. Boole devised a branch of algebra that deals with logical relationships. Today it is known as *boolean algebra,* but its electronic usefulness lay dormant from 1851 until it was applied to the logic design of computers. Modern programming languages make extensive use of boolean expressions as part of their control mechanisms.

Chapter Contents

Any programming construct that chooses one out of a number of alternative actions is called a *branching mechanism.* The `if-then` and the `if-then-else` statements are two examples of branching mechanisms. In this chapter we expand our description of the `if` statement to include the `elsif` clause. Also, the full class of boolean expressions, which can be used to control branching, is included. We then go on to describe boolean variables and how they are used as a programming tool. Ada has one additional branching statement, called the `case` statement, that we introduce in this chapter. We also explore problem solving and programming techniques for designing branches in particular and programs in general. We begin with a discussion of how Ada branching statements may be nested within other branching statements to produce complex program instructions.

Nested Statements

An **if-then-else** or **if-then** statement can contain simple statements within it. Thus far we have used simple statements such as assignment statements as the substatement. In fact any statement at all can be used. In particular, we can use an **if-then** statement within an **if-then** statement.

recursive (circular) definitions

This nesting of statements inside of statements points out one peculiarity in the definitions of the **if** statement. The definitions say that it can contain any sort of statement, including one of the same kind, as illustrated in Figure 6.1. This way of defining statements may seem circular and, in fact, it is. Circular definitions and even circular program instructions are common in computer science. In computer science, however, circular definitions and instructions are usually referred to by the word *recursive* rather than the word *circular.*

It is not always wrong or even undesirable to give a circular definition. The same thing happens in English grammar, but there we seldom notice that it is circular. We can make two sentences into one sentence by joining them with the word *and* or with a semicolon. Hence, if we were to write out the grammar rules for English sentences, the definition of *sentence* would refer to sentences and so would be recursive (i.e., circular). For instance, a complete definition of English sentences would begin something like: ''A *sentence* is any string of words formed according to the following rules.'' One of the rules would read, ''A *sentence* can be formed by taking any *sentence* followed by the word *and* followed by any other *sentence* (and for written sentences, adjusting periods and capitalization appropriately).''

how to formulate recursive definitions

Recursive definitions do require a bit of care in how they are formulated. For such a definition to be meaningful, it should contain some clauses that are not circular. In the case of Ada statements, this general rule means that some statements may qualify for statementhood because some subpart (or subparts) is itself a statement, and that substatement may similarly contain a subpart that is a statement, and so forth. Eventually this chain of substatement, sub-substatement, and so forth, must bottom out with a statement that does not contain any substatements. This bottoming out is what saves these circular or recursive definitions from going on endlessly and meaninglessly when you try to use them. For example, an **if-then** statement can contain another **if-then** statement, and that **if-then** statement can contain yet another **if-then** statement, and so on for any number of times. Eventually, however, this must end, and the innermost **if-then** statement must contain something simple like an assignment statement or an input/output statement, as shown in Figure 6.1.

```
if AGE < 40 then
    if CHOLESTEROL < 180 then
         PUT ( "age < 40 and cholesterol < 180 " );
         NEW_LINE;
    end if;
end if;
```

Figure 6.1 Nesting an if-then statement within an if-then statement.

recursive syntax diagrams

The recursive nature of the definition of Ada statements can be seen in their syntax diagrams. If you look at the syntax diagrams in Appendix B, you will see that a statement can be formed in a number of ways. Some of the diagrams, such as the one labeled *if statement,* involve reference back to the diagram for *statement.* On the other hand, the diagrams for other clauses, such as *assignment statement* and *procedure call,* do not refer to the diagram labeled *statement* either directly or indirectly. When using syntax diagrams to verify the correctness of a statement, a successful check must ultimately involve one of the clauses that do not refer back to the diagram labeled *statement.*

Elsif Clause

An additional feature of the `if` statement in Ada is the **`elsif`** clause. The reserved word **`elsif`** is pronounced as if it were two words, *else if,* and in fact it is used to represent the combination of an **`else`** followed by an **`if`**. It can often be used when there is a second (or third, or fourth, and so on) condition (boolean expression) that must be tested. The following nested **`if`** statement

```
if boolean__expression__1 then
      statements__1
else
      if boolean__expression__2 then
            statements__2
      else
            if boolean__expression__3 then
                  statements__3
            else
                  statements__4
            end if;
      end if;
end if;
```

can be rewritten using the **`elsif`** clause as follows:

```
if boolean__expression__1 then
      statements__1
elsif boolean__expression__2 then
      statements__2
elsif boolean__expression__3 then
      statements__3
else
      statements__4
end if;
```

The boolean expressions are evaluated in order until one is found to be *true.* The statements corresponding to the first true boolean expression are executed. If none of the boolean expressions are true and there is a final **`else`**, then the statements after the final **else** are executed. If none of the boolean expressions are true and there is no final **else**, then nothing happens; execution of the program continues with the next statement.

Figure 6.2 is an example program that tests AGE and DRIVERS_EDUCATION. The first boolean expression tests if AGE is less than 16. If that is true the first PUT statement is the only statement executed. However, if the first boolean expression is false, then the second boolean expression (the one following the **elsif**) is evaluated. The statements following the second **then** and before the **else** are executed only if the first boolean expression is false and the second boolean expression is true. The statement following the **else** is executed only if the first and second boolean expressions both evaluate to false. Although there are two boolean expression they are both in the same **if** statement, so only one **end if** is required. An **end if** is used to terminate each **if** statement. The **end if** is not associated with the **elsif**.

Program

```
with I_O; use I_O;
procedure MAIN is
--                  Input  : An integer age and a code (Yes or No)
--                           for drivers education.
--                  Output : Statements about driving and insurance.
--                  Description : The program tests for a legal
--                                driving age and for an insurance
--                                discount for drivers education.
    AGE : INTEGER;
    DRIVERS_EDUCATION : CHARACTER;
begin -- Main
    PUT ( "Enter your age." ); NEW_LINE;
    GET ( AGE ); SKIP_LINE;
    PUT ( "Have you had drivers education? (Enter Yes or No)" );
    NEW_LINE;
    GET ( DRIVERS_EDUCATION ); SKIP_LINE;
    if AGE < 16 then
        PUT ( "Sorry, you are too young to drive." );
    elsif DRIVERS_EDUCATION = 'Y' then
        PUT ( "Congratulations, you get a discount on your insurance."
    else
        PUT ( "Drive very carefully." );
    end if;
    NEW_LINE;
end MAIN;
```

Sample Dialogue

```
Enter your age.
18
Have you had drivers education? (Enter Yes or No)
Yes
Congratulations, you get a discount on your insurance.
```

Figure 6.2 Program with an `elsif` clause.

The syntax diagrams in Figure 6.3 show that the **`elsif`** clause is optional and may be repeated as often as necessary. The **`else`** clause of the **`if`** statement is also optional, but it may not be repeated. When the **`else`** clause is used, it must always be the last clause of the **`if`** statement.

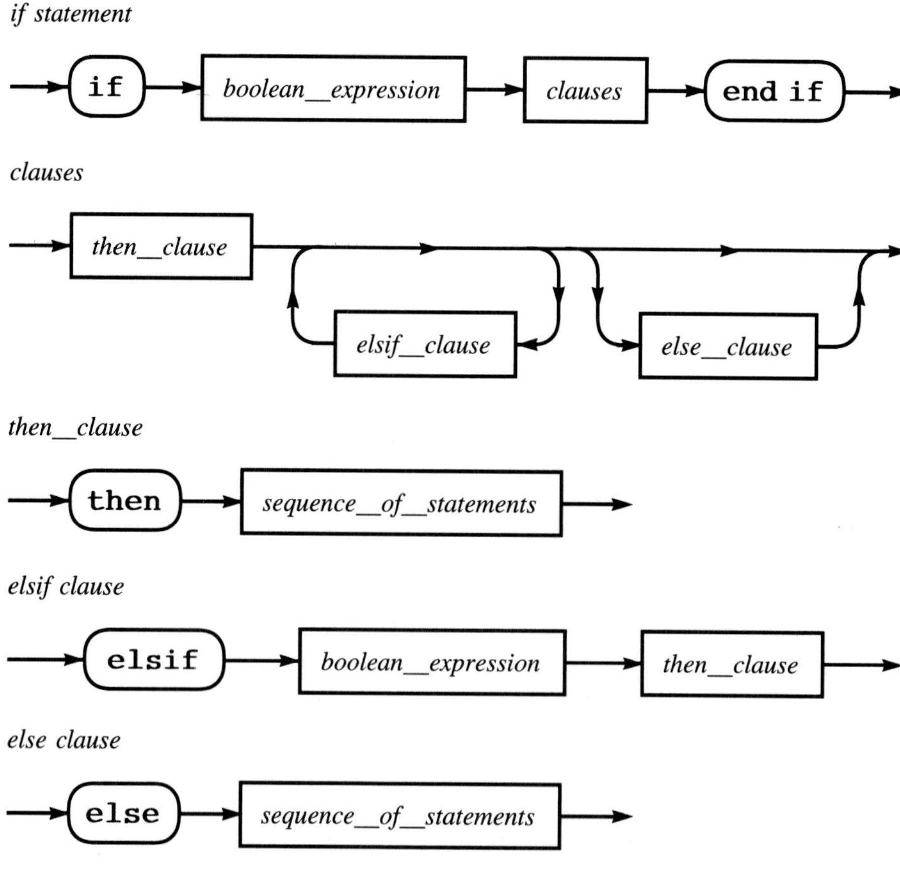

Figure 6.3 Extended `if` statement syntax diagram.

Complex Boolean Expressions

An Ada expression that is either true or false is called a *boolean expression*. For example, we have been using simple boolean expressions such as **AGE < 40** within **if** statements. You can form more complicated boolean expressions out of these simple boolean expressions by combining them with the operators **and**, **or**, **xor**, and **not**. These operators work very much as they do in English, combining simpler boolean expressions to yield a new, complex boolean expression.

and

A large boolean expression can be formed from two smaller boolean expressions by joining them with an **and**. The larger expression evaluates to TRUE, provided that both subexpressions evaluate to TRUE; otherwise, it evaluates to FALSE. For example,

```
AGE > 15 and DRIVERS_EDUCATION = 'Y'
```

evaluates to TRUE if both the value of AGE is greater than the value **15** and the value of DRIVERS_EDUCATION is equal to the value '**Y**'; otherwise, its value is FALSE.

In mathematics, pairs of inequalities are usually expressed as follows:

MERCURY < EARTH < JUPITER

Expressions with such chains of interlocking comparisons are not allowed in Ada. Instead you must break them into parts and connect these parts with **and**'s.

```
MERCURY < EARTH and EARTH < JUPITER
```

These complex boolean expressions are used in the same way as the simple boolean expressions we introduced in Chapter 3. For example, the program in Figure 6.4 uses complex boolean expressions to determine if the user's zodiac sign is Scorpio.

Program

```
with I_O; use I_O;
procedure MAIN is
--                INPUT  : Birthday (month and day)
--                OUTPUT : A message about the zodiac sign Scorpio
--                DESCRIPTION : Determines if the user is a Scorpio:
--                              birthday between October 24th and
--                              November 22nd, inclusive.
    DAY,
    MONTH : INTEGER;
begin -- Main
    PUT ( "Enter your month and day" ); NEW_LINE;
    PUT ( "of birth, as two integer numbers." ); NEW_LINE;
    GET ( MONTH ); GET ( DAY ); SKIP_LINE;
```

```
    if MONTH = 10
    and DAY >= 24 then
        PUT ( "You're an October Scorpio." );
    else
        PUT ( "You're not an October Scorpio." );
    end if;
    NEW_LINE;
    if MONTH = 11
    and DAY <= 22 then
        PUT ( "You're a November Scorpio." );
    else
        PUT ( "You're not a November Scorpio." );
    end if;
    NEW_LINE;
    PUT ( "I knew it!" ); NEW_LINE;
end MAIN;
```

Sample Dialogue 1

```
Enter your month and day
of birth, as two integer numbers.
10 25
You're an October Scorpio.
You're not a November Scorpio.
I knew it!
```

Sample Dialogue 2

```
Enter your month and day
of birth, as two integer numbers.
10 21
You're not an October Scorpio.
You're not a November Scorpio.
I knew it!
```

Figure 6.4 Boolean expressions using and.

The syntax for expressions involving **or** is similar to what we described for **and**. For example:

```
AGE > 18 or HIGH_SCHOOL_GRADUATE = 'Y'
```

or This expression is TRUE provided the value of AGE is greater than the value **18**, or the value of HIGH_SCHOOL_GRADUATE is 'Y', *or both* are TRUE. This is the so-called "inclusive" meaning of the word *or.* This inclusive meaning is always used in mathematics, but it is not always used in ordinary conversation. Ordinary conversational English has trouble coping with situations where two true statements are joined by the word *or.* Ada and mathematical disciplines in general have no such problem. In Ada, if two things are connected by an **or**, then the resulting expression is TRUE provided one or both subexpressions are TRUE; otherwise, its value is FALSE.

xor

Ada has the so-called "exclusive or" as well as the "inclusive or," which we just discussed. In Ada the "exclusive or" is written **xor** to distinguish it from **or**. Two boolean expressions joined by **xor** produce a larger boolean expression that is TRUE provided one, but not both, of the two subexpressions are TRUE. For example,

```
AGE < 30 xor RANK > 5
```

is TRUE provided the value of AGE is less than 30 and the value of RANK is *not* greater than 5. It is also TRUE if the value of RANK is greater than 5 and the value of AGE is *not* less than 30. However, it is FALSE if the value of AGE is less than 30 and the value of RANK is greater than 5. Of course, it is also FALSE if the value of AGE is not less than 30 and the value of RANK is not greater than 5.

not

The boolean operator **not** reverses truth values, much as the word *not* does in English. However, the Ada syntax for **not** is quite different from English. In Ada the **not** is always placed in front of the expression being negated. As examples, consider the following boolean expressions:

```
Not ( 'A' = 'Z' )                Not ( 2 < 3 )
```

Since **not** changes TRUE to FALSE and FALSE to TRUE, the first of these two boolean expressions evaluates to TRUE and the second to FALSE.

nested expressions

As illustrated by the following two examples, we can repeat this method of combining boolean expressions with **and**, **or**, and **not** to obtain even more complex expressions.

```
   ( ( MONTH = 10 ) and ( DAY >= 24 ) )
or ( ( MONTH = 11 ) and ( DAY <= 22 ) )

    ( TIME < 60 )
and ( not ( ( ANSWER = 'N' ) or ( ANSWER = 'n' ) ) )
```

The first of these sample expressions could be used in a program similar to that in Figure 6.4. It would be TRUE if the values of MONTH and DAY indicate a Scorpio (October 24 through November 22) of any kind.

parentheses

Most of the examples we have constructed thus far have been fully parenthesized to show exactly what two expressions each **and** or **or** applies to. If both **and** and **or** appear in the same boolean expression, parentheses must be included to show exactly which boolean expressions are associated with the logical operator. If there is more than one **and** but no **or**'s appear in an expression, parentheses may not be necessary. The same is true for multiple **or**'s without any **and**'s. Thus, one place parentheses can safely be omitted is in a simple string of **and**'s or **or**'s, but not where there is a mixture of the two. Parentheses may not be required around most expressions that involve any relational operators (=, >, etc.), unless the logical **not** operator is used. The logical operator **not** can also appear in boolean expressions. The **not** operator always takes precedence over **and**, **or**, and any of the relational operators. Thus, it is good practice to include most parentheses to make the expression easier to understand. The following expressions are acceptable in terms of both the Ada compiler and readability:

```
( MONTH = 10 and DAY >= 24 ) or ( MONTH = 11 and DAY <= 22 )
TIME < 60 and not ( ANSWER = 'N' or ANSWER = 'n' )
( AGE < 100 ) and ( ANSWER /= 'N' ) and ( ANSWER /= 'n' )
```

There are many ways to format complex boolean expression to enhance readability. One way is to fully parenthesize the expression. When they are included in more complicated expressions, the parentheses around simple boolean expressions, such as `( AGE < 100 )`, are optional. If they are omitted, the compiler will use the precedence rules established in the language. A second method is to put each boolean expression on a separate line, as in the following examples:
Example 1:

```
( MONTH = 10
and DAY >= 24 )
or
( MONTH = 11
and DAY <= 22 )
```

Example 2:

```
( MONTH = 10
and
DAY >= 24 )
or
( MONTH = 11
and
DAY <= 22 )
```

Both examples are evaluated in exactly the same way; the difference is simply a matter of writing style.

Many high-level programming languages have boolean expressions that are formed and used in much the same way as they are in Ada. Such minor details as the placement of parentheses will vary from language to language, but the general ideas are the same for most programming languages. A summary of the precedence of Ada operators used thus far is given in Figure 6.5.

highest precedence operators	**	**not**	**abs**			
multiplying operators	*	/	**rem**			
unary adding operators	+	-				
binary adding operators	+	-				
relational operators	=	/=	<	<=	>	>=
logical operators	**and**	**or**	**xor**			

Figure 6.5 Precedence of Ada operators.

Evaluating Boolean Expressions

Boolean expressions such as

```
( X > 0 ) and ( Y < Z )
```

are evaluated and have a value of either TRUE or FALSE. The computer obtains values for these boolean expressions in a way analogous to how we normally evaluate arithmetic expressions.

By way of review, consider the following arithmetic expression:

```
( 1 + 2 ) * ( 2 + 3 )
```

To evaluate this arithmetic expression, we evaluate the two sums to obtain the values 3 and 5, and then we combine the 3 and the 5 using multiplication to obtain 15 as the value of the entire expression. When determining the value of the expression, we do not multiply the *expressions* (1 + 2) and (2 + 3). Instead, we multiply the *values* of the expressions. We use 3; we do not use (1 + 2).

The computer evaluates boolean expressions in a similar way. Subexpressions are evaluated to obtain values each of which is either TRUE or FALSE. These values of TRUE or FALSE are then combined according to the rules in the table shown in Figure 6.6. For example, consider the boolean expression

```
not ( ( X > 0 ) or ( X < 7 ) )
```

and suppose that the value of **X** is 5. In this case **(X > 0)** and **(X < 7)** both evaluate to TRUE, so the expression is equivalent to

```
not ( TRUE or TRUE )
```

Consulting the tables for **or**, the computer sees that the expression inside the parentheses evaluates to TRUE, so the entire expression is equivalent to **not** (TRUE). Again consulting the tables, it sees that **not** (TRUE) evaluates to FALSE, so it concludes that FALSE is the value of the original boolean expression.

Expression	Value	Expression	Value
TRUE **and** TRUE	TRUE	TRUE **or** TRUE	TRUE
TRUE **and** FALSE	FALSE	TRUE **or** FALSE	TRUE
FALSE **and** TRUE	FALSE	FALSE **or** TRUE	TRUE
FALSE **and** FALSE	FALSE	FALSE **or** FALSE	FALSE
TRUE **xor** TRUE	FALSE	**not** TRUE	FALSE
TRUE **xor** FALSE	TRUE	**not** FALSE	TRUE
FALSE **xor** TRUE	TRUE		
FALSE **xor** FALSE	FALSE		

Figure 6.6 Truth tables.

Pitfall

Undefined Boolean Expressions

Boolean expressions are evaluated by first evaluating the subexpressions and then combining those values, as we described in the previous section. This method of evaluation gives rise to one subtle problem. In all implementations of Ada, if two subexpressions are connected by **and** or by **or**, then the computer first evaluates *both* of these subexpressions and *then* uses these two values to determine the value of the full expression. This means that the two subexpressions must be well defined and capable of being evaluated. As an example, consider the following reasonable looking statement:

```
if ( KIDS /= 0 ) and ( PIECES / KIDS >= 2 ) then
    PUT ( "Each child may have two pieces!" );
end if;
```

undefined subexpressions

If the value of KIDS is not zero, this statement performs fine. However, suppose the value of KIDS is zero. Then we might expect the boolean expression to evaluate to FALSE. After all, the first subexpression evaluates to FALSE, and using an **and** to combine FALSE with any other value will yield a value of FALSE. The computer will try to evaluate *both* subexpressions *before* it applies the **and**. This will produce an error because / is being asked to divide by zero, and this error can cause the program to terminate abnormally at this point.

One way to avoid this problem is to use the following statement:

```
if KIDS /= 0 then
    if PIECES / KIDS >= 2 then
        PUT ( "Each child may have two pieces!" );
    end if;
end if;
```

In this version, the second boolean expression is not evaluated when the value of KIDS is zero.

Ada provides a way to accomplish the above without nested **if** statements. The **and** and **or** operations can be extended, with the addition of **then** and **else**, to provide what is called *short-circuit evaluation*. The short-circuit evaluation of the **and** operation is accomplished by using **and then** instead of just **and**. The short-circuit evaluation of the **or** operation is accomplished by using **or else**. With short-circuit evaluation, Ada stops evaluating subexpressions as soon as it has enough information to "get the answer."

The precise definition of

boolean_expression_1 **and then** *boolean_expression_2*

is that if *boolean_expression_1* evaluates to FALSE, then *boolean_expression_2* is not evaluated, and FALSE is the value of the **and then** operation; otherwise, it evaluates like the ordinary **and**.

The definition of

boolean_expression_1 **or else** *boolean_expression_2*

is that if *boolean_expression_1* evaluates to TRUE, then *boolean_expression_2* is not evaluated, and TRUE is the value of the **or else** operations; otherwise, it evaluates like the ordinary **or**.

Ada puts the control of the evaluation in the hands of the programmer. If you want both boolean expressions evaluated, use **and** or **or**. If you want short-circuit evaluation, use **and then** or **or else**.

The best way to write the **if** statement above, therefore, is as follows:

```
if ( KIDS /= 0 ) and then ( PIECES / KIDS >= 2 ) then
    PUT ( "Each child may have two pieces!" );
end if;
```

Exercises

Self-Test Exercises

1. What output will be produced by the following program:

```
with I_O; use I_O;
procedure MAIN is
begin -- Main
    PUT ( "Start" ); NEW_LINE;
    if 2 <= 3 then
        if 0 /= 1 then
            PUT ( "First put" ); NEW_LINE;
        else
            PUT ( "Second put" ); NEW_LINE;
        end if;
    end if;
    PUT ( "Next" ); NEW_LINE;
    if 2 > 3 then
        if 0 = 1 then
            PUT ( "Third put" ); NEW_LINE;
        else
            PUT ( "Fourth put" ); NEW_LINE;
        end if;
    end if;
    PUT ( "Enough" ); NEW_LINE;
end MAIN;
```

2. Determine the value, TRUE or FALSE, of each of the following boolean expressions:

```
( 0 = 1 ) and ( 2 < 3 )
( 0 = 1 ) or ( 2 < 3 )
not ( 0 = 1 )
( 'Y' = 'y' ) and ( INTEGER'LAST = 65535 )
not ( ( 4.5 < 12.9 ) and ( 6 * 2 <= 13 ) )
not ( ( 31 rem 15 ) /= 1 )
```

3. Translate the following English and mathematics expressions into Ada boolean expressions:

- two plus two equals four
- *x* plus seven is more than one hundred or else it is less than fifty
- the value of the variable *z* (of type CHARACTER) is not one of the first three (uppercase) letters of the alphabet
- *x* is not evenly divisible by 3
- either *x* is not evenly divisible by 3 or *y* is evenly divisible by 5
- $x < y + 2 \leq z$

4. The expression (A **or** B) evaluates to TRUE provided that the value of either *or both* of the variables is TRUE. Design a boolean expression that evaluates to TRUE provided that the value of *exactly one* of the two variables is TRUE.

Programming with Boolean Variables

the type boolean

The values TRUE and FALSE form a complete list of values for the data type called BOOLEAN. TRUE and FALSE are literals of the type BOOLEAN. As we have seen, a boolean expression, like an arithmetic expression, yields a value. In the case of an arithmetic expression, the value is either INTEGER or FLOAT. In the case of a boolean expression, the value is of type BOOLEAN. This value of type BOOLEAN can be stored in a variable, just as the value of an arithmetic expression can be stored in a variable, except that a variable that contains a value of TRUE or FALSE must be of type BOOLEAN. Hence, if NUMBER is a variable of type INTEGER, and SENTINEL is a variable of type BOOLEAN, then the following is perfectly meaningful in Ada and sets the value of SENTINEL to FALSE.

```
NUMBER := 2;
SENTINEL := NUMBER > 10 or NUMBER < 0;
```

setting boolean variables

At first such assignment statements look strange, but you quickly adjust to them. The rules are the same as they are for variables of other types: The expression on the right-hand side of the assignment operator is evaluated (since it is a boolean expression, this value will be either TRUE or FALSE); after that, the value of the boolean variable is set equal to this value of TRUE or FALSE. In the preceding example, the value of NUMBER is not greater than **10**, nor is it less than zero, so the boolean expression evaluates to FALSE, and SENTINEL has its value changed to FALSE.

Variables of type BOOLEAN are declared in the same place and in the same way as other types of variables. A hypothetical program might start out

```
with I_O; use I_O;
procedure MAIN is
    TEMPERATURE : FLOAT;
    ANSWER : CHARACTER;
    RAINING, DRY : BOOLEAN;
```

The program might then contain the following statement:

```
RAINING := (ANSWER = 'y') or (ANSWER = 'Y');
```

If the value of ANSWER is either **'Y'** *or* **'y'**, then this statement sets the value of RAINING equal to TRUE; otherwise, it sets it equal to FALSE. Hence, this assignment statement is equivalent to the following longer and somewhat inefficient statement:

```
if (ANSWER = 'y') or (ANSWER = 'Y') then
    RAINING := TRUE;
else
    RAINING := FALSE;
end if;
```

The longer statement, which was given only to help explain the assignment statement, is poor programming style.

why use boolean variables

Boolean variables can be used to remember a condition that may change later or that will not be easy to check later on. An equally important use of boolean variables is to make the meaning of a program more apparent. In the program fragment below, the boolean variable RAINING frees the programmer from having to remember the exact wording of the question "Is it raining?". The question might have been "Has it stopped raining?", and the programmer who forgets the exact wording of the question can easily misinterpret the meaning of ANSWER, even if the value of ANSWER does not change.

```
PUT ( "Is it raining?" ); NEW_LINE;
GET ( ANSWER ); SKIP_LINE;
RAINING := ANSWER = 'y' or ANSWER = 'Y';
if RAINING then
    PUT ( "Too bad." );
else
    PUT ( "Would you like to go for a walk?" );
end if;
NEW_LINE;
```

The use of boolean variables is illustrated in the program given in Figure 6.7.

Program

```
with I_O; use I_O;
procedure MAIN is
    ANSWER : CHARACTER;
    RAINING : BOOLEAN;
begin -- Main
    PUT ( "Good day. My name is Ronald Gollum." ); NEW_LINE;
    PUT ( "I'm stuck in this box until quitting time." ); NEW_LINE;
    PUT ( "Please chat with me about the outside." ); NEW_LINE;
    PUT ( "Is it raining out now?" ); NEW_LINE;
    GET ( ANSWER ); SKIP_LINE;
    RAINING := ANSWER = 'Y' or ANSWER = 'y';
    if not RAINING then
        PUT ( "Too bad. We need rain." ); NEW_LINE;
    end if;
    PUT ( "Do you think it will rain tomorrow?" ); NEW_LINE;
    GET ( ANSWER ); SKIP_LINE;
    if ANSWER = 'Y' or ANSWER = 'y' then
        PUT ( "I'll worry about that tomorrow." ); NEW_LINE;
    end if;
    PUT ( "It's finally quitting time! Good bye." ); NEW_LINE;
    if RAINING then
        PUT ( "You brightened up this rainy day." ); NEW_LINE;
    else
        PUT ( "I want to work on my tan." ); NEW_LINE;
    end if;
end MAIN;
```

Sample Dialogue 1

```
Good day. My name is Ronald Gollum.
I'm stuck in this box until quitting time.
Please chat with me about the outside.
Is it raining out now?
no
Too bad. We need rain.
Do you think it will rain tomorrow?
yes
I'll worry about that tomorrow.
It's finally quitting time! Good bye.
I want to work on my tan.
```

Sample Dialogue 2

```
Good day. My name is Ronald Gollum.
I'm stuck in this box until quitting time.
Please chat with me about the outside.
Is it raining out now?
YES
Do you think it will rain tomorrow?
NO
It's finally quitting time! Good bye.
You brightened up this rainy day.
```

Figure 6.7 Program using a boolean variable.

Many other common programming languages do not have boolean variables. In these languages, programmers frequently simulate boolean variables by some trick, such as pretending that the integer value 1 means true and that zero means false.

Boolean Input and Output

Reading in a value of type BOOLEAN can be done directly. The input can be spelled in any combination of upper- and lowercase letters. The same is true for the display of BOOLEAN type variables to the screen; however, the output will be all uppercase. For example

```
with I_O; use I_O;
procedure MAIN is
    DRY : BOOLEAN;
begin -- Main
    PUT ( "There was no rain today. (TRUE or FALSE)" );
    NEW_LINE;
    GET ( DRY ); SKIP_LINE;
    PUT ( "Was it dry today? " );
    PUT ( DRY );
    NEW_LINE;
end MAIN;
```

Dialogue

```
There was no rain today. (TRUE or FALSE)
TrUe
Was it dry today? TRUE
```

Boolean Valued Functions

A function may return a value of type BOOLEAN. A call to the function can then be used anyplace that a boolean expression is allowed. This can often help to make a program easier to read. By means of a function body declaration, we can associate a complex boolean expression with a meaningful name and use that name as the boolean expression in an **if** or an **exit when** statement. The result can often make a program read rather like English. For example, the statement

```
if   ( RATE >= 10
and    RATE < 20 )
or     RATE = 0 then
         .
         .
end if;
```

can be written

```
if APPROPRIATE ( RATE ) then
      .
      .
end if;
```

provided the following boolean function has already been defined:

```
function APPROPRIATE ( RATE : INTEGER ) return
BOOLEAN is
begin -- Appropriate
    return ( RATE >= 10
       and   RATE < 20 )
        or   RATE = 0;
end APPROPRIATE;
```

Case Study

Calculating Leap Years

Problem Definition

We want to write a program that will take a year as input and will provide output that tells whether or not that year is a leap year.

Discussion

For most years it is very easy to decide if the year is a leap year. If the year is divisible by four, then it is a leap year. So 2004 is a leap year, but 2001 is not. This rule is based on the fact that it takes 365 ¼ days for the earth to revolve around the sun. Every fourth year we add up the four extra quarter days and insert an extra full day in February. Unfortunately for calendar makers, the earth actually takes a bit less than 365 ¼ days to complete its trip around the sun, so leap years should add a bit less than one full day. This is not practical, so a full day is added, and then after a few centuries a leap year day is skipped, which effectively subtracts a day and makes things balance out. The exact rule says that if a year is divisible by 100, then it is not a leap year unless it is also divisible by 400, so 2200 is divisible by 4 but will not be a leap year. Our algorithm will include subalgorithms for two separate calculations, one for most years and the other for years divisible by 100.

Subalgorithms

NON_CENTURY_CALCULATION
--Precondition: the year is not divisible by 100.
if the year is divisible by **4**, then it is a leap year;
otherwise it is not.
CENTURY_CALCULATION
--Precondition: the year is divisible by 100.
if the year is divisible by **400**, then it is a leap year,
otherwise it is not.

Since the year does not change and there is but one output value, we will implement both of these subalgorithms as functions with parameters NON_CENTURY_YEAR and CENTURY_YEAR for the year. Recall that all parameters for functions are **in** parameters, and by convention we do not show the mode in function specifications. The complete program is given in Figure 6.8.

Program

```
with I_O; use I_O;
procedure MAIN is
--                  INPUT  : A year.
--                  OUTPUT : Displays an appropriate message as
--                           to whether the year is a leap year.
--                  DESCRIPTION : Determines if the year is a
--                                century year and calls the proper
--                                function to determine if the
--                                year is a leap year.
    YEAR : INTEGER;
    LEAP_YEAR : BOOLEAN;
    function NON_CENTURY_CALCULATION ( NON_CENTURY_YEAR : INTEGER )
                                             return BOOLEAN is
--                  INPUT  : A year that is predetermined not
--                           to be a century year.
--                  OUTPUT : TRUE is a leap year, otherwise FALSE
--                  DESCRIPTION : Test if this noncentury year
--                                is also a leap year.
```

```
    begin -- Non_Century_Calculation
        return NON_CENTURY_YEAR rem 4 = 0;
    end NON_CENTURY_CALCULATION;
    function CENTURY_CALCULATION ( CENTURY_YEAR : in INTEGER )
                                        return BOOLEAN is
--                  INPUT  : A year that is predetermined to be
--                           a century year.
--                  OUTPUT : TRUE is a leap year, otherwise FALSE
--                  DESCRIPTION : Test if this century year
--                                is also a leap year.
    begin -- Century_Calculation
        return CENTURY_YEAR rem 400 = 0;
    end CENTURY_CALCULATION;
begin -- Main
    PUT ( "Enter a year." ); NEW_LINE;
    GET ( YEAR ); SKIP_LINE;
    if YEAR rem 100 = 0 then
        LEAP_YEAR := CENTURY_CALCULATION ( YEAR );
    else
        LEAP_YEAR := NON_CENTURY_CALCULATION ( YEAR );
    end if;
    PUT ( YEAR );
    if LEAP_YEAR then
        PUT ( " is a leap year!" );
    else
        PUT ( " is not a leap year!" );
    end if;
    NEW_LINE;
end MAIN;
```

Sample Dialogue 1

```
Enter a year.
1900
 1900 is not a leap year!
```

Sample Dialogue 2

```
Enter a year.
2000
 2000 is a leap year!
```

Sample Dialogue 3

```
Enter a year.
2004
 2004 is a leap year!
```

Figure 6.8 Leap year program.

Case Study

Designing Output

Problem Definition

In Chapter 4 we produced a program to determine the number of coins needed to give an amount of change from 1 to 99 cents. That program produced outputs such as the following:

```
  27 cents can be given as:
1 quarters
0 dimes and
2 pennies
```

This sort of output is frequently acceptable, but it would be nicer to have output that is grammatically correct and that does not contain pointless information. Ideally, the output should look like

```
27 cents can be given as:
one quarter and 2 pennies
```

In this section we will design a procedure to produce this sort of output. We will design it for output that includes the possibility of nickels so that it would work for the enhanced version of the program which uses the redesigned procedures given in Figure 4.7. As in the original program, we will assume that the total amount of change is between 1 and 99 cents. The procedure will receive the amount and the coin counts as **in** parameters.

Discussion

When you stop to think of all the grammatical details we do automatically when writing phrases such as the desired sample output, you quickly realize that designing output can be a complicated task. The program must somehow ignore coin amounts of zero, it needs to decide between singular and plural forms, it must place the *and* correctly, and it needs to insert commas if three or more types of coins are used, as in

```
32 cents can be given as:
one quarter, one nickel and 2 pennies
```

(There are two accepted ways of inserting commas in such expressions. To simplify the problem, we are using the rule that does not place a comma before the *and*.)

The **in** parameters for the total amount and the counts of quarters, dimes, nickels, and pennies will be AMOUNT, NUMBER_OF_QUARTERS, NUMBER_OF_DIMES, NUMBER_OF_NICKELS, and NUMBER_OF_PENNIES. We will use a very straightforward decomposition of this problem into subproblems:

subproblems

begin
1. Write the heading.
2. If the number of quarters is not zero, then write it out.
3. If the number of dimes is not zero, then write it out preceded by a comma or *and* as appropriate.
4. If the number of nickels is not zero, then write it out preceded by a comma or *and* as appropriate.
5. If the number of pennies is not zero, then write it out preceded by a comma or *and* as appropriate.

end

flags

To determine whether it should output a comma or *and,* the program needs some way to test if there were any previous coins output and if there are more coins to output. We will use a boolean variable PREVIOUS_COINS. This variable will be initialized to FALSE and will have its value changed to TRUE as soon as a nonzero number of coins is output. The value of PREVIOUS_COINS is the data that is passed from one subtask to another. A variable, such as PREVIOUS_COINS, that changes value to indicate that some event has taken place is often called a *flag* or *sentinel.* In this sample, ''when the flag goes up'' or ''when you see the sentinel fire,'' it is time to insert a comma or *and.* The pseudocode for outputting dimes is given below.

Algorithm

```
--                    PREVIOUS_COINS is true
--                      if some number of quarters has been output.

if NUMBER_OF_DIMES > 0 then
    if PREVIOUS_COINS then
        if there are more coins to follow then
            output a comma and appropriate spaces
        else -- Dimes will be the last type of coin.
            output the word and and appropriate spaces;
    Write out the number of dimes;
    PREVIOUS_COINS := TRUE
```

The test for more coins to follow can be accomplished with the boolean expression:

```
NUMBER_OF_NICKELS > 0
or
NUMBER_OF_PENNIES > 0
```

The complete procedure embedded in a test program is displayed in Figure 6.9. Since it was not used outside of the procedure, we made the boolean variable PREVIOUS_COINS a local variable.

Program

```
with I_O; use I_O;
procedure MAIN is
    AMOUNT,
    NUMBER_OF_DIMES,
    NUMBER_OF_NICKELS,
    NUMBER_OF_PENNIES,
    NUMBER_OF_QUARTERS : INTEGER;
    procedure OUTPUT_COINS ( CHANGE,
                             QUARTERS,
                             DIMES,
                             NICKELS,
                             PENNIES : in INTEGER ) is
--                     INPUT  : 0 < change <= 99 cents and
--                              the appropriate number of each coin.
--                     OUTPUT : None
--                     DESCRIPTION : Displays a collection of coins
--                                   that total to change cents.
        COMMA : constant STRING := ", ";
        LAST_COIN : constant STRING := " and ";
        PREVIOUS_COINS : BOOLEAN := FALSE;
        procedure OUTPUT_QUARTERS ( NUMBER_OF_QUARTERS : in INTEGER;
                                    PREVIOUS_COINS : in out BOOLEAN ) i
        begin -- Output_Quarters
            if NUMBER_OF_QUARTERS > 0 then
                if NUMBER_OF_QUARTERS = 1 then
                    PUT ( "one quarter" );
                else
                    PUT ( NUMBER_OF_QUARTERS, 1 ); PUT ( " quarters" )
                end if;
                PREVIOUS_COINS := TRUE;
            end if;
        end OUTPUT_QUARTERS;
        procedure OUTPUT_DIMES ( NUMBER_OF_DIMES : in INTEGER;
                                 NUMBER_OF_NICKELS : in INTEGER;
                                 NUMBER_OF_PENNIES : in INTEGER;
                                 PREVIOUS_COINS : in out BOOLEAN ) is
        begin -- Output_Dimes
            if NUMBER_OF_DIMES > 0 then
                if PREVIOUS_COINS then
                    if NUMBER_OF_NICKELS > 0
                    or NUMBER_OF_PENNIES > 0 then
```

```
                PUT ( COMMA );
                PUT ( LAST_COIN );
            end if;
        end if;
        if NUMBER_OF_DIMES = 1 then
            PUT ( "one dime" );
        else
            PUT ( NUMBER_OF_DIMES, 1 ); PUT ( " dimes" );
        end if;
        PREVIOUS_COINS := TRUE;
    end if;
end OUTPUT_DIMES;
procedure OUTPUT_NICKELS ( NUMBER_OF_NICKELS : in INTEGER;
                           NUMBER_OF_PENNIES : in INTEGER;
                           PREVIOUS_COINS : in out BOOLEAN ) is
begin -- Output_Nickels
    if NUMBER_OF_NICKELS > 0 then
        if PREVIOUS_COINS then
            if NUMBER_OF_PENNIES > 0 then
                PUT ( COMMA );
            else
                PUT ( LAST_COIN );
            end if;
        end if;
        if NUMBER_OF_NICKELS = 1 then
            PUT ( "one nickel" );
        else
            PUT ( NUMBER_OF_NICKELS, 1 ); PUT ( " nickels" );
        end if;
        PREVIOUS_COINS := TRUE;
    end if;
end OUTPUT_NICKELS;
procedure OUTPUT_PENNIES ( NUMBER_OF_PENNIES : in INTEGER;
                           PREVIOUS_COINS : in out BOOLEAN )
                           is
begin -- Output_Pennies
    if NUMBER_OF_PENNIES > 0 then
        if PREVIOUS_COINS then
            PUT ( LAST_COIN );
        end if;
        if NUMBER_OF_PENNIES = 1 then
            PUT ( "one penny" );
        else
            PUT ( NUMBER_OF_PENNIES, 1 ); PUT ( " pennies" );
        end if;
    end if;
end OUTPUT_PENNIES;
```

```
    begin -- Output_Coins
        PUT ( CHANGE, 2 );
        PUT ( " cents can be given as: " );
        NEW_LINE;
        OUTPUT_QUARTERS ( QUARTERS, PREVIOUS_COINS );
        OUTPUT_DIMES ( DIMES,
                       NICKELS,
                       PENNIES,
                       PREVIOUS_COINS );
        OUTPUT_NICKELS ( NICKELS,
                         PENNIES,
                         PREVIOUS_COINS );
        OUTPUT_PENNIES ( PENNIES,
                         PREVIOUS_COINS );
        NEW_LINE;
    end OUTPUT_COINS;
begin -- Main
    PUT ( "Enter: Quarters, Dimes, Nickels, Pennies:" ); NEW_LINE;
    GET ( NUMBER_OF_QUARTERS );
    GET ( NUMBER_OF_DIMES );
    GET ( NUMBER_OF_NICKELS );
    GET ( NUMBER_OF_PENNIES );
    SKIP_LINE;
    AMOUNT := 25 * NUMBER_OF_QUARTERS
            + 10 * NUMBER_OF_DIMES
            +  5 * NUMBER_OF_NICKELS
            +      NUMBER_OF_PENNIES;
    OUTPUT_COINS ( AMOUNT,
                   NUMBER_OF_QUARTERS,
                   NUMBER_OF_DIMES,
                   NUMBER_OF_NICKELS,
                   NUMBER_OF_PENNIES );
end MAIN;
```

Sample Dialogue

```
Enter: Quarters, Dimes, Nickels, Pennies:
1 0 1 2
32 cents can be given as:
one quarter, one nickel and 2 pennies
```

Figure 6.9 Enhanced procedure to output coins.

Boolean Constants and Debugging Switches

true
false

The two values of type BOOLEAN can be named using the two predefined literals TRUE and FALSE. These constants can be used anyplace that a boolean expression is allowed. So the following, although pointless, is allowed. It always causes the second PUT to be executed.

```
if FALSE then
    PUT ( "I know truth." );
else
    PUT ( "I know falsehood." );
end if;
NEW_LINE;
```

An identifier that has been given a boolean value in a constant declaration can be used in the same way, and its use is not always pointless. The following declaration makes DEBUGGING a synonym for TRUE.

```
DEBUGGING : constant BOOLEAN := TRUE;
```

A boolean constant such as DEBUGGING can be used as a switch to change a program into one of two forms. To switch from one form of the program to the other, the named boolean constant in the declarations is changed from TRUE to FALSE, or vice versa. This is particularly useful when debugging large programs.

Large programs are often written with trace statements and other debugging diagnostics written into the program. Often one wants to retain the debugging features even after the program is released for use, either because it will be changed or because you expect the users to discover new bugs. If the program is to be used, or even observed, without these debugging messages being sent to the screen, some method must be found for turning them off. One method is a boolean switch.

If you include a constant declaration such as the sample one we displayed for DEBUGGING, then you can use it as a switch to turn on debugging statements like the following one that traces two variables:

```
if DEBUGGING then
    PUT ( "amount = " ); PUT ( AMOUNT ); NEW_LINE;
    PUT ( "amount_left = " ); PUT ( AMOUNT_LEFT ); NEW_LINE;
end if;
```

To turn off the debugging features, just reset the boolean constant by changing the constant declaration to

```
DEBUGGING : constant BOOLEAN := FALSE;
```

The Null Statement

Ada has a statement that does absolutely nothing; it is called the *null statement*. The syntax of the null statement is simply the reserved word **null**. It may sound like a joke, but nonetheless it does have a number of serious purposes. Believe it or not, there are times when you want to tell the computer to do nothing. It is often used during program development, but there are other uses. Figure 6.13, an example program using the **case** statement (which is covered next), uses the **null** statement.

During program development the **null** statement often appears simply to satisfy the syntax of the language and allows you to compile and test a partially completed program. Here are two examples:

1. The **if** statement syntax requires that the **then** and the **else** be followed by at least one statement in each branch. Say that you have not worked out all of the details of the **then** branch, but you want to see if the rest of your program compiles. Write

```
if COUNT > 0 then
    null;
else
    PUT ( "count must be greater than zero" );
    NEW_LINE;
end if;
```

2. You are working on a team, and one member of the team is to write a particular procedure, but it isn't completed. You must have something in your code so you can continue. Write

```
procedure SOMETHING is
begin
    null;
end SOMETHING;
```

A similar thing can be done with a function, except it must contain a **return** statement.

```
function ANYTHING return SOME_TYPE is
begin
    return SOME_TYPE_VALUE;
end ANYTHING;
```

The Case Statement

An **if-then-else** statement chooses one of two alternative actions. A *case statement* is a different kind of Ada statement that can choose from a list of any number of actions. The **case** statement is a complex statement made up from other simpler statements. When the **case** statement is executed, one (and only one) of the simpler statements is selected and executed. As usual, an example is likely to be more enlightening that an abstract discussion.

Consider the program shown in Figure 6.10. The five lines starting with the reserved word **case** and ending with **end case** compose a **case** statement. The **case** statement contains four substatements: one labeled by the pair **'A'** | **'B'**, one labeled by the literal **'C'**, one labeled by the pair **'D'** | **'F'** and the last labeled with an **others**. When the **case** statement is executed, exactly one of these four substatements will be executed; which one depends on the value of the object GRADE. When the case statement is executed, the value of GRADE is checked, and then the substatement labeled by that value is executed. Hence, if the value of GRADE is either **'A'** or **'B'**, then the PUT following that pair will be executed. If instead the value of GRADE is **'C'**, then the PUT following the **'C'** will instead be executed. If the value of GRADE is either **'D'** or **'F'**, then the third PUT is executed. If the value of GRADE is anything other than **'A'**, **'B'**, **'C'**, **'D'**, or **'F'**, then the fourth PUT is executed.

Program

```
with I_O; use I_O;
procedure MAIN is
GRADE : CHARACTER;
begin -- Main
    PUT ( "What grade did you receive?" ); NEW_LINE;
    GET ( GRADE ); SKIP_LINE;
    case GRADE is
       when 'A' | 'B' => PUT ( "Very Good!" );
       when 'C' => PUT ( "Passing." );
       when 'D' | 'F' => PUT ( "Too bad." );
       when others => PUT ( "Invalid letter grade." );
    end case;
    NEW_LINE;
    PUT ( "I have to go study. Goodbye." ); NEW_LINE;
end MAIN;
```

Sample Dialogue 1

```
What grade did you receive?
A
Very Good!
I have to go study. Goodbye.
```

Sample Dialogue 2

```
What grade did you receive?
F
Too bad.
I have to go study. Goodbye.
```

Figure 6.10 Program with a `case` statement.

The syntax of a **case** statement is given in Figure 6.11, and the meaning of a **case** statement is given in Figure 6.12. A **case** statement may have any number of alternatives to choose from. Each alternative consists of one or more statements. Each statement must be prefaced by a **when**, followed by one or more choices that are separated by a vertical bar (|), and followed by the arrow symbol (=>). Each choice is made up of a value, from what is called a *static expression,* or a *range* of such values. A static expression is an expression made up of things that do not change, like numbers, constants, and literals. A range is specified by using a double dot (. .)

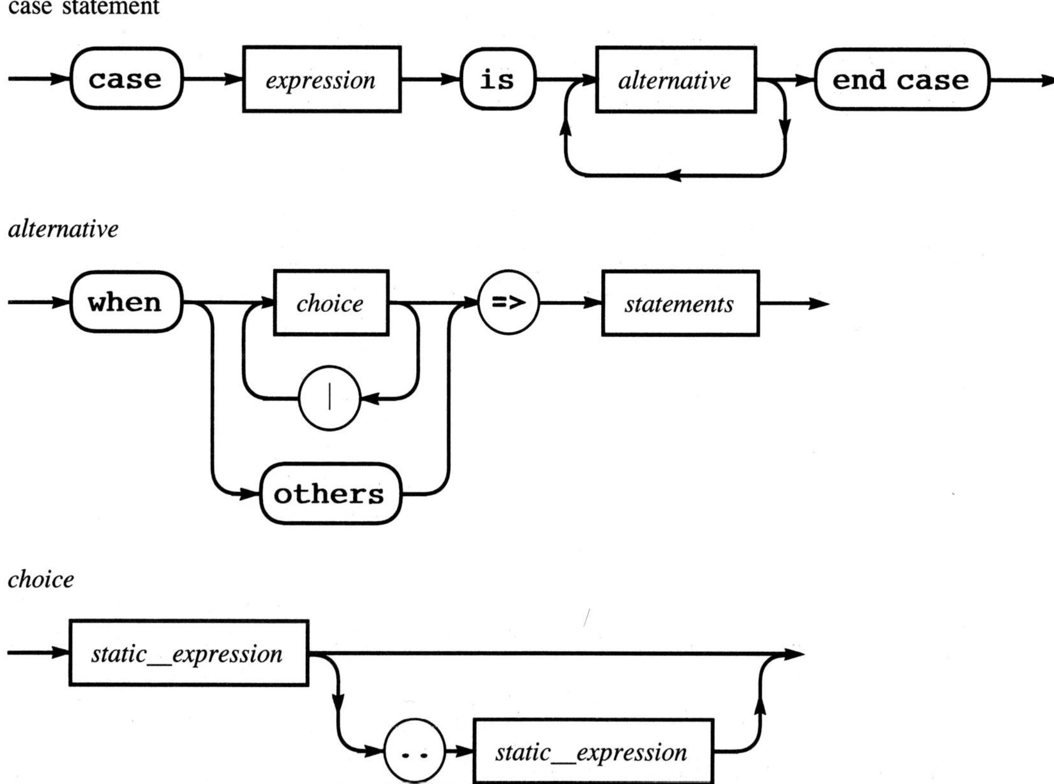

Figure 6.11 Syntax of a `case` statement.

```
statement_1;
case expression is
    when choice_list A => statement(s)_2A;
    when choice_list B => statement(s)_2B;

    when choice_list N => statement(s)_2N;
end case;
statement 3;
```

```
                    statement_1
                         |
                 evaluate expression
                         |
   choice_list_A    choice_list_B    choice_list_N
         |                |                |
statement(s)_2A  statement(s)_2B  statement(s)_2N
                         |
                    statement_3
```

Figure 6.12 Behavior of a case statement.

to separate two values. The values in the range must be of the same type, and the first value in the range must be less than or equal to the second value. Any given choice may not appear in more than one list of choices, since that would produce an ambiguous instruction. Stated another way, the choices must be *mutually exclusive*. All possible choices for the expression in the **case** statement must be enumerated in the choices or accounted for by a **when others** alternative. The **when others**, if it appears, must be the last alternative. The **when others** alternative accounts for all other possible choices for that type of expression that do not appear in the previous choices. The entire **case** statement is terminated by an **end case**.

The expression that follows the word **case** need not be a simple object. You can use any *discrete expression* to control a **case** statement. A discrete expression is an expression that evaluates to a discrete type. INTEGER, CHARACTER, and BOOLEAN are three examples of discrete types, but the types FLOAT and STRING are not discrete. Therefore, you cannot use expressions or objects of the types FLOAT or STRING to control a **case** statement. When the **case** statement is executed, the expression is evaluated and then the alternative statement(s) associated with that value is executed. Hence, the choices that label the alternative substatements must match this expression type.

Figure 6.13 includes a **case** statement with a more complicated controlling expression. The program in that figure calculates leap years using the following rule: Leap years are those years that are evenly divisible by four. This rule works for all years except century years like 1900 or 2000.

Program

```
with I_O; use I_O;
procedure MAIN is
--                  Input  : An integer year.
--                  Output : A message relating to the year.
--                  Description : Determines if the year input or
--                                the next year is a leap year.
--                                Only works for years which are not
--                                divisible by 100.
    YEAR : INTEGER;
begin
    PUT ( "Enter a year." ); NEW_LINE;
    GET ( YEAR ); SKIP_LINE;
    case YEAR rem 4 is
        when 0 => PUT ( "That year is a leap year." );
        when 3 => PUT ( "The following year is a leap year." );
        when 1 | 2 => PUT ( "That year is not a leap year." );
        when others => null;
    end case;
    NEW_LINE;
end MAIN;
```

Sample Dialogue 1

```
Enter a year.
1964
That year is a leap year.
```

Sample Dialogue 2

```
Enter a year.
2001
That year is not a leap year.
```

Figure 6.13 Program with case and a range.

You will quickly realize that using just one simple statement for each alternative is rather weak, and that it is desirable to have each alternative consist of a list of statements. This is in fact possible. All statements listed after the arrow and before the next **when** are executed in order if the expression evaluates to one of the choices in the alternative. An example of this is shown in Figure 6.13.

The **when others** ensures that the expression in a **case** statement evaluates to one of the alternatives. It is safest to enumerate as many choices as is realistic to do. For example, the program in Figure 6.14 includes lowercase as well as uppercase letters in the choice lists. This helps to ensure that the value of GRADE will always be among the specified choices.

Program

```
with I_O; use I_O;
procedure MAIN is
    GRADE : CHARACTER;
begin -- Main
    PUT ( "What grade did you receive?" ); NEW_LINE;
    GET ( GRADE ); SKIP_LINE;
    case GRADE is
        when 'A' | 'a' | 'B' | 'b' =>
            PUT ( GRADE & " is very good!" ); NEW_LINE;
            PUT ( "I wish I could do as well." );
        when 'C' | 'c' =>
            PUT ( "Passing." );
        when 'D' | 'd' | 'F' | 'f' =>
            PUT ( "Too bad." ); NEW_LINE;
            PUT ( GRADE & " is not very good." );
        when others =>
            PUT ( "Invalid letter grade." );
    end case;
    NEW_LINE;
    PUT ( "Have to go study. Goodbye." ); NEW_LINE;
end MAIN;
```

Sample Dialogue

```
What grade did you receive?
A
A is very good!
I wish I could do as well.
I have to go study. Goodbye.
```

Figure 6.14 Sample use of a case statement.

Programming Multiple Alternatives

The **case** statement chooses one of several statements to execute, but it is somewhat restricted in its use. The choice of which statement to execute must be made on the basis of a list of single values or ranges of values. The choice can not be based on a relational operator. Sometimes an **if** statement with **elsif** clauses can be a more versatile way of implementing multiple alternative branches.

For example, suppose you are designing a game-playing program in which the user must guess the value of some number. The number can be named NUMBER, and the guess can be called GUESS. If you wish to give a hint after each guess, you might design the following subalgorithm:

```
PUT ( "Too high." ), provided GUESS > NUMBER
PUT ( "Too low." ), provided GUESS < NUMBER
PUT ( "Correct!" ), provided GUESS = NUMBER
```

Any time a branching action is described as a list of mutually exclusive conditions and corresponding actions, as in this example, the branching action can be implemented in Ada by using an **if** statement. For example, the above pseudocode translates to

```
if GUESS > NUMBER then
    PUT ( "Too high." );
elsif GUESS < NUMBER then
    PUT ( "Too low." );
else -- guess = number
    PUT ( "Correct!" );
end if;
NEW_LINE;
```

Since the conditions are mutually exclusive, the test for equality is superfluous and can be omitted, but it is usually best to include it in a comment.

Case Study

State Income Tax

Problem Definition

We will design a function to compute state income tax from net income (computed to the nearest dollar) according to the following formula:

1. No tax is paid on the first $15,000 of net income.
2. A tax of 5% is assessed on each dollar of net income from $15,001 to $32,000.
3. A tax of 10% is assessed on each dollar of net income over $32,000.

Discussion

If we let FIRST_CHUNK name the amount of income that is taxed at the 5% rate and let SECOND_CHUNK name the amount of income taxed at the 10% rate, then our algorithm to compute FIRST_CHUNK follows directly from the problem specification:

Algorithm

```
FIRST_CHUNK := 0, provided NET_INCOME <= 15000
FIRST_CHUNK := NET_INCOME - 15000,
      provided 15000 < NET_INCOME <= 32000
FIRST_CHUNK := 17000, provided NET_INCOME > 32000
```

A similar piece of pseudocode can be written for computing SECOND_CHUNK. The total tax is then 5% of the first figure plus 10% of the second figure. Once the pseudocode has been written it is routine to translate it into an Ada function like the one in Figure 6.15.

Program

```
with I_O; use I_O;
procedure MAIN is
    INCOME : INTEGER;
    function COMPUTE_STATE_TAX ( NET_INCOME : INTEGER )
                                  return FLOAT is
        FIRST_CHUNK,
        SECOND_CHUNK : INTEGER;
    begin -- Compute_State_Tax
        if NET_INCOME <= 15_000 then
            FIRST_CHUNK := 0;
        elsif NET_INCOME > 15_000
          and NET_INCOME <= 32_000 then
            FIRST_CHUNK := NET_INCOME - 15_000;
        else
            FIRST_CHUNK := 17_000;
        end if;
        if NET_INCOME <= 32_000 then
            SECOND_CHUNK := 0;
        else
            SECOND_CHUNK := NET_INCOME - 32_000;
        end if;
        return 0.05 * FLOAT ( FIRST_CHUNK )
              + 0.10 * FLOAT ( SECOND_CHUNK );
    end COMPUTE_STATE_TAX;
```

```
begin -- Main
    PUT ( "Enter net income:" ); NEW_LINE;
    GET ( INCOME ); SKIP_LINE;
    PUT ( "Your state tax is " );
    PUT ( COMPUTE_STATE_TAX ( INCOME ), 3, 2, 0 );
    NEW_LINE;
end MAIN;
```

Figure 6.15 Function including multiple alternative actions.

In Operator

The **in** operator tests for *membership*. It tests to see if a variable or expression is a member of a range or a subtype. The general form for a *range* is

expression . . expression

where the value of the first expression is less than or equal to the value of the second expression.

A *subtype* has not been covered yet, but it is basically a subrange of an existing type. There is a predefined subtype called POSITIVE, and it is a subrange of the type INTEGER that represents all positive integer values. So we could test to see if a value is positive, that is, N **in** POSITIVE.

The result of a membership test is a value of type BOOLEAN; thus the **in** operator is a form of relational operator. The **in** operator has a complementary form, **not in**. If N **in** 1 . . 10 is TRUE, then N **not in** 1 . . 10 is FALSE; for example:

```
if SONG in 1 . . 10 then
     PUT ( "This song is in the top ten!" );
end if;

NUMBER := 5;
loop
    exit when NUMBER not in POSITIVE;
              .
              .
              .
    NUMBER := NUMBER - 1;
end loop;

GET ( LETTER );
if LETTER in 'a' . . 'z' then
    PUT ( "The letter is lowercase." );
end if;
```

The function COMPUTE_STATE_TAX from Figure 6.15 could have used the membership operator to test NET_INCOME to see what range of values it fits into. The following is that function using the **in** operator:

```
function COMPUTE_STATE_TAX ( NET_INCOME : INTEGER )
                                         return FLOAT is
    FIRST_CHUNK,
    SECOND_CHUNK : INTEGER;
begin -- Compute_State_Tax
    if NET_INCOME in 0..15_000 then
        FIRST_CHUNK := 0;
    elsif NET_INCOME in 15_001..32_000 then
        FIRST_CHUNK := NET_INCOME - 15_000;
    else
        FIRST_CHUNK := 17_000;
    end if;
    if NET_INCOME in 0..32_000 then
        SECOND_CHUNK := 0;
    else
        SECOND_CHUNK := NET_INCOME - 32_000;
    end if;
    return 0.05 * FLOAT ( FIRST_CHUNK )
         + 0.10 * FLOAT ( SECOND_CHUNK );
end COMPUTE_STATE_TAX;
```

Exception

An *exception* in Ada is a reaction to an exceptional or unusual situation, or what we sometimes call an error. In fact what we have been calling run-time errors up till now have really been Ada exceptions. The run-time error messages that you got probably said something about an unhandled exception. So in Ada, run-time errors are called exceptions. Each different kind of exception in Ada has a name, called, as you might expect, an *exception name.* Exception names are identifiers, and they follow the same rules of formation as any other identifier.

Thus we can add exception identifiers to our list of different kinds of identifiers. As a quick review, first there are identifiers called reserved words, then variable identifiers, constant identifiers, type identifiers, procedure identifiers, function identifiers, and now exception identifiers.

predefined exceptions

In Ada, there are five predefined exception names:

- CONSTRAINT_ERROR
- NUMERIC_ERROR
- PROGRAM_ERROR
- STORAGE_ERROR
- TASKING_ERROR

Beside these, there is a group of input-output exceptions packaged together and called IO_EXCEPTIONS. You may have already encountered one of the IO_EXCEPTIONS, namely, DATA_ERROR. Most of the IO_EXCEPTIONS deal with errors that arise when dealing with files and will be covered later.

raise exception

The term that is used in Ada to indicate that an error or unusual situation has occurred is to say that an exception has been *raised,* much like one might raise a white flag to indicate surrender or raise the American flag to indicate the beginning of a sporting event. Just like these two flags, an exception signals a change to the current pattern of events. In the case of the white flag, fighting is suspended. In the case of the American flag, the warm-up period is over and it is time to start the game. When an exception in Ada is raised, the normal sequential execution of statements is stopped.

Different things cause different exceptions to be raised. We will start from the beginning of our list shown above and discuss each. A CONSTRAINT_ERROR is raised if we attempt to assign to a variable a value that is outside the range of acceptable values for that variable. As an example, suppose the following declarations are made in a subprogram:

```
subtype ZERO_TO_TEN is INTEGER range 0 . . 10;
RATING : ZERO_TO_TEN;
```

and that in the body of that subprogram the following statements are executed:

```
GET ( RATING );
RATING := RATING + 3;
```

Now if the value typed in for RATING is greater than 7, CONSTRAINT_ERROR will be raised when an attempt is made to assign RATING the value of the sum of RATING plus 3. The sum of RATING plus 3 will be greater then 10. Since RATING is of subtype ZERO_TO_TEN, which is *constrained* to the range 0 . . 10, any attempt to assign a value to RATING that is greater than 10 (or less than 0 for that matter) will cause CONSTRAINT_ERROR to be raised. In future chapters we will discover other things that will also cause CONSTRAINT_ERROR to be raised.

The exception NUMERIC_ERROR is raised as the result of a numeric operation that cannot give a correct result. NUMERIC_ERROR will be raised if the computer is instructed to compute a FLOAT value larger than FLOAT'LAST or smaller than FLOAT'FIRST. The first example is sometimes called *floating point overflow*; similarly, the latter is called *floating point underflow.*

All Ada functions must have a **return** statement that includes an expression of the type specified in the function heading. The following example meets that qualification, but it is possible to execute the function without executing the **return** statement.

```
function GOTCHA ( ARGUMENT : INTEGER )
         return FLOAT is
begin -- Gotcha
    if ARGUMENT > 0 then
         return FLOAT ( ARGUMENT );
    end if;
end GOTCHA;
```

If the following statements appear in the main procedure

```
INDEX : INTEGER;

INDEX := 5;
loop
    exit when INDEX < -5
    PUT ( GOTCHA ( INDEX ), 1, 1, 0 );
    NEW_LINE;
    INDEX := INDEX - 1;
end loop;
```

the output would be

```
5.0
4.0
3.0
2.0
1.0
*** Unhandled PROGRAM_ERROR
```

The sixth time GOTCHA is called, the value of the argument is **0** and the **return** statement is not executed. After failing the **if** test, the function comes to its **end**. If a function reaches the **end** for the function, PROGRAM_ERROR is raised. The actual error message will vary from system to system, but the result will be the same: The program will terminate because of PROGRAM_ERROR.

It is unlikely that you will ever raise STORAGE_ERROR as the result of a program written in this course, but if you do it will be because the computer does not have enough internal memory to continue with the execution of the program.

The last of the predefined exceptions is called TASKING_ERROR. It is included for completeness sake and is beyond the scope of this text.

Exception Handler

The error message ''Unhandled *exception name*'' indicates that your program failed to *handle* the exception. This implies that there must have been a way to handle the exception, whatever *handle* means. Handling a raised exception does not mean correcting the error and continuing normal execution of the program. What *handle* means is to do something about a raised exception so that your program does not terminate with an unhandled exception message. An Ada exception is handled by an *exception handler*. An exception handler can appear as an optional part of any block statement or a subprogram body. For purposes of discussion about exceptions, the LRM calls this construct a *frame*. An exception handler, if it appears, is placed immediately before the reserved word **end** in any procedure or function. The syntax for an exception handler is the reserved word **exception** followed by a list of individual exception choices. The syntax for an exception choice starts with the reserved word **when** followed by a list of exception names, each separated by a vertical bar (|), followed by an arrow (=>), followed by a sequence of statements. Figure 6.16 gives the complete syntax diagram for an exception handler.

One of the options in an exception handler is the **when others**, which serves as a catch all. If the exception is not handled explicitly by one of the exception choices, the **when others** will handle it, no matter what exception has been raised. If the exception is handled in an exception handler, the exception is no longer raised, and execution continues with whatever statement would normally be executed after the procedure or function call.

exception raised

What exactly happens when an exception is raised? When an exception is raised the execution of the sequence of statements stops and control is transferred to the exception handler in the frame in which it is raised. If the name of the exception that is raised appears in the exception handler, the statements after the arrow are executed, the exception is "lowered," and execution continues at the **end** of the frame. If the name of the exception that is raised does not appear in the exception handler and if

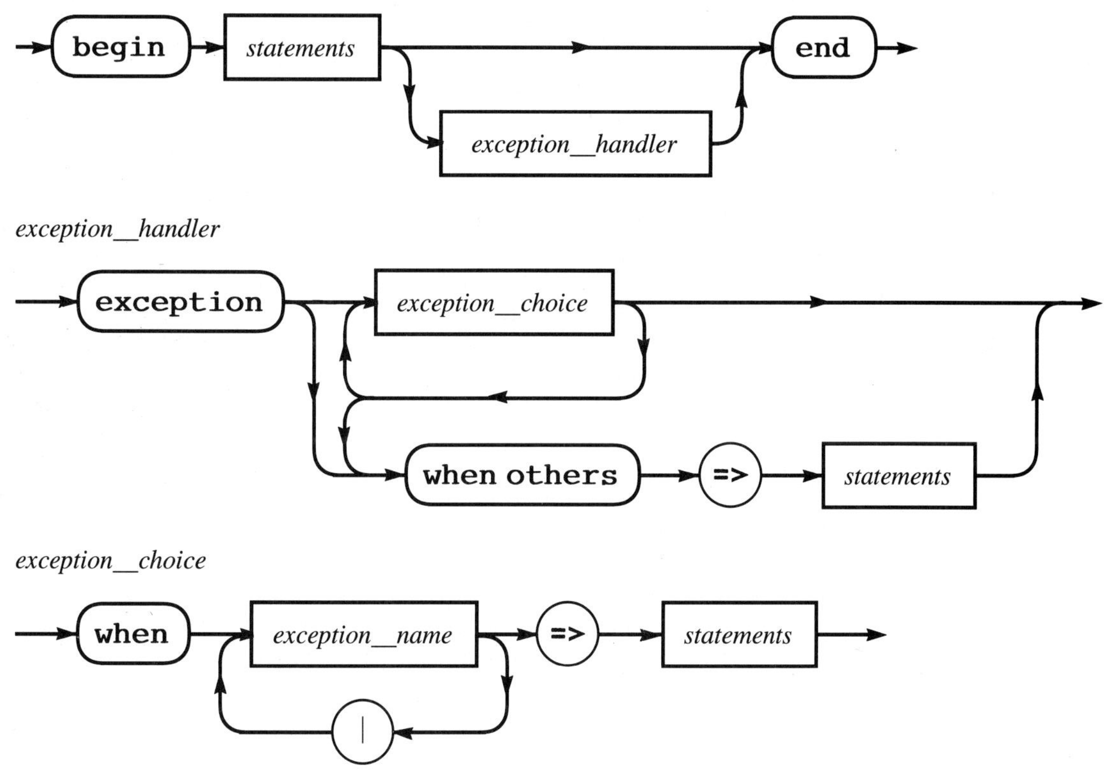

Figure 6.16 Syntax diagram for an exception handler.

there is no **when others**, the exception is not handled and the procedure or function is terminated with the exception still raised.

Whether or not the exception is handled, the subprogram terminates and control passes back to where the subprogram is called. If the subprogram is a procedure, control goes to the statement after the call. If the subprogram is a function, control goes back to the expression from which the function was called. A return from a subprogram with an exception raised causes the calling subprogram to transfer control to its exception handler. This process continues until the exception is handled or control comes back to the main procedure.

main procedure

If a raised exception reaches the main procedure or is raised in the main procedure, control is transferred to the main procedure's exception handler. If the exception is handled, the statements in the handler are executed and the program terminates normally. If the exception is not handled in the exception handler of the main procedure, a run-time error message is displayed on the screen and the program terminates.

If there are no exception handlers in any of the frames, which is the case for all of the programs we have written until now, the program will always terminate with a run-time error message if an exception is raised.

That may seem very complicated. Let's try again, this time using pseudocode:

```
begin execution
loop
    if exception raised then
        suspend normal execution
        if exception handler in this frame
        And then ( exception name or a when others in exception handler)
            lower exception
            execute statement(s) after =>
        end if
        transfer to end of this frame
    elsif exception handler next thing in the frame then
        skip over exception handler to end of this frame
    else
        execute the next instruction
    end if
    if end of this frame then
        if in main procedure then
            if exception raised then
                display error message
            end if
            exit
        else
            return to calling subprogram
        end if
    end if
end loop
Stop execution
```

It has been said that "a picture is worth a thousand words," so this time we will use a diagram as one more form of explanation before some examples.

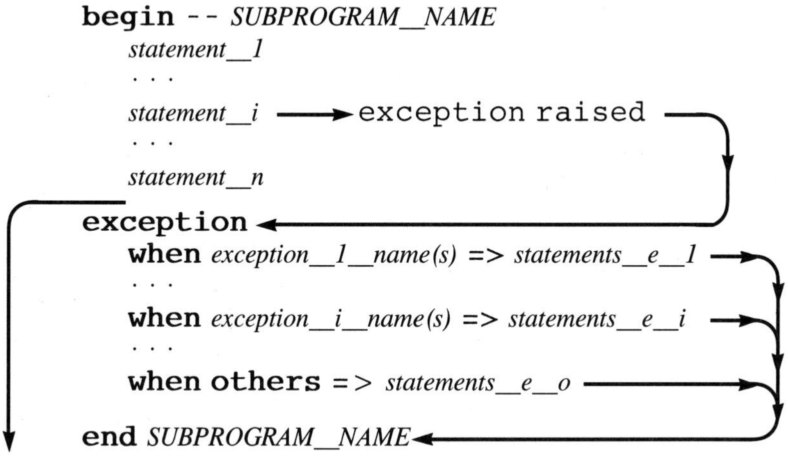

```
begin -- SUBPROGRAM_NAME
   statement_1
   . . .
   statement_i ——> exception raised ——┐
   . . .                               ↓
   statement_n                         │
exception <────────────────────────────┘
   when exception_1_name(s) => statements_e_1 ──┐
   . . .                                        ↓
   when exception_i_name(s) => statements_e_i ──┤
   . . .                                        ↓
   when others => statements_e_o ───────────────┤
                                                ↓
end SUBPROGRAM_NAME <───────────────────────────┘
```

Now the "thousand words" to explain the diagram. If an exception is raised during the execution of the *i*th statement, execution is transferred to the exception handler (if it exists). If the exception name is found in one of the individual handlers, the exception is "lowered," the statements after the arrow are executed, and we go to the **end** of the subprogram. If the *n*th statement is executed without raising an exception, we skip over the exception handler and **end** the subprogram.

Exception Examples

The program in Figure 6.17 has an exception handler in the procedure GET_RATING. The exception handler will be invoked if any exception is raised in this input procedure. The exception handler will take action, however, only if that exception is CONSTRAINT_ERROR. We know what an exception handler does: it "lowers" the exception and executes the statements in the handler. The question is, what should those statements do? The purpose of having an exception handler is to allow the program to continue. The MAIN procedure in this case is expecting a value for RATING. Thus, the exception handler must assign a value to RATING that is within the range; in this case we chose a value in the middle of the range. Since the program is interactive, the exception handler should also inform the user that an exception was raised and what was done as a result of the exception.

Program

```
with I_O; use I_O;
procedure MAIN is
    subtype ZERO_TO_TEN is INTEGER range 0 . . 10;
    RATING : ZERO_TO_TEN;
    procedure GET_RATING ( RATING : in out ZERO_TO_TEN ) is
    begin -- Get_Rating
        GET ( RATING ); SKIP_LINE;
        RATING := RATING + 3;
    exception
        when CONSTRAINT_ERROR =>
            PUT ( "Rating is outside the range" ); NEW_LINE;
            PUT ( "Setting rating to 5" ); NEW_LINE;
            RATING := 5;
    end GET_RATING;
begin
    loop
        PUT ( "What is your rating?" ); NEW_LINE;
        GET_RATING ( RATING );
        PUT ( "The inflated rating is " );
        PUT ( RATING ); NEW_LINE ( 2 );
    end loop;
end MAIN;
```

Sample Dialogue

```
What is your rating?
5
The inflated rating is        8
What is your rating?
8
Rating is outside the range
Setting rating to 5
The inflated rating is        5
What is your rating?
11
Rating is outside the range
Setting rating to 5
The inflated rating is        5
```

Figure 6.17 Example program using an exception handler

The sample dialogue first has an input of **5**, which gives RATING a value that is within the range as the result of both the GET and the assignment. The second input, **8**, is okay for the GET, but CONSTRAINT_ERROR is raised when an attempt is made to assign the value of **8 + 3** to RATING. The third input of **11** causes CONSTRAINT_ERROR to be raised as a result of attempting to give RATING a value outside the range in the GET statement.

Programmer-Defined Exceptions

A programmer can define exception names for use within a program. These exception names are declared in the declaration part of any procedure or function. The syntax for an exception declaration is a list of identifiers separated by commas, followed by a colon, followed by the reserved word **exception**, and terminated with a semicolon. The declaration looks quite similar to any object declaration and can be intermingled with other object declarations, as shown in the following example:

```
DANGER, HIGH_TEMPERATURE : exception;
INDEX : INTEGER;
LOW_COOLANT_LEVEL : exception;
ROOT, RADICAND : FLOAT;
```

The exception identifiers are not objects in the same sense as those of type INTEGER, FLOAT, BOOLEAN, or CHARACTER. Exceptions cannot be assigned a value; in fact they have no value. Exceptions cannot be interrogated; in other words, they cannot be referenced in an **if** statement. To say **if** DANGER **then** makes no sense because DANGER is not a BOOLEAN. In some ways exceptions may look like BOOLEANs in that they are either ''raised'' or ''lowered,'' where BOOLEANs are TRUE or FALSE, but that is where the similarity ends.

Raise Statement

An exception can be referenced in only two places. One is in an exception handler, as in this example:

```
exception
     when DANGER => PUT ( "Call for help" );
```

The second place is in a **raise** statement. Predefined exceptions can be raised by the run-time system during the execution of the program. Predefined exceptions can also be raised via a **raise** statement. Programmer-defined exceptions can be raised only by the execution of a **raise** statement.

The syntax for the raise statement is quite simple.

raise statement

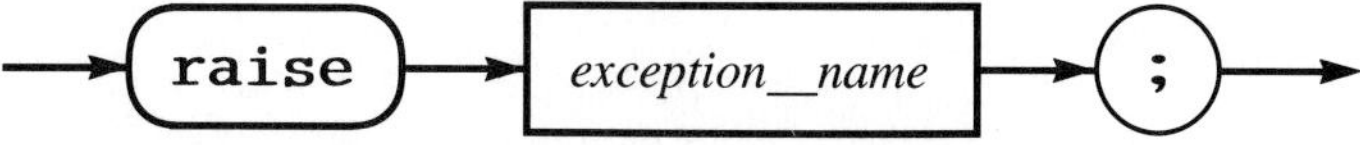

The **raise** statement can be used in a program wherever a statement is allowed. Often times a **raise** statement will appear as part of an **if** statement; for example:

```
if TEMPERATURE > 5000 then
    raise HIGH_TEMPERATURE;
end if;
```

The same thing happens if the system raises one of the predefined exceptions or if the program raises either a predefined or programmer-defined exception. When an exception is raised, normal execution stops and control is transferred to the exception handler for the frame in which the exception was raised. If there is no exception handler in that frame, control passes to the exception handler for the calling subprogram. This process continues until the exception is handled or the program terminates because no exception handler can be found.

The **raise** statement does have other forms, but its use is restricted. The reserved word **raise** can appear alone as a statement, but only in an exception handler. This form of the **raise** statement ''reraises'' the exception that got the program into the exception handler in the first place. The effect is to pass control to the calling subprogram's exception handler with the exception raised again; for example:

```
exception
    when DANGER => PUT ( "Call for HELP!" );
                   raise;
```

Block Statement

To make the exception example in Figure 6.19 complete, we need to introduce one more Ada construction. The block statement is an Ada construct that can be used anywhere a statement can be used. The block statement is simply a sequence of statements and an optional exception handler, all enclosed in a **begin/end** pair. The syntax for the block statement is given in Figure 6.18. Beside the use of a block statement in Figure 6.19, a further example of the use of the block statement appears in the next chapter as part of a discussion of robustness.

We hope the following example program (Figure 6.19) will clarify some of the mystery surrounding exceptions, exception handlers, and **raise** and block statements. The MAIN procedure simulates the reading of temperatures in a plant reactor of some kind. Each time around the loop in the MAIN procedure, a new temperature value will be input from the keyboard as if it were a reading from a temperature-measuring device. MAIN calls a procedure (REACTOR) to process that temperature reading and take any appropriate action. The numbers on the right-hand edge of the program are there for reference purposes and are used in the narrative that traces through the program following the sample dialogue.

block__statement

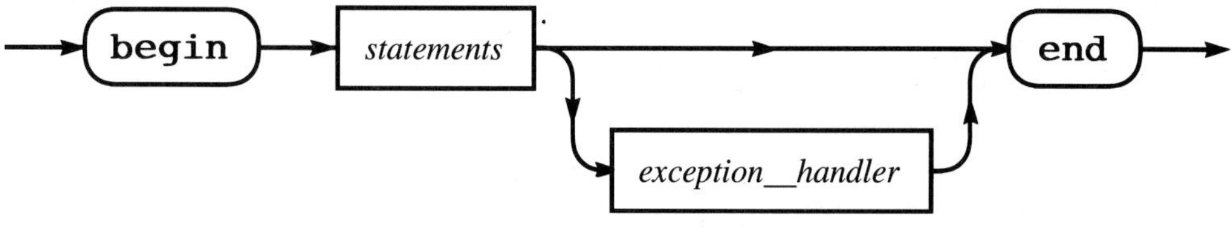

Figure 6.18 Syntax for the block statement.

Program

```
with I_O; use I_O;
procedure MAIN is
    subtype FAHRENHEIT is INTEGER range -25 .. 525;
    PEOPLE : BOOLEAN := TRUE;
    TEMPERATURE : FAHRENHEIT;
    procedure REACTOR ( TEMPERATURE : in out FAHRENHEIT;
                        EMPLOYEES : in BOOLEAN ) is
        CRITICAL_TEMPERATURE,
        DANGER : exception;
        MAXIMUM_TEMPERATURE : constant FAHRENHEIT := 500;
        TEMPERATURE_RATIO : FAHRENHEIT;
        procedure ADD_COOLANT ( TEMPERATURE : out FAHRENHEIT ) is
        begin
            PUT ( "Adding cooling material" ); NEW_LINE;
            TEMPERATURE := MAXIMUM_TEMPERATURE;
        end ADD_COOLANT;
    begin -- Reactor
        if TEMPERATURE > MAXIMUM_TEMPERATURE then
            raise CRITICAL_TEMPERATURE;
        end if;
        TEMPERATURE := FAHRENHEIT ( FLOAT ( TEMPERATURE ) * 1.1 );
        begin -- Inner Block
            TEMPERATURE_RATIO := MAXIMUM_TEMPERATURE / TEMPERATURE;
            TEMPERATURE := TEMPERATURE + 15;
            if TEMPERATURE > MAXIMUM_TEMPERATURE then
                raise CRITICAL_TEMPERATURE;
            end if;
        exception
            when CRITICAL_TEMPERATURE =>
                if EMPLOYEES then
                    raise DANGER;
                end if;
        end; -- Inner Block
```

```
    exception
        when CRITICAL_TEMPERATURE =>
            PUT ( "REDUCE TEMPERATURE IMMEDIATELY!" ); NEW_LINE;
            ADD_COOLANT ( TEMPERATURE );
        when CONSTRAINT_ERROR =>
            PUT ( "TEMPERATURE OVER 463!" ); NEW_LINE;
        when DANGER =>
            PUT ( "CLEAR THE AREA!" ); NEW_LINE;
    end REACTOR;
begin -- Main
    loop
        PUT ( "Enter new temperature" ); NEW_LINE;
        GET ( TEMPERATURE ); SKIP_LINE;
        PUT ( "The new temperature is " );
        PUT ( TEMPERATURE ); NEW_LINE;
        exit when TEMPERATURE < 0;
        REACTOR ( TEMPERATURE, PEOPLE );
    end loop;
exception
    when NUMERIC_ERROR =>
        PUT ( "Don't divide by zero." ); NEW_LINE;
end MAIN;
```

Sample Dialogue

```
Enter new temperature
300
The new temperature is    300
Enter new temperature
450
The new temperature is    450
CLEAR THE AREA!
Enter new temperature
465
The new temperature is    465
TEMPERATURE OVER 463!
Enter new temperature
510
The new temperature is    510
REDUCE TEMPERATURE IMMEDIATELY!
Adding cooling material
Enter new temperature
0
The new temperature is      0
Don't divide by zero.
```

Figure 6.19 Program with exception handler.

Execution of the program begins with the **loop** statement in the MAIN procedure, which is on line number 44. The first temperature reading (300) is input through the GET statement on line 46. A call to the REACTOR procedure is made at line 50, and control passes to the beginning of the procedure at line 18. A temperature reading of 300 causes no exceptions to be raised. None of the statements in any of the exception handlers is executed. Control simply passes over the exception handlers as if they did not exist. The complete sequence of lines is 18, 20, 21, 22, 23, 24, 25, 27, 33, 42. The procedure terminates normally through line 42, and control passes back to the MAIN procedure at line 51.

The second time around the loop in the MAIN procedure, a temperature reading of 450 is input via line 46. Control passes to line 18 in the REACTOR procedure via the procedure call in line 50. The temperature passes the first test and is recomputed in line 21 (450 * 1.1 = 495). Execution continues into the "Inner Block," where 15 is added to the temperature, making it now 510. Since the temperature is now greater than 500, which is the MAXIMUM_TEMPERATURE constant, the exception CRITICAL_TEMPERATURE is raised in line 26. At this point normal execution of the program sequence is stopped and control is passed to the exception handler in line 28. An exception handler for CRITICAL_TEMPERATURE is found in line 29. There is also an exception handler for CRITICAL_TEMPERATURE in line 35, but it is in a different frame, and the exception handler in line 29 handles the exception. As soon as an exception handler is found for the raised exception, the exception is "lowered." Execution picks up again at line 30, and in line 31 another exception is raised (DANGER). Normal execution stops, and control is passed to the exception handler in the next outer frame, which in this case turns out to be line 34. An exception handler for DANGER is found in line 40, and execution continues with line 41. Control passes out of the exception handler to line 42 where the procedure terminates and passes control to line 51 in the MAIN procedure.

The third time around the loop, a temperature value of 465 is input, and control passes to the REACTOR procedure again (line 18). Nothing happens as a result of the test in line 18, and in line 21 the temperature is changed to 512 (465 * 1.1 = 512). Execution continues normally until line 24. The value 15 is added to the temperature giving a resultant value of 527. When an attempt is made to assign 527 to TEMPERATURE, CONSTRAINT_ERROR is raised because TEMPERATURE is of the **subtype** FAHRENHEIT, which is restricted to INTEGER values between -25 and 525. The raising of CONSTRAINT_ERROR by the computer causes normal execution to stop and control to be transferred to the exception handler at line 28. Since there is no handler for CONSTRAINT_ERROR in this exception handler, control is passed to the exception handler in the next outer frame at line 34. Here a handler for CONSTRAINT_ERROR is found, and execution picks up again at line 39. Once the statements in the handler for this particular exception have been executed, control passes to the end of the procedure at line 42. The procedure terminates normally and control is passed to line 51.

The fourth time around the loop, the value 510 is input. A call to the procedure REACTOR continues execution at line 18. The value of temperature (510) is greater than MAXIMUM_TEMPERATURE (500), and the exception CRITICAL_TEMPERATURE is raised in line 19. Normal execution stops, and control is passed to the exception handler for this frame, which is at line 34. Notice that control does not go to the exception handler at line 28 because that exception handler is inside the "Inner Block." The exception handler at line 34 has a handler for CRITICAL_TEMPERATURE, so execution continues with the statement in line 35. At line 37 control is passed to line 14 because of the call to the procedure ADD_COOLANT. When the procedure is completed, control is back to the exception handler. The procedure call to ADD_COOLANT is the last statement in this specific exception handler, so control transfers to the end of the REACTOR procedure at line 42. The procedure terminates normally and control returns to the main procedure.

What proves to be the last time around the loop, the value of 0 is input for TEMPERATURE. Control goes to the REACTOR procedure and into the "Inner Block," where at line 23 the exception NUMERIC_ERROR is raised by the computer because the resultant value from the divide (/) operation cannot give a proper value for that operation (MAXIMUM_TEMPERATURE / TEMPERATURE is 500 / 0). Control passes to the exception handler in the "Inner Block" at line 28. But there is no handler for the exception NUMERIC_ERROR in this frame, so control passes to the exception handler at line 34. Again, there is no handler for NUMERIC_ERROR, so control passes to the exception handler for the calling procedure MAIN at line 52. The exception is handled here, and a message is displayed admonishing the user for attempting to divide by zero. The exception has been handled, and control passes to the end of the MAIN procedure, which then terminates normally without any system run-time error message.

Summary of Problem Solving and Programming Techniques

- A boolean variable can be used within a program as a flag to record whether or not some specific action has taken place.
- A boolean constant can be used as a switch to turn program features off and on by changing the constant declaration. One such use of this feature is in trace statements for debugging.
- One approach to solving a problem or subproblem is to write down conditions and corresponding actions that need to be taken under each condition. This can be implemented in Ada as a series of nested **if** statements.

Summary of Ada Constructs

`if` statement with `elsif` clause

Syntax:

```
if boolean__expression__1 then
      statement(s)__1
elsif boolean__expression__2 then
      statement(s)__2
elsif boolean__expression__3 then
      statement(s)__3
      :
else
      statement(s)__N
end if
```

Example:

```
if X = 0 then
     PUT ( "value of x is equal to zero" );
elsif X < 0 then
     PUT ( "value of x is less than zero" );
elsif X >= 25 then
     PUT ( "value of x is 25 or greater" );
else
     PUT ( "value of x is greater than zero, " );
     PUT ( "but less than 25" );
end if;
```

statement(s)__1, statement(s)__2, statement(s)__3, . . . statement(s)__N may be any Ada statements. *boolean__expression__1, boolean__expression__2, boolean__expression__3,* . . . may be any boolean expression. If *boolean__expression__1* evaluates to TRUE, then only *statement(s)__1* is executed. If *boolean__expression__2* evaluates to TRUE and *boolean__expression__1* has been evaluated to FALSE, then only *statement(s)__2* is executed. If *boolean__expression__3* evaluates to TRUE, then only *statement(s)__3* is executed. *statement(s)__N* is executed only if all of the boolean expressions evaluate to FALSE. The **elsif** clause may be repeated as many times as is necessary. The **else** clause is optional, but may appear at most once and only as the last clause.

the type boolean

Syntax:

```
BOOLEAN
```

Example:

```
RAINING : BOOLEAN;
```

This Ada type has exactly two values: TRUE and FALSE. An Ada program can have variables, constants, and expressions of type BOOLEAN. The LRM defines BOOLEAN in the following manner:

```
type BOOLEAN is ( FALSE, TRUE );
```

use of and

Syntax:

boolean__expression__1 **and** *boolean__expression__2*

Examples:

```
( X < 1 ) and ( X /= Y )
( abs X < 10.7 ) and ( Y > 0 )
```

This is one way to make a larger boolean expression out of two smaller boolean expressions. If both *boolean__expression__1* and *boolean__expression__2* evaluate to TRUE, then the entire expression evaluates to TRUE. If at least one of *boolean__expression__1* and *boolean__expression__2* evaluates to FALSE, then the entire expression evaluates to FALSE. Both *boolean__expression__1* and *boolean__expression__2* will be evaluated, regardless of results. (It is sometimes necessary, and usually wise, to place parentheses around the subexpressions.)

use of and then

Syntax:

boolean__expression__1 **and then** *boolean__expression__2*

Examples:

```
( X < 1 ) and then ( X /= Y )
( abs X < 10.7 ) and then ( Y > 0 )
```

The **and then** performs the same logical operation as the **and**. The difference is that if *boolean__expression__1* is FALSE, then *boolean__expression__2* is not evaluated and FALSE is the value of the **and then** operation. In all other cases the **and then** and the **and** do the same thing.

use of or

Syntax:

boolean__expression__1 **or** *boolean__expression__2*

Example:

```
( ANSWER = 'Y') or ( NUMBER = 7 )
```

This is one way to make a larger boolean expression out of two smaller boolean expressions. If at least one of *boolean__expression__1* and *boolean__expression__2* evaluate to TRUE, then the entire expression evaluates to TRUE. If both *boolean__expression__1* and *boolean__expression__2* evaluate to FALSE, then the entire expression evaluates to FALSE. (It is sometimes necessary, and usually wise, to place parentheses around the subexpressions.)

use of or else

Syntax:

boolean__expression__1 **or else** *boolean__expression__2*

Example:

```
( ANSWER = 'Y' ) or else ( NUMBER = 7 )
```

The **or else** performs the same logical operation as the **or**. The difference is that if *boolean__expression__1* is TRUE, then *boolean__expression__2* is not evaluated and TRUE is the value of the **or else** operation. In all other cases the **or else** and the **or** do the same thing.

use of not

Syntax:

not (*boolean__expression* **)**

Examples:

```
not ( X < 0 )
not ( ( X < 1 ) and ( Y < 0 ) )
```

This is one way to make a larger boolean expression out of a smaller one. The **not** reverses boolean values. If *boolean__expression* evaluates to TRUE, then the expression with the **not** evaluates to FALSE. If *boolean__expression* evaluates to FALSE, then the expression with the **not** evaluates to TRUE. If *boolean__expression* is a boolean variable (or certain other boolean expressions described later in this book), then the parentheses around the expression are not required.

case statement

Syntax:

```
case expression is
      when choice(s)__1 => statement(s)__1;
      when choice(s)__2 => statement(s)__2;
                  .
                  .
      when others => statement(s)__n;
end case;
```

Example:

```
case N is
      when 2 => PUT ( "Value of n is 2" );
                NEW_LINE;
      when 7 . . 9 | 4 => PUT ( "Value of n is 7, 8, 9 or 4" );
                          NEW_LINE;
      when others => null; -- Do nothing
end case;
```

expression must evaluate to something of type INTEGER or type CHARACTER. (Later we will discover other allowable types.) It cannot be of type FLOAT. The choices must be lists or ranges of values of the same type as that of *expression,* and all these values must be different. The statements may be any Ada statements. When the **case** statement is executed, *expression* is evaluated and the statement with that value in its choices is executed.

raise statement

Syntax:

```
raise exception_name;
or
raise;
```

Example:

```
raise DANGER;
```

The **raise** statement with an *exception_name* in it causes that exception to be raised, and the system then transfers control to the exception handler of that name. If there is no exception handler for the raised exception, the program terminates with a message indicating that there was an unhandled exception.

The **raise** statement without an *exception_name* may only appear in an exception handler. This statement "reraises" the exception that caused the transfer to this exception handler.

exception handler

Syntax:

```
exception
      when exception_name_1 => sequence_of_statements
      when exception_name_2 => sequence_of_statements
                .
                .
      when others => sequence_of_statements
```

Example:

```
exception
    when DANGER => PUT ( "Call 911" ); NEW_LINE;
                   raise;
    when DATA_ERROR => PUT ( "Bad data, try again" ); NEW_LINE;
    when others => PUT ( "Don't know how I got here." ); NEW_LINE;
```

An exception handler "lowers" the exception that caused the program to branch to this exception handler. Any sequence of statements can appear in an exception handler. This sequence of statements may also include a **raise** statement which "reraises" the exception that was just handled.

block statement

Syntax:

```
begin
    sequence_of_statements
exception
    exception_handler(s)
end;
```

Example:

```
loop
   begin
        GET ( DATA );
        SKIP_LINE;
        exit;
   exception
        when DATA_ERROR => PUT ( "Try again" ); NEW_LINE;
                           SKIP_LINE;
   end;
end loop;
```

A block statement is a grouping of statements that allows exception handlers to be embedded inside the **begin** / **end** pair. If the exception DATA_ERROR is raised during the GET statement, control is transferred to the exception handler where a message is displayed and all remaining data on the present input line is ignored. If no exception is raised during the GET or SKIP_LINE the loop is exited, and the exception handler is ignored.

Exercises

Self-Test Exercises

5. What is the output produced by the following code, when embedded in a complete program in which SMALL is declared to be a variable of type BOOLEAN:

```
if TRUE then
     PUT ( "First Put" );
     NEW_LINE;
else
     PUT ( "Second Put" );
     NEW_LINE;
end if;
SMALL := ( 1 < 2 ) and ( 4 < 3 );
if SMALL then
     PUT ( "Third Put" );
else
     PUT ( "Fourth Put" );
end if;
NEW_LINE;
```

6. Write a program that reads in three integers and outputs a message telling whether or not they are in numeric order.

7. Write a nested **if-then-else** statement that classifies an integer NUMBER into one of the following categories and writes out an appropriate message:

NUMBER < 0   0 <= NUMBER =< 100   NUMBER >= 100

8. We have seen four types thus far in our discussion of the Ada language: INTEGER, FLOAT, CHARACTER, and BOOLEAN. Which of these types are allowed as the type for the controlling expression in a **case** statement; that is, what can the type of *expression* be in a **case** statement that begins with

case *expression* **is**

9. Write a program whose input is a month entered as a number from 1 to 12 and whose output is the number of days in that month.

10. The following four boolean expressions divide into two groups with two equivalent expressions in each group. What are the two groups? (Two expressions are equivalent if they evaluate to the same value of TRUE or FALSE for each possible way of setting FOOT_LOOSE and FANCY_FREE to TRUE or FALSE.)

```
not FOOT_LOOSE and not FANCY_FREE
not ( FOOT_LOOSE ) or not ( FANCY_FREE )
not ( FOOT_LOOSE and FANCY_FREE )
not ( FOOT_LOOSE or FANCY_FREE )
```

Interactive Exercises

11. Embed the following code in a complete program and run it several times using different input values each time:

```
PUT ( "Type in three integers:" ); NEW_LINE;
GET ( FIRST ); GET ( SECOND ); GET ( THIRD ); SKIP_LINE;
if FIRST > 0 then
     PUT ( "The first value is greater than zero" );
elsif SECOND > 0 then
     PUT ( "The second value is greater than zero" );
elsif THIRD > 0 then
     PUT ( "The third value is greater than zero" );
else
     PUT ( "They are all zero or negative" );
end if;
NEW_LINE;
```

Predict the output before you run the program.

12. Write a program that reads in three integers and outputs a message telling whether exactly two of them are greater than 10. There is no need to be fancy. It is perfectly all right to use a long boolean expression that tests all possible pairs of variables.

13. Write a program whose input is a one-digit number and whose output is that number written as a word. For example, an input of 5 should produce an output of `five`.

Programming Exercises

14. Enhance the program from Exercise 9 so that the month is input as a name, such as `January`, and not as a number. If the month is `February`, the program also asks the year in order to determine whether it is a leap year. The program in Figure 6.8 can be modified into a subprogram to determine if a year is a leap year. The program should allow the month to be spelled with any combination of upper- and lowercase letters. It should accept misspelled months as long as the first three letters are correct.

15. Write a program that computes state income tax according to the following formula: Net income is gross income minus deductions (both given as input). Tax is as follows:

    3% on each dollar of net income up to $8,000 plus
    5% on each dollar of net income from $8,001 to 15,000 plus
    8% on each dollar of net income over $15,000.

16. Write a program that guesses the user's height. The program makes a first guess and then asks the user if it is too high or too low. The program continues to guess and ask the user until the user says the guess is correct or for three tries, whichever comes first.

17. Write a program to determine grades in a course with three quizzes, each scored on a basis of 10 points. Grades are determined according to the following rules: A is an average of 9.0 or better; B is an average of 8.0 or better (up to 9.0); C is an average of 7.0 or better; D is an average of 6.0 or better; less than 6.0 is an F.

18. A bicycle salesperson is offered a choice of wage plans: (a) a straight salary of $300 per week; (b) $3.50 per hour for 40 hours plus a 10% commission on sales; (c) a straight 15% commission on sales with no other salary. Write a program that takes as input the salesperson's expected weekly sales, outputs the expected wages paid under each plan, and announces the best paying plan.

19. Write a program to compute the interest due, total amount due, and the minimum payment for a revolving credit account. The program accepts the account balance as input and then adds on the interest to get the total amount due. The rate schedules are as follows: The interest is 1.5% on the first $1,000 and 1% on any amount over that. The minimum payment is the total amount due if that is $10 or less; otherwise, it is $10 or 10% of the total amount owed, whichever is larger.

20. Write a program to give a student's final grade in a course with the following grading scheme: three quizzes worth 10 points each, a midterm worth 100 points, and a final worth 100 points. The grade is based on the following weights: 50% on the final exam, 25% on the midterm, and 25% on the quiz average. (Be sure to normalize the quiz average to 100 by multiplying by 10.) The grade is determined from the weighted average in the traditional way: 90 or over is an A, below 90 down to 80 is a B, below 80 to 70 is a C, below 70 to 60 is a D, below 60 is an F.

21. Write a program that computes the cost of postage on a first-class letter according to the following rate scale: 29 cents for the first ounce or fraction of an ounce, 23 cents for each additional half ounce, plus a $5 service charge if the customer desires special delivery.

22. Write a program that reads in a time of day in 24-hour notation and outputs it in 12-hour notation. For example, if the input is 13:45, then the output should be

```
1:45 PM
```

The program should instruct the user to always type in exactly five characters. So nine o'clock should be input as

```
09:00
```

23. Write a program that accepts dates written in the usual way and then outputs them as three numbers. For example, the input

```
February 15, 1961
```

should produce the output

```
2 15 61
```

24. Write a program that accepts a "three-digit" number written in words and then outputs it as a value of type `INTEGER`. The input is terminated with a period. For example, the input

```
two hundred thirty-five.
```

should produce the output

```
235
```

25. Write a program that reads in the radius of a circle and then outputs one of the following, depending on what the user requests: circumference of the circle, area of the circle, or diameter of the circle.

26. Write a program to score the "paper-rock-scissors" game. Each of two users types in either **'P'**, **'R'**, or **'S'**, and the program announces the winner as well as the basis for determining the winner: "paper covers rock," "rock breaks scissors," "scissors cut paper," or "nobody wins." Be sure to allow the users to use lower- as well as uppercase letters (if they are available on your machine).

27. Write a program that accepts a year written as a four-digit Arabic (ordinary) numeral and outputs the year written in Roman numerals. Important Roman numerals are V for 5, X for 10, L for 50, C for 100, D for 500, and M for 1000. Recall that some numbers are formed by using a kind of subtraction of one Roman "digit"; for example, IV is 4 produced as V minus I, XL is 40, CM is 900, etc. A few more sample years: MCM is 1900, MCML is 1950, MCMLX is 1960, MCMXL is 1940, MCMLXXXIX is 1989. Assume the year is between 1000 and 3000.

28. Write an astrology program. The user types in his or her birthday and the program responds with the user's sign and horoscope. The month may be entered as a number from 1 to 12. Use a newspaper horoscope section for the horoscopes and dates of each sign. Then enhance your program so that if the user is only one or two days away from an adjacent sign, then the program announces that the user is on a "cusp" and also outputs the horoscope for that nearest adjacent sign. For a nicer but harder program, let the user type in the month as a word rather than as a number.

29. Write a program that accepts a number written as a Roman numeral and outputs the equivalent Arabic (ordinary) numeral. Assume that the Roman numeral is 50 or smaller (Roman numeral L or smaller.) See Exercise 27 for a review of Roman numerals.

CHAPTER

7

PROBLEM SOLVING USING LOOPS

Claude E. Shannon

The stage was set for the development of the electronic computer when Shannon applied the algebra of Boole to electronic circuits. Shannon's switching algebra was the forerunner of modern switching theory that made today's computers possible. He also made contributions to communications with his mathematical theory of information.

Chapter Contents

One very common sort of algorithm instruction requires some action to be repeated a number of times. A program that reads in a list of numbers may repeat the same sequence of prompt and input statements until all the numbers are read in. A program to calculate change may repeat its entire calculation, computing change for different amounts until the user is through with the program. A program to update an inventory list may repeat the update process as many times as the user specifies.

Any program instruction that repeats some sequence of statements a number of times is called a *loop*. In this chapter we will describe a number of techniques for designing algorithms and programs that use loops. We will review the **loop** and **exit when** statements and then introduce the other looping mechanisms available in the Ada language.

Basic Loop Considerations

loop body, loop iteration

The simple **loop** statements that we have already seen are examples of loops. The sequence of statements to be repeated in a loop is called the *body* of the loop, and each repetition of the loop body is called an *iteration* of the loop. The two main design questions when constructing loops are What should be in the body? and How many times should the loop be repeated? Another way to phrase the second of these two design questions is How will the loop stop?

The Loop Statement

A simplified form of the **loop** statement was introduced in Chapter 3. That form of the **loop** statement used only simple comparisons in the **exit when** statement to control the number of loop iterations. However, any boolean expression whatsoever may be used in an **exit when** statement. For example, the following loop will be iterated until the values of the variables ALPHA and BETA are both positive:

```
loop
   exit when ALPHA > 0
          and BETA > 0;
   ALPHA := ALPHA + 1;
   BETA := BETA + 1;
end loop;
```

(The variables ALPHA and BETA must, of course, be given some value before the **loop** statement is executed.) For the sake of completeness and review, we next give the complete definitions of **loop** and **exit when** statements.

syntax

Syntax diagrams for the **loop** and **exit when** statements are shown in Figure 7.1. The **loop** syntax consists of the reserved word **loop**, followed by a sequence of statements (called the *body* of the loop), followed by the two reserved words **end loop**. As with all statements, the **loop** terminates with a semicolon. When the loop is executed, the sequence of statements will be executed some number of times, depending on the values of the boolean expression in the **exit when**. The boolean expression may be any of the boolean expressions described in Chapter 6.

In our examples up to now, the first statement in the body has always been an **exit when** statement. (Later in this chapter, we will explore additional placements of the **exit when**.) The **exit when** syntax is also quite simple and consists of the two reserved words **exit when**, followed by a boolean expression, and terminated with a semicolon. The use of the **exit when** is restricted to the body of a loop only.

In the jargon of the Ada language, the **loop**, along with **if** and **case** statements, is called a *compound statement*. All other statements we have looked at so far (assignment, procedure call, **exit when**) are called *simple statements*.

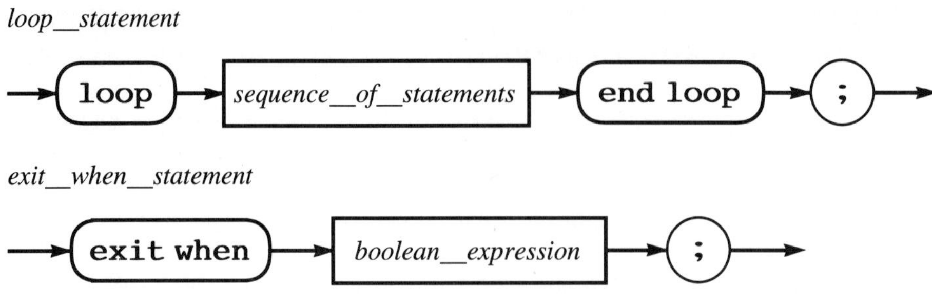

Figure 7.1 Syntax diagrams for `loop` and `exit when` statements.

action of a loop statement

When an **`exit when`** statement inside a loop is executed, the first thing that happens is that the boolean expression is evaluated. If it evaluates to `TRUE`, the program "jumps" out of the loop and proceeds with the next statement after the **`end loop`**. If the boolean expression evaluates to `FALSE`, the exit is ignored and the program proceeds with the statement after the **`exit when`**. This process is iterated again and again as long as the boolean expression remains `FALSE`. When the program reaches the **`end loop`**, it goes back to the **`loop`** and starts all over again. Each time the program reaches the **`exit when`**, the boolean expression is reevaluated. If it is `TRUE`, then the program jumps out of the loop; otherwise, the loop continues.

executing the body zero times

With the **`exit when`** as the first statement in the body of the loop, the boolean expression is evaluated before any other statements in the body. If the boolean expression evaluates to `TRUE` the first time into the loop, the rest of the body is never executed at all. It may seem pointless to execute the rest of the body of a loop *zero times.* After all, that has no effect whatsoever on any values or output. However, it is sometimes the desired action. In the next case study, we will design a loop to add a list of numbers. If the numbers are homework scores, it might turn out that a student did absolutely no homework, so the list of scores will be empty. To get the correct sum (and grade) of zero, the loop body must be executed zero times. As another example, suppose the numbers are the values of the checks you have written in a month. You might take a month's vacation in which you write no checks at all. In that case there are zero numbers to sum, so the loop is iterated zero times.

Case Study

Summing a List of Numbers

loop body

Suppose we wish to sum a list of numbers typed in at the keyboard. For example, they may be homework scores or sales figures. The obvious way to accomplish this is to read in the numbers and keep a running total of all the numbers seen so far. To hold this running sum, we use a variable called SUM. The variable SUM is set equal to zero, and then each time the program reads in a number, SUM is increased by adding in that number. After initializing SUM to zero, the program will repeat the following action for each of the numbers in the list:

```
GET ( NUMBER );
SUM := SUM + NUMBER;
```

This repeated action indicates that we can use a loop. The above two statements will form the body of our loop, or at least part of the body of our loop.

stopping the loop

When adding a list of numbers with a loop, we somehow need to determine the number of numbers to be added. We somehow need to ''stop'' the loop. In this example we will use a very simple strategy: We will first ask the user how many numbers there are and then iterate the loop that number of times. To count the number of iterations, we will use a variable called LEFT_TO_READ, which is initialized to the number of numbers to be read in and is then decreased by 1 each time the loop is iterated. This adds one more statement to the loop body:

```
LEFT_TO_READ := LEFT_TO_READ - 1;
```

The complete pseudocode for our algorithm that includes this loop is given in Figure 7.2. Figure 7.3 shows how we can realize this algorithm as a complete program using a **loop** statement. Be sure to notice that the variables SUM and LEFT_TO_READ are initialized before the loop.

```
    Prompt the user for number of integers in the list
    Get that number of integers
    left_to_read := number_of_integers
    sum := 0
--  The loop starts here
        Do the following until there are no more LEFT_TO_READ.
        In other words get out of the loop when LEFT_TO_READ = 0
        Input a number
        Add that number to the SUM
        Decrease LEFT_TO_READ by 1
--  The loop ends here
    Report the number of integers read in and their sum
```

Figure 7.2 Pseudocode for summing a list of numbers.

Program

```
with I_O; use I_O;
procedure MAIN is
--                  INPUT  : The number of integers in a list
--                           followed by the list of integers.
--                  OUTPUT : The number of integers in a list
--                           and the sum of the integers.
--                  DESCRIPTION : Computes the sum of a list of integers.
    LEFT_TO_READ : INTEGER;
    NUMBER_OF_INTEGERS : INTEGER;
    NUMBER : INTEGER;
    SUM : INTEGER := 0;
begin -- Main
    PUT ( "The program adds a list of integers." ); NEW_LINE;
    PUT ( "How many integers will there be in the list?" ); NEW_LINE;
    GET ( NUMBER_OF_INTEGERS ); SKIP_LINE;
    PUT ( "Now type in the " ); PUT ( NUMBER_OF_INTEGERS );
    PUT ( " integers." ); NEW_LINE;
    LEFT_TO_READ := NUMBER_OF_INTEGERS;
    loop
        exit when LEFT_TO_READ <= 0;
        GET ( NUMBER );
        SUM := SUM + NUMBER;
        LEFT_TO_READ := LEFT_TO_READ - 1;
    end loop;
    PUT ( "The sum of the " ); PUT ( NUMBER_OF_INTEGERS );
    PUT ( " numbers is " ); PUT ( SUM ); NEW_LINE;
end MAIN;
```

Sample Dialogue 1

```
The program adds a list of integers.
How many integers will there be in the list?
3
Now type in the      3 integers.
4 6 2
The sum of the      3 numbers is       12
```

Sample Dialogue 2

```
The program adds a list of integers.
How many integers will there be in the list?
0
Now type in the      0 integers.
The sum of the      0 numbers is       0
```

Figure 7.3 Program for summing a list of numbers.

Pitfall

Uninitialized Variables

The program in Figure 7.3 sums a list of numbers by adding one number to the value of SUM on each loop iteration. Changing one or more variables in some incremental way is a typical kind of loop body. When designing such a loop, you can easily become so concerned with designing the loop body that you forget to initialize the variables used in the loop. A statement such as the following will produce unpredictable results unless the variable SUM is first given a value:

```
SUM := SUM + NUMBER;
```

If this statement is used in a loop to sum a list of numbers, then the variable SUM should be initialized to zero before the loop is executed. To see that zero is the correct initial value, simply note that zero plus the first number is that number, which is the correct value for a sum of one number.

Do not assume that zero is always the correct initial value for a variable used in a loop. Different situations require different initial values. For instance, the following computes the product of a list of numbers:

```
LEFT_TO_READ := NUMBER_OF_INTEGERS;
PRODUCT := 1;
loop
    exit when LEFT_TO_READ = 0;
    GET ( NUMBER );
    PRODUCT := PRODUCT * NUMBER;
    LEFT_TO_READ := LEFT_TO_READ - 1;
end loop;
```

To see why PRODUCT should be initialized to 1, note that 1 times the first number yields that number, which gets things started correctly. Any other value will produce problems. In particular, if PRODUCT is initialized to zero, its value would remain zero no matter how many times the loop is iterated.

What happens when you fail to initialize a variable varies from system to system, but it almost always produces problems. Even worse, the problem may not be apparent. One common situation is that uninitialized variables simply receive some leftover value that was stored in memory by a previously run program. This sets the value of the variables to some unpredictable values. The values may even vary from one run of the program to another. Anytime a program is run twice with *absolutely* no changes and with *identical* input and yet produces different outputs, you should suspect an uninitialized variable of some sort. The problem can even occur if there is no loop. Every variable must be explicitly given a value before it can appear on the right-hand side of an assignment statement, or anyplace else that expects it to have a value.

Pitfall

Unintended Infinite Loops

Some loops are not required to end. For example, an airline reservation system might simply repeat a loop that allows the user to add or delete reservations. The program and the loop run forever, or at least until the computer breaks or the airline goes bankrupt. More often a loop is designed to compute a value or small list of values and should end after finding the value(s). For example, our sample loop to add up a list of numbers ends after summing all the numbers. A loop that repeats forever is called an *infinite loop.* An unintended infinite loop is a common error that should be guarded against.

Consider the following loop, which displays the interest produced by the value of AMOUNT for some sample interest rates in the range from 10% to 20%.

```
RATE := 10;
loop
    exit when RATE = 20;
    INTEREST := FLOAT ( RATE ) * 0.01 * AMOUNT;
--          The 0.01 changes percent to a
--          fraction
    PUT ( RATE ); PUT ( "% yields $" );
    PUT ( INTEREST ); ( " in interest." );
    NEW_LINE;
    RATE := RATE + 2;
end loop;
```

Now suppose we wish to change the display so that it shows changes of 3% rather than 2%. If we change the last line of the loop body to the following we will produce an infinite loop.

```
RATE := RATE + 3;
```

The problem is that the value of RATE now changes from **19** to **22** and is never equal to **20**. So the boolean expression never changes its value to TRUE. The correct boolean expression is

```
RATE >= 20
```

It would be safer to use this expression even in the original version of the loop, which increased percents by **2** and so did happen to terminate correctly. That way the loop would be robust enough to perform correctly even if we need to change it slightly.

dangers of equality

As a general rule, it is safer to terminate a loop with a test that involves greater-than or less-than rather than a test for exact equality or a test using the inequality operator **/=**. In the case of FLOAT values, this is an absolute rule. Since FLOAT values are stored as approximate quantities, a test for equality of FLOAT values is meaningless. Controlling a loop with a boolean expression that tests two FLOAT values for equality is virtually guaranteed to end the loop too soon or not at all. Always arrange to test FLOAT values using one of the relations **<**, **<=**, **>**, or **>=**.

Exercises

Self-Test Exercises

1. What is the output of the following program?

```
with I_O; use I_O;
procedure MAIN is
    SPACE : INTEGER := 3;
    TIME : INTEGER := 10;
begin
    loop
        exit when TIME <= 0
              or SPACE <= 0;
        TIME := TIME - SPACE;
    end loop;
    PUT ( TIME ); NEW_LINE;
end MAIN;
```

2. What output would be produced by the code in Exercise 1 if SPACE were initialized to −3 instead of 3?

3. What is the output of the following program?

```
with I_O; use I_O;
procedure MAIN is
    TIME : INTEGER := 10;
begin
    loop
        exit when TIME <= 0;
        TIME := TIME + 3;
    end loop;
    PUT ( TIME ); NEW_LINE;
end MAIN;
```

4. The following is supposed to output all the positive odd numbers less than 10. It contains mistakes. What are they and how can they be corrected?

```
with I_O; use I_O;
procedure MAIN is
    ODD : INTEGER;
begin
    loop
        exit when ODD = 10;
        ODD := ODD + 2;
        PUT ( ODD );
    end loop;
end MAIN;
```

Terminating an Input loop

If your program is reading in a list of values with a loop, it must include some kind of mechanism to terminate the loop. If the program runs out of input, the program will stop, but if no provisions are made for the program to explicitly terminate the loop, then the result will be an error condition that terminates the program abnormally. There are four commonly used methods for terminating an input loop:

1. Asking the user before iterating a list of values
2. Heading the list with its size
3. Ending the list with a sentinel value
4. Running out of input

We will discuss them in order.

asking user before iterating

The first method is simply to ask the user, as in the following program:

```
SUM := 0;
PUT ( "Are there any numbers in the list? (y/n)" ); NEW_LINE;
GET ( ANSWER ); SKIP_LINE;
loop
    exit when ANSWER = 'n'
          or ANSWER = 'N';
    GET ( NUMBER ); SKIP_LINE;
    SUM := SUM + NUMBER;
    PUT ( "Are there more numbers? (y/n)" ); NEW_LINE;
    GET ( ANSWER ); SKIP_LINE;
end loop;
```

This is sometimes acceptable and is very useful in situations other than reading in a list. However, for a long list this is very tiresome. Imagine typing in a list of 100 numbers this way. The user is likely to progress from happy to sarcastic to angry and frustrated. Also, when the user must type in long lists, it is preferable to include only one stopping signal.

heading list with its size

On those occasions when the user naturally and easily knows the size of the list beforehand, the program can ask the user for the size of the list. This is the method we used in our sample program in Figure 7.3.

ending list with sentinel value

Perhaps the neatest way to terminate a loop that reads a list of values is with a *sentinel value*. A sentinel value is one that is somehow distinct from all the possible values on the list and so can be used to signal the end of the list. For example, if the loop reads in a list of positive numbers, then a negative number can be used as a sentinel value to indicate the end of the list. A loop such as the following can be used to add a list of nonnegative numbers:

```
SUM := 0;
loop
     GET ( NUMBER );
     exit when NUMBER < 0;
     SUM := SUM + NUMBER;
end loop;
```

Notice that the last number in the list is read but is not added into SUM. To add up the numbers 1, 2, and 3, the user adds a negative number to the end of the list, like so:

```
1    2    3    -1
```

The final **-1** is read in but not added into the sum.

Also notice that when using a sentinel value, we reverse the order of reading and testing within our loop. With a sentinel value we want the loop to end as soon as the sentinel value is read, so the loop needs to have the GET statement just prior to the **exit when**. This is the first example in which the **exit when** was not the first thing inside the **loop**. The **exit when** can be placed anywhere inside the loop, as we will see later in this chapter.

Use of a sentinel value in the way just discussed does require that the list of values be known to exclude at least one value of the data type in question. If the list consists of integers that might be any value whatsoever, there is no value left to serve as a sentinel value. In this situation you must use some other method to terminate the loop.

running out of input

As already noted, a loop that simply runs out of input will terminate with an error condition. However, in some situations when special provisions are made within the program, it is possible to test for running out of input and to end a loop gracefully on this condition. The next section discusses one way to do this.

END_OF_LINE

Using the special boolean function END_OF_LINE, an Ada program can detect the end of a line. This allows a user to mark the end of a list by simply pressing the return key. This is not very convenient for long lists, but it does work well for lists short enough to fit comfortably on one line. The identifier END_OF_LINE is a boolean function that tells the program when it is at the end of a line. When the program still has input available on the line that is currently being read, the boolean END_OF_LINE has the value FALSE, but when the end of a line is encountered, the value of END_OF_LINE changes from FALSE to TRUE. Less formally, END_OF_LINE is TRUE when the program gets to the end of a line of input and is FALSE otherwise.

The program in Figure 7.4 is designed to determine the number of nonblank characters in a given input line of textual matter. This version uses END_OF_LINE to detect the end of a line rather than asking the user how many characters there will be coming into the program.

Program

```
with I_O; use I_O;
procedure MAIN is
--                   INPUT  : A line of text.
--                   OUTPUT : The number of nonblank characters.
--                   DESCRIPTION : Computes the number of nonblank
--                                 characters in a line of text.
    BLANK : constant CHARACTER := ' ';
    A_CHARACTER : CHARACTER;
    NUMBER_OF_NONBLANKS : INTEGER := 0;
begin -- Main
    PUT ( "Enter a line of text" ); NEW_LINE;
    PUT ( "and then press the return key." ); NEW_LINE;
    PUT ( "I will compute the number of nonblanks." ); NEW_LINE;
    loop
        exit when END_OF_LINE;
        GET ( A_CHARACTER );
        if A_CHARACTER /= BLANK then
            NUMBER_OF_NONBLANKS := NUMBER_OF_NONBLANKS + 1;
        end if;
    end loop;
    PUT ( "The number of nonblank characters in the line is " );
    PUT ( NUMBER_OF_NONBLANKS );
    NEW_LINE;
end MAIN;
```

Sample Dialogue 1

```
Enter a line of text
and then press the return key.
I will compute the number of nonblanks.
Jean Ichbiah led the team that developed Ada.
The number of nonblank characters in the line is          38
```

Sample Dialogue 2

```
Enter a line of text
and then press the return key.
I will compute the number of nonblanks.
Augusta Ada Lovelace worked with Charles Babbage.
The number of nonblank characters in the line is          43
```

Figure 7.4 Program using END_OF_LINE.

end-of-line character

The exact description of how to determine the value of END_OF_LINE involves a special character called the *end-of-line character.* When the user presses the return key, the *end-of-line character* is sent to the computer as input. The character is not shown on the screen, but its presence is indicated by the start of a new line. When the program has read all the data on one line, the next character of input is this end-of-line character. When the program executes a SKIP_LINE, this end-of-line character is skipped over. The boolean END_OF_LINE has the value TRUE whenever the next input character is the end-of-line character; otherwise, its value is FALSE. Normally one can simply think of END_OF_LINE as being TRUE when the computer is "at the end of a line," but in some subtle situations you may need to think in terms of the end-of-line character.

As a precaution, END_OF_LINE should be used only when reading character information; it should not be used when reading numeric data. When reading numeric data and testing for END_OF_LINE, the simple addition of a space character after the last number on a line may cause your program to terminate unexpectedly when it attempts to read past the end-of-line character to find the next number.

Off-Line Data and a Preview of END_OF_FILE (Optional)

Data is sometimes prepared ahead of time rather than entered by the user one piece of data at a time from the keyboard. This is sometimes called *off-line data.* For example, the data might consist of experimental data collected over a long period of time and given to a program for statistical analysis. Such data is likely to be read by the program directly from some electronic media. In Chapters 13 and 16, we discuss methods for reading data off-line. Some systems have other methods for entering data that has been prepared ahead of time. In all these cases there is no need to give prompt lines like the following since there is nobody to read them:

```
PUT ( "Enter a list of nonnegative integers" ); NEW_LINE;
PUT ( ' and I will compute their sum." ); NEW_LINE;
PUT ( 'Place a negative number after the list" ); NEW_LINE;
```

Since the data is known to be ready and waiting, there is no need for any prompt lines at all.

Also, there is no point in asking the user to reenter the data if the data is not appropriate; there is nobody there to follow the instructions. In the case of off-line data, all the data must be carefully prepared to be certain that it is in the form expected by the program.

With such programs the output is also in a different format. Since the output is not given in a dialogue with the user, the output should be annotated carefully to indicate which output is paired with which input. When the output is read by the user, the input will not be at hand automatically, so the output should include sufficient information about the input to allow the user to interpret the output data. For example, the output might write the corresponding inputs and outputs next to each other.

end_of_file

Off-line data is stored in units called *files*. When data is read off-line from one of these files, the end of the file can be detected by an Ada program in much the same way that it detects the end of a line. The predefined boolean function END_OF_FILE is FALSE as long as there is any input left and changes to TRUE as soon as the program has read all the input. The use of END_OF_FILE is similar to that of END_OF_LINE. For example, the following loop sums a list of numbers that are read off-line. The numbers are stored one per line.

```
SUM := 0;
loop
    exit when END_OF_FILE;
    GET ( NUMBER ); SKIP_LINE;
    SUM := SUM + NUMBER;
end loop;
```

It is safest to use a GET followed by a SKIP_LINE when using END_OF_FILE with numeric data. This does, of course, require that the numbers being input be stored one per line in the file.

text files

You must somehow specify that a program is using off-line data. Some systems have special instructions that apply to one specific installation or system. You should check your local installation to see if there is a simple way to specify that data is to be read off-line. In Chapter 13 we discuss one method that works for all Ada systems. If you want to cover some of the material earlier than that, you can read some of Chapter 13, which introduces a form of off-line data called *text files*. It can be read and understood without the material that precedes it. You can then return to this point and continue reading.

Modifying an Algorithm

One way to solve a problem is to modify a solution for a similar problem. Earlier we used a sentinel loop to compute the sum of a list of numbers. A simple modification can change it into a program to compute the average of a list of numbers. The modification is to add a variable COUNT to the loop. This variable will count the number of times the loop is iterated and hence will end with a value equal to the number of numbers read in. To obtain the average, the program simply divides the sum by COUNT. The modified program is given in Figure 7.5.

All of the loops we have used in previous chapters have had the **exit when** as the first thing inside the loop. This form of loop statement is called a pretest loop. Not only can we have pretest loops, but we also can have *midtest loops* where **exit when** can appear in the middle of the loop. In fact the **exit when** can be placed anywhere within the loop and as often as it is needed. In our next case study, we will see exactly how to take advantage of the free placement of the **exit when** inside a loop. In another example later in this chapter, we also will use multiple exits.

Program

```
with I_O; use I_O;
procedure MAIN is
--                  INPUT  : A list of integers.
--                  OUTPUT : The average of a list of integers.
--                  DESCRIPTION : Computes the average of
--                                a list of integers, not including
--                                the last value, which is negative.
    AVERAGE : FLOAT;
    COUNT   : INTEGER := 0;
    NUMBER  : INTEGER;
    SUM : INTEGER := 0;
begin -- Main
    PUT ( "Enter a list of integers all on one line" ); NEW_LINE;
    PUT ( "The last number should be a negative value." ); NEW_LINE;
    PUT ( "I will compute their average." ); NEW_LINE;
    loop
        GET ( NUMBER );
        exit when NUMBER < 0;
        SUM := SUM + NUMBER;
        COUNT := COUNT + 1;
    end loop;
    if COUNT = 0 then
        PUT ( "No numbers read in." ); NEW_LINE;
    else
        AVERAGE := FLOAT ( SUM ) / FLOAT ( COUNT );
        PUT ( COUNT ); PUT ( " numbers read in." ); NEW_LINE;
        PUT ( "The average is " ); PUT ( AVERAGE, 2, 2, 0 ); NEW_LINE;
    end if;
end MAIN;
```

Sample Dialogue

```
Enter a list of integers all on one line.
The last number should be a negative value.
I will compute their average.
90 88 73 50 100 -1
     5 numbers read in.
The average is 80.20
```

Figure 7.5 Averaging program.

Case Study

Finding the Largest and Smallest Values on a List

You often will want to end a loop part way through the body of the loop. For example, on the last iteration of a loop that has three statements, you might want the loop to execute only the first one or the first two statements and then end. This can be done quite easily in Ada by simply placing the **exit when** wherever it needs to be in the body of the loop; for example

```
loop
      leading__statements
      exit when boolean__expression;
      trailing__statements
end loop;
```

In this "Case Study" we will illustrate a technique for doing exactly that.

Problem Definition

As a sample design problem, consider the problem of writing a program to determine the largest and smallest value on a list of positive numbers. We will assume that the list is not empty and that it is followed by a negative number that serves as a sentinel value marking the end of the input list.

Discussion

One approach is to use two variables, LARGEST_VALUE and SMALLEST_ VALUE, to hold the largest and smallest values read in so far. After each number is read in, it is compared to LARGEST_VALUE and SMALLEST_VALUE to see if this new number is a new low or a new high value. The basic operations in the loop body are as follows.

Algorithm

first version

```
loop
    Get the next__number
    if next__number > largest__value
        largest__value := next__number
    elsif next__number < smallest__value
        smallest__value := next__number
    end if
end loop
```

Since the loop body uses the values of LARGEST_VALUE and SMALLEST_VALUE, they must be initialized so that they do have a value the first time through the loop. After processing the first number, the values of both LARGEST_VALUE and SMALLEST_VALUE should be equal to this number, because at that point it is both the largest and the smallest number seen so far. One way to initialize LARGEST_VALUE and SMALLEST_VALUE is to process one number before starting the loop. The following statements placed before the loop will initialize values correctly:

initializing variables

```
GET ( NEXT_NUMBER );
LARGEST_VALUE := NEXT_NUMBER;
SMALLEST_VALUE := NEXT_NUMBER;
```

Another approach is to take advantage of knowing the largest and smallest possible integer value that the computer will allow.

```
LARGEST_VALUE : INTEGER := INTEGER'FIRST; -- smallest integer
SMALLEST_VALUE : INTEGER := INTEGER'LAST; -- largest integer
```

This may look backwards, but by setting LARGEST_VALUE to the smallest possible integer, the algorithm above assures that it will be changed if any value larger than the smallest possible integer is input. A similar result is true for SMALLEST_VALUE.

At this point we are almost through designing the algorithm and even the Ada code. All we need to do is design the Ada code so the loop stops as soon as a negative number is read in. This does not present a problem in Ada. If we choose either approach, all we have to do is place the **exit when** after the GET in the loop. The complete program using the second approach is given in Figure 7.6.

stopping part way through the loop body

A Posttest Loop

A variation of the **loop** statement places the **exit when** just prior to the **end loop**. For example, the following loop is almost equivalent to the loop in Figure 7.3:

```
loop
     GET ( NUMBER );
     SUM := SUM + NUMBER;
     LEFT_TO_READ := LEFT_TO_READ - 1;
     exit when LEFT_TO_READ <= 0;
end loop;
```

This construction of a **loop** statement is called a *posttest loop*. It is called a posttest loop because the exit test is made after all the other statements in the body of the loop. The loops constructed as we have used them previously were called *pretest loops* or *midtest loops*. In a pretest loop the **exit when** test comes before anything else in the loop. A midtest loop has statements before and after the **exit when**.

Program

```
with I_O; use I_O;
procedure MAIN is
--                  INPUT  : A list of positive integers.
--                  OUTPUT : The largest and smallest integer.
--                  DESCRIPTION : Finds the largest and smallest
--                                integer from a list of integers.
    LARGEST  : INTEGER := INTEGER'FIRST;
    NEXT     : INTEGER;
    SMALLEST : INTEGER := INTEGER'LAST;
begin -- Main
    PUT ( "This program finds the largest and smallest" ); NEW_LINE;
    PUT ( "values on a list of positive integers." ); NEW_LINE;
    PUT ( "Enter a list of positive integers." ); NEW_LINE;
    PUT ( "Place a negative number at the end." ); NEW_LINE;
    loop
      GET ( NEXT );
      exit when NEXT < 0;
      if NEXT > LARGEST then
          LARGEST := NEXT;
      elsif NEXT < SMALLEST then
          SMALLEST := NEXT;
      end if;
    end loop;
    PUT ( "The largest is " ); PUT ( LARGEST ); NEW_LINE;
    PUT ( "The smallest is " ); PUT ( SMALLEST ); NEW_LINE;
end MAIN;
```

Sample Dialogue

```
This program finds the largest and smallest
values on a list of positive integers.
Enter a list of positive integers.
Place a negative number at the end.
3 2 7 5 -1
The largest is      7
The smallest is     2
```

Figure 7.6 Program to compute largest and smallest numbers.

With a posttest loop the loop body is always executed at least once. When a posttest loop is executed, the first thing that happens is that all of the statements in the loop body are executed. The boolean expression in the **exit when** is evaluated last. If it evaluates to FALSE, the loop body is repeated and the boolean expression is evaluated one more time. After each iteration of the loop body, the boolean expression is reevaluated. If the boolean expression evaluates to TRUE, the loop is ended and the program proceeds to the next statement.

action of a posttest loop

Comparison of Pretest and Posttest Loops

There is no syntactic difference between a pretest and a posttest loop. It is simply a matter of placing the **exit when** as the first statement (pretest) or the last statement (posttest) in the sequence of statements that make up the body of a loop. There is no difference in the **exit when** statement itself. It works exactly the same for both pretest and posttest loops. If the boolean expression evaluates to TRUE, the program exits the loop; otherwise, it does not and the loop repeats.

The main difference between the two types of **loop** statements is that with a posttest loop, the body of the loop is always executed at least once. A pretest loop is more general and allows the possibility that the rest of the loop body may not be executed at all. Hence, if we use the sample posttest loop of the previous section to replace the pretest loop in Figure 7.3, then the program will no longer be able to cope with empty lists. You cannot use a posttest loop unless you are certain that, under all circumstances, the entire loop body should be executed at least once.

Exercises

Self-Test Exercises

5. What is the output of the following program?

```
with I_O; use I_O;
procedure MAIN is
    THRICE : INTEGER := 10;
begin -- Main
    loop
        THRICE := THRICE - 3;
        exit when THRICE <= 0;
    end loop;
    PUT ( THRICE ); NEW_LINE;
end MAIN;
```

6. What is the biggest difference between a posttest loop and a pretest loop?

7. Write a program that reads in a line of text and then echoes just the last letter. The characters are read one at a time into a variable of type CHARACTER using a loop. The loop is terminated using END_OF_LINE, and then the last character read in is echoed. So for the input

pineapple pasta

the output is the single letter *a*.

Case Study

Testing a Procedure

We have advocated testing procedures separately by writing a small test program for each procedure. To add to our confidence in the correctness of the procedure, we need to test it with a number of different parameter values. A posttest loop in the test program will allow us to test the procedure as often as we wish without having to rerun the test program.

For example, in Chapter 6 we wrote a program to test a procedure named OUTPUT_COINS. That program tested one set of parameter values and then terminated. If we add a posttest loop, as shown in Figure 7.7, then we can test the input on several different sets of parameter values without having to rerun the program.

Program

```
with I_O; use I_O;
procedure MAIN is
    ANSWER : CHARACTER;
    AMOUNT,
    NUMBER_OF_DIMES,
    NUMBER_OF_NICKELS,
    NUMBER_OF_PENNIES,
    NUMBER_OF_QUARTERS : INTEGER;
    procedure OUTPUT_COINS ( CHANGE,
                             QUARTERS,
                             DIMES,
                             NICKELS,
                             PENNIES : in INTEGER ) is
--                    INPUT  : 0 < change <= 99 cents and
--                             the appropriate number of each coin.
--                    OUTPUT : None
--                    DESCRIPTION : Displays a collection of coins
--                                  that total to change cents.
--  The rest of the procedure is shown in Figure 6.9
```

```
begin -- Main
    loop
        PUT ( "Enter: Quarters, Dimes, Nickels, Pennies:" ); NEW_LINE;
        GET ( NUMBER_OF_QUARTERS );
        GET ( NUMBER_OF_DIMES );
        GET ( NUMBER_OF_NICKELS );
        GET ( NUMBER_OF_PENNIES );
        SKIP_LINE;
        AMOUNT := 25 * NUMBER_OF_QUARTERS
                + 10 * NUMBER_OF_DIMES
                +  5 * NUMBER_OF_NICKELS
                +      NUMBER_OF_PENNIES;
        OUTPUT_COINS ( AMOUNT,
                       NUMBER_OF_QUARTERS,
                       NUMBER_OF_DIMES,
                       NUMBER_OF_NICKELS,
                       NUMBER_OF_PENNIES );
        PUT ( "Do you want to test again? (y/n)" ); NEW_LINE;
        GET ( ANSWER ); SKIP_LINE;
        exit when ANSWER = 'n'
              or ANSWER = 'N';
    end loop;
    PUT ( "End of testing" ); NEW_LINE;
end MAIN;
```

Sample Dialogue

```
Enter: Quarters, Dimes, Nickels, Pennies:
1 0 1 2
32 cents can be given as:
one quarter, one nickel and 2 pennies
Do you want to test again? (y/n)
y
Enter: Quarters, Dimes, Nickels, Pennies:
2 0 1 2
57 cents can be given as:
2 quarters, one nickel and 2 pennies
Do you want to test again? (y/n)
n
End of testing
```

Figure 7.7 Testing a procedure.

When you read Figure 7.7, you need not look back at the previous chapter to see the body of the procedure. The procedure heading and the comment are all you need in order to understand the loop. The sample dialogue is short due to space limitations. This procedure should be tested on many more than the two sets of values shown.

Multiple Exit Loop

It is possible to have a loop with a pretest and a posttest. That means that an **exit when** would appear just after the word **loop** and another would appear just before the **end loop.**

```
loop
     exit when condition_1;
     .
     .
     exit when condition_2;
end loop;
```

As an example of when you might need both pretest and posttest loops, assume we wish to read in numbers until we reach the end of the file but no more than say 10 values.

```
SUM := 0;
COUNT := 0;
loop
     exit when END_OF_FILE;
     GET ( NUMBER ); SKIP_LINE;
     COUNT := COUNT + 1;
     exit when COUNT = 10;
end loop;
```

In this example, once COUNT has been incremented to **10**, an **exit when** tests that fact and terminates the loop. There is no reason to go back to the beginning of the loop and test END_OF_FILE again.

Some experts feel that the multiple exit loop is poor programming style. However, the multiple exit loop is really very similar to the **case** statement in that there are multiple exit paths from the statement. There are applications in which the multiple exit loop is very useful.

The Exit Statement

There is another cleaner way to accomplish the same thing: use an **exit** statement. The **exit when** is called a *conditional* exit, because the exit of the loop occurs only if the condition (the boolean expression) is TRUE. The **exit** statement is *unconditional*; when the statement is executed, the loop in which it appears is finished and execution of the program takes up with the statement after the **end loop**. The following is an example of how to use the **exit** to help clean up the READ_CHECK procedure.

```
VALUE : INTEGER;
loop
    PUT ( "Enter an amount in the range of 0 to 100." );
    NEW_LINE;
    GET ( VALUE ); SKIP_LINE;
    if VALUE in 0 . . 100 then
        exit;
    else
        PUT ( "Error, try again." ); NEW_LINE ( 2 );
    end if;
end loop;
AMOUNT := VALUE;
```

At first glance a **loop** statement without an **exit when** looks like the dreaded infinite loop. Upon closer inspection you see an **exit** statement nested inside an **if** statement. This is the normal way that the **exit** is used. If the input value is in the range 0 to 100, we exit the loop and assign AMOUNT the input value. If the input value is not in the proper range, we output an error message and continue by repeating the loop. The only way out of this loop is to get the correct input.

Designing Robust Programs

A program that aborts or does something useless because the user made a slight typing mistake can be maddening to use. To the extent that it is possible you should design your programs so that they can cope with minor mistakes on the part of the user. A program should be *robust* enough to perform correctly despite some minor abuse. Thus, if possible, a program should adapt itself to the user rather than the other way around. Such easy-to-use programs are often referred to as *user friendly,* a pleasant term for a pleasant concept.

upper- and lowercase letters in input

For example, if the user is supposed to enter a letter, the program should accept either an uppercase or lowercase letter. If the letter is used to control a **case** statement, then both upper- and lowercase letters should normally be used in the lists of choices.

```
case LETTER is
    when 'A' | 'a' => . . .
```

If the user is supposed to type in **y** for yes, the program test should read something like

```
if ANSWER = 'y'
or ANSWER = 'Y' then . . .
```

We have already used these techniques in the programs in Figures 6.7 and earlier in this chapter when discussing asking the user. If the idea is not clear, you may want to review these programs.

retry input Another helpful feature is to echo input and let the user retype the input if it has been entered incorrectly. Sometimes the program can check the data for appropriateness. The procedure in Figure 7.8 reads in an integer and allows the user to retry until it is in the desired range.

```
procedure READ_CHECK ( AMOUNT : out INTEGER ) is
--                    INPUT  : None
--                    OUTPUT : An amount in the range 0 . . 100.
--                    DESCRIPTION : Prompts the user and requires
--                                  retries until the value read in
--                                  is in the range of 0 to 100.
    VALUE : INTEGER;
begin -- Read_Check
    PUT ( "Enter an amount in the range of 0 to 100." ); NEW_LINE;
    GET ( VALUE ); SKIP_LINE;
    loop
        exit when VALUE in 0 . . 100;
        PUT ( "Error, try again." ); NEW_LINE;
        PUT ( "Enter an amount in the range of 0 to 100." ); NEW_LINE;
        GET ( VALUE ); SKIP_LINE;
    end loop;
    AMOUNT := VALUE;
end READ_CHECK;
```

Figure 7.8 Robust input procedure.

The one exception in the group of IO_EXCEPTIONS that we will discuss at this point is DATA_ERROR. It would be surprising if you had not already encountered it. DATA_ERROR will be raised if the value input as the result of executing a GET statement is not of the same type as the variable in the GET statement. For example, assume the variable E is of type FLOAT and the statement GET (E); is executed. Now suppose that you intend to type in **2.79**, but you type a comma instead of a period and hit the enter key with **2,79** appearing on the screen. Since the GET is expecting a floating point value and what you gave it is not, DATA_ERROR will be raised and your program will terminate with "Unhandled DATA_ERROR" appearing on the screen.

To improve the robustness of a program, we could give the user a chance to verify the input. We could put the input statement in a loop along with output statements to echo the input and ask if it was okay, or the program could test the input to see if the value was within the proper range. These definitely would be an improvement, but it still would not work if the user input was out-of-range or simply unacceptable characters. As we have just seen, there is a method that will allow us to trap bad data. Now we will show you how you can combine the echoing technique used previously and exception handlers to make the input procedure basically bulletproof. To accomplish this we must first introduce one more construct.

Figure 7.9 is an input procedure used with an exception handler in a block statement to trap improper data. The procedure GET_INPUT assumes the following declaration in the main procedure:

```
subtype ZERO_TO_100 is INTEGER range 0 . . 100;
```

The procedure in Figure 7.9 has an infinite loop that allows the user to try and try again until the input is acceptable. The only way the user can get out of the loop is by indicating satisfaction with the value. Note the **exit** that is nested inside the **if**. Only when the user answers 'y' will the loop terminate and AMOUNT be assigned a value.

Procedure

```
procedure GET_INPUT ( AMOUNT : out ZERO_TO_100 ) is
    ANSWER : CHARACTER;
    VALUE : ZERO_TO_100;
begin -- Get_Input
    loop
        PUT ( "Input a value in the range 0 to 100" ); NEW_LINE;
        begin
            GET ( VALUE ); SKIP_LINE;
            PUT ( "Is this value correct? (y/n) " );
            PUT ( VALUE ); NEW_LINE;
            GET ( ANSWER ); SKIP_LINE;
            if ANSWER = 'y' then
                exit;
            end if;
        exception
            when DATA_ERROR =>
                SKIP_LINE;
                PUT ( "Bad character in input, try again." );
                NEW_LINE;
            when CONSTRAINT_ERROR =>
                SKIP_LINE;
                PUT ( "Input out of the range 0 to 100, " );
                PUT ( "try again." ); NEW_LINE;
        end;
    end loop;
    AMOUNT := VALUE;
end GET_INPUT;
```

Sample Dialogue

```
Input a value in the range 0 to 100
o
Bad character in input, try again.
Input a value in the range 0 to 100
1000
Input out of the range 0 to 100, try again.
Input a value in the range 0 to 100
100
Is this value correct? (y/n)  100
n
Input a value in the range 0 to 100
50
Is this value correct? (y/n)   50
y
```

Figure 7.9 Bulletproof input procedure.

Also inside the loop is a block statement that begins just prior to the GET statement and ends just prior to the end of the loop. The block statement has an exception handler that handles two different exceptions. The first exception handler is for bad data, when the user has entered characters that are not acceptable as integer values, such as 'o' instead of '0'. The second exception handler is for trapping values that are not in the range 0 to 100, such as 101 or 1000. Both of the exception handlers have as their first statement a SKIP_LINE. The SKIP_LINE is there to clear any other characters that might have been entered before the **enter** key was pressed. The SKIP_LINE also assures that the user will be starting with a clean input line the next time around the loop.

The sample dialogue demonstrates the action of the procedure GET_INPUT. When the character **o** is entered after the prompt line appears on the screen, the exception DATA_ERROR is raised. Normal execution stops with the statement GET (VALUE);. Control transfers to the exception handler in the block where the exception is raised. There is an exception handler for the exception DATA_ERROR in the block statement inside the procedure. Thus the exception is lowered, and execution continues with the statements after the arrow in the exception handler for DATA_ERROR. The three statements

```
SKIP_LINE;
PUT ( "Bad character is input, try again." );
NEW_LINE;
```

are executed. Execution skips over the other exception handler to the end of the block statement to the end of the loop and around to the prompt line again.

The second time around the loop the value **1000** is input, which raises the exception CONSTRAINT_ERROR. The exception is raised because the value is outside the range of the variable VALUE, which is of the **subtype** ZERO_TO_100. The three statements

```
SKIP_LINE;
PUT ( "Input out of the range 0 to 100, " );
PUT ( "try again." );
NEW_LINE;
```

in the exception handler for CONSTRAINT_ERROR are executed, and around the loop we go again.

The third time the loop is executed, the value **100** is input. No exception is raised and the question is displayed on the screen. The answer **n** is given, so around the loop we go one more time.

The fourth time the value **50** is input. No exception is raised. The answer **y** is given so we exit the loop and assign AMOUNT the value **50**. The procedure is now terminated and control is transferred to the calling procedure.

Loop Statement Prefix—While and For

The **loop** statement, with its various exit capabilities, is the only looping mechanism that is really needed to make the language complete. Ada does however provide for two **loop** statement prefixes that serve as control mechanisms for the loop. These two prefixes are named for the reserved words with which they begin: **while** and **for**. Neither of these preclude the use of any exit from inside the loop, as we have done in previous examples.

while loop

The **while** prefix for the **loop** statement really adds little new to the power of the language and is basically a holdover from previous computer programming languages from which Ada was derived. It is included here for the sake of completeness.

The loop with a **while** prefix is a pretest loop similar to what we have previously discussed, but slightly different in appearance and control strategy. First, we deal with appearance.

The syntax for the loop with a **while** prefix is as follows:

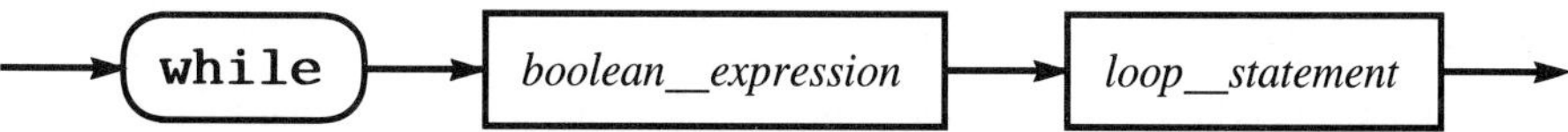

Now you can see why it is called a loop prefix, for it is something that can appear before a loop statement. The *loop_statement* is the same **loop** statement we have been discussing so far in this chapter. The *boolean_expression* that controls the repeating of the loop appears outside the loop, but don't let that fool you; it is still reevaluated at the beginning of each iteration of the loop.

The other difference is the value of the boolean expression that causes the loop to repeat. You can read it this way: "While the boolean expression is true, repeat the loop." In other words, if the boolean expression evaluates to TRUE, execute the loop statement; otherwise, do not execute the **loop** statement, but continue execution of the program with the statement immediately following the **end loop**. The following examples point out the syntactic difference between the **while** and the equivalent standard pretest loop:

```
loop
    exit when END_OF_FILE;
    GET ( LETTER );
    .
    .
end loop;
```

```
while not END_OF_FILE
loop
    GET ( NUMBER );
    .
    .
end loop;
```

```
GET ( NUMBER );
loop
    exit when NUMBER < 0;
    SUM := SUM + NUMBER;
    GET ( NUMBER );
end loop;
```

```
GET ( NUMBER );
while NUMBER >= 0
loop
    SUM := SUM + NUMBER;
    GET ( NUMBER );
end loop;
```

for loop

There is one sort of loop that is so common that Ada includes a special "tailor-made" **loop** statement prefix for it. In performing numeric calculations, it is common to do a calculation with the number 1, then with 2, then with 3, and so forth, until some last value is reached. For example, to write out the "2 times table," we want the computer to perform the following:

```
PUT ("2 times " ); PUT ( number ); PUT ( " is " );
PUT ( 2 * number ); NEW_LINE;
```

first with NUMBER equal to **1**, then with NUMBER equal to **2**, and so forth up to, say, **9**. One way to do this is with a pretest loop statement such as

```
NUMBER := 1;
loop
    exit when NUMBER > 9;
    PUT ("2 times " ); PUT ( NUMBER ); PUT ( " is " );
    PUT ( 2 * NUMBER ); NEW_LINE;
    NUMBER := NUMBER + 1;
end loop;
```

Although a pretest loop will do here, this sort of situation is just what the *for prefix* was designed for. The above piece of code will produce the same output as the following **loop** statement with a **for** prefix:

```
for NUMBER in 1 . . 9
loop
    PUT ("2 times " ); PUT ( NUMBER ); PUT ( " is " );
    PUT ( 2 * NUMBER ); NEW_LINE;
end loop;
```

Not only does it produce the same output, but it does exactly the same things. NUMBER is initialized to 1 at the outset, then tested for greater than 9, and at the end of the loop, it is incremented by 1 before the loop is repeated again.

syntax

The **for** prefix for the **loop** statement comes in two very similar varieties. The above example is one variety. The other variety contains the reserved word **reverse**; we will talk more about it later. The general form of the **for** prefix is

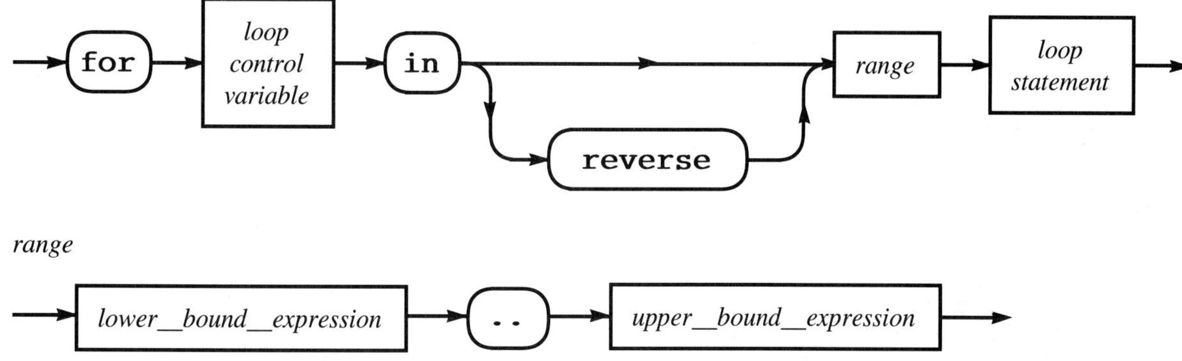

loop control variable

The *loop statement* is the same **loop** statement that we have studied throughout this chapter. The *loop__control__variable* is an identifier. The term *variable,* though, is slightly misleading. The loop control variable in a **for** loop is different from other variables in a program in several ways:

- It is not explicitly declared in the beginning of a procedure with the other variables, and it exists only within the loop. Thus it cannot be referenced outside of the loop.
- While it does take on different values during the execution of the loop, you may not write any statement that would change that value. You may use the value at any time, as you would use a constant or an **in** parameter, but you may not change the value.
- The computer takes complete control of changing the value of the loop control variable.
- The type of the loop control variable is the same type as that of the expressions in the *range.* Both expressions of the range must be of the same type.

As a quick review, remember that a range is made up of the lower bound of the range, followed by double dot, followed by the upper bound of the range (e.g., 1 . . 9).

In the examples we will start with, the expressions in the range will be of type INTEGER. Eventually we will see how to use other types for the control variable, but the idea is clearest in the case of INTEGER variables.

behavior of for loops

When the **for** loop is executed, both *lower__bound__expression* and *upper__bound__expression* are evaluated to obtain the initial and final values for the *loop__control__variable.* After that, *loop statement* is executed, with *loop__control__variable* equal to the lower bound value, then again with *loop__control__variable* equal to the value of *lower bound expression* plus 1, and again with *loop__control__variable* equal to the value of *lower__bound__expression* plus 2, and so on, increasing the value of *loop__control__variable* by **1** each time. The last time through, *loop statement* is executed with *loop__control__variable* equal to the value that was obtained from *upper__bound__expression.* This behavior is diagrammed in Figure 7.10.

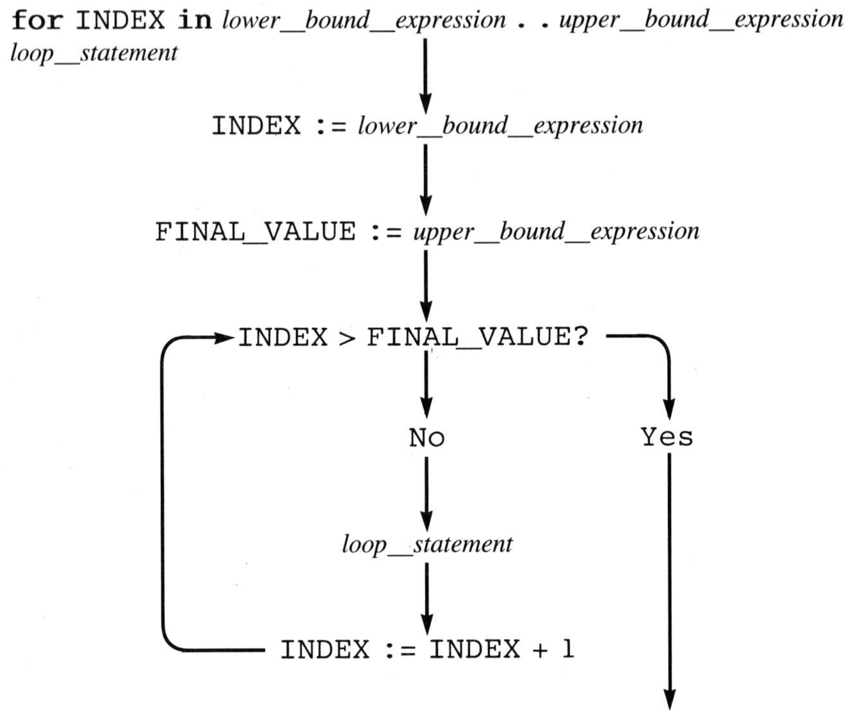

Figure 7.10 Behavior of one type of `for` loop.

A **`for`** loop need not start with 1; it can start or end at any value. However, if the loop is to start with a negated integer literal value and the `FINAL_VALUE` is a positive integer literal value, as in

```
for NUMBER in -9 . . 9
```

a compiler error will be produced. The problem deals with type incompatibility. It may seem obscure, but the fact is that integer literals are of a special type called *universal__integer.* The result of any arithmetic operation on a value of type *universal__integer* (e.g., `-9`, unary minus operation on 9) produces an `INTEGER` result. Thus `-9`, an `INTEGER`, is not compatible with 9, a *universal__integer.* Rewriting it in one of the following forms will correct the problem.

```
MINUS_NINE : INTEGER := -9;
PLUS_NINE : INTEGER := 9;

for NUMBER in MINUS_NINE . . PLUS_NINE
```

or

```
for NUMBER in INTEGER range -9 . . 9
```

or

```
for NUMBER in -9 . . INTEGER ( 9 )
```

An example of when one might want to use a negative starting value would be to give the "2 times table" for all values from negative 9 up to positive 9:

```
MINUS_NINE : INTEGER := -9;
PLUS_NINE  : INTEGER := 9;

for NUMBER in MINUS_NINE . . PLUS_NINE
loop
    PUT ("2 times " ); PUT ( NUMBER ); PUT ( " is " );
    PUT ( 2 * NUMBER ); NEW_LINE;
end loop;
```

The loop control variable is automatically increased by 1 each time through. There is no need to include anything like the following in the body of the loop:

```
NUMBER := NUMBER + 1;
```

In fact it is an error to do so. The **loop** statement is not allowed to change the loop control variable in any way. Recall that the loop control variable is a named constant to the user. The **loop** statement can use the value of the loop control variable, but it cannot change it.

restrictions on loop control variable

A loop control variable is intended to be used to control the **for** loop and nothing else. The loop control variable is declared for the user by the computer, and that declaration holds only inside the loop statement itself. The loop control variable does not exist before or after the loop. One could think of the loop control variable as a local identifier that is local to the loop statement. The loop control variable is not explicitly declared in a declaration statement as other variables are. The computer always declares the loop control variable for you.

It is natural to wonder what happens when the value of *lower_bound_expression* is greater than that of *upper_bound_expression.* In Ada when this happens, the loop statement is not executed at all, and the program goes on to the next thing. That means that in Ada it is impossible to write a **for** loop that is an infinite loop.

The **loop** statement cannot change the number of times it is iterated by changing the value of *upper_bound_expression.* The technical explanation of what happens is as follows: Both *lower_bound_expression* and *upper_bound_expression* are evaluated once at the start of the loop, and those two values are used to control the loop.

One cultural point that is of some significance to the design of readable programs has to do with names of loop control variables. Many **for** loops use **i**, **j**, and **k** as loop control variables. The reasons are historical, but it comes mainly from mathematics and its influence on early computer programming languages in general and FORTRAN in particular. Those letters carry no mnemonic value. The custom is so well ingrained that it may seem pointless to fight it, but since we intend to use meaningful identifiers in all cases, and since these letters carry no mnemonic value, we will not use them in this text. Of course, it is up to you, but if you *can* come up with good mnemonic names of **for** loop control variables, that is always the better way.

in reverse

The second version of the **for** prefix to the **loop** statement is very similar to the first. The only difference in syntax is that **reverse** is placed after the **in**. This minor syntactic change causes a major change when the loop is executed. The loop control variable is initialized to the value of *upper_bound_expression* and the loop control variable is decreased by 1 each time through. The **loop** statement terminates after it is executed with the loop control variable equal to *lower_bound_expression.* The loop control variable steps through the *range* **in reverse** order. In this case the value of *lower_bound_expression* is still typically less than or equal to that of *upper_bound_expression,* and if it is not, then the loop statement is not executed at all and the program proceeds to the next statement. The words **in reverse** are two separate reserved words, and they must be separated by at least one space.

other increment sizes

In Ada a **for** loop control variable is always changed to either the next larger value in the range or the next smaller value when **in reverse** is used. Other programming languages allow it to change by any specified amount. At first this looks like a real limitation in Ada, but it is easy to program around this limitation. To output the even numbers 0, 2, 4, 6, 8, 10, the following trick works:

```
for INDEX in 0 . . 5
loop
    PUT ( 2 * INDEX );
end loop;
```

Of course, this same loop problem can be handled with an ordinary loop, which may be more straightforward.

```
INDEX := 0;
loop
    exit when INDEX > 10;
    PUT ( INDEX );
    INDEX := INDEX + 2;
end loop;
```

This same sort of trick can be used to get something equivalent to increments of fractional size as well. To see the effect of small changes in interest rates, one might use a **for** loop such as the following:

```
for COUNT in 10 . . 200
loop
    RATE := 0.001 * FLOAT ( COUNT );
    INTEREST := AMOUNT * RATE;
```

```
        PUT ( "A rate of " );
        PUT ( RATE * 100.0, 2, 1, 0 );
        PUT ( " percent, yields " );
        PUT ( " in interest" );
        NEW_LINE;
    end loop;
```

Again the use of an ordinary loop in the following example, which produces the same output, might be more straightforward:

```
    RATE := 1.0;
    loop
        exit when RATE > 20.0;
        INTEREST := AMOUNT * ( RATE / 100.0 );
        PUT ( "A rate of " ); PUT ( RATE, 1, 2, 0 );
        PUT ( " percent, yields " ); PUT ( INTEREST, 3, 2, 0 );
        PUT ( " in interest" ); NEW_LINE;
        RATE := RATE + 0.1;
    end loop;
```

Example—Summing a Series

Figure 7.11 contains a complete program that includes a **for** loop. The program computes the average number of times you need to flip a coin to get the coin to come up heads. The program uses the following formula to approximate the average:

$$\frac{1}{2^1} + \frac{2}{2^2} + \frac{3}{2^3} + \ldots + \frac{n}{2^n}$$

We need not concern ourselves with deriving the formula. We will simply assume that it works. Like many such formulas it yields an approximation to the desired value rather than the exact value. As the number of terms in the equation (**n**) is increased, we get better approximations to the true value of this average. When the number of terms equals 100, it is more than large enough to give as much accuracy as most computers are capable of delivering, and so the program uses the formula with **n** set equal to 100.

sums versus products

Notice that SUM is initialized to zero, while POWER_OF_TWO is initialized to 1. This is because SUM will contain a sum of numbers, while POWER_OF_TWO will contain a product of numbers. One way to check that these are the correct initial values is to see what would happen in the assignment statement

```
    POWER_OF_TWO := POWER_OF_TWO * 2.0;
```

if you were to initialize POWER__OF__TWO to zero.

Program

```
with I_O; use I_O;
procedure MAIN is
--                 INPUT  : None.
--                 OUTPUT : The average number of coin tosses to
--                          get a head.
--                 DESCRIPTION : Sums a series to compute the
--                               average number of coin tosses
--                               required to get a head
--                               the first time.
--                               The series is the sum of
--                               i / 2 to the power of i
--                               as i goes from 1 to 100.
    NUMBER_OF_TERMS : constant INTEGER := 100;
    POWER_OF_TWO : FLOAT := 1.0;
    SUM : FLOAT := 0.0;
begin
    for INDEX in 1 .. NUMBER_OF_TERMS
    loop
        POWER_OF_TWO := POWER_OF_TWO * 2.0;
        SUM := SUM + FLOAT ( INDEX ) / POWER_OF_TWO;
    end loop;
    PUT ( "On the average it will take " );
    PUT ( SUM, 1, 3, 0 );
    NEW_LINE;
    PUT ( "tosses of a balanced coin" ); NEW_LINE;
    PUT ( "to get heads the first time." ); NEW_LINE;
end MAIN;
```

Figure 7.11 Summing a series.

Also notice that POWER_OF_TWO is declared to be of type FLOAT, even though its value is conceptually an integer. The reason for this is that the value of POWER_OF_TWO becomes extremely large and on most systems would produce NUMERIC_ERROR caused by integer overflow; that is, its value quickly would become larger than INTEGER'LAST. Since computers can store much larger FLOAT values than they can INTEGER values, the change to type FLOAT overcomes this problem. When doing numeric calculations with **for** loops, this can be a common problem. We will have more to say about this problem in Chapter 15.

Repeat N Times

One often encounters a section of pseudocode similar to the following:

```
repeat the following loop body n times
loop
    Get a number
    add it to sum
end loop
```

Some programming languages have a loop construct that corresponds exactly to this type of loop. Ada does not, but it is easy to construct the equivalent of "repeat the loop body **n** times." Our first example of a program with a loop, shown in Figure 7.3, illustrates one way to do this with a pretest loop, but the easiest way to implement it is with a **for** loop.

```
for COUNTER in 1 . . NUMBER_OF_TIMES
loop
    GET ( NUMBER );
    SUM := SUM + NUMBER;
end loop;
```

At first this may seem strange since the loop control variable (in this case COUNTER) does not appear in the loop body. There is nothing wrong with that. It is perfectly legitimate to use it for nothing other than counting the number of loop iterations.

What Kind of Loop to Use

The choice of which type of Ada **loop** statement to use is best postponed until the end of the design process. First design the loop using pseudocode, and then translate the pseudocode into Ada code. At that point it is easy to decide what type of Ada **loop** statement to use.

If the loop involves a numeric calculation that is repeated a fixed number of times using a value that is changed by equal amounts each time through the loop, then use a **for** loop. In fact any time you have a loop for a numeric calculation, you should consider using a **for** loop. It will not always be possible, but in many cases of numeric calculations it is the clearest and easiest loop to use. A **for** loop is also the easiest way to construct the equivalent of an instruction that says "repeat the loop body **n** times."

In most other cases, you will probably use a pretest or a posttest loop. It is fairly easy to decide whether to use a pretest or a posttest loop. If you want to insist that the loop body will be executed at least once, then you may use a posttest loop. If there are circumstances in which the loop body should not be executed at all, then you cannot use a posttest loop, and you must use a pretest loop. A common situation that demands a pretest loop is when there is a possibility of no data at all. For example, if the program reads in a list of exam scores, there may be cases of students who have taken no exams, so the input loop may be faced with an empty list. This calls for a pretest loop.

Nested Loops

Figure 7.12 contains a program that writes out the times table. The **for** loop in the main body of the program writes out one line for each value of ROW_NUMBER from zero to nine using the procedure called PRINT_ROW (ROW_NUMBER). The procedure PRINT_ROW writes out the number ROW to label the row and then writes the table entries for ROW times the COLUMN numbers zero to nine.

The body of a loop may contain any kind of statement, so it is possible to have loops nested within loops. The program in Figure 7.12 contains a loop within a loop. Normally we do not think of it as containing a nested loop, because the inner loop is contained within a procedure, and it is the procedure call that is contained in the outer loop. There is a lesson to be learned from these unobtrusively nested loops: Nested loops are no different than any other loops. Figure 7.13 is another version of the times table program, with the nested loop explicitly displayed. The nested loop in Figure 7.13 is executed once for each value of ROW from zero to nine. For each such iteration of the outer **for** loop, there is one complete execution of the inner **for** loop.

Program

```
with I_O; use I_O;
procedure MAIN is
--                  INPUT  : None.
--                  OUTPUT : Multiplications table.
--                  DESCRIPTION : Computes and outputs a multiplication
--                                table for values 0 through 9.
    WIDTH : constant INTEGER := 4;
    procedure PRINT_HEADINGS is
--                   INPUT  : None.
--                   OUTPUT : Headings.
--                   DESCRIPTION : Displays the headings for the
--                                 multiplication table and a line
--                                 of digits from 0 to 9.
    begin -- Print_Headings
        PUT ( " The Multiplication Table" ); NEW_LINE;
        PUT ( " *" );
        for COLUMN in 0 .. 9
        loop
            PUT ( COLUMN, WIDTH );
        end loop;
        NEW_LINE;
    end PRINT_HEADINGS;
```

```
    procedure PRINT_ROW ( ROW : in INTEGER ) is
--                     INPUT  : The row number for the table.
--                     OUTPUT : The row number followed by
--                              the values in the table for that row.
--                     DESCRIPTION : Computes and prints the values
--                                   row*0, row*1, row*2, . . . row*9
    begin -- Print_Row
        PUT ( ROW, WIDTH );
        for COLUMN in 0 . . 9
        loop
            PUT ( ROW * COLUMN, WIDTH );
        end loop;
        NEW_LINE;
    end PRINT_ROW;

begin -- Main
    PRINT_HEADINGS;
    for ROW_NUMBER in 0 . . 9
    loop
        PRINT_ROW ( ROW_NUMBER );
    end loop;
end MAIN;
```

Output

```
           The Multiplication Table
*    0    1    2    3    4    5    6    7    8    9
0    0    0    0    0    0    0    0    0    0    0
1    0    1    2    3    4    5    6    7    8    9
2    0    2    4    6    8   10   12   14   16   18
3    0    3    6    9   12   15   18   21   24   27
4    0    4    8   12   16   20   24   28   32   36
5    0    5   10   15   20   25   30   35   40   45
6    0    6   12   18   24   30   36   42   48   54
7    0    7   14   21   28   35   42   49   56   63
8    0    8   16   24   32   40   48   56   64   72
9    0    9   18   27   36   45   54   63   72   81
```

Figure 7.12 Times table program, one version.

The two versions of our times table program are equivalent, but many people find the version in Figure 7.12 easier to understand because the loop body is a procedure. This is an example of procedural abstraction. When considering the outer loop, we think of printing a row as a single operation and not as a loop. When writing or reading explicitly displayed nested loops, like the one in Figure 7.13, one should think of the loop body as a unit in this way, whether or not it is encased in a procedure.

procedural abstraction

```
with I_O; use I_O;
procedure MAIN is
--                 INPUT  : None.
--                 OUTPUT : Multiplications table.
--                 DESCRIPTION : Computes and outputs a multiplication
--                               table for values 0 through 9.
    WIDTH : constant INTEGER := 4;
    procedure PRINT_HEADINGS is
--                    INPUT  : None.
--                    OUTPUT : Headings.
--                    DESCRIPTION : Displays the headings for the
--                                  multiplication table and a line
--                                  of digits from 0 to 9.
    begin -- Print_Headings
        PUT ( " *" );
        for COLUMN in 0 . . 9
        loop
                PUT ( COLUMN, WIDTH );
        end loop;
        NEW_LINE;
    end PRINT_HEADINGS;

begin -- Main
    PRINT_HEADINGS;
    for ROW_NUMBER in 0 . . 9
    loop
        PUT ( ROW_NUMBER, WIDTH );
        for COLUMN in 0 . . 9
        loop
                PUT ( ROW_NUMBER * COLUMN, WIDTH );
        end loop;
        NEW_LINE;
    end loop;
end MAIN;
```

Figure 7.13 Nested `for` loop.

Exit from Nested Loops

The **`exit`** and **`exit when`** statements are limited in scope. The execution of either form of exit causes a transfer of control to the statement immediately after the **`end loop`** for the **`loop`** in which the exit resides.

Thus if loops are nested inside one another, the execution of an exit in the inner loop does not take you out of the entire loop structure but only to the end of the loop where the exit is. Consider the following example of nested loops. When *inner__condition* is `TRUE` and the statement **`exit when`** *inner__condition* is executed, the next statement to be executed will be *statement__outer__2*. That is the statement immediately after **`end loop;`** `-- Inner`. When *outer__condition* is `TRUE` and the statement **`exit when`** *outer__condition* is executed, the next__statement to be executed will be *next__statement,* the statement after **`end loop;`** `-- Outer`.

```
loop -- Outer
    statement__outer__1
    loop -- Inner
        statement__inner__1
        . . .
        exit when inner__condition
        statement__inner__n
        . . .
    end loop; -- Inner
    statement__outer__2
    exit when outer__condition
        . . .
    statement__outer__n
end loop; -- Outer
next__statement
```

Debugging Loops

common errors

No matter how carefully a program is designed, sometimes mistakes will occur. In the case of loops, there is a pattern to the kinds of mistakes most often made. Most loop errors involve the first or last iteration of the loop. If you find that your loop does not perform as expected, check to see if the loop is iterated one too many or one too few times. Loops that iterate one too many or one too few times are among the most common loop bugs. Be sure that you are not confusing less-than with less-than-or-equal. Be sure that you have initialized the loop correctly. Check the possibility that the loop may sometimes need to be iterated zero times, and check that your loop handles that possibility correctly.

off-by-one errors

infinite loops

Infinite loops usually result from a mistake in the boolean expression of the **`exit when`**. Check to see that you have not reversed an inequality, confusing less-than with greater-than. Terminating a loop with a test for equality rather than something involving greater-than or less-than is another common source of infinite loops.

If you check and recheck your loop and can find no error, but the program still misbehaves, then you need to do some more sophisticated testing. First, make sure the mistake is indeed in the loop. Just because the program is performing incorrectly does not mean the bug is where you think it is. If your program was designed to be modular and is divided into procedures, then it should be easy to locate the approximate location of the bug or bugs. Once you have decided that the bug is in a particular loop, you should trace some key variables in the loop.

tracing

Tracing was introduced in Chapter 3. It consists of adding some extra PUT statements to output intermediate results so you can watch the program working. For example, consider the following piece of code:

```
SUM := 10;
COUNTER := 10;
loop
     exit when COUNTER <= 1;
     SUM := SUM + COUNTER;
     COUNTER := COUNTER - 1;
end loop;
--                 The value of sum is the sum of all integers
--                 from 10 down to 1.
```

The comment explains what the value of SUM is supposed to be. If you run this code, you will find that it does not set SUM to a value of 55, as one might expect. The value of SUM will be larger than it is supposed to be, namely 64. The loop can be tested by tracing the variable SUM; that is, by writing out its value after each iteration of the loop. Suitable output statements to do the job are shown in Figure 7.14. Notice that the temporary output statements are written in all lowercase letters. This is done so they are easy to spot as temporary statements, not part of the regular completed program, and thus are easy to find when it comes time to remove them.

```
    SUM := 10;
    COUNTER := 10;
--                    temporary output
    put ( "counter = " ); put ( counter ); new_line;
    put ( "sum = " ); put ( sum ); new_line;
    put ( "before loop" ); new_line;
    loop
         exit when COUNTER <= 1;
         SUM := SUM + COUNTER;
         COUNTER := COUNTER - 1;
--                    temporary output
         put ( "counter = " ); put ( counter );
         new_line;
         put ( "sum = " ); put ( sum ); new_line;
    end loop;
--                    temporary output
    put ( "after loop" ); new_line;
    put ( "counter = " ); put ( counter ); new_line;
    put ( "sum = " ); put ( sum ); new_line;
```

Figure 7.14 Tracing a loop.

If the loop with the trace statement is embedded in a program and run, then the source of the error will immediately become apparent. The first two values of SUM will be **10** and **20,** but the value of SUM after one iteration of the loop should be **10** + **9** or **19,** rather than **20.** Thus we can immediately see that the value of COUNTER is the source of the problem. After we discover this, it is easy to see that COUNTER should be added into SUM after it is decremented, rather than before. In other words, the correct order for the statements in the loop body is:

```
COUNTER := COUNTER - 1;
SUM := SUM + COUNTER;
```

It may seem that the trace statements that precede and follow the loop are not needed. In this case they were not, but remember that you are using trace statements because you do not know where the error is. It is dangerous to leave any possibility unchecked. A good practice is to place one trace statement before the loop, one after the loop, and one or more inside the body of the loop, even if some of these traces are ''clearly'' redundant.

long loops

The idea of tracing the loop through each iteration will work fine on a loop that is iterated 10 times, but if the loop is iterated 1000 times, it is likely to produce too much information to digest. For example, the following will produce nothing but a blur of light on a video display screen:

```
for INDEX in 0 . . 1_000
loop
    SUM := SUM + INDEX;
    PUT ( SUM ); PUT ( INDEX ); NEW_LINE;
end loop;
```

A better approach is to take a smaller sample, say

```
for INDEX in 0 . . 10
```

or by doing the following:

```
    for INDEX in 0 . . 1_000
    loop
        SUM := SUM + INDEX;
--                TEMPORARY OUTPUT
        if index rem 100 = 0 then
            put ( sum ); put ( index ); new_line;
        end if;
    end loop;
```

This will output a trace statement every time INDEX is a multiple of **100**. There is a possibility that such a uniform sampling technique will fail to detect certain kinds of periodic problems. If a trace like the above yields no insights, then try a different sampling technique such as using

```
INDEX rem 100 = 1
```

This will sample every one hundredth iteration, but the value of INDEX will not be a ''round'' number. If that fails, change **100** to some other number.

Case Study

Testing for Primes (Optional)

Problem Definition

In this section we will design a function that has one integer parameter that is tested to see if the integer is a prime number or not. The function will return TRUE if it is prime and FALSE if it is not. A *prime* number is an integer, greater than one, that has no divisors other than itself and 1. In other words, the prime numbers are the positive integers (other than 1) that cannot be factored. For example, 12 can be factored into 2 times 6 and so is not prime. The first few primes are 2, 3, 5, 7, 11, and 13. As is common when discussing prime numbers, we will confine our attention to positive integers.

Discussion

We must first design an algorithm to test a positive integer for primality. A candidate number is prime provided it has no divisors other than itself and 1. Obviously we cannot check all the positive integers to see if any of them divide into the candidate number. Fortunately for us, we know that any divisor of the number must be less than or equal to the number, so we need only test those integers that are less than the candidate number. This observation yields the heart of our algorithm:

Algorithm
first version

1. **for** each NUMBER such that 1 < NUMBER < PRIME_CANDIDATE, test **if** NUMBER divides evenly into the PRIME_CANDIDATE.
2. **if** *any such* NUMBER is a divisor of PRIME_CANDIDATE **then** report that PRIME_CANDIDATE *is not* a prime;. **if** there is *no such* NUMBER for PRIME_CANDIDATE **then** report that PRIME_CANDIDATE *is* a prime.

special cases

This function, like many functions, has some parameters that are special cases. For example, the definition of primes makes a special case of 1. It has no divisor other than 1 and itself. Yet by definition, it is not a prime. (The reason has to do with the theory of numbers and is not a topic for this book.) Although 1 is not a prime, it technically satisfies the basic test that will become the heart of our algorithm. Substituting 1 for PRIME_CANDIDATE, we see that there are no values for NUMBER such that

1 < NUMBER < 1

and such that NUMBER divides 1; in fact there is no NUMBER that even satisfies the inequality, and so certainly none that both satisfies the inequality and divides 1. Hence, we must add a special case for the parameter 1, or else our function would incorrectly claim that it is a prime. Our algorithm will include a special check to see if its parameter is 1, and if it is, it will return the value FALSE.

That leaves us with the numbers 2 and greater. One should always test the extreme values used by an algorithm to see if they are special cases. The parameter 2 is a special case. If we look at the heart of our algorithm and apply it to the number 2, it says to test all integers NUMBER such that

1 < NUMBER < 2

Since there is no such NUMBER, the test is suspect. The number 2 is a prime, and if applied rigorously, the heart of our algorithm will say that it is a prime. However, to make it easier to understand our algorithm, we will make a special case of 2. Parameter values of 3 and larger behave normally with no subtleties when we apply the heart of our algorithm to them. So our algorithm now takes shape in more detail:

Algorithm second version

1. **if** PRIME_CANDIDATE is 1 **then** it is not a prime.
2. **if** PRIME_CANDIDATE is 2 **then** it is a prime.
3. **if** PRIME_CANDIDATE > 2 **then** do the following:
   a. **for** each NUMBER such that
      1 < NUMBER < PRIME_CANDIDATE,
      test if NUMBER is a divisor of PRIME_CANDIDATE.
   b. **if** *any such* NUMBER that divides evenly into PRIME_CANDIDATE, **then** report that PRIME_CANDIDATE *is not* a prime. **if** there is *no such* NUMBER of PRIME_CANDIDATE, **then** report that PRIME_CANDIDATE *is* a prime.

refining the algorithm

The following boolean expression is TRUE if NUMBER is a divisor of PRIME_CANDIDATE and is FALSE otherwise:

```
PRIME_CANDIDATE rem NUMBER = 0
```

So step 3 can be rewritten as

```
for NUMBER in 2 . . PRIME_CANDIDATE - 1
loop
    if PRIME_CANDIDATE rem NUMBER = 0
        it is not prime, so return
end loop
no divisor for prime__candidate
it is prime, so return
```

As soon as you find any number that divides evenly into PRIME_CANDIDATE and returns FALSE, there is no reason to continue. The **return** statement terminates the function and returns a value for the function. If there is no divisor of PRIME_CANDIDATE, the loop terminates normally and you can return the fact that PRIME_CANDIDATE is indeed a prime number. The complete function body declaration embedded in a test program is displayed in Figure 7.15.

Program

```
with I_O; use I_O;
procedure MAIN is
--                 INPUT   : A positive integer.
--                 OUTPUT : A message stating whether the input
--                          number is a prime number.
--                 DESCRIPTION : Determines if the number is prime.
    NUMBER : INTEGER;
    function PRIME ( PRIME_CANDIDATE : POSITIVE )
            return BOOLEAN is
--                 INPUT   : prime_candidate > 0
--                 OUTPUT : TRUE if prime_candidate is prime
--                          otherwise FALSE.
--                 DESCRIPTION : Determines if a prime_candidate
--                               is a prime.
--                               Uses the subtype Positive and
--                               a Case with a nested For loop
--                               with a nested If.
    begin -- Prime
        case PRIME_CANDIDATE is
            when 1 => return FALSE;
            when 2 => return TRUE;
            when others =>
                for NUMBER in 2 . . PRIME_CANDIDATE - 1
                loop
                    if PRIME_CANDIDATE rem NUMBER = 0 then
                        return FALSE;
                    end if;
                end loop;
--                  no divisor for prime_candidate
                return TRUE;
        end case;
    end PRIME;
begin -- Main
    PUT ( "Enter a positive integer and" ); NEW_LINE;
    PUT ( "I will tell you if it is prime." ); NEW_LINE;
    PUT ( "Enter a zero to quit." ); NEW_LINE;
```

```
    loop
        PUT ( "Enter an integer:" ); NEW_LINE;
        GET ( NUMBER ); SKIP_LINE;
        exit when NUMBER <= 0;
        PUT ( NUMBER );
        if PRIME ( NUMBER ) then
            PUT ( " is a prime." );
        else
            PUT ( " is not a prime." );
        end if;
        NEW_LINE;
    end loop;
    PUT ( "End of program." ); NEW_LINE;
end MAIN;
```

Sample Dialogue

```
Enter a positive integer and
I will tell you if it is prime.
Enter a zero to quit.
Enter an integer:
15
    15 is not a prime.
Enter an integer:
17
    17 is a prime.
Enter an integer:
0
End of program.
```

Figure 7.15 A boolean function that tests for prime numbers.

Summary of Problem Solving and Programming Techniques

- There are four commonly used methods for terminating an input loop: asking the user before iterating the list, heading the list with its size, ending the list with a sentinel value, and running out of input. (The last one can be dangerous if not handled correctly.)
- Using the boolean END_OF_LINE or END_OF_FILE is one good way to end a loop by ''running out of input.''
- One way to design an algorithm is to modify a known algorithm that solves a related problem.

- It is usually best to design loops in pseudocode that do not specify a choice of an Ada looping mechanism. Once the algorithm has been designed, the choice of which Ada loop statement to use is usually clear.
- A posttest loop should not be used unless you are certain that the loop should always be iterated at least once.
- A **for** loop can be used to obtain the equivalent of the instruction "repeat the loop body N times."
- One way to simplify reasoning about nested loops is to make the loop body a procedure. Any **exit** or **exit when** must still be in the loop body and not in the procedure.
- Programs should be designed to be robust enough to perform adequately, even if the user makes a slight mistake in entering input.
- Always check a loop to be sure that the variables used by the loop are properly initialized before the loop begins.
- Never terminate a loop with a test of FLOAT values for equality. Tests for equality are dangerous with other types as well.
- Always check loops to be certain they are not iterated one too many or one too few times.
- When debugging loops always check the first and last iteration of the loop body.
- When debugging loops it helps to trace key variables in the loop body.
- If a program or algorithm is very difficult to understand or performs very poorly, do not try to fix it. Instead, throw it away and start over.

Summary of Ada Constructs

loop statement

Syntax:

loop *sequence_of_statements* **end loop;**

The *sequence_of_statements* can consist of any Ada statements and is sometimes referred to as the *body* of the loop.

exit when statement

Syntax:

exit when *boolean_expression;*

Example:

```
SUM := 0;
   GET ( NUMBER );
loop
   exit when NUMBER < 0;
   SUM := SUM + NUMBER;
   GET ( NUMBER );
end loop;
```

The **exit when** statement can appear only inside the body of a loop. When the **exit when** is executed, the *boolean_expression* is evaluated first. If the condition is TRUE, the loop is terminated and execution continues with the statement after the **end loop**. If the condition is FALSE, the loop continues.

exit statement

Syntax:

```
exit;
```

Example:

```
loop
     GET ( VALUE );
     SKIP_LINE;
     if VALUE in 1 .. 100 then
          exit;
     else
          PUT ( "Error" );
          NEW_LINE;
     end if;
end loop;
```

The **exit** statement can appear only in the body of a loop. It is normally in an **if** statement, that is nested inside a **loop** statement. When the **exit** statement is executed, the loop is terminated and the program continues with the execution of the next statement immediately following the **end loop**.

pretest loop

Syntax:

```
loop
     exit when boolean__expression;
     sequence__of__statements
end loop;
```

Example:

See **exit when** example above.

The first thing that happens in a pretest loop is the evaluation of the *boolean__expression* in the **exit when**. If the *boolean__expression* is TRUE, the loop terminates and none of the *sequence__of__statements* is executed. If it is FALSE, the *sequence__of__statements* is executed. The next time around the loop, the same thing happens. The *boolean__expression* is evaluated every time around the loop.

posttest loop

Syntax:

```
loop
     sequence__of__statements
     exit when boolean__expression;
end loop;
```

Example:

```
loop
     SUM := SUM + NEXT;
     GET ( NEXT );
     exit when NEXT <= 0;
end loop;
```

When a **posttest** loop is executed, the statements are executed in order, and then the *boolean__expression* is evaluated. If it evaluates to TRUE, the **loop** statement is over and the program goes on to the statement immediately after **end loop**. If the *boolean__expression* evaluates to FALSE, then the statements are repeated again. The *sequence__of__statements* is repeated again and again until the *boolean__expression* evaluates to TRUE. At that point the **loop** statement is complete, and the program goes on to the statement after **end loop**.

midtest loop

Syntax:

```
loop
    sequence__of__statements
    exit when boolean__expression;
    sequence__of__statements
end loop;
```

Example:

```
SUM := 0;
loop
    GET ( NUMBER );
    exit when NUMBER < 0;
    SUM := SUM + NUMBER;
end loop;
```

The first *sequence__of__statements* is executed the first time, regardless of the value of the *boolean__expression*. If the *boolean__expression* evaluates to TRUE, the second *sequence__of__statements* is not executed and the loop is finished. As long as the *boolean__expression* is FALSE, both *sequence__of__statements* are executed repeatedly.

while loop prefix

Syntax:

```
while boolean__expression
loop
    sequence__of__statements
end loop;
```

Example:

```
while COUNT < 3
  and TALLY < 3
loop
     COUNT := COUNT + 1;
     TALLY := TALLY + 1;
end loop;
```

When the **while** prefix is used, the *boolean__expression* is evaluated first. If it evaluates to TRUE, then the body of the loop is executed. If the *boolean__expression* instead evaluates to FALSE, then nothing more happens. Each time the *boolean__expression* evaluates to TRUE, the body of the loop is executed. The first time it evaluates to FALSE, the **loop** statement terminates and the program goes on to the next statement.

for loop prefix

Syntax:

for *loop__control__variable* **in** *optional__reverse range*
loop
    sequence__of__statements
end loop;

range is *lower__bound__expression* **. .** *upper__bound__expression*
Example:

```
for INDEX in 20 . . 500
loop
     SUM := SUM + INDEX;
     PUT ( SUM );
     NEW_LINE;
end loop;
```

The *loop__control__variable* will be a variable of the type that matches the expressions in the range. For now that type is INTEGER (other types are possible and will be discussed in Chapter 8.) Both *lower__bound__expression* and *upper__bound__expression* must be expressions that evaluate to the same type, which will in turn be the type for the *loop__control__variable.* The body of the loop may be any Ada statements. When the **for** prefix is executed, *lower__bound__expression* and *upper__bound__expression* are first evaluated. The **loop** statement terminates without doing anything if the value of *upper__bound__expression* is less than that of *lower__bound__expression.* If the value of *lower__bound__expression* is less than or equal to the value of *upper__bound__expression,* then the body of the loop is executed first with the value of *loop__control__variable* set equal to the value of *lower__bound__expression,* then with the value of *loop__control__variable* increased by one, then with *loop__control__variable* increased by one more, and so forth. The last time the body of the loop is executed, the value of *loop__control__variable* is equal to the value obtained when *upper__bound__expression* was evaluated initially. *The loop__control__variable* may not be changed by the body of the loop; it must be treated as a named constant inside the loop. The *loop__control__variable* is declared by the computer and exists only within the confines of the loop itself.

for loop prefix with optional_reverse

Syntax:

```
for loop_control_variable in reverse range
loop
     sequence_of_statements
end loop;
```

Example:

```
for COUNT in reverse 20 . . 500
loop
     SUM := SUM + COUNT;
     PUT ( SUM );
     NEW_LINE;
end loop;
```

It is similar to the previous kind of **for** loop prefix, except that with this kind the *loop_control_variable* starts at the value of *upper_bound_expression* and is decreased by one on each iteration of the loop. If the value of *upper_bound_expression* is less than that of *lower_bound_expression,* then the **loop** statement terminates without doing anything.

end-of-line

Syntax:

```
END_OF_LINE
```

Example:

```
loop
     GET ( A_CHARACTER);
     SUM := SUM + 1;
     exit when END_OF_LINE;
end loop;
```

This is known as the end-of-line boolean. Its value becomes TRUE after the program reads the last value on a line using a GET statement. Executing a SKIP_LINE statement resets it to FALSE (provided there is some input data on the next line). See the explanation of *end-of-line character* in the chapter text for a more precise description of END_OF_LINE.

end-of-file

Syntax:

```
END_OF_FILE
```

Example:

```
loop
     exit when END_OF_FILE;
     GET ( NUMBER );
     SUM := SUM + NUMBER;
end loop;
```

The END_OF_FILE has a boolean value. This form of loop is used primarily with off-line data. The last thing in an off-line data file is an end-of-file marker. END_OF_FILE is normally FALSE. When all the data has been read from the file, END_OF_FILE will become TRUE.

Exercises

Self-Test Exercises

8. What is the output of the following program fragment (when embedded in a complete program)?

```
MINUS_THREE : INTEGER := -3;

for INDEX in MINUS_THREE . . 11
loop
     PUT ( 2 * INDEX );
end loop;
```

9. What is the output of the following program fragment (when embedded in a complete program)?

```
for COUNT in reverse 1 . . 10
loop
     PUT ( COUNT );
end loop;
```

10. Write a program that outputs all the even numbers between **1** and **25**.

11. What is the output of the following program fragment (when embedded in a complete program)?

```
LIMIT := 3;
NUMBER := 1;
loop
     exit when NUMBER > LIMIT;
     PUT ( NUMBER );
     PUT ( LIMIT );
     NEW_LINE;
     LIMIT := 2;
     NUMBER := NUMBER + 1;
end loop;
```

12. Predict the output of the following nested **for** loops.

```
for OUTER in reverse 1 . . 10
loop
     for INNER in 1 . . 10
     loop
          PUT ( INNER );
          PUT ( " times " );
```

```
            PUT ( OUTER );
            PUT ( " equals " );
            PUT ( INNER * OUTER );
            NEW_LINE;
        end loop;
    end loop;
```

13. For each of the following situations, which type of loop (pretest, posttest, or **for**) would work best?

(a) Summing a series.
(b) Reading in the list of exams scores for one student in a class.
(c) Reading in the number of days of sick leave taken by employees in a department. The input consists of a list of numbers giving the number of days missed by each employee who took sick leave.
(d) Testing a procedure for different values of the parameters.

Interactive Exercises

14. Replace the pretest loop in Figure 7.3 with the "almost equivalent" posttest loop given in the section called "A Posttest Loop." Then run the modified program. Since the posttest loop is not completely equivalent to the pretest loop, the program will not perform correctly on an empty list. Try running the program on both nonempty and empty lists of numbers. (For the empty list, think of the program as adding the list of sales commissions earned by a lazy salesman for a month in which he only went fishing and never saw a customer.)

15. Embed the nested loop from Exercise 12 in a program and run the program. Try changing the various numbers and running the program again. In each case predict the output before running the program.

16. Modify any one of the programming exercises you did for Chapter 6 by adding a loop so that the calculation can be repeated again and again with new input as long as the user desires. Do it once with a posttest loop. Do it again with a pretest loop, and this time allow the user to change his/her mind and not do the calculation even once.

Programming Exercises

17. Write a program to read in a list of test scores and output the highest score, the lowest score, and the average score. Most of the solution can be found in Figures 7.5 and 7.6.

18. Write a program to list the numbers from 0 to 25, their squares, square roots, fourth power, and fourth root. The output should be in a neat five-column format. (The square root procedure was given in Chapter 3, Figure 3.14.)

19. Write a program that will read in a number UPPER and then output the sum of the squares of the numbers from **1** to UPPER. For example, if the input is 3, the output should be **14**, because

$$1^2 + 2^2 + 3^2 = 1 + 4 + 9 = 14$$

The program should allow the user to repeat this process with different values for UPPER as often as desired.

20. Modify the program in Exercise 19 to input the numbers LOWER and UPPER. Have the number LOWER replace the 1.

21. Write a program to determine the largest value of UPPER such that your computer can compute the factorial of UPPER, written mathematically as UPPER!, before it attempts to exceed INTEGER'LAST. The factorial is the product of all positive numbers less than or equal to UPPER. For example, 3! = 1 times 2 times 3 = 6. By convention 0! is set equal to 1.

22. Write a program that takes one FLOAT value as input and computes the first integer POWER such that 2^{POWER} is greater than or equal to the input value. The program should output both POWER and 2^{POWER}.

23. Write a program that outputs the balance of an account after each succeeding year. The input is the initial balance, the interest rate, the first year, and the last year. Assume the deposit is made on January 1 and that the interest for the past year is calculated and paid once each year on January 1. Next modify the program so that it shows three different balances for three different ways of calculating the interest: simple interest, compounded semiannually, and compounded quarterly.

24. Modify the program in the previous exercise (or do it from scratch) so that interest is compounded monthly (and not any other way, such as semiannually) and so that the output shows the interest at the end of each month. You should insert a SKIP_LINE to stop the output at the end of each year. When the user hits the return key, the figures for the following year are displayed. If this were not done, the user would not have time to read the output. After that enhance the program so that the calculation can be made as often as desired with different inputs.

25. Interest on a loan is paid on a declining balance, and hence a loan with an interest rate of, say, 14% can cost significantly less than 14% of the balance. Write a program that takes a loan amount and interest rate as input and then outputs the monthly payments and balance of the loan until the loan is paid off. Assume that the monthly payments are 1/20 of the original loan amount and that any amount in excess of the interest is credited toward decreasing the balance due. Thus, on a loan of $20,000, the payments would be $1000 a month. If the interest rate is 10%, then each month the interest is 1/12 of 10% of the remaining balance. The first month (10% of $20,000)/12 or $166.67 would be paid in interest, and the remaining $833.33 would decrease the balance to $19,166.67. The following month the interest would be (10% of $19,166.67)/12, and so forth. Also, have the program output the total interest paid over the life of the loan. Finally, determine what simple annualized percentage of the original loan balance was paid in interest. For example, if $1000 was paid in interest on a $10,000 loan and it took two years to pay it off, then the annualized interest is $500, which is 5% of the $10,000 loan amount.

26. Write a program that reads in a FLOAT number RADICAND and outputs the integer CUBE_ROOT closest to the cube root of RADICAND. Assume that RADICAND is always nonnegative.

27. A *perfect number* is a positive integer that is equal to the sum of all those positive integers (excluding itself) that divide it evenly. The first perfect number is 6, because its divisors (excluding itself) are 1, 2, 3, and because 6 = 1 + 2 + 3. Write a program to find the first three perfect numbers (including 6).

28. The second order Fibonacci numbers $\mathbf{F_n}$ are defined as follows: $\mathbf{F_1}$ is **1**, $\mathbf{F_2}$ is **1**, and $\mathbf{F_{i+2}} = \mathbf{F_i} + \mathbf{F_{i+1}}$, **for** i = 1, 2, . . The first few Fibonacci numbers are 1, 1, 2, 3, 5, 8.

Note that each number in the sequence is the sum of the previous two numbers. One place where these numbers occur is as certain population growth rates. If a population has no deaths, then the series shows the increase in population after each generation. A generation is the time it takes a member to reach reproducing age. The formula applies most straightforwardly to asexual reproduction at a rate of one offspring per generation. In any event, the green crud population grows at that rate and produces one generation every five days. Hence, if a green crud population starts out as 10 pounds of crud, then in 5 days there is still 10 pounds of crud; in 10 days there is 20 pounds of crud, in 15 days 30 pounds, in 20 days 50 pounds, and so forth. Write a program that takes the initial size of a green crud population (in pounds) and a number of days and then outputs the number of pounds of green crud after that many days. Assume that the population size is the same for four days and then increases every fifth day.

29. Write a program to find all integer solutions to the equation

$$4x + 3y - 9z = 5$$

for values of **x**, **y**, and **z** between zero and 100.

30. Write a program that will read in and evaluate expressions such as the following:

```
+15+90-100-7+36end
```

The expression is a sequence of integers each preceded by a sign. The expression is terminated with the word *end*. There are no blanks in the expression.

31. The value e^x can be approximated by the sum

```
1 + x + x²/2! + x3/3! + . . . + xⁿ/n!
```

Write a program that takes a value **x** as input and outputs this sum for **n** taken to be each of the values **1** to **100**. The program should repeat the calculation for new values of **x** until the user says he/she is through. Use variables of type FLOAT to store the factorials, or you are likely to produce integer overflow.

32. Write a procedure that returns one **out** parameter of type INTEGER that has a value read from the keyboard. The procedure reads the input as a string of characters, and it checks and recovers from input typing mistakes as follows: It skips over all characters other than the 10 digits; for example, it interprets the input **$12**%5** as the number **125**. It then echos the integer value and allows the user to try again if it is not correct.

CHAPTER 8

MORE DATA TYPES AND AN INTRODUCTION TO PACKAGES

John von Neumann

An outstanding mathematician, von Neumann (1903–1957) introduced the *stored program concept* for computers. In a report written in 1945 titled "Preliminary Discussion of the Logical Design of an Electronic Computing Instrument," von Neumann defined a computer using the concept of a stored program. This machine is known today as the *von Neumann machine.* Central to the design of this machine is the principle that instructions and data are to be stored together in a common storage medium.

Chapter Contents

We begin this chapter by classifying the simple data types that we used up to this point. Then we describe how some new kinds of data types can be defined within an Ada program. In addition to the predefined types, Ada allows the programmer to define types. In this chapter we introduce some of the simpler kinds of programmer-defined data types and show how they can be very helpful in making programs more readable and more representative of the real world.

Next we introduce a new and very powerful Ada concept called a *package*. A package gives the programmer the capability to group together a number of related declarations and subprograms. We discuss the idea of grouping these packages together and storing them in a library for later reference. (In later chapters we will continue to explore additional uses of packages.) In this part of the chapter we also uncover some of the previously hidden information that has surrounded the input and output of textual material and discover that all text I/O is done through a predefined package called **TEXT_IO**.

Discrete Types

The most straightforward way to specify the values of a data type is to list them. In the case of the type BOOLEAN, that is easy to do because there are just two values: FALSE and TRUE. In the case of the type CHARACTER the list is much longer: . . . , **'A'**, **'B'**, **'C'**, ... In the case of INTEGER the list is so long that it would be unrealistic to write it out, but in principle all the values could be listed. In Ada a type whose values are specified by a list is called a *discrete type.* The types INTEGER, BOOLEAN, and CHARACTER are all discrete types.

integer
boolean

Since the items of any list are ordered, the values of a discrete type have an order determined by their order in the list. The operation **<** can be used to test this ordering. Relational operations are defined for all Ada discrete types, and it always yields a boolean value. The most obvious case of this is the discrete type INTEGER. In that case the order is the usual less-than ordering on the integers. For example, **1 < 2** and **-5 < -3** both evaluate to TRUE. In the case of the type BOOLEAN, the value of FALSE is considered to be less than TRUE. There is little intuitive meaning to that ordering; it is completely arbitrary. Nonetheless, it is the prescribed ordering, so **FALSE < TRUE** evaluates to TRUE.

character

The ordering of the type CHARACTER is more or less the obvious one. Letters are ordered alphabetically. So **'A' < 'B'** and **'A' < 'Z'** both evaluate to TRUE, while **'Z' < 'X'** evaluates to FALSE. Digits are ordered as you would expect. For example, **'1' < '2'** and **'0' < '9'** both evaluate to TRUE, while **'3' < '2'** evaluates to FALSE. The ordering of digits reflects the ordering of the numbers they stand for. What about the character pairs that do not have a traditional ordering? Is the semicolon less than or greater than the comma? Is uppercase **'A'** less than or greater than lowercase **'a'**? Ada is very specific about these cases. The type CHARACTER is not only predefined, but that predefinition specifies the exact order of all characters permitted in the type. Figure 8.1 shows the Ada definition for the type CHARACTER. This is the ASCII (American Standard Code for Information Interchange) character set. The first 32 and the last 1 (all shown in italics) are not really identifiers, but rather they are *control characters.* The characters in the list are ordered lowest to highest.

```
type CHARACTER is ( nul,  soh,  stx,  etx,  eot,  enq,  ack,  bel,
                    bs,   ht,   lf,   vt,   ff,   cr,   so,   si,
                    dle,  dc1,  dc2,  dc3,  dc4,  nak,  syn,  etb,
                    can,  em,   sub,  esc,  fs,   gs,   rs,   us,

                    ' ',  '!',  '"',  '#',  '$',  '%',  '&',  ''',
                    '(',  ')',  '*',  '+',  ',',  '-',  '.',  '/',
                    '0',  '1',  '2',  '3',  '4',  '5',  '6',  '7',
                    '8',  '9',  ':',  ';',  '<',  '=',  '>',  '?',
```

```
'@',  'A',  'B',  'C',  'D',  'E',  'F',  'G',
'H',  'I',  'J',  'K',  'L',  'M',  'N',  'O',
'P',  'Q',  'R',  'S',  'T',  'U',  'V',  'W',
'X',  'Y',  'Z',  '[',  '\',  ']',  '^',  '_',

'`',  'a',  'b',  'c',  'd',  'e',  'f',  'g',
'h',  'i',  'j',  'k',  'l',  'm',  'n',  'o',
'p',  'q',  'r',  's',  't',  'u',  'v',  'w',
'x',  'y',  'z',  '{',  '|',  '}',  '~',  del );
```

Figure 8.1 Definition of the type `CHARACTER`.

The ordering properties of discrete types can be used in a program. For example, it is sometimes useful to test two letters to determine if they are in alphabetic order. An obvious example of this would be in a program that alphabetizes a list of words. We have already seen that there are numerous reasons why a program might compare two integer values.

When comparing two values of a discrete type, the variations on the **<** operations, namely **<=**, **>**, and **>=**, are all available and have the obvious interpretation.

float

Of all the types we have seen so far in this chapter, only `FLOAT` is not a discrete type. (The type `STRING`, used in examples in previous chapters but not discussed in detail until Chapter 9, is also not a discrete type.) This is a consequence of the abstract model of real numbers that is used in mathematics. In that model the real numbers cannot be listed. Computers can represent only a finite number of `FLOAT` values that represent real numbers in Ada, so the `FLOAT` values for any particular implementation can, in principle, be listed. However, the definition of Ada does not specify the list; moreover, we do not normally think of `FLOAT` values as being on a list. For these reasons the type `FLOAT` is not a discrete type. As we have seen, the relational operators, like **<**, can be applied to values of type `FLOAT` in the same fashion as they can be applied to values of discrete types.

scalar types

In many, but not all, ways the type `FLOAT` is like a discrete type. The unifying term *scalar type* is used to mean any type that is either a representation of the real numbers or a discrete type. The type `FLOAT` is both important and troublesome. All of Chapter 15 is devoted to discussing this type.

Enumeration Types

There is one other kind of discrete type: an *enumeration type*. An enumeration type is just a list of values named by identifiers or values as character literals (a character literal is a character value represented by a character enclosed in single quotes). The values of an enumeration type, called *enumeration literals,* have no properties other than their order and their names. Despite their simple nature, enumeration types can be useful. By choosing the identifiers to be meaningful names, they sometimes can be used to make a program easier to read and understand. For example, the following type declaration declares the names of four kinds of vehicles to be an enumeration type:

```
type VEHICLE is ( MOTORCYCLE, CAR, BUS, TRUCK );
```

This type has four values named by the four identifiers in the list. These four identifiers represent the literals or the set of values of a new type called VEHICLE. They are not variables or named constants; they are values of this new type. The predefined type BOOLEAN is declared in the same manner:

```
type BOOLEAN is ( FALSE, TRUE );
```

The identifiers FALSE and TRUE are the literals of the type BOOLEAN. If you refer back to the previous section (Figure 8.1), you will see that the declaration of the type CHARACTER is an enumeration type also.

The declaration of an enumeration type then is the declaration of a new type, and the list enclosed in parentheses defines the values of this new type.

declaration

All type declarations are given in the declaration part of a program, which is that part of a procedure or function after the formal parameter list and before the **begin/end** section. It is permissible to intermix declarations of subtypes, enumerations, and other yet-to-be-introduced types. They can even be intermixed with constant and variable object declarations, as long as the type is declared before an object of that type. There is an occurrence of the reserved word **type** or **subtype** before every type identifier name. The syntax for all type declarations is as follows:

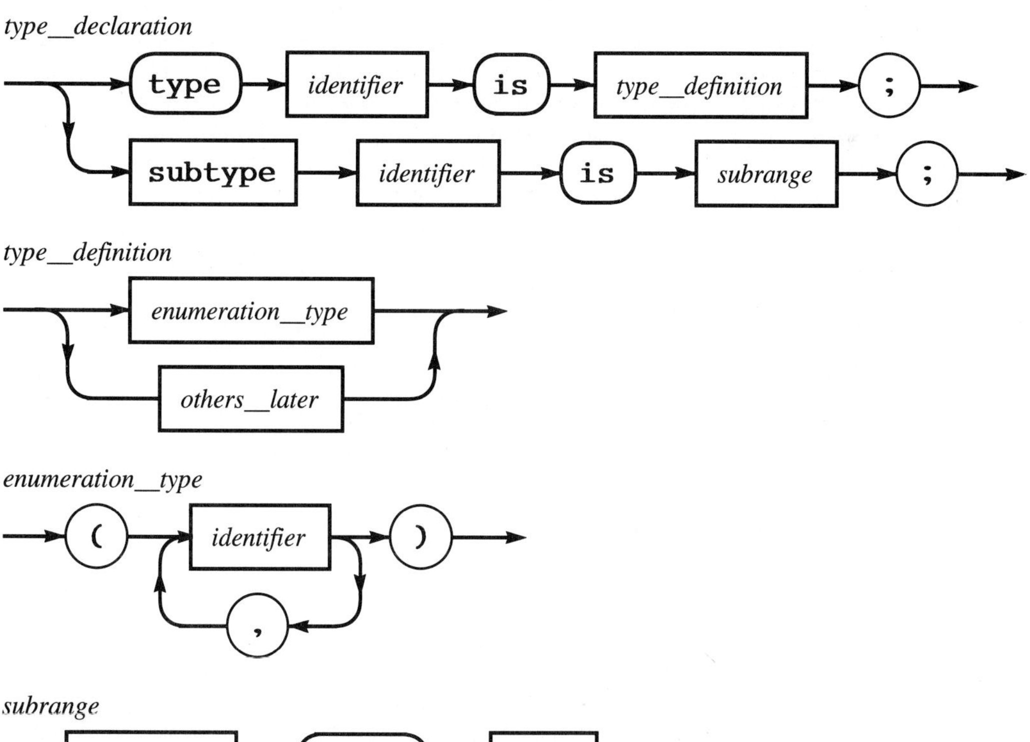

For an enumeration type, the *type_definition* follows the previous examples for VEHICLE and BOOLEAN. The definition consists of a list of identifiers and/or character literals enclosed in parentheses. The list of identifiers consists of the names of the values of that type, and they are ordered as in the list. It is an ordered list of distinct values.

variables

Just like other types, there can be variables of an enumeration type. For example, the following declares CLASS to be of type VEHICLE:

```
CLASS : VEHICLE;
```

Variables of an enumeration type and their values behave much like those of any other type. For example, the following makes BUS the value of the variable CLASS:

```
CLASS := BUS;
```

uses of enumeration types

One common use of enumeration types is in **case** statements, such as

```
case CLASS is
    when MOTORCYCLE => TOLL := 0.25;
    when CAR        => TOLL := 0.50;
    when TRUCK | BUS => TOLL := 1.00;
end case;
```

The enumeration type serves two purposes here: It makes the program meaning clearer, and it guarantees that the **case** statement is almost always defined. (You do not need to use a **when others** choice to trap extraneous values.) The variable CLASS cannot take on a value that is not on some statement's choice list. The only way the **case** statement could be undefined is if the variable CLASS were never initialized. Of course, a similar thing can sometimes be done with a subtype of integers (1 . . 4) or characters ('a' . . 'd'), for example, but an enumeration type allows more flexibility in choosing names.

It is important to note that the literals in an enumeration type are not strings but values represented by identifiers. Later in this chapter we will show you how enumeration types can be either read in or written out by a program. In a program with the above declarations, it will be possible to have the following output statement, for instance:

```
PUT ( TRUCK );
```

Figure 8.2 shows a program that uses an enumeration type for the days of the week. Also note the use of a subrange for the subtype HOURS. Since there are no more than 24 hours in one day, this subtype ensures that the hours worked for a given day fall within the range of 0 to 24.

Program

```
with I_O; use I_O;
procedure MAIN is
--                  INPUT  : The basic pay rate and the hours worked
--                           for each day of the week Sun thru Sat.
--                  OUTPUT : The wages earned for the week.
--                  DESCRIPTION : Applies additional factors to
--                                the basic pay rate for weekend work.
--                                The program then computes the total
--                                wages for the week.
    AFTER : constant INTEGER := 2;
    BEFORE : constant INTEGER := 5;
    EXPONENT : constant INTEGER := 0;
    SATURDAY_FACTOR : constant FLOAT := 1.5;
    SUNDAY_FACTOR : constant FLOAT := 2.0;
    subtype HOURS is INTEGER range 0 .. 24;
    type WEEK_DAYS is ( SUN, MON, TUE, WED, THU, FRI, SAT );

    BASE_RATE : FLOAT;
    HOURS_WORKED : HOURS;
    WAGES : FLOAT := 0.0;

    function RATE ( BASE_RATE : FLOAT; DAY : WEEK_DAYS )
            return FLOAT is
--                    INPUT  : The base rate of pay
--                             and the day of the week.
--                    OUTPUT : The pay rate for a day of the week.
--                    DESCRIPTION : Applies additional factors to
--                                  the basic pay rate for weekend work.
    begin -- Rate
        case DAY is
            when SUN => return BASE_RATE * SUNDAY_FACTOR;
            when MON .. FRI => return BASE_RATE;
            when SAT => return BASE_RATE * SATURDAY_FACTOR;
        end case;
    end RATE;
begin -- Main
    PUT ( "Enter the basic hourly wage rate:" ); NEW_LINE;
    GET ( BASE_RATE ); SKIP_LINE;
    PUT ( "Enter the hours worked" ); NEW_LINE;
    PUT ( "for Sunday through Saturday:" ); NEW_LINE;
```

```
    for DAY in SUN . . SAT
    loop
        GET ( HOURS_WORKED );
        WAGES := WAGES
              + FLOAT ( HOURS_WORKED ) * RATE ( BASE_RATE, DAY );
    end loop;
    SKIP_LINE;
    PUT ( "Wages for the week total: $" );
    PUT ( WAGES, BEFORE, AFTER, EXPONENT );
    NEW_LINE;
end MAIN;
```

Sample Dialogue

```
Enter the basic hourly wage rate:
10.00
Enter the hours worked
for Sunday through Saturday:
2 8 8 8 8 8 0
Wages for the week total: $ 440.00
```

Figure 8.2 Program using an enumeration type.

The Attributes PRED, SUCC, POS, and VAL

pred
succ

Since the values of a discrete type are ordered in a list, a programmer may find it useful to refer to the value preceding a given value or to the value following a given value in a list. Ada provides two attributes, PRED (short for *predecessor*) and SUCC (short for *successor*), for exactly those purposes. Given a discrete type as a prefix and some expression of that type as a parameter, the attribute PRED returns the preceding value of that type; for example:

```
INTEGER'PRED ( 18 )
```

returns **17**. Similarly the attribute SUCC returns the next value in the ordering of that type; for example:

```
INTEGER'SUCC ( 18 )
```

returns **19**.

Think of attributes as predefined functions. They work exactly as function calls do; they return a value as part of an expression. They look a little different because they have a prefix followed by a separating single quote. We previously encountered the attributes FIRST and LAST.

The attributes PRED and SUCC work for any prefix type that is a discrete type. Thus CHARACTER'SUCC ('B') returns **'C'** and, in the program in Figure 8.2, WEEK_DAYS'PRED (MON) returns SUN.

pos

Since the values of a discrete type are listed in some order, we can meaningfully ask where a specific value is located on the list. The Ada attribute POS provides a way of doing this (POS is short for *position*). The positions in discrete types are numbered starting with zero rather than 1. So POS applied to the first value of a discrete type returns **0**, applied to the second value it returns **1**, and so forth. The type INTEGER is the sole exception to this numbering scheme. The attribute POS applied to any value of type INTEGER simply returns that value, which makes POS an uninteresting attribute to apply to integers.

All attributes follow these syntax rules:

attribute call

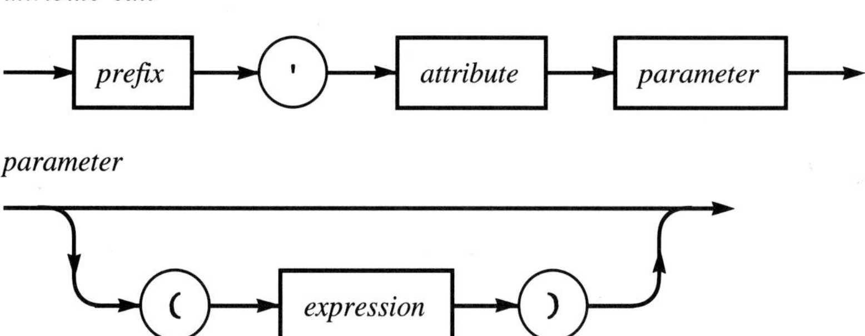

val

The inverse of the attribute POS is VAL (short for *value*). When given a nonnegative parameter, the attribute VAL returns the value of the prefix type that is in the parameter's position in the list. In the program in Figure 8.2, WEEK_DAYS'VAL (2) returns TUE. When used with the type CHARACTER, CHARACTER'VAL (65) returns the character 'A'. Go back to the earlier definition for CHARACTER (Figure 8.1) and count, starting with zero, to verify that 'A' is indeed in the 65th position in the enumeration of characters.

These various attributes, which depend on the ordering of enumeration types, are very useful, as we will see in an upcoming example program. These attributes will become even more useful as we continue to use enumeration types in the description of more complex data types in future chapters.

nonprintable characters

Another use for the VAL attribute has to do with nonprintable characters. A computer has the ability to send messages to the video screen output device that mean things like "clear the screen," "ring the bell," or some other manipulation of the output device other than simply writing a letter on the screen. These signals are considered to be values of type CHARACTER. For example, the "character" that rings the bell on a teletype machine (and causes a "beep" on a video terminal) is in position **7**, according to the encoding in type CHARACTER. Therefore, the following statement will ring the bell (or sound the beep) on a terminal:

```
PUT ( CHARACTER'VAL ( 7 ) );
```

Subtypes Revisited

The simplest kind of user-defined type that can be defined within an Ada program is a *subtype*. Subtypes are crucially important in constructing other more complicated and very useful types that we will introduce in Chapter 9. They are also useful in their own right as an automatic error-checking facility. But before discussing their uses, we must describe what these subtypes are.

base type

A subtype is obtained from a scalar type by specifying two simple expressions (often constants, but not always) of that type. The type from which the two expressions are chosen is called the *base type*. The values of the subtype consist of the values of the two specified expressions, plus all the values of the base type that fall between the values of the two specified expressions. A subtype is essentially a subset or subrange of a scalar type, and the values are ordered in the same way as they are in the base type. A subtype definition is a declaration and so goes in the declarative part of a program using the reserved word **subtype**. For example, a program might start as follows:

```
procedure SAMPLE is
    PI : constant FLOAT := 3.14159;
    subtype SMALL_INTEGER is INTEGER range -10 . . 10;
    BIG : INTEGER;
    LITTLE : SMALL_INTEGER;
    REAL, IMAGINARY : FLOAT;
```

type declaration

The third line is called a *subtype declaration*. The subtype SMALL_INTEGER is defined to be all INTEGER values between **-10** and **10**, including the end points. The variable LITTLE is defined to be of type SMALL_INTEGER, so it can take on values from **-10** to **+10**. Hence, the following is an Ada statement that might legitimately appear in this program:

```
LITTLE := 4;
```

However, the following would raise an exception when the program is compiled:

```
LITTLE := 11; -- Not allowed
```

The subtype definition uses a subrange that consists of two expressions separated by two periods (called a *double dot*). The two expressions must evaluate to the same scalar type, and the first expression value must be less than or equal to the second. You can define any number of subranges as subtypes. The reserved word **subtype** precedes each subrange declaration. It is included with every one, no matter how many subtypes are declared.

type compatibility

Subtypes and their base types are compatible in the sense that any value of a subtype is also considered to be of the base type. For example, using the preceding program specification, any value of type SMALL_INTEGER is also of type INTEGER. So in this program, the following is a legitimate statement:

```
BIG := LITTLE;
```

The following program code is also legitimate:

```
GET ( BIG );
LITTLE := BIG;
```

However, if the GET statement sets the value of BIG to a value outside the range of the subtype SMALL_INTEGER, then the assignment statement will precipitate the raising of the exception CONSTRAINT_ERROR.

The subtype *inherits* all the operations of its base type. For example, a program with types declared as above could add or subtract two things of type SMALL_INTEGER.

error checking

One important use of subtypes is as a device to detect certain programming errors. If you expect a variable to always take on values within a certain range, then that variable should be declared as having a subtype. That way if an error does cause it to take on a value outside of the specified range, then an error message will be produced. Otherwise, the error might go undetected. For example, if a variable DATA is expected to hold only positive integers, then the following declarations will serve to declare DATA in such a way that nonpositive values will produce an error message:

```
DATA : POSITIVE;
```

Recall that POSITIVE is a predefined subtype with range 1 to INTEGER'LAST.

As another example, assume FINAL is supposed to hold a letter grade in a classroom grading program. Furthermore assume that the possible grades are A, B, C, D, and F. Then FINAL should be declared as follows:

```
subtype GRADES is CHARACTER range 'A' .. 'F';
FINAL : GRADES;
```

With the variable FINAL declared to be of a subrange of the type CHARACTER as shown, the computer will give an error message if for some reason the value of FINAL is set to, say, **'G'**. There is a limit to how much of this type checking can be handled by subtypes. A **subtype** is a subrange of a type that consists of *all* the values between the two limits. Hence, the above declaration does not provide for an error message in the event that the value of GRADES is set to **'E'**.

The For and Case Statements Revisited

Discrete types are made up of enumeration types and integer types. Enumeration types are like the integers in the sense that they can be listed. Given two bounds, we can proceed from the lower bound to the next value in the ordered list, then the next, and so forth until we reach the upper bound. This is the only property of the type INTEGER that the **for** statement uses. It thus seems natural to allow the loop control variable in a **for** statement to be of any discrete type. Ada does just that. Naturally the expressions that give the initial and final values of the loop control variable must be of the same discrete type. Recall that the loop control variable is, in essence, declared within the loop, and its type will be the same discrete type as the bounds for the range of values. As an example, the following is a perfectly legitimate Ada statement:

```
for INDEX in 'a' .. 'z'
loop
     PUT ( INDEX );
end loop;
```

The loop control variable INDEX is automatically declared by the system to be a subtype of CHARACTER, and this code segment will output the lowercase alphabet. The loop control variable will not take on values outside the range 'a' to 'z'.

We could also define 'a' to 'z' as a subtype,

```
subtype LOWER_CASE is CHARACTER range 'a' .. 'z';
```

and then write the above loop as follows:

```
for INDEX in LOWER_CASE
loop
     PUT ( INDEX );
end loop;
```

case Now that we have defined the discrete types, we can define the **case** statement more completely and compactly. The expression that governs a **case** statement may be of any discrete type. The choice lists must, of course, consist of values of that discrete type.

Allowable Parameter Types

Procedures and functions may have parameters of any type whatsoever, including all the types we have seen so far and all the defined types we will introduce in succeeding chapters. However, a procedure or function specification must use type names. It cannot use type definitions. The following is thus an illegal procedure specification:

```
procedure WRITE_GRADES ( QUIZ_1, QUIZ_2 : in 0 .. 100 )
-- Not Allowed
```

Instead you must declare a name for the defined type and use the name in the formal parameter list, as follows:

```
subtype SCORES is INTEGER range 0 .. 100;
procedure WRITE_GRADES ( QUIZ_1, QUIZ_2 : in SCORES )
```

type returned by a function The same rule applies to the type returned by a function. You must use a type name or subtype name, not a type or subtype definition, in the function specification. There are no restrictions on what types may be used as parameters to functions, and there are no restrictions on what types may be returned. All the types and subtypes we have seen thus far and will see in the future are allowed as the type of the value returned by a function.

Pitfall

Parameter Type Conflicts

The rules for matching parameters say that the formal and actual parameters must be of the same *base type*. Thus a subtype of the type INTEGER can be passed to an INTEGER parameter, and vice versa. As an example, recall the procedure EXCHANGE defined in Chapter 5. All the information we need to know about the procedure is given in the procedure specification. This as well as some other declarations that might appear in a program are

```
subtype RATING is INTEGER range 0 .. 10;
YOU, ME : RATING;
procedure EXCHANGE ( LEFT, RIGHT : in out INTEGER ) is
```

In a program with these declarations it is possible to include a procedure call such as

```
   EXCHANGE ( YOU, ME );
```

The formal parameters are of type INTEGER, whereas the actual parameters are of subtype RATING. This will not raise an exception, even though the formal and actual parameters are of different types. The reason is that the formal and actual parameter types do have the same base type. The only time a problem would be created would be if the procedure EXCHANGE were to attempt to assign a value that was outside the range of the subtype RATING to one of the parameters. At this point an exception would be raised (CONSTRAINT_ERROR) and the procedure would terminate.

Random Number Generators
(Optional)

Suppose you flip a coin, write down 0 if it comes up heads, and write down 1 if it comes up tails. You have just made a *random* choice between 0 and 1. If you roll a single die and count the number of dots on the top face, you will get a random number between 1 and 6. These are two ways of generating random numbers. There are numerous occasions when a computer program needs, or at least can profitably use, a source of random numbers. Perhaps the most obvious example is that of game-playing programs. Random numbers are also used in simulation programs. A program to model the performance of a proposed new highway interchange would typically use a random number generator to model the arrival times of vehicles. A program to write poetry might use a random number generator to guide the choice of words. These are just a few of the numerous uses for random number generators.

pseudorandom numbers

An exact definition of what constitutes a *true random number generator* is a matter of significant philosophical debate. However, the examples of the coin flip and the die provide an adequate feel for the concept. Computer programs typically do not use true random number generators. Instead they use procedures or functions that generate sequences of numbers that *appear* to be random. Since these sequences are generated by procedures or functions, they are not "truly random." Hence, these generators are referred to as *pseudorandom number generators.*

For most applications, these pseudorandom number generators are close enough to an approximation of a true random number generator. In fact, they are usually preferable to a true random number generator. A pseudorandom number generator has one important advantage over a true random number generator: The sequence of numbers it produces is repeatable. If run twice with the same initial conditions, a pseudorandom number generator will always produce exactly the same sequence of numbers. This can be very handy for a number of purposes. It is very useful for debugging. When an error is discovered, the proposed program changes can be tested with the *same* sequence of pseudorandom numbers that exposed the error. Similarly, a particularly interesting run of a simulation program may be reproduced, provided a pseudorandom number generator was used. With a true random number generator, every run of the program is likely to be different.

linear congruence method

seed

The most common method of generating pseudorandom numbers is the *linear congruence method.* This method starts out with a number called the *seed.* For each individual run of the program, the seed is usually chosen by the user. It completely determines the sequence of numbers produced. There are three other numbers called the MULTIPLIER, the INCREMENT, and the MODULUS, which are named constants. The formula for generating what we hope are random-looking numbers is quite simple. The first number is

(MULTIPLIER * (*the seed*) + INCREMENT) **rem** MODULUS.

The $n + 1st$ number is

(MULTIPLIER * (*the n-th number*) + INCREMENT) **rem** MODULUS.

For example, suppose we take the MULTIPLIER to be 2, the INCREMENT to be 3, and the MODULUS to be 5. With a seed value of 1, that produces the following sequence of numbers:

```
( 2 * 1 + 3 ) rem 5 = 0,
( 2 * 0 + 3 ) rem 5 = 3,
( 2 * 3 + 3 ) rem 5 = 4,
( 2 * 4 + 3 ) rem 5 = 1,
( 2 * 1 + 3 ) rem 5 = 0, . . .
```

The pattern of numbers produced is thus 0, 3, 4, 1, 0, 3, 4, 1, 0, 3, 4, 1, ...

Something is not right. This formula should produce a sequence that looks like a sequence of randomly chosen integers between zero and one less than the modulus. In this example the numbers should range from 0 to 4. But the above pattern is a repeating pattern and does not contain 2. So the value 2 will never be produced. Changing the seed will not help much. If we use 2 as the seed, we obtain the sequence: 2, 2, 2, 2, 2 . . . . That certainly produces the value 2, but it generates no other numbers. The problem is in the choice of the other constants, not in the choice of the seed.

Any choice of values for the constants in our pseudorandom number generator will produce a sequence that ultimately falls into a repeating pattern. However, if the constants are chosen carefully, the pattern will be large and will appear to be random. The values given in Figure 8.3 should work reasonably well on any implementation whose value of INTEGER'LAST is 32767 or larger. With those constants, the random number generator will produce 729 numbers before repeating a number.

```
SEED := 1;
function RANDOM return INTEGER is
    INCREMENT  : constant INTEGER := 3641;
    MODULUS    : constant INTEGER := 729;
    MULTIPLIER : constant INTEGER := 40;
begin
    SEED := ( MULTIPLIER * SEED + INCREMENT ) rem MODULUS;
    return SEED;
end RANDOM;
```

Figure 8.3 A pseudorandom number generator.

Notice that the function RANDOM has a global variable called SEED that it uses to remember one number. The initial value of this variable is 1. Each time the function is called, this global variable is changed, which violates our guideline that functions should not have side effects. This is one of those rare occasions when it is acceptable to violate the guideline. In this case a global variable seems necessary. The generator must somehow remember the last value it produced, since that determines the next value it will produce. Later we will show an example of how it would look as a procedure, which would not violate our own rule about a function returning more than one value.

Using Pseudorandom Numbers
(Optional)

changing the range

Very few programs require an integer chosen at random from the range zero through 728 (the value of MODULUS − 1). Usually it is a different and typically smaller range. For example, a program might need a pseudorandom integer between zero and 10. One possibility is to use the following formula:

```
RANDOM rem 11
```

because for any value RANDOM, the value of the expression is guaranteed to fall in the range 0 . . 10. The function ZERO_TO_TEN in Figure 8.4 uses this formula. The program shown there uses the pseudorandom numbers to produce random-looking output.

Program

```
with I_O; use I_O;
procedure MAIN is
    WIDTH : constant INTEGER := 2;
    ANSWER : CHARACTER;
    SEED : INTEGER;
    function ZERO_TO_TEN return INTEGER is
        function RANDOM return INTEGER is
            INCREMENT  : constant INTEGER := 3641;
            MODULUS    : constant INTEGER := 729;
            MULTIPLIER : constant INTEGER := 40;
        begin -- Random
            SEED := ( MULTIPLIER * SEED + INCREMENT )
                   rem MODULUS;
            return SEED;
        end RANDOM;
    begin -- Zero_To_Ten
        return RANDOM rem 11;
    end ZERO_TO_TEN;
begin -- Main
    Put ( "Hi, my name is Gollum." ); NEW_LINE;
    PUT ( "I'm a perfect 10. What are you?" ); NEW_LINE
    PUT ( "Answer with a number between 0 and 10." );
    NEW_LINE;
    GET ( SEED ); SKIP_LINE;
    if SEED > 7 then
        PUT ( "Not bad." );
    else
        PUT ( "Oh well." );
    end if;
    NEW_LINE;
```

```
    loop
        PUT ( "Would you like to rate somebody else? (yes/no)" );
        NEW_LINE;
        GET ( ANSWER ); SKIP_LINE;
        exit when ANSWER = 'n'
                or ANSWER = 'N';
        PUT ( "You name somebody and I'll give a rating." );
        NEW_LINE;
        SKIP_LINE;
        PUT ( "That individual is a " );
        PUT ( ZERO_TO_TEN, WIDTH );
        NEW_LINE;
    end loop;
    PUT ( "Before I leave, let me rate you." ); NEW_LINE;
    PUT ( "I'd say you were a " );
    PUT ( ZERO_TO_TEN, WIDTH );
    NEW_LINE;
end MAIN;
```

Sample Dialogue

```
Hi, my name is Gollum.
I'm a perfect 10. What are you?
Answer with a number between 0 and 10.
10
Not bad.
Would you like to rate somebody else? (yes/no)
yes
You name somebody and I'll give a rating.
Joseph Cool
That individual is a 0
Would you like to rate somebody else? (yes/no)
yes
You name somebody and I'll give a rating.
Bo Derek
That individual is a 10
Would you like to rate somebody else? (yes/no)
yes
You name somebody and I'll give a rating.
Batman
That individual is a 4
Would you like to rate somebody else? (yes/no)
no
Before I leave, let me rate you.
I'd say you were a 4
```

Figure 8.4 Program using a pseudorandom number generator.

Random numbers can be scaled by additive constants. One way to get a pseudorandom number in the range **1** to **10** is to add 1 to an expression that yields numbers in the range **0** to **9**. The following is one such expression:

```
( RANDOM rem 10 ) + 1
```

pseudorandom floats

The function RANDOM shown in Figure 8.4 will produce a pseudorandom number in the range **0** to **728**. But what if you want a FLOAT value in the range zero to 1? Simply divide by the largest value that our random number generator produces. The function RANDOM_FLOAT shown in Figure 8.5 uses this technique to return a pseudorandom value between zero and 1. To get a FLOAT value in any other range, multiply by an appropriate factor and, if need be, add an appropriate constant.

```
SEED : INTEGER := 1;
function RANDOM return INTEGER is
     INCREMENT  : constant INTEGER := 3641;
     MODULUS    : constant INTEGER :=  729;
     MULTIPLIER : constant INTEGER :=   40;
begin
     SEED := ( MULTIPLIER * SEED + INCREMENT )
               rem MODULUS;
     return SEED;
end RANDOM;
function RANDOM_FLOAT return FLOAT is
begin -- Random_Float
     return FLOAT ( RANDOM ) / 728.0;
end RANDOM_FLOAT;
```

Figure 8.5 A random number generator for floating point values.

Designing a good pseudorandom number generator is not an easy task. It frequently needs some sort of "tuning" to keep it from producing a sequence of numbers that looks blatantly nonrandom. The pseudorandom number generators in this section will work reasonably well on virtually any system. However, some systems have been extended to include a predefined generator that has been carefully tuned to run efficiently and to produce the most "random-looking" sequences possible, given the limitations of the particular computer system. If your system includes such a predefined function, it makes sense to use it rather than the one given in Figure 8.3.

better scaling of random numbers

To produce pseudorandom numbers in some specified range requires some scaling of the values produced by the function RANDOM. The methods of scaling that we have already seen will work well in most situations. However, they do occasionally produce unsatisfactory sequences, so we will discuss another slightly more complicated, but preferable, method of scaling that avoids such problems. Before discussing the solution, however, we will illustrate the problem.

Sequences of pseudorandom numbers produced by the linear congruence method have a pattern that can become apparent when the numbers are scaled in certain innocent-looking ways. For example, one way to obtain a pseudorandom number chosen from the three values **0**, **1**, and **2** is to use the following formula:

```
RANDOM rem 3
```

If this formula is used with SEED initialized to the value of **100**, then the resulting sequence will be: **0**, **2**, **1**, **0**, **2**, **1**, **0**, **2**, **1**, ... The sequence repeats after just three numbers.

Patterns like the unfortunate one we just saw frequently depend on the last digits of the numbers. One way to break the pattern is to discard the last digit. The following formula yields pseudorandom numbers produced by the generator RANDOM but with the last digit discarded:

```
RANDOM / 10
```

For example, if SEED has a value of **100**, then RANDOM produces a value of **114**, which yields a final value of **11** after applying the / operator.

If we combine the two tricks of discarding the last digit and then scaling by applying a **rem**, we get the following formula for producing pseudorandom numbers in the range **0** to **2**:

```
( RANDOM / 10 ) rem 3
```

Again starting with a seed value of **100**, this more complicated formula produces a more random looking sequence that starts out

2, 0, 1, 2, 0, 2, 2, 2, 0, 1, ...

As promised, the random number generator can be written not only as a function but also as a procedure (see below) with one parameter (the seed). The parameter comes in as the seed for the next random number and returns not only as that random number but the seed for the next random number.

```
procedure RANDOM ( SEED : in out INTEGER ) is
     INCREMENT   : constant INTEGER := 3641;
     MODULUS     : constant INTEGER := 729;
     MULTIPLIER : constant INTEGER := 40;
begin
     SEED := ( MULTIPLIER * SEED + INCREMENT )
               mod MODULUS;
end RANDOM;
```

The use of the procedure RANDOM would be slightly different:

```
RANDOM ( SEED );
```

The variable SEED could be used in a call to the function ZERO_TO_TEN or RANDOM_FLOAT by adding a parameter. Note the following example function,

```
function RANDOM_FLOAT ( RANDOM_INTEGER : INTEGER )
        return FLOAT is
begin -- Random_Float
    return FLOAT ( RANDOM_INTEGER ) / 728.0;
end RANDOM_FLOAT;
```

and its use as

```
RANDOM ( SEED );
PUT ( RANDOM_FLOAT ( SEED ) );
```

In either case, procedure or function, a global variable is required that serves as the seed for the next random number.

Packages

library unit

Ada allows the grouping or bundling together of related entities such as object and type declarations and also including subprograms, all of which can be used by outside units. This group of entities is encapsulated and protected in what Ada calls a *package.* These packages are stored in a library—a library not unlike your college library with its shelves of books. We'll make the analogy between books in the college library and packages in your computer library. You go to your college library and find a book that you want and take it *with* you. You then *use* all or parts of the book to help you complete an assignment. The words *with* and *use* were italicized to help emphasize those words, because those are the exact words you will use in an Ada program when you want to take advantage of the capabilities of a package in your computer library. The packages in the computer library are also known as *library units.*

You have been taking advantage of library packages already in your programs without even knowing about it. For instance, there is a package named STANDARD that the compiler will automatically **with** and **use** every time you compile a program. The specifications of package STANDARD are available to the user in human readable form in Appendix C of the *Language Reference Manual* (LRM) and are also included in this text as Appendix C. Package STANDARD is used to define the types BOOLEAN, INTEGER, FLOAT, CHARACTER, and STRING. It also defines what operations are available in the language for each of these types. Package STANDARD also contains the declarations for the five predefined exceptions that were covered in a previous chapter. Two additional predefined subtypes (NATURAL and POSITIVE) that we have used previously are also declared in package STANDARD.

The scheme that we have been using to perform input and output operations has hidden from you the fact that all of these I/O operations are specified in a package called TEXT_IO. TEXT_IO is a shorthand way of saying "the input and output of textual (meaning *character*) information." It is called *textual* information because it appears on the keyboard and the screen as characters, as it would in a textbook. Package TEXT_IO includes the procedures SKIP_LINE and NEW_LINE and the functions END_OF_LINE and END_OF_FILE. The procedures GET and PUT, as used for characters and strings, are also specified in package TEXT_IO.

The reason for hiding the information from you was an attempt to reduce the confusion of getting started with programming. In the beginning you had never heard of a procedure or a function, let alone a package. Now that you have a better feel for procedures and functions and how they work to help you solve problems on the computer, we are telling you "the rest of the story."

Inside package TEXT_IO there are four special kinds of packages that help us perform input and output operations on objects of type INTEGER, FLOAT, FIXED, and any enumeration type. The type FIXED is mentioned here only for completeness, but it is not part of the material covered in this book. These special packages also allow us to perform I/O operations on subtypes of the just listed types. These packages are examples of a class of packages called *generic packages.* More details about TEXT_IO and generic packages will be provided later. For now we will concentrate on user-compiled packages.

User-Compiled Packages

One of the nice features of the Ada programming language is that it allows a programmer to write packages that can be put in his or her own library for use with other programs that might be written in the future. What that basically means is that operations such as N_FACTORIAL, SQUARE_ROOT, and RANDOM_NUMBER can be bundled together in an Ada package. We will call this package MATH_LIBRARY. Any time you need any of these operations in any other program, you will not have to rewrite it or even copy it into your program. You will simply **with** MATH_LIBRARY as part of your program, and the compiler will go to your computer library and get it. All you will have to do is then **use** MATH_LIBRARY, and all the things in the package can be used in your program.

Package Syntax

A package is made up of two parts, the *specification* and the *body*. The *package specification* declares all of the things that are available to your program when you **with** and **use** a package that is in your library. The *package body* contains all the details of exactly how the operations in the package specification are implemented. The package body will be hidden from view of the program that **with**s the package. The specifications basically say "Here's what's available for use in this package." The body contains all of the implementation details that the user of the package, for the most part, couldn't care less about. Another way of looking at it is to say, "Once I've written that SQUARE_ROOT operation and checked it out, all I want to do is use it. Hide it away and protect it and don't bore me with the details again."

The syntax diagram for a *package__specification* and a *package__body* are given in Figure 8.6. Notice that in the *package__specification* there are *basic__declarations*, and in the *package__body* there are *declarations*. The *declarations* used in the *package__body* are the same as any declarations that you have used in any of the programs written to date in this book. The *basic__declarations* are a restricted subset of *declarations*. The primary restriction is that *subprogram__specification* can appear in the *basic__declarations*, but the entire *subprogram__body* must appear in the *declarations* of the package body. The *subprogram__specification* includes everything in the *subprogram__declaration* up to the semicolon. The *subprogram__body* includes everything in the declaration of a subprogram from the reserved word **procedure** or **function** to the **end** subprogram name.

package__specification

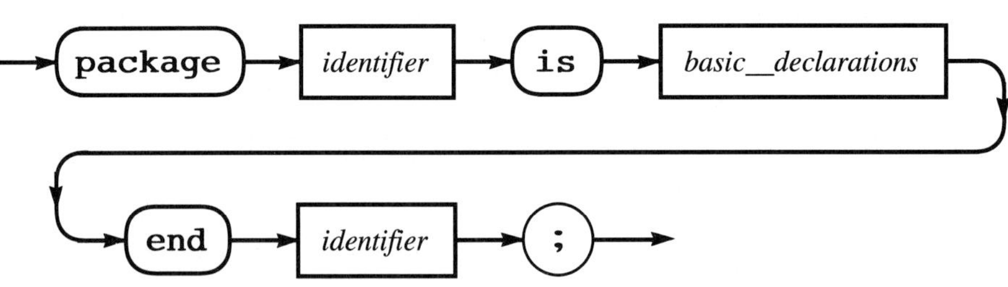

basic__declarations

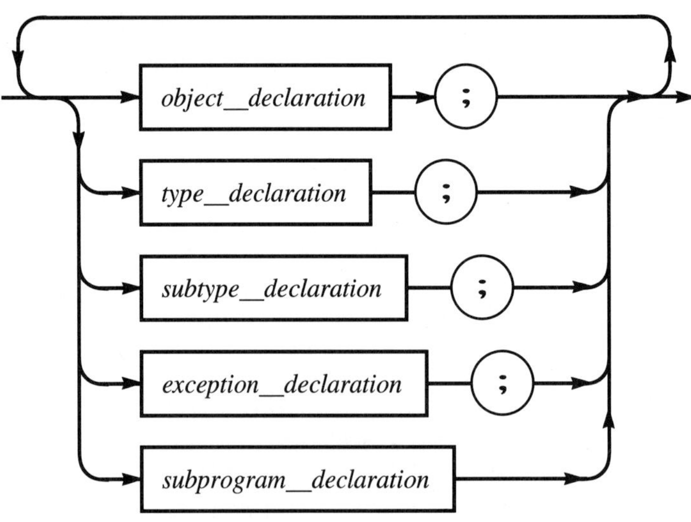

subprogram__declaration

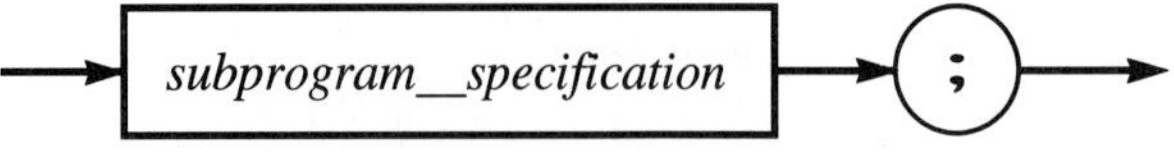

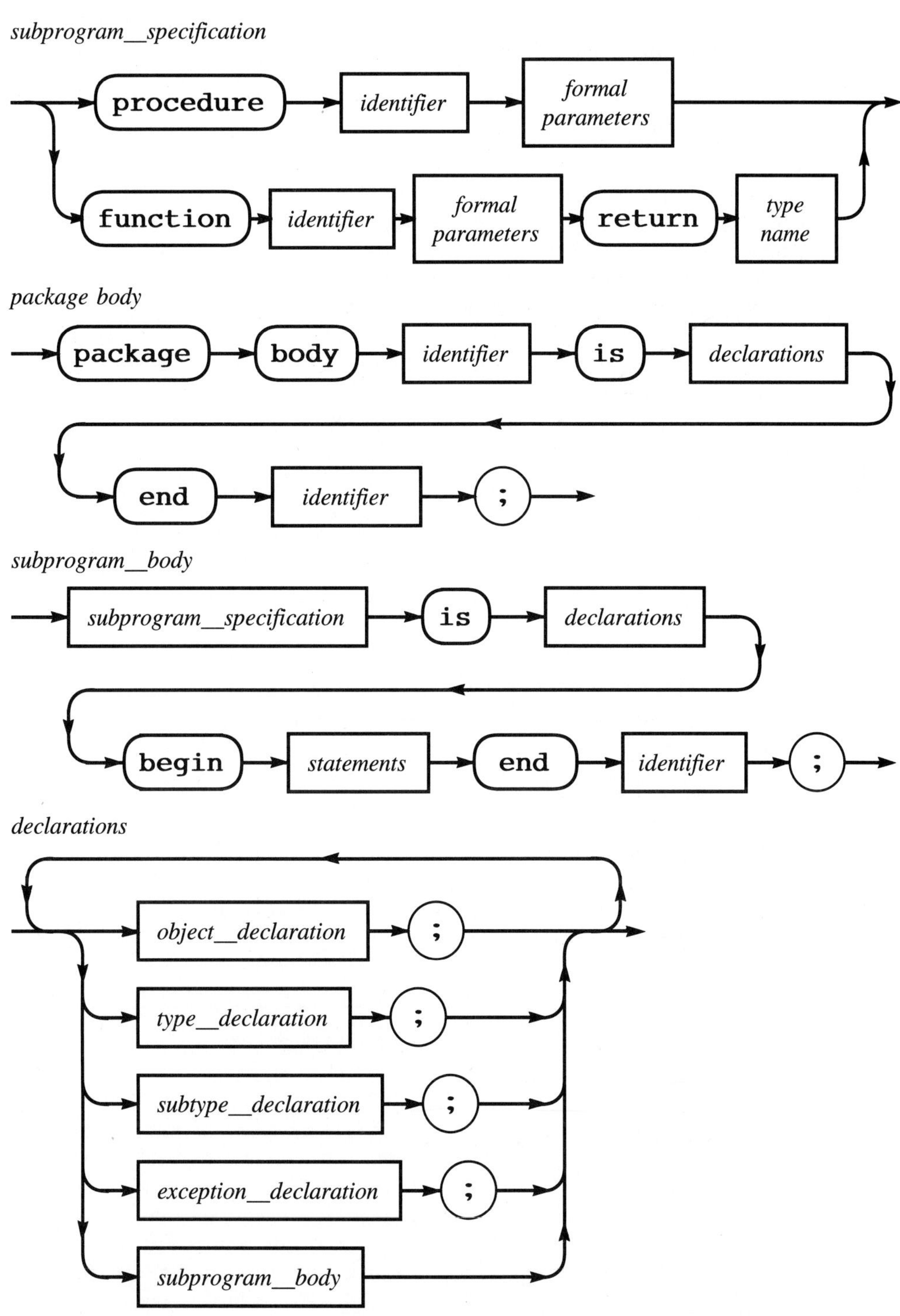

Figure 8.6 Syntax diagrams for a package.

Case Study

Math Library

We wish to write an Ada package that contains a collection of useful mathematical functions: n!, square root, random number, and sine. We will also include in this math library package the useful constants for PI (3.14159) and E (2.71828), the base of the natural logarithms.

package specification The package specification for the math library package must include the constant object declarations for PI and E and the function subprogram declarations. The package body must include the function subprogram bodies for all of the functions specified in the package specification. The package body may include any other declaration needed to fully implement all of the functions in the package specification. As an example, we will include the seed for the random number generator as an object in the package body. This hides the seed away from the user of the package and helps protect the integrity of the random number generator from any intentional or inadvertent tampering with the random number generator seed. Figure 8.7 gives the complete package specification for the math library. Figure 8.8 gives the complete package body for the math library.

```
package MATH_LIBRARY is
    PI : constant FLOAT := 3.14159;
    E  : constant FLOAT := 2.71828;
    N_FACTORIAL_TOO_LARGE : exception;
    NEGATIVE_RADICAND     : exception;
    function N_FACTORIAL ( N : NATURAL ) return NATURAL;
    function SQUARE_ROOT ( RADICAND : FLOAT ) return FLOAT;
    function RANDOM_NUMBER return INTEGER;
    function SIN ( RADIAN : FLOAT ) return FLOAT;
end MATH_LIBRARY;
```

Figure 8.7 Package specification for a math library.

exceptions Note that the specifications for the MATH_LIBRARY package also contain the declaration of two exceptions, N_FACTORIAL_TOO_LARGE and NEGATIVE_RADICAND. Both of these exceptions are available to whatever program **with**s the MATH_LIBRARY package. These exceptions will be raised by the functions N_FACTORIAL and SQUARE_ROOT, respectively. The first of these exceptions, N_FACTORIAL_TOO_LARGE, will be raised if the value of N! is larger than can be represented by the computer system. The second will be raised if the parameter RADICAND of the SQUARE_ROOT function is passed a negative value. By mathematical definition, the square root of a negative value is "imaginary" and cannot be properly represented by the SQUARE_ROOT function.

Both of these exceptions are there because we want to protect our programs from so-called impossible situations. We know that we cannot expect the computer to compute values for large factorials of N, nor can we expect it to compute the square root of a negative value. Just because we know these facts does not stop some programmer, either intentionally or inadvertently, from making such calls to these functions.

impossible situations

In the case of the N_FACTORIAL function, as shown in Figure 8.8, when the expression PRODUCT * INDEX produces an incorrect value, the system raises NUMERIC_ERROR. The function handles the NUMERIC_ERROR exception and in turn raises N_FACTORIAL_TOO_LARGE. This is done because it provides better information to the user of the package than simply allowing NUMERIC_ERROR to be propagated out of the package into the user's program. The exception N_FACTORIAL_TOO_LARGE provides more specific information to the user of the package than does the more general NUMERIC_ERROR. The exception is allowed to propagate, however, because there is no reason to allow the function to terminate normally; after all, what possible meaningful value would the function return?

The SQUARE_ROOT function (Figure 8.8) tests the RADICAND upon entry to the function. If the value of RADICAND is negative, the exception NEGATIVE_RADICAND is raised. Again, there is no reason to allow the function to terminate normally, as there is no possible value of type FLOAT that can represent the square root of a negative value.

The function RANDOM_NUMBER (Figure 8.8) is the same function we used in a previous optional section and appears there in Figure 8.3. If you did not cover that section, it should suffice to say that it generates a number at random.

The SIN function (Figure 8.8) is something we have not seen before. *Sine* is a trigonometric function that represents the ratio of the length of two sides of a right triangle. (A *right triangle* is one in which one of the three angles is a square angle, called a 90-degree angle.) The sine of either of the other two angles of a triangle is represented as the ratio of the length of the side opposite the angle to the length of the hypotenuse. (The *hypotenuse* of a triangle is the longest of the three sides of a triangle.) The value of the sine of an angle expressed in radians can be computed using the following formula

$$\sin x = x - x^3 / 3! + x^5 / 5! - x^7 / 7! \ldots$$

To implement this formula, the function SIN uses the function N_FACTORIAL, which is part of the same MATH_LIBRARY package. Any of the subprograms in a package body can use any of the other subprograms whose specifications appear in a package specification.

```
package body MATH_LIBRARY is
    RANDOM_SEED : INTEGER := 10;
    function N_FACTORIAL ( N : NATURAL ) return NATURAL is
        PRODUCT : NATURAL := 1;
```

```
    begin -- N_Factorial
        for INDEX in 2 . . N
        loop
            PRODUCT := PRODUCT * INDEX;
        end loop;
        return PRODUCT;
    exception
        when NUMERIC_ERROR =>
            raise N_FACTORIAL_TOO_LARGE;
    end N_FACTORIAL;
    function SQUARE_ROOT ( RADICAND : FLOAT ) return FLOAT is
        ERROR    : FLOAT := 0.001;
        ESTIMATE : FLOAT := RADICAND;
        ROOT     : FLOAT := RADICAND / 2.0;
    begin -- Square_Root
        if RADICAND < 0.0 then
            raise NEGATIVE_RADICAND;
        else
            loop
                exit when abs ( ESTIMATE - ROOT ) <= ROOT * ERROR;
                ESTIMATE := ROOT;
                ROOT := ( ESTIMATE + RADICAND / ESTIMATE ) / 2.0;
            end loop;
            return ROOT;
        end if;
    end SQUARE_ROOT;
    function RANDOM_NUMBER return INTEGER is
        INCREMENT  : constant INTEGER := 3641;
        MODULUS    : constant INTEGER := 729;
        MULTIPLIER : constant INTEGER := 40;
    begin -- Random_Number
        RANDOM_SEED := ( MULTIPLIER * RANDOM_SEED + INCREMENT )
                       rem MODULUS;
        return RANDOM_SEED;
    end RANDOM_NUMBER;
    function SIN ( RADIAN : FLOAT ) return FLOAT is
    begin -- Sin
        return RADIAN
            - ( RADIAN ** 3 ) / FLOAT ( N_FACTORIAL ( 3 ) )
            + ( RADIAN ** 5 ) / FLOAT ( N_FACTORIAL ( 5 ) )
            - ( RADIAN ** 7 ) / FLOAT ( N_FACTORIAL ( 7 ) );
    end SIN;
end MATH_LIBRARY;
```

Figure 8.8 Package body for a math library.

compilation unit

The two parts of the package are intentionally shown as two separate figures (Figures 8.7 and 8.8) because they actually are two separate *compilation units.* A compilation unit is a group of Ada code that can be compiled separately from any other Ada code. The programs we have written to this point have all been compilation units. A package specification is a compilation unit. A package body is a compilation unit. There is a restriction on the order in which compilation units must be compiled. A package specification must be compiled before its package body can be compiled. Any program that **with**s a package must be compiled after the package specification is compiled. The program cannot be linked and executed, however, before the package body has been compiled.

A package is not executable like a program. You never execute a package. That is not to say that the code written in a package body cannot be executed; it can. A package is placed in a computer library and can be referenced only by a program that **with**s the package. The procedures and functions that are declared in the package body can be executed only by calls to those subprograms from programs that have **with**ed that package.

Programs and Packages

We will now show how two programs can be written to take advantage of the MATH_LIBRARY package. The first one is one that we have previously written; we will show how it can be rewritten to use the capabilities available from MATH_LIBRARY.

random number generator

We used a random number generator in the program presented in Figure 8.4. Figure 8.9 shows how that same program would be written using the MATH_LIBRARY package. The programs in Figure 8.4 and 8.9 will produce exactly the same output, given the same input as shown in the **Sample Dialogue** in Figure 8.4.

Program

```
with MATH_LIBRARY;
use MATH_LIBRARY;
with I_O; use I_O;
procedure MAIN is
    subtype RATING_SCALE is INTEGER range 0 . . 10;
    WIDTH : constant INTEGER := 2;
    ANSWER : CHARACTER;
    SEED : RATING_SCALE;
    function ZERO_TO_TEN return RATING_SCALE is
    begin -- Zero_To_Ten
        return RANDOM_NUMBER rem 11;
    end ZERO_TO_TEN;
begin -- Main
    PUT ( "Hi, my name is Gollum." );NEW_LINE;
    PUT ( "I'm a perfect 10. What are you?" ); NEW_LINE;
    PUT ( "Answer with a number between 0 and 10." );
```

```
    NEW_LINE;
    GET ( SEED ); SKIP_LINE;
    if SEED > 7 then
        PUT ( "Not bad." );
    else
        PUT ( "Oh well." );
    end if;
    NEW_LINE;
    loop
        PUT ( "Would you like to rate somebody else? (yes/no)" );
        NEW_LINE;
        GET ( ANSWER ); SKIP_LINE;
        exit when ANSWER = 'n'
              or ANSWER = 'N';
        PUT ( "You name somebody and I'll give a rating." );
        NEW_LINE;
        SKIP_LINE;
        PUT ( "That individual is a " );
        PUT ( ZERO_TO_TEN, WIDTH );
        NEW_LINE;
    end loop;
    PUT ( "Before I leave, let me rate you." ); NEW_LINE;
    PUT ( "I'd say you were a " );
    PUT ( ZERO_TO_TEN, WIDTH );
    NEW_LINE;
end MAIN;
```

Figure 8.9 Program using random number generator.

polynomial roots

The second example involves solving for the roots of a second order polynomial. A *second order polynomial* is an equation that has a variable raised to the second power. The general form for a second order polynomial is

$$\mathbf{a\,x^2 + b\,x + c}$$

The value of **x** can be found given the values of **a**, **b**, and **c**. The formula for finding the values of **x** is called the *quadratic equation* and is given below:

$$\mathbf{x = \frac{-b \pm \sqrt{b^2 - 4ac}}{2a}}$$

Notice that in order to write a program to implement the quadratic equation, you must be able to take the square root of a quantity called the *discriminant,* which is

$$\mathbf{b^2 - 4ac}$$

Furthermore, if the roots of the equation are real, the discriminant must be positive. Also notice that the quadratic equation is really two equations in one. The quadratic equation has a $\pm$ sign in front of the square root of the discriminant.

Our program will ask the user to input the values of **a**, **b**, and **c** and apply the values to the quadratic equation. If the discriminant is negative, the SQUARE_ROOT function will raise the NEGATIVE_RADICAND exception and display an appropriate message on the screen. If the discriminant is positive, the SQUARE_ROOT function will return a value that the program will use to compute the values of **x**.

The pseudocode for the main procedure is

1. Get the values for a,b,c.
2. Display the polynomial.
3. Compute the roots of the polynomials.
4. Display the roots.
5. Repeat steps 1 through 4.

Notice that the first four steps of the pseudocode become procedure calls in the program in Figure 8.10. This is part of the top-down design that we have talked about previously. All programs should be designed so there is as little code as absolutely necessary in the main procedure aside from procedure calls. The procedure calls in the main procedure should show the ''big picture'' of what the program does.

block statement

The block statement in the MAIN procedure contains the exception handler for NEGATIVE_RADICAND, and it encloses only those portions of the program that are affected by a negative discriminant. If the exception NEGATIVE_RADICAND is raised in the SQUARE_ROOT function, which is called from the COMPUTE_ROOTS procedure, then the procedure DISPLAY_ROOTS is not called. When NEGATIVE_RADICAND is raised the execution of SQUARE_ROOT is terminated, the execution of COMPUTE_ROOTS is terminated, the call to DISPLAY_ROOTS is not made, and execution continues with the code in the exception handler for NEGATIVE_RADICAND, which is in the MAIN procedure.

Program

```
with MATH_LIBRARY;
use MATH_LIBRARY;
with I_O; use I_O;
procedure MAIN is
    ANSWER : CHARACTER;
    A, B, C : FLOAT;
    ROOT_1, ROOT_2 : FLOAT;
    procedure GET_COEFFICIENTS ( A, B, C : out FLOAT ) is
    begin -- Get_Coefficients
```

```
    loop
        PUT ( "To find the roots for the polynomial" );
        NEW_LINE;
        PUT ( " a * x ** 2 + b * x + c = 0" );
        NEW_LINE;
        PUT ( "Input floating point values for a, b, c " );
        PUT ( "all on one line." );
        NEW_LINE;
        begin
            GET ( A ); GET ( B ); GET ( C ); SKIP_LINE;
            exit;
        exception
            when DATA_ERROR =>
                SKIP_LINE;
                PUT ( "Bad character is input, try again." );
                NEW_LINE;
        end;
    end loop;
end GET_COEFFICIENTS;
procedure DISPLAY_POLYNOMIAL ( A, B, C : in FLOAT ) is
begin -- Display_Polynomial
    PUT ( A, 1, 3, 0 );
    PUT ( " * x ** 2 + " );
    PUT ( B, 1, 3, 0 );
    PUT ( " * x + " );
    PUT ( C, 1, 3, 0 );
    PUT ( " = 0.0" );
    NEW_LINE;
end DISPLAY_POLYNOMIAL;
procedure COMPUTE_ROOTS ( A, B, C : in FLOAT;
                          ROOT_1, ROOT_2 : out FLOAT ) is
    DISCRIMINANT_ROOT : FLOAT
                    := SQUARE_ROOT ( B ** 2 - 4.0 * A * C );
    DIVISOR : FLOAT := 2.0 * A;
begin -- Compute_Roots
    ROOT_1 := ( -B + DISCRIMINANT_ROOT ) / DIVISOR;
    ROOT_2 := ( -B - DISCRIMINANT_ROOT ) / DIVISOR;
end COMPUTE_ROOTS;
procedure DISPLAY_ROOTS ( ROOT_1, ROOT_2 : in FLOAT ) is
begin -- Display_Roots
    PUT ( "The roots to the above polynomial are " );
    PUT ( ROOT_1, 1, 3, 0 );
    PUT ( " and " );
    PUT ( ROOT_2, 1, 3, 0 );
    NEW_LINE ( 2 );
end DISPLAY_ROOTS;
```

```
begin -- Main
    loop
        GET_COEFFICIENTS ( A, B, C );
        DISPLAY_POLYNOMIAL ( A, B, C );
        begin -- Inner_Block
            COMPUTE_ROOTS ( A, B, C, ROOT_1, ROOT_2 );
            DISPLAY_ROOTS ( ROOT_1, ROOT_2 );
        exception
            when NEGATIVE_RADICAND =>
                PUT ( "There are no real roots to this polynomial." );
                NEW_LINE ( 2 );
        end; -- Inner_Block
        PUT ( "Do you want the roots of another polynomial? (y/n)" );
        NEW_LINE;
        GET ( ANSWER );
        exit when ANSWER /= 'y';
    end loop;
end MAIN;
```

Sample Dialogue

```
To find the roots for the polynomial
    a * x ** 2 + b * x + c = 0
Input floating point values for a, b, c all on one line.
1.0 1.0 -12.0
1.000 * x ** 2 + 1.000 * x + -12.000 = 0.0
The roots to the above polynomial are 3.000 and -4.000

Do you want the roots of another polynomial? (y/n)
y
To find the roots for the polynomial
    a * x ** 2 + b * x + c = 0
Input floating point values for a, b, c all on one line.
1.0 2.0 3.0
1.000 * x ** 2 + 2.000 * x + 3.000 = 0.0
There are no real roots to this polynomial.

Do you want the roots of another polynomial? (y/n)
y
To find the roots for the polynomial
    a * x ** 2 + b * x + c = 0
Input floating point values for a, b, c all on one line.
2.5 3.078 -4.678
2.500 * x ** 2 + 3.078 * x + -4.678 = 0.0
The roots to the above polynomial are 0.884 and -2.116

Do you want the roots of another polynomial? (y/n)
n
```

Figure 8.10 Program for a quadratic equation.

There is also a block statement in the procedure GET_COEFFICIENTS. The block statement contains an exception handler for the exception DATA_ERROR. This input procedure is designed in a similar manner to the "bulletproof" input procedure shown in Chapter 7 (Figure 7.9). If the user of the program makes a mistake during the input of the coefficients for the polynomial, the program will not "bomb," and the user will be given as many chances as necessary to get it right.

Package Text_IO

The entire specification for the package TEXT_IO is given in Appendix E. Here, in Figure 8.11, we give you only the portions of TEXT_IO that we have used up to this point. The reduced version is presented because there are many things in TEXT_IO that have not been discussed yet, and any attempt at this point to cover everything will only blur the points we need to make at this time.

overloading

One of the first things you notice in the partial specification for package TEXT_IO is that there are two GET procedures.

```
procedure GET ( ITEM : out CHARACTER );
procedure GET ( ITEM : out STRING );
```

How is this possible? How can you have two procedures with the same name? How does the system know which one you intend to call? Isn't this an ambiguous situation?

```
with IO_EXCEPTIONS;
package TEXT_IO is
    procedure NEW_LINE;
    procedure SKIP_LINE;
    function END_OF_LINE return BOOLEAN;
    function END_OF_FILE return BOOLEAN;
    procedure GET ( ITEM : out CHARACTER );
    procedure GET ( ITEM : out STRING );
    procedure PUT ( ITEM : in CHARACTER );
    procedure PUT ( ITEM : in STRING );
    generic
        type NUM is range <>;
    package INTEGER_IO is
        GET ( ITEM : out NUM );
        PUT ( ITEM : in NUM );
    end INTEGER_IO;
```

```
    generic
        type NUM is digits <>;
    package FLOAT_IO is
        GET ( ITEM : out NUM );
        PUT ( ITEM : in NUM );
    end FLOAT_IO;
    generic
        type ENUM is (<>);
    package ENUMERATION_IO is
        GET ( ITEM : out ENUM );
        PUT ( ITEM : in ENUM );
    end ENUMERATION_IO;
end TEXT_IO;
```

Figure 8.11 Partial specification for package TEXT_IO.

With the advent of the use of library packages, it is inevitable that the situation will arise where two different packages **with**ed by the same program will have the same procedure names. What we have here is called *overloading* of procedure names. Overloading is asking the same name to mean or do two or more different things. We have seen overloading before, but we didn't call it that or make a big deal of it. For instance, we have been overloading the numeric operators from the beginning. We use the plus symbol (+) to do addition of both INTEGER and FLOAT values. Integer addition is not the same in the computer as floating point addition. How does the system know which operation you want it to do? Your reply is, ''That's simple; it looks at the types of the operands and then does the appropriate kind of addition.''

That is exactly what the system does with the two GET procedures in TEXT_IO. It looks at the type of the parameter and then calls the appropriate procedure. This process is called *disambiguation*; it is the method used to resolve an apparent ambiguous situation. If the parameter is of type CHARACTER, the procedure

```
procedure GET ( ITEM : out CHARACTER );
```

is called. If the parameter is of type STRING, the procedure

```
procedure GET ( ITEM : out STRING );
```

is called.

Can the compiler always disambiguate? No! For example, assume that a program **with**s and **use**s three packages: YOUR_PACKAGE, MY_PACKAGE, and ANOTHER_PACKAGE. Also assume that in all three of those packages there is a procedure called DELIVER. Further assume that all three of the DELIVER procedures has one **out** parameter of type INTEGER. If the program makes a call to the procedure such as DELIVER (CODE_NUMBER), there is no way to disambiguate. There is no way to resolve the conflict without some help from the programmer.

When this situation arises, the programmer must specify which DELIVER procedure is to be called by prefacing the procedure call with the name of the package and connecting the two with a dot. Hence, MY_PACKAGE.DELIVER(CODE_NUMBER) would direct the compiler to call the DELIVER procedure in the package called MY_PACKAGE.

Some experts say that you should "never use **use**." If you do not **use**, then any reference to anything in the package specification of a **with**ed package must have this form:

prefix.identifier

The following is a very simple example program in which TEXT_IO is **with**ed but not **use**d.

```
with TEXT_IO;
procedure PREFIX is
    NAME : STRING( 1 . . 10 );
begin -- Prefix
    TEXT_IO.PUT ( "Input your name." );
    TEXT_IO.NEW_LINE;
    TEXT_IO.PUT
            ( "Make the input exactly 10 characters." );
    TEXT_IO.NEW_LINE;
    TEXT_IO.GET ( NAME );
    TEXT_IO.SKIP_LINE;
    TEXT_IO.PUT ( "Welcome to the world of package " );
    TEXT_IO.PUT ( NAME );
    TEXT_IO.NEW_LINE;
end PREFIX;
```

Notice that the line **with I_O** is missing from the above example. As mentioned earlier, until now we have been hiding all of TEXT_IO from you. Now that it is out in the open, we no longer need this "crutch."

Generic Packages

generic parameters

Inside the portion of package TEXT_IO given in Figure 8.11 are three additional packages. These packages, INTEGER_IO, FLOAT_IO, and ENUMERATION_IO, are called *generic_packages*; note the reserved word **generic** just two lines prior to **package**. The type declaration between **generic** and **package** is called a *generic_formal_parameter*.

box

The symbol **<>** is called the *box* and is used to represent some yet unknown range of values. In package TEXT_IO, above, the box is used in association with another symbol (**range**, **digits**, and parentheses). For package INTEGER_IO you see **range <>**, which means that an integer type must be supplied by the user. For package FLOAT_IO you see **digits <>**, which means that a float type must be supplied by the user. For ENUMERATION_IO you see **(<>)**, which means that a discrete type must be supplied by the user.

instantiation

Think of a generic package as a template for a potential package. Like any template, we can make as many copies of the package as we need. Each copy of a given generic package is called an *instance* of that package. The process of making a copy is called an *instantiation.* When a package is instantiated, *actual_generic_parameters* must be supplied. These actual generic parameters replace the formal generic parameters for that instance of the generic package. The process of instantiation creates a new package with a new name. Once a generic package has been instantiated, the newly named instantiated package can be used by a program, just like a nongeneric package is used by a program. The following is an example of instantiations of package `INTEGER_IO`:

```
package WHOLE_NUMBER_IO is new INTEGER_IO ( INTEGER );
package POSITIVE_IO is new INTEGER_IO ( POSITIVE );
subtype FIVE_TO_FIVE is INTEGER range -5 . . 5;
package FIVE_IO is new INTEGER_IO ( FIVE_TO_FIVE );
```

The program in Figure 8.12 is the same program as in Figure 8.9, except that the **with I_O** and the **use** `MATH_LIBRARY` have been removed, and an instantiation of `INTEGER_IO` has been added.

Program

```
with MATH_LIBRARY;
with TEXT_IO;
use TEXT_IO;
procedure MAIN is
    subtype RATING_SCALE is INTEGER range 0 . . 10;
    WIDTH : constant INTEGER := 2;
    ANSWER : CHARACTER;
    SEED : RATING_SCALE;
    package RATING_IO is new INTEGER_IO ( RATING_SCALE );
    function ZERO_TO_TEN return RATING_SCALE is
    begin -- Zero_To_Ten
        return MATH_LIBRARY.RANDOM_NUMBER rem 11;
    end ZERO_TO_TEN;
begin -- Main
    PUT ( "Hi, my name is Gollum." );NEW_LINE;
    PUT ( "I'm a perfect 10. What are you?" ); NEW_LINE;
    PUT ( "Answer with a number between 0 and 10." );
    NEW_LINE;
    RATING_IO.GET ( SEED ); SKIP_LINE;
    if SEED > 7 then
        PUT ( "Not bad." );
    else
        PUT ( "Oh well." );
    end if;
```

```
    NEW_LINE;
    loop
        PUT ( "Would you like to rate somebody else? (yes/no)" );
        NEW_LINE;
        GET ( ANSWER ); SKIP_LINE;
        exit when ANSWER = 'n'
              or ANSWER = 'N';
        PUT ( "You name somebody and I'll give a rating." );
        NEW_LINE;
        SKIP_LINE;
        PUT ( "That individual is a " );
        RATING_IO.PUT ( ZERO_TO_TEN, WIDTH );
        NEW_LINE;
    end loop;
    PUT ( "Before I leave, let me rate you." ); NEW_LINE;
    PUT ( "I'd say you were a " );
    RATING_IO.PUT ( ZERO_TO_TEN, WIDTH );
    NEW_LINE;
end MAIN;
```

Figure 8.12 Program that instantiates INTEGER_IO.

Case Study

Calendar Display

Problem Definition

We wish to design a procedure that outputs the traditional calendar display of a month. To simplify the problem we will assume that the user tells the program how many days there are in the month and what day of the week the month starts on. The day of the week will be input as SUN, MON, TUE, and so forth. For example, an input of **30** (for number of days) and WED (for Wednesday) should produce the following output:

```
 SUN  MON  TUE  WED  THU  FRI  SAT
                  1    2    3    4
   5    6    7    8    9   10   11
  12   13   14   15   16   17   18
  19   20   21   22   23   24   25
  26   27   28   29   30
```

Discussion

One approach to this problem is the following outline of an algorithm:

```
Output a heading with the names SUN, MON, TUE, etc.
Output blanks up to the first day of the month.
Output the rest of the first week.
for each remaining week do the following:
    output the numbers for the week;
    start a new line
```

A straightforward refinement of the above algorithm would produce the following pseudocode:

```
Output a heading with the names SUN, MON, TUE, etc.
for day in SUN . . first_day - 1
    write some blanks
for day in first_day . . SAT
    output date (numeric form for day)
Start a new line
date := 7 - first_day;
Repeat
    for day In SUN . . SAT
        output date + numeric form for day
    Start a new line
    date := date + 7
until date > (the number of days in the month)
```

false starts

It may not be obvious at first, but by close inspection we can observe a number of things wrong with our approach. First, the pseudocode does not work. The second **7** should be an **8** or else one number will be output twice. Fixing that will make the code look strange, but it will eliminate one problem. However, even after that "patch," the output will not be correct. Unless the last week happens to end on a Saturday, it will output that week incorrectly. Another "patch" can make it work, but that will make the code even more complicated and even less understandable. The real problems are that the code is unclear and is too complicated for the job it is accomplishing. In a situation like this, it is best to try starting over.

rethinking the problem

Let us look at the problem in a different way: All we want the program to do is to output the numbers `1` through the number of the last day and to insert `NEW_LINE` at the end of each week. The first of these chores is trivial:

```
for DATE in 1 . . (the number of the last day)
    PUT ( DATE )
```

To accomplish the second problem we can add a test for the end of the week inside of the `for` loop:

```
for DATE in 1 . . (the number of the last day)
     PUT ( DATE )
     if end of a week then
          NEW_LINE
```

To complete our second (and successful) attempt at designing our program, we need only design a test for the end of a week. A first, careless guess might be

```
if DATE rem 7 = 0 then
     NEW_LINE
```

This will work provided the month starts on a Sunday, but again look back at our sample of what we want for output. That week starts on a Wednesday, so the program should have a NEW_LINE after the first four days. The above test will produce output that begins

```
SUN  MON  TUE  WED  THU  FRI  SAT
                 1    2    3    4    5    6    7
  8    9   10   11   12   13   14
```

To determine where the NEW_LINE statements should be, the program must know when the day is Saturday. To do this we will use another variable, called DAY, that starts on the FIRST_DAY of the month. Every day, DAY is assigned the next day of the week, and when DAY is Saturday, it is the end of the week and time to insert a NEW_LINE. The correct pseudocode is as follows:

Algorithm

```
Output a heading with the names SUN, MON, TUE, etc.
Output the initial blanks.
day := first_day;
for date in 1 . . (the number of the last day)
     put ( date );
     if day is Saturday
          insert a NEW_LINE
          set day to Sunday
     else
          day is set to the next day
NEW_LINE;
```

The use of an enumeration for the days of the week and the use of ENUMERATION_IO will permit us to output the headings and input the first day of the month in a very natural way.

```
type WEEK_DAYS is ( SUN, MON, TUE, WED, THU, FRI, SAT );
package DAY_IO is new ENUMERATION_IO ( WEEK_DAYS );
use DAY_IO;
```

Also, establishing a **subtype** for the days of the month

```
subtype MONTH_DAYS is POSITIVE range 1 . . 31;
```

will help us ensure proper input. A discussion on good input procedures follows the complete display procedure, which is embedded in a test program and shown in Figure 8.13.

Program

```
with TEXT_IO; use TEXT_IO;
procedure MAIN is
--                      INPUT  : The number of days in a month and
--                               the first day of the month.
--                               Uses SUN, MON, etc
--                      OUTPUT : A calendar for the month.
--                      DESCRIPTION : Repeated prompts user information
--                                    and establishes format for a
--                                    calendar.
     subtype MONTH_DAYS is POSITIVE range 1 . . 31;
     type WEEK_DAYS is ( SUN, MON, TUE, WED, THU, FRI, SAT );
     package POSITIVE_IO is new INTEGER_IO ( POSITIVE );
     use POSITIVE_IO;
     package DAY_IO is new ENUMERATION_IO ( WEEK_DAYS );
     use DAY_IO;
     ANSWER : CHARACTER;
     FIRST_DAY : WEEK_DAYS;
     NUMBER_OF_DAYS : MONTH_DAYS;
     procedure GET_NUMBER_OF_DAYS
               ( NUMBER_OF_DAYS : out MONTH_DAYS ) is
--                      INPUT  : None
--                      OUTPUT : The number of days in the month.
--                      DESCRIPTION : Prompt the user to input the
--                                    number of days in the month.
     begin -- Get_Number_Of_Days
          PUT ( "Enter the number of days in the month:" );
          NEW_LINE;
          GET ( NUMBER_OF_DAYS );
          SKIP_LINE;
     end GET_NUMBER_OF_DAYS;

     procedure GET_FIRST_DAY ( FIRST_DAY : out WEEK_DAYS ) is
--                      INPUT  : None
--                      OUTPUT : The first day of the month.
--                      DESCRIPTION : Prompt the user to input the
--                                    first day of the month.
     begin -- Get_First_Day
          PUT ( "Enter the first day of the month:" ); NEW_LINE;
          PUT ( "SUN, MON, etc." ); NEW_LINE;
```

```
        GET ( FIRST_DAY ); SKIP_LINE;
    end GET_FIRST_DAY;

    procedure DISPLAY_MONTH ( NUMBER_OF_DAYS : in MONTH_DAYS;
                              FIRST_DAY : in WEEK_DAYS ) is
--                   INPUT   : The number of days in a given month
--                             and the first day of that month.
--                   OUTPUT : None.
--                   DESCRIPTION : Displays a calendar
--                                 for the given month.
        DAY : WEEK_DAYS := FIRST_DAY;
        FOUR_BLANKS : constant STRING := "    ";
        WIDTH : constant INTEGER := 4;
    begin -- Display_Month
        for DAY in WEEK_DAYS
        loop
            PUT ( ' ' ); PUT ( DAY );
        end loop;
        NEW_LINE;
        for BLANK_DAYS in MON . . FIRST_DAY
--                            SUN . . Week_Day'Pred ( first_day )
--                            makes more sense here, but unfortunately
--                            there is no predecessor if first_day is SUN
        loop
            PUT ( FOUR_BLANKS );
        end loop;
        for DATE in 1 . . NUMBER_OF_DAYS
        loop
            PUT ( DATE, WIDTH );
            if DAY = SAT then
                DAY := SUN;
                NEW_LINE;
            else
                DAY := WEEK_DAYS'SUCC ( DAY );
            end if;
        end loop;
        NEW_LINE;
    end DISPLAY_MONTH;

begin -- Main
    PUT ( "I will display the calendar of a month." ); NEW_LINE;
    loop
        GET_NUMBER_OF_DAYS ( NUMBER_OF_DAYS );
        GET_FIRST_DAY ( FIRST_DAY );
        DISPLAY_MONTH ( NUMBER_OF_DAYS, FIRST_DAY );
        PUT ( "Do you wish to see another month?" ); NEW_LINE;
        PUT ( "(yes or no):" ); NEW_LINE;
```

```
            GET ( ANSWER ); SKIP_LINE;
            exit when ANSWER = 'n'
                   or ANSWER = 'N';
        end loop;
        PUT ( "Have a good month!" ); NEW_LINE;
    end MAIN;
```

Sample Dialogue

```
I will display the calendar of a month.
Enter the number of days in the month:
31
Enter the first day of the month:
SUN, MON, etc.
TUE
SUN  MON  TUE  WED  THU  FRI  SAT
                1    2    3    4    5
  6    7    8    9   10   11   12
 13   14   15   16   17   18   19
 20   21   22   23   24   25   26
 27   28   29   30   31
Do you wish to see another month?
(yes or no):
no
Have a good month!
```

Figure 8.13 Calendar program.

User-Friendly Input

The input procedures (GET_NUMBER_OF_DAYS and GET_FIRST_DAY) were intentionally quite simple so we could concentrate on the problem of how to get the NEW_LINE at the correct place. Now let's apply the techniques of robustness and friendliness that we learned in a previous section.

The GET_NUMBER_OF_DAYS procedure in Figure 8.13 allows the user to choose any value within the range of 1 to 31. Many of these values are inappropriate, for we know that the number of days for any given month fall within a very narrow range. You may remember the old saying "30 days has September, April, June, and November; all the rest have 31, except February, which has 28, or 29 if it's a leap year." Thus we can test the number of days that the user inputs with a simple membership test (MONTH_LENGTH **in** 28 . . 31). This is done in Figure 8.14, and an exception is raised if the value is out of the proper range. The first prompt makes no mention of the range of acceptable values, for there is no reason to insult the user's intelligence. It isn't until the user makes a mistake that he or she is given a reminder. The exception handler is designed to trap any exception, not just the one raised if the value is smaller than 28. The user could input a large positive or negative value, or the user could inadvertently hold the shift key down and strike 30, which would be #). In either case the exception handler would catch the mistake and allow the user to try again and again until it is done correctly. Thus the procedure is not only user-friendly, but also it is robust in that incorrect input will not cause the program to terminate.

```
procedure GET_NUMBER_OF_DAYS
          ( NUMBER_OF_DAYS : out MONTH_DAYS ) is
--                    INPUT   : None
--                    OUTPUT : The number of days in the month.
--                    DESCRIPTION : Prompt the user to input the
--                                  number of days in the month.
    MONTH_LENGTH : MONTH_DAYS;
begin -- Get_Number_Of_Days
    loop
        begin
            PUT ( "Enter the number of days in the month:" );
            NEW_LINE;
            GET ( MONTH_LENGTH ); SKIP_LINE;
            if MONTH_LENGTH in 28 .. 31 then
                exit;
            else
                raise CONSTRAINT_ERROR;
            end if;
        exception
            when others =>
                SKIP_LINE;
                PUT ( "Bad input, " );
                PUT ( "enter a value between 28 and 31." );
                NEW_LINE;
        end;
    end loop;
    NUMBER_OF_DAYS := MONTH_LENGTH;
end GET_NUMBER_OF_DAYS;
```

Figure 8.14 Friendlier input procedure for the calendar program.

User-friendliness is applied to the procedure GET_FIRST_DAY also. The inclusion of ENUMERATION_IO in the package TEXT_IO allows the user to input a string of characters that the program will interpret as one of the values of an enumeration. There is no need to ask the user to input a numeric value that the program maps into a day of the week. Even with a string of characters as input, the program does not have to inspect the individual characters in the string and somehow map them into the correct value in the enumeration. With the proper choice of an enumeration and the instantiation of ENUMERATION_IO for that enumeration, the input is easy and natural for both the user and the programmer. It is user-friendly also because in this case the prompt shows the user the form of the expected input (SUN, MON, etc.), yet it does not bore the user with the entire list of possibilities until a mistake is made.

The example in Figure 8.15 applies not only user-friendliness but also robustness. It is user-friendly because the user input is natural and also because ENUMERATION_IO allows normal user input in upper- or lowercase. It displays robustness by allowing the user to correct any input mistakes, because the exception handler catches any kind of input errors.

```
procedure GET_FIRST_DAY ( FIRST_DAY : out WEEK_DAYS ) is
--                      INPUT   : None
--                      OUTPUT : The first day of the month.
--                      DESCRIPTION : Prompt the user to input the
--                                    first day of the month.
begin -- Get_First_Day
    loop
        begin
            PUT ( "Enter the first day of the month:" ); NEW_LINE;
            PUT ( "SUN, MON, etc." ); NEW_LINE;
            GET ( FIRST_DAY ); SKIP_LINE;
            exit;
        exception
            when others =>
                SKIP_LINE;
                PUT ( "Bad input, " );
                PUT ( "enter three letters for the day." );
                NEW_LINE;
                PUT ( "SUN, MON, TUE, WED, THU, FRI, or SAT" );
                NEW_LINE;
        end;
    end loop;
end GET_FIRST_DAY;
```

Figure 8.15 Friendlier and more robust input procedure for the calendar program.

Starting Over

The previous case study illustrates an important engineering design principle. If a program or algorithm is very difficult to understand or performs very poorly, do not try to fix it; instead throw it away and start over. This will result in a program that is clearer to read and less likely to contain hidden errors. What may not be so obvious is that by throwing out the poorly designed code and starting over, you will produce a working program faster than if you try to repair the old code (or old pseudocode.) It may seem like wasted effort to throw out all the code that you worked so hard on, but that is the most efficient way to proceed. The work that went into the discarded code is not wasted. The lessons you learned by writing it will help you design a better program and do so faster than if you started with no experience. The code itself is unlikely to help at all.

Case Study

Complete Calendar Program

Problem Definition

We want to embed the calendar display procedure from Figure 8.13 in a complete calendar program. The calendar program will accept a month and year in a natural manner and will then output the calendar display for that particular month and year.

refining the definition

Calendars are now taken for granted, so we tend to forget that they are a complicated computational task. Historically they have presented society with a serious problem, a problem that has not always been completely solved. The calendar design has changed more than once. So a date like January 1, 1132, has more than one possible interpretation, since the calendar used then was different than what we use now (which makes one wonder exactly what time is referred to by the word *then*). As we indicated in Chapter 7, calculating leap years is complicated enough to require a special computation for some century years. Moreover, if we go back far enough in history or go forward far enough into the future, that algorithm will not work accurately enough, and we will need to complicate the calculation even more. To eliminate all these problems, we will require only that the program apply to years in the relatively recent past and the relatively near future—specifically the years 1901 through 2999. For those years, a year is a leap year if it is divisible by four, and no additional corrections are needed. This rule even works correctly for the century year 2000, although it would not work correctly for the years 1900 and 3000.

Discussion

As the previous paragraph indicated, this is likely to be a complicated and delicate computational problem. A hastily constructed solution will probably give incorrect results as well as the frustration that results from wasted effort. This problem will require more care and more inspiration than the other problems we have seen, so we will precede slowly and methodically.

The problem of displaying the calendar for a given month can be divided into three main subproblems:

FIRST_DAY: Determine what day of the week (Sunday, Monday, etc.) the first day of the month falls on.
TOTAL_DAYS: Determine how many days there are in the month.
DISPLAY_MONTH: Call the procedure given in Figure 8.13.

enumeration type

The only meaningful values for the variable MONTH are the values JAN through DEC. Hence, we can declare an enumeration type for the months of the year. This is better than a subtype **1 . . 12** because it is a more natural way of assigning MONTH a value. Either approach is certainly better than simply making MONTH an INTEGER type, which would allow the user and the programmer to assign any positive or negative integer value to MONTH. The use of an enumeration is more natural and far less error prone. Similarly, the variable YEAR can be declared to be of the subtype **1901 . . 2999**, which we name YEARS. In this case numeric values are the natural way to go, and the subtype ensures that we are working with values that are within the values of the program design.

The function TOTAL_DAYS will return the number of days in a month. We could use the type INTEGER as the type of the value returned, but it would be preferable to use a subtype as an additional check for mistakes in the function computation. We will therefore define a subtype MONTH_DAYS as **1 . . 31** and use this as the type of the value returned by the function. Thus, our program will include the following enumeration and subtype declarations.

```
type MONTHS is ( JAN, FEB, MAR, APR, MAY, JUN,
                 JUL, AUG, SEP, OCT, NOV, DEC );
subtype MONTH_DAYS is INTEGER range 1 . . 31;
subtype MONTH_NUMBERS is INTEGER range 1 . . 12;
type WEEK_DAYS is ( SUN, MON, TUE, WED, THU, FRI, SAT );
subtype YEARS is INTEGER range 1901 . . 2999;
```

Algorithm for TOTAL_DAYS

The function TOTAL_DAYS is one part of the program that is easy to construct. The procedure specification shows the subtype that is returned:

```
function TOTAL_DAYS ( MONTH : MONTHS; YEAR : YEARS )
         return MONTH_DAYS
```

The computation is carried out by a single **case** statement:

```
case MONTH is
    when SEP | APR | JUN | NOV => return 30;
    when FEB => if LEAP_YEAR ( YEAR ) then
                    return 29;
                else
                    return 28;
                end if;
    when others => return 31;
end case;
```

In designing this **case** statement, we followed the old mnemonic saying, "Thirty days has September, April, June, and November (note the first **when**); all the rest have 31 (note the **when others**), except February, which has 28, or 29 if it's a leap year (note the case for FEB and the test of the LEAP_YEAR function)." This is an attempt to make our program look as much like the real world as possible. Programs that closely represent real-world problems are easier to solve and debug. The complete function body declaration is trivial to produce by combining these two items.

As a side issue, notice the use of multiple return statements in the preceding code segment. Some experts also consider this poor programming style because it allows multiple exits from a construction. Many of the same experts also consider multiple exits from a loop as poor style for the same reason. Most of the experts do allow the use of the **case** statement, which has multiple exits from its construction. The authors do not wish to engage in a philosophical discussion of what constitutes a construction. In our view the block of a function is a construction just as a loop or case is a construction, and we will use multiple returns from functions. Your instructor may have a different opinion.

Discussion of FIRST_DAY

The function FIRST_DAY is the complicated part of this programming assignment. It takes two arguments, MONTH and YEAR, and should return the day of the week (Sunday, Monday, etc.) for the given month of the specified year. For this purpose, we used the enumeration type called WEEK_DAYS.

```
type WEEK_DAYS is ( SUN, MON, TUE, WED, THU, FRI, SAT );
```

January 1 1901

Our approach to this problem will be to take a fixed date for which we know the day of the week and to calculate days of the week by counting forward from this day. January 1, 1901, was a Tuesday. We will define a constant JANUARY_FIRST_1901 to be TUE. We will also use the attributes POS and VAL as part of our computation. The calculation for any values of the arguments MONTH and YEAR will proceed in two stages:

NEW_YEARS_DAY: Calculate the day of the week for January 1 of YEAR.

FIRST_DAY: Use the result of the first stage to calculate the day of the week for the first day of the MONTH in that YEAR. (This will require knowing how many days there are in each month from January up to MONTH.)

Discussion of NEW_YEARS_DAY

To obtain the algorithm for the first stage, note that all years are either 365 days long or, in the case of leap years, 366 days long. Now if you look at the calendars for two successive years, you will see that if a year has 365 days, then January 1 moves ahead one weekday the next year. (If you do not have two calendars handy, you can figure this out from the fact that 365 **rem** 7 is equal to 1.) Hence, since January 1, 1901, is a Tuesday (WEEK_DAY'POS(TUE) = 2), January 1, 1902, must be a Wednesday (weekday 3), and January 1, 1903, must be a Thursday (weekday 4). Although 1904 is a leap year, January 1, 1904, occurs before the extra leap year day is inserted, so it is a Friday (weekday 5). January 1, 1905, falls after the extra day inserted in February, 1904, so January 1, 1905, falls on a Sunday (WEEK_DAY'VAL(0) = SUN, the zero was obtained as (5 + 2) **rem** 7).

To obtain the day of the week for any January first after 1901, we can start with the day JANUARY_FIRST_1901, add 1 for each 365-day year, and add 2 for each leap year up to the desired year. All this addition is performed counting by sevens, so that 7 is the same as 0; in other words, we apply the operator **rem** 7 to our calculations. Hence, our first try at an algorithm for the function NEW_YEARS_DAY is to return the value

```
( JANUARY_FIRST_1901
+ (number of non leap years)
+ 2 * (the number of leap years) )
rem 7
```

An alternative and easier algorithm is to add 1 for *every* year and then add another 1 (for a total of 2) for the leap years. That leads to the following code:

Algorithm for NEW_YEARS_DAY

```
        JANUARY_FIRST_1901 : constant WEEK_DAYS := TUE;
        ELAPSED_YEARS : INTEGER := YEAR - YEARS'FIRST;
        LEAP_YEAR_COUNT : INTEGER := ELAPSED_YEARS / 4;
    begin -- New_Years_Day
        return WEEK_DAYS'VAL
                ( ( WEEK_DAYS'POS ( JANUARY_FIRST_1901 )
                  + ELAPSED_YEARS
                  + LEAP_YEAR_COUNT )
                  rem 7 );
    end NEW_YEARS_DAY;
```

All that remains is to construct the algorithm for the function FIRST_DAY. The function has two arguments for the MONTH and the YEAR. The computation starts with the value NEW_YEARS_DAY (YEAR) and then adds in the number of days in every month up to MONTH to obtain an integer called DAY_COUNT. The week-day for the first day of the specified month is then computed as

```
WEEK_DAYS'VAL ( DAY_COUNT rem 7)
```

The complete program, including this function, is given in Figure 8.16. Notice that, since an enumeration type is a discrete type, it can be the type of a **for** loop control variable.

Program

```
with TEXT_IO; use TEXT_IO;
procedure MAIN is
--                   INPUT  : A month (JAN to DEC)
--                            and a year (1901 to 2999).
--                   OUTPUT : A calendar for the given month.
--                   DESCRIPTION : Computes the first day of the month
--                                 in the given year and displays a
--                                 calendar for that month.
--                                 The program is an example that
--                                 uses enumerations, ENUMERATION_IO
--                                 and subtypes.
    type MONTHS is ( JAN, FEB, MAR, APR, MAY, JUN,
                     JUL, AUG, SEP, OCT, NOV, DEC );
    subtype MONTH_DAYS is POSITIVE range 1 . . 31;
    type WEEK_DAYS is ( SUN, MON, TUE, WED, THU, FRI, SAT );
    subtype YEARS is POSITIVE range 1901 . . 2999;
    package MONTH_IO is new ENUMERATION_IO ( MONTHS );
    use MONTH_IO;
    package POSITIVE_IO is new INTEGER_IO ( POSITIVE );
    use POSITIVE_IO;
    package DAY_IO is new ENUMERATION_IO ( WEEK_DAYS );
    use DAY_IO;
    ANSWER : CHARACTER;
    MONTH : MONTHS;
    YEAR : YEARS;
    procedure GET ( MONTH : out MONTHS; YEAR : out YEARS ) is
--                  INPUT  : None
--                  OUTPUT : The month and the year for the calendar.
--                  DESCRIPTION : Prompt the user for the month and
--                                year for the calendar desired.
--                                Forces the user to input proper
--                                values through use of an exception
--                                handler.
```

```
    begin -- GET
        loop
            begin
                PUT ( "Enter month (JAN to DEC) " );
                PUT ( "and year (1901 to 2999):" );
                NEW_LINE;
                GET ( MONTH ); GET ( YEAR ); SKIP_LINE;
                exit;
            exception
                when others =>
                    SKIP_LINE;
                    PUT ( "Bad input, try again!" ); NEW_LINE;
            end;
        end loop;
    end GET;
    function NEW_YEARS_DAY ( YEAR : YEARS )
            return WEEK_DAYS is
--                  INPUT  : A year in the range of 1901 to 2999.
--                  OUTPUT : The first day of the given year.
--                  DESCRIPTION : Begins with the fact that the first
--                                day of 1901 was a Tuesday, adds on
--                                the intervening years, adjusts for
--                                leap years,and computes the first
--                                day of the given year.
        JANUARY_FIRST_1901 : constant WEEK_DAYS := TUE;
        ELAPSED_YEARS : INTEGER := YEAR - YEARS'FIRST;
        LEAP_YEAR_COUNT : INTEGER := ELAPSED_YEARS / 4;
    begin -- New_Years_Day
        return WEEK_DAYS'VAL ( ( WEEK_DAYS'POS ( JANUARY_FIRST_1901 )
                               + ELAPSED_YEARS
                               + LEAP_YEAR_COUNT )
                               rem 7 );
    end NEW_YEARS_DAY;
    function LEAP_YEAR ( YEAR : YEARS )
            return BOOLEAN is
--                  INPUT  : A calendar year between 1901 and 2999.
--                  OUTPUT : TRUE if a leap year, otherwise FALSE.
--                  DESCRIPTION : Uses Rem to see if the year is
--                                evenly divisable by 4.
    begin -- Leap_Year
        return YEAR rem 4 = 0;
    end LEAP_YEAR;
    function TOTAL_DAYS ( MONTH : MONTHS; YEAR : YEARS )
            return MONTH_DAYS is
--                  INPUT  : The month and the years in question.
--                  OUTPUT : The number of days in the given month.
```

```
--                 DESCRIPTION : Uses the old saying
--                               "30 days has September, April,
--                               June, and November; all the rest
--                               have 31, except February, which
--                               has 28,or 29 if it's a leap year"
--                               to determine the number of days
--                               in the given month.
    begin -- Total_Days
        case MONTH is
            when SEP | APR | JUN | NOV => return 30;
            when FEB => if LEAP_YEAR ( YEAR ) then
                                return 29;
                            else
                                return 28;
                            end if;
            when others => return 31;
        end case;
    end TOTAL_DAYS;
    function FIRST_DAY ( MONTH : MONTHS; YEAR : YEARS )
             return WEEK_DAYS is
--                 INPUT   : The month and the year for the calendar.
--                 OUTPUT : The first day of the given month.
--                 DESCRIPTION : Uses the New_Years_Day function
--                               to determine the first day of
--                               January for the given year.
--                               Counts the total number of days
--                               up to the given month.
--                               Uses Rem 7 to get the first day
--                               for the month.
    DAY_COUNT : INTEGER;
    begin -- First_Day
        if MONTH = JAN then
            return NEW_YEARS_DAY ( YEAR );
        else
            DAY_COUNT := WEEK_DAYS'POS ( NEW_YEARS_DAY ( YEAR ) );
            for PAST_MONTH in JAN . . MONTHS'PRED ( MONTH )
            loop
                DAY_COUNT := DAY_COUNT
                           + TOTAL_DAYS ( PAST_MONTH, YEAR );
            end loop;
        end if;
        return WEEK_DAYS'VAL ( DAY_COUNT rem 7 );
    end FIRST_DAY;
    procedure DISPLAY_MONTH ( NUMBER_OF_DAYS : in MONTH_DAYS;
                              FIRST_DAY : in WEEK_DAYS ) is
```

```
--                  INPUT  : The number of days in a given month
--                           and the first day of that month.
--                  OUTPUT : None.
--                  DESCRIPTION : Displays a calendar
--                                for the given month.
        DAY : WEEK_DAYS := FIRST_DAY;
        FOUR_BLANKS : constant STRING := "    ";
        WIDTH : constant INTEGER := 4;
    begin -- Display_Month
        for DAY in WEEK_DAYS
        loop
            PUT ( ' ' ); PUT ( DAY );
        end loop;
        NEW_LINE;
        for BLANK_DAYS in MON . . FIRST_DAY
--                          SUN . . Week_Day'Pred ( first_day )
--                          makes more sense here, but unfortunately
--                          there is no predecessor if first_day is SUN
        loop
            PUT ( FOUR_BLANKS );
        end loop;
        for DATE in 1 . . NUMBER_OF_DAYS
        loop
            PUT ( DATE, WIDTH );
            if DAY = SAT then
                DAY := SUN;
                NEW_LINE;
            else
                DAY := WEEK_DAYS'SUCC ( DAY );
            end if;
        end loop;
        NEW_LINE;
    end DISPLAY_MONTH;
begin -- Main
    PUT ( "This program will display the calendar for" ); NEW_LINE;
    PUT ( "any month from the years 1901 to 2999." ); NEW_LINE;
    loop
        GET ( MONTH, YEAR );
        SET_COL ( 10 );
        PUT ( MONTH ); PUT ( YEAR, 8 ); NEW_LINE;
        DISPLAY_MONTH ( TOTAL_DAYS ( MONTH, YEAR ),
                        FIRST_DAY ( MONTH, YEAR ) );
        PUT ( "Do you want to see another month? (y/n)" );
        NEW_LINE;
        GET ( ANSWER ); SKIP_LINE;
        exit when ANSWER = 'n'
              or ANSWER = 'N';
        end loop;
```

```
    PUT ( "Have a good month!" ); NEW_LINE;
end MAIN;
```

Sample Dialogue

```
This program will display the calendar for
any month from the years 1901 to 2999.
Enter month (JAN to DEC) and year (1901 to 2999):
JUN 1944
              JUN         1944
  SUN  MON  TUE  WED  THU  FRI  SAT
                        1    2    3
    4    5    6    7    8    9   10
   11   12   13   14   15   16   17
   18   19   20   21   22   23   24
   25   26   27   28   29   30
Do you want to see another month? (y/n)
no
Have a good month!
```

Figure 8.16 Complete calendar program.

Use of Subtypes for Error Detection

A common mistake when calling a function or procedure is to give the parameters in an incorrect order. For example, if the function FIRST_DAY is declared as in Figure 8.13, then the following will evaluate to the first day of February, 1950:

```
FIRST_DAY ( FEB, 1950 )
```

Suppose that we accidently reverse the first two digits in the second argument:

```
FIRST_DAY ( FEB, 9150 )
```

Since we used a subtype for the formal parameter, the computer will detect an error and raise CONSTRAINT_ERROR. The computer will see that the value **9150** is not of the subtype YEARS, which is defined as **1901 . . 2999**, and will alert us to a problem. If the parameter had instead been defined to be of type INTEGER, then the function might simply return an incorrect value. Such a mistake is likely to go unnoticed if you do not use subtypes. (Do you know what day of the week February 1, 1950, fell on?) Even if the computer does catch this mistake in some other way, it is not likely to find the correct location of the mistake unless you use subtypes.

Summary

enumeration type

Syntax:

```
type type__name is ( enumeration__list ) ;
```

Example:

```
type AUTOMOBILE is ( FORD, CHEVY, DODGE, HONDA, TOYOTA );
CAR : AUTOMOBILE;
```

This new type is an enumeration called AUTOMOBILE and its *enumeration__list* consists of 5 enumeration literals. The *enumeration__list* is an ordered list of distinct values, in that FORD < CHEVY < DODGE < HONDA < TOYOTA. The object CAR is of type AUTOMOBILE and it can contain any *one* of the values in the *enumeration__list.*

subtype

Syntax:

```
subtype identifier is type__name range range ;
```

Example:

```
subtype ZERO_TO_TEN is INTEGER range 0 . . 10;
subtype U_S_AUTO is AUTOMOBILE range FORD . . DODGE;
```

The subtype *identifier* can be used as a type name in declarations and formal parameter lists. The *type__name* in the subtype declaration is any discrete type or subtype. A subtype is a subrange of a larger type or subtype.

package specification

Syntax:

```
package identifier is basic__declarations end identifier ;
```

Example:

```
package AUTO_PACKAGE is
    type AUTOMOBILE is ( FORD, CHEVY, DODGE, HONDA, TOYOTA );
    procedure MANUFACTURE ( CAR : out AUTOMOBILE );
    function REPAIR ( CAR : AUTOMOBILE ) return AUTOMOBILE;
end AUTO_PACKAGE;
```

A package specification can contain object, type, and subprogram declarations. All declarations in a package specification are visible to any program that **with**s the package. A package specification is a library unit that is compiled separately.

package body

Syntax:

package body *identifier* **is** *declarations* **end** *identifier* **;**

Example:

```
package body AUTO_PACKAGE is
    procedure MANUFACTURE ( CAR : out AUTOMOBILE ) is
    begin
       . . .
    end MANUFACTURE;
    function REPAIR ( CAR : AUTOMOBILE ) return AUTOMOBILE is
        A_CAR : AUTOMOBILE := CAR;
    begin
        . . .
        return A_CAR;
    end REPAIR;
end AUTO_PACKAGE;
```

A package body may contain object, type, and subprogram declarations. A package body *must* contain subprogram bodies for all subprogram declarations given in the package specification. None of the declarations in a package body is visible to any user of the package. The package body is the implementation of the package specification.

generic package

Syntax:

generic *generic__parameters package__specification*

A generic package is a template for a package. A package is created from a generic package by instantiating the generic package with specific *generic__parameters.* One of the generic packages in package TEXT_IO is ENUMERATION_IO; the following is an example of an instantiation of ENUMERATION_IO.

```
package AUTO_IO is new ENUMERATION_IO ( AUTOMOBILE );
```

Exercises

Programming Exercises

1. Add a function called COS to the MATH_LIBRARY package using the following formula:

$$\text{Cos } x = 1 - \frac{x^2}{2!} + \frac{x^4}{4!} - \frac{x^6}{6!} \ldots$$

Write a program that **with**s MATH_LIBRARY and tests the COS function.

2. Add a second SIN function to MATH_LIBRARY. This one has a single INTEGER parameter that represents the angle in degrees.

PI radians = 180 degrees

Write a program that **with**s MATH_LIBRARY and tests the newly added SIN function.

3. Add a second RANDOM_NUMBER function to MATH_LIBRARY that returns a floating point value in the range 0.0 . . 1.0. Write a program that **with**s MATH_LIBRARY and tests the newly added RANDOM_NUMBER function.

4. Add a function called DEGREE that takes in a floating point value representing radians and returns an integer value that is equal to the corresponding **in** value in degrees. Write a program that **with**s MATH_LIBRARY and tests the newly added DEGREE function.

5. Add a function called RADIAN that takes in an integer value representing degrees and returns a floating point value that is equal to the corresponding **in** value in radians. Write a program that **with**s MATH_LIBRARY and tests the newly added RADIAN function.

6. Write a program to verify the following trigonometric identities using MATH_LIBRARY:

(a) $1 = \text{Cos}^2\ x + \text{Sin}^2\ x$
(b) $\text{Cos}^2\ x - \text{Sin}^2\ x = 1 + 2 * \text{Sin}\ x * \text{Cos}\ x$
(c) $\text{Cos}^4\ x - \text{Sin}^4\ x = 1 - 2 * \text{Sin}^2\ x$

7. Generate 100 random numbers in the range 0.0 . . 1.0. Use 10 frequency count elements. The values in each element should represent the number of random numbers generated in 0.1 increments.

8. Print a horizontal histogram using the values in the frequency count found from Exercise 7. Would you say that the numbers are uniformly distributed in each subrange?

9. Print the above histogram with a vertical orientation.

C H A P T E R

9

ARRAYS FOR PROBLEM SOLVING

Electronic Numerical Integrator and Calculator

The ENIAC was the first large-scale, all-electronic digital computer. Its co-inventors, J. Presper Echert and John Mauchly, built the machine at the Moore School of Electrical Engineering, University of Pennsylvania, in 1946. The machine required 1500 square feet of space, weighed 30 tons, had 18,000 vacuum tubes, and drew 130 kw of power. It could perform 5000 operations per second and ran successfully for nine years.

Chapter Contents

In this chapter we introduce a common and extremely useful class of defined data types known as *arrays.* These will be our first examples of *composite types* and will serve to introduce both the idea of a composite type and the importance of these types to problem solving. A composite type can be described briefly as a complex type built up from simpler types. A more detailed discussion of the concept is included in this chapter.

Introduction to Arrays

Suppose we wish to write a program that reads in five test scores and performs some manipulations on these scores. For instance, the program might compute the highest test score and then output the amount by which each score falls short of the highest score. The highest score is not known until all five scores are read in. Hence, all five scores must be retained in storage so that after the highest score is computed each individual score can be compared to it. To retain the five scores, we need something equivalent to five variables of type `INTEGER`. We could use five individual variables of type `INTEGER`, but five variables are hard to keep track of, so this is not an elegant solution. We could make the program more readable by giving the variables related names, such as `SCORE_1`, `SCORE_2`, and so forth, but this solution becomes absurd if the number of scores is very large. Imagine doing this if there were 100 scores instead of just five. The solution we will propose is similar to the idea of using a list of variables, but it handles the details in a much neater fashion.

To solve this dilemma we introduce a new Ada construct known as an *array.* An array is rather like a list of objects, each of which has a two-part name. One part of the name is the same for each of these objects, which collectively constitute the array. The other part is different for each object. For example, the five names for the five individual objects we need might be `SCORE( 1 )`, `SCORE( 2 )`, `SCORE( 3 )`, `SCORE( 4 )`, and `SCORE( 5 )`. The part that does not change, in this case SCORE, is the name of the array. In this example the part that can change is an integer in the range `1 .. 5`.

In Ada the type and object declarations for an array of the kind we just described can be given as follows:

```
type SMALL_ARRAY is array( 1 .. 5 ) of INTEGER;
SCORE : SMALL_ARRAY;
```

component type

The type given after the word **`of`**, such as `INTEGER` in the above declaration, is called the *component type.* This declaration is like declaring the following five variable objects all to be of type `INTEGER`:

```
SCORE( 1 ), SCORE( 2 ), SCORE( 3 ), SCORE( 4 ), SCORE( 5 )
```

indexed components

Objects like the above five that are derived from an array name are called *indexed components,* to distinguish them from the sort of objects we have seen up to now. These five indexed names are not valid Ada identifiers since they contain the parentheses symbols **( )**, so they may not look like objects. However, they have all the properties of objects. An indexed component like `SCORE( 1 )` can be used *anyplace* that an ordinary object of type `INTEGER` can be used. (There is one exception. While indexed components can be, and often are, used as actual parameters, they cannot be used as formal parameters.) For example, with `SCORE` declared in this way, all of the following are possible:

```
GET ( SCORE( 1 ) ); GET ( SCORE( 5 ) ); SKIP_LINE;
PUT ( SCORE( 1 ) ); PUT ( SCORE( 5 ) ); NEW_LINE;
EXAM_SCORE := SCORE( 5 );
SCORE( 4 )  := PROGRAM_SCORE;
--   exam_score and program_score are of type Integer
```

In addition to having all the properties of objects, these indexed components have additional properties that objects do not have. The most important of these properties is that a literal, a variable, or a more complicated expression can be used inside the parentheses.

index

The expression inside the parentheses is called the *index expression* or, more simply, the *index*. These indexes have some similarity to the subscripts on the subscripted variables used in mathematics, like the **i** in $\mathbf{x_i}$; hence, some programmers use the term *subscript* as a synonym for index. These array indexes are truly INTEGER values. For our sample array SCORE, any integer expression that evaluates to a value in the range **1 . . 5** can be placed inside the parentheses. This provides the program with a way to manipulate indexed components. For example, the following code sets the value of SCORE(2) to **99** and displays it on the screen twice:

```
INDEX := 2;
SCORE( INDEX ) := 99;
PUT ( SCORE( INDEX ) );
PUT ( SCORE( 2 ) );
NEW_LINE;
```

The variable INDEX may be of a subtype **1 . . 5** or of type INTEGER. Figure 9.1 presents a summary of the terms used in discussing indexed objects.

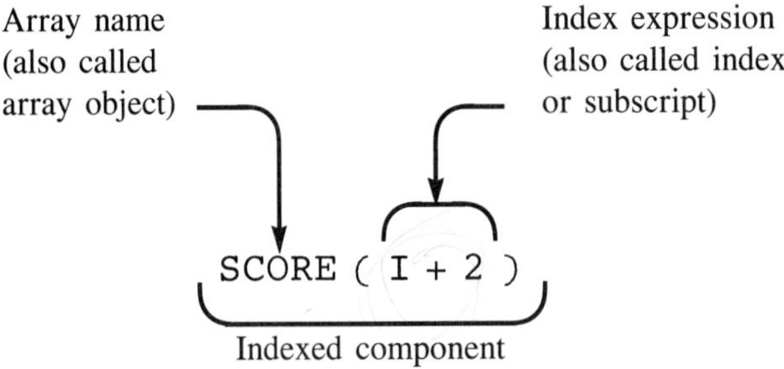

Figure 9.1 Indexed component.

Two things should be observed in the preceding piece of code. First, the array index can be a variable. This allows the program to say things equivalent to ''do the following to the **indexth** indexed component.'' Second, the identity of an indexed component, such as SCORE(INDEX), is determined by the value of its index (and, of course, the array name, like SCORE). In the example of the previous paragraph, SCORE(2) and SCORE(INDEX) are the same indexed component because the value of INDEX is 2. Similarly, since the value of INDEX is 2, the indexed component SCORE(INDEX + 3) is the same component as SCORE(5).

elements

Figure 9.2 gives an explanation of how a sample piece of Ada code manipulates the indexes and components of the array SCORE.

SCORE(1)	SCORE(2)	SCORE(3)	SCORE(4)	SCORE(5)
9	6	2	10	7

Value of array components before code is executed

Sample Code

```
PUT ( SCORE( 2 ) ); -- Display value of score( 2 ) = 6
SCORE( 2 ) := 9;    -- Change value of score( 2 ) to 9
INDEX := 2;
SCORE( INDEX + 3 ) := 8; -- Change value of score( 5 ) to 8
SCORE( 1 ) := SCORE( 4 ) - 6; -- Change value of score( 1 ) to 4
                              -- 10 - 6 = 4
```

SCORE(1)	SCORE(2)	SCORE(3)	SCORE(4)	SCORE(5)
4	9	2	10	8

Values of array components after code is executed

Figure 9.2 Manipulating array components.

As you can see from the figure, each component of an array has a single value, and all components of the array are of the same type.

For another example, suppose the value of INDEX is 2, and EXAMPLE is a procedure with one formal parameter of type INTEGER. Then the procedure call

indexed components as parameters

```
EXAMPLE ( SCORE( INDEX ) );
```

is equivalent to

```
EXAMPLE ( SCORE( 2 ) );
```

Hence, when an indexed component is an actual parameter, the index expression is always evaluated before the indexed component is copied into the formal parameter.

type declaration

component type

An array type is declared in the same place and in the same general manner as other user types. As with any type declaration, the declaration for an array type consists of the reserved word **type**, followed by the type name, the reserved word **is**, the type definition, and a semicolon. The form of an array type definition is given by the syntax diagram in Figure 9.3. For example, consider the declaration for the array SCORE given earlier in this section. The identifier SMALL_ARRAY is declared to be an array type. In that declaration we used **1 . . 5** as an *index constraint.* An index constraint can be any discrete range or any discrete subtype definition, such as a previously declared name of a discrete type or subtype. As the component type, we used the type INTEGER. Any Ada type, including the types we will introduce in later chapters, may be used as the component type.

index type

The syntax diagram in Figure 9.3 indicates that you can use any discrete range or type (or subtype) name to specify the index type of an array. Hence, you can use the types BOOLEAN and CHARACTER as index types. Whatever the index type is, an array with that index type has one indexed component for each value of the index type. Therefore, it is not practical to use the type INTEGER as the index type of an array, even though it is a discrete type, because it would create an array with thousands of components. (The exact number is machine and implementation dependent.) INTEGER'FIRST . . INTEGER'LAST would, in effect, be the *discrete_range* of the array if INTEGER were used as the index type. For other examples, consider the following declarations:

```
type NAME_1 is array( BOOLEAN ) of INTEGER;
type NAME_2 is array( 0 . . 2 ) of CHARACTER;
type NAME_3 is array( 'a' . . 'c' ) of FLOAT;
APPLE, BAKER : NAME_1;
COBBLER : NAME_3;
PIE : NAME_2;
```

The arrays APPLE and BAKER each have two indexed components,

```
APPLE( FALSE )
APPLE( TRUE )
BAKER( FALSE )
BAKER( TRUE )
```

array_type_definition

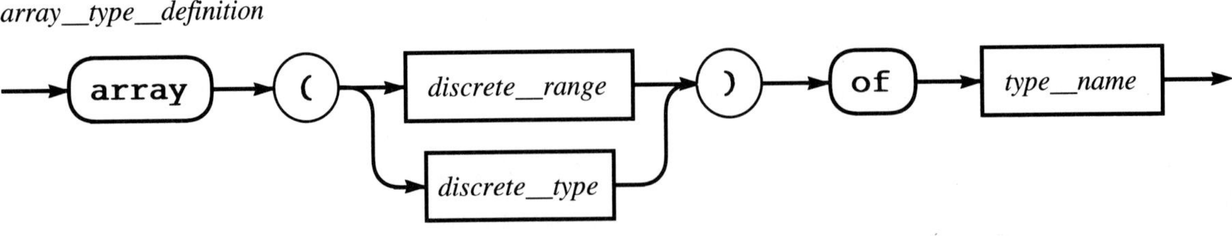

Figure 9.3 Syntax diagram for an array type definition.

each capable of holding one integer. The array PIE has three indexed components,

```
PIE( 0 )
PIE( 1 )
PIE( 2 )
```

each capable of holding one character value. The array COBBLER also has three indexed components,

```
COBBLER( 'a' )
COBBLER( 'b' )
COBBLER( 'c' )
```

each capable of holding one value of type FLOAT.

Notice that once an array type name has been declared, a particular array is declared just like an object. Neither the parentheses nor the index expression is included in the declaration of the array object.

Figure 9.4 is a complete program that uses an array to display scores in the manner we described in the opening discussion of this section. The algorithm for finding the largest value is essentially the same as that used for the program in Figure 7.6.

Program

```
with TEXT_IO; use TEXT_IO;
procedure MAIN is
--                    INPUT   : Five integer scores.
--                    OUTPUT  : Five integer scores and their
--                              difference from the highest.
--                    DESCRIPTION : Find the highest score.
    type SMALL_ARRAY is array( 1 . . 5 ) of INTEGER;
    HIGHEST_SCORE : INTEGER;
    SCORE : SMALL_ARRAY;
    package SCORE_IO is new INTEGER_IO ( INTEGER );
    use SCORE_IO;
begin -- Main
    PUT ( "Enter five scores:" ); NEW_LINE;
    GET ( SCORE( 1 ) );
    HIGHEST_SCORE := SCORE( 1 );
    for INDEX in 2 . . 5
    loop
        GET ( SCORE( INDEX ) );
        if SCORE( INDEX ) > HIGHEST_SCORE then
            HIGHEST_SCORE := SCORE( INDEX );
        end if;
    end loop;
```

```
    PUT ( "The highest score is " ); PUT ( HIGHEST_SCORE ); NEW_LINE;
    PUT ( "The scores and" ); NEW_LINE;
    PUT ( "their differences from the highest are:" ); NEW_LINE;
    for INDEX in 1 . . 5
    loop
        PUT ( SCORE( INDEX ) );
        PUT ( " off by " );
        PUT ( HIGHEST_SCORE - SCORE(INDEX ) );
        NEW_LINE;
    end loop;
end MAIN;
```

Sample Dialogue

```
Enter five scores:
5 9 2 10 6
The highest score is      10
The scores and
their differences from the highest are:
     5 off by       5
     9 off by       1
     2 off by       8
    10 off by       0
     6 off by       4
```

Figure 9.4 Program using an array.

Pitfall

Use of Plurals in Array Definitions

An array of floats contains more than one number. Hence the following type declaration seems natural:

```
type LIST is array( 1 . . 25 ) of FLOATS;
```

As innocent as it may look, it will produce an error message. There is no type named FLOATS. The **S** that seems so natural to speakers of English is incomprehensible to the compiler. If you delete the **S**, the declaration is correct. In array type definitions, the component type name is used unchanged, even though that may violate your sense of English grammar.

Type Declarations—A Summary

Type declarations may appear anywhere in the declaration part of a procedure, as long as they are declared before the type name is used in the declaration of an object of that type. Types may be defined in terms of named constants and in terms of other types. In fact, it can aid readability to do so. For example, a program might open as follows:

```
procedure SAMPLE is
     START : constant INTEGER := 0;
     STOP  : constant INTEGER := 100;
     subtype INDEX is INTEGER range START . . STOP;
     type LIST is array( INDEX ) of FLOAT;
     PI, E : FLOAT;
     SUBSCRIPT : INDEX;
     TEMPERATURE, DISTANCE : LIST;
```

Notice that no type name is used before it is defined.

local types

Just like the other kinds of declarations, type declarations may be local to a procedure. The need for local type declaration may not occur often, but types, like variables, should be declared where they are used. Do not assume that all type declarations should be at the outer level.

parameter types

It is possible to use an array type definition directly instead of first defining a type name. Hence, the following is a legal program opening:

```
procedure MAIN is
   A, B : array( 1 . . 100 ) of FLOAT;
```

This is called an *anonymous* array declaration. It is called anonymous because the type has no known name, hence it is anonymous. Arrays are the only anonymous data type covered in this textbook. (Anonymous task types also are allowed in Ada, but tasks are beyond the scope of this textbook.) A problem with anonymous arrays is that variables declared of a common anonymous type do not have the same type name. In our example above, A and B do not have the same type name because the type name is not known. Thus the assignment `A := B;` is not legal.

It is better to declare names for array types and to refer to the array types by name. When specifying a type for a procedure or function parameter, it is absolutely necessary to use a type name. A formal parameter list cannot contain any type definitions, only type names. More often than not you will want to pass an array as a parameter, and if the array is an anonymous type, you will have to go back and give it a name. You might as well get in the habit of giving names to all array definitions.

Input and Output with Arrays

You cannot use an entire array as a parameter for any of the GET or PUT procedures in TEXT_IO. For instance, if the array SCORE is declared as in Figure 9.4, then the following is not allowed:

```
GET( SCORE ) -- NOT ALLOWED if SCORE is an array type
```

Similarly it is not possible to output an array with a statement like

```
PUT( SCORE ) -- NOT ALLOWED if SCORE is an array type
```

Typically input and output is done with **for** loops, as in Figure 9.4, or in loops with an **exit when** END_OF_FILE.

Partially Filled Arrays

Often the exact size needed for an array is not known at the time a program is written. Sometimes the required size will differ from one run of the program to another. Many programming languages, including Ada, allow the size of an array to be determined by some sort of input at the time that the program is run. Examples of unconstrained arrays and arrays with expressions in the discrete range of the index will be covered later in this chapter. For now we will assume that the size of all arrays must be declared at the time the program is written. Thus, if we do not know how large an array must be, we must declare the array to be of the largest size the program could possibly need. Then the program is free to use as much or as little of the array as necessary.

Partially filled arrays require some special care. The program must keep track of how much of the array is used and must not reference any indexed component that has not been given a value. To illustrate the point, consider the program in Figure 9.4. That program works fine provided there are exactly five scores, but suppose that the number of scores will vary from one run of the program to another. Perhaps different students who have taken different numbers of exams will be using the program. If we know the maximum number of scores possible, then we can declare the array to be that large. If the maximum number is 10, then the following declarations will do:

```
MAXIMUM_SIZE : constant INTEGER := 10;
subtype INDEX_CONSTRAINT is INTEGER range 1 . . MAXIMUM_SIZE;
type SMALL_ARRAY is array( INDEX_CONSTRAINT ) of INTEGER;
SCORE : SMALL_ARRAY;
LAST, INDEX : INDEX_CONSTRAINT;
```

Since there may be less than the maximum number of scores, the program needs to keep track of which indexed components have been used. This can be accomplished with a variable LAST to record the last index used, as illustrated in Figure 9.5. The scores are read into the array SCORE, and every time another number is entered into the array, the value of LAST is increased by one. A complete program that illustrates this technique is displayed in Figure 9.6. Notice that, when writing out the array, the program only outputs those components that have a value.

SCORE (1)	SCORE (2)	SCORE (3)	SCORE (4)	SCORE (5)	SCORE (6)	SCORE (7)	SCORE (8)	SCORE (9)	SCORE (10)
5	9	2	10	6	?	?	?	?	?

LAST = 5

Array with last-used position recorded

SCORE (1)	SCORE (2)	SCORE (3)	SCORE (4)	SCORE (5)	SCORE (6)	SCORE (7)	SCORE (8)	SCORE (9)	SCORE (10)
5	9	2	10	6	3	?	?	?	?

LAST = 6

Array with one more array element value

Figure 9.5 Partially filled array.

Program

```
with TEXT_IO; use TEXT_IO;
procedure MAIN is
--                    INPUT  : At least 1 and up to 10 integer scores.
--                             The input is terminated with a -1.
--                    OUTPUT : Each score input and its difference
--                             from the highest score.
--                    DESCRIPTION : Store the scores in an array.
--                                  Find the highest score.
--                                  Compare all scores to the highest.
    MAXIMUM_SIZE : constant INTEGER := 10;
    subtype INDEXES is INTEGER range 1 . . MAXIMUM_SIZE;
    type SMALL_ARRAY is array( INDEXES ) of INTEGER;
    INPUT_VALUE : INTEGER;
    HIGHEST_SCORE : INTEGER := 0;
    LAST : INDEXES := 1;
    SCORE : SMALL_ARRAY;
    package SCORE_IO is new INTEGER_IO ( INTEGER );
    use SCORE_IO;
begin -- Main
    PUT ( "Enter up to " ); PUT ( MAXIMUM_SIZE, 1 );
    PUT ( " scores." ); NEW_LINE;
    PUT ( "Terminate the input with a -1 and a return." );
    NEW_LINE;
```

```
loop
    GET ( INPUT_VALUE );                              -- SCORE( LAST )
    if INPUT_VALUE < 0 then                           -- SCORE( LAST )
        LAST := LAST - 1;
        exit;
    elsif INPUT_VALUE > HIGHEST_SCORE then -- SCORE( LAST )
        HIGHEST_SCORE := INPUT_VALUE;
    end if;
    SCORE ( LAST ) := INPUT_VALUE;
    if LAST = MAXIMUM_SIZE then
        PUT ( "The array was filled with the input of " );
        PUT ( INPUT_VALUE, 1 );                       -- SCORE( LAST )
        NEW_LINE;
        PUT ( "Additional values were ignored." );
        NEW_LINE;
        exit;
    else
        LAST := LAST + 1;
    end if;
end loop;
PUT ( "The highest score is " ); PUT ( HIGHEST_SCORE );
NEW_LINE;
PUT ( "The scores and " );
PUT ( "their differences from the highest score are:" );
NEW_LINE;
for INDEX in 1 . . LAST
loop
    PUT ( SCORE( INDEX ) ); PUT ( " off by " );
    PUT ( HIGHEST_SCORE - SCORE( INDEX ) );
    NEW_LINE;
end loop;
end MAIN;
```

Sample Dialogue

```
Enter up to 10 scores.
Terminate the input with a -1 and a return.
5 9 2 10 6 3 -1
The highest score is 10
The scores and their differences from the highest score are:
     5 off by      5
     9 off by      1
     2 off by      8
    10 off by      0
     6 off by      4
     3 off by      7
```

Figure 9.6 Program using a partially filled array.

It is more efficient to use scalar objects than indexed objects. Fewer machine instructions are required to access scalar objects than index objects, so execution is faster. In the four lines of code below, which were extracted from the program in Figure 9.6, the scalar variable `INPUT_VALUE` was used instead of `SCORE ( LAST )`. The comment, `-- SCORE( LAST )`, was inserted on those lines only to draw your attention to the fact that a substitution had been made.

efficient code

```
GET ( INPUT_VALUE );                              -- SCORE( LAST )
if INPUT_VALUE < 0 then                           -- SCORE( LAST )
elsif INPUT_VALUE > HIGHEST_SCORE then            -- SCORE( LAST )
PUT ( INPUT_VALUE, 1 );                           -- SCORE( LAST )
```

We all know that there is "no free lunch," so what did this substitution cost? The cost was space for the simple variable `INPUT_VALUE` and the time to execute the assignment statement

```
SCORE( LAST ) := INPUT_VALUE;
```

For small arrays such an improvement is hardly worth the cost. However, if the array had been of size 10,000 or 30,000, the program would run very significantly faster with the simple variable substituted for the index variable. This is particularly true if the index variable is referenced several times inside a loop. If a loop contains only one or two references to an index variable, it is not worth making a substitution.

The sample program in Figure 9.6 has no need to allow for an empty list of scores. However, in other situations a program may have to cope with an empty list of data items. For example, a list of sales figures might be empty if no sales were made. In these cases a program may need to record the fact that no array elements were used. If the index type is `1 . . MAXIMUM_SIZE` and the variable `LAST` records the last index used, then an empty list can be indicated by setting `LAST` equal to **0**. If this is done, then the type of `LAST` cannot be the index type of the array, since `LAST` may assume a value outside that range. In this situation `LAST` would have to be declared to be of type `INTEGER` or of subtype `0 . . MAXIMUM_INDEX`. We will use this technique in a program later in this chapter (Figure 9.9).

empty arrays

Although we have assumed for now that the size of an array cannot be determined by the user, we can write our programs so the array sizes can be increased or decreased by making only minor changes in the program. If we declare one or both bounds on the index type to be defined constants, like `MAXIMUM_SIZE` in our sample, then we can write the program in such a way that a simple change in these defined constants will produce a correct program for different-sized arrays.

providing for array expansion

Pitfall

Array Index Out of Range

The most common programming error made when using arrays is attempting to reference a nonexistent index. If the array index subtype is `1 . . MAXIMUM_SIZE` for the array `SCORE`, and `INDEX` is of type `INTEGER`, then a

constraint_error

reference to SCORE(INDEX), when the value of INDEX is either less than **1** or greater than MAXIMUM_SIZE, is meaningless and will cause the exception CONSTRAINT_ERROR to be raised. This is particularly likely to happen as the first or last step of a loop that processes the entire array. If possible, the type of any variable used to index a component of an array should be of the same subtype as was used in the index portion of the array declaration. This was done in Figure 9.6.

A more subtle and related problem can arise when the index to an array is an expression, not just a simple variable. Consider the following declarations:

```
subtype INDEXES is INTEGER range 1 . . MAXIMUM_SIZE;
type POSITIVE_ARRAY is array( INDEXES ) of POSITIVE;
INPUT_VALUE : INDEXES;
LAST : INDEXES := 1;
LIST : POSITIVE_ARRAY;
OFFSET : INTEGER;
```

and the following assignment statement:

```
LIST ( LAST - OFFSET ) := INPUT_VALUE - 5;
```

Assume CONSTRAINT_ERROR is raised at this statement. Was it caused by the index (LAST - OFFSET) being out of range, or was it caused by the assignment of the value of the expression (INPUT_VALUE - 5), which is negative? If the exception is not handled and the program terminates, some systems may give you a clue as to the value that caused the exception. If that does not happen, it may take some detective work in the form of output debug statements to find the cause of the problem.

exceeding array capacity

When reading input into an array with a loop, one way to guard against a CONSTRAINT_ERROR is by testing to see if the array is full, and then terminating the loop if the array is full. The following section of code taken from Figure 9.6 was written to account for this situation:

```
if LAST = MAXIMUM_SIZE then
   PUT ( "The array was filled with the input of " );
   PUT ( INPUT_VALUE, 1 );                -- score( last )
   NEW_LINE;
   PUT ( "Additional values were ignored." );
   NEW_LINE;
   exit;
else
   LAST := LAST + 1;
end if;
```

Be sure to notice that we have inserted code to output a warning if the array is too small. Without such a warning message we would avoid a CONSTRAINT_ERROR, but we would likely produce an even worse situation: an undetected error. If we omit the warning message and there is too much input for the array, then the user might not notice that something is wrong.

Exercises

Self-Test Exercises

1. Which of the following are legal type or subtype declarations?

```
type ANSWER_LIST is array( 0 . . 10 ) of BOOLEAN;
subtype INDEX is INTEGER range -100 . . -50;
type LIST is array( INDEX ) of FLOAT;
type COUNT is array( CHARACTER ) of INTEGER;
subtype NON_NEGATIVE is INTEGER range 0 . . INTEGER'LAST;
type TALLY is array( 'a' . . 'z' ) of NON_NEGATIVE;
type ANSWER_TYPE is array( BOOLEAN ) of NON_NEGATIVE;
type TEMPORARY_COUNT is array( FLOAT ) of INTEGER;
type GRADE_TALLY is array ( 0.0 . . 4.0 ) of INTEGER;
```

2. Write suitable type declarations for each of the following:

(a) An array to hold 100 scores, each between zero and 10.
(b) An array of floats indexed by the type 'a'.. 'z'.
(c) An array of characters whose smallest index is **−5** and whose largest index is **19.**

3. Give suitable type and object declarations for data of each of the following kinds:

(a) A list of 100 or fewer scores, each a whole number in the range zero to 10.
(b) An array to record, for each letter of the alphabet, the number of students in a class whose last name starts with that letter.
(c) An array to record which students have completed graduation requirements. The students are numbered 1 through 100. The array records whether or not they can graduate and nothing else.

4. The following piece of code is supposed to add all the elements in an array A with 100 elements. It does not work. What is wrong with it, and how should it be fixed?

```
SUM := 0;
for ELEMENT in A( 1 ) . . A( 100 )
loop
    SUM := SUM + ELEMENT;
end loop;
```

5. Write code to initialize an array CENTIGRADE declared as follows so that each element has value zero:

```
type TEMPERATURE_LIST is array( 0 . . 100 ) of FLOAT;
CENTIGRADE : TEMPERATURE_LIST
```

6. If CENTIGRADE is declared as in the previous exercise, is the following legal?

```
CENTIGRADE := 0;
```

7. The following piece of code is supposed to test an array of elements to see if they are in order. It contains a bug. What is it?

```
IN_ORDER : BOOLEAN := TRUE;
type LIST is array( FIRST . . LAST ) of INTEGER;
ELEMENT : LIST;
   . . .
for INDEX in FIRST . . LAST
loop
    if ELEMENT( INDEX ) > ELEMENT( INDEX + 1 ) then
        IN_ORDER := FALSE;
    end if;
end loop;
```

8. Write code that reads exactly six letters into an array and then outputs them in reverse order. The array is declared as follows:

```
type WORD is array( 1 . . 6 ) of CHARACTER;
LETTER : WORD;
```

9. Write code that reads a list of up to 10 positive integers into the array NUMBERS, declared as shown below, and then writes the integers back to the screen. The input list is terminated with a negative number. The negative number is not written back out.

```
type LIST is array( 1 . . 10 ) of POSITIVE;
NUMBERS : LIST;
```

The Notion of a Data Type

The word *data,* in its most general sense, refers to anything that can be manipulated by a computer program. A *data type* is a particular type or kind of data, together with some rules for how these data items can be manipulated. The types INTEGER, FLOAT, CHARACTER, and BOOLEAN are provided automatically in the Ada language. Additionally we have seen how subtypes and array types can be defined within an Ada program.

One way to think of a data type is as a description of the values that an object of that type can have. A data type is defined by specifying the values of that type and the operations that are allowed on those values. For example, the values of the Ada type INTEGER are all the negative integers greater than or equal to the smallest negative integer the computer can handle (INTEGER'FIRST), the integer zero, and all the positive integers less than or equal to INTEGER'LAST. The operations that are provided include addition, subtraction, multiplication, division quotient, division remainder, and the relational operators such as = and <. The subtype 1 . . 5 has the same operations but a different set of values, namely, 1, 2, 3, 4, and 5. They are said to *inherit* the operations from the parent type or base type. The type BOOLEAN consists of the two values, TRUE and FALSE, together with the operations on those values. The operations consist of **and**, **or**, **xor**, **not**, and all the comparison operations.

The discussion in the previous paragraph is easy to apply to simple data types such as INTEGER or BOOLEAN. However, at first reading it may not be apparent that it also applies to array types. In the next section we will see that, when viewed properly, it does.

Arrays as a Composite Type

One can consider an array to be a collection of indexed components that are named in a convenient and uniform way. For instance, the array LIST, declared as follows, can be thought of as five indexed components, LIST(0), LIST(1), and so forth, each capable of holding one value of type FLOAT.

```
type FLOAT_ARRAY is array ( 0 . . 4 ) of FLOAT;
LIST, VECTOR : FLOAT_ARRAY;
```

This point of view is often adequate. However, to understand the complete nature of arrays, you must also take another view.

An array can also be viewed as a single object of a complex type. Our array LIST can be thought of as a single variable whose value is a list of five floating point numbers, such as

```
2.3, 4.0, 3.6, 2.8, 3.6
```

To emphasize this point of view, objects like LIST are called *array objects.* Do not confuse the terms *array object* and *indexed component*; LIST is an array object; LIST(3) is an indexed component. Figure 9.7 illustrates the various terms and presents one way to visualize arrays and array values.

Since an array object can be viewed as a single object with a single compound value, you can often treat it just like any other object. For example, with the array objects LIST and VECTOR declared as above, the following assignment statement is perfectly valid:

```
VECTOR := LIST;
```

This statement sets the value of VECTOR equal to the value of LIST. After this statement the value of VECTOR(0) will be the same as that of LIST(0), that of VECTOR(1) the same as LIST(1), and so forth for each component of the array VECTOR.

array parameters

We have already noted that an indexed component such as LIST(1) can be used as a parameter in a procedure call. It is also possible to use an entire array, such as VECTOR, as a single parameter to a procedure or function. In such cases the array is treated as a single object with a single compound value. The formal parameter in the procedure specification and the actual parameter in the procedure call are specified by giving the array name without parentheses or indexes. For example, if the array type FLOAT_ARRAY is declared as above, then the following is a legitimate procedure specification:

```
procedure SAMPLE ( LIST : in FLOAT_ARRAY;
                   VECTOR : in out FLOAT_ARRAY )
```

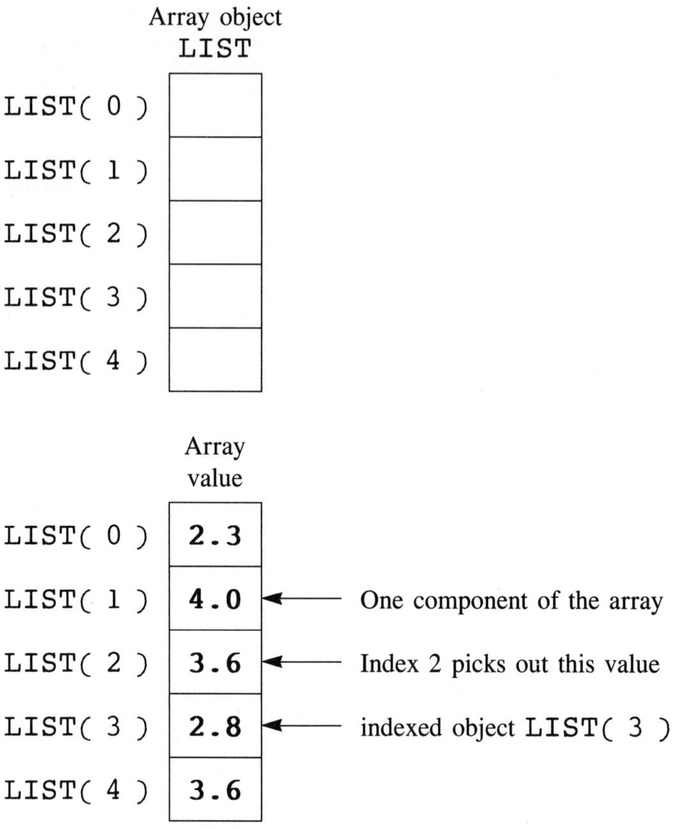

Figure 9.7 Array and array value.

If TEMPERATURE and PRESSURE are declared to be of type FLOAT_ARRAY, the following is a legitimate procedure call:

```
SAMPLE ( TEMPERATURE, PRESSURE );
```

A complete example of array parameters is given in the next "Case Study."

Be sure to note the difference between using an array object as a parameter and using an indexed component as a parameter. To illustrate this let us continue to assume that LIST is an array of type FLOAT_ARRAY, as in the previous discussion. When the entire array is passed as a parameter, then the parameter type must be FLOAT_ARRAY and the actual parameter is LIST, written without any parentheses or indexes. When only one indexed component is passed, such as LIST(3), then the parameter type must be FLOAT and both parentheses and an index are used when the actual parameter is given. For example, consider the following procedure specification:

```
procedure SECOND_SAMPLE ( VALUE : in FLOAT;
                          ELEMENT : out FLOAT )
```

A possible procedure call is

```
SECOND_SAMPLE ( LIST( 3 ), LIST( 1 ) );
```

In this case we want only indexed components, not entire arrays, as actual parameters. In the previous case we wanted entire arrays as actual parameters.

composite types

Array types are a good illustration of the notion of a *composite type*. All the types introduced in previous chapters are scalar types. Scalar types, whether predefined by Ada or defined by the programmer, have values that intuitively are indivisible units. The character `'A'` cannot be meaningfully decomposed into parts. The real number `2.34` intuitively could be decomposed in a few different ways, but we usually think of it as a single item, and the Ada language treats it as a single item. The same holds for the other simple types. In addition to these simple types, Ada, as well as most other programming languages, allows the programmer to define more complicated types whose values are compound items composed of a number of values of some simpler type or types. These sorts of compound types are called *composite types* because, unlike the simple types, they have a structure that can be meaningfully decomposed by operations provided within the programming language. For example, to reference one element, as opposed to an entire array, we can combine an index and an array object to obtain an indexed component such as `VECTOR( 2 )`.

Allowable Function Types

Viewing an array as a single value naturally leads to the conclusion that a function can return an array as a value. This conclusion is correct for the Ada language. In Ada the value returned by a function can be an array type. In fact the value returned by a function may be any user-defined or predefined type.

Case Study

Searching an Array

As an example of the use of array parameters, we will construct an algorithm to search a partially filled array for a particular value and then implement it as a boolean-valued Ada function with an array parameter.

Problem Definition

The array type is as follows:

```
MAXIMUM_SIZE : constant INTEGER := 10;
subtype EXTENDED_INDEXES is INTEGER range 0 . . MAXIMUM_SIZE;
subtype INDEXES is EXTENDED_INDEXES range 1 . . MAXIMUM_SIZE;
type INTEGER_ARRAY is array( INDEXES ) of INTEGER;
```

where EXTENDED_INDEXES is a subtype of INTEGER, and INDEXES is a subtype of EXTENDED_INDEXES.

Our function will be given three pieces of data: an array ELEMENT of type INTEGER_ARRAY, an index value LAST, and one integer VALUE. The function is supposed to tell us whether or not the integer VALUE is one of the components in the array:

```
ELEMENT( 1 ), ELEMENT( 2 ), . . . ELEMENT( last )
```

For example, the list of numbers might be a list of invalid credit card numbers, so the function could be used to find out if a given credit card should or should not be accepted by a merchant. Since there are exactly two possible outcomes, we will design the function to return a boolean value. If VALUE is equal to one of the elements, then our function will return TRUE; otherwise, it will return FALSE.

Discussion

brute force method

To accomplish this task our algorithm will simply try all possible values for the index. The approach of trying all possibilities is called the *brute force approach.* It is not always efficient, but it is straightforward and effective.

Algorithm

serial search

If the possibilities are stored in an array, then the natural way to try all possibilities is to proceed through the array serially, from the first to the last index. This *serial search* algorithm proceeds as follows:

```
for INDEX in first_index . . last_index
     test whether VALUE = ELEMENT( INDEX )
```

If we name our boolean function FOUND, then the heart of the code for our function body will be the following realization of our serial search algorithm:

```
for INDEX in 1 . . LAST
loop
    if VALUE = ELEMENT( INDEX ) then
        return TRUE;
    end if;
end loop;
return FALSE;
```

This is an example of the *innocent if not proven guilty* technique. We need to test a list to see if it is "guilty" of containing an element equal to VALUE. The program starts out making no assumptions that the list is innocent or guilty. It is proven "guilty" (i.e., **return** TRUE) only if it discovers VALUE in the list.

innocent if not proven guilty

The complete procedure embedded in a demonstration program is shown in Figure 9.8. Notice that the variable LAST is declared to be of type EXTENDED_INDEXES to allow it to be initialized to zero. If we had declared LAST to be of type INDEXES, we would have caused CONSTRAINT_ERROR to be raised and an error message to display when it is set equal to zero. This also allows us to represent the empty list with a value of zero. By using EXTENDED_INDEXES as the type of the function parameter, we can accommodate an empty list. If you check the code, you will see that for an empty list the function correctly returns the value FALSE.

Program

```
with TEXT_IO; use TEXT_IO;
procedure MAIN is
--                   INPUT  : None up to 10 integer scores.
--                            The input is terminated with a -1.
--                            Also input a value to be searched for.
--                   OUTPUT : A statement indicating whether the
--                            searched for value is in the list
--                            or not.
--                   DESCRIPTION : Uses a linear search of the array
--                                 to see if the searched for value
--                                 is in the array.
    MAXIMUM_SIZE : constant INTEGER := 10;
    subtype EXTENDED_INDEXES is INTEGER range 0 . . MAXIMUM_SIZE;
    subtype INDEXES is EXTENDED_INDEXES range 1 . . MAXIMUM_SIZE;
    type INTEGER_ARRAY is array( INDEXES ) of INTEGER;
    INPUT_VALUE : INTEGER;
    LAST        : EXTENDED_INDEXES := 0;
    LIST        : INTEGER_ARRAY;
    NUMBER      : INTEGER;
    package SCORE_IO is new INTEGER_IO ( INTEGER );
    use SCORE_IO;
    function FOUND ( VALUE : INTEGER;
                     ELEMENT : INTEGER_ARRAY;
                     LAST : EXTENDED_INDEXES )
                     return BOOLEAN is
    begin -- Found
        for INDEX in 1 . . LAST
        loop
            if VALUE = ELEMENT( INDEX ) then
                return TRUE;
            end if;
        end loop;
```

```
        return FALSE;
    end FOUND;
begin -- Main
    PUT ( "Enter up to " ); PUT ( MAXIMUM_SIZE, 1 );
    PUT ( " scores." ); NEW_LINE;
    PUT ( "Terminate the input with a -1 and a return." );
    NEW_LINE;
    loop
        GET ( INPUT_VALUE );
        exit when INPUT_VALUE < 0;
        LAST := LAST + 1;
        LIST ( LAST ) := INPUT_VALUE;
    end loop;
    PUT ( "Enter a number to be searched for:" ); NEW_LINE;
    GET ( NUMBER ); SKIP_LINE;
    if FOUND ( NUMBER, LIST, LAST ) then
        PUT ( "Yep, it's on the list." );
    else
        PUT ( "Nope, it's not on the list." );
    end if;
    NEW_LINE;
end MAIN;
```

Sample Dialogue 1

```
Enter up to 10 scores.
Terminate the input with a -1 and a return.
11 1 2 3 4 5 6 7 8 10 -1
Enter a number to be searched for:
9
Nope, it's not on the list.
```

Sample Dialogue 2

```
Enter up to 10 scores.
Terminate the input with a -1 and a return.
8 7 6 5 4 3 2 1 -1
Enter a number to be searched for:
3
Yep, it's on the list.
```

Sample Dialogue 3

```
Enter up to 10 scores.
Terminate the input with a -1 and a return.
-1
Enter a number to be searched for:
3
Nope, it's not on the list.
```

Figure 9.8 Searching a partially filled array.

array parameters

In the program in Figure 9.8, the entire array LIST is passed as the actual parameter in the function call

```
if FOUND ( NUMBER, LIST, LAST ) then
```

When this function call is executed in the first sample run of the program, the formal parameter NUMBER is set equal to the value of the actual parameter VALUE, so it is set equal to 9. In exactly the same manner, the formal parameter ELEMENT is set equal to the value of the actual parameter LIST, so it is set equal to

```
11, 1, 2, 3, 4, 5, 6, 7, 8, 10
```

The entire array value is passed as a single unit.

Note that in the second dialogue the array is allowed as a parameter even though it is not completely filled. This is permitted, but the function should not attempt to access any of the undefined elements. In this case it does not, so there are no problems.

Pitfall

Type Mismatches with Array Parameters

As we noted in the last chapter, two Ada types are not the same unless they have the same name. This can cause problems if anonymous types are used when declaring arrays. Consider the following:

```
type FIRST_NAME is array( 1 . . 10 ) of INTEGER;
GIVEN_NAME : array( 1 . . 10 ) of INTEGER;
```

With these declarations, the array GIVEN_NAME cannot be used as an actual parameter of type FIRST_NAME. The way to avoid this problem is always to declare a unique name for each array type and always to refer to it by that name.

Array Example with Noninteger Indexes

As we already noted, the index type of an array need not be a subrange of the integers; it can be a subrange type of any discrete type. The program in Figure 9.9 illustrates the use of the subrange type `'a' . . 'z'`, both as an array index type and as the type of a **for** loop control variable. That program reads in a sentence and then uses an array indexed by `'a' . . 'z'` to count the number of occurrences of `'a'`, `'b'`, and so forth in the sentence. The program assumes that the lowercase letters are contiguous (that is, there are no symbols between any two alphabetically consecutive lowercase letters). This assumption holds because that is the way type CHARACTER is defined (see Figure 8.1).

Program

```
with TEXT_IO; use TEXT_IO;
procedure MAIN is
    subtype LETTER is CHARACTER range 'a' .. 'z';
    type LETTER_COUNTER is array( LETTER ) of INTEGER;
    COUNT : LETTER_COUNTER := ( others => 0 );
    package COUNT_IO is new INTEGER_IO ( INTEGER );
    use COUNT_IO;
    procedure READ_SENTENCE ( FREQUENCY : in out LETTER_COUNTER ) is
        SYMBOL : CHARACTER;
    begin -- Read_Sentence
        loop
            exit when END_OF_LINE;
            GET ( SYMBOL );
            if SYMBOL in LETTER then
                FREQUENCY( SYMBOL ) := FREQUENCY( SYMBOL ) + 1;
            end if;
        end loop;
        SKIP_LINE;
    end READ_SENTENCE;
    procedure DISPLAY_COUNT ( COUNT : in LETTER_COUNTER ) is
        BLANK : constant CHARACTER := ' ';
    begin -- Display_Count
        for SYMBOL in LETTER
        loop
            if COUNT( SYMBOL ) > 0 then
                PUT ( COUNT( SYMBOL ) );
                PUT ( BLANK );
                PUT ( SYMBOL );
                NEW_LINE;
            end if;
        end loop;
    end DISPLAY_COUNT;
begin -- Main
    PUT ( "Enter a sentence and press return." ); NEW_LINE;
    PUT ( "All lowercase letters please." ); NEW_LINE;
    READ_SENTENCE ( COUNT );
    PUT ( "Your sentence contains:" ); NEW_LINE;
    DISPLAY_COUNT ( COUNT );
end MAIN;
```

Sample Dialogue

```
Enter a sentence and press return.
All lowercase letters please.
may the hair on your toes grow long and curly.
Your sentence contains:
      3 a
      1 c
      1 d
      2 e
      2 g
      2 h
      1 i
      2 l
      1 m
      3 n
      5 o
      4 r
      1 s
      2 t
      2 u
      1 w
      3 y
```

Figure 9.9 Program using 'a'..'z' as an index type.

Initialization of Arrays

The elements of an array can be given an initial value when an array object is declared. This is done in a manner very similar to that used for initializing simple objects. Note the following declaration taken from the program in Figure 9.9:

```
COUNT : LETTER_COUNTER := ( others => 0 );
```

All elements of the array COUNT are given the value of **0** via the assignment `:= ( others => 0 )`. This is a shorthand way of listing all 26 values, which is a legal possibility, as follows:

```
COUNT : LETTER_COUNTER := ( 0, 0, 0, 0, 0, 0, 0, 0, 0, 0,
                            0, 0, 0, 0, 0, 0, 0, 0, 0, 0,
                            0, 0, 0, 0, 0, 0 );
```

These two methods can also be used in combination with one another, as long as the **others** part comes last. The following array would have the first five elements initialized to 1, 2, 3, 4, and 5, respectively, with all of the **others** given the value of 0.

```
COUNT : LETTER_COUNTER := ( 1, 2, 3, 4, 5, others => 0 );
```

aggregate

One cannot partially initialize an array; it is either all or nothing at all. These methods of initializing an array use what is called an *aggregate.* An aggregate is a list of array components, each separated by a comma, with the entire list enclosed in parentheses. In the examples above, an aggregate was used as part of a declaration. An aggregate can be used as an actual parameter, a generic parameter, the result expression of a function, and as the expression following the assignment operator.

The array could also have been initialized by executing the following code segment:

```
for INDEX in 'a' .. 'z'
loop
    COUNT( INDEX ) := 0;
end loop;
```

Random Versus Sequential Array Access

The **for** loop code above illustrates a method for accessing array elements. The array elements of the array COUNT are initialized to zero by stepping through the array indexes in order. This method is called *sequential access.*

Another method of array access is used when the letters of the sentence are read in and counted in procedure READ_SENTENCE in Figure 9.9. If the letter 'a' is read in, then the first array element is changed; if the letter 'z' is accessed, then the last array element is changed; if the letter 'd' is read, then the fourth element is changed. This is referred to as *random access,* since the order of the elements accessed cannot be determined beforehand.

Array Indexes with Semantic Content

The indexes of an array allow us to access individual elements in an organized fashion. Often they serve no purpose other than that of an arbitrary numbering of the array elements, as in our first sample program with a list of five scores (Figure 9.4). Frequently the array indexes can carry some meaning. For example, in our letter-counting program, the index 'a' is not arbitrary. It stands for the letter 'a', and the indexed component COUNT('a') has a vâlue equal to the number of times the letter 'a' appears. Choosing array indexes with semantic content can often simplify a program. In our letter-counting program, this allowed for random access to the array. The program did not have to search a list of letters to find the location for, say, 'm'; it went directly to FREQUENCY('m') by using thc indcx 'm'.

Integers are typically used when we need arbitrary indexes without any particular meaning. Often they also can have meaning. In a list of students, they might serve as the students' identification numbers. In a list of checks, they may serve as the check numbers.

Enumeration_IO and Enumerated Types as Array Index Types

Since they are discrete types, enumerated types and subranges of enumerated types may be used as the index types of arrays. For example, the following declares SALES to be an array of integers indexed by an enumerated type for the days of the week:

```
type WEEKDAY is ( SUN, MON, TUE, WED, THU, FRI, SAT );
type SALES_LIST is array ( WEEKDAY ) of INTEGER;
SALES : SALES_LIST;
```

The array might be used to keep track of the number of automobiles sold by an auto dealer's sales force. Once the array has been filled, the weekly sales can be totaled as follows:

```
TOTAL : INTEGER := 0;

for DAY in WEEKDAY
loop
     GET ( SALES( DAY ) );
     TOTAL := TOTAL + SALES( DAY );
end loop;
```

Figure 9.10 shows these details embedded in a complete program that reads in daily sales and then echoes them back with each day marked as above average (+), below average (−), or average (0).

The program also has two relatively new things that were introduced in Chapter 8: the use of ENUMERATION_IO for the output of the days of the week, and the use of SET_COL as an aid to formatting the output. As mentioned in Chapter 8, ENUMERATION_IO is a generic package inside TEXT_IO. To be able to access the I/O operations in a generic package, the package must first be *instantiated*. The process of instantiation provides an *instance* or copy of the generic template for a particular purpose. The following two lines instantiate ENUMERATION_IO for the type WEEKDAY and make its operation available to the program:

```
package DAY_IO is new ENUMERATION_IO ( WEEKDAY );
use DAY_IO;
```

The identifier DAY_IO is the name of the actual package that is **use**d for the output of the constants of the type WEEKDAY.

The procedure SET_COL (short for Set Column) is used to move the output cursor to a specific column on the output line. SET_COL has one parameter of type POSITIVE_COUNT. POSITIVE_COUNT is a subtype of the type COUNT. The type COUNT is a new type and is declared in much the same manner as INTEGER, but they are not the same types and are therefore incompatible. Both of these types, COUNT and POSITIVE_COUNT, as well as SET_COL are declared inside the package TEXT_IO, as shown below:

```
type COUNT is 0 . . implementation_dependent;
subtype POSITIVE_COUNT is COUNT range 1 . . COUNT'LAST;

procedure SET_COL ( COLUMN : POSITIVE_COUNT );
```

The calls to SET_COL shown below and used in the program in Figure 9.10 have an INTEGER computation enclosed in a call to the conversion function POSITIVE_COUNT. POSITIVE_COUNT converts the integer parameter to a value of type POSITIVE_COUNT. This type conversion may seem pointless, but it is required. Type conversions of this kind are necessary to prevent inadvertent type mismatches and provide an important safety feature.

```
SET_COL ( POSITIVE_COUNT
          ( WEEKDAY'POS ( DAY ) * WIDTH + ( WIDTH - 2 ) ) );
SET_COL ( POSITIVE_COUNT
          ( WEEKDAY'POS ( DAY ) * WIDTH + WIDTH ) );
```

The formula used to determine the proper column position uses the attribute POS and is based on the value of the constant WIDTH as it is declared in the program. The formula works for all positive value of WIDTH, assuming that WIDTH is at least large enough to accommodate the values to be printed.

The first series of calls to SET_COL is used in the loop to print out the days of the week. The first time through the loop, DAY has the value SUN, which is the first value in the enumeration of the type WEEKDAY. The position (POS) of SUN in that enumeration is **0**. (Recall that the positions in an enumeration start at **0** and go up.) Thus

```
WEEKDAY'POS ( DAY ) * WIDTH + ( WIDTH - 2 )
             0      *   6   + (   6   - 2 )
```

evaluates to **4**. The printing of SUN begins in print position 4. The value MON will be printed starting in position 10 (1 * 6 + (6 − 2)).

The second series of calls to SET_COL is used to position the printer for printing the **+**, **−**, or **0**. The formula is a small variation of one used in the first calls to SET_COL. If the constant WIDTH were changed to, say, **10** and the program were to be recompiled, the output would still be properly aligned.

Program

```
with TEXT_IO; use TEXT_IO;
procedure MAIN is
--                    INPUT  : Units sold for each day of the week.
--                    OUTPUT : Units sold and
--                             whether above or below average.
--                    DESCRIPTION : Compute the average sales.
    WIDTH : constant INTEGER := 6;
    type WEEKDAY is ( SUN, MON, TUE, WED, THU, FRI, SAT );
    package DAY_IO is new ENUMERATION_IO ( WEEKDAY );
    use DAY_IO;
    type SALES_LIST is array ( WEEKDAY ) of INTEGER;
    AVERAGE : FLOAT;
    SALES   : SALES_LIST;
    TOTAL   : INTEGER := 0;
    package SALES_IO is new INTEGER_IO ( INTEGER );
    use SALES_IO;
begin -- Main
    PUT ( "Welcome to the sales meeting." ); NEW_LINE;
    PUT ( "Enter units sold for Sunday through Saturday:" );
    NEW_LINE;
    for DAY in WEEKDAY
    loop
        GET ( SALES( DAY ) );
        TOTAL := TOTAL + SALES( DAY );
    end loop;
    SKIP_LINE;
    AVERAGE := FLOAT ( TOTAL ) / 7.0;
    PUT ( "Daily sales compared to average:" ); NEW_LINE;
    for DAY in WEEKDAY
    loop
        SET_COL ( POSITIVE_COUNT
            ( WEEKDAY'POS ( DAY ) * WIDTH + ( WIDTH - 2 ) ) );
        PUT ( DAY );
    end loop;
    NEW_LINE;
    for DAY in WEEKDAY
    loop
        PUT ( SALES( DAY ), WIDTH );
    end loop;
    NEW_LINE;
```

```
    for DAY in WEEKDAY
    loop
        SET_COL ( POSITIVE_COUNT
            ( WEEKDAY'POS ( DAY ) * WIDTH + WIDTH ) );
        if FLOAT ( SALES( DAY ) ) > AVERAGE then
            PUT ( '+' );
        elsif FLOAT ( SALES( DAY ) ) < AVERAGE then
            PUT ( '-' );
        else
            PUT ( '0' );
        end if;
    end loop;
    NEW_LINE;
    PUT ( "Go get 'em!" ); NEW_LINE;
end MAIN;
```

Sample Dialogue

```
Welcome to the sales meeting.
Enter units sold for Sunday through Saturday:
6 7 10 9 8 5 11
Daily sales compared to average:
   SUN MON TUE WED THU FRI SAT
     6   7  10   9   8   5  11
     -   -   +   +   0   -   +

Go get 'em!
```

Figure 9.10 Enumerated type as an index type.

Case Study

Production Graph

Problem Definition

The Apex Plastic Spoon Manufacturing Company has commissioned you to write a program that will display a bar graph showing the productivity of each of their four manufacturing plants for any given week. Each plant keeps separate production figures for each department, such as the teaspoon department, soup spoon department, plain cocktail spoon department, colored cocktail spoon department, and so forth. Moreover, each plant has a different number of departments. For example, only one plant manufactures colored cocktail spoons.

The input is entered plant by plant and consists of a list of numbers giving the production for each department in that plant. The output will consist of a bar graph in the following form:

```
Plant # 1 **********
Plant # 2 *************
Plant # 3 ********************
Plant # 4 *****
```

Each asterisk represents 1000 units of output.

Notice that the output is in 1000s of units; hence, the output must be scaled by dividing it by 1000. This presents a problem since the computer must display some whole number of asterisks. It cannot display 1.6 asterisks for 1600 units. We will thus round to the nearest number of 1000s, so 1600 will be the same as 2000 and produce two asterisks.

refining the problem definition

Discussion

We will use an array called UNITS, which will be indexed by plant numbers **1 . . 4** and will hold the total output of each plant. For example, `UNITS( 3 )` will be set equal to the total output of plant number three. Since the output is in 1000s of units, the program will scale the values of the array elements. So if the value of `UNITS( 3 )` is **2040**, then it will be scaled to **2**, and eventually two asterisks will be output.

If the company had given names to each of its plants instead of a number to identify them, the index type would have been an enumeration of the plants names instead of a subrange of the integers. It would have no effect on the solution of the problem. This will be left as one of the programming exercises.

The problem can be divided into the following subprograms:

1. GET_DATA: For each plant INDEX, read input and set UNITS(INDEX) equal to the total production for plant number INDEX.

2. SCALE: For each INDEX change the value of UNITS(INDEX) to the correct number of asterisks for plant number INDEX.

3. GRAPH: Output the bar graph.

GET_DATA

The program receives separate input figures for each department within a plant, but output is in terms of the total output for a plant. Hence, the program must total the output of all departments in a plant to get the appropriate figure for that plant. These observations lead us to the following basic outline of the algorithm for `GET_DATA`:

Algorithm

```
for all plants
loop
    Read in all the data for this plant number,
    total the numbers and set units( plant )
    equal to that total.
end loop
```

adapting another algorithm

The body of the **for** loop sums a list of numbers and leaves the value of UNITS(PLANT) equal to this sum. In other contexts we have designed code for just this task. If we wanted the sum stored in a variable called TOTAL instead of in UNITS(PLANT), then we would know how to proceed. To store a sum of input numbers in the variable TOTAL, we would use the following:

```
TOTAL := 0;
loop
    GET ( UNITS_PRODUCED );
    exit when UNITS_PRODUCED < 0;
    TOTAL := TOTAL + UNITS_PRODUCED;
end loop;
```

If instead we want the total to be in UNITS(PLANT), then all we need do is assign UNITS(PLANT) the value of TOTAL outside the inner loop, and we will obtain code for the body of our **for** loop:

```
for PLANT in INDEXES
loop
    TOTAL := 0;
    loop
        GET ( UNITS_PRODUCED );
        exit when UNITS_PRODUCED < 0;
        TOTAL := TOTAL + UNITS_PRODUCED;
    end loop;
    SKIP_LINE;
    UNITS( PLANT ) := TOTAL;
end loop;
```

The final SKIP_LINE is needed to advance to the next input line, so the next iteration of the **for** loop starts at the beginning of a line.

Scale

To scale the numbers to an integral number of 1000s, we want to divide by 1000 and then round up to the nearest integer. Integer division, however, does not round up, so simply dividing by 1000 will not produce the desired result. Fortunately, the conversion from FLOAT to INTEGER does round to the nearest integer value; so to scale UNITS(PLANT), the following does produce the desired value:

```
UNITS( PLANT ) := INTEGER ( FLOAT ( UNITS( PLANT ) ) / 1000.0 );
```

We can use a **for** loop to scale each element of the entire array. The final procedure body is given in Figure 9.11.

Graph Algorithm

The algorithm for the procedure GRAPH is straightforward:

```
for PLANT in INDEXES
loop
    PUT ( "Plant #" ); PUT ( plant, 2 );
    repeat the following UNITS( PLANT ) number of times
        PUT ( '*' );
    NEW_LINE;
end loop;
```

The "repeat *n* number of times" loop can be implemented in the standard fashion using a **for** loop. The complete procedure is included in the final program given in Figure 9.11.

Program

```
with TEXT_IO; use TEXT_IO;
procedure MAIN is
--                  INPUT : Production data (units) from 4 plants
--                  OUTPUT : A bar graph of production vs plant
--                  DESCRIPTION : After the data is input it is
--                                scaled down to fit the screen
--                                before the graph is displayed.
    NUMBER_OF_PLANTS : constant INTEGER := 4;
    subtype INDEXES is INTEGER range 1 . . NUMBER_OF_PLANTS;
    type LIST is array ( INDEXES ) of INTEGER;
    UNITS : LIST;
    package UNIT_IO is new INTEGER_IO ( INTEGER );
    use UNIT_IO;
    procedure GET_DATA ( UNITS : out LIST ) is
--                  INPUT : Array whose values are all 0.
--                  OUTPUT : Number of units for each plant.
--                  DESCRIPTION : Unit(I) contains the production
--                                from all departments of plant I.
        TOTAL : INTEGER;
        UNITS_PRODUCED : INTEGER;
```

```
begin -- Get_Data
    for PLANT in INDEXES
    loop
        TOTAL := 0;
        NEW_LINE;
        PUT ( "Enter number of units produced for" ); NEW_LINE;
        PUT ( "each department in plant number " );
        PUT ( PLANT, 1 ); NEW_LINE;
        PUT ( "End by entering a -1 and pressing return." );
        NEW_LINE;
        loop
            GET ( UNITS_PRODUCED );
            exit when UNITS_PRODUCED < 0;
            TOTAL := TOTAL + UNITS_PRODUCED;
        end loop;
        SKIP_LINE;
        UNITS( PLANT ) := TOTAL;
    end loop;
end GET_DATA;
procedure SCALE ( UNITS : in out LIST ) is
--                  INPUT  : Number of units for each plant.
--                  OUTPUT : Scaled units for each plant.
--                  DESCRIPTION : Change value of units so that it
--                                records 1000s of units.
--                                Round to the nearest 1000, e.g.,
--                                5020 is changed to 5, but
--                                5900 is changed to 6.
begin -- Scale
    for PLANT in INDEXES
    loop
        UNITS( PLANT ) :=
            INTEGER ( FLOAT ( UNITS( PLANT ) ) / 1000.0 );
    end loop;
end SCALE;
procedure GRAPH ( UNITS : in LIST ) is
--                  INPUT  : Number of units to nearest thousand
--                           for each plant.
--                  OUTPUT : A bar graph for each plant.
--                  DESCRIPTION : Display an asterisk for every
--                                thousand units for each plant.
begin -- Graph
    NEW_LINE;
    PUT ( "Units produced in thousands of units." ); NEW_LINE;
```

```
        for PLANT in INDEXES
        loop
            PUT ( "Plant #" ); PUT ( PLANT, 2 );
            for ASTERISK in 1 . . UNITS( PLANT )
            loop
                PUT ( '*' );
            end loop;
            NEW_LINE;
        end loop;
    end GRAPH;
begin -- Main
    PUT ( "This program displays a graph showing" ); NEW_LINE;
    PUT ( "production for each plant in the company." ); NEW_LINE;
    GET_DATA ( UNITS );
    SCALE ( UNITS );
    GRAPH ( UNITS );
end MAIN;
```

Sample Dialogue

```
This program displays a graph showing
production for each plant in the company.
Enter number of units produced for
each department in plant number 1
End by entering a -1 and pressing return.
2000 3000 1000 -1
Enter number of units produced for
each department in plant number 2
End by entering a -1 and pressing return.
2050 3002 1300 -1
Enter number of units produced for
each department in plant number 3
End by entering a -1 and pressing return.
5000 4020 500 4348 -1
Enter number of units produced for
each department in plant number 4
End by entering a -1 and pressing return.
2507 6050 1809 -1
Units produced in thousands of units.
Plant # 1******
Plant # 2******
Plant # 3**************
Plant # 4**********
```

Figure 9.11 Production graph program.

Off-Line Data
(Optional)

Arrays are often used to process large amounts of data. If the data set is very large, then it is impractical to enter the data interactively from the keyboard. For example, suppose that in the previous case study each plant had hundreds of departments instead of a few, as in the sample dialogue. In that case it would make sense to read the data off-line in the manner discussed in the optional section of Chapter 7 entitled "Off-Line Data and a Preview of END_OF_FILE." The general method of reading in the data would be the same, except there is no point in display instructions and no need for the sentinel **-1**. The data is prepared before the program is run and must be in a format that matches what the program expects. If it does not match, then either the data must be reformated or the program must be changed to accommodate the data.

Case Study

Sorting

Problem Definition

One of the most widely encountered programming problems, and certainly the most thoroughly studied, is that of sorting a list of values. For example, the list might consist of exam scores, and we may want to see them sorted from lowest to highest or from highest to lowest; the list might consist of words that we have misspelled, and we may want to see them in alphabetical order. In this section we will consider lists of integers and design a procedure that sorts a list into the order smallest to largest. The list will be stored in an array of the following type, where MAXIMUM_SIZE is a defined constant:

```
subtype EXTENDED_INDEXES is INTEGER range 0 .. MAXIMUM_SIZE;
subtype INDEX_TYPE is EXTENDED_INDEXES range 1 .. MAXIMUM_SIZE;
type INTEGER_ARRAY is array( INDEX_TYPE ) of INTEGER;
LIST : INTEGER_ARRAY;
```

Since we want to accommodate partially filled arrays, we will use a variable LAST to record the last array index used, and we will write our procedure to sort the elements LIST(1) through LIST(LAST) and ignore array locations with indexes greater than LAST.

Discussion

first design idea

One way to design an algorithm is to rely on the definition of the problem. In this case the problem is to sort an array, such as LIST, from smallest to largest. That means rearranging the values so that LIST(1) is the smallest, LIST(2) the next smallest, and so forth. That definition yields an outline for a straightforward algorithm:

```
for INDEX in 1 . . LAST
    put the indexth smallest element into LIST( INDEX )
```

exploring the problem

There are many ways to realize this general approach. The details can be developed using two arrays and copying the elements from one array to the other in sorted order. However, one array should be both adequate and economical, so we decide to develop the algorithm using only one array. To help in exploring the problem, we will use the concrete example described in Figure 9.12 as the original array value, and we will consider sorting that array using pencil and eraser. (In Figure 9.12, the array is full, so LAST = MAXIMUM_SIZE = **10**.) When we search the array to find the smallest element, we discover that it is the value of LIST(4) = 2. We next want to set LIST(1) equal to this value of **2**. However, in doing so we must be careful to not lose the original value **8** of LIST(1). A simple assignment statement like the following would destroy the **8**:

```
    LIST( 1 ) := LIST( 4 );
  -- No good: destroys the original value of LIST( 1 )
```

Now that we understand some of the problems involved in this example, we can begin to formulate a strategy for handling these problems.

interchange sorting

We wish to set the value of LIST(1) equal to the value of the index component with the smallest value, which is the value of LIST(4). When we do that we must preserve the old value of LIST(1) so it can be inserted into the array at some later time. This is illustrated in the second snapshot of the array shown in Figure 9.12. The algorithm must do something with the displaced value **8** that was the original value of LIST(1). Fortunately we have an array location in which to store it. We place it in the only vacant position. Since the value **2** has "left" LIST(4), the algorithm can place the **8** there. In other words the values of LIST(1) and LIST(4) are simply interchanged. A similar thing is done with LIST(2), as shown in the figure. The entire array can be sorted by a series of interchanges such as these two. Any sorting algorithm that is based on interchanging elements is referred to as an *interchange sort.*

Algorithm

selection sort

The simplest interchange sorting algorithm is called a *selection sort,* and this is the one we obtained by proceeding as we did with our sample array values. In outline form it is as follows:

```
for POSITION in 1 . . LAST - 1
    EXCHANGE ( LIST( POSITION ), LIST( suitable_index ) );
```

(LIST(LAST) will automatically be in place, once the previous elements are sorted.)

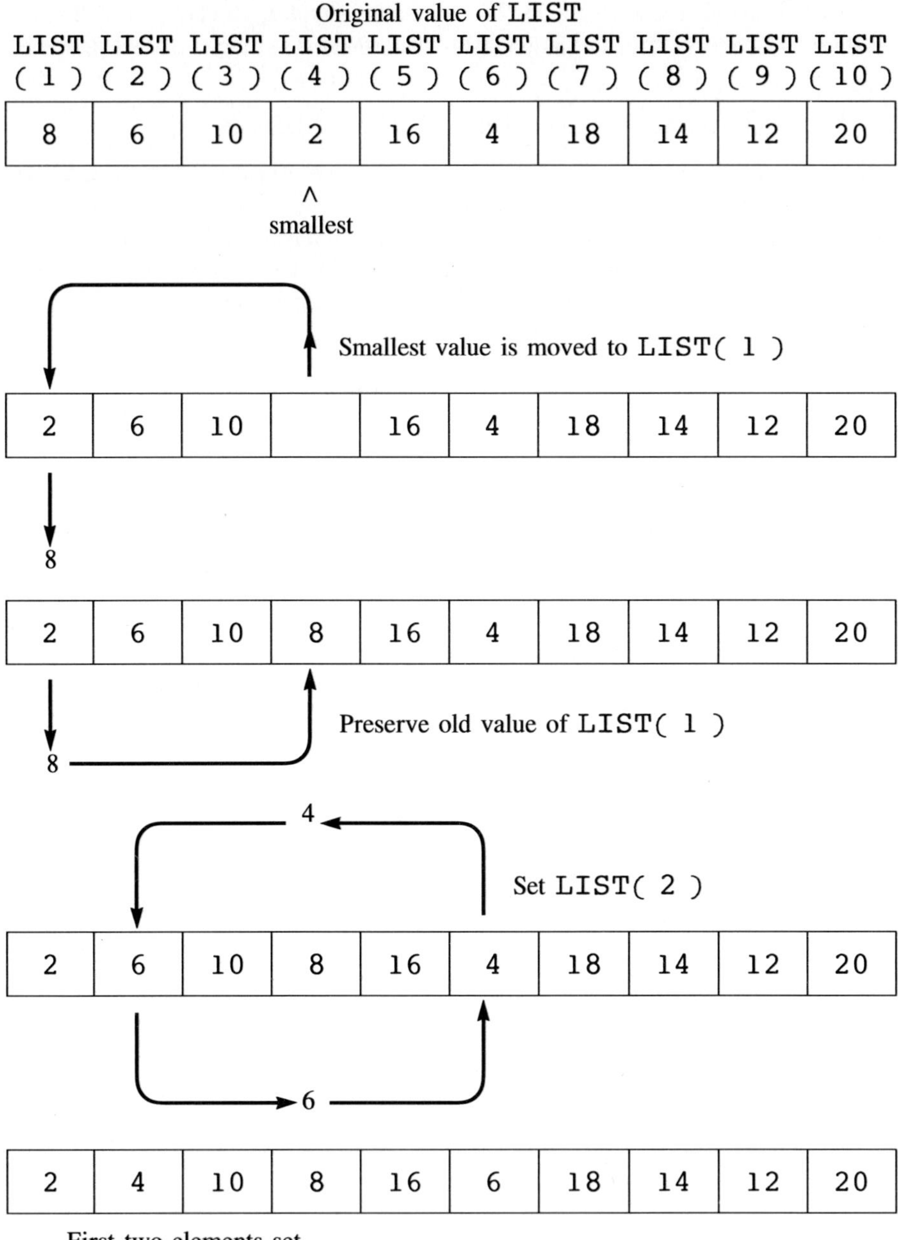

Figure 9.12 Interchange sorting.

All that remains is to calculate the expression *suitable__index*. When the loop considers LIST(POSITION) and looks for a suitable interchange, the indexed components with smaller indexes already contain the correct values for a sorted array. So the sought-after index is the index of the smallest of the remaining elements LIST(POSITION), LIST(POSITION + 1), . . . LIST(LAST). Since this index is a single value, we can define a function to return the index. The value of *suitable__index* will be INDEX_OF_SMALLEST (ELEMENTS, POSITION, LAST), where INDEX_OF_SMALLEST is as declared in Figure 9.13. The complete sorting algorithm is implemented by the procedure SELECTION_SORT, which is also declared in Figure 9.13.

Program

```
with TEXT_IO; use TEXT_IO;
procedure MAIN is
--                  INPUT  : A list of numbers, terminated with -1
--                  OUTPUT : A list of numbers, sorted low to high
--                  DESCRIPTION : Tests the selection sort.
    MAXIMUM_SIZE : constant INTEGER := 10;
    subtype EXTENDED_INDEXES is INTEGER range 0 . . MAXIMUM_SIZE;
    subtype INDEX_TYPE is EXTENDED_INDEXES range 1 . . MAXIMUM_SIZE;
    type INTEGER_ARRAY is array( INDEX_TYPE ) of INTEGER;
    INPUT_VALUE : INTEGER;
    LAST        : EXTENDED_INDEXES := 0;
    LIST        : INTEGER_ARRAY;
    NUMBER      : INTEGER;
    package LIST_IO is new INTEGER_IO ( INTEGER );
    use LIST_IO;
    procedure SELECTION_SORT ( ELEMENTS : in out INTEGER_ARRAY;
                               LAST     : EXTENDED_INDEXES ) is
--                  INPUT  : A list of numbers and
--                           an index to the last one.
--                  OUTPUT : A list of numbers, sorted low to high
--                  DESCRIPTION : Sorts the partially filled array
--                                into increasing order using the
--                                selection sort algorithm.
        procedure EXCHANGE ( ITEM_1, ITEM_2 : in out INTEGER ) is
--                  INPUT : Two integer values.
--                  OUTPUT : Two integer values.
--                  DESCRIPTION : Interchanges the two values.
            TEMPORARY : INTEGER;
        begin -- Exchange
            TEMPORARY := ITEM_1;
            ITEM_1 := ITEM_2;
            ITEM_2 := TEMPORARY;
        end EXCHANGE;
```

```
        function INDEX_OF_SMALLEST ( LIST : INTEGER_ARRAY;
                                     START, LAST : INDEX_TYPE )
                                     return INDEX_TYPE is
--                 INPUT  : A list of numbers and indexes to the
--                          start and the last of the numbers.
--                 OUTPUT : Index to the smallest value.
--                 DESCRIPTION : Finds the smallest value in the
--                               list between the indexes
--                               start and last.
            SMALLEST_ELEMENT : INTEGER := LIST( START );
            SMALLEST_INDEX : INDEX_TYPE := START;
        begin -- Index_Of_Smallest
            for INDEX in START + 1 . . LAST
            loop
                if LIST( INDEX ) < SMALLEST_ELEMENT then
                    SMALLEST_ELEMENT := LIST( INDEX );
                    SMALLEST_INDEX := INDEX;
                end if;
            end loop;
            return SMALLEST_INDEX;
        end INDEX_OF_SMALLEST;
    begin -- Selection_Sort
        for POSITION in 1 . . LAST - 1
        loop
            EXCHANGE ( ELEMENTS( POSITION ),
                       ELEMENTS( INDEX_OF_SMALLEST ( ELEMENTS,
                                                     POSITION,
                                                     LAST ) )
                                                     );
        end loop;
    end SELECTION_SORT;
begin -- Main
    PUT ( "Enter a list of positive integers." );
    NEW_LINE;
    PUT ( "I will take up to " ); PUT ( MAXIMUM_SIZE, 1 );
    PUT ( " numbers." ); NEW_LINE;
    PUT ( "Terminate the input with a -1 and a return." );
    NEW_LINE;
    loop
        GET ( INPUT_VALUE );
        exit when INPUT_VALUE < 0;
        LAST := LAST + 1;
        LIST ( LAST ) := INPUT_VALUE;
    end loop;
    SKIP_LINE;
```

```
    SELECTION_SORT ( LIST, LAST );
    PUT ( "In sorted order the numbers are:" ); NEW_LINE;
    for INDEX in 1 . . LAST
    loop
        PUT ( LIST( INDEX ) );
    end loop;
    NEW_LINE;
end MAIN;
```

Sample Dialogue

```
Enter a list of positive integers.
I will take up to 10 numbers.
Terminate the input with a -1 and a return.
80 10 50 70 60 90 20 30 40 -1
In sorted order the numbers are:
    10    20    30    40    50    60    70    80    90
```

Figure 9.13 Selection sort.

Summary of Problem Solving and Programming Techniques

- An array type can be used to produce a unified naming scheme for a collection of related values.
- A big advantage of array types is that a program can manipulate the array index, to compute the name of an indexed component.
- An array indexed component can be used anyplace that a variable of the array's component type can be used, except as a formal parameter.
- It is a good idea to use defined constants for one or both bounds on an array index type. That way the array size can be changed by simply changing the constant declarations.
- A common bug in programs that use arrays is to attempt to use an index value outside the defined range for an array's indexes.
- You may often need a variable that takes on values one step beyond the index range of an array. In these cases do not declare the variable to be of the index type. Instead declare it to be of a larger subrange subtype or of the host type (such as `INTEGER`).
- A **for** loop is a natural way to proceed sequentially through an array.
- The "brute force" method of looking at every element of an array can be used to search an array for almost any property. It can be inefficient, but it is simple and effective.
- The "innocent until proven guilty" technique can be used to check if some element of an array has a given property (is "guilty"). An example of this technique was seen in the case study on searching an array. A boolean variable can be used to implement this technique in an Ada program.

- One way to design an algorithm is to think about how you would solve the problem using pencil and paper, and then design the algorithm to do that, or some variation on that.
- Array indexes can carry information that serves to identify the corresponding elements of the array. For example, the indexes might be student identification numbers or check numbers or the letters of the alphabet.
- Array elements may be accessed either sequentially, as with a **for** loop, or in a "random" order by computing the desired index.
- There are two different ways of viewing an array: as a collection of indexed components of the component type and as a single object with a single compound value consisting of a list of values of the component type. Sometimes it is more productive to take one view; other times the alternative view is more productive.
- An array variable without subscripts may be used in an assignment statement, as in `A := B`.
- Either a single array component or an entire array may be passed as a parameter to a procedure. In the first case the formal parameter type must be the component type of the array; in the second case it must be the array type.
- If an indexed component is used as an actual parameter to a procedure, the index expression is evaluated before the actual parameter is substituted for the formal parameter.
- It is good practice to declare a name for each array type definition (or any other type definition) and to use the type name, rather than the type definition, when declaring array objects. Both formal and actual parameters of an array type must always be specified by a type name.
- Arrays consume large quantities of storage, and some care should be taken to not use excessive storage when dealing with arrays.

Summary of Ada Constructs

type declaration

Syntax:

```
type type_name is type_definition;
subtype identifier is type_name range subrange;
```

Example:

```
subtype INDEX is INTEGER range 0 . . 100;
type LIST is array( INDEX ) of CHARACTER;
```

The type names are identifiers chosen by the programmer. The type definitions can be any of the type definitions described in this book. The declaration of type(s) comes after the formal parameters of a procedure and before the **begin**/**end**. The reserved word **type** or **subtype** is used before every type declaration.

array types

Syntax:

```
array( index_type ) of component_type
```

Examples:

```
array( 0 .. 100 ) of INTEGER
array( INDEX ) of CHARACTER
```

The *index_type* must be either a discrete type, a discrete range, or the definition of a subtype of a discrete type. For example, it could be the name of a predefined discrete type, such as CHARACTER, or a range or subtype of CHARACTER. The type INTEGER can be used as an *index_type*, but it is unwise and may cause STORAGE_ERROR to be raised. A subrange of the INTEGER type is much preferred. The *component_type* may be any Ada type.

array declaration

Syntax:

array_variable_name : *array_type_name*;

Example:

```
HOURLY_TEMPERATURES : LIST;
```

The way to declare an array variable. It is just like declaring a variable of any other type. Note that the array variable is declared without appending any parentheses or indexes. An array type definition may be used in place of an array type name, but it is usually preferable to use a defined type name. (The sample array type LIST is defined in the first entry of this summary.)

indexed component

Syntax:

array_name(*index_expression*)

Example:

```
LIST( INDEX + 1 )
```

An indexed component of the array *array_name*. The *index_expression* may be any expression that evaluates to a value whose type is the index type of the array. An indexed component can be used any place that a variable of the component type of the array can be used.

Exercises

Self-Test Exercises

10. Write suitable array type declarations for each of the following:
    (a) An array to record the number of students who received a grade of 0 on a quiz, the number who received a grade of 1, and so forth, up to the maximum grade of 10.
    (b) The number of children in a school for each of the ages from 5 to 13.
    (c) An array to hold the amount of each check you wrote this month, recorded so that you can deduct the amount given the number of the check. Check numbers range from 661 to 753.

11. Write a suitable enumerated type definition for all the days of the week and for the days Monday through Friday. Also write two array type declarations, one for an array to record the hours worked on each day from Monday through Friday and one for the number of hours reserved for play on each day of the week, including Saturday and Sunday.

12. Give a simpler way of accomplishing the following:

```
for INDEX in 0 . . 10
loop
    APPLE( INDEX ) := BERRY( INDEX );
end loop;
```

where APPLE and BERRY are of type **array**(0 . . 10) **of** INTEGER.

13. The following is an alternative to the loop used in the function declaration in Figure 9.10. It does not work correctly. What is wrong?

```
for INDEX in 1 . . LAST
loop
    if NUMBER = LIST( INDEX ) then
        return TRUE;
    else
        return FALSE;
end loop;
```

14. Write a procedure that reverses the order of the elements in an array of the following type:

```
type LABEL is array( 0 . . 100 ) of CHARACTER;
```

15. What changes do you need to make to the procedure SELECTION_SORT in Figure 9.13 so that it sorts numbers in the order largest to smallest rather than smallest to largest?

16. What changes do you need to make to the procedure SELECTION_SORT in Figure 9.13 so that it sorts a list of numbers of type FLOAT rather than a list of numbers of type INTEGER?

17. What changes do you need to make to the procedure SORT in Figure 9.13 so that it sorts a list of lowercase letters into alphabetical order instead of a list of numbers into numeric order?

Interactive Exercises

18. Run the following two programs in order to see what error messages your system gives:

```
with I_O; use I_O;
procedure MAIN is
    INDEX := INTEGER := 0;
    VECTOR : array( 1 . . 10 ) of INTEGER;
```

```
    begin
        VECTOR( INDEX ) := 1;
--                    array index too small
    end MAIN;

    with I_O; use I_O;
    procedure MAIN is
        subtype ONE_TO_TEN is INTEGER range 1 . . 10;
        PINS : ONE_TO_TEN;
    begin
        PINS := 0;
--                    value assigned too small
    end MAIN;
```

19. Write a program that allows the user to type in up to 10 positive numbers and then echoes back the numbers typed in, but in reverse order. Have the user terminate the list with a negative number. The answer to Exercise 9 might be of some help.

Programming Exercises

20. Write a program that reads 10 integers into an array, then computes the average and the largest and smallest numbers in the array, and finally outputs the numbers plus the amount that each one differs from the smallest, the largest, and the average.

21. Write a program to keep a budget. There are five numbered budget categories: 1 for food, 2 for housing, 3 for clothing, 4 for utilities, and 5 for entertainment. The program displays the categories showing the number of each category, and then the user and the program refer to categories by number rather than name. The user may name any category by number and then enter an amount. The program records the amount spent and keeps track of the total amount spent in each category. When the user indicates that he/she wants to see the totals, the program prints out the amount spent in each category and the total amount spent in all categories combined. The user may enter more amounts after seeing the total and may ask for a new total later on.

22. Redo, or do for the first time, Exercise 20 using an enumeration type for the budget categories.

23. Write a program that computes grades for a class of up to 50 students. The program reads in a score in the range `0 . . 100` for each student and then outputs the grades identifying the student by number. The first student read in is student number 1, the next student number 2, and so forth. Grades are to be determined as follows: Any student who receives 10 points below the average receives an F. Any student who receives a score above that and at most 10 points above the average receives a C. Any student who receives a score above that receives an A. There are no D's or B's. To use your program for larger classes, you should not need to change anything except the constant declaration section.

24. Write a program to read in four letters and then output all 24 permutations of these letters. Use an array to hold the four letters. Do not cut corners in designing this one; it can be confusing.

25. Write a program to play Nim using five piles of sticks. Use an array to store the size of the piles. The game is explained in Exercise 27 of Chapter 8. Use the random number generator in the package `MATH_LIBRARY` from Chapter 8.

26. Write a procedure body for a procedure called DEAL that sets an **`out`** parameter to a value that represents a card chosen at random from a standard 52-card deck. The procedure should also keep track of the cards already dealt out so it does not deal a card twice. For example, after dealing out four aces, it should not deal out a fifth ace at any later time. Use an array parameter to keep track of the cards already dealt out. There is no need to keep track of suits (clubs, hearts, etc.).

27. Write a program that reads in two lists of 10 or fewer numbers each into one of two arrays. The input is assumed to be in numeric order. The program then outputs a list of all (up to 20) numbers in numeric order. This is called *merging* the lists.

28. It is probably unrealistic to assume that `INTEGER'LAST` on your computer can contain values up to 10 digits. However, you should be able to write procedures to read in two numbers of 10 or fewer digits and output their sum. The numbers can be read in, as character values, one digit at a time using a variable of type `CHARACTER`, then converted into numbers (use `POS`) and stored in two arrays of 10 integer values each. If the number is less than 10 digits long, then leading zeros should be added to the array. An addition procedure is then called to calculate the sum and store it in a third array. If the sum would be more than 10 digits long, then the program issues an ''integer overflow'' message by raising an exception. If the sum is less than 10 digits long, then the two numbers read in and their sum are output.

References for Further Reading

P. Helman and R. Veroff, *Intermediate Problem Solving and Data Structures—Walls and Mirrors* (Redwood City, CA: The Benjamin/Cummings Publishing Co., 1986). Contains more information on sorting.

CHAPTER

10

COMPLEX ARRAY STRUCTURES

Jay Forrester

Forrester is best known for the development of the *magnetic core memory.* This development revolutionized computer internal memory and was used in most computers built between 1951 and 1964. A team at M.I.T., with Forrester at the head, built the Whirlwind computer. The Whirlwind is considered by many to be most influential in terms of today's commercial computers.

Chapter Contents

Like other composite types that we will introduce in succeeding chapters, arrays may be declared so they form a hierarchy. The hierarchy consists of an array of arrays. Other ways of structuring data involve the way we use arrays rather than the way the array type is defined. Two or more arrays or an array and one or more variables may form a conceptual unit for handling a particular kind of data. These data types and combinations of data types are called *data structures* and are the topic of this chapter. Most of these topics require no new Ada constructs, but they do represent significantly new ways of reasoning about the tools we already have on hand. We do introduce one new Ada concept, namely the multidimensional array, which is an array whose indexed variables have two or more indexes instead of a single index, as in the arrays we saw in the last chapter. We open with an important application using one of the simple array types we introduced in the last chapter.

The Predefined Type String

One way to represent a string of characters, such as a word or a name or a line of text, is as an array of characters, such as the array variable LINE declared as follows:

```
MAXIMUM_LENGTH : constant INTEGER := 20;
type CHARACTER_STRING is array( 1 . . MAXIMUM_LENGTH ) of CHARACTER;
LINE : CHARACTER_STRING;
```

There is, however, in package STANDARD a predefined type named STRING with the following syntax:

```
type STRING is array ( POSITIVE range <>) of CHARACTER;
```

This declaration is not the standard sort of array declaration that we have used in the past. This kind of array declaration is called an *unconstrained array*. It means that the type STRING is an array of characters with indexes that must be only within the POSITIVE **range.** For this type of array to be useful in a program, the array must be constrained first. When objects of type STRING are declared, the indexes must be specified. A few examples follow:

```
NAME : STRING( 1 . . 25 );
SENTENCE : STRING( 1 . . 120 );
MAXIMUM_LENGTH : constant INTEGER := 20;
subtype CHARACTER_STRING is STRING( 1 . . MAXIMUM_LENGTH );
LINE : CHARACTER_STRING;
```

From these declarations you can see that NAME is an array of 25 characters, and SENTENCE is an array of 120 characters. A subtype of STRING called CHARACTER_STRING is also declared, as well as the object LINE, which is of type CHARACTER_STRING. Objects of type CHARACTER_STRING inherit all the properties of the type STRING.

The three objects (NAME, SENTENCE, and LINE) are not *anonymous* arrays, as would be the case in the following examples:

```
BUFFER : array( 1 . . 85 ) of CHARACTER;
CITY : array( 1 . . 20 ) of CHARACTER;
```

In the second example BUFFER and CITY are not of the same type, for their type names are unknown but they are different. The advantage to the first set of examples is that LINE, NAME, and SENTENCE can be passed as actual parameters to any subprogram that has a formal parameter of type STRING. For example, there are two procedures in package TEXT_IO that allow us to input values of type STRING and two that allow us to output values of type STRING.

```
GET ( ITEM : out STRING );
GET_LINE ( ITEM : out STRING, LAST : out NATURAL );
PUT ( ITEM : in STRING );
PUT_LINE ( ITEM : in STRING );
```

With these procedures, we could

```
GET ( SENTENCE );
PUT_LINE ( NAME );
```

but we could not use these procedures with the objects BUFFER and CITY. To do input and output for these anonymous arrays, we would have to have a loop and read one character at a time. There would have to be two separate loops for each of the objects of the anonymous types.

Some caution must be used when using GET and GET_LINE. If you use GET (NAME), for example, the program expects exactly 25 characters, no more and no less. If you give it more than 25 characters, it will take the first 25 characters and leave the rest in the input buffer. If you give it less than 25 characters, it will simply stop and wait on you until it has all 25 characters. The program will not continue until you give it all 25 characters.

The procedure GET_LINE has a second parameter, and it will allow you to give it less than the 25 characters for a GET_LINE (NAME, NUMBER_OF_CHARACTERS). It will report to you via the second parameter (NUMBER_OF_CHARACTERS) exactly how many characters were put into NAME. If you give it three characters followed by a return, it will put those three characters into the first three locations of NAME and assign NUMBER_OF_CHARACTERS the value of 3. None of the other positions in NAME will be changed. Positions 4 through 25 of NAME will be exactly the same as they were before the GET_LINE.

GET_LINE has one additional annoying characteristic. If you use GET_LINE (NAME, NUMBER_OF_CHARACTERS) and give it less than 25 characters, it will consume the end-of-line character that is input when the return is pressed. If you give it 25 or more characters, the end-of-line is not consumed. The problem this presents is, do you need a SKIP_LINE after a GET_LINE? The answer is, only if NUMBER_OF_CHARACTERS is 25. As a result, the code for GET_LINE often looks like

```
GET_LINE ( NAME, NUMBER_OF_CHARACTERS );
if NUMBER_OF_CHARACTERS = 25 then
    SKIP_LINE;
end if;
```

operators for type String

There are a few predefined operators for objects of type STRING. The predefined operators for this type are the standard relational operators (<, =, >, etc.) and the catenation operator **&**. The catenation operator allows us to catenate two strings together, making a new string that contains all the characters of the left operand string, followed by all the characters of the right operand string. The operation can be useful in PUT statements, as follows:

```
PUT ( STRING_1 & ' ' & STRING_2 );
```

The output from this PUT statement would be all of the characters of STRING_1, followed by a blank, followed by all of the characters of STRING_2. Note in the above example that we have catenated STRING_1 with the single character ' '.

The **&** operator has the flexibility to accept the left and/or right operand as either of type `STRING` or type `CHARACTER`. The result of the operation, however, is always of type `STRING`.

The relational operators can be particularly useful. Say that your program is required to read in a list of 10 names and print them back out in alphabetic order. We know what happens when we apply the relational operators to objects of type `CHARACTER`. The type `CHARACTER` is an enumeration with the relationship between individual characters clearly defined. For example, we know that `'a'` is less than `'z'`, but is `"Charles"` clearly less than `"Walter"`? What about `"John"` and `"Johan"`?

The rule for comparing objects of type `STRING` is that the relational operator is applied to the first nonequal pair of characters starting from index position 1. Thus, `"Charles"` is less than `"Walter"` because `'C' < 'W'`. If we write

```
if "John" < "Johan" then
     PUT ( "John");
else
     PUT ( "Johan" );
end if;
NEW_LINE;
```

The output display will be `"Johan"` because `'n' < 'a'` is `FALSE`. The first three characters of the strings were the same: `"Joh"` and `"Joh"`. The first non-equal pair of characters starting from index position 1 is `'n'` and `'a'`. Thus, the relational operator is applied as `'n' < 'a'`, producing a `FALSE`.

Strings Package—First Version

We will start with the following declarations:

```
MAXIMUM_LENGTH : constant POSITIVE := 20;
subtype INDEX_RANGE is POSITIVE range 1 . . MAXIMUM_LENGTH;
subtype CHARACTER_STRING is STRING( INDEX_RANGE );
 LINE : CHARACTER_STRING;
```

To read in a line typed at the keyboard, we can use

```
for INDEX in 1 . . MAXIMUM_LENGTH
loop
     GET ( LINE( INDEX ) );
end loop;
SKIP_LINE;
```

padding with blanks

As mentioned earlier, there is one annoying feature of reading strings in this way: The string input must be exactly as long as the array. There must be one character for each indexed variable. For our sample declarations, the string of characters must always be exactly 20 characters long. If it is not, the user must type in extra blanks to fill the extra indexed variables. Filling the extra array positions with blanks is called *padding with blanks*. Typing in the extra blanks is burdensome to the user. We can avoid this by using the following:

```
GET_LINE ( LINE, NUMBER_OF_CHARACTERS );
if NUMBER_OF_CHARACTERS = 20 then
    SKIP_LINE;
end if;
```

However, if less than 20 characters are input, the remaining characters in LINE have whatever they had before GET_LINE was called. Thus if you output LINE via

```
for INDEX in 1 . . MAXIMUM_LENGTH
loop
    PUT ( LINE( INDEX ) );
end loop;
NEW_LINE;
```

or more simply with

```
PUT_LINE ( LINE );
```

the output could appear with some unexpected characters on the end of the line.

A better alternative is to use the GET_LINE, and then have the program fill the extra positions with blanks. We can accomplish this by assigning the end portion of the array to all blank characters. We could use a loop and insert blank characters into the remainder of the array, as follows:

```
for INDEX in NUMBER_OF_CHARACTER + 1 . . INDEX_RANGE'LAST
loop
   LINE( INDEX ) :=' ';
end loop;
```

slice

There is an even better way. The Ada term for a portion of an array is called a *slice*. A slice can be used any time a portion of any one-dimensional array is needed. A slice need not only be the last so many components, as it is in the **for** loop example above. It can be any range within the bounds of the array. The general form for the *slice* is

array__variable(beginning__of__slice . . end__of__slice)

To assign a slice or all of the components the same value, we use an array aggregate, as we did in Chapter 9 when initializing an array. For example, note that the procedure GET_STRING in Figure 10.1 has the following statement:

```
ITEM( NUMBER_OF_CHARACTERS + 1 . . ITEM'LAST ) := ( others => ' ' );
```

The *beginning__of__slice* is NUMBER_OF_CHARCTERS + 1 and *end__of__slice* is ITEM'LAST in this example, and all the components in this range are set equal to the blank by this assignment statement. A slice will be used several places in this and following chapters.

The package called STRINGS, shown in Figure 10.1, contains the declaration for the type CHARACTER_STRING and two input/output operations, GET_STRING and PUT_STRING. This package will be used again and expanded as part of the solution to several of the upcoming programming problems. The GET_STRING procedure has an additional feature in that it displays a message if the user inputs more than 20 characters. It does this by testing for END_OF_LINE.

Figure 10.1 also has a small test program that demonstrates how to use the STRINGS package. Note the use of

```
with TEXT_IO; use TEXT_IO;
```

This requires that we instantiate a package called INDEX_IO to help display a message that references the value of ITEM'LAST. To accomplish this instantiation we added the following two lines to the package body:

```
package INDEX_IO is new INTEGER_IO ( POSITIVE );
use INDEX_IO;
```

Because INDEX_IO is instantiated inside the body of package STRINGS, it is not visible to the test program TEST_STRINGS. (We can call the program by whatever meaningful name we wish instead of having to always call it MAIN.) Thus, we must instantiate another I/O package, which we also call INDEX_IO, as follows:

```
package INDEX_IO is new INTEGER_IO ( NATURAL );
use INDEX_IO;
```

Thus, the test program can output the string of digits

```
12345678901234567890
```

to help show the length of the input string.

Package

```
package STRINGS is
   MAXIMUM_LENGTH : constant POSITIVE := 20;
   subtype INDEX_RANGE is POSITIVE range 1 . . MAXIMUM_LENGTH;
   subtype CHARACTER_STRING is STRING( INDEX_RANGE );
   procedure GET_STRING ( ITEM : out CHARACTER_STRING );
   procedure PUT_STRING ( ITEM : in CHARACTER_STRING );
end STRINGS;

with TEXT_IO; use TEXT_IO;
package body STRINGS is
   package INDEX_IO is new INTEGER_IO ( POSITIVE );
   use INDEX_IO;
   procedure GET_STRING ( ITEM : out CHARACTER_STRING ) is
--                    INPUT  : Nothing.
--                    OUTPUT : A string of characters.
```

```
--                      DESCRIPTION : Reads in a string of characters,
--                                    truncated at MAXIMUM_LENGTH
--                                    characters or padded with blanks.
--                                    Displays a message
--                                    if the input is truncated.
        NUMBER_OF_CHARACTERS : NATURAL;
    begin -- GET_STRING
        GET_LINE ( ITEM, NUMBER_OF_CHARACTERS );
        if NUMBER_OF_CHARACTERS = ITEM'LAST then
            if END_OF_LINE then
                SKIP_LINE;
            else
                SKIP_LINE;
                PUT ( "Only");
                PUT ( ITEM'LAST );
                PUT ("characters read in." );
                NEW_LINE;
            end if;
        else
            ITEM( NUMBER_OF_CHARACTERS + 1 . . ITEM'LAST )
                := ( others => ' ' );
        end if;
    end GET_STRING;
    procedure PUT_STRING ( ITEM : in CHARACTER_STRING ) is
--                      INPUT   : A string of characters.
--                      OUTPUT : Nothing.
--                      DESCRIPTION : Displays the entire character string.
    begin -- PUT_STRING
        PUT_LINE ( ITEM );
    end PUT_STRING;
end STRINGS;
```

Program

```
with STRINGS;
use STRINGS;
with TEXT_IO;
use TEXT_IO;
procedure TEST_STRINGS is
--                    INPUT   : Lines of characters.
--                    OUTPUT : Same lines of characters.
--                    DESCRIPTION : Test the Get_Line
--                                  and Put_Line procedures.
    package INDEX_IO is new INTEGER_IO ( NATURAL );
    use INDEX_IO;
    ANSWER : CHARACTER;
    LINE    : CHARACTER_STRING;
```

```
begin -- TEST_STRINGS
    loop
        PUT ( "Enter a string and press return." ); NEW_LINE;
        for INDEX in INDEX_RANGE
        loop
            PUT ( INDEX rem 10, 1 );
        end loop;
        NEW_LINE;
        GET_STRING ( LINE );
        PUT ( "The line contains:" ); NEW_LINE;
        PUT_STRING ( LINE );
        PUT ( "More? (y/n)" ); NEW_LINE;
        GET ( ANSWER ); SKIP_LINE;
        exit when ANSWER = 'n'
              or ANSWER = 'N';
    end loop;
    PUT ( "End of test." ); NEW_LINE;
end TEST_STRINGS;
```

Sample Dialogue

```
Enter a string and press return.
12345678901234567890
Do Be Do
The line contains:
Do Be Do
More? (y/n)
y
Enter a string and press return.
12345678901234567890
Life is a jelly doughnut. Isn't it?
Only     20 characters read in.
The line contains:
Life is a jelly doug
More? (y/n)
n
End of test.
```

Figure 10.1 A package to read and write strings of characters.

The technique that was used in the design of this package is called *object-oriented design*. It gets its name from the fact that the package is designed around (or oriented around) an object. The object in this case is a string of characters. Once the data type has been designed, then the operations that are to be performed on this object are designed. The object and its operations are then *encapsulated* in a package. That, in a nutshell, is object-oriented design.

object-oriented design

Arrays of Arrays

The component type of an array may be any Ada type whatsoever. In particular, it can be an array type. Thus, we can have an array of arrays. A common situation that requires an array of arrays is an array of strings. The array variable NAME, when declared as follows, can be used to keep a list of names:

```
type CHARACTER_STRING is array( 1 . . MAXIMUM_LENGTH ) of CHARACTER;
subtype INDEX_RANGE is POSITIVE range 1 . . LARGEST_INDEX;
type STRING_LIST is array( INDEX_RANGE ) of CHARACTER_STRING
NAME : STRING_LIST;
```

MAXIMUM_LENGTH and LARGEST_INDEX are defined as constants. Figure 10.2 illustrates a list of names stored in the array NAME. In that figure MAXIMUM_LENGTH is set equal to 17.

nested indexes

With arrays of arrays such as these arrays of strings, the notation can get a bit complicated, but there are no new rules involved. Just read or write the expressions from left to right carefully and with courage. For example, consider the following expression:

```
NAME( 6 ) ( 3 )
```

NAME (6) is an indexed variable of type CHARACTER_STRING and in our example would contain the sixth name on our list of names. The type CHARACTER_STRING is an array of characters, so it makes sense to add an index to it. By adding **(3)** we obtain the third indexed variable of this array of characters. If we put this all together, we see that the above expression is the location of the third letter in the sixth name on our list.

Expressions such as the one we just discussed usually need not be used at all. Instead it is preferable to think of NAME (6) as a unit and to manipulate it as a unit using procedures. For example, the following procedure call will read a string from the keyboard and store it in the array NAME (6). (The procedure declaration is in the package STRINGS in Figure 10.1.)

```
GET_STRING ( NAME ( 6 ) );
```

It is true that when NAME (6) is copied into the formal parameter ITEM in the procedure declaration, it will produce, in effect, an expression such as

```
NAME ( 6 ) ( NUMBER_OF_CHARACTERS + 1 . . NAME ( 6 ) 'LAST )
            := ( others => ' ' );
```

However, you need never think about that expression. The procedure GET_STRING reads a string into an array of type CHARACTER_STRING, and NAME (6) is an array of that type. The procedure takes NAME (6) as a single unit, gives it a value consisting of a string of characters, and then returns it to the calling program or procedure as a single unit. Once the procedure is written, you need not be aware of the details of how it accomplishes its task. You need not even be aware of the existence of any indexing or slicing. That is the beauty of procedural abstraction.

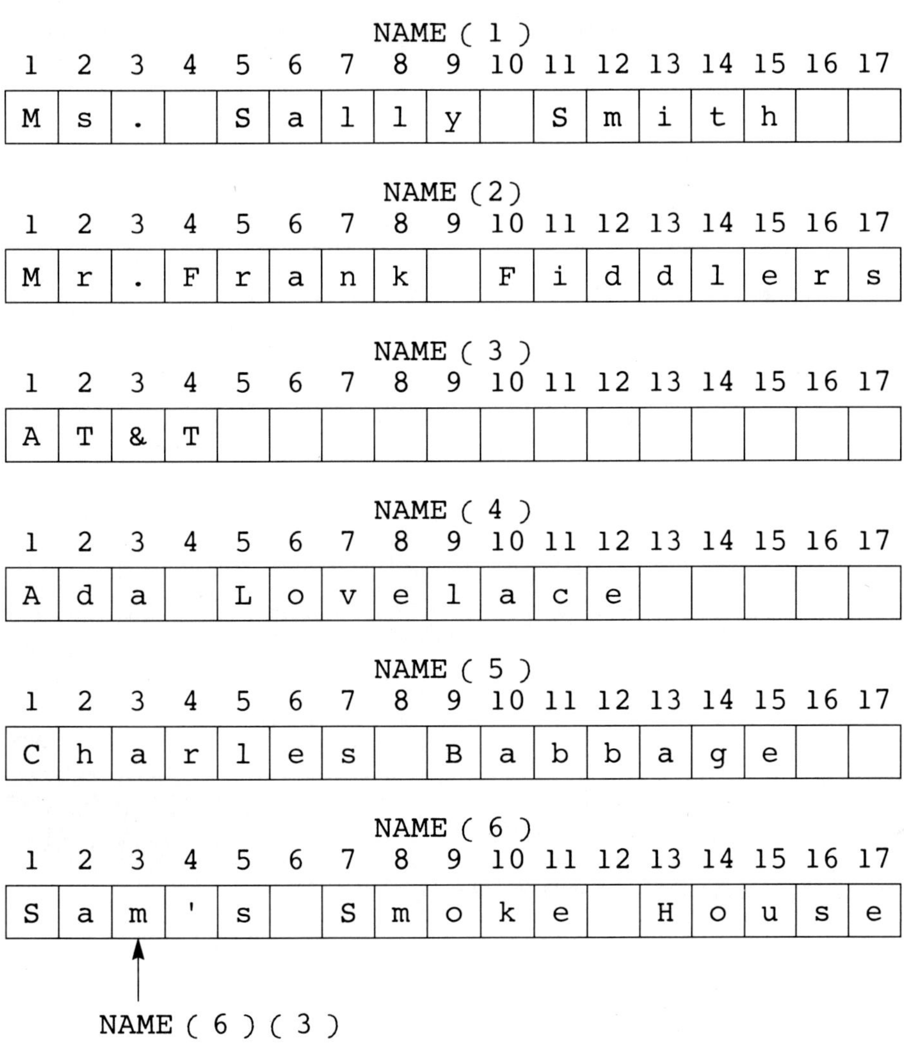

Figure 10.2 An array of strings.

Exercises

Self-Test Exercises

1. What is the output of the following program?

```
with I_O; use I_O;
procedure MAIN is
     MAXIMUM : constant INTEGER := 5;
```

```
        WORD : array( 1 . . MAXIMUM ) of CHARACTER;
    begin -- Main
        WORD( 1 ) := 'a';
        for INDEX in 2 . . MAXIMUM
        loop
            WORD( INDEX ) := 'b';
        end loop;
        for POSITION in 1 . . MAXIMUM
        loop
            PUT ( WORD( POSITION ) );
        end loop;
        NEW_LINE;
    end MAIN;
```

2. The procedure PUT_STRING in Figure 10.1 always ends by going to the next line. Hence, it cannot be used to write a variable of type CHARACTER_STRING, followed by a string literal, followed by a number all on one line. Write a procedure called PUT (without "_LINE") that could be added to the package that writes a value of type CHARACTER_STRING but does not advance to the next line. Thus, the complete output of the following will appear on one line:

```
PUT ( NAME( INDEX ) );
PUT ( " is numbered " );
PUT ( INDEX );
```

3. Give suitable type declarations for the family records for the children in a large family. The family is so large that the children are numbered **1** through **17.** The following information is available on each child: name, year of birth, and whether or not the child has been vaccinated against the flu.

The Notion of a Data Structure

The notion of a data structure and the notion of a data type are very intimately intertwined, so we will preface our discussion of data structures with a review of the notion of a data type. Recall that a data type is a collection of values together with some operations on those values. For example, the values of the type INTEGER are **0**, **1**, **-1**, **2**, and so forth. The operations include addition, subtraction, multiplication, division (/ and **rem**), and the comparison relations such as < and =. The data type FLOAT has a different set of values and a different set of operations, although some operations like addition may be considered to apply to both data types. Certain operations relate two or more data types. For example, the function FLOAT when applied to a value of type INTEGER produces a value of type FLOAT. The function INTEGER when applied to a value of type FLOAT produces a value of type INTEGER.

Yet another data type is the following array type:

```
type LIST is array( 0 . . 4 ) of FLOAT;
```

The values of this data type are a list of five numbers indexed by the numbers zero through four. The operations on this data type do not combine two values of this type but instead combine a value of this array type with a value of the subrange type **0 . . 4** to produce a value of type FLOAT. If PAYRATE is of type LIST, then PAYRATE combined with **0** yields an indexed variable PAYRATE(0). In this case the operation is **( )**. The syntax is a bit unorthodox for an operation, and the result is strictly speaking not a value but a variable. However, it is an operation, and it does produce a value of type FLOAT, namely, the value of the indexed variable PAYRATE(0).

Like the data types INTEGER, FLOAT, and CHARACTER, the type LIST is a data type with values and operations. However, it clearly is a different sort of type. It is what we call a *composite type*. It is called *composite* because it is made up of a grouping or composite of other smaller parts. In the above case a list of numbers can be decomposed into parts, namely, the individual FLOAT numbers, by means of operations using **( )** to produce indexed variables like PAYRATE(0).

composite type

A data structure is almost the same thing as a composite data type. Every composite data type is a data structure, and given any data structure, we could redesign the Ada language to include it as a data type. A *data structure* is a way of structuring data. It organizes the data into composite items and provides operations for manipulating the items. Data types are in the declarative part of the program or package. Data structures are in the mind of the programmer and might or might not also occur as composite data types in the declarative part of the program.

Data Abstraction

We have already discussed the concept of procedural abstraction. It consists of forgetting the unessential details of a procedure. Wise use of procedural abstraction means that, once we have finished writing and testing a procedure, we can forget how the procedure works and concern ourselves only with what it does. Once we have written (or somebody else has written) the procedure PUT_STRING in Figure 10.1, we need not constantly return to the code to see how it works. We only need to remember that it fills an array of type CHARACTER_STRING with characters read from the keyboard and that it pads the string with blanks to make it 20 characters long. There is no need to remember whether it uses a **for** loop or a pretest loop or even to remember whether it uses any loop at all. This forgetting frees the mind of unessential details and so frees mental energy for the larger details of program writing. This technique of abstraction can be applied to data structures as well as procedures.

Data abstraction is a similar kind of judicious forgetfulness, but this time it is applied to data structures. To realize a data structure within Ada, or any other programming language, we may need to specify some details which, while necessary in the particular language, are not a necessary part of our intuitive thinking about the data structure. For example, the type CHARACTER_STRING discussed earlier in this chapter was designed to hold strings of 20 or fewer characters. A natural way to do this is with an array. This required that we specify an index type. We chose to specify **1 . . 20**.

We could just as well have chosen **0 . . 19**. Some authorities would argue vigorously that that would have been a better choice for an index type. Nobody is likely to argue for **100 . . 119** as the index type, but it would be adequate. Since the index type matters so little, it would seem safe to just forget about it. That is exactly what data abstraction is all about: forgetting the unessential details of a data structure. The productive way to view the type CHARACTER_STRING is as a string of 20 or fewer characters and not as an array type with some arbitrary index type. You should think about designing algorithms that manipulate strings. Do not waste mental energy memorizing the particular numbers used to index the characters.

Data abstraction and procedural abstraction go hand in hand. Once a data structure like the type CHARACTER_STRING has been designed and once the procedures for the basic operations like GET_LINE and PUT_LINE have been written, we can forget the unessential details of both the data structure and the procedures. At that point we are reading and writing strings of characters, not arrays of characters, and we are doing it with procedures, not with **for** loops. Of course, you must remember the details long enough to write the basic procedures, but after that you can forget the details. Of course it is no sin to remember the index type or other details if you happen to be able to comfortably fit them into your memory, but there comes a time when you should not emphasize them in your thinking.

Case Study

Automated Drill and Practice

Problem Definition

We want to produce an automated drill and practice program. The program will accept input and build parallel arrays, and it will drill the user to see if the user knows the birth date of the composers. It will first clear the screen. After that it will ask the user to input a composer and birth date and will check to see whether or not the birth date is correct. It repeats this drill as often as the user desires.

Discussion

The following is an outline for the program:

1. Input data and fill the parallel arrays.
2. Clear the screen.
3. Do the following as often as the user wants:
   3a. Read a composer's name.
   3b. Search the list of names to find the composer.
   3c. Read the candidate year for birth date.
   3d. Output an appropriate response.

This program can be written by using operations that we have already designed and that are part of the STRINGS package. The input and filling of the parallel arrays require a loop and the use of one index that is used for both arrays. The procedure to clear the screen will simply consist of a call to NEW_LINE (*blank_lines*) to produce enough blank lines to fill the screen. The input of the composer's name and candidate birth year are standard, as is the output message. Only the search algorithm seems to present anything new, but even that can be adapted from previous algorithms.

Algorithm

The search algorithm will search an array of names. We will again use the array type CHARACTER_STRING from the package STRINGS. The type definition is reproduced below:

serial search

```
MAXIMUM_LENGTH : constant INTEGER := 20;
subtype INDEX_RANGE is INTEGER range 1 . . MAXIMUM_LENGTH;
type CHARACTER_STRING is array( STRING_RANGE ) of CHARACTER;
```

The search must return the index of the name if the name is found or indicate that the name is not on the list. Thus, we are led to the following procedure heading:

```
   procedure SEARCH ( PATTERN  : in CHARACTER_STRING;
                      NAME     : in NAME_LIST;
                      LAST     : in LIST_RANGE;
                      POSITION : out LIST_RANGE ) is
--                 INPUT  : A pattern for which to search a name
--                          list. Also the number of names in
--                          the name list (last).
--                 OUTPUT : The index or position of the pattern
--                          in the name list.
--                 DESCRIPTION : The procedure performs a serial
--                               search of the name list.
--                               Exception composer_not_found
--                               is raised if the pattern is not
--                               found in the name list.
```

In Chapter 9 we used a serial search algorithm to search an array of integers. That algorithm used no special properties of integers, so it can be used to search any list, including a list of arrays. Although NAME(INDEX) and PATTERN are entire arrays, we can view them as variables with complex values and compare them with the usual equality operator:

```
   PATTERN = NAME( INDEX )
```

The serial search algorithm tests each element of the array to see if PATTERN is present:

```
for INDEX in 1 . . LAST
loop
    if PATTERN = NAME( INDEX ) then
        POSITION := INDEX;
        return;
    end if;
end loop;
raise COMPOSER_NOT_FOUND;
```

If the PATTERN is found in NAME(INDEX) the index is assigned to POSITION, which is returned when the procedure terminates as the result of the **return** statement. If the loop terminates it is because the pattern was not found; at this point the exception COMPOSER_NOT_FOUND is raised. The exception is raised only if the loop fails to find the pattern in the list. The complete program is given in Figure 10.3.

Program

```
with STRINGS; use STRINGS;
with TEXT_IO; use TEXT_IO;
procedure DRILL_DATES is
   package YEAR_IO is new INTEGER_IO ( POSITIVE );
   use YEAR_IO;
   LARGEST_INDEX : constant POSITIVE := 10;
   SCREEN_SIZE   : constant POSITIVE_COUNT := 26;
   subtype LIST_RANGE is POSITIVE range 1 . . LARGEST_INDEX;
   type NAME_LIST is array( LIST_RANGE ) of CHARACTER_STRING;
   type DATE_LIST is array( LIST_RANGE ) of POSITIVE;
   ANSWER : CHARACTER;
   DATE   : DATE_LIST;
   LAST   : LIST_RANGE;
   NAME   : NAME_LIST;
   YEAR   : POSITIVE;
   procedure READ_LIST ( NAME : out NAME_LIST;
                         DATE : out DATE_LIST;
                         LAST : out LIST_RANGE ) is
      INDEX : LIST_RANGE := LIST_RANGE'FIRST;
   begin -- Read_List
      loop
         PUT ( "Name?" ); NEW_LINE;
         GET_STRING ( NAME( INDEX ) );
         PUT ( "Year of birth?" ); NEW_LINE;
         GET ( DATE( INDEX ) ); SKIP_LINE;
         exit when INDEX = LIST_RANGE'LAST;
         PUT ( "More? (y/n)" ); NEW_LINE;
         GET ( ANSWER ); SKIP_LINE;
         exit when ANSWER = 'n'
              or ANSWER = 'N';
         INDEX := INDEX + 1;
      end loop;
```

```
      LAST := INDEX;
   end READ_LIST;
   procedure CLEAR_SCREEN is
   begin -- Clear Screen
       NEW_LINE ( SCREEN_SIZE );
   end CLEAR_SCREEN;
   procedure TEST_MEMORY ( NAME : in NAME_LIST;
                           DATE : in DATE_LIST;
                           LAST : in LIST_RANGE ) is
      COMPOSER_NOT_FOUND : exception;
      LOCATION : LIST_RANGE;
      PATTERN : CHARACTER_STRING;
      YEAR : POSITIVE;
      procedure SEARCH ( PATTERN  : in CHARACTER_STRING;
                         NAME     : in NAME_LIST;
                         LAST     : in LIST_RANGE;
                         POSITION : out LIST_RANGE ) is
--              INPUT  : A pattern for which to search a name
--                       list. Also the number of names in
--                       the name list (last).
--              OUTPUT : The index or position of the pattern
--                       in the name list.
--              DESCRIPTION : The procedure performs a linear
--                            search of the name list.
--                            Exception composer_not_found
--                            is raised if the pattern is not
--                            found in the name list.
      begin -- Search
         for INDEX in 1 .. LAST
         loop
            if PATTERN = NAME( INDEX ) then
                POSITION := INDEX;
                return;
            end if;
         end loop;
         raise COMPOSER_NOT_FOUND;
      end SEARCH;
   begin -- Test_Memory
      PUT ( "Enter composer's name:" ); NEW_LINE;
      GET_STRING ( PATTERN );
      SEARCH ( PATTERN, NAME, LAST, LOCATION );
      PUT ( "Year of birth?" ); NEW_LINE;
      GET ( YEAR ); SKIP_LINE;
      if YEAR = DATE( LOCATION ) then
          PUT ( "You're right!" ); NEW_LINE;
```

```
            else
                PUT ( "Sorry, you are wrong." ); NEW_LINE;
                PUT_STRING ( NAME( LOCATION ) );
                PUT ( "was born in");
                PUT ( DATE ( LOCATION ) );
                NEW_LINE;
            end if;
        exception
            when COMPOSER_NOT_FOUND =>
                PUT ( "Sorry, no record of that composer." );
                NEW_LINE;
        end TEST_MEMORY;
    begin -- Drill_Dates
        PUT ( "Enter the composers and years of birth:" ); NEW_LINE;
        READ_LIST ( NAME, DATE, LAST );
        CLEAR_SCREEN;
        PUT ( "Do you want to test your memory of dates? (y/n)" );
        NEW_LINE;
        loop
            GET ( ANSWER ); SKIP_LINE;
            exit when ANSWER = 'n'
                  or ANSWER = 'N';
            TEST_MEMORY ( NAME, DATE, LAST );
            PUT ( "Again? (y/n)" ); NEW_LINE;
        end loop;
        PUT ( "End of drill." ); NEW_LINE;
    end DRILL_DATES;
```

Sample Dialogue

```
Enter the composers and years of birth:
Name?
Bloch
Year of birth?
1880
More? (y/n)
y
Name?
J. S. Bach
Year of birth?
1685
More? (y/n)
y
Name?
Beethoven
```

```
Year of birth?
1770
More? (y/n)
n
-- Screen is cleared

Do you want to test your memory of dates? (y/n)
y
Enter composer's name:
Beethoven
Year of birth?
1776
Sorry, you are wrong.
Beethoven
was born in 1770
Again? (y/n)
y
Enter composer's name:
Bach
Sorry, no record of that composer.
Again? (y/n)
y
Enter composer's name:
J. S. Bach
Year of birth?
1685
You're right!
Again? (y/n)
n
End of drill.
```

Figure 10.3 Automated drill program.

Using an Existing Package

The previous case study illustrates one very important programming technique. Problems can be often solved with the aid of previously written packages. Also before trying to construct an algorithm from scratch, it always pays to see if the problem is similar to one you solved at some previous time. It could be that the solution is in a previously written package in your library. If the previously written program is well documented, this will be easy to do. It may even be possible to use operations from previously written, well-documented packages.

Case Study

Pattern Matching

The sample dialogue for the program in Figure 10.3 points out one shortcoming of that program: The name must be spelled exactly the same as the name in the array or the program will consider it a mismatch. To that program ''Bach,'' ''Johann Sebastian Bach,'' and ''J. S. Bach'' are three different composers. In this section we will design a pattern-matching algorithm that will check for the occurrence of one string within another string. We can then use that algorithm to check for ''Bach'' and it will match any variation on Bach's name. (Those who are concerned about accommodating the other composers in the Bach family are encouraged to do Exercise 13 after reading this section.)

Problem Definition

Both the pattern, like ''Bach,'' and the string to which it is compared, like ''J. S. Bach,'' will be stored in arrays of characters of the type CHARACTER_STRING, which we used in the last Case Study and is part of the STRINGS package. We want to design a boolean-valued function that will return TRUE if the pattern occurs as a substring in the, typically larger, target string. However, there is a problem with trailing blanks. The string ''Bach,'' if read in by the procedure GET_STRING, will be stored as ''Bach'' followed by sixteen blanks. Our pattern-searching function will somehow need to disregard any trailing blanks. The function we want can be described by the following heading:

```
function SUBPATTERN ( PATTERN, TARGET : CHARACTER_STRING )
                           return BOOLEAN is
--               INPUT  : A pattern string and a target string.
--               OUTPUT : TRUE if the pattern is in the target,
--                           otherwise FALSE.
--               DESCRIPTION : Any trailing blanks in the pattern
--                                are ignored.
```

Discussion

Suppose the array PATTERN contains the string ''Bach'' in indexed components PATTERN(1) through PATTERN(4), followed by trailing blanks. We want to know if ''Bach'' occurs anyplace in the array TARGET. One way to approach the problem is to assume that the arrays are strips of paper containing the strings and to visualize how we might compare the two strings using the strips of paper. This approach to the problem is diagrammed in Figure 10.4. For each position in the target array,

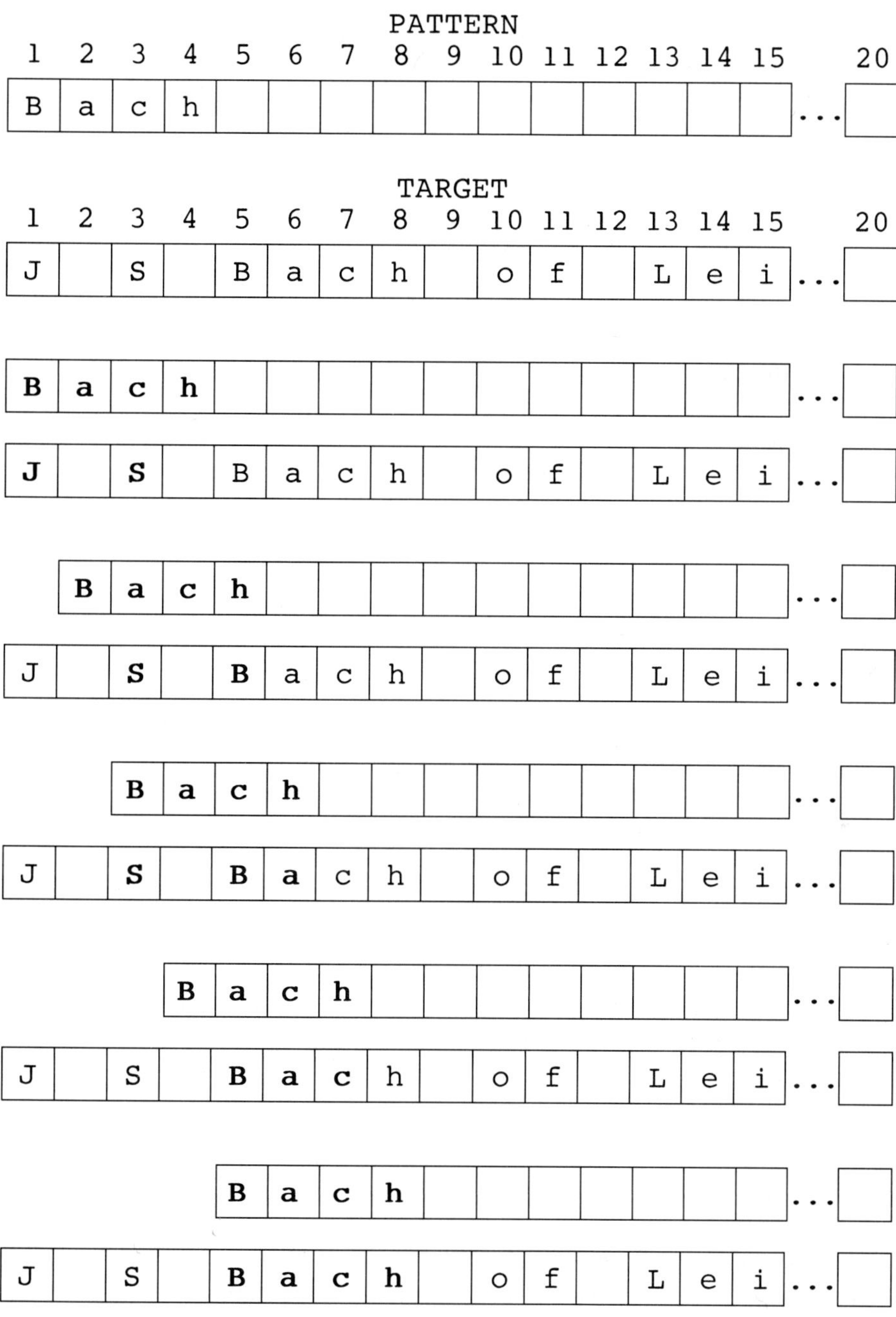

Figure 10.4 Technique for finding a pattern.

we compare the pattern to the substring beginning at that position. This is nothing other than a more involved version of the serial search algorithm we used earlier, and it translates to the following algorithm outline:

Algorithm

```
for index in 1 . . length_of_pattern
    Begin testing at target( start_of_target )
    and compare pattern(1) though pattern(length_of_pattern)
    to target ( start_of_target ),
       target ( start_of_target + 1 ),
       target ( start_of_target + 2), etc.
    if any character doesn't match then
         the pattern is not found
    if all characters match then
         the pattern is found
```

If the pattern string is ''Bach,'' our algorithm needs to know that there are four letters in ''Bach.'' It will also need to be able to compare ''Bach'' to any four successive elements of the target array. We will need to design functions or procedures for each of these two subproblems: one to find the length of the pattern and another to match the pattern array to a portion of the target array.

Expanding the Strings Package

length function The length of the pattern will be computed by the function described in the following heading:

```
function LENGTH ( ITEM : CHARACTER_STRING )
                  return INDEX_RANGE is
--              INPUT  : A character string with at least one
--                       nonblank character in it.
--              OUTPUT : The number of nonblank characters
--                       in the string.
--              DESCRIPTION : Computes the length (number of
--                            nonblank characters in the string).
--                            Raises empty_string if all
--                            characters are blanks.
```

The most obvious approach is to count the characters, starting at the beginning of the string and stopping when we encounter a blank. However, this approach will not work for strings that contain blanks, such as ''Vaughan Williams.'' To accommodate such strings, we will instead count backwards from the end of the array until we find a nonblank character. We count by decrementing a variable COUNT as follows:

```
for COUNT in reverse ITEM'FIRST . . ITEM'LAST
loop
    if ITEM( COUNT ) /= BLANK then
        return COUNT;
```

In this example the attributes FIRST and LAST are applied to the array variable ITEM. The attribute FIRST, when applied to an array variable, returns the index to the very first element of the array. Similarly, the attribute LAST when applied to an array variable returns the index to the very last element of the array. The advantage of using these attributes in this case is that we don't need to know what the exact index range of ITEM is. The code works regardless of the range of the indexes for the array. If we later change the declaration for CHARACTER_STRING so it has a different range of indexes, we will not have to rewrite the code for the function LENGTH. The complete function declaration for LENGTH can be found in Figure 10.5.

Function

```
function LENGTH ( ITEM : CHARACTER_STRING ) return INDEX_RANGE is
--               INPUT  : A character string with at least one
--                        nonblank character in it.
--               OUTPUT : The number of nonblank characters
--                        in the string.
--               DESCRIPTION : Computes the length (number of
--                             nonblank characters in the string).
--                             Raises empty_string if all characters
--                             are blanks.
   BLANK : constant CHARACTER := ' ';
begin -- Length
   for COUNT in reverse ITEM'FIRST . . ITEM'LAST
   loop
      if ITEM( COUNT ) /= BLANK then
         return COUNT;
      end if;
   end loop;
   raise EMPTY_STRING;
end LENGTH;
```

Figure 10.5 The function LENGTH.

match function

We now turn to the task of comparing the pattern to a portion of the array TARGET. In other words we want to design a module with some parameters that can perform any one of the various comparisons illustrated in Figure 10.4. For our parameters we will want meaningful names. Figure 10.6(a) illustrates our problem and presents our naming conventions. The identifier LENGTH_OF_PATTERN is the value LENGTH(PATTERN). START_OF_TARGET is the index of TARGET where the comparison begins. If START_OF_TARGET has value 3, as in Figure 10.6(a), the comparison will fail. If it has value 5, and if the other values are as shown in Figure 10.6(a), then the comparison will succeed. Our module will compare the two lists of characters:

```
PATTERN(1),PATTERN(2), . . . , PATTERN( LENGTH_OF_ PATTERN )
TARGET(START_OF_TARGET), TARGET(START_OF_TARGET +1), etc.
```

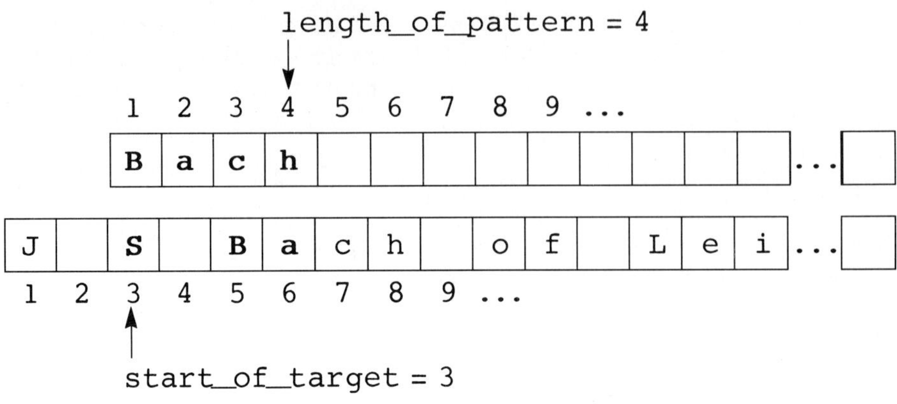

Figure 10.6(a) Parameters for the procedure MATCH.

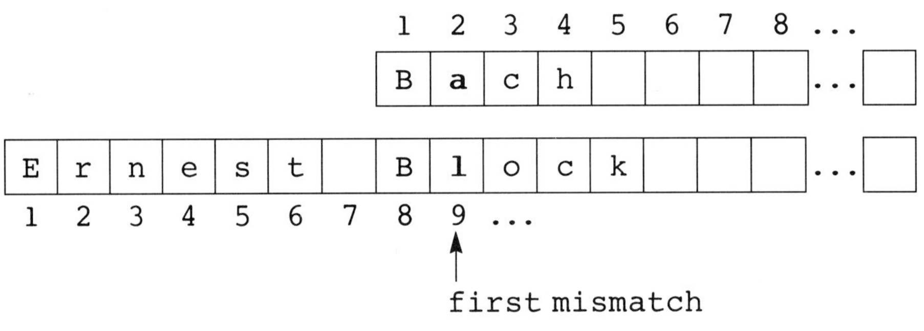

Figure 10.6(b) Technique for procedure MATCH.

A natural way to do this is with a boolean-valued function that behaves as indicated below:

```
function MATCH ( PATTERN, TARGET : CHARACTER_STRING;
                 LENGTH_OF_PATTERN,
                 START_OF_TARGET : INDEX_RANGE )
                 return BOOLEAN is
--             INPUT  : A pattern and name string, along
--                      with the length of the pattern and
--                      the starting point in the target.
--             OUTPUT : FALSE is returned if the pattern is
--                      longer than the rest of the target.
--                      TRUE if there is a match,
--                      otherwise FALSE.
```

```
--                DESCRIPTION : The matching begins with the
--                              first of the pattern and the
--                              starting point in the target.
```

We will be applying the function MATCH even if the index position START_OF_TARGET is too large to allow a match. For example, if we try to compare a pattern of length 4 to the last three or fewer symbols in the target array, the pattern cannot possibly match, so FALSE is returned. The following code segment will do the trick:

no precondition

```
if LENGTH_OF_PATTERN >
    INDEX_RANGE'LAST - START_OF_TARGET + 1 then
        return FALSE;
```

begin matching characters

If LENGTH_OF_PATTERN is **2** and START_OF_TARGET is the last character in the target, and thus equal to INDEX_RANGE'LAST, then the comparison is **2 > 1** and FALSE is returned. If LENGTH_OF_PATTERN is **1** and START_OF_TARGET is the last character in the target, then the comparison is **1 > 1**, which fails the test, and the matching-of-characters part of the algorithm is executed.

To find if the pattern exists in the TARGET string, we need to compare the entire pattern with a portion of TARGET. The key word there is *portion,* and in Ada that means a "slice" of TARGET. Thus, we can compare to see if PATTERN is equal to some suitable slice of TARGET. Recall that a slice is specified with a range, so our comparison could be specified as

algorithm for match

PATTERN(1 . . LENGTH_OF_PATTERN) = TARGET(*suitable__range*)

The technique is illustrated in Figure 10.6(b), where the *suitable__range* is 8 . . 11. The lower bound for the TARGET slice is START_OF_TARGET, and we know that the length or size of the slice is LENGTH_OF_PATTERN. From this we might be tempted to say that *suitable__range* is

START_OF_TARGET . . LENGTH_OF_PATTERN

This is proven incorrect with a simple example. What if START_OF_TARGET is **10** but LENGTH_OF_PATTERN is only **3**?
A second choice might be

START_OF_TARGET . . START_OF_TARGET + LENGTH_OF_PATTERN

The length of any range is found as

upper__bound – *lower__bound* + 1

When applying our second choice to this formula, we find that

upper__bound	–	*lower__bound*	+ 1
START_OF_TARGET + LENGTH_OF_PATTERN	–	START_OF_TARGET	+ 1

is equal to LENGTH_OF_PATTERN + 1. The correct slice is thus

START_OF_TARGET . . START_OF_TARGET + LENGTH_OF_PATTERN – 1

Thus, for this part of the algorithm, we could write the code as

```
if PATTERN ( 1 . . LENGTH_OF_PATTERN )
    = TARGET ( START_OF_TARGET
            . . START_OF_TARGET + LENGTH_OF_PATTERN - 1 ) then
    return TRUE;
else
    return FALSE;
end if;
```

or more simply as

```
return PATTERN ( 1 . . LENGTH_OF_PATTERN )
    = TARGET ( START_OF_TARGET
            . . START_OF_TARGET + LENGTH_OF_PATTERN - 1 );
```

In the complete function declaration, which can be found in Figure 10.7(b), the two tests are combined into a single **return** using an **and then**. The MATCH function, along with the LENGTH function, is added to the body of the STRINGS package. The specifications for both functions are added to the specification part of the STRINGS package. The new package specification is shown in Figure 10.7(a).

Package

```
package STRINGS is
    MAXIMUM_LENGTH : constant POSITIVE := 20;
    subtype INDEX_RANGE is POSITIVE range 1 . . MAXIMUM_LENGTH;
    EMPTY_STRING : exception;
    subtype CHARACTER_STRING is STRING( INDEX_RANGE );
    function LENGTH ( ITEM : CHARACTER_STRING ) return INDEX_RANGE;
    function MATCH  ( PATTERN, TARGET : CHARACTER_STRING;
                      LENGTH_OF_PATTERN,
                      START_OF_TARGET : INDEX_RANGE )
                      return BOOLEAN;
    procedure GET_STRING ( ITEM : out CHARACTER_STRING );
    procedure PUT_STRING ( ITEM : in CHARACTER_STRING );
end STRINGS;
```

Figure 10.7(a) The revised specification part of package STRINGS.

```
function MATCH  ( PATTERN, TARGET : CHARACTER_STRING;
                  LENGTH_OF_PATTERN,
                  START_OF_TARGET : INDEX_RANGE )
                  return BOOLEAN is
--              INPUT  : A pattern and name string, along
--                         with the length of the pattern and
--                         the starting point in the target.
```

```
--                    OUTPUT : FALSE is returned if the pattern is
--                             longer than the rest of the target.
--                             TRUE if there is a match,
--                             otherwise FALSE.
--                    DESCRIPTION : The matching begins with the
--                                  first of the pattern and the
--                                  starting point in the target.
begin -- Match
    return LENGTH_OF_PATTERN
        <= INDEX_RANGE'LAST - START_OF_TARGET + 1
    and then
          PATTERN ( 1 .. LENGTH_OF_PATTERN )
        = TARGET ( START_OF_TARGET
                  .. START_OF_TARGET + LENGTH_OF_PATTERN - 1 );
end MATCH;
```

Figure 10.7(b) The complete MATCH function.

The program in Figure 10.8 is designed to use the revised STRINGS package and to test the functions MATCH and LENGTH.

Program

```
with TEXT_IO; use TEXT_IO;
with STRINGS; use STRINGS;
procedure TEST_MATCH is
    ANSWER : CHARACTER;
    PATTERN : CHARACTER_STRING;
    START_OF_TARGET : INDEX_RANGE;
    TARGET : CHARACTER_STRING;
    package INDEX_IO is new INTEGER_IO ( NATURAL );
    use INDEX_IO;
begin -- Test_Match
    loop
        PUT ( "Enter a target string and press return." );
        NEW_LINE;
        for INDEX in 1 .. MAXIMUM_LENGTH
        loop
            PUT ( NATURAL ( INDEX ) rem 10, 1 );
        end loop;
        NEW_LINE;
        GET_STRING ( TARGET );
        PUT ( "Enter a pattern string and press return." );
        NEW_LINE;
        GET_STRING ( PATTERN );
        PUT ( "Enter the index of where you want" ); NEW_LINE;
        PUT ( "to try matching the target." ); NEW_LINE;
```

```
        GET ( START_OF_TARGET ); SKIP_LINE;
        if MATCH ( PATTERN, TARGET,
                   LENGTH ( PATTERN ),
                   START_OF_TARGET ) then
            PUT ( "The pattern was FOUND at index");
        else
            PUT ( "The pattern was NOT FOUND at index");
        end if;
        PUT ( START_OF_TARGET );
        NEW_LINE ( 2 );
        PUT ( "More? (y/n)" ); NEW_LINE;
        GET ( ANSWER ); SKIP_LINE;
        exit when ANSWER = 'n'
             or ANSWER = 'N';
    end loop;
    PUT ( "End of test." ); NEW_LINE;
end TEST_MATCH;
```

Sample Dialogue

```
Enter a target string and press return.
12345678901234567890
J S Bach of Leizig
Enter a pattern string and press return.
Bach
Enter the index of where you want
to try matching the target.
3
The pattern was NOT FOUND at index 3

More? (y/n)
y
Enter a target string and press return.
12345678901234567890
J S Bach of Leipzig
Enter a pattern string and press return.
Bach
Enter the index of where you want
to try matching the target.
5
The pattern was FOUND at index 5
More? (y/n)
n
End of test.
```

Figure 10.8 Program to test the function MATCH.

Strings Package Expanded Again

We are now ready to piece together the complete pattern-matching algorithm for the function SUBPATTERN. The basic algorithm is another example of the "innocent if not proven guilty" technique and can be realized as follows:

first version of subpattern

```
for INDEX in 1 . . INDEX_RANGE'LAST - LENGTH ( PATTERN ) + 1
loop
    if MATCH ( PATTERN, TARGET,
               LENGTH ( PATTERN ), INDEX ) then
        return TRUE;
    end if;
end loop;
return FALSE;
```

You should always check that a loop is not executed one too few or one too many times. In designing the above code you might be tempted to use the following as the final value of the loop control variable:

check boundary values

```
INDEX_RANGE'LAST - LENGTH ( PATTERN )
```

However a careful check will reveal that that would stop the loop one iteration too early. This is easiest to see if you consider some concrete values. Recall that INDEX_RANGE'LAST is **20** and suppose that the length of the pattern is **4**. Then the value of the above expression (without the plus one) is **16**. Yet if we try **17** we will see that it is possible to fit in a pattern of four letters, starting with index variable **17**:

```
TARGET(17) = 'B'
TARGET(18) = 'a'
TARGET(19) = 'c'
TARGET(20) = 'h'
```

Hence, we see that in fact we need the expression with the plus one as shown in our **for** loop, otherwise we will miss one possible location for the pattern.

The algorithm described in our pseudocode will work for the function SUBPATTERN, and it is efficient. Once the pattern is found, there is no need to perform any more checking, so we immediately return TRUE and the function terminates. There is no need, however, to compute the length of the pattern every time around the loop; the length of the pattern will not change inside the function. For the sake of additional efficiency, we use a local variable called LENGTH_OF_PATTERN to hold the value LENGTH(PATTERN), so the program need only compute that value once. The function SUBPATTERN is now added to the body of the STRINGS package. The package specification is updated to include the specifications for the function. The revised version of the specification part of the package is given in Figure 10.9(a) and, the complete SUBPATTERN function is shown in Figure 10.9(b).

efficiency

Package

```
package STRINGS is
    MAXIMUM_LENGTH : constant POSITIVE := 20;
    subtype INDEX_RANGE is POSITIVE range 1 . . MAXIMUM_LENGTH;
    type CHARACTER_STRING is array( INDEX_RANGE ) of CHARACTER;
    EMPTY_STRING : exception;
    function LENGTH ( ITEM : CHARACTER_STRING ) return INDEX_RANGE;
    function MATCH  ( PATTERN, TARGET : CHARACTER_STRING;
                      LENGTH_OF_PATTERN,
                      START_OF_TARGET : INDEX_RANGE )
                      return BOOLEAN;
    procedure GET_STRING ( ITEM : out CHARACTER_STRING );
    function SUBPATTERN ( PATTERN, TARGET : CHARACTER_STRING )
                            return BOOLEAN;
    procedure PUT_STRING ( ITEM : in CHARACTER_STRING );
end STRINGS;
```

Figure 10.9(a) The re-revised specification part of package STRINGS.

```
    function SUBPATTERN ( PATTERN, TARGET : CHARACTER_STRING )
                            return BOOLEAN is
--                  INPUT  : A pattern and target string.
--                  OUTPUT : TRUE if they match, otherwise FALSE.
--                           Returns FALSE if pattern is longer
--                           than the target.
--                  DESCRIPTION : The function compares the pattern
--                                to the target, character by character
--                                To ensure a perfect match.
        LENGTH_OF_PATTERN : INDEX_RANGE := LENGTH ( PATTERN );
    begin -- Subpattern
        for INDEX in 1 . . INDEX_RANGE'LAST - LENGTH_OF_PATTERN + 1
        loop
            if MATCH ( PATTERN, TARGET,
                       LENGTH_OF_PATTERN, INDEX ) then
                return TRUE;
            end if;
        end loop;
        return FALSE;
    end SUBPATTERN;
```

Figure 10.9(b) The complete SUBPATTERN function.

The program in Figure 10.10 uses the re-revised STRINGS package to test the SUBPATTERN function.

Program

```
with TEXT_IO; use TEXT_IO;
with STRINGS; use STRINGS;
procedure TEST_SUBPATTERN is
    ANSWER : CHARACTER;
    PATTERN,
    TARGET : CHARACTER_STRING;
begin -- Test_Subpattern
    loop
        PUT ( "Enter a target string and press return." ); NEW_LINE;
        GET_STRING ( TARGET );
        PUT ( "Enter a pattern string and press return." ); NEW_LINE;
        GET_STRING ( PATTERN );
        if SUBPATTERN ( PATTERN, TARGET ) then
            PUT ( "The pattern was FOUND." );
        else
            PUT ( "The pattern was NOT FOUND." );
        end if;
        NEW_LINE ( 2 );
        PUT ( "More? (y/n)" ); NEW_LINE;
        GET ( ANSWER ); SKIP_LINE;
        exit when ANSWER = 'n'
              or ANSWER = 'N';
    end loop;
    PUT ( "End of test." ); NEW_LINE;
end TEST_SUBPATTERN;
```

Sample Dialogue

```
Enter a target string and press return.
Ernest Bloch
Enter a pattern string and press return.
Bach
The pattern was NOT FOUND.

More? (y/n)
y
Enter a target string and press return.
J S Bach of Leipzig
Enter a pattern string and press return.
Bach
The pattern was FOUND.
```

```
More? (y/n)
n
End of test.
```

Figure 10.10 Finding a pattern.

use of subpattern

Using the function SUBPATTERN, we can rewrite the function SEARCH used in the drill program in Figure 10.3. The rewritten version of SEARCH is given in Figure 10.11. If this rewritten version is used in the program in Figure 10.3, then the user can enter "Bach" during the automated drill and the composer will be recognized as being on the list, even if the composer's name was originally entered as "J S Bach." All we have to do is **with** and **use** the STRINGS package, and SUBPATTERN is at our disposal.

Procedure

```
procedure SEARCH ( PATTERN   : in CHARACTER_STRING;
                   NAME      : in NAME_LIST;
                   LAST      : in LIST_RANGE;
                   POSITION : out LIST_RANGE ) is
--             INPUT  : A pattern for which to search a name
--                      list. Also the number of names in
--                      the name list (last).
--             OUTPUT : The index or position of the pattern
--                      in any position of the name list.
--             DESCRIPTION : The procedure performs a linear
--                           search of the name list.
--                           Exception composer_not_found
--                           is raised if the pattern is not
--                           found in the name list.
begin -- Search
    for INDEX in 1 . . LAST
    loop
        if SUBPATTERN ( PATTERN, NAME( INDEX ) ) then
            POSITION := INDEX;
            return;
        end if;
    end loop;
    raise COMPOSER_NOT_FOUND;
end SEARCH;
```

Figure 10.11 Procedure SEARCH rewritten to use the function SUBPATTERN.

Design by Concrete Example

When designing a program or procedure, it is often more fruitful to think in terms of a concrete example rather than an abstract characterization. In the previous example, it helped to think of locating the pattern "Bach" in the target string "J S Bach of Leipzig." This allowed us to visualize the problem and to try out our ideas immediately. Once we know how to find "Bach" in "J S Bach of Leipzig," we can then replace "Bach" with an arbitrary array PATTERN and "J S Bach of Leipzig" with another arbitrary array TARGET. When using this technique you should consider one concrete case to represent each of the major possibilities. In this case either the pattern is found or it is not. Hence, we want to also look at a value for TARGET that does not contain the pattern "Bach." For this we used the target string "Ernest Bloch." Just because you have an algorithm that works for a few special cases, you are not guaranteed that you have the correct algorithm, but you do have some inspiration. Once you have some inspiration and a candidate algorithm, you must determine if the algorithm works for all cases, and if not, you must modify it so that it does.

This technique of using concrete data is particularly fruitful when determining the exact form of an arithmetic expression. In designing the algorithm for the procedure SUBPATTERN, we needed to know the last index of TARGET that allowed sufficient room to hold a pattern of size LENGTH(PATTERN). Clearly the number is approximately

```
INDEX_RANGE'LAST - LENGTH ( PATTERN )
```

but such expressions can often be off by one in either direction. When we considered the concrete examples of 4 for the pattern length and 20 for INDEX_RANGE'LAST, we immediately saw that we needed to add 1 to obtain the correct expression. When you are deciding on the exact form of an arithmetic expression, nothing clarifies your thinking as much as a concrete example.

Time Efficiency

Computers work amazingly fast. Each program we have seen to date takes a negligible amount of time to run. Now that we are considering arrays, processing time becomes more significant. We are now writing programs that may take many seconds to run on some machines. As they get more complicated, they will take longer to run. There is no need to be obsessive about making your programs run more quickly, but take care to avoid the extreme cases of inefficiency. Seconds add up, and 30 seconds can seem like an endless amount of time when you are waiting for the computer to answer. Moreover, many computer installations charge for time and storage, just as the electricity company charges for electricity.

To illustrate some sources of inefficiency, consider the pattern-matching example we recently discussed. When we call the procedure MATCH, it will usually find a mismatch within the first few symbols. Hence, we terminate the loop as soon as a mismatch is found. If we did not terminate the loop as soon as a mismatch is found, then the procedure would go on to make many useless comparisons. This waste of time is compounded by the fact that MATCH is called numerous times by the function SUBPATTERN. With a pattern of length four and an array size of 20, MATCH would be called 17 times if the pattern does not occur in the target array. Hence, any inefficiency might be multiplied seventeenfold. The fact that array processing can include repeated computations for all (or many) elements of an array can make small inefficiencies multiply and produce noticeably slow programs.

Making a program efficient can often complicate the program. This complication increases the chance of introducing program bugs. Whenever you tune a program to make it more efficient, be certain that the program is still correct. Reject any changes that are not certain to produce a correct program. Incorrect output is useless, no matter how rapidly it is produced.

Exercises

Self-Test Exercises

4. How must the data type CHARACTER_STRING and the procedures GET_LINE and PUT_LINE of package STRINGS in Figure 10.1 be modified to accommodate strings of length up to 40 characters?

5. Given the declaration

```
WORD : STRING( 1 . . 5 );
```

which of the following are allowed?

```
WORD := "Stuff";
PUT ( WORD );
PUT_LINE ( WORD );
GET ( WORD );
WORD := "Hi!";
```

Multidimensional Arrays

multiple indexes

An index often contains some sort of information about how the array elements are most naturally organized. For some situations, one index is not sufficient to organize the elements in an ideal fashion. As an example, suppose we wish to hold a page of text in an array. We could number the characters of the text consecutively and use a larger array index range. If there are 100 characters per line and 30 lines per page, we could make it an array of characters indexed by the type `1 . . 3000`. However, it would be much more convenient to use two different indexes, one for the line and one for the character on that line. In Ada, and most other high-level programming languages, this is possible. It is possible to have an array, for example, called PAGE that has two indexes, one for the line and one for the characters in that line. Although Ada does not insist on it, it is traditional to make the first index count the lines and the second index count the position in the line. The array declaration in this case would be written

```
type ONE_PAGE is array( 1 . . 30, 1 . . 100 ) of CHARACTER;
PAGE : ONE_PAGE;
```

With PAGE declared this way, the first character of the first line can be stored as the value of PAGE(1 , 1), that of the second character on the first line as the value of PAGE(1 , 2), and so forth. As another example, the value of PAGE(5 , 38) is the thirty-eighth character on the fifth line. To write out the entire fifth line to the screen, the following will do:

```
for INDEX in 1 . . 100
loop
    PUT ( PAGE ( 5, INDEX ) );
end loop;
NEW_LINE;
```

two-dimensional example

An array with more than one index is called a *multidimensional array*. The diagram in Figure 10.12 may help to explain this choice of terminology. The array AVERAGE diagrammed there contains a list of average grades for a small class with four students numbered **1** through **4**. The array can be thought of as a simple list. Such lists are one-dimensional objects. The array GRADE shows more details of the class grading. It gives three quiz scores for each of the four students. This can be visualized as a two-dimensional arrangement, with one row for each student and one column for each quiz.

sample declarations

Multidimensional arrays are declared in the same way as the one-dimensional arrays we have been studying until now. The syntax for a multidimensional type definition is described in Figure 10.13. Just as in the one-dimensional case, the index types must be discrete or subrange types. The various index types need not be subranges of the same type. There may be any number of indexes, so long as there is at least one. (If there is just one, then we have the one-dimensional case.) As with one-dimensional arrays, the component type can be any Ada type. Some sample multidimensional array type declarations are

```
type MATRIX is array( 1 . . 10, 1 . . 5 ) of FLOAT;
type COUNT is array( 1 . . 100, 'A' . . 'Z' ) of INTEGER;
type PICTURE is array( 0 . . 4, 0 . . 9 ) of CHARACTER;
```

sample applications

Arrays of the first type, MATRIX, might hold floating point numbers for some scientific or engineering calculation. The type COUNT can be used in text processing. For example, suppose FREQUENCY is declared as

```
FREQUENCY : COUNT;
```

The array FREQUENCY might be used to count occurrences of each letter in a 100-line text. With the two-dimensional array, the program can easily keep a separate count for each line. The number of occurrences of, say, **'M'** on line 20 would be the value of FREQUENCY(20, 'M'). Arrays of type PICTURE might be used to hold

```
AVERAGE : array( 1 . . 4 ) of FLOAT;
```

Layout

Student 1	AVERAGE(1)
Student 2	AVERAGE(2)
Student 3	AVERAGE(3)
Student 4	AVERAGE(4)

Sample Values

Student 1	10.0
Student 2	1.0
Student 3	7.7
Student 4	7.7

```
subtype GRADE_RANGE is NATURAL range 0 . . 10;
GRADE : array( 1 . . 4, 1 . . 3 ) of GRADE_RANGE;
```

Layout

	Quiz 1	Quiz 2	Quiz 3
Student 1	GRADE(1,1)	GRADE(1,2)	GRADE(1,3)
Student 2	GRADE(2,1)	GRADE(2,2)	GRADE(2,3)
Student 3	GRADE(3,1)	GRADE(3,2)	GRADE(3,3)
Student 4	GRADE(4,1)	GRADE(4,2)	GRADE(4,3)

Sample Values

	Quiz 1	Quiz 2	Quiz 3
Student 1	10	10	10
Student 2	2	0	1
Student 3	8	6	9
Student 4	8	5	10

Figure 10.12 One- and two-dimensional arrays.

patterns consisting of five lines of ten characters each, which, when displayed on the screen, form a geometric pattern.

Aside from the fact that they may have more than one index, indexed variables of multidimensional arrays have the same properties as those of one-dimensional arrays.

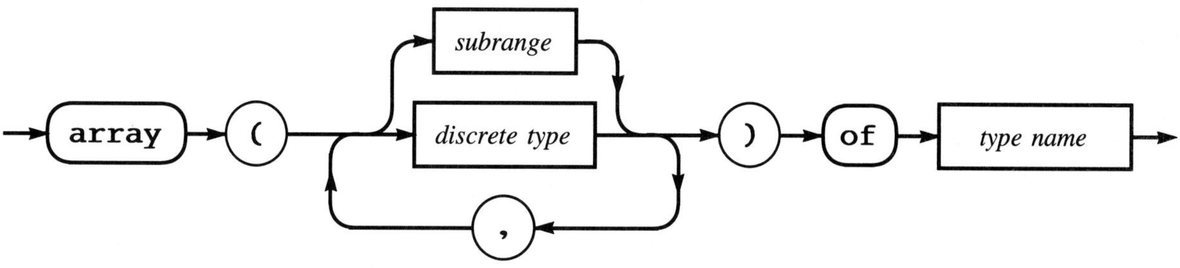

Figure 10.13 Syntax of array type declarations.

Case Study

Grading Program

To illustrate the use of multidimensional arrays, we will solve a simple class grading problem. The program we design will compute student averages and display the individual quiz grades and the averages for each student in the class. The program could be used by an instructor to obtain an overview of class grades. To give a perspective on how difficult each individual quiz was, the program will also display the class average for each quiz.

Problem Definition

The quiz scores are to be read into the computer. A screen display is then written out consisting of each student's identification number, followed by the student's average grade and a list of all the quiz scores for that student. The program will also display the average of all the students for each individual quiz.

Discussion

data structure

We need to devise some method for keeping track of each student's score. A natural way to do this is with a two-dimensional array, such as the array GRADE illustrated in Figure 10.12. One index can be the student number; the other index can be the quiz number. If the array is called `GRADE`, then `GRADE( STUDENT, QUIZ )` will contain the grade that student number STUDENT received on quiz number QUIZ. If NUMBER_OF_STUDENTS and NUMBER_OF_QUIZZES are constants equal to the number of students and the number of quizzes, and if each quiz is scored on a basis of zero to 10 points, then the declaration for the two-dimensional array GRADE can be

```
subtype SCORE is NATURAL range 0 . . 10;
subtype QUIZ_INDEX is POSITIVE range 1 . . NUMBER_OF_QUIZZES;
subtype STUDENT_INDEX is POSITIVE range 1 . . NUMBER_OF_STUDENTS;
type GRADE_ARRAY is array( STUDENT_INDEX, QUIZ_INDEX ) of SCORE;
type STUDENT_AVERAGE_ARRAY is array( STUDENT_INDEX ) of FLOAT;
type QUIZ_AVERAGE_ARRAY is array( QUIZ_INDEX ) of FLOAT;
GRADE : GRADE_ARRAY;
STUDENT_AVERAGE : STUDENT_AVERAGE_ARRAY;
QUIZ_AVERAGE : QUIZ_AVERAGE_ARRAY;
```

Figure 10.12 illustrates one possible set of values for GRADE. There, and in our program, NUMBER_OF_STUDENTS is set to **4** and NUMBER_OF_QUIZZES is set to **3**.

parallel arrays

We will use two one-dimensional arrays to hold the averages. The array STUDENT_AVERAGE will hold the averages of each student, and the array QUIZ_AVERAGE will hold the class average for each quiz. The relation between these two arrays and the array GRADE is illustrated in Figure 10.14. The arrays STUDENT_AVERAGE and QUIZ_AVERAGE are not absolutely necessary for this simple problem, but they would be needed if we were to expand the program to do more complicated things, such as displaying the student averages in sorted order or showing how much each score differs from the class average.

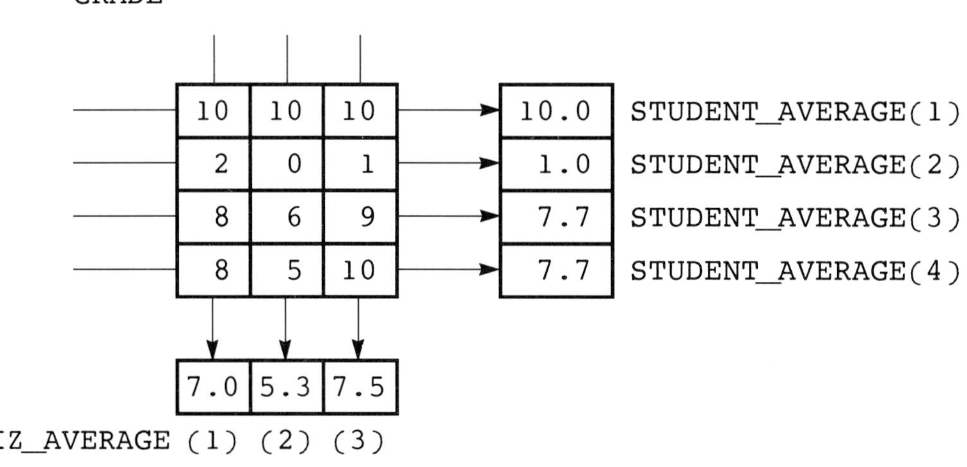

Figure 10.14 Relationship of arrays for grading program.

The problem to be solved by this program can be decomposed into four subproblems:

1. Read in the quiz grades.
2. Compute the average for each quiz.
3. Compute the average for each student.
4. Display the grades and the averages.

Each subproblem is accomplished by a separate procedure. The complete program is shown in Figure 10.15. Note that one I/O package, GRADE_IO, is instantiated for the values of type NATURAL and another, AVERAGE_IO, for the values of type FLOAT.

Program

```
with TEXT_IO; use TEXT_IO;
procedure SHOW_GRADES is
    NUMBER_OF_QUIZZES    : constant POSITIVE := 3;
    NUMBER_OF_STUDENTS   : constant POSITIVE := 4;

    subtype SCORE is NATURAL range 0 . . 10;
    subtype QUIZ_INDEX is POSITIVE range 1 . . NUMBER_OF_QUIZZES;
    subtype STUDENT_INDEX is POSITIVE range
    1 . . NUMBER_OF_STUDENTS;
    type GRADE_ARRAY is array( STUDENT_INDEX, QUIZ_INDEX ) of
    SCORE;
    type STUDENT_AVERAGE_ARRAY is array( STUDENT_INDEX ) of FLOAT;
    type QUIZ_AVERAGE_ARRAY is array( QUIZ_INDEX ) of FLOAT;

    package GRADE_IO is new INTEGER_IO ( NATURAL );
    use GRADE_IO;
    package AVERAGE_IO is new FLOAT_IO ( FLOAT );
    use AVERAGE_IO;

    GRADE : GRADE_ARRAY;
    STUDENT_AVERAGE : STUDENT_AVERAGE_ARRAY;
    QUIZ_AVERAGE : QUIZ_AVERAGE_ARRAY;

    procedure READ_QUIZZES ( GRADE : out GRADE_ARRAY ) is
    begin -- Read_Quizzes
        for STUDENT in STUDENT_INDEX
        loop
            PUT ( "Enter the" );
            PUT ( NUMBER_OF_QUIZZES, 3 );
            PUT ( "quiz scores" );
            NEW_LINE;
            PUT ( "for student number");
            PUT ( STUDENT, 3 );
            NEW_LINE;
```

```
        for QUIZ in QUIZ_INDEX
        loop
            GET ( GRADE( STUDENT, QUIZ ) );
        end loop;
        SKIP_LINE;
    end loop;
end READ_QUIZZES;

procedure QUIZ_AVERAGES
              ( GRADE : in GRADE_ARRAY;
                QUIZ_AVERAGE : out QUIZ_AVERAGE_ARRAY ) is
    SUM : NATURAL;
begin -- Quiz_Averages
    for QUIZ in QUIZ_INDEX
    loop
        SUM := 0;
        for STUDENT in STUDENT_INDEX
        loop
            SUM := SUM + GRADE( STUDENT, QUIZ );
        end loop;
        QUIZ_AVERAGE( QUIZ )
            := FLOAT ( SUM ) / FLOAT ( NUMBER_OF_STUDENTS );
    end loop;
end QUIZ_AVERAGES;

procedure STUDENT_AVERAGES
              ( GRADE : in GRADE_ARRAY;
                STUDENT_AVERAGE : out STUDENT_AVERAGE_ARRAY ) is
    SUM : NATURAL;
begin -- Student_Averages
    for STUDENT in STUDENT_INDEX
    loop
        SUM := 0;
        for QUIZ in QUIZ_INDEX
        loop
            SUM := SUM + GRADE( STUDENT, QUIZ );
        end loop;
        STUDENT_AVERAGE( STUDENT )
            := FLOAT ( SUM ) / FLOAT ( NUMBER_OF_QUIZZES );
    end loop;
end STUDENT_AVERAGES;

procedure DISPLAY ( GRADE : in GRADE_ARRAY;
                    STUDENT_AVERAGE : in STUDENT_AVERAGE_ARRAY;
                    QUIZ_AVERAGE : in QUIZ_AVERAGE_ARRAY ) is
```

```
    begin -- Display
        PUT (" Student Avg Quizzes" ); NEW_LINE;
        for STUDENT in STUDENT_INDEX
        loop
            PUT ( STUDENT, 10 );
            PUT ( STUDENT_AVERAGE( STUDENT ), 3, 1, 0 );
            SET_COL ( 20 );
            for QUIZ in QUIZ_INDEX
            loop
                PUT ( GRADE( STUDENT, QUIZ ), 5 );
            end loop;
            NEW_LINE;
        end loop;
        PUT ( "Quiz Averages =" );
        SET_COL ( 20 );
        for QUIZ in QUIZ_INDEX
        loop
            PUT ( QUIZ_AVERAGE( QUIZ ), 3, 1, 0 );
        end loop;
        NEW_LINE;
    end DISPLAY;

begin -- Show_Grades
    READ_QUIZZES ( GRADE );
    QUIZ_AVERAGES ( GRADE, QUIZ_AVERAGE );
    STUDENT_AVERAGES ( GRADE, STUDENT_AVERAGE );
    DISPLAY ( GRADE, STUDENT_AVERAGE, QUIZ_AVERAGE );
    PUT ( "Now you know the scores!" ); NEW_LINE;
end SHOW_GRADES;
```

Sample Dialogue

```
Enter the   3 quiz scores
for student number   1
10 10 10
Enter the 3   quiz scores
for student number   2
 2  0  1
Enter the   3 quiz scores
for student number   3
 8  6  9
Enter the   3 quiz scores
for student number   4
 8  5 10
```

```
Student  Avg          Quizzes
      1 10.0      10    10    10
      2  1.0       2     0     1
      3  7.7       8     6     9
      4  7.7       8     5    10
Quiz Averages =  7.0   5.2   7.5
Now you know the scores!
```

Figure 10.15 Program using two-dimensional arrays.

nested for loops

As illustrated in the procedure DISPLAY, the usual and natural way to step through all the elements of a multidimensional array is to use **for** loops nested inside one another. Each **for** loop steps through one of the array indexes.

The order of the nesting of **for** loops determines the order of processing. In Figure 10.15, since QUIZ_INDEX specifies the range for the inner loop, all quizzes for the first student are processed before the quizzes for the second student, and so on. If inner loop had the range specified by STUDENT_INDEX and the outer loop was QUIZ_INDEX, then each student would be processed for the first quiz, followed by each student for the second quiz, and so on.

The order of the indexes when referencing an array component of a multidimensional array (e.g., GRADE(STUDENT, QUIZ)) is *not* determined by the nesting of loops, but rather by the order in which the ranges appear in the array declaration.

Pitfall

Exceeding Storage Capacity

It is very easy to use unreasonably large amounts of storage when programming with multidimensional arrays. Even a modest-looking multidimensional array declaration can sometimes cause the computer to use a huge amount of storage. For example, consider the following reasonable-looking array declaration:

```
THREE_D : array( 0 . . 50, 0 . . 50, 0 . . 50 ) of INTEGER;
```

The compiler must allocate storage for 51 times 51 times 51 integers, which equals 132,651 integers. Many computer installations simply will not have enough storage available to accommodate such a program.

Summary of Problem Solving and Programming Techniques

- When you are designing an algorithm, it often helps to clarify your thinking by working with some specific sample data.
- Drawing a picture can often reveal the structure of a problem and lead to an algorithmic solution.
- You often can adapt a previously designed algorithm to solve a new, but similar, problem.
- When designing an algorithm one of your first tasks is to decide on a data structure to represent the data that will be manipulated by the algorithm.
- Data abstraction allows us to forget the unessential details about a data structure and concentrate on the substantive issues of algorithm design. In this way it is like, and in fact goes hand in hand with, procedural abstraction.
- If you need a list of arrays, then you can use an array of arrays.
- If you desire more than one index for each array element, then you can use a multidimensional array type.
- Arrays are often processed sequentially. If the array is large, this can be time consuming. You can save time by terminating array processing as soon as the relevant information has been obtained. For example, when looking for something in an array, the processing can stop when the item or condition is found.
- One way to help find the correct index expression for array processing is to try specific numbers in place of the variables and see if the expression yields the correct value.

Summary of Ada Constructs

array type declaration

Syntax:

```
type identifier
   is array ( range_1, range_2, . . . , range_n ) of component_type;
```

Example:

```
type ARRAY_NAME is array( 0 . . 5, 'A' . . 'F' ) of FLOAT;
```

The *n* index ranges must be discrete type or subtype names or subranges of discrete types or subtypes. There may be any number of index ranges as long as there is at least one. The component type may be any Ada type, including the defined types introduced in later chapters.

predefined type STRING

Syntax:

```
type STRING is array( POSITIVE range <> ) of CHARACTER;
```

Example:

```
   subtype CHARACTER_STRING is STRING( 1 . . 20 );
   NAME : CHARACTER_STRING;
   LINE : STRING( 1 . . 65 );
```

The type STRING is an unconstrained array of characters. A string array of characters is like an ordinary array of characters, but the index must be constrained before it can be used. STRING type is provided with some additional properties by the packages TEXT_IO and STANDARD. You can read or write part or all of a string with a procedure call to GET, GET_LINE, PUT, or PUT_LINE, all found in TEXT_IO. Package STANDARD provides the relational operators and the catenation operator **&**, all of which can be applied to STRING objects. There are no other built-in string manipulating functions or procedures.

Exercises

Self-Test Exercises

6. The variable SCREEN declared below can be used to hold a page or screen of text consisting of 20 lines with 50 characters per line.

```
type ONE_SCREEN is array( 1 .. 20, 1 .. 50 ) of CHARACTER;
SCREEN : ONE_SCREEN;
```

Write code to do each of the following tasks:

(a) Write the first character of each line to the screen.
(b) Write the last line to the screen.
(c) Write the entire page of text to the screen.

Interactive Exercises

7. Write a program to read in a list of 10 numbers and letters that are typed in one letter and one number per line. The program should then echo the input back in the same format. Use two parallel arrays to hold the data.

8. Write a program to fill a two-dimensional array called TWO_D of the following type:

```
array( 1 .. 3, 1 .. 2 ) of INTEGER
```

Display it to the screen in the natural way, and then allow the user to type in any pair of indexes called FIRST_INDEX and SECOND_INDEX. Have the program write out the value of TWO_D(FIRST_INDEX, SECOND_INDEX). Include a loop to let the user enter different values of FIRST_INDEX and SECOND_INDEX for as long as the user wishes. The procedures READ_QUIZZES and DISPLAY from Figure 10.15 can be used as models for the general method of reading in the array and displaying the array. They will not work without changes, but they do give the general idea of what is to be done.

Programming Exercises

9. Write a program that reads in a person's name in the format

First_name Middle_name_or_initial_or_nothing Last_name

Assume there is a single blank between part of the name.

The program should then output the name in the format:

Last_name First_name Middle_initial.

If the person inputs no middle name or initial, then the output should, of course, omit the middle initial. The program should work the same whether or not the user places a period after the middle initial. You may find it helpful to use more than one array. The program should work as long as each name is at most 10 characters long. If a name is over 10 characters long, then the program should use the first 10 letters of the name and should also issue an output statement saying that it did not use all the letters in some name.

10. Write a program that reads in a sentence of up to 50 characters and then outputs the sentence with letters corrected for capitalization. In other words the output sentence should start with an uppercase letter but contain no other uppercase letters. Do not worry about proper names. For example, the input

```
the Answer IS 42.
```

should produce the output

```
The answer is 42.
```

(This program can be written more cleanly using material in the section of Chapter 8 entitled "The Attributes `PRED`, `SUCC`, `POS`, and `VAL`."

11. Write a program that reads in a line of text and then outputs a list of all the letters that occur in the text, together with the number of times each letter occurs in the line. The letters should be listed in order beginning with the most frequently occurring letter, followed by the next most frequently occurring letter, and so forth. Use two parallel arrays with the index type `1 .. 26`. One array will hold letters and the other will hold the number of times that the corresponding letter occurs. Your program should consider upper- and lowercase versions of a letter to be equal, so the input line

```
DO be do
```

should produce output similar to

```
letter: number of occurrences:
  d             2
  o             2
  b             1
  e             1
```

12. Write a checkbook balancing program. The program reads in the following for all checks that were not cashed as of the last time you balanced your checkbook: the number of each check, the amount of the check, and whether or not it has been cashed yet. Use three parallel arrays, one for the numbers, one for the amounts, and one to record whether the check was cashed. The program also reads in the deposits, as well as the old and the new account balance. The new account balance should be the old balance, plus all deposits, and minus all checks that have been cashed. The program outputs what the total of the checks cashed is, the total of the deposits, what the new

balance should be, and how much this figure differs from what the bank says the new balance is. It also outputs two lists of checks: the checks cashed since the last time you balanced your checkbook and the checks still not cashed. Both lists are sorted by check number.

13. Modify the automated drill and practice program in Figure 10.3 so it can account for families with more than one composer in them. The most notable example is the Bach family. The very famous Johann Sebastian Bach had four sons who were composers: Wilhelm Friedemann Bach, Karl Philipp Emanuel Bach, Johann Christoph Freidrich Bach, and Johann Christian Bach. Your modified program will look for multiple matches, and if it finds more than one match for, say ''Bach'', it will test to see if the date matches any one of them. If dates do match, it will consider it a correct answer. If no dates match, it will output all composers whose names contain the subpattern, along with the date for each composer.

14. A queue is a list that is used in a restricted way. Items are always added to the end of the list. For example, when X is added to A, B, C, the result is A, B, C, X. Items can only be removed from the front of the list. To remove C from the list, A and B must first be removed. Write a set of procedures for treating an array of characters as a queue. There should be procedures for insertion and deletion. The limits of the array index should be defined constants of type INTEGER. Allow the possibility that the number of elements in the queue is less than the size of the array.

15. Telephone dials and push buttons have letters as well as numbers. Hence, some phone numbers spell words. For example 452-4357 is also 452-HELP. Write a program to help people find words for phone numbers. The program should read in the last four digits of a phone number and then output all possible letter versions of that number. For example, 4357 can be HELP. It can also be GDJP. It can also be other letter combinations. Use three arrays indexed by **0 . . 9** to hold the three letters that correspond to each number. There are no letters for **0** or **1**. Do something graceful with those digits. If you prefer, you can use **1 . . 9** or **2 . . 9** as the array index type.

16. Write a program that does the following: asks the user to type in nine numbers in three rows of three numbers each, reads the numbers into a two-dimensional array, computes the sum of each row and each column, and then outputs the array as well as the row and column sums in the following format:

```
              ARRAY: ROW SUMS:
              1 2 3     6
              3 3 3     9
              3 2 1     6

COLUMN SUMS:  7 7 7
```

17. Write a program to assign passenger seats in an airplane. Assume a small airplane with seat numbering as follows:

```
1 A B   C D
2 A B   C D
3 A B   C D
4 A B   C D
5 A B   C D
6 A B   C D
7 A B   C D
```

The program should display the seat pattern, with an 'X' marking the seats already assigned. For example, after seats 1A, 2B, and 4C are taken, the display should look like

```
1 X B   C D
2 A X   C D
3 A B   C D
4 A B   X D
5 A B   C D
6 A B   C D
7 A B   C D
```

After displaying the seats available, the program prompts for the seat desired, the user types in a seat, and then the display of available seats is updated. This continues until all seats are filled or until the user signals that the program should end. If the user types in a seat that is already assigned, then the program should say that seat is occupied and ask for another choice.

18. Write a program that accepts input like the program in Figure 9.13 and that outputs a bar graph like the one in that figure, except your program outputs the bars vertically rather than horizontally. A two-dimensional array may be useful.

19. A graph with NUMBER_OF_VERTICES can be represented by an array of the type

```
GRAPH : array( 1 . . NUMBER_OF_VERTICES,
               1 . . NUMBER_OF_VERTICES ) of BOOLEAN;
```

If GRAPH(SOURCE, DESTINATION) has value TRUE, that means that there is an arc from node SOURCE to node DESTINATION. Write a program that takes as input the array representation of a graph and two nodes in the graph and outputs a path from the first node to the second or else announces that no path exists. Assume that the arcs are "one-way" arrows, so if there is an arc from SOURCE to DESTINATION, then the path can go from SOURCE to DESTINATION but not necessarily in the other direction.

20. The game of *Life*, invented by J. H. Conway, is played by choosing an arrangement of marks on a rectangular grid and watching them change according to the following rule: If two or three of the four immediately neighboring positions are marked, then the mark is left; otherwise, it disappears. An unmarked cell becomes marked if exactly three of its immediately neighboring positions are marked. Write a program that accepts a pattern and then shows the series of patterns it produces. Have the program stop after the pattern stabilizes or after 10 changes if it does not stabilize by then. Use a grid size of at least 10 by 10. All changes occur simultaneously, so the program

will need two copies of the configuration, one for the old pattern and one for the new one.

21. Write a program that does the following: reads in a screen display consisting of 20 lines of 20 characters each, writes the display out rotated on its side (the horizontal lines become vertical lines), writes another display rotated until it is upside down, writes a third display rotated to three quarters of a complete rotation, and finally writes a display rotated back to its original orientation.

22. An *n* by *m* matrix is a rectangular array of numbers. For example, the following is a 4 by 3 matrix:

```
1   2   3
0   5   9
1   3   9
6  -3   5
```

The entries of a matrix are normally numbered by two subscripts, one for the row and one for the column. The following illustrates the numbering of a 4 by 3 and a 3 by 2 matrix:

$$\begin{matrix} a_{11} & a_{12} & a_{13} \\ a_{21} & a_{22} & a_{23} \\ a_{31} & a_{32} & a_{33} \\ a_{41} & a_{42} & a_{43} \end{matrix} \qquad \begin{matrix} b_{11} & b_{12} \\ b_{21} & b_{22} \\ b_{31} & b_{21} \end{matrix}$$

The product of an *m* by *n* matrix with entries a_{ij} and an *n* by *p* matrix with entries b_{ij} is an *m* by *p* matrix whose entries c_{ij} are defined as follows:

$$c_{ij} = a_{i1}b_{1j} + a_{i2}b_{2j} + \ldots + a_{in}b_{nj}$$

Write a program that reads in an *m* by *n* matrix row by row, then reads in an *n* by *p* matrix row by row, and then computes the product matrix and displays the two matrices as well as their product matrix on the screen. Use integer values for the matrix entries. Use 3, 4, and 5 for the values of *m, n,* and *p,* respectively, but declare constant names for them so they can easily be changed.

23. Write a program that reads an *n* by *n* matrix into a two-dimensional array **A** and then determines which, if any, of the following special classes the matrix falls into:

- Symmetric: **A(I,J)** = **A(J,I)** for all indexes **I** and **J**.
- Diagonal: **A(I,J)** = **0** whenever **I** and **J** are different.
- Upper triangular: **A(I,J)** = **0** whenever **I < J**.
- Lower triangular: **A(I,J)** = **0** whenever **I > J**.

Use 6 as the value of *n*.

24. Write a program that allows two users to play tic-tac-toe. The program should ask for moves alternately from player X and player O. The program displays the game positions as follows:

```
1   2   3
4   5   6
7   8   9
```

The players enter their moves by entering the position number. After each move, the program displays the changed board. A sample board configuration is

```
X  X  O
4  5  6
O  8  9
```

25. Redo Exercise 24, but this time have the computer be one of the two players.

26. Write a program that allows the user to make a pattern on the screen using the keyboard and then stores the pattern in a two-dimensional array and echoes it back to the user. It continues to do this until the user indicates that the program should end. Use any array dimensions that are convenient, but allow at least a four by four pattern of characters.

CHAPTER 11

RECORDS AND OTHER DATA STRUCTURES

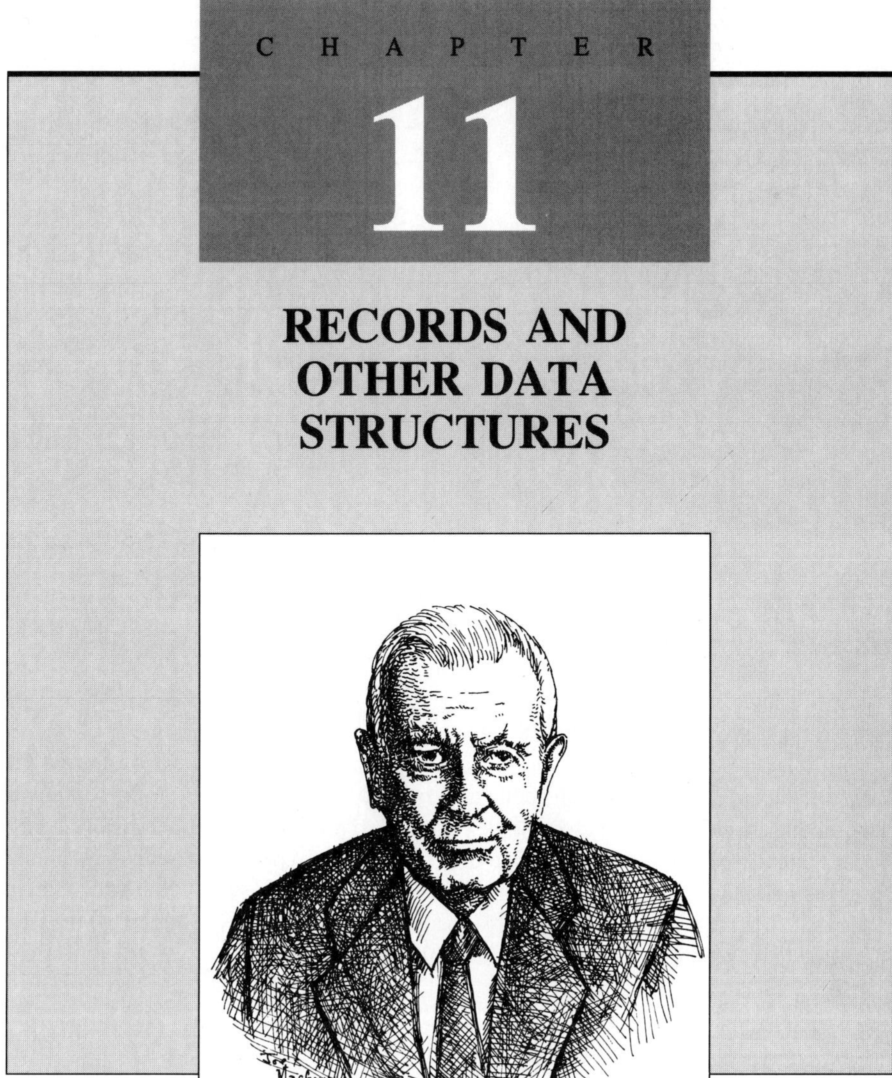

Thomas J. Watson

Watson was president of the IBM corporation until 1952. He was known as a superior salesman of business machines. His motto was "THINK." Ironically, he didn't think there would be a big demand for computers. His son, Thomas Jr., guided the company into its leadership position in the computer industry.

Chapter Contents

In Chapters 9 and 10 we discussed the notion of a data structure and introduced arrays as our first example of a composite type. In this chapter we introduce another class of composite types called *record types*. Record data types allow us to combine data of different types to obtain a single complex type that holds diverse components in a single compound value. We discuss techniques for using this data type as well as techniques for deciding which of all the data types we have seen is best suited to particular applications.

Introduction to Records

Sometimes it is useful to have a single name for a collection of values that may be of diverse types. For example, an inventory for a mail-order house might contain the following entry:

```
atomic clock
item #2001
price $1,999.99
```

In this example each inventory record consists of a name, a stock number, and a price. Although the record is conceptually a unit, the components are items of different data types. In Ada it is possible to define a composite type consisting of a number of components, each of a possibly different type. These kinds of composite types are called *records.*

component

The individual entries in a record are commonly referred to as *components.* Each component has a name, called a *component identifier,* that is some identifier chosen by the programmer when the record type is declared. Each component also has a type, which is specified when the record type is declared. Each component may also be assigned an optional initial value in the type declaration. A possible record declaration for the inventory record mentioned in the last paragraph is the type STOCK_ITEM, defined below:

```
type STOCK_ITEM is record
                        NAME : STRING( 1 . . 15 );
                        NUMBER : INTEGER := 0;
                        PRICE : FLOAT;
                    end record;
```

NAME, NUMBER, and PRICE are the component identifiers. STOCK_ITEM is the name of the type. A component of a record can be given an initial value in the same manner as any other object can be given an initial value. Notice that the NUMBER component of STOCK_ITEM has been given an initial value of **0**. In a program with the above type declaration, variables of type STOCK_ITEM are declared in the usual way:

```
ITEM_1, ITEM_2 : STOCK_ITEM;
```

The NUMBER component of both ITEM_1 and ITEM_2 has an initial value of **0**.

component values

A value of a record type is a collection of values, each of which is of some simpler type. The record has one value in the collection for each component. The type of each of these values is the type specified for that component in the record type declaration. For example, a value of type STOCK_ITEM is composed of three simpler values: one is an array of characters, one is of type INTEGER, and one is of type FLOAT. These individual values are called the *component values* of the record. The situation for the sample record type STOCK_ITEM is illustrated in Figure 11.1.

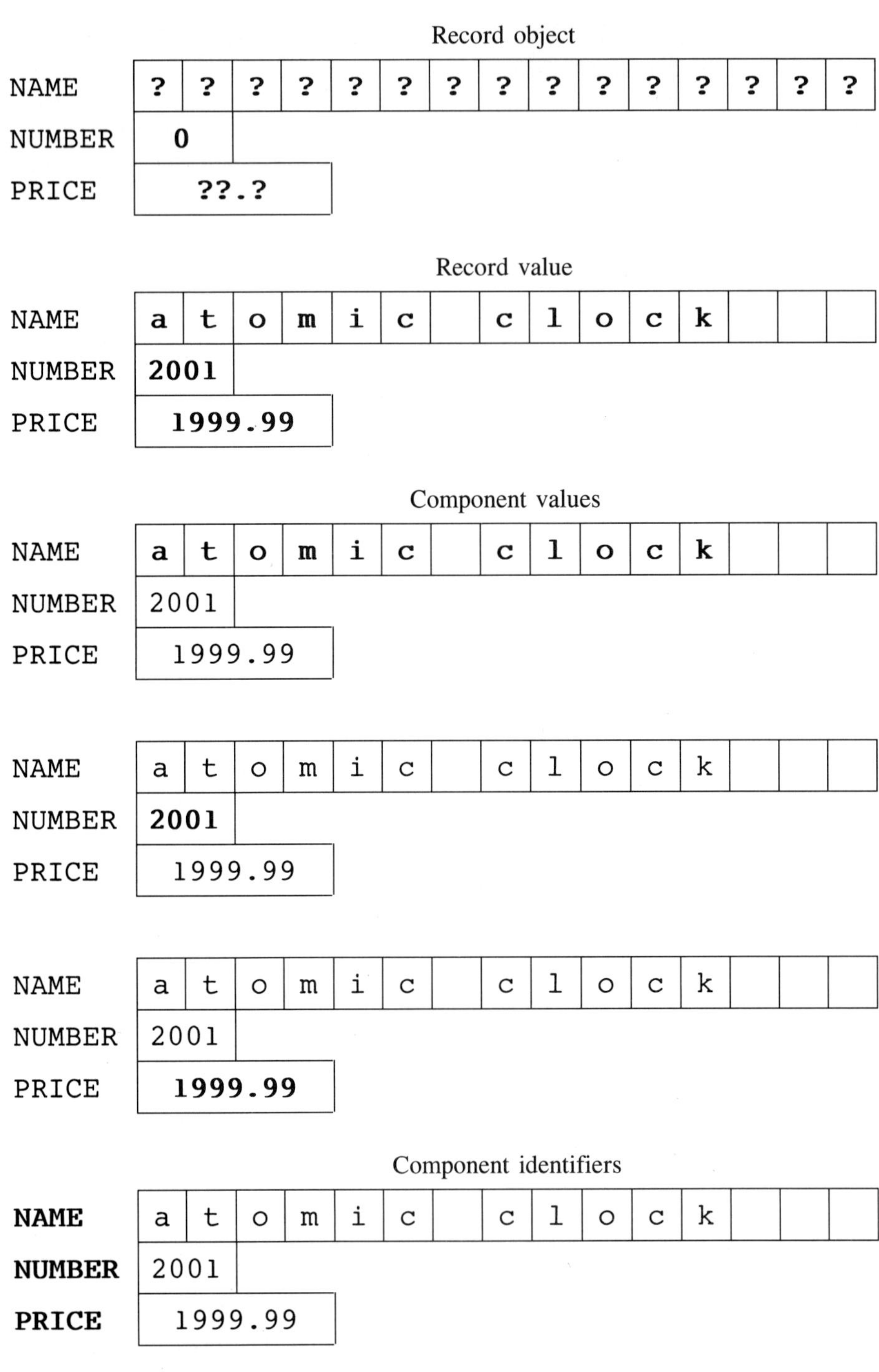

Figure 11.1 A record object.

The component identifiers of a record are similar to the indexes of an array. They provide a way to name each individual value in the collection of values that make up the record. By adding the component name to a record object, we can specialize the object to one of its components. A component of a record object is, as you might expect, called a *record component.* To specify a record component, a period and the component identifier are appended to the record object. (The period is usually pronounced "dot.") For instance, the record component of ITEM_1 named by the component identifier PRICE is written as follows:

record component

```
ITEM_1.PRICE
```

It is a variable of type FLOAT and can be used just like any other variable of type FLOAT. For example, the following will assign it the FLOAT value **9.95:**

```
ITEM_1.PRICE := 9.95;
```

Similarly the record component ITEM_1.NUMBER is a variable of type INTEGER, and the record component ITEM_1.NAME is an array of characters. These record components are illustrated in Figure 11.2.

```
type STOCK_ITEM is record
                        NAME : STRING( 1 . . 15 );
                        NUMBER : INTEGER := 0;
                        PRICE : FLOAT;
                    end record;
ITEM_1 : STOCK_ITEM;
```

When reading expressions involving records and arrays, always proceed from left to right. For instance, consider the following expression:

```
ITEM_1.NAME(4)
```

The identifier ITEM_1 names a record variable of type STOCK_ITEM. By adding the component identifier, we specify a particular record component. So ITEM_1.NAME denotes the record component called NAME. As specified in the type declaration, that is an array, so we can add an array index to it. The complete expression thus refers to the fourth indexed variable of this array. To be very concrete, it refers to the fourth letter in the name of the item with this inventory record. This notation is pictured in the last record illustrated in Figure 11.2.

Figure 11.3 presents an Ada procedure that fills a record variable of type STOCK_ITEM, and it illustrates the basic technique for manipulating record variables. Also note that we have overloaded the procedure name GET, which appears several places in package TEXT_IO. We use the name GET here because it makes sense to do so. The complier can disambiguate the situation because of the type of the parameter.

```
type STOCK_ITEM is record
                        NAME : STRING( 1 . . 15 );
                        NUMBER : INTEGER := 0;
                        PRICE : FLOAT;
                    end record;
```

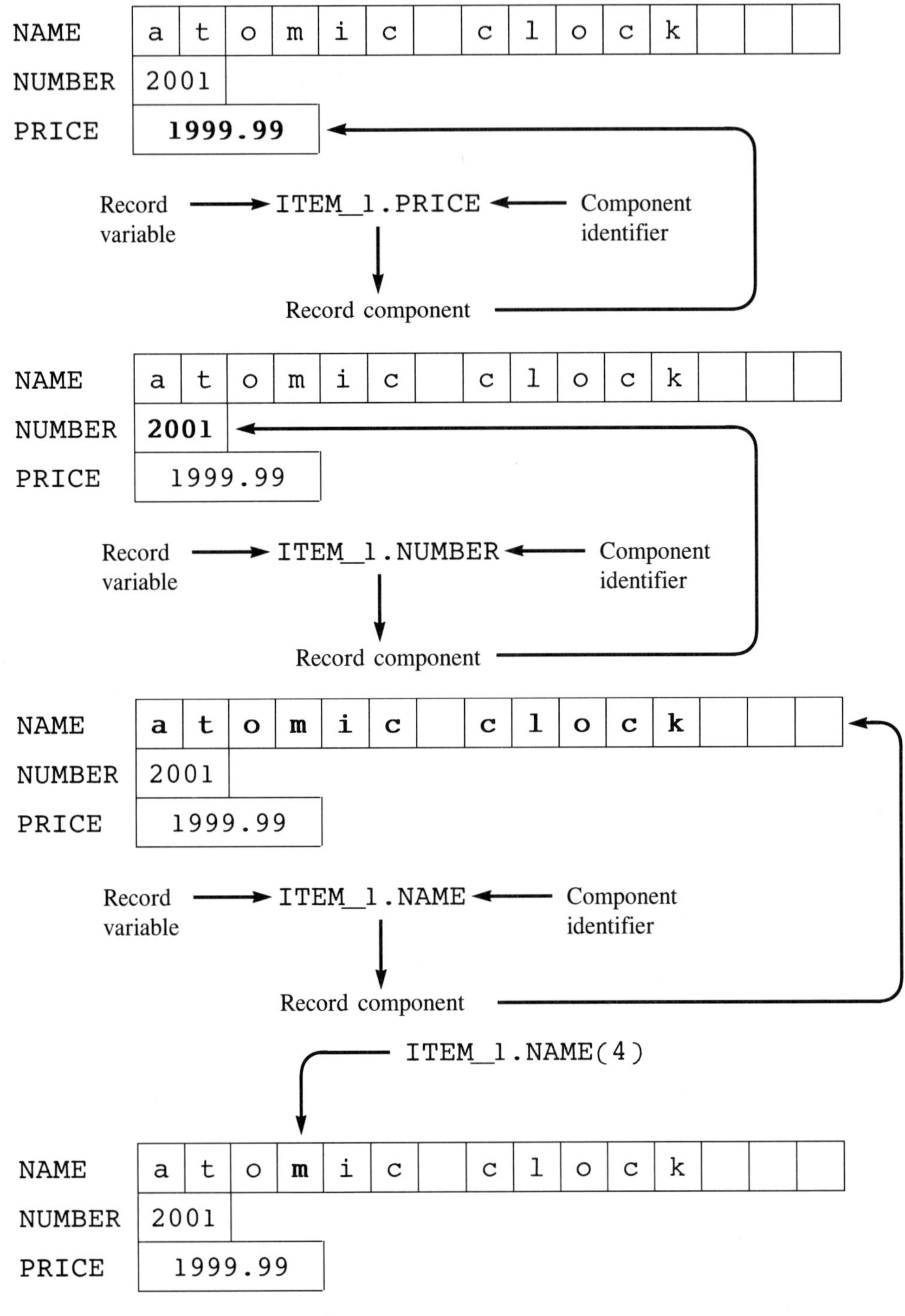

Figure 11.2 Record components.

```
procedure GET ( ITEM : out STOCK_ITEM ) is
--               INPUT  : None
--               OUTPUT : A stock item.
--               DESCRIPTION : Sets the value of each component
--                             variable of item to a value read
--                             in from the keyboard.
begin -- Get
    PUT ( "Enter name of item. Add blanks" ); NEW_LINE;
    PUT ( "to make it 15 characters long." ); NEW_LINE;
    PUT ( "Extra blanks are OK." ); NEW_LINE;
    GET ( ITEM.NAME ); SKIP_LINE;
    PUT ( "Enter stock number." ); NEW_LINE;
    GET ( ITEM.NUMBER ); SKIP_LINE;
    PUT ( "Enter price." ); NEW_LINE;
    PUT ( "Do not include a dollar sign." ); NEW_LINE;
    GET ( ITEM.PRICE ); SKIP_LINE;
end GET;
```

Figure 11.3 Procedure to fill a record variable.

records as single values

A value of a record type is composed of a group of values of the component types specified in the declaration of that record type. This group can sometimes be treated as a single composite value. For example, a procedure parameter of a record type is written without any component identifiers. The situation is similar to that of arrays. Also, the value of an entire record variable can be set by a single assignment statement.

For example, suppose ITEM_1 and ITEM_2 are record variables of the type STOCK_ITEM, which is declared in Figure 11.3. The following two statements consist of a procedure call, followed by an assignment:

```
GET ( ITEM_1 ); -- GET is defined in Figure 11.3
ITEM_2 := ITEM_1;
```

If the declarations are as we gave them in Figure 11.3, then the first statement is a procedure call that sets the value of the record variable ITEM_1 by setting the value of each record component. The second statement sets the value of each record component of ITEM_2 equal to the value of the corresponding component of ITEM_1.

aggregate assignment

All the components of a record can also be assigned values in an assignment statement by using an *aggregate*. An aggregate is enclosed in parentheses and contains a list of values. To assign values to components of a record via an aggregate, values for all of the components must be listed, and they must appear in the order in which the components appear in the record description. The example below shows how the components of ITEM_1 of type STOCK_ITEM can be assigned using an aggregate:

```
ITEM_1 := ( "atomic clock    ", 2001, 1999.95 );
```

This single assignment statement accomplishes the same as the following three assignment statements.

```
ITEM_1.NAME   := "atomic clock    ";
ITEM_1.NUMBER := 2001;
ITEM_1.PRICE  := 1999.95;
```

operations on records

A data type is specified by describing both the values that can be held by the variables of that type and the operations on those values. In the case of records, the values are collections of simpler values, each indexed by a component identifier. The ''dot'' operation combines a record object and a component identifier to obtain a component value. For example, the record variable ITEM_1 and the component identifier PRICE can be combined to obtain the record component ITEM_1.PRICE, which contains the component value specified by the name PRICE. Additionally the usual operations on variables may be used with record variables, such as ITEM_1, and with record components, like ITEM_1.PRICE. Either may be used with the assignment statement, and either may be used as a parameter to a procedure. All this makes a record sound very much like an array. As we will see in the next section, arrays and records are very similar, but they also have important differences.

Comparison of Arrays and Records

Records and arrays are similar in many ways. They both provide a way to give a single name to a collection of values. They both refer to elements of the collection by means of some sort of name. In the case of an array, the name is an index. In the case of a record, the name is a component identifier. An object of either type can be thought of as a collection of objects of the component types.

On the other hand, arrays and records do have some important differences. All elements in an array list must be of the same type. The component values of a record may be of different types. The index of an array may be computed by the program. If the index type is **1 . . 50**, then a variable of this type may be used as the index. So the name of an array index variable (such as GRADE(INDEX)) may be computed by the program (by computing the value of INDEX). The name of a component of a record (such as ITEM_1.PRICE) must include a component identifier (such as PRICE), and there is no way for the program to compute a component identifier. The programmer must write it into the program.

The Syntax of Simple Records

Type definitions of records follow the pattern of the inventory record in the opening section of this chapter. The list of component identifiers is enclosed within the reserved words **record** and **end record**. Each component identifier is followed by a colon and the type of that component. A component type may be any Ada type. In particular, it can be a composite type, such as an array or even another record type. Each of the component parts is terminated with a semicolon. If two successive component identifiers are of the same type, their declarations may be combined by separating them with commas and only listing the component type once. For instance, the following two type declarations are equivalent:

```
type EMPLOYEE is record
                    NUMBER : INTEGER;
                    BASE_RATE : FLOAT;
                    OVERTIME_RATE : FLOAT;
                 end record;
type EMPLOYEE is record
                    NUMBER : INTEGER;
                    BASE_RATE,
                    OVERTIME_RATE : FLOAT;
                 end record;
```

Of course, you may not use the same component identifier to name two different components within the same record type. However, component names from two different record types may be the same. So the following is allowed:

```
type ITEM is record
                NUMBER   : INTEGER;
                QUANTITY : NATURAL;
                PRICE    : FLOAT;
             end record;
type TEMPERATURE is record
                NUMBER : FLOAT;
                SCALE  : CHARACTER;
             end record;
```

The syntax for a record type declaration is summarized in Figure 11.4.

Notice that components within a record may be given an initial value. This is done in the same manner as in a variable declaration: after the type name the component is assigned a value. As the syntax diagram in Figure 11.4 demonstrates, the assigning of initial values to components of a record is done with a **:=**, followed by an expression. The expression is evaluated at the time the record is declared. Using the ITEM example from above, the QUANTITY component could be given an initial value of **0**, as shown below:

```
type ITEM is record
                NUMBER   : INTEGER;
                QUANTITY : NATURAL := 0;
                PRICE    : FLOAT;
             end record;
```

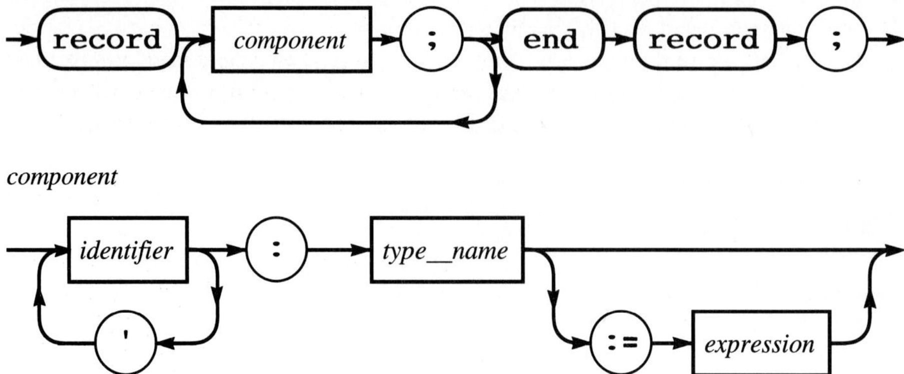

Figure 11.4 Syntax for simple record type definitions.

Exercises

Self-Test Exercises

1. Consider the following type declarations:

```
type PLASMA is record
                    QUANTITY   : NATURAL;
                    BLOOD_TYPE : CHARACTER;
                end record;
DONOR_1,
DONOR_2 : PLASMA;
```

What will the output of the following piece of code be (provided that it is embedded in a complete Ada program that includes the preceding type declarations and the instantiation of INTEGER_IO)?

```
DONOR_1 := ( 5, 'A' );
PUT ( DONOR_1.QUANTITY );
PUT ( DONOR_1.BLOOD_TYPE );
DONOR_2 := DONOR_1;
DONOR_2.QUANTITY := 6;
PUT ( DONOR_2.QUANTITY );
PUT ( DONOR_2.BLOOD_TYPE );
```

2. Write a type declaration for a record type called SAM with one component of type INTEGER, one of type FLOAT, and one of type CHARACTER.

3. Write a program to fill (with data read from the keyboard) one record of the type described in Exercise 2, and then display the record to the screen.

4. Write a type declaration for a student record that contains one component for the name; room for ten quiz scores between zero and ten; a midterm, a final exam score, and a final numeric grade, all in the range zero to 100; and also a final letter grade.

Records Within Records

Sometimes it makes sense to structure a record in a hierarchical way by making some component or components records themselves. For example, a record to hold the name and birth date of an individual might be of the following type:

```
subtype MONTH_RANGE is POSITIVE range 1 . . 12;
subtype DAY_RANGE is POSITIVE range 1 . . 31;
type DATE is record
                MONTH : MONTH_RANGE;
                DAY   : DAY_RANGE;
                YEAR  : POSITIVE;
            end record;
type INFORMATION is record
                      NAME : STRING( 1 . . 20 );
                      BIRTHDAY : DATE;
                  end record;
```

A record variable might then be declared as follows:

```
PERSON : INFORMATION;
```

If this record variable PERSON has its value set to record a person's birth date, then the year he or she was born is

```
PERSON.BIRTHDAY.YEAR
```

As always, the way to read these expressions is very carefully, from left to right. PERSON is a record variable. The component with name BIRTHDAY is

```
PERSON.BIRTHDAY
```

This component variable is itself a record of type DATE. Hence, it has three components, one of which is called YEAR.

Arrays of Records

Simple record types are seldom used by themselves. More often records are grouped into larger units, such as arrays of records. For example, if STOCK_ITEM is the record type defined in our introduction to records, then we are likely to use the records in an array of records. If there are 100 items in the inventory, a likely additional declaration would be the following:

```
type LIST is array( 1 . . 100 ) of STOCK_ITEM;
INVENTORY : LIST;
```

The complete list of the inventory could be read into the array by the following code:

```
for INDEX in 1 . . 100
loop
    PUT ( "Next_Item:" ); NEW_LINE;
    GET ( INVENTORY( INDEX ) );
end loop;
```

The procedure GET is described in Figure 11.3.

syntax for nested structures

When programming with these nested structures, such as an array of records, expressions can sometimes get quite complicated. To interpret them correctly, you must patiently work your way through them from left to right. As a sample, review the declaration of the type `STOCK_ITEM`, and then try to figure out the following expression before reading on:

```
INVENTORY(2).NAME(3)
```

The expression is interpreted as follows: `INVENTORY` is an array of records of type `STOCK_ITEM`. Hence, each indexed variable of that array is a record of that type. `INVENTORY(2)` is the second indexed variable of this array and hence is a record variable of type `STOCK_ITEM`. Since it is of this record type, it makes sense to refer to the component called `NAME`. The way to specify a component variable of any record variable is to append a period followed by the component name. In this case the following is the component variable of the record variable `INVENTORY(2)` that has the component name `NAME`:

```
INVENTORY(2).NAME
```

The component named `NAME` is an array of characters. Hence, the above is an array of characters whose third indexed variable is

```
INVENTORY(2).NAME(3)
```

This expression is an indexed variable of type `CHARACTER`. Its value is the third letter in the name of the second item on the inventory list.

records as a unit

To truly master records and data structures, you must be able to unravel and understand expressions such as the one we just discussed. However, once you have mastered the notation, it is often best to avoid such complicated expressions. By treating a record as a unit and by using procedures that manipulate these units, we can simplify both our reasoning and our notation. The loop code given earlier in this section filled an array of records, but it did not mention any details about record components. It filled record number `INDEX` of the array with one simple procedure call, as follows:

```
GET ( INVENTORY( INDEX ) );
```

Sample Program Using Records

As an example of how arrays of records are used, Figure 11.5 presents a version of the grading program in Figure 10.15. This time we use an array of records rather than parallel arrays. To shorten the example, this version does not compute class averages for the quizzes.

Program

```
with TEXT_IO; use TEXT_IO;
procedure GRADE_AVERAGE is
    NUMBER_OF_QUIZZES : constant POSITIVE := 3;
    NUMBER_OF_STUDENTS : constant POSITIVE := 4;
    subtype SCORE is NATURAL range 0 . . 10;
    subtype STUDENT_INDEX is POSITIVE range 1 . . NUMBER_OF_STUDENTS;
    subtype QUIZ_INDEX is POSITIVE range 1 . . NUMBER_OF_QUIZZES;
    type SCORE_ARRAY is array( QUIZ_INDEX ) of SCORE;
    type STUDENT is record
                      QUIZ : SCORE_ARRAY;
                      AVERAGE : FLOAT;
                  end record;
    type GRADE_BOOK is array( STUDENT_INDEX ) of STUDENT;
    HISTORY : GRADE_BOOK;
    package GRADE_IO is new INTEGER_IO ( NATURAL );
    use GRADE_IO;
    package AVERAGE_IO is new FLOAT_IO ( FLOAT );
    use AVERAGE_IO;
    procedure GET ( HISTORY : out GRADE_BOOK ) is
    begin-- Get
        for STUDENT in STUDENT_INDEX
        loop
            PUT ( "Enter the ");
            PUT ( NUMBER_OF_QUIZZES, 3 );
            PUT (" quiz scores." );
            NEW_LINE;
            PUT ( "for student number ");
            PUT ( STUDENT, 3 );
            NEW_LINE;
            for INDEX in QUIZ_INDEX
            loop
                GET ( HISTORY( STUDENT ).QUIZ( INDEX ) );
            end loop;
            SKIP_LINE;
        end loop;
    end GET;
```

```
    procedure COMPUTE_AVERAGE ( HISTORY : in out GRADE_BOOK ) is
        SUM : INTEGER;
    begin -- Compute_Average
        for STUDENT_NUMBER in STUDENT_INDEX
        loop
            SUM := 0;
            for QUIZ_NUMBER in QUIZ_INDEX
            loop
                SUM := SUM +
                      HISTORY( STUDENT_NUMBER ).QUIZ( QUIZ_NUMBER );
            end loop;
            HISTORY( STUDENT_NUMBER ).AVERAGE :=
                FLOAT ( SUM ) / FLOAT ( NUMBER_OF_QUIZZES );
        end loop;
    end COMPUTE_AVERAGE;
    procedure DISPLAY ( HISTORY : in GRADE_BOOK ) is
        SPACE : constant CHARACTER := ' ';
    begin -- Display_Average
        PUT (" Student  Avg  Quizzes" ); NEW_LINE;
        for STUDENT in STUDENT_INDEX
        loop
            PUT ( STUDENT, 8 );
            PUT ( HISTORY( STUDENT ).AVERAGE, 3, 1, 0 );
            SET_COL ( 17 );
            for INDEX in QUIZ_INDEX
            loop
                PUT ( HISTORY( STUDENT ).QUIZ( INDEX ), 3 );
            end loop;
            NEW_LINE;
        end loop;
    end DISPLAY;
begin -- Grade_Average
    GET ( HISTORY );
    COMPUTE_AVERAGE ( HISTORY );
    DISPLAY ( HISTORY );
    PUT ( "Now you know the scores!" ); NEW_LINE;
end GRADE_AVERAGE;
```

Sample Dialogue

```
Enter the    3 quiz scores.
for student number    1
10 10 10
Enter the    3 quiz scores.
for student number    2
1 0 0
```

```
Enter the    3 quiz scores.
for student number    3
7 8 5
Enter the    3 quiz scores.
for student number    4
9 7 9
Student  Avg    Quizzes
      1 10.0    10 10 10
      2  0.3     1  0  0
      3  6.7     7  8  5
      4  8.3     9  7  9
Now you know the scores!
```

Figure 11.5 Grading program using records.

Choosing a Data Structure

data structures

A *data structure* is a way of organizing data values. The various composite types that we have seen, such as arrays and records, are all data structures. Even simple variables of types such as INTEGER or CHARACTER could be considered data structures, although of a particularly simple kind. We now have a number of data structures available. We will eventually learn how to create other data structures within an Ada program. When designing a program, the choice of an appropriate data structure is a critically important part of the design process.

parallel arrays versus arrays of records

Frequently we have a choice of structures. For example, we presented two versions of a grading program: The one in Figure 10.15 used parallel arrays as the data structure. The one in Figure 11.5 used an array of records as the data structure. The array of records data structure is closer to our intuition of how grade information is naturally kept and organized, so it is often preferable to the two parallel arrays GRADE and QUIZ_AVERAGE we used for the same data in Figure 10.15. This is a general phenomenon. Whenever parallel arrays are appropriate, an array of records is often also appropriate and usually is a preferable data structure.

In some situations other array structures are more appropriate than an array of records. The program in Figure 10.15 uses a two-dimensional array and computes two kinds of averages: student averages and quiz averages. The program in Figure 11.5 uses an array of records but computes only student averages. With the two-dimensional array we have a symmetry between students and quizzes. With the array of student records it is very easy to do calculations for each student, but calculations for one particular quiz are awkward without an array for each quiz. Which data structure we choose depends on the problem. For the output in Figure 10.15, a two-dimensional array and two one-dimensional arrays served best. For the simpler problem in Figure 11.5, an array of records is more natural.

When designing a program, the choice of a data structure can be just as important as the design of an algorithm for the program. The efficiency and clarity of a program can depend heavily on what data structures are used. Unfortunately there is no algorithm for choosing a data structure. There are, however, a few useful guidelines.

Always consider the possibility of alternative data structures. Just because you find one that works does not mean that you have found the best one. All other things being equal, choose the one that is easiest to understand and manipulate.

hierarchical data structures

Just as hierarchical control structures make a program easier to understand, so do hierarchical data structures. It pays to combine the basic data structuring techniques to obtain hierarchical structures, such as arrays of records, records of arrays, arrays of records of arrays, and so forth.

There are some rules that apply to choosing between the various options for array types and/or record types. If all the items to be stored are of the same simple type, then a single array with that simple type as its base type can be used. If the items are of different types, then an array of records type can be used. An alternative to using the array of records data structure is using parallel arrays, that is, a collection of arrays with the same indexes.

The Declare Block and Renames Clause

Look back at the procedure COMPUTE_AVERAGE given in Figure 11.5. The entire procedure deals with the single record HISTORY(STUDENT_NUMBER). Every component identifier refers to HISTORY(STUDENT_NUMBER). Every time around the quiz number loop, the computer has to compute the address of HISTORY(STUDENT_NUMBER), even though it does not change until the next time around the student number loop. It would be convenient to have a way to say that all references to a record of type STUDENT are references to the record HISTORY(STUDENT_NUMBER) and will be referenced using a simple variable called HISTORY_STUDENT or even perhaps more simply as PUPIL. Then we could simply write PUPIL followed by a dot, followed by the component identifier, and we would not have to write HISTORY(STUDENT_NUMBER) each time. The **renames** clause in conjunction with a *declare block* lets us do just that. But before dealing with arrays, we will first look at the **declare** block and the **renames** clause within a simpler context.

The **declare** block is simply an optional extension of the *block* statement that we have used earlier. A **declare** block has the reserved word **declare** followed by any declaration just before the **begin** in a block statement.

Consider the following declarations:

```
type PRODUCT is record
                        PART_NUMBER : INTEGER;
                        CODE        : CHARACTER;
                   end record;
SAMPLE : PRODUCT;
```

Compare the two code segments that follow: the first is the way we have used it in the past, and the second uses a block statement with a **declare** and a **renames**. They both produce the same output.

```
SAMPLE.PART_NUMBER := 5;
SAMPLE.CODE := 'a';
PUT ( SAMPLE.PART_NUMBER );
PUT ( SAMPLE.CODE );

declare
    ITEM : PRODUCT renames SAMPLE;
begin
    ITEM.PART_NUMBER := 5;
    ITEM.CODE := 'a';
    PUT ( ITEM.PART_NUMBER );
    PUT ( ITEM.CODE );
end;
```

What we have done in the second example is to make the name ITEM mean the same thing as the name SAMPLE. When one name means the same as another, it is called an alias. Thus ITEM and SAMPLE are aliases. The second example looks like a lot of work for little benefit, and in this context that is true. However, when we realize that the type PRODUCT could be part of a much larger structure and that the object name SAMPLE could have been a more complex reference, such as an array element or a record component or any combination of the two, there can be some real advantage to shortening the name. This is also a more efficient way to write code if the alias is referenced several times within the **begin/end** pair. This is particularly true if the alias is used inside a loop.

Having mastered a simple example, we can now use a **declare** block statement to rewrite the procedure COMPUTE_AVERAGE so that the record name HISTORY(STUDENT_NUMBER) needs to be written only once. The procedure in Figure 11.6 does this and is equivalent to the one in Figure 11.5.

```
procedure COMPUTE_AVERAGE ( HISTORY : in out GRADE_BOOK ) is
   SUM : INTEGER;
begin -- Compute_Average
    for STUDENT_NUMBER in STUDENT_INDEX
    loop
        declare
            PUPIL : STUDENT renames HISTORY( STUDENT_NUMBER );
        begin
            SUM := 0;
            for QUIZ_NUMBER in QUIZ_INDEX
            loop
                SUM := SUM + PUPIL.QUIZ( QUIZ_NUMBER );
            end loop;
```

```
            PUPIL.AVERAGE :=
                FLOAT ( SUM ) / FLOAT ( NUMBER_OF_QUIZZES );
        end;
    end loop;
end COMPUTE_AVERAGE;
```

Figure 11.6 Procedure COMPUTE_AVERAGE rewritten using renames.

The syntax for a **declare** block statement and the **renames** clause are summarized in Figure 11.7.

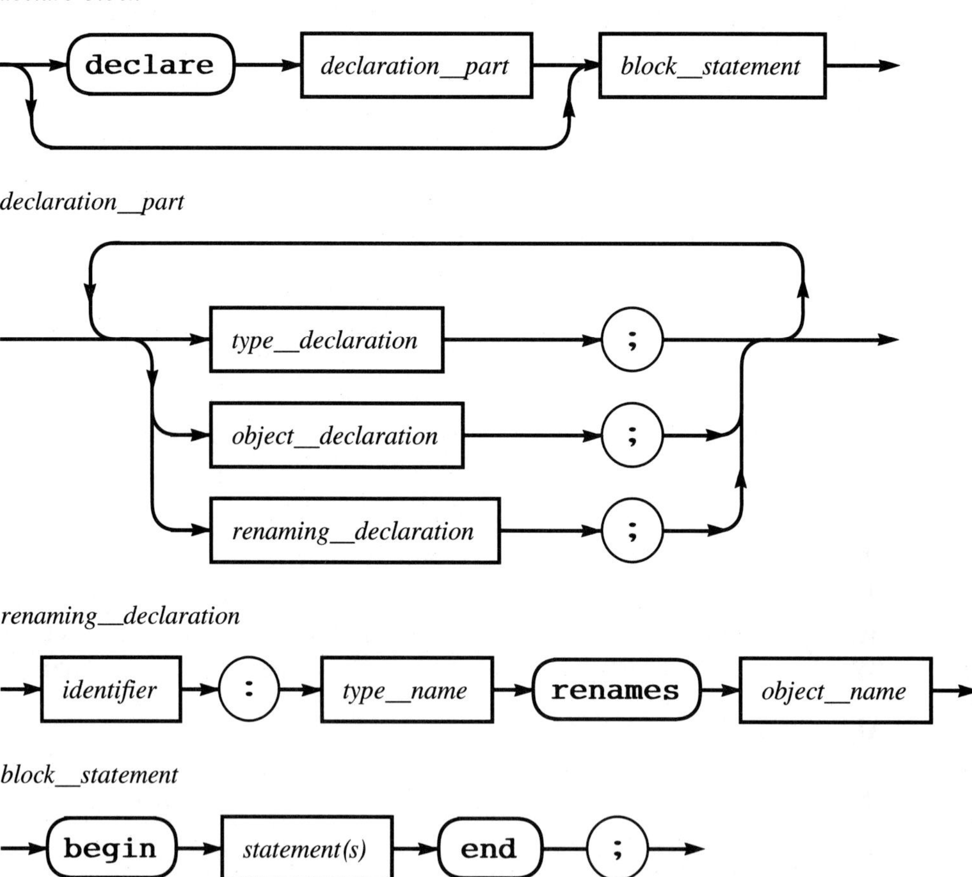

Figure 11.7 Syntax for declare and renames.

Case Study

Sales Report

Problem Definition

The program we wrote for the Apex Plastic Spoon Company (in Chapter 9) has helped them to organize and optimize production. However, their annual company report shows that profits are falling despite increases in plant efficiency. The company decides that the problem is with their sales force and commissions us to write another, totally different program that will evaluate the performance of their sales force. For each salesperson, the program reads in the salesperson's total sales for the month and also the total value of goods that were sold by that person but were returned for credit during the month. The program outputs the net yield (sales minus returns) for each member of the sales force as well as the differences between each person's net yield and the average net yield.

Discussion

The first step is to decide on a data structure for the program. The information for each salesperson is naturally kept in a record.

data structure

```
type INFORMATION is record
                       NAME : STRING( 1 . . MAXIMUM_LENGTH );
                       SALES,
                       RETURNS,
                       NET,
                       COMPARISON : INTEGER;
                    end record;
```

The data consists of a list of records and so is most naturally represented as an array of records.

```
subtype PEOPLE_INDEX is POSITIVE range 1 . . NUMBER_OF_PEOPLE;
type INFORMATION_LIST is array( PEOPLE_INDEX ) of INFORMATION;
```

Algorithm

The problem breaks down in a standard way into three main subprograms:

1. GET__DATA: Input the data.
2. COMPUTE__RESULTS.
3. WRITE__TABLE: Output the results.

Subprogram 2 can be further broken down as follows:

2a. Compute the net yield for each person.
2b. Compute the average net yield.
2c. Compute the difference between each person's net yield and the average net yield.

The complete program is given in Figure 11.8. Since subtasks 2a and 2b are both performed by a loop that processes each record, and since they are each very simple, we have combined the two subproblems and used a single **for** loop to perform both calculations. Subproblem 2c requires a separate loop.

Program

```
with STRINGS; use STRINGS;
with TEXT_IO; use TEXT_IO;
procedure SALES_REPORT is
    MAXIMUM_LENGTH : constant POSITIVE := 20;
    NUMBER_OF_PEOPLE : constant POSITIVE := 3;
    WIDTH : constant POSITIVE := 12;
    type INFORMATION is record
                          NAME : STRING( 1 . . MAXIMUM_LENGTH );
                          SALES,
                          RETURNS,
                          NET,
                          COMPARISON : INTEGER;
                      end record;
    subtype PEOPLE_INDEX is POSITIVE range 1 . . NUMBER_OF_PEOPLE;
    type INFORMATION_LIST is array( PEOPLE_INDEX ) of INFORMATION;
    AVERAGE_YIELD : INTEGER;
    SALESPERSON : INFORMATION_LIST;
    TOTAL : INTEGER := 0;
    package INFORMATION_IO is new INTEGER_IO ( INTEGER );
    use INFORMATION_IO;
    procedure GET_DATA ( PERSONNEL : out INFORMATION_LIST ) is
    begin -- Get_Data
        PUT ( "Enter names, sales, and returns" ); NEW_LINE;
        PUT ( "one person at a time:" ); NEW_LINE;
        for PEOPLE in PEOPLE_INDEX
        loop
            declare
                PERSONNEL_INFORMATION : INFORMATION
                    renames PERSONNEL( PEOPLE );
            begin
                PUT ( "Enter name of salesperson:" ); NEW_LINE;
                GET_STRING ( PERSONNEL_INFORMATION.NAME );
                PUT ( "Enter Sales and Returns:" ); NEW_LINE;
                GET ( PERSONNEL_INFORMATION.SALES );
```

```
            GET ( PERSONNEL_INFORMATION.RETURNS );
            SKIP_LINE;
        end;
    end loop;
end GET_DATA;
procedure COMPUTE_RESULTS
          ( SALESPERSON : in out INFORMATION_LIST;
            AVERAGE_YIELD : in out INTEGER ) is
begin -- Compute_Results
    for PEOPLE in PEOPLE_INDEX
    loop
        declare
            A_PERSONS : INFORMATION renames SALESPERSON( PEOPLE );
        begin
            A_PERSONS.NET := A_PERSONS.SALES - A_PERSONS.RETURNS;
            TOTAL := TOTAL + A_PERSONS.NET;
        end;
    end loop;
    AVERAGE_YIELD :=
        INTEGER ( FLOAT ( TOTAL ) / FLOAT ( NUMBER_OF_PEOPLE ) );
    for PEOPLE in PEOPLE_INDEX
    loop
        declare
            A_PERSONS : INFORMATION renames SALESPERSON( PEOPLE );
        begin
            A_PERSONS.COMPARISON := A_PERSONS.NET - AVERAGE_YIELD;
        end;
    end loop;
end COMPUTE_RESULTS;
procedure WRITE_TABLE ( PERSONNEL : in INFORMATION_LIST;
                        AVERAGE_YIELD : in INTEGER ) is
begin -- Write_Table
    SET_COL ( 18 );
    PUT ( "Sales Summary" ); NEW_LINE;
    PUT ( "Name" ); NEW_LINE;
    PUT ("          Sales             Returns              Net +/-Average" );
    NEW_LINE;
    for PEOPLE in PEOPLE_INDEX
    loop
        declare
            A_PERSONS : INFORMATION renames PERSONNEL( PEOPLE );
        begin
            PUT_STRING ( A_PERSONS.NAME );
            PUT ( A_PERSONS.SALES, WIDTH );
            PUT ( A_PERSONS.RETURNS, WIDTH );
            PUT ( A_PERSONS.NET, WIDTH );
```

```
                PUT ( A_PERSONS.COMPARISON, WIDTH );
                NEW_LINE;
            end;
        end loop;
        PUT ( "Average net yield of all personnel =" );
        PUT ( AVERAGE_YIELD, WIDTH );
        NEW_LINE;
    end WRITE_TABLE;
begin -- Sales_Report
    GET_DATA ( SALESPERSON );
    COMPUTE_RESULTS ( SALESPERSON, AVERAGE_YIELD );
    WRITE_TABLE ( SALESPERSON, AVERAGE_YIELD );
end SALES_REPORT;
```

Sample Dialogue

```
Enter names, sales, and returns
one person at a time:
Enter name of salesperson:
Charles Steak
Enter Sales and Returns:
2000 100
Enter name of salesperson:
Dusty Rhodes
Enter Sales and Returns:
3000 200
Enter name of salesperson:
Rock Garden
Enter Sales and Returns:
1000 500
                  Sales Summary
Name
       Sales         Returns        Net    +/-Average
Charles Steak
        2000             100       1900           167
Dusty Rhodes
        3000             200       2800          1067
Rock Garden
        1000             500        500         -1233
Average net yield of all personnel =             1733
```

Figures 11.8 Sales report program.

Searching by Hashing
(Optional)

Suppose we want to store inventory records so we can later retrieve any particular record by specifying its stock number. To be specific, suppose the records are of the following form, with the stock number stored in the STOCK_NUMBER component:

```
MAXIMUM_INDEX : constant POSITIVE := 50;
subtype INDEX_RANGE is POSITIVE range 1 . . MAXIMUM_INDEX;
type ITEM is record
                  STOCK_NUMBER : INTEGER := 0;
                  PRICE   : FLOAT      := 0.0;
                  RATING : CHARACTER := 'X';
              end record;
ONE_ITEM :    ITEM;
```

If the records have STOCK_NUMBER components with the values **1** through **50**, then we could store them in an array of the following type, placing record number **n** in indexed variable LIST(N):

```
type ITEM_LIST is array( INDEX_RANGE ) of ITEM;
LIST : ITEM_LIST;
```

The record numbered **n** can be retrieved immediately since we know it will be in LIST(N).

But suppose the numbers do not form a neat range like **1 . . 50**. Suppose we know there will be 50 or fewer numbers, but they will be distributed in the range **1** through **5000**. We could use an array with index type **1 . . 5000**, but that would be extremely wasteful of storage, since only a very small fraction of the indexed variables would be used. Hence, it appears that we have no alternative but to store the records in an array with 50 elements and to use a serial search through the array whenever we wish to find a particular record. Things are not that bad. If we are clever we can store the records in an array with relatively few (well under 200) indexed variables and yet retrieve records much faster than we would by serial search. In fact, there is more than one way to achieve this goal. In Chapter 15 we will present one method that depends on the array being sorted. In this section we will present a method that does not require sorting the array.

To illustrate the trick involved, suppose that somebody tells us that the 50 numbers will turn out to be the following:

100, 200, 300, 400, . . . ,4900, 5000

In that case, we can store the records in an array LIST with index type **1 . . 50**. The record with its STOCK_NUMBER component equal to **n** is stored in indexed variable

```
LIST( N / 100 )
```

With the aid of the / operation, we can make do with the index type **1 . . 50**, even though the numbers become as large as 5000. If we want record number 700, we compute **700 / 100** and obtain the index **7.** The record is stored in indexed variable LIST(7).

key

hash function

This general technique is called *hashing*. One component of the record type, called the *key*, is singled out to serve as the name of the record. In our example this was the STOCK_NUMBER component. A function HASH, called the *hash function*, maps key values to array indexes. In our example, if KEY is the value of the STOCK_NUMBER component of a record, then that record is stored in array position LIST(HASH (KEY)). The function HASH must be chosen so that HASH (KEY) is always within the index range of the array. The hash function HASH can be either a declared Ada function or an arithmetic expression. In our example HASH (KEY) was KEY / 100.

collisions

In our example every KEY produced a different value of HASH (KEY). That is perfect, but one cannot always find a perfect hash function. Suppose we change the example by substituting 399 for 400. Then record number 300 will be placed in LIST(3), as before. Record number 399 is supposed to be placed in LIST(399 / 100); in other words, record number 399 is also supposed to be placed in LIST(3). There are now two different records that belong in LIST(3). This situation is known as a *collision*. In this case we could redefine the hash function to avoid the collision. In practice you usually do not know the exact numbers that will occur as record keys, so you cannot design a hash function that is guaranteed to be free of collisions. Something must be done to cope with collisions.

Typically you do not know what numbers will be used as the key values, but you do know an upper bound on how many there will be. The usual approach is to use an array size that is larger than is needed, typically two to three times as large as the number of records to be stored. The extra array positions make collisions less likely. A good hash function will distribute the key values uniformly through the index range of the array. If the array index type is **1 . . 100**, then you might use the following hash function to produce an array index for the record whose STOCK_NUMBER component is equal to KEY:

```
( KEY rem 100 ) + 1
```

coping with collisions

One way to deal with a collision is with the following algorithm:

Given the KEY,

1. Compute the index HASH (KEY).

2. **if** LIST(HASH (KEY)) does not already contain a record, **then** store the record in LIST(HASH (KEY)) and end the algorithm.

3. **if** LIST(HASH (KEY)) already contains a record, **then** use LIST (HASH (KEY) + 1); **if** that contains a record, use LIST(HASH (KEY) + 2), and so forth, until a vacant position is found. (When the highest numbered array position is reached, simply go to the start of the array. For example, if the index type is **1 . . 100**, and **99** is full, try **100**, **1**, **2**, etc., in that order.)

This requires the array to be initialized so the program can test to see if an array position already contains a record. For example, if the key will always be a positive integer, then the key component of each array element can be initialized to **0**. As long as it has a value of **0**, the program knows that it does not contain a record. It is not necessary, however, to have a procedure to *initialize* the elements of the array. Ada allows components of a record to be assigned an initial value (note the record description for ITEM in Figure 11.9). If a component of a record is given an initial value and the record is an element of an array, then all the elements of the array will have that record component initialized to that initial value.

Figure 11.9 contains procedures to store and retrieve records using this technique. The next few paragraphs explain the details of how these procedures work.

```
    MAXIMUM_INDEX : constant POSITIVE := 50;
    subtype INDEX_RANGE is POSITIVE range 1 . . MAXIMUM_INDEX;
    type ITEM is record
                 STOCK_NUMBER : INTEGER := 0;
                 PRICE   : FLOAT      := 0.0;
                 RATING : CHARACTER := 'X';
             end record;
    type ITEM_LIST is array( INDEX_RANGE ) of ITEM;
    ANSWER     : CHARACTER;
    ARRAY_FULL : exception;
    LIST       : ITEM_LIST;
    ONE_ITEM   : ITEM;
    function HASH ( VALUE : INTEGER ) return INDEX_RANGE is
    begin -- Hash
        return ( VALUE rem MAXIMUM_INDEX ) + 1;
    end HASH;
```

Figure 11.9(a)
HASH function.

```
procedure INSERT ( LIST : in out ITEM_LIST;
                   ONE_ITEM : in ITEM ) is
    HASH_VALUE : INDEX_RANGE := HASH ( ONE_ITEM.STOCK_NUMBER );
    POSITIONS_TRIED : POSITIVE := 1;
begin -- Insert
    loop
        if LIST( HASH_VALUE ).STOCK_NUMBER = 0 then
--              Position unoccupied, insert item and leave.
                LIST( HASH_VALUE ) := ONE_ITEM;
                exit;
        elsif LIST( HASH_VALUE ).STOCK_NUMBER
               = ONE_ITEM.STOCK_NUMBER then
                  PUT ( "Already have an entry for item number ");
                  PUT ( ONE_ITEM.STOCK_NUMBER );
                  NEW_LINE;
                  exit;
        elsif POSITIONS_TRIED = INDEX_RANGE'LAST then
--            The array is full,there is no place to put it.
              raise ARRAY_FULL;
```

```
        else
            HASH_VALUE := ( HASH_VALUE rem MAXIMUM_INDEX ) + 1;
            POSITIONS_TRIED := POSITIONS_TRIED + 1;
--              Go to the next position in the array
--              The rem allows the hash_value to wrap around
--              from MAXIMUM_INDEX to 1.
        end if;
    end loop;
end INSERT;
```

Figure 11.9(b) INSERT procedure.

```
procedure FIND ( LIST : in ITEM_LIST; KEY : in INTEGER ) is
    HASH_VALUE : INDEX_RANGE := HASH ( KEY );
    POSITIONS_TRIED : POSITIVE := 1;
--              Used to determine if all positions
--              have been tried, thus the array is full
begin -- Find
    loop
        if LIST( HASH_VALUE ).STOCK_NUMBER = KEY then
--              Found the record with this key,
--              display it and get out of Dodge
            PUT ( LIST( KEY ) );
            exit;
        elsif LIST( HASH_VALUE ).STOCK_NUMBER = 0
        or else POSITIONS_TRIED = INDEX_RANGE'LAST then
--              All positions have been tried.
            PUT ( "Record is not in the array." ); NEW_LINE;
            exit;
        else
            HASH_VALUE := ( HASH_VALUE rem MAXIMUM_INDEX ) + 1;
--              Try the next position,
--              wrap around if necessary
            POSITIONS_TRIED := POSITIONS_TRIED + 1;
        end if;
    end loop;
end FIND;
```

Figure 11.9(c) FIND procedure.

Figure 11.9 INSERT and FIND procedures using hashing.

The procedure INSERT, shown in Figure 11.9(b), will insert record ONE_ITEM into array ITEM_LIST by hashing the key value ONE_ITEM.STOCK_NUMBER and handle collisions. (The hash function is called HASH and is shown in Figure 11.9(a).) *Insert*

You should always plan on things not going smoothly. Therefore, the procedure in Figure 11.9(b) includes a number of checks. It checks to see if the array already contains a record with the specified item number; if it does, then it tells this to the user. It also counts the loop iterations to see if it has inspected the entire array. If it inspects the entire array without finding a vacant position, it raises the exception ARRAY_FULL.

The procedure FIND, shown in Figure 11.9(c), searches an array LIST to see if it contains a record whose STOCK_NUMBER component is equal to KEY. It assumes that the array has been initialized in the declaration and then changed only by the procedure INSERT. *Find*

If the record is in the array when the loop terminates, HASH_VALUE will be set so that LIST (HASH_VALUE) contains the record. If the record is not in the array, then the above code would search the entire array before it stops looking for the record. That is more work than is needed.

If the record is not in the array, then the loop can usually terminate much sooner. Recall that if there is a record with its STOCK_NUMBER component equal to KEY, then it should be in position HASH (KEY) or else in the first available position after that. The loop starts the search at array index HASH (KEY). Should a vacant position ever be encountered, we know that if the record had been inserted, then it would have been inserted at or before that position. Hence, we know we have looked at every place that the record could possibly be. The final version of the procedure FIND tests for a vacant position and terminates the loop if it finds one.

Another technique for coping with collisions is to use two different hash functions. If a collision occurs, the program uses the second hash function to compute a number *n,* and then, rather than going to the next location, it goes to the location that is *n* places after the location given by the first hash function. This is called *double hashing.* *double hashing*

We have been discussing hashing for the case where the key is an integer. The same techniques apply if the key is of some other type. For example, the key might be a name. One approach to designing a hash function for such a key would be to assign a number to each letter of the alphabet. (One such function is the attribute POS discussed in the section "The Attributes" PRED, SUCC, POS, and VAL in Chapter 8.) The hash function can then add up the numbers associated with each letter of the name to obtain a number and then proceed as if it had a numeric key. *nonnumeric keys*

Case Study

Strings Implemented with Discriminated Records

We have already seen how to represent strings of characters as an array of characters. In Chapter 10 and in the previous "case study," a string of up to 20 characters was represented as an array of type STRING in the following form:

```
type STRING is array( POSITIVE range <> ) of CHARACTER;
```

The constant MAXIMUM_LENGTH was set equal to **20** to constrain the array as follows:

```
NAME : STRING( 1 . . MAXIMUM_LENGTH );
```

Typically the strings we encountered were less than the full 20 characters. So, when we used arrays of type STRING, we filled the remaining array positions with the blank symbol. When we computed the length of the string in subprograms such as the one for pattern matching, we discarded these trailing blanks. (See Figure 10.8 for a detailed example of this.) There is a blatant inefficiency in this practice of adding blanks only to later remove them. It often makes more sense to treat the array as partially filled and have one variable to record the last array position used, that is, to record the length of the string.

Using a record we can combine into one unit both the array to hold the string and a variable to record the length of the string. This will have the added advantage of letting us more easily store and manipulate a string that ends with a blank. With a type STRING declared as in the last chapter, the strings **"Bach"** and **"Bach "** (with one blank before the final quotation mark) would be stored in the same way and so would be indistinguishable. Trailing blanks like that are not often relevant, but occasionally they can be useful. For example, they can be a convenient way to ensure that there will be a space between any two words that we might later join together.

new type Character_String

Our definition of a new type CHARACTER_STRING is a record with two components. One component is an array of characters that normally will be only partially filled. The other component is a positive variable that records the last array position used and so records the length of the string. The type declaration is as follows:

```
type CHARACTER_STRING( MAXIMUM_LENGTH : POSITIVE ) is
        record
            SYMBOLS : STRING( 1 . . MAXIMUM_LENGTH );
            LENGTH  : NATURAL;
        end record;
```

parameterized record

This is a new type, even though we are using the same type name, CHARACTER_STRING, as we did in the previous chapter. Although it is a new type, it serves the same purpose as our old type CHARACTER_STRING. The "new, improved" CHARACTER_STRING type is represented by what looks like a record with a parameter. Some have called it a *parameterized record,* but its official Ada term is *discriminated record.* The reason it sometimes is called a parameterized record is that a parameter (discriminant) in a record description serves the same purpose as a parameter in the function declaration. A parameter in a function allows the same actions to be performed with different input values. In a discriminated record, the discriminant allows the same general type description to be customized to a particular application. In the discriminated record description above, the discriminant allows the same type description to be used for different string lengths. The declaration of any objects of type CHARACTER_STRING must include a value for MAXIMUM_LENGTH. This

discriminated record

record discriminant is used to constrain the STRING array. The following examples demonstrate how to declare objects of type CHARACTER_STRING:

```
NAME, CITY : CHARACTER_STRING( 15 );
DESCRIPTION : CHARACTER_STRING ( 25 );
```

Some sample string values for NAME of this redefined type are diagrammed in Figure 11.10.

To use this new type CHARACTER_STRING, we must rewrite the basic string-manipulating procedures that we used in our STRINGS package. Again we will use the idea of object-oriented design. The objects will be of type CHARACTER_STRING, and the operations on those objects will be encapsulated in a package called STRING_PACKAGE.

A New String Package

The beauty of the use of a discriminated record as our *abstract data type* is that we can rewrite the operations so they will work properly, regardless of the value of the parameter in the object declaration. The operations on the data structure take advantage of the attributes FIRST and LAST. When the attribute FIRST is associated with an array variable (i.e., NAME'FIRST), it returns the index value of the *first* element of the array. Likewise, when the attribute LAST is associated with an array variable (i.e., NAME'LAST), it returns the index value of the *last* element of the array. The entire package, including the rewritten operations, is given in Figure 11.11(a).

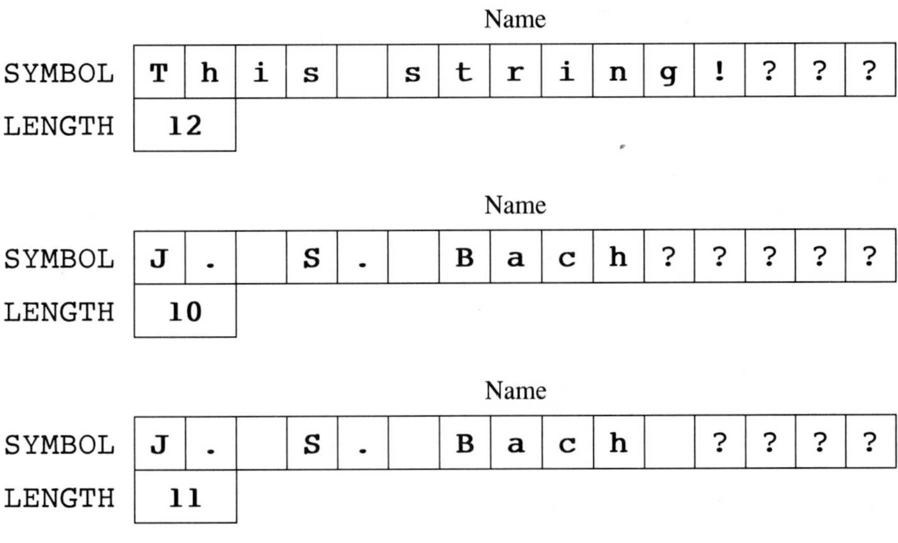

Figure 11.10 Strings as records.

A test procedure that uses STRING_PACKAGE is given in Figure 11.11(b). We have used this test program to demonstrate that the **use** clause is not necessary. When **use** is not used, the identifier in the program that references things in a package must have a *prefix* that is the package name. This prefix takes the same form as used to reference a component of a record, namely an identifier followed by a "dot." (See Figure 11.11(b) for examples.)

Notice that, since we now keep a record of the length of a string, we need not fill unused symbol positions with blanks. Also notice that the LENGTH function is now trivial to declare. However, in order to think of the abstract notion of a string and not have to worry about details of component specifications, we still include a length function. The new type CHARACTER_STRING and the new basic procedures PUT_STRING, GET_STRING, LENGTH, MATCH, and SUBPATTERN can be used anyplace we used the ones defined in Chapter 10. In particular, these new type, procedure, and function declarations can be used in place of the ones we used in Figure 10.10 by using the STRING_PACKAGE; nothing else in the program will need to change.

Package

```
package STRING_PACKAGE is
    type CHARACTER_STRING ( MAXIMUM_LENGTH : POSITIVE ) is
            record
                SYMBOL : STRING( 1 . . MAXIMUM_LENGTH );
                LENGTH : NATURAL;
            end record;
    EMPTY_STRING : exception;
    function LENGTH ( ITEM : CHARACTER_STRING ) return POSITIVE;
    function MATCH  ( PATTERN, TARGET : CHARACTER_STRING;
                      START_OF_TARGET : POSITIVE )
                      return BOOLEAN;
    procedure GET_STRING ( ITEM : out CHARACTER_STRING );
    function SUBPATTERN ( PATTERN, TARGET : CHARACTER_STRING )
                          return BOOLEAN;
    procedure PUT_STRING ( ITEM : in CHARACTER_STRING );
end STRING_PACKAGE;

with TEXT_IO;
use TEXT_IO;
package body STRING_PACKAGE is
    package POSITIVE_IO is new INTEGER_IO ( POSITIVE );
    use POSITIVE_IO;
    function LENGTH ( ITEM : CHARACTER_STRING ) return POSITIVE is
--                    INPUT  : A character string with at least one
--                             character in it.
--                    OUTPUT : The number of characters
--                             in the string.
```

```
--                DESCRIPTION : Computes the length (number of nonblank
--                              characters in the string).
--                              Raises empty_string if the string is
--                              empty.
begin -- Length
    if ITEM.LENGTH = 0 then
        raise EMPTY_STRING;
    else
        return ITEM.LENGTH;
    end if;
end LENGTH;
function MATCH ( PATTERN, TARGET : CHARACTER_STRING;
                 START_OF_TARGET : POSITIVE )
                 return BOOLEAN is
--             INPUT : A pattern and name string, along
--                     with the length of the pattern and
--                     the starting point in the target.
--             OUTPUT : FALSE is returned if the pattern is
--                     longer than the rest of the target.
--                     TRUE if there is a match,
--                     otherwise FALSE.
--             DESCRIPTION : The matching begins with the
--                           first of the pattern and the
--                           starting point in the target.
    LENGTH_OF_PATTERN : NATURAL := PATTERN.LENGTH;
begin -- Match
    return LENGTH_OF_PATTERN <= TARGET.SYMBOL'LAST - START_OF_TARGET + 1
    and then
          PATTERN.SYMBOL ( 1 .. LENGTH_OF_PATTERN )
          =
          TARGET.SYMBOL ( START_OF_TARGET
                    .. START_OF_TARGET + LENGTH_OF_PATTERN - 1 );
end MATCH;
procedure GET_STRING ( ITEM : out CHARACTER_STRING ) is
--              INPUT  : Nothing.
--              OUTPUT : A string of characters.
--              DESCRIPTION : Reads in a string of characters,
--                            truncated at MAXIMUM_LENGTH
--                            characters.
--                            Displays a message,
--                            if the input is truncated.
    POSITION : NATURAL;
```

```
    begin -- GET_STRING
        GET_LINE ( ITEM.SYMBOL, POSITION );
        ITEM.LENGTH := POSITION;
        if POSITION = ITEM.SYMBOL'LAST then
            if END_OF_LINE then
                SKIP_LINE;
            else
                SKIP_LINE;
                PUT ( "Only ");
                PUT ( POSITION );
                PUT ( " characters read in." );
                NEW_LINE;
            end if;
        end if;
    end GET_STRING;
    function SUBPATTERN ( PATTERN, TARGET : CHARACTER_STRING )
                            return BOOLEAN is
        LENGTH_OF_PATTERN : POSITIVE := LENGTH ( PATTERN );
    begin -- Subpattern
        for INDEX in 1 . . PATTERN.SYMBOL'LAST - LENGTH_OF_PATTERN + 1
        loop
            if MATCH ( PATTERN, TARGET, INDEX ) then
                return TRUE;
            end if;
        end loop;
        return FALSE;
    end SUBPATTERN;
    procedure PUT_STRING ( ITEM : in CHARACTER_STRING ) is
--                      INPUT  : A string of characters.
--                      OUTPUT : Nothing.
--                      DESCRIPTION : Displays LENGTH characters.
    begin -- PUT_STRING
        PUT_LINE ( ITEM.SYMBOL( ITEM.SYMBOL'FIRST . . ITEM.LENGTH ) );
    end PUT_STRING;
end STRING_PACKAGE;
```

Figure 11.11a Strings reimplemented as records.

Program

```
with TEXT_IO;
with STRING_PACKAGE;
procedure TEST_STRING_PACKAGE is
    STRING_SIZE : constant POSITIVE := 20;
    ANSWER : CHARACTER;
    LINE : STRING_PACKAGE.CHARACTER_STRING( STRING_SIZE );
```

```
    package NUMBER_IO is new TEXT_IO.INTEGER_IO ( NATURAL );
begin -- Test_String_Package
     loop
         TEXT_IO.PUT ( "Enter a string and press return." );
         TEXT_IO.NEW_LINE;
         for POSITION in 1 . . STRING_SIZE
         loop
             NUMBER_IO.PUT ( POSITION rem 10, 1 );
         end loop;
         TEXT_IO.NEW_LINE;
         STRING_PACKAGE.GET_STRING ( LINE );
         TEXT_IO.PUT ( "String contains the ");
         NUMBER_IO.PUT ( STRING_PACKAGE.LENGTH ( LINE ) );
         TEXT_IO.PUT ( " symbols:" );
         TEXT_IO.NEW_LINE;
         STRING_PACKAGE.PUT_STRING ( LINE );
         TEXT_IO.PUT ( "More? (y/n)" ); TEXT_IO.NEW_LINE;
         TEXT_IO.GET ( ANSWER ); TEXT_IO.SKIP_LINE;
         exit when ANSWER = 'n'
              or ANSWER = 'N';
    end loop;
    TEXT_IO.PUT ( "End of test." ); TEXT_IO.NEW_LINE;
end TEST_STRING_PACKAGE;
```

Sample Dialogue

```
Enter a string and press return.
12345678901234567890
Do Be Do
String contains the 8 symbols:
Do Be Do
More? (y/n)
y
Enter a string and press return.
12345678901234567890
Life is a jelly doughnut. Isn't it?
Only      20 characters read in.
String contains the 20 symbols.
Life is a jelly doug
More? (y/n)
n
```

Figure 11.11b Testing STRING__PACKAGE.

Case Study

Sorting Records

In Chapter 9 we developed a method for sorting an array of integers. In this section we will adapt the original sorting algorithm from Chapter 9 again. This time we will derive an algorithm to sort records according to the values in one particular component. For example, you may want to sort inventory records by price from the least expensive to the most expensive. We will adapt the sorting procedure from Figure 9.13 so that it sorts inventory records according to price.

Problem Definition

Before we begin to adapt our sorting procedure, let us be sure that we understand exactly what kind of records our procedure will need to sort. Rather than use the inventory type that opened this chapter, we will use the following new type definition in order to have yet another sample type:

```
type ITEM ( MAXIMUM_LENGTH : POSITIVE ) is
    record
        NAME     : CHARACTER_STRING( MAXIMUM_LENGTH );
        QUANTITY : INTEGER;
        PRICE    : FLOAT;
    end record;
subtype LIST_RANGE is POSITIVE range 1 . . MAXIMUM_LIST;
type ITEM_LIST is array( LIST_RANGE ) of ITEM( STRING_SIZE );
```

The type CHARACTER_STRING is defined in STRING_PACKAGE.

Suppose the array STOREROOM is of type ITEM_LIST. We wish to sort the records in STOREROOM so the price components of the records are in increasing order. If the first array index is **1**, then we want the following to hold:

```
STOREROOM(1).PRICE <= STOREROOM(2).PRICE <= STOREROOM(3).PRICE . . .
```

Discussion

In Chapter 9 we used the following algorithm to sort a simple array of integers named LIST:

```
for INDEX in first_index . . LAST - 1 loop
    EXCHANGE ( LIST(INDEX)), LIST( suitable_index );
end loop;
```

where LAST records the last array index used. To adapt this code to an array of records named STOREROOM, we need to do the following:

1. Replace the simple array LIST, with the array of records STOREROOM.
2. Write a procedure like EXCHANGE that applies to records of type ITEM.
3. Design an algorithm to compute *suitable__index*.

Subproblems 1 and 2 are trivial. The version of EXCHANGE that applies to records is called EXCHANGE. It is shown in Figure 11.13, and it is exactly the same as the procedure EXCHANGE, except that the type INTEGER is replaced by the type ITEM.

Index__Of__Smallest

Subproblem 3 will be accomplished by adapting the procedure INDEX_OF_SMALLEST from Figure 9.13. The version shown there worked for an array of positive integers, LIST, so it compared array values LIST(INDEX). This version will apply to all the records in our array of records, STOREROOM, but only the PRICE component will be used to determine the ordering. Hence, comparisons involving the record STOREROOM(INDEX) are made using STOREROOM (INDEX).PRICE. However, once the function INDEX_OF_SMALLEST determines *suitable__index,* procedure EXCHANGE interchanges the entire record STOREROOM(INDEX) with the entire record indexed by *suitable__index.* This distinction between testing one component and moving the entire record is illustrated in Figure 11.12.

Since it is irrelevant to the issues at hand, the internal structure of the strings is not diagrammed. The complete program is given in Figure 11.13.

STOREROOM

(1)	(2)	(3)
Coffee	Tea	Milk
30	50	20
6.98	3.95	**0.97**

Find the smallest value of STOREROOM.PRICE

STOREROOM

(1)	(2)	(3)
Milk	Tea	**Coffee**
20	50	**30**
0.97	3.95	**6.98**

Interchange entire records

Figure 11.12 Test and interchange for sorting records.

```
with STRING_PACKAGE; use STRING_PACKAGE;
with TEXT_IO; use TEXT_IO;
procedure SORT_RECORDS is
    STRING_SIZE : constant POSITIVE := 20;
    MAXIMUM_LIST : constant POSITIVE := 10;
    type ITEM ( MAXIMUM_LENGTH : POSITIVE ) is
        record
            NAME     : CHARACTER_STRING( MAXIMUM_LENGTH );
            QUANTITY : INTEGER;
            PRICE    : FLOAT;
        end record;
    subtype LIST_RANGE is POSITIVE range 1 . . MAXIMUM_LIST;
    type ITEM_LIST is array( LIST_RANGE ) of ITEM( STRING_SIZE );
    LAST : LIST_RANGE := 1;
    STOREROOM : ITEM_LIST;
    package QUANTITY_IO is new INTEGER_IO ( INTEGER );
    use QUANTITY_IO;
    package PRICE_IO is new FLOAT_IO ( FLOAT );
    use PRICE_IO;
    procedure EXCHANGE ( LEFT, RIGHT : in out ITEM ) is
        TEMPORARY : ITEM( STRING_SIZE ) := LEFT;
    begin
        LEFT := RIGHT;
        RIGHT := TEMPORARY;
    end EXCHANGE;
    function INDEX_OF_SMALLEST ( INVENTORY : ITEM_LIST;
                                 START,
                                 LAST      : LIST_RANGE )
                                 return LIST_RANGE is
        LOWEST_PRICE : FLOAT := INVENTORY( START ).PRICE;
        SMALLEST_INDEX : LIST_RANGE := START;
    begin
        for INDEX in START + 1 . . LAST
        loop
            if INVENTORY( INDEX ).PRICE < LOWEST_PRICE then
                LOWEST_PRICE := INVENTORY( INDEX ).PRICE;
                SMALLEST_INDEX := INDEX;
            end if;
        end loop;
        return SMALLEST_INDEX;
    end INDEX_OF_SMALLEST;
    procedure SORT ( INVENTORY : in out ITEM_LIST;
                     LAST      : in LIST_RANGE ) is
    begin
        for INDEX in 1 . . LAST - 1
```

```
    loop
        EXCHANGE ( INVENTORY( INDEX ),
                   INVENTORY( INDEX_OF_SMALLEST ( INVENTORY,
                                                  INDEX,
                                                  LAST ) ) );
    end loop;
end SORT;
procedure GET_INVENTORY ( INVENTORY : out ITEM_LIST;
                          LAST : out LIST_RANGE ) is
    ANSWER : CHARACTER;
begin
    for INDEX in LIST_RANGE
    loop
        declare
            ONE_ITEM : ITEM renames INVENTORY( INDEX );
        begin
            PUT ( "Enter name of inventory item:" ); NEW_LINE;
            GET_STRING ( ONE_ITEM.NAME );
            PUT ( "Enter quantity and price:" ); NEW_LINE;
            GET ( ONE_ITEM.QUANTITY );
            GET ( ONE_ITEM.PRICE );
            SKIP_LINE;
        end;
        if INDEX < LIST_RANGE'LAST then
            PUT ( "More? (y/n)" ); NEW_LINE;
            GET ( ANSWER ); SKIP_LINE;
            if ANSWER = 'n'
            or else ANSWER = 'N' then
                LAST := INDEX;
                exit;
            end if;
        else
            LAST := INDEX;
        end if;
    end loop;
end GET_INVENTORY;
procedure DISPLAY ( INVENTORY : in ITEM_LIST;
                    LAST : in LIST_RANGE ) is
begin
    for INDEX in 1 . . LAST
    loop
        declare
            ONE_ITEM : ITEM renames INVENTORY( INDEX );
        begin
            PUT_STRING ( ONE_ITEM.NAME );
            PUT ( ONE_ITEM.QUANTITY, 5 );
```

```
                    PUT ( ONE_ITEM.PRICE, 5, 2, 0 );
                    NEW_LINE;
                end;
            end loop;
        end DISPLAY;
begin
    GET_INVENTORY ( STOREROOM, LAST );
    SORT ( STOREROOM, LAST );
    DISPLAY ( STOREROOM, LAST );
end SORT_RECORDS;
```

Figure 11.13 Program for sorting an array of records.

Algorithm Abstraction

In Chapter 9 we developed an algorithm for sorting an array of integers. In the previous section we adapted that algorithm to obtain an algorithm for sorting an array of records. There is a sense that those two algorithms are the same. There is a level of abstraction that captures them both. Instead of writing those two algorithms, we could have written a single algorithm to sort an array of some unspecified type according to some unspecified operator for "less than." The algorithm would step through the array and place the smallest element in the first array location, such as INVENTORY(1) in the procedure SORT of Figure 11.13, the next smallest in the next array location, such as INVENTORY(2) in that procedure, and so forth. To understand the algorithm we do not need to know the component type of the array. We also do not need to know the exact details of the "less than" relation. We can formulate an algorithm with these details left unspecified. If we then specify that the component type of the array is the type INTEGER and that "less than" is to be the normal less-than operator on the integers, we obtain the algorithm we presented in Chapter 9. If instead we specify that the component type of the array is the record type ITEM given in Figure 11.13 and that "less than" is defined by considering only the PRICE components of the records compared, then we obtain the algorithm we derived in the previous section. This is what is meant by *algorithm abstraction.* If we design our algorithms at a more abstract level, then we can reuse them in a variety of situations. If we think in terms of the more abstract algorithm, then we need not rederive the algorithm every time we want to sort an array of some different type.

The idea of changing the component type of the array and using the same abstract algorithm may seem quite obvious. A less obvious but equally useful change is to change the meaning of "less than." If we define "less than" to mean "greater than," we still get a sorting algorithm, but now it sorts the entries from the largest to the smallest, rather than from the smallest to the largest. By thinking in terms of a single more abstract algorithm, we do not need to derive separate algorithms to sort into increasing order and to sort into decreasing order. They are the same algorithm but with different relations for what we have been calling "less than." If it helps to eliminate confusion, you might call the unspecified relation in your abstract algorithm something other than "less than," such as "goes before" or "relation X." You also might use some phrase other than "the smallest element" to designate the element that belongs in the first array position; for example, you might instead use the phrase "first with respect to the relation." This eliminates any prejudice against "greater than" relations. The important point is to think of the relation as being unspecified so it can later be specialized to any relation that defines an ordering, such as less-than on integers, greater-than on integers, alphabetical on words, reverse alphabetical on words, and so on. Once we have the abstract algorithm, we can write programs to sort any kind of array into almost any kind of order by making only routine adaptations to our basic abstract algorithm.

ADTs—Abstract Data Types

In this book we have discussed procedural abstraction, data abstraction, and now algorithm abstraction. If you experience a bit of trouble distinguishing between these three techniques, do not be too concerned. They are not totally distinct concepts. They overlap and interrelate with each other. The key idea in all three of these programming techniques is abstraction. *Abstraction* means the hiding of certain details so as to allow more general thinking and to allow the separation of problems into independent subproblems. For example, we have seen that an abstract treatment of sorting an array might hide the component type of the array elements and the definition of when one element is "less than" another.

Abstract data types, which we will introduce in this section, provide us with a systematic technique for hiding information and so help us with all the forms of abstraction that we have discussed. Many newer programming languages, including Ada, have facilities to implement abstract data types directly. An *abstract data type* (abbreviated *ADT*) is a data structure (or data structures) and a collection of operations on the data structure defined in a particular way. In an abstract data type the specification of what effects the operations have on the data structure must be separated from the details of how the data structure and the operations are implemented. Moreover, any details of a data structure or operation that are left unspecified in an abstract data type must be clearly noted so that they can easily be filled in when the abstract data type is used in a program. An example is likely to be more informative than this wordy definition, so let us go directly to an example.

Figure 11.11 shows a specification for the abstract data type `CHARACTER_STRING`. The values of this type consist of strings of characters. The operations on this type are reading a value from the keyboard and writing a value to the screen. One other operation that is not explicitly mentioned since it comes automatically with all types is that of placing a value in a variable. In practice we might want to add a number of other operations, but these few will suffice to illustrate the concept of an ADT.

String Package with Private Section

The specification of our ADT for CHARACTER_STRING is divided into two subparts. One subpart, called the *package specification,* gives all the information that a programmer needs to know in order to use the ADT. The other section, called the *package body,* contains the complete code to implement the data type CHARACTER_STRING and the operations like GET_STRING and PUT_STRING. Let us look at each of these two subparts in more detail.

package specification

The *package specification* in Figure 11.14 contains the name of the type CHARACTER_STRING, a description of the type, and the specifications for the procedures that manipulate values of that type. However, it marks type declaration for CHARACTER_STRING as **private** and initially provides no other details. The package specification does not contain complete procedure bodies for the procedures that manipulate values of this type. The user of this ADT does not need to know those details to use the ADT. This package specification is slightly different than the one in Figure 11.11, because it contains a section labeled **private**. The items above the **private** section are the things that a programmer who uses the ADT has available for use. The declarations in the **private** section complete the declarations of the items marked previously as **private**. The items in the **private** section are not available to the user of the package. A program that **with**s the package does not have access to this information, it is hidden from the user. For example, a program that **with**s the STRING_PACKAGE with these package specifications can declare objects of type CHARACTER_STRING, but it cannot reference the record components SYMBOL or LENGTH.

Package Specification

```
package STRING_PACKAGE is
    type CHARACTER_STRING ( MAXIMUM_LENGTH : POSITIVE ) is private;
    EMPTY_STRING : exception;
    function LENGTH ( ITEM : CHARACTER_STRING ) return POSITIVE;
    function MATCH  ( PATTERN, TARGET : CHARACTER_STRING;
                      START_OF_TARGET : POSITIVE )
                      return BOOLEAN;
    procedure GET_STRING ( ITEM : out CHARACTER_STRING );
    function SUBPATTERN ( PATTERN, TARGET : CHARACTER_STRING )
                          return BOOLEAN;
    procedure PUT_STRING ( ITEM : in CHARACTER_STRING );
private
    type CHARACTER_STRING ( MAXIMUM_LENGTH : POSITIVE ) is
            record
                SYMBOL : STRING( 1 . . MAXIMUM_LENGTH );
                LENGTH : NATURAL;
            end record;
end STRING_PACKAGE;
```

Figure 11.14 Package specification with Private section.

A package specification is thus expanded to include a **private** section. The syntax for a package specification with an optional **private** section is shown in Figure 11.15. Figure 11.15 also includes the syntax for a private__type__declaration, as is used in the visible part of the package specification in Figure 11.14.

exported

The items available to a program that **with**s the package are sometimes said to be *exported* by the package. A programmer who uses this ADT can use the type CHARACTER_STRING, the procedures GET_STRING and PUT_STRING, and the functions LENGTH, MATCH, and SUBPATTERN. A programmer cannot use any of the details about these items that are given in the package body. For example, a user of the ADT cannot use the details of the type definition to access individual characters of a string. If accessing individual characters is a desired operation, then the ADT should have a procedure or function for doing so added to the ADT and listed in the package specification. Like the other exported procedures, this one would be described in the package specification, and the complete declaration would only be given in the package body.

imported

Information that is necessary for a program to actually use the package is sometimes said to be *imported* by the package. In this example, the only item imported is the value of MAXIMUM_LENGTH. Imported items must be defined before the ADT can be used. However, a user of the ADT does not need to know how they are defined. In this example the values of MAXIMUM_LENGTH must be defined by the user when objects of type CHARACTER_STRING are declared; for examples:

```
LINE : CHARACTER_STRING( 80 );
WORD : CHARACTER_STRING( 10 );
```

private__type__declaration

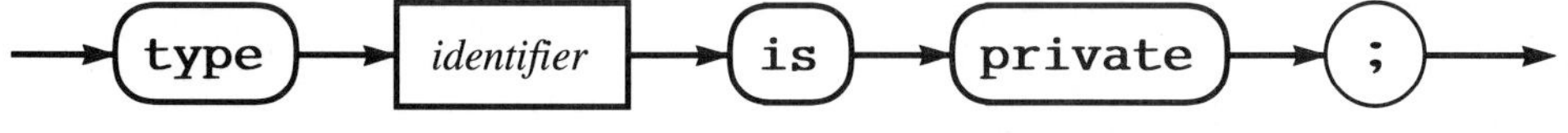

package__specification

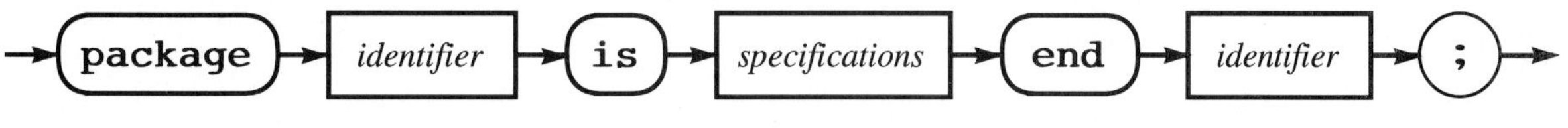

specifications

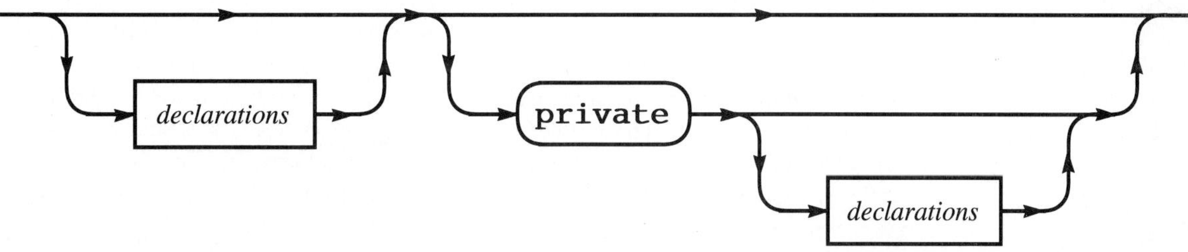

Figure 11.15 Syntax for expanded package specification.

Beyond this point the user of the ADT should program as if he or she did not know what integer values were supplied in the declaration.

package body The package body contains the full bodies for all the subprogram specifications that are described in the package specification. Refer to Figure 11.11(a) for an example of a package body. In order to use the ADT, a program need only **with** the package and provide the necessary imported information. The compiler goes to the library and, in effect, attaches the package to the front end of your program.

The package specification and body for the ADTs are written and compiled separately and then stored in a library of ADTs that any program can use.

why use ADTs? What do we get for all this effort of dividing things into packages? We have gained generality and modularity. We can have several programs that use this ADT, and we need to write it only once. We can design algorithms that depend only on what is defined in the package specification and apply them in a number of different settings. This generality is a result of hiding information. This hiding of information also produces modularity.

If this were part of a group project, we might first write only the package specification. After that, one programmer could be assigned to write the main part of the program, and another programmer could be assigned to write the package body of the ADT. We have separated these two jobs by putting a wall between them so that each programmer need only see what is on his or her side of the wall. There are advantages to be gained from this separation of interface (specification) from implementation (body), even if all the programming is done by only one programmer. For one thing, you are free to change the package body if you want to later. If you discover a more efficient way to write the procedures in the package body, then you can change that section and you need not worry about changing the rest of the program. As long as you make your declarations consistent with what is said in the package specification, you need not worry about changing the program that uses your ADT.

Variant Records
(Optional)

It is frequently convenient and natural to have records in which the component identifiers and component types vary from record to record. For example, a list of publications might naturally be thought of as an array of records. Normally the records would contain slightly different entries for articles and for books. Records for both articles and books would include authors, titles, and dates. A book normally also has a publisher and city, while an article normally has a journal name, volume number, and pages. Ada allows records which have some components that vary from record to record. These sorts of records are called *variant records.* They are most often used in conjunction with enumeration types. (If you have not read the section in Chapter 8 on enumeration types, you should go back and read it before reading the rest of this section.)

```
subtype DATE_RANGE is POSITIVE range 1900 . . 2000;
type FORM is ( BOOK, ARTICLE );
type PUBLICATION ( KIND : FORM := BOOK ) is
        record
            AUTHOR,
            TITLE : STRING( 1 . . 20 );
            DATE  : DATE_RANGE;
            case KIND is
                when BOOK =>
                    PUBLISHER,
                    CITY : STRING( 1 . . 10 );
                when ARTICLE =>
                    JOURNAL : STRING( 1 . . 20 );
                    VOLUME,
                    FIRST_PAGE,
                    LAST_PAGE : POSITIVE;
            end case;
        end record;
```

Figure 11.16 A variant record type.

The syntax of a variant record type declaration uses something analogous to a **case** statement to specify the components that vary from record to record. For example, Figure 11.16 defines two types. The type FORM is an enumeration type. The type PUBLICATION is a variant record type for records that are entries for either a book or an article.

discriminant part

The part in parentheses after the record name and before the reserved word **is** is called the *discriminant part.* It contains a declaration of the *discriminant* that will be used later in the *variant part.* It may also be given an optional default value, as in the example above, where KIND was assigned the value BOOK. It is called a *default value* because if a value is not given in an object declaration, the system will give it the value specified in the type declaration.

fixed part

The part before the reserved word **case** is called the *fixed part.* The fixed part is just like the record types we have seen. By way of illustration, suppose we have the following variable declaration:

```
THIS_PUBLICATION : PUBLICATION;
```

Then the following component variables are exactly like the ones we have seen for the ordinary records discussed in previous sections:

```
THIS_PUBLICATION.AUTHOR
THIS_PUBLICATION.TITLE
THIS_PUBLICATION.DATE
```

variant part

discriminant

The part of the type declaration that starts with the identifier **case** is called the *variant part.* The identifier KIND is called the *discriminant.* It is an object of type FORM, as declared in the discriminant part. Every record has this component. Hence, THIS_PUBLICATION.KIND can be referenced as an ordinary component variable. However, this component has an additional property. The value of the component KIND determines the form of the rest of the record. If the value of KIND is BOOK, then the record will have the following additional two components:

```
THIS_PUBLICATION.PUBLISHER
THIS_PUBLICATION.CITY
```

If the value of KIND had been initialized to ARTICLE, then these two components will not exist; instead, the following four components will be present:

```
THIS_PUBLICATION.JOURNAL
THIS_PUBLICATION.VOLUME
THIS_PUBLICATION.FIRST_PAGE
THIS_PUBLICATION.LAST_PAGE
```

In all cases the types of the components are the ones specified in the declaration.

changing discriminant value

The only way to change the value of the discriminant and, hence, the configuration of the record is to declare all values of the record in an aggregate. For example, assume

```
PAPER : PUBLICATION;
```

is by default a record with a discriminant value of BOOK. To change the discriminant value to ARTICLE, we need to list all values in the record in order of declaration as follows:

```
PAPER := ( ARTICLE,
           "Walter J Savitch    ",
           "Doctor in your lab? ",
           1990,
           "Journal of Ada, etc.",
           17,
           1990,
           1990 );
```

A complete syntax diagram for record type definitions that can include a variant part is given in Figure 11.17. Notice that there is only one **case** type structure, and it always comes last. (There can be a **case** within a **case**, but such nesting is rare.) All the various component identifiers must be distinct. The *discriminant* is a normal component identifier. The *type name* associated with the *discriminant* may name any discrete type or subrange. It must be a type name; it cannot be a type definition, such as **1 . . 4**.

omitting discriminant value

It is possible to omit the assignment of a default value to the discriminant. In Figure 11.16, that would be done by replacing

```
type PUBLICATION ( KIND : FORM := BOOK ) is
```

by

```
type PUBLICATION ( KIND : FORM ) is
```

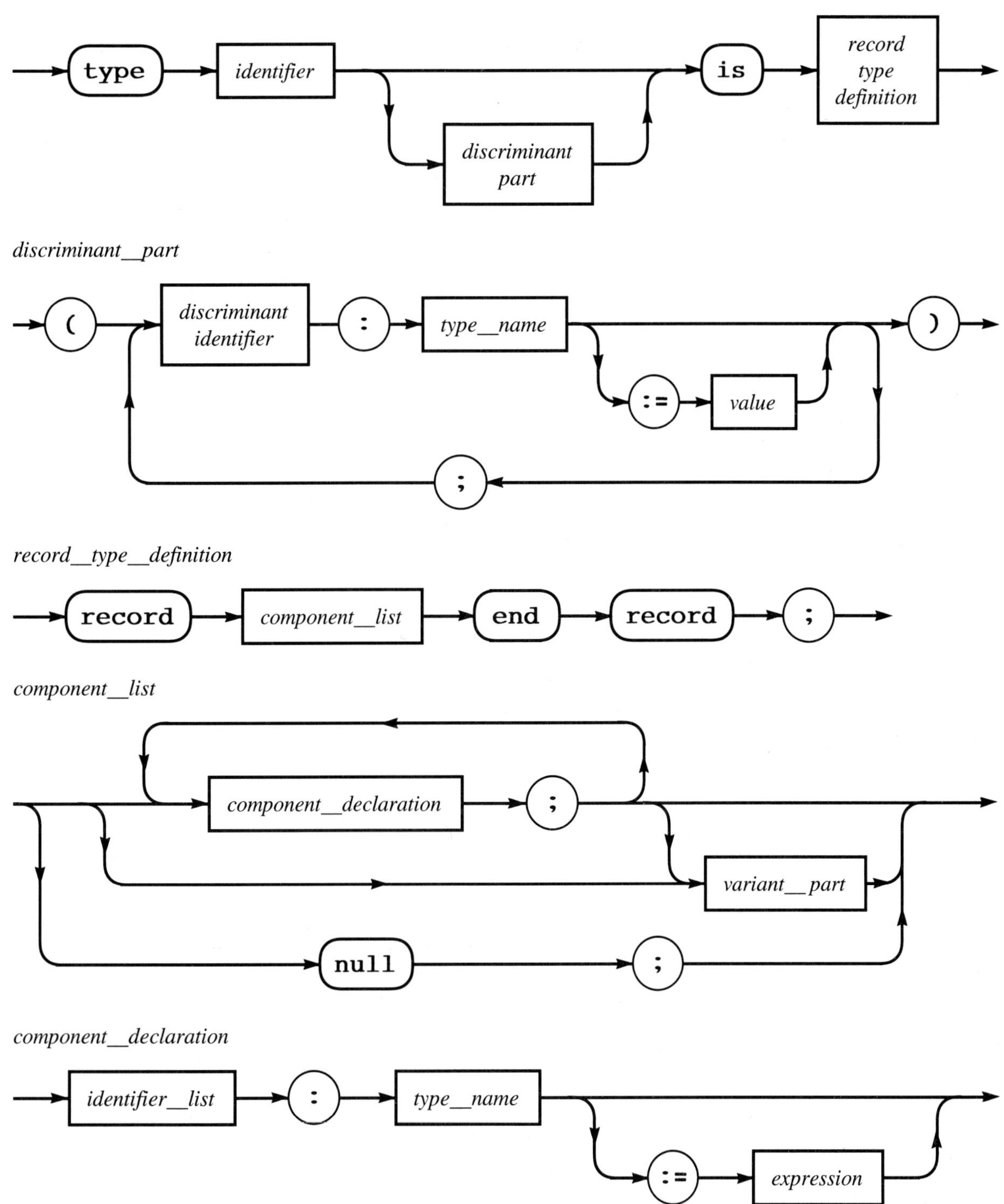
type
identifier
discriminant part
is
record type definition
discriminant__part
(
discriminant identifier
:
type__name
:=
value
)
;
record__type__definition
record
component__list
end
record
;
component__list
component__declaration
;
variant__part
null
;
component__declaration
identifier__list
:
type__name
:=
expression

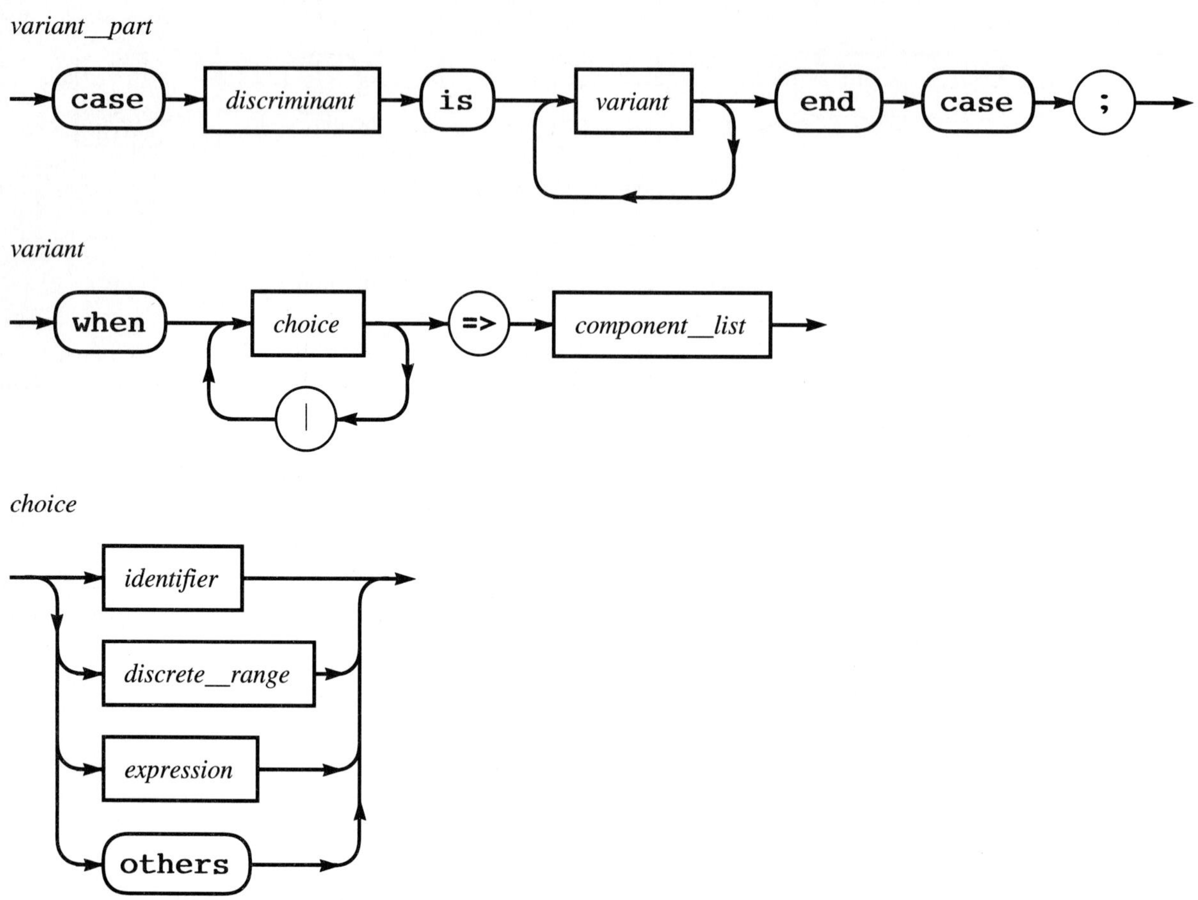

Figure 11.17 Complete syntax diagram for record type declaration.

If this is done, the component called KIND has no default value. The programmer must provide the information when objects of type PUBLICATION are declared. Using the above examples, the object declaration would appear as follows:

```
THIS_PUBLICATION : PUBLICATION ( BOOK );
PAPER : PUBLICATION ( ARTICLE );
```

If records are declared in this manner where the discriminant is assigned a value via the declaration, then it is not possible to change, in any manner, the value of the discriminant for that object. The discriminant for THIS_PUBLICATION will be BOOK throughout its scope of declaration; similarly, PAPER is always an ARTICLE. The syntax diagram in Figure 11.17 describes all the possible variations.

Variant records are not absolutely necessary. For example, we could have defined the type PUBLICATION to have all 10 possible components and then write the program so that it uses whatever components are needed. However, on most systems the variant record form will use less storage because the same storage is used for the BOOK components as for the ARTICLE components. Hence, the storage needed is the maximum of the two cases rather than the sum of the two. This kind of storage allocation is illustrated in Figure 11.18.

storage efficiency

Figure 11.19 contains a sample program using a variant record type. In that program, the discriminant SHAPE is set to either RECTANGLE or CIRCLE. In the first case there will be two additional components called HEIGHT and WIDTH. In the second case there will be just one additional component called RADIUS. In the GET_DATA procedure, we used an optional form of aggregate assignment in which the components of the record are explicitly named. This form of assignment is called *named association.* If this form is used, the order in which the components appear in the assignment do not have to coincide with their order of occurrence in the record itself. The form we have used in previous examples is called *positional association.* It is called positional association because the values are associated with the various components of the record by their position within the record.

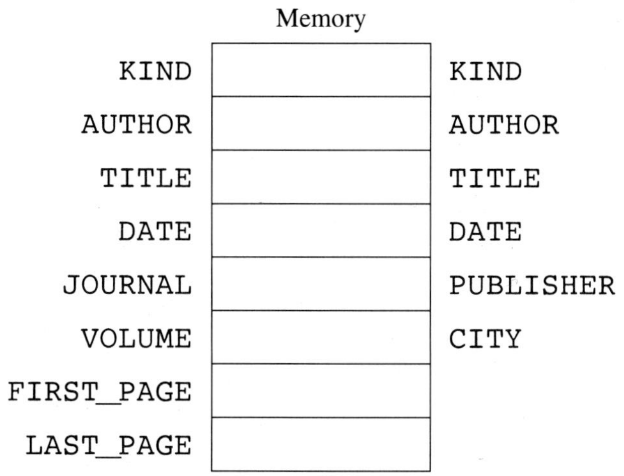

named association

positional association

	Memory	
KIND		KIND
AUTHOR		AUTHOR
TITLE		TITLE
DATE		DATE
JOURNAL		PUBLISHER
VOLUME		CITY
FIRST_PAGE		
LAST_PAGE		

Figure 11.18 Memory allocation for a variant record.

Program

```
with TEXT_IO;
procedure AREA_COMPUTATION is
    PI : constant FLOAT := 3.14159;
    type KIND is ( RECTANGLE, CIRCLE );
    type FIGURE ( SHAPE : KIND := RECTANGLE ) is
            record
                AREA : FLOAT;
                case SHAPE is
                    when RECTANGLE =>
                        HEIGHT,
                        WIDTH : FLOAT;
                    when CIRCLE =>
                        RADIUS : FLOAT;
                end case;
            end record;
    FORM : FIGURE;
    FORM_AREA : FLOAT;
    FORM_SHAPE : KIND;
    FORM_HEIGHT,
    FORM_RADIUS,
    FORM_WIDTH : FLOAT;
    package KIND_IO is new TEXT_IO.ENUMERATION_IO ( KIND );
    package DIMENSION_IO is new TEXT_IO.FLOAT_IO ( FLOAT );
    procedure GET_DATA ( SHAPE : KIND; FORM : out FIGURE ) is
    begin -- Get_Data
        case SHAPE is
            when RECTANGLE =>
                TEXT_IO.PUT ( "Enter height and width:" );
                TEXT_IO.NEW_LINE;
                DIMENSION_IO.GET ( FORM_HEIGHT );
                DIMENSION_IO.GET ( FORM_WIDTH );
                TEXT_IO.SKIP_LINE;
                FORM := ( SHAPE  => RECTANGLE,
                          HEIGHT => FORM_HEIGHT,
                          WIDTH  => FORM_WIDTH,
                          AREA   => FORM_HEIGHT * FORM_WIDTH
                          );
            when CIRCLE =>
                TEXT_IO.PUT ( "Enter radius:" );
                TEXT_IO.NEW_LINE;
                DIMENSION_IO.GET ( FORM_RADIUS );
                TEXT_IO.SKIP_LINE;
                FORM := ( SHAPE  => CIRCLE,
                          RADIUS => FORM_RADIUS,
                          AREA   => PI * FORM_RADIUS ** 2 );
        end case;
```

```
    end GET_DATA;
    procedure DISPLAY ( FORM : in FIGURE ) is
    begin -- Display
        TEXT_IO.PUT ( "The figure's form is " );
        KIND_IO.PUT ( FORM.SHAPE );
        TEXT_IO.NEW_LINE;
        TEXT_IO.PUT ( "Area = " );
        DIMENSION_IO.PUT ( FORM.AREA, 2, 1, 0 );
        TEXT_IO.NEW_LINE;
        case FORM.SHAPE is
            when CIRCLE =>
                TEXT_IO.PUT ( "For radius = " );
                DIMENSION_IO.PUT ( FORM.RADIUS,2, 1, 0 );
                TEXT_IO.NEW_LINE;
            when RECTANGLE =>
                TEXT_IO.PUT ( "For dimensions " );
                DIMENSION_IO.PUT ( FORM.HEIGHT, 2, 1, 0 );
                TEXT_IO.PUT ( " by " );
                DIMENSION_IO.PUT ( FORM.WIDTH, 2, 1, 0 );
                TEXT_IO.NEW_LINE;
        end case;
    end DISPLAY;
begin -- Area_Computation
    loop
        TEXT_IO.PUT ( "Enter type of figure:" );
        TEXT_IO.NEW_LINE;
        TEXT_IO.PUT ( "(RECTANGLE or CIRCLE)" );
        TEXT_IO.NEW_LINE;
        begin
            KIND_IO.GET ( FORM_SHAPE );
            exit;
        exception
            when others => TEXT_IO. PUT_LINE ( "Bad input, try again." );
        end;
    end loop;
    TEXT_IO.SKIP_LINE;
    GET_DATA ( FORM_SHAPE, FORM );
    DISPLAY ( FORM );
end AREA_COMPUTATION;
```

Sample Dialogue 1

```
Enter type of figure:
(RECTANGLE or CIRCLE)
RECTANGLE
Enter height and width:
1.0 2.0
```

```
The figure's form is RECTANGLE
Area = 2.0
For dimensions 1.0 by 2.0
```

Sample Dialogue 2

```
Enter type of figure:
(RECTANGLE or CIRCLE)
CIRCLE
Enter radius:
2.0
The figure's form is CIRCLE
Area = 12.6
For radius = 2.0
```

Figure 11.19 Program using variant records.

Generic Sets Package

We often want a program to check whether a value is on some list. For example, the program might ask the user to type in the letter **'Y'** or **'N'** for "yes" or "no" and then read the answer into the variable ANSWER. The user might get confused and type in something else, such as **"OK"**. In this situation you may want the program to make sure the value of ANSWER is either **'Y'** or **'N'** before going on.

Is_In

Wouldn't it be nice if we had a boolean function that would tell us if the ANSWER was **'Y'** or **'N'**. Assume for the moment that we have an object named YES_OR_NO that contains the values **'Y'** and **'N'**. Also assume for the moment that we have a boolean function named IS_IN that would tell us if the ANSWER was in the object YES_OR_NO. The code would look like

```
IS_IN ( ANSWER, YES_OR_NO )
```

It may read a little funny unless you think of IS_IN as an operator and read the above code as

```
ANSWER IS_IN YES_OR_NO -- NOT Ada syntax
```

This boolean expression means just what you naturally expect it to mean. It evaluates to TRUE if the value of ANSWER is equal to **'Y'** or **'N'**. In other words it is exactly equivalent to the boolean expression

```
ANSWER = 'Y' or ANSWER = 'N'
```

When the list consists of only two or three values, you can just as well use an expression with **or** like the above, but when the list of values is four or more, the new kind of boolean expression could be very handy. For example, if we assume YES_OR_NO contained **'Y'**, **'y'**, **'N'**, and **'n'**, then the following boolean expressions are completely equivalent. However, the first one using IS_IN is easier to write and easier to read.

```
IS_IN ( ANSWER, YES_OR_NO )
ANSWER = 'Y' or ANSWER = 'y' or ANSWER = 'N' or ANSWER = 'n'
```

This concept can be expanded to include any grouping of letters or other entities. This grouping can be described as a set of values.

sets

A list of discrete values is called a *set.* Ada does not have a predefined type called SET. That need not deter us, for we can design an abstract data type (*ADT*) for a set of discrete values. An ADT describes a data type and then a group of operations that we wish to perform on values of this data type. We can then encapsulate this ADT in an Ada package and put it in our library for use anytime we have the need to use sets in a program. First, let's make sure we know a little more about sets.

ADT

sets versus lists

A *set* is almost identical to what most people call a *list.* However, there are some differences. The elements of a list have an order, and that order is part of the identity of the list. So the following two lists are different:

1, 3, 5

and

1, 5, 3

A set is like a list except the order in which the elements are named is unimportant. For example, the following two sets are equal:

1, 3, 5

and

1, 5, 3

One other difference between sets and lists is that, unlike a list, a set cannot have any repetitions. The following example is not a set:

1, 3, 5, 3

because the value **3** appears more than once.

set types

What sort of data structure can we use to describe the characteristics of sets? A set can be described as an array whose indexes are the elements of the set. This array could have elements of type BOOLEAN to tell us if the element of the set is in the array. Abstractly then, our data type SET could be described in the following manner:

elements

```
type SET is array( SET_ELEMENT ) of BOOLEAN;
```

This description implies that we can define a type called SET_ELEMENT that is a discrete range of values, all of the same type. The following are some examples of how SET_ELEMENT might be defined:

```
type SET_ELEMENT is INTEGER range 0 . . 100;
type SET_ELEMENT is CHARACTER range 'a' . . 'z';
type AUTO is ( FORD, CHEVY, DODGE, MERCURY, CADILLAC, EAGLE );
subtype SET_ELEMENT is AUTO range FORD . . DODGE;
```

Naturally we need the ability to insert elements into a set, to remove or delete elements from a set, or remove all elements from a set to create an empty set. Traditionally there is a group of mathematical operations performed on sets, such as the *union* of two sets, the *intersection* of two sets, and the *difference* between two sets. Figure 11.20 describes what these terms mean with respect to sets. We might also want to test for equality (=), size of, and so on.

Operation	Value Returned
`Union ( set_1, set_2 )`	The set returned contains all elements that are in set__1 or set__2 or both.
`Intersection ( set_1, set_ 2 )`	The set returned contains those elements that are in both set__1 and set__2.
`Difference ( set_1, set_2 )`	The set returned contains those elements that are in set__1 but not in set__2

Figure 11.20 Some set operations.

Before going any further, it is best that we review what we learned about generic packages back in Chapter 8. Recall that a generic package is like a template that we can use to make copies of called instances. In Chapter 8 we discussed the generic packages that were part of package `TEXT_IO`, in particular `INTEGER_IO`, `FLOAT_IO`, and `ENUMERATION_IO`. In the preceding chapters, we have used these generic packages by instantiating (from the word *instance*) them as we needed them. This is the first time that we will write our own generic package. Recall that the syntax for a generic package is very similar to a nongeneric package. The only difference in appearance is that the specification for a generic package starts with the reserved word **generic**, followed by any generic parameters. Figure 11.21 is the specification for a generic package that encapsulates the ADT for a set.

```
generic
    type SET_ELEMENT is ( <> );
package SET_PACKAGE is
    type SET is private;
    procedure INSERT ( ELEMENT : SET_ELEMENT; A_SET : in out SET );
    procedure DELETE ( ELEMENT : SET_ELEMENT; A_SET : in out SET );
    function IS_IN ( ELEMENT : SET_ELEMENT; A_SET : SET )
            return BOOLEAN;
    function IS_EMPTY ( A_SET : SET ) return BOOLEAN;
    function EMPTY_SET return SET;
    function SIZE_OF ( A_SET : SET ) return NATURAL;
    function EQUAL ( LEFT, RIGHT :SET ) return BOOLEAN;
```

```
    function UNION ( LEFT, RIGHT : SET ) return SET;
    function INTERSECTION ( LEFT, RIGHT : SET ) return SET;
    function DIFFERENCE ( LEFT, RIGHT : SET ) return SET;
    function COMPLEMENT ( A_SET : SET ) return SET;
private
    type SET is array ( SET_ELEMENT ) of BOOLEAN;
end SET_PACKAGE;
```

Figure 11.21 Package specification describing the abstract data type SET.

For completeness sake, the package body for SET_PACKAGE is included as Figure 11.23. However, an understanding of its exact implementation is not necessary for us to use SET_PACKAGE. Before we use the package, we will discuss some of the Ada features of a generic package that are used in this example.

First, we use a generic package so we do not need a separate package for every imaginable discrete type for which we may want to use sets. The generic parameter

```
    type SET_ELEMENT is ( <> );
```

says that SET_ELEMENT is a type name that must be supplied by the user when the package is instantiated. The *box* enclosed in parentheses, **(<>)**, says that the type supplied by the user in the instantiation must be a discrete type.

The first statement inside the package specification is the declaration of the type SET, and it is declared to be **private**. The user of SET_PACKAGE can declare objects of type SET, as is done in the sample program in Figure 11.22. However, any operations on the type SET are restricted to those defined in the package specification and thus are held privately by the package. This precludes any program statement from affecting the objects of type SET, except through the declared operations. This protects the integrity of the set.

Following the declaration of the type SET, all the operations that can change, use, or test a set are listed in the form of functions and procedures. The equals operation is not listed because the '=' relation exists for all types. You can always test if two objects of a given type are equal, or not equal for that matter.

The **private** section of the package specification is required to complete the declaration of any type that was previously declared to be of type **private**. The **private** section of the package specification in this case declares the type SET to be a boolean array whose indexes are the complete range of all values of the generic parameter SET_ELEMENT.

It would not be a good idea to instantiate SET_PACKAGE with the type INTEGER, for the range of indexes would be from INTEGER'FIRST to INTEGER'LAST. You could instantiate the package, however, with a smaller subset of the integers by declaring a **subtype** subrange of the integers, say 1 to 100, and using that subtype name as the generic parameter during instantiation. The following are a couple of examples of instantiations of SET_PACKAGE:

```
subtype ONE_TO_HUNDRED is INTEGER range 1 . . 100;
package NUMBER_SET is new SET_PACKAGE ( ONE_TO_HUNDRED );

type AUTO is ( FORD, CHEVY, DODGE, MERCURY, CADILLAC, EAGLE );
package AUTO_SET is new SET_PACKAGE ( AUTO );
```

The program in Figure 11.22 uses the SET_PACKAGE to determine what uppercase letters appear in a given input sentence. Notice that there is no **use** for SET_PACKAGE. Generic packages are merely templates for the real package that is created at the point of instantiation. The program has two objects of type SET. The first, CHARACTER_SET, is declared in the main procedure, and the second, TERMINATORS, is declared in the input procedure READ_SENTENCE. EMPTY_SET, a function in the package, is used in two places in the READ_SENTENCE procedure to ensure that there is nothing in a set: first in the declaration of TERMINATORS and later to ensure that CHARACTER_SET is empty just before any characters are read in and inserted into the set.

Program

```
with TEXT_IO; use TEXT_IO;
with SET_PACKAGE;
procedure LETTERS is
    package SET_OF_CHARACTER is new SET_PACKAGE ( CHARACTER );
    use SET_OF_CHARACTER;
    CHARACTER_SET : SET;
    procedure READ_SENTENCE ( CHARACTER_SET : in out SET ) is
        A_CHARACTER : CHARACTER;
        TERMINATORS : SET := EMPTY_SET;
    begin -- Read_Sentence
        PUT ( "Enter a sentence. End it with" ); NEW_LINE;
        PUT ( "a '?', '!', or a period." ); NEW_LINE;
        INSERT ( '?', TERMINATORS );
        INSERT ( '!', TERMINATORS );
        INSERT ( '.', TERMINATORS );
        CHARACTER_SET := EMPTY_SET;
        loop
            GET ( A_CHARACTER );
            exit when IS_IN ( A_CHARACTER, TERMINATORS );
            INSERT ( A_CHARACTER, CHARACTER_SET );
        end loop;
        SKIP_LINE;
    end READ_SENTENCE;
    procedure WRITE_LETTERS ( CHARACTER_SET : in SET ) is
        BLANK : constant CHARACTER := ' ' ;
    begin -- Write_Letters
        for A_CHARACTER in 'A' . . 'Z'
        loop
            if IS_IN ( A_CHARACTER, CHARACTER_SET ) then
```

```
                PUT ( A_CHARACTER );
                PUT ( BLANK );
            end if;
        end loop;
        NEW_LINE;
    end WRITE_LETTERS;
begin -- Letters
    READ_SENTENCE ( CHARACTER_SET );
    PUT ( "Your sentence contains the" ); NEW_LINE;
    PUT ( "following uppercase letters:" ); NEW_LINE;
    WRITE_LETTERS ( CHARACTER_SET );
end LETTERS;
```

Sample Dialogue

```
Enter a sentence. End it with
a '?', '!', or a period.
Buy Low and Sell HIGH!
Your sentence contains the
following uppercase letters:
B G H I L S
```

Figure 11.22 A program using a set package.

The body for SET_PACKAGE is shown for the sake of completeness and to show how easy it is to implement the operations on the type SET. The idea, as you can see, is quite simple. If the element is in the set, the value in the array that the element indexes is set to TRUE. If it is not in the set, the value is FALSE.

```
package body SET_PACKAGE is

    procedure INSERT ( ELEMENT : SET_ELEMENT; A_SET : in out SET ) is
    begin
        A_SET( ELEMENT ) := TRUE;
    end INSERT;

    procedure DELETE ( ELEMENT : SET_ELEMENT; A_SET : in out SET ) is
    begin
        A_SET( ELEMENT ) := FALSE;
    end DELETE;

    function IS_IN ( ELEMENT : SET_ELEMENT; A_SET : SET )
            return BOOLEAN is
    begin
        return A_SET( ELEMENT );
    end IS_IN;
```

```
    function IS_EMPTY ( A_SET : SET ) return BOOLEAN is
        EMPTY_SET : constant SET := ( others => FALSE );
    begin
        return A_SET = EMPTY_SET;
    end IS_EMPTY;

    function EMPTY_SET return SET is
        EMPTY : constant SET := ( others => FALSE );
    begin
        return EMPTY;
    end EMPTY_SET;

    function SIZE_OF ( A_SET : SET ) return NATURAL is
        COUNT : NATURAL := 0;
    begin
        for INDEX in SET_ELEMENT loop
            if A_SET( INDEX ) then
                COUNT := COUNT + 1;
            end if;
        end loop;
        return COUNT;
    end SIZE_OF;

    function EQUAL ( LEFT, RIGHT :SET ) return BOOLEAN is
    begin
        return LEFT = RIGHT;
    end EQUAL;

    function UNION ( LEFT, RIGHT : SET ) return SET is
    begin
        return LEFT or RIGHT;
    end UNION;

    function INTERSECTION ( LEFT, RIGHT : SET ) return SET is
    begin
        return LEFT and RIGHT;
    end INTERSECTION;

    function DIFFERENCE ( LEFT, RIGHT : SET ) return SET is
    begin
        return LEFT and not RIGHT;
    end DIFFERENCE;

    function COMPLEMENT ( A_SET : SET ) return SET is
    begin
        return not A_SET;
    end COMPLEMENT;

end SET_PACKAGE;
```

Figure 11.23 The body for the set package.

Summary of Problem Solving and Programming Techniques

- Records can be used to combine data of different types into a single compound value of a record type.
- A component variable of a record variable can be used anyplace that a simple variable of the component type can be used.
- A record variable without a component specifier may be used in an assignment statement like `ITEM_1 := ITEM_2`.
- Either a record component or an entire record may be passed as a parameter to a procedure. In the first case the formal parameter type must be a component type of the record; in the second case it must be the record type.
- Just as hierarchical control structures make a program easier to understand, so do hierarchical data structures. It pays to combine the basic data structure types to obtain hierarchical structures such as arrays of records, records of arrays, arrays of records of arrays, and so forth.
- When manipulating arrays of records (and other hierarchical data structures) it simplifies notation and reasoning to use procedures that have a record value (or variable) as a parameter or parameters, and to manipulate the records with procedures. This is a form of data and procedural abstraction that eliminates notational detail from the body of the program.
- Always consider the possibility of alternative data structures. Just because you find one that works does not mean that you have found the best one.
- Parallel arrays and arrays of records are data structures that serve the same function. Which one you choose for a particular application will depend on the details of that application.

Summary of Ada Constructs

simple record type declaration

Syntax:

```
type type__name is
        record
            component__ident__1 : component__type__1;
            component__ident__2 : component__type__2;
                                .
                                .
                                .
            component__ident__n : <component__type__n;
        end Record;
```

Example:

```
type PERSON is record
                    NAME : STRING( 1 . . 20 );
                    AGE  : AGE_RANGE;
                    HEIGHT : FLOAT;
```

```
                    WEIGHT : FLOAT;
                end record;
type SAMPLE is record
                    A : INTEGER;
                    B : CHARACTER;
                end record;
```

The *type_name* is an identifier that will name the record type. The component identifiers *component_ident_1, component_ident_2, . . . component_ident n* can be any non-reserved-word identifiers. All these identifiers must be different. The component types may be any Ada types and may be different from one another. If two component identifiers are of the same type, then their declaration may be combined by separating them with commas and only listing the component type once, like so:

```
type PERSON is record
                    NAME : STRING( 1 . . 20 );
                    AGE  : AGE_RANGE;
                    HEIGHT,
                    WEIGHT : FLOAT;
                end record;
```

The above type declaration is equivalent to the first type declaration given in the examples.

record variable declaration

Syntax:

variable_name (, *variable_name*) : *type_name* ; -- (optional repeat)

Example:

```
MS_X, MR_Y : PERSON;
SAM : SAMPLE;
```

This is the same form as any other variable declaration. Note that no component identifiers are used.

component variable of a record_variable

Syntax:

record_variable.component_identifier

Example:

```
MS_X.HEIGHT
```

This is a variable of the type given after *component_identifier* in the type definition for the type of the *record_variable*.

variant_record (optional)

Syntax:

```
type type_name ( discriminant : type_name [ := expression]) is -- [optional]
     record
          component_ident_1 : component_type_1;
          component_ident_2 : component_type_2;
                  .
                  .
                  .
          component_ident_n : component_type_n;
          case discriminant is
               When choice_1 => variant_description_1;
               When choice_2 => variant_description_2;
                    .
                    .
                    .
               when others => variant_description_m;
          end case;
     end record;
```

Example:

```
subtype MMDDYY is STRING( 1 . . 6 );
subtype NAME_TYPE is STRING( 1 . . 25 );
type STATUS_TYPE is ( DIVORCED, MARRIED, SINGLE, WIDOWED );
type SEX_TYPE is ( FEMALE, MALE );
type PERSON ( MARITAL_STATUS : STATUS_TYPE := SINGLE ) is
     record
          NAME                 : NAME_TYPE;
          SEX                  : SEX_TYPE;
          DATE_OF_BIRTH        : MMDDYY;
          NUMBER_OF_DEPENDENTS : NATURAL;
          case MARITAL_STATUS is
               when DIVORCED => DATE_OF_DIVORCE : MMDDYY;
               when MARRIED  => SPOUSE_NAME     : NAME_TYPE;
               when SINGLE   => null;
               when WIDOWED  => DATE_OF_DEATH   : MMDDYY;
          end case;
     end record;
```

The *discriminant* is any nonreserved-word identifier. The *type__name* that follows is the type name of a subrange or discrete type. It is the type for the component named *discriminant*. The fixed part is the same as in a simple record type definition, which is described in the first entry of this summary. The *choice__i* are each constants or discrete ranges or it can be a list of constants or discrete ranges of the type of the discriminant. Each *variant__description__i* is a list of component identifiers, followed by their types, with colons and semicolons inserted as in the fixed part. All the component identifiers must be different.

renames clause

Syntax:

identifier : *type__name* **renames** *variable*;

Example:

```
ELEMENT : INTEGER renames VECTOR( INDEX );
```

The **renames** clause allows the programmer to provide an alias for any variable. This is particularly helpful if the variable involves an array index computation or a record component that is referenced often in the code that follows or is in a loop that is repeated many times.

Exercises

Self-Test Exercises

5. Suppose WAREHOUSE is declared as follows, where the type is declared as in Figure 11.13:

```
WAREHOUSE : ITEM_LIST;
```

Write Ada expressions for each of the following:

(a) The third item on the list
(b) The price of the third item on the list WAREHOUSE
(c) The sixth letter of the name of the tenth item on the list
(d) The length of the name of the second item on the list

6. The inventory of a shoe store lists shoes by stock numbers. With each stock number there is associated a style number in the range 0 to 50, the number of pairs in each size (sizes range from 3 to 14), and a price. A program is to be written to keep track of the inventory. Give type declarations for two different ways to structure the inventory data: as parallel arrays and as an array of records.

7. (This is for the optional section on sets.) Determine the value returned by each of the following calls to functions in the SET_PACKAGE:

(a) Assume SET__1 has the value 7, 8, 9 and SET__2 has 8, 1, 3:

```
UNION ( SET_1, SET_2 )
INTERSECTION ( SET_1, SET_2 )
```

(b) Assume SET__1 has the value 7, 8, 9 and SET__2 is empty:

```
UNION ( SET_1, SET_2 )
```

(c) Assume SET__1 has the value 7, 8, 9 and SET__2 is 31, 19:

```
INTERSECTION ( SET_1, SET_2 )
```

(d) Assume SET__1 has the value 7, 8, 9 and SET__2 is 8, 9:

```
DIFFERENCE ( SET_1, SET_2 )
```

(e) Assume SET_1 has the value 7, 8, 9 and SET_2 is 8, 9, 7:

```
SET_1 = SET_2
```

(f) Assume SET_1 has the value 7, 8, 9 and SET_2 is 1, 2, 3:

```
SET_1 = SET_2
```

(g) Assume SET_1 has the value 7, 8, 9 and SET_2 is 1, 2, 3:

```
SET_1 /= SET_2
```

Interactive Exercises

8. Write a program to read data from the keyboard into a record of the type given below and then echo the data back to the screen.

```
type SAMPLE is record
                      CODE  : CHARACTER;
                      VALUE : INTEGER;
                 end record;
```

9. Redo Exercise 8, but this time replace the type CHARACTER with the type `CHARACTER_STRING`, which is declared in Figure 11.11a.

10. Write a program to fill (with data read from the keyboard) one record of the type `ITEM_LIST`, which is declared in Figure 11.13. Use a **renames** clause.

Programming Exercises

11. Write a program that keeps the inventory for a shoe store in an array of records. Use the type declaration from Exercise 6. (See Answers to Self-Test Exercises in the back of the book.) The user is given the following choices: enter a new record, display a record, change the price of a stock item, or change the number on hand. When specifying a record, the user may give either the stock number or the style number. The array index can be used as a stock number. If the user decides to change the stock on hand, the program should ask which sizes will have their stock on hand changed. The program should be designed to run indefinitely, keeping track of changes in stock.

12. Write an inventory program for items whose record descriptions are of type `ITEM`, which is given in Figure 11.13. The program reads in a list of records entered at the keyboard and stores them in an array of records. The program then allows the user to inquire about records. The user can ask to see all records with a given component name or all records in a given price range, such as $5.00 to $9.99, or all records of a given quantity range, such as over 100, under 2, or between 10 and 20.

13. Write a grading program for a class with the following grading policies:

(a) There are three quizzes, each graded on the basis of 10 points.
(b) There is one midterm exam and one final exam, each graded on the basis of 100 points.

(c) The final exam counts for 50% of the grade, the midterm counts for 25%, and the quizzes count for 25%. (Do not forget to normalize the quiz scores. They should be converted to a percent before they are averaged in.) Grades are determined by the following rules: 90 . . 100 is an 'A', 80 . . 89 is a 'B', 70 . . 79 is a 'C', 60 . . 69 is a 'D', below 60 is an 'F'.

The program reads in the student's name and various scores and outputs a table of all students showing each student's name, all scores, average numeric score, and final letter grade. The program also outputs the class average for the final numeric score.

14. Modify the previous exercise in the following ways:

(a) The table of students also shows the difference between each student's final numeric score and the class average.
(b) The program also calculates the median value of the final numeric scores. (The median score is the score that has as many scores located above it on the list as below it; that is, the "midpoint" score. If there is an even number of scores, there are two scores in the middle. In that case the median is the average of those two scores.)
(c) The table of students also shows the difference between each student's final numeric score and the median score.

15. Write a program that reads a line of text into an array of records of type CHARACTER_STRING, as defined in Figure 11.11a. Each word is read into one record of the array. Each punctuation symbol such as a comma, colon, and so forth is also read into a single record. (You may assume that the only punctuation symbols are commas, colons, periods, exclamation marks, and question marks.) The sentence is then output with correct spaces and capitalization. For example, the input

```
hi , How are yOU?
```

should produce the output

```
Hi, how are you?
```

You need not be concerned about capitalizing proper names. If "John" is changed to "john," that will be acceptable. You will want to write a procedure PUT that is like PUT_STRING except it does not advance to the next line. (The code is the same except that the final NEW_LINE is omitted.) You will probably want to design a special procedure for reading single words rather than use the procedure GET_STRING.

16. Write string-manipulating procedures for strings of the type `CHARACTER_STRING`, as declared in Figure 11.11a. There should be a catenation function; for example, the catenation of "do be" and "do" is "do bedo." There should be a pattern-searching function like the function `SUBPATTERN` given in Figure 10.10, but you need to make it applicable to this new definition of the type CHARACTER_STRING. The function `SUBPATTERN` that you design should return the location where the first symbol of the pattern is found in the target; if the pattern is not found, an exception should be raised. There should also be a procedure to delete a substring specified by symbol positions; for example, the procedure should be capable of deleting symbols number 2 to 4 from "abcdefg" to obtain "afg." The string being manipulated should be a variable parameter that is changed by the procedure. There should be a procedure to insert a string at a position; for example, the procedure should be capable

of accepting instructions equivalent to insert ''sam'' after location 2 in ''dobedo'' to deliver the string ''dosambedo.'' The string like ''dobedo'' is an `in out` parameter whose value is changed to the new value like ''dosambedo.'' Embed these procedures in the `STRING_PACKAGE` and write a test program.

17. Write a program to play ''clock patience,'' displaying the game configurations on the screen. ''Clock patience'' is a solitaire card game played as follows: The cards in a 52-card deck are shuffled and dealt into 12 piles of 4 each in a ''clock'' circle, with the remaining four cards in the middle. A move consists of taking a card from a pile and placing it under the pile where it belongs, and this pile provides the card for the next move. (Cards are ordered clockwise: ace for one, then two, three, etc., to queen.) The center pile is for the kings. The game terminates when the four kings have been placed on the center pile. The game is considered successful if all the other cards are correctly placed.

18. (You should know about random number generators to do this exercise. They are covered in Chapter 8.) Write a procedure declaration for a procedure called DEAL that sets the values of a variable parameter of a record type to values that represent a card chosen at random from a standard 52-card deck. The function should also keep track of the cards already dealt out so it does not deal a card twice. A card will be represented as two component values, one for the ''value'' (ace, two, etc.) and one for the suit (diamonds, clubs, etc.). Use an array of records parameter to keep track of the cards already dealt out.

19. Write a program to score five-card poker hands into one of the following categories: nothing, one pair, two pairs, three of a kind, straight (in order), flush (all the same suit), full house (one pair and three of a kind), four of a kind, and straight-flush (both straight and flush). Use an array of records to store the hand. The array index type is `1 .. 5`, the records have one component for the value and one for the suit of a card.

20. (You should know about random number generators to do this exercise. They are covered in Chapter 8. The exercises 18 and 19 in this chapter should be done before this one is done.) Write a program to play five-card draw poker with the user. The user and the program each get five cards. They may discard and receive replacements for up to three cards. The hands are then scored according to the order given in Exercise 19. Do not forget to keep track of the cards already dealt so that no card is dealt twice. In the easy version only the above ordering is used. So any two hands with three of a kind, for example, are equal. In the harder version the hands are compared further; for example, three aces beat three jacks.

References for Further Reading

A. Aho, J. Hopcroft, and J. Ullman, *Data Structures and Algorithms* (Reading, MA: Addison-Wesley, 1983).

M. B. Feldman, *Data Structures with Ada* (Reston, VA: Reston Publishing Company Inc., 1985).

C. A. R. Hoare, ''Notes on Data Structuring,'' in O. J. Dahl, E. W. Dijkstra, and C. A. R. Hoare, *Structured Programming* (New York: Academic Press, 1972).

C H A P T E R

12

PROGRAMMING DESIGN METHODOLOGY

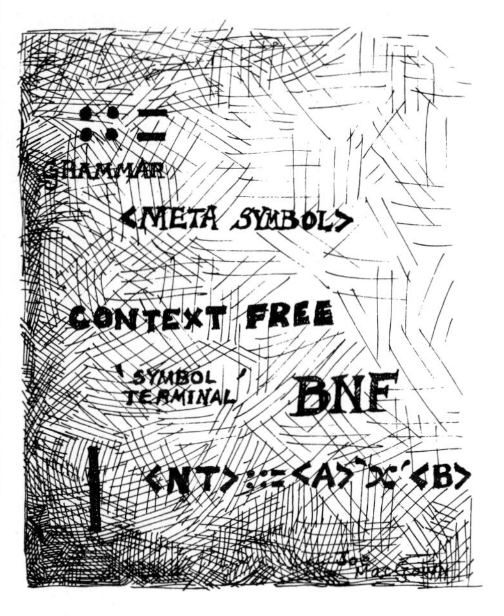

Backus-Naur Form

John Backus devised a notation for describing the syntax of a programming language. Peter Naur suggested some changes in the notation, and it was used to describe the syntax of the programming language ALGOL 60. ALGOL 60 was the forerunner of modern block-structured languages, including Ada. This simple notation, which uses a combination of only four symbols (< > : : = |), became known as Backus-Naur Form.

Chapter Contents

The production of a program can be divided into two phases: the problem solving phase, including problem definition and algorithm design, and the implementation phase, during which the actual program code is produced. Testing and debugging takes place during both of these phases. Throughout this book we have described a number of techniques to apply at various points in this process. In this chapter we summarize these techniques and then go on to discuss a few other issues connected with the design and maintenance of computer programs.

Some Guidelines for Designing Algorithms

If we could provide you with a method that is guaranteed to lead you to a correct algorithm for any problem you might encounter, then programming would be a very simple task. However, neither this nor any other book can provide such a method. There is no algorithm for writing algorithms. Designing algorithms is a creative process. There are, however, some guidelines that can sometimes help in your search for algorithms. These guidelines have some similarity to an algorithm for writing algorithms. They do, however, fall short of being an algorithm for producing algorithms in two ways: the steps are not precisely defined, and they are not guaranteed to produce a correct algorithm. The guidelines are listed in Figure 12.1, and each step is discussed in the paragraphs that follow.

Some Guidelines for Algorithm Design

1. Formulate a precise statement of the problem to be solved by the algorithm.
2. See if somebody has already formulated an algorithm to solve the problem.
3. See if any standard techniques can be used to solve the problem.
4. See if the problem is a slight variation of a problem for which somebody has already formulated an algorithm. If so, try to adapt that known algorithm to the new problem.
5. Design a data structure to organize the data involved.
6. Break the problem into subproblems and apply this method to each of the subproblems.
7. If all else fails, simplify the problem and apply this method to the simplified problem. When you obtain a solution to the simplified problem, try to adapt the algorithm to fit the real problem. If that fails, or if the algorithm produced is unclear, incorrect, or inappropriate to the real problem, then discard this first attempt and start the process all over again at step 1. (You should then have a better feel for the problem and a better chance of success.)

Figure 12.1 Guidelines.

defining the problem

The original formulation of a problem is typically imprecise, incomplete, or both. Before attempting to formulate an algorithm for a problem, be sure the problem definition has been made complete and precise. In particular be certain that

- You have complete and precise specifications for the inputs that will be needed.
- You have complete and precise specifications for the output.
- You know how the program must react to incorrect data: Is it required to issue an error message? Must it be able to continue computing, or may it end when it encounters input of the wrong type or in the wrong format?
- You know when the program should end and how the program will know when it is time to end.

using known algorithms

The algorithm may be produced at any point after step 1 of our guidelines. The earlier the better. For example, suppose you are asked to write a program to sort a list. There are a number of well-known algorithms for the problem, such as the sorting algorithm discussed in Chapter 10. You can simply use that algorithm and perhaps even a modified version of the code given there. If you take an existing algorithm that has stood the test of time, it is likely to be more efficient and less likely to contain any subtle errors. You may wish to solve these problems on your own as a training exercise, but in a ''real-world'' situation, where it is the performance of the program that counts, you should always see what algorithms others have produced.

using standard techniques

Step 3 requires that you cultivate a ''bag of tricks,'' or do a search of the literature, or both. A number of tricks are well known to experienced programmers. In Chapter 7 we gave a number of well-known techniques for terminating a loop that reads in input data. An example of one of the techniques we presented there was the use of a sentinel value to mark the end of a list of input numbers. Other more complicated techniques are discussed throughout this book. Frequently these so-called ''tricks'' offer rare and brilliant insights that are easy to understand and use but difficult to discover on your own.

adapting another algorithm

As a simple example of step 4, consider the following code for computing the sum of the numbers stored in an array `LIST`:

```
SUM := 0;
for INDEX in LIST'FIRST . . LIST'LAST
loop
     SUM := SUM + LIST( INDEX );
end loop;
```

If instead we wish to compute the product of all the numbers in the array, we can adapt the algorithm by substituting multiplication for addition and by substituting 1 for zero. If we also rename the variable SUM to PRODUCT, that yields

```
PRODUCT := 1;
for INDEX in LIST'FIRST . . LIST'LAST
loop
     PRODUCT := PRODUCT * LIST( INDEX );
end loop;
```

A more complicated example is given in Chapter 11, where we take an algorithm for sorting arrays of numbers and adapt it to obtain a procedure to sort arrays of records.

If there is no existing algorithm or standard techniques that can be applied to the problem, then you must design an algorithm from scratch. But before going on to design the algorithm, you must first design a suitable data structure. Steps 5 and 6 are not unrelated. The choice of a data structure will influence the algorithm you design, and vice versa. As you design an algorithm it may prove convenient to go back and change the data structure. Do not feel that you are irrevocably committed to a data structure and that all the details of the data structure must be determined before you begin the algorithm design. You should, however, have some data structure designed before you design your algorithm. Chapters 9, 10, and 11 discuss the design of data structures composed of arrays and/or records. Other data structures are discussed in Chapters 13, 14, and 17.

choosing a data structure

Step 6 is the top-down design strategy that we have been using and advocating throughout this book. The subproblems are attacked by these same guidelines, starting with step 1. Eventually a subproblem becomes so small that its solution is obvious or one of the other steps applies, such as when there is a well-known solution to the subproblem.

using top-down design

Sometimes step 7 can be a variation on step 6. First design an algorithm with some features missing, then design embellishments for the missing features. The change-making program we designed earlier in this book is an example of this technique. In Chapter 4 we designed the basic program for calculating change. In Chapter 6 we showed how to enhance it to have much neater and clearer output. Step 7 is also the step to use when you are completely stumped by a problem and need a way to overcome a mental block. If you cannot solve the problem at hand, solve a related and simpler problem as a practice exercise. That should give you some new insights. Then throw out the practice algorithm and start over. Do not be reluctant to throw out an algorithm or a program. It is usually faster and easier to design an algorithm from scratch than to salvage a poor design.

when all else fails

These are all just guidelines. You should always consider them, but you need not adhere to them rigidly. In particular, the order of steps (especially the order of steps 3 through 6) is certainly not rigid. Moreover, these steps certainly do not make a complete list of known techniques. They are merely a general plan of attack that can and should be augmented with other design techniques. In Chapter 7 (particularly in the optional sections), we discussed some additional techniques that apply to the design of loops. Those techniques can be used in conjunction with the plan of attack given in Figure 12.1.

Writing Code

When a program is divided into subproblems, the algorithms for the subproblems can and should be coded and tested separately. Even when simply coding somebody else's algorithm, divide the algorithm into subparts and code the subparts separately. That way they can be tested and debugged separately. It is relatively easy to find a mistake in a small procedure. It is nearly impossible to find all the mistakes in a large, untested program that was coded and tested as a single large unit rather than as a collection of well-defined modules. The rules we have been advocating for indenting and documentation all apply to the task of writing code. In fact they apply even earlier. Pseudocode should have an indenting pattern and a collection of comments that will carry over with only minor changes to the final Ada code.

Abstraction and ADTs

Programs should have a conspicuously modular design. A program should be divided into self-contained subpieces. These subpieces, which are usually implemented as procedures, are a natural consequence of top-down design. Each procedure should include a header comment explaining what the procedure does. This comment should be all you need to know to use the procedure. If the procedure is designed with this in mind, then the details of how the procedure performs its task can safely be forgotten. This form of selective forgetting is called *procedural abstraction.* Using procedural abstraction you can build up a library of procedures whose internal structure may be very complicated but which are, nonetheless, straightforward to use. For example, to use the procedure `SELECTION_SORT` in Figure 9.13, you do not need to read the code. All you need to know is that it does somehow sort an array of integers.

This same method of *abstraction* may be applied to data structures and algorithms as well as procedures. When thinking about a data structure, such as an array, it is often productive to ignore certain details, such as the exact bounds on the index type. This is often referred to as *data abstraction.* When designing an algorithm, such as one for sorting, you can obtain a more general algorithm by leaving some details, such as the type of the elements being sorted, unspecified. This is often referred to as *algorithm abstraction.*

One tool that can aid in all these abstraction techniques is the use of *abstract data types (ADTs).* An *ADT* is a data structure and a collection of operations on the data structure defined so as to separate the details that a programmer using the data structure needs to know from the details of how the data structure and operations are implemented. ADTs are easily implemented in Ada using packages. The package specification contains the description of the data type and lists the available operations and their interfaces (parameters). The package body contains the implementation of the operations. The package specification is visible to the using program, while the package body containing the details of the operations is hidden. A more detailed discussion of ADTs can be found in Chapter 11.

Testing and Debugging

When you are producing a program, the natural sequence of events is first algorithm design, then coding, and then testing and debugging. However, the divisions are not, or at least should not be, very rigid. Some coding and debugging for some programs can be done before the complete algorithm is derived. When a problem is broken into subproblems, some simple testing can and usually should be done immediately. If the subproblems are well defined and fit together simply enough, then a pencil-and-paper simulation of the algorithm can be used to test this formulation of the problem. If the test cannot be carried out with pencil and paper, then a skeleton of a program can be written to see if the pieces will fit together. If the pieces do not fit together, then there is no point in proceeding to derive algorithms for the subproblems.

example of early testing

For example, consider the following problem. Suppose we wish to gather statistics on how much time student programmers spend at the terminal during any one session. Perhaps this will be used to help redesign the chairs so that students will be more comfortable while coding up their homework assignments. To get a good profile of usage, we want a program that will compute the average time per session for each individual student, as well as the average session length for all sessions used by all students. The input will consist of a list of students, with each student's name followed by a list of the times that student spent in each individual session. Dividing this problem into subproblems might produce the following pseudocode:

1. Compute each student's average time per session.
2. Output the averages.
3. Compute the average of student averages obtained in 1.
4. Output the overall average.

The presence of a logical flaw in this algorithm can be discovered by testing, even before algorithms for the subproblems are designed. Consider the following sample data:

Joseph Cool:
    10 min., 10 min.

Sally Workhard:
    60 min., 60 min., 60 min., 60 min.,
    60 min., 60 min., 60 min., 60 min.

We do not need a computer to simulate the pseudocode on this simple data. The two student averages are trivially seen to be 10 and 60 min. Now step 3 of the pseudocode says to average these two numbers, which yields

(10 + 60) / 2 = 35 min.

The algorithm's computation of the average session length is wrong. Using pencil and paper, or a little bit of mental arithmetic, or a hand-held calculator will show that the average length of a session is really

(2 * 10 + 8 * 60) / 10 = 50 min.

As it turns out, the average length of a session is not the average of the individual student averages.

All programs should be divided into procedures, and the procedures, as well as the interaction between procedures, should be tested separately. This general technique was described in more detail in the section of Chapter 5 entitled "Testing Procedures." Below we give some hints on how to test and debug the individual procedures.

syntax errors

Programming errors can be divided into three classes: syntax errors, run-time errors, and logical errors. A *syntax error* occurs when a portion of the program violates the syntax rules of the programming language, for example, omitting a required semicolon or an **end**. These are usually easy to find. The compiler will discover them and produce an error message. The error message may not accurately describe the nature or location of the error, but it definitely does indicate an error, and the location given is very likely to be the approximate location of the error.

run-time errors

Run-time errors (also called unhandled exceptions) are also errors that result from the program violating the rules of the language. However, unlike syntax errors, run-time errors are not discovered by the compiler. As illustrated in Figure 12.2, the two types of errors are discovered at different stages of program processing. A run-time error is only detected when the program is run. For example, the statement below will produce a run-time error if the value of DIVISOR is zero:

```
INVERSE := 1 / DIVISOR
```

Whether or not it is an error depends on running the program to see if DIVISOR does receive the value zero. A run-time error also produces an error message that gives some hint of the location and nature of the error. Run-time errors are harder to find than syntax errors but still have the advantage that they will produce an error message. They are hard to find because they may only occur for certain inputs and not for others. For example, the above line of code will not produce a run-time error on those inputs that cause DIVISOR to take on any value other than zero.

logical errors

The third type of error is the hardest to locate. *Logical errors* are errors in the algorithm or in the translation of the algorithm from pseudocode to Ada. They are difficult to find because the computer does not give any error message. They can occur in a perfectly valid Ada program that performs a perfectly valid computation and gives out an answer. The problem is that the answer is sometimes wrong. For example, the

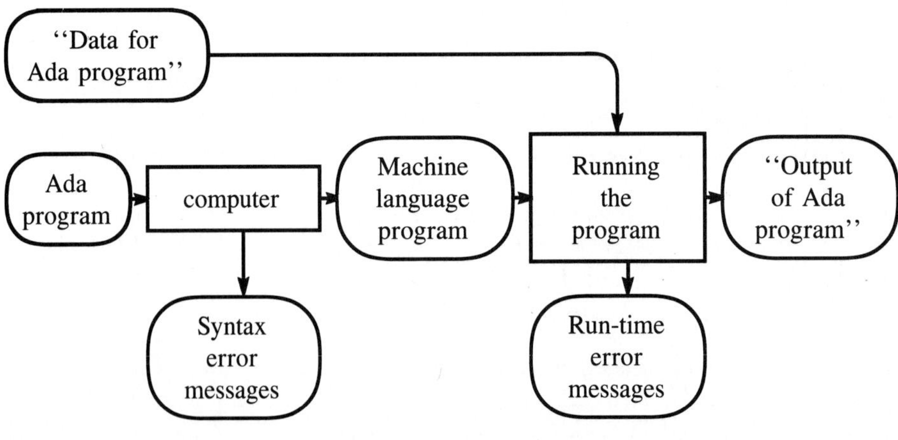

Figure 12.2 Syntax and run-time errors.

following piece of code is supposed to output the average of the elements in the array `LIST` of type `array( 0 . . 10 ) of INTEGER`:

```
SUM := 0;
for INDEX in 0 . . 10
loop
    SUM := SUM + LIST( INDEX );
end loop;
PUT ( SUM / 10 );
NEW_LINE;
```

This is a perfectly valid piece of Ada code and will run with no problems or error messages. For most values of the array elements, the answers will even look ''about right.'' However, there is a logical error. Since the array bounds go from **0** to **10**, there are 11 elements and not 10 elements. Hence the PUT statement should be

```
PUT ( SUM / 11 );
```

When a logical error is discovered, it is usually not too difficult to fix. The problem is finding logical errors. Since the computer produces no error messages for logical errors, it is difficult to be certain that a program contains no logical errors.

Correcting run-time and logical errors is a three-stage process. The first stage is error avoidance. If a program is carefully designed along the lines we have suggested in this book, then the number of such errors should be few. The second stage is testing. In the testing stage the program is checked to see if it contains any mistakes. Testing procedures separately also serves to tell you which procedures contain mistakes. The last stage is debugging. In that stage the exact nature of the error is determined and the error is corrected. (Additional discussion of these three types of errors can be found in the section of Chapter 3 entitled ''Testing and Debugging'' and in Chapter 6 in the section entitled ''Exception.'')

choosing test data

When testing a procedure, you want to find some input values or parameter values that will expose possible errors. One way to catch an error is to find input values for which you know the correct output—perhaps by doing the calculation in some other way or by looking up the answer. Then you can run the procedure or program on those values. If the procedure's answer differs from the correct answer, then you know there is a mistake in the procedure. However, always remember that just because a procedure or program works correctly on 10 or even 100 test cases, this is not a guarantee that it does not contain an error. It might make a mistake on the next input that is tried.

boundary values

One other technique to increase your confidence in a program is to use a variety of different types of test data. For example, if the data is an integer, try a large positive number, a small positive number, zero, a small negative number, a large negative number, and any other categories that come to mind. For loops, try data that will cause the loop to be executed zero times, one time, and more than one time (or as many of those cases as are possible for the loop in question). Be sure to use a representative sample of the possible *boundary values* as test data. There is no precise definition of the notion of a boundary value, but you should develop an intuitive feel for what it means. If a loop will be executed some number of times between one and ten, depending on the data, then be sure to have a test run that executes it one time and one that executes the loop ten times. If a procedure does something to only one element of an array, always test the first and last elements of the array. Of course, you should also test a "typical" (nonboundary) value.

fully exercising code

Still another testing technique consists of *fully exercising* the procedure or program. This technique consists of using a collection of test cases that will cause each part of the procedure to be executed. That means executing each statement and substatement, and also making each boolean expression that controls a loop assume the value TRUE at least once and assume the value FALSE at least once. For example, consider the following piece of code:

```
if OVERTIME > 0 then
     PROCEDURE_1;
elsif BONUS <= 0 then
     PROCEDURE_2;
elsif SICK_LEAVE >= 0 then
     PROCEDURE_3;
else
     PROCEDURE_4;
end if;
```

The call to PROCEDURE_4 will never take place unless the test data causes OVERTIME to be less than or equal to zero, while at the same time it causes BONUS to be greater than zero and SICK_LEAVE to be less than zero. The call to PROCEDURE_3 will never take place unless the test data causes OVERTIME to be less than or equal to zero, while at the same time it causes BONUS to be greater than zero and SICK_LEAVE to be greater than or equal to zero. Fully exercising a program is difficult to do. However, if the program is divided into procedures and the procedures are small, then it is possible to fully exercise each procedure separately. Figure 12.3 illustrates some other examples of fully exercising code.

```
if boolean__expression then
    sequence__of__statements
else
    sequence__of__statements
end if;
```

To test both sequences of statements requires at least two test runs, one that makes *boolean__expression* TRUE and one that makes it FALSE.

```
loop
    exit when boolean__expression;
    sequence__of__statements
end loop;
```

There should be at least two test runs: one that makes *boolean__expression* TRUE and so skips the loop, and one that makes it FALSE and so executes at least one iteration of the loop.

Figure 12.3 Fully exercising code.

An even better test of a program can be obtained with a technique called *testing all paths*. In testing all paths, the tests not only cause each statement to be executed at least once but also cause each possible combination of branch and loop behaviors to take place. Some combinations may be impossible to achieve, but the test set should cause all other combinations to occur.

testing all paths

To see the difference between fully exercising a piece of code and testing all paths, consider the following code:

```
if SALES > 0 then
     BONUS := BIG;
else
     BONUS := SMALL;
end if;
if OVERTIME > 0 then
     TAX := BIG;
else
     TAX := SMALL;
end if;
```

This piece of code can be fully exercised with two inputs, one in which both SALES and OVERTIME are positive, and one in which they are both negative. To test all paths requires four tests, as shown in Figure 12.4. Testing all paths is a good testing strategy. Unfortunately it is often difficult to find a set of test cases that will test all paths. Frequently you must settle for fully exercising the procedure and then testing as many paths as you reasonably can.

debugging

Testing can tell you that a program or procedure contains an error. Moreover, if it is done correctly, it will tell you which procedure contains the error, but it usually will not tell you what the error is. Once you know that a procedure contains an error, you still must correct the error. That is the debugging stage. At that stage frustrated programmers are sometimes tempted to make random changes, in the hope that these random changes will magically correct the errors. Random changes seldom correct the errors, and moreover, they make the program even less understandable. The way to correct an error is to test and analyze until you have located the exact cause of the error. Once the cause is located, the cure is usually easy to find.

tracing

One of the best ways to find the exact location of an error is to watch the procedure while it performs its calculation, that is, to watch the values of the various variables changing. This is called *tracing*. When a variable is traced, its value is written out either every time it is changed or at some other specified times. Some systems provide special debugging facilities for doing this automatically. If your system does not, then you can use temporary PUT statements in the manner we described in the section of Chapter 7 entitled "Debugging Loops."

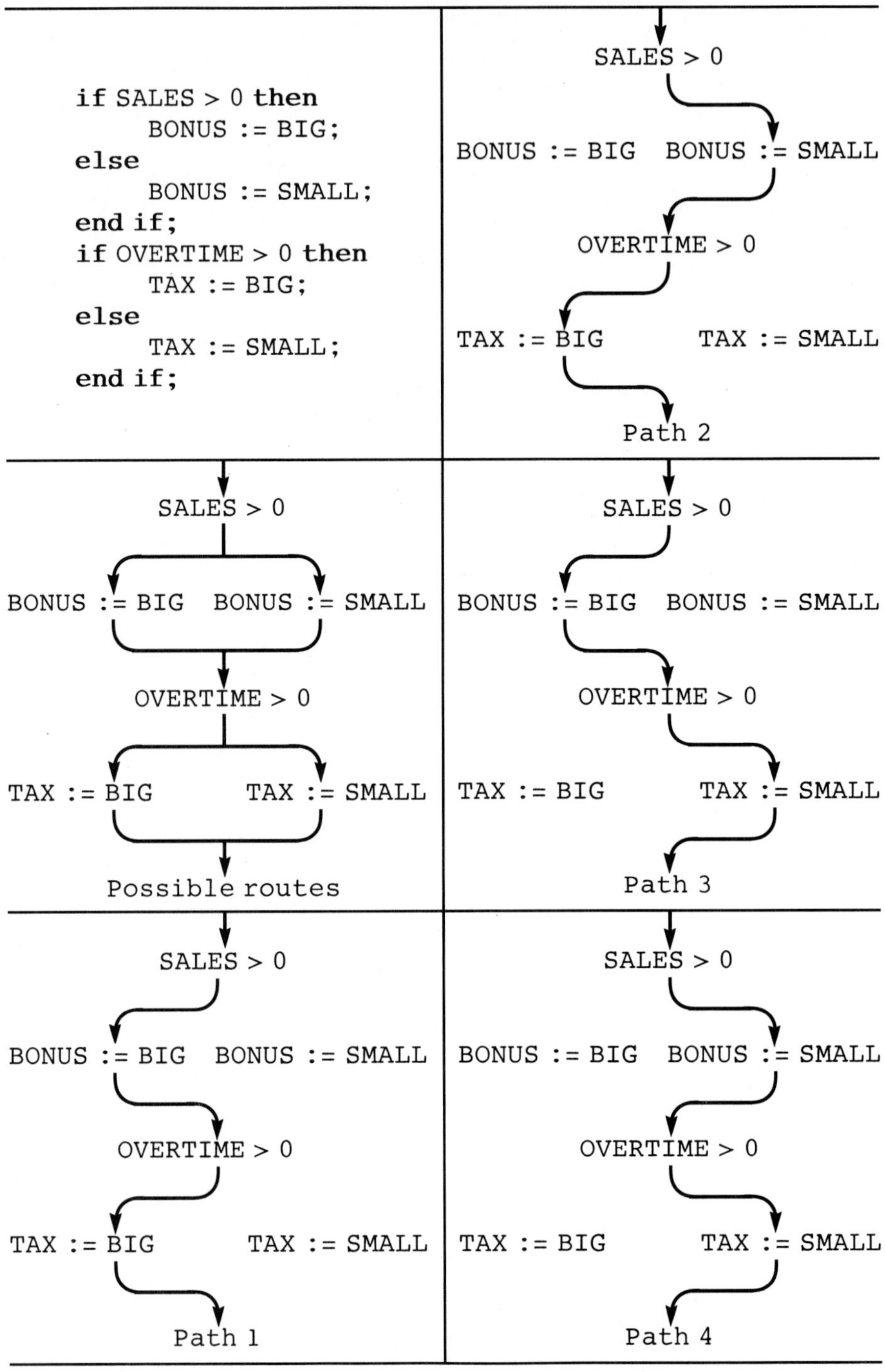

Figure 12.4 Testing all paths.

Verification

In the ideal world there would be no need for testing and debugging, because all programs would be correct. In the ideal world the programmer would prove the correctness of a program in much the same way a mathematician proves a theorem. Proving the correctness of a program, that is, proving that it does what the specifications say it is supposed to do, is called program *verification.*

Whether or not it is practical to prove the correctness of large programs is still a hotly debated issue. In practice, testing and debugging will never be completely eliminated, but they may become less necessary, and program verification may become a more common practice than it is today. For small programs verification is usually a realizable task. The debate arises when the discussion turns to large programs. There certainly is little hope of verifying a large program, such as a compiler, if you are given just the program code (without very extensive comments) and the specifications. On the other hand, if the top-down design strategy is used and each piece is verified separately, then it may be a tractable task. In this scenario the verification takes place as the program is written, not after it is finished.

The debate over verification is one of degree. How formal should the verification be, and to what extent can it be relied on? Certainly a programmer should always make a serious attempt to somehow demonstrate (at least to oneself) that the algorithms are correct and that the code accurately represents the algorithm. Code should never be designed by simply writing down something that ''looks like it might work'' and then running a few test cases ''to see if it works.''

Portability

A *portable* program is one that can be moved from one computer system to another with little or no changes. Since programs represent a large investment in programmer time, it pays to make them portable.

standard language

One way to make a program portable is to adhere closely to a *standard version* of the programming language. There are national and international organizations that set standards for the syntax and other details of programming languages. We are fortunate that with the use of the Ada programming language, there is a single definitive standard. *The Language Reference Manual* (LRM), ANSI/MIL-STD-1815A-1983, defines the language and is published by the Department of Defense (DoD). Furthermore, all Ada compilers must be tested against a validation suite of programs. No subset nor superset compiler will meet the validation test. The compiler implementation must meet all of the standards, and no extensions of the language are allowed.

The standard's initials and numbers (ANSI/MIL-STD-1815A-1983) have the following meanings: ANSI stands for the American National Standards Institute; MIL-STD stands for Military Standard; 1815 is the standard number and also the year Ada Lovelace was born; the A after 1815 means this is the first version of the standard; and 1983 is the year the LRM was approved. As impressive as all those initials and numbers may look, it is still not true that all the Ada programs will run on any system that claims to follow the Ada standards. Unfortunately there are still differences among compilers and the computers on which they run. There are a number of things in the LRM that are stated as *implementation_dependent.* As a simple example, the value of INTEGER'LAST is usually dependent on the number of bits in a word of memory for computers on which the program is run. Also, there is no way that the validation suite can test all possible combinations of language features. Despite Ada's language standard (the LRM), the disallowing of subset and superset compilers, and a validation test, there is no guarantee that an Ada program will be portable to every conceivable compiler or computer system. Because of all of these safeguards, however, Ada programs are probably more portable than programs written in any other language. Standards do serve a purpose.

Efficiency

time and storage

The *efficiency* of a program is a measure of the amount of resources consumed by the program. Traditionally the only resources considered have been time and/or storage. The less time it uses, the more time-efficient a program is. The less storage it uses, the more storage-efficient it is.

When running small programs of the type you encounter when first learning to program, efficiency is not usually an issue. If the user waits a few extra seconds for an answer, that is insignificant. A small program is also unlikely to use more than a very small fraction of the available storage. Moreover, if the program is run just a few times, then the savings are likely to be minimal at best. However, when running large programs repeatedly over a long period of time, the amount of time and storage saved can be significant. Computer time and storage cost money. Hence, if a program can be changed so that it runs faster or uses less storage, then, *all other things being equal,* the program should be changed.

In some specialized settings, efficiency is critically important. If a computer is controlling a hospital patient-monitoring system, a delay of just a fraction of a second may mean a patient's life. A very sophisticated storm-predicting program is useless if it takes two hours to predict that a tornado will arrive in one hour. A program to work in a small wrist calculator or a small satellite may have to make do with very little storage.

example searching an array

To illustrate the notion of efficiency, consider the task of searching an array of integers to see whether or not a particular integer is in the array. If the array is called VALUE and the integer being searched for is called KEY, then the following loop will accomplish the search:

```
INDEX := VALUE'FIRST;
loop
    exit when KEY = VALUE( INDEX );
    INDEX := INDEX + 1;
    exit when INDEX = VALUE'LAST;
end loop;
```

```
PUT ( KEY );
if KEY = VALUE( INDEX ) then
    PUT (" is in the array." );
else
    PUT (" is not in the array." );
end if;
NEW_LINE;
```

The loop checks successive elements of the array until it either finds the value KEY or gets to the end of the array without finding KEY.

Now let us suppose that we know the array elements are ordered as follows:

```
VALUE(VALUE'FIRST) < VALUE(VALUE'FIRST+1) < . . . < VALUE(VALUE'LAST)
```

In this case we can make the loop run more efficiently, in the sense of taking less time. If we know the list is ordered, then we can stop looking for the value KEY as soon as the following holds:

```
KEY <= VALUE( INDEX )
```

This works because, if KEY equals VALUE(INDEX), we have found the value of KEY, and if KEY is less than VALUE(INDEX), we know that KEY is smaller than all the array elements that follow and so cannot possibly equal any of them. Hence, assuming the list is ordered, we can replace the boolean expression in the first **exit when** in the loop with the following:

```
exit when KEY <= LIST( INDEX )
```

With this altered boolean expression, the loop will frequently perform fewer iterations. If the value of KEY is in the array, then the two loops perform exactly the same number of iterations. If KEY is not in the array, then "on the average" the second loop will perform a little more than half the number of iterations than the first loop. A precise definition of what we mean by "on the average" is beyond the scope of this book. However, the important thing to observe is that the second version does save a large fraction of time on a large number of inputs. The program in Figure 12.5 illustrates the savings for one particular set of values.

Program

```
with TEXT_IO;
use TEXT_IO;
procedure COMPARE_SORTS is
--                      INPUT  : A list of integers
--                               and a key for which to search.
--                      OUTPUT : A message reporting the success or
--                               failure of the search.
--                               The number of iteration completed.
--                      DESCRIPTION : The primary purpose is to compare
--                                    two searching algorithms.
```

```
type LIST is array( 1 . . 10 ) of INTEGER;
NUMBER : LIST;
KEY : INTEGER;
package NUMBER_IO is new INTEGER_IO ( INTEGER );
use NUMBER_IO;
procedure SEARCH_1 ( VALUE : in LIST; KEY : in INTEGER ) is
    INDEX : INTEGER;
begin -- Search_1
    INDEX := VALUE'FIRST;
    loop
        exit when KEY = VALUE( INDEX );
        INDEX := INDEX + 1;
        exit when INDEX = VALUE'LAST;
    end loop;
    PUT ( KEY );
    if KEY = VALUE( INDEX ) then
        PUT ( " is in the array." );
    else
        PUT ( " is not in the array." );
    end if;
    NEW_LINE;
    PUT ("Search 1 executed " );
    PUT ( INDEX - VALUE'FIRST );
    PUT ( " iterations." );
    NEW_LINE;
end SEARCH_1;
procedure SEARCH_2 ( VALUE : in LIST; KEY : in INTEGER ) is
    INDEX : INTEGER;
begin -- Search_2
    INDEX := VALUE'FIRST;
    loop
        exit when KEY <= VALUE( INDEX );
        INDEX := INDEX + 1;
        exit when INDEX = VALUE'LAST;
    end loop;
    PUT ( KEY );
    if KEY = VALUE( INDEX ) then
        PUT (" is in the array." );
    else
        PUT (" is not in the array." );
    end if;
    NEW_LINE;
    PUT ( "Search 2 executed " );
    PUT ( INDEX - VALUE'FIRST );
    PUT ( " iterations." );
    NEW_LINE;
end SEARCH_2;
```

```
begin -- Compare_Sorts
    PUT ( "Enter 10 integers in ascending order:" ); NEW_LINE;
    for INDEX in NUMBER'FIRST . . NUMBER'LAST
    loop
        GET ( NUMBER( INDEX ) );
    end loop;
    SKIP_LINE;
    PUT ( "Enter a KEY to search for:" ); NEW_LINE;
    GET ( KEY ); SKIP_LINE;
    SEARCH_1 ( NUMBER, KEY );
    SEARCH_2 ( NUMBER, KEY );
end COMPARE_SORTS;
```

Sample Dialogue

```
Enter 10 integers in ascending order:
2 4 6 8 10 12 14 16 18 2001
Enter a KEY to search for:
11
    11 is not in the array.
Search 1 executed      9 iterations.
    11 is not in the array.
Search 2 executed      5 iterations.
```

Figure 12.5 Comparing two algorithms.

Occasionally, a simple change like the one we just described can improve efficiency significantly. More often, however, the savings gained by a minor change are correspondingly minor. To make substantial savings, a completely new and more complicated algorithm is usually required. In the next section we discuss the advisability of using a complicated, efficient algorithm as opposed to a simple, less efficient one.

You should also be aware of the fact that the first algorithm works regardless of the ordering of the list. The second algorithm only works if the list was previously sorted.

Efficiency Versus Clarity

The current trend is to pay less attention to time and storage efficiency. The reason for this switch is that computer time and storage have become less expensive, while programmer time has become more costly. It simply does not make sense to pay thousands of dollars (or even much less) in programmer salaries to realize a few dollars in savings in computer usage.

Frequently there are also other hidden costs in making a program very "efficient." A typical way to arrive at an "efficient" program is to start with a simple, easy-to-understand, correctly running program and then to make changes to the program so it runs faster or uses less storage. In the process of doing so, a number of unfortunate things can happen. The changes may introduce an error. Ultimately that produces an inefficient program. Getting the wrong answer quickly is never a bargain. Changing a program to make it run faster may make the program harder to understand. Sometime later, when the program needs to be changed, this will increase the time needed to change it and will make errors more likely. Large programs typically have a life span in which they are modified numerous times by a series of different programmers. In that situation, clarity is the critically important consideration. When the choice is between clarity and efficiency, it usually pays to choose clarity.

A good strategy is the following: First, make sure the program is clear and correct. Second, within those constraints and the constraints of available programmer time, it may pay to make the program more time and storage efficient.

Software Engineering

Software engineering is that branch of science and engineering that deals with the production and maintenance of large software systems. Like all engineering endeavors it is concerned with both the quality of its products and the economies of their production and use. It is a "real-world" discipline concerned with the production of reliable, economical products for the use of its customers. Since this makes it sound like it is concerned more with the performance of the final product than with the appearance of the product, you might think it is not concerned with niceties of style and technique, such as commenting rules, top-down design, and the use of abstraction. However, one indication of how very useful software engineering techniques are is that they become even more important when designing a large system or any system for a real-world application. Software engineering is concerned with all the design principles that we have advocated throughout this text. It is also concerned with other considerations that only come into play when producing large software systems.

what is "large"?

The programs presented in an introductory programming book are extremely small compared to the programs that professional programmers typically work on. One widely used Ada compiler consists of more than 50,000 lines of high-level-language code. If written as small as the text of this book, that program would occupy over 900 pages! Programs that large are qualitatively as well as quantitatively different from the sorts of small programs we have seen. It has been said that "you can't taste beer with a sip." Using that as a metaphor, we can say that the typical reader of this book has had only a "sip" of programming. The reader who completes this book and writes programs from the exercises in each chapter will have tasted programming. However, large programs really do have a different flavor from small programs. For one thing, they are produced by teams of programmers rather than single programmers working alone or almost alone.

group effort

A program as large as a compiler or a complete operating system is not written by a single person. The effort is too large for any individual. To take an extreme case, F. P. Brooks reports that the design of the IBM OS/360 operating systems consumed 5000 "man-years" (see "References" at the end of this chapter). That figure includes support staff and probably would be lower today. However, it is clear that the job is too large for any one programmer. The production of a piece of software of that size requires a major organizational effort. It is a management feat as well as a design feat. The book by Brooks, cited at the end of this chapter, gives a good description of the management problems involved in designing large programs. Most of the book is understandable to anyone who has read the first few chapters of this book.

software life cycle

Development of large software systems is a long-term process. A large amount of planning needs to be done before any code is written. Moreover, the release of a finished system for customers to use does not end the development process. The system must be continually maintained and updated. This entire development process is often referred to as the *software life cycle.* This life cycle can be divided into the following six phases:

1. Analysis and specification of the task
2. Design of the software
3. Implementation (coding)
4. Testing
5. Maintenance and evolution of the system
6. Obsolescence

analysis phase

The first step in the production of a software system is to decide exactly what the system is supposed to do. You might be inclined to think that this analysis phase is the easiest part of the process. After all, the system is supposed to do what the customers want it to do, so all that needs be done is to ask the customers what they want. Unfortunately, it is not that simple. The end user of the system typically has only a vague, high-level idea of what the system should do. The user's characterization of the task is likely to be a general statement such as ''keep my books,'' or ''produce an automated testing system for my class,'' or ''give me an interactive design environment,'' or some other equally nonspecific description. The end user typically does not know exactly what he or she wants the system to do. Hence, the software analyst must interact with the user to find out what the user *will* want the system to do. At this stage questions such as the following must all be asked and answered: What should the input and output look like? What should the system do when the user makes errors in input? Who will be using the system, trained specialists or casual users? How fast must the system be? How often and in what ways will it be necessary to change the system after it is delivered?

specifications

The end result of the analysis phase is a specification of the software's requirements. This specification must tell not only what the input and output is to look like, but must also specify exactly what machine environment(s) it must work in, how much data the system must accommodate, how many users it must serve, what specific tests the system must successfully pass, what kind of documentation will accompany the system, what future modifications the system must accommodate, and numerous other details on the capacity of the system. This specification is the definition of the system. It states what the software team is promising to deliver. The final product will be measured against this yardstick.

design phase

The specification for a software system tells *what* the system should do. The design of the system tells *how* it is to be done. For a very small system, the design phase can be as simple as actually writing the algorithm in pseudocode. For a very large system, this phase still involves designing the algorithm, but it includes the design and interaction of a number of different algorithms, often only specified in outline form, as well as a strategy for filling in the details and producing the code. In this phase, the software team formulates its plan of attack. The difficult problems are likely to be organizational. Most software design teams use a collection of known algorithms or variations on known algorithms rather than producing breakthrough discoveries of new and clever algorithm techniques. However, the integration and adaptation of a number of known algorithms to a very large task is a formidable challenge. In fact it is so formidable that many large, well-funded, and highly trained teams have failed to perform their tasks successfully. Most of the classic design tools of software engineering, such as top-down design and abstraction, were formulated primarily to facilitate this design phase.

coding

Coding is far from the most difficult of the six phases in the software life cycle. However, the size of the task does present problems that do not arise when coding the short programs encountered in introductory programming classes. Since coding of a large software system is a team effort, questions of style must be made explicit to ensure a consistent style. All programmers must know what conventions are being used for choosing identifier names, layout style, commenting style, size of subprograms, parameter-passing conventions, and a host of other conventions. The work must be divided among the members of the programming team. This division of labor is not simply a matter of assigning one person to each of the subtasks produced by top-down design. There are overall tasks to be divided. Somebody needs to be in charge. Somebody typically serves as librarian to keep the records on documentation and back-up copies of software.

testing

Testing a large software system is a major undertaking. One cannot simply run the entire system, note the error messages, and then look through the code in hopes of finding and fixing bugs. The first testing absolutely must be performed on smaller submodules so as to localize the search for bugs. In addition to the testing that is designed and carried out by the programming team, large software systems must also undergo acceptance testing. After the system is completed and tested by the software production team, it is given to the user for acceptance testing. In acceptance testing the software may be run on a collection of bench mark programs or on a test suite. A *bench mark program* is a program whose run time and other statistics are known so that the system's efficiency can be compared to that of other systems. A *test suite* is something like a large bench mark program or a collection of bench mark programs that systematically exercise each of the different functions that the system is supposed to satisfy to see if the system performs correctly and efficiently. If a test suite is reliable enough, that would be the end of the testing process, but no test suite can guarantee that the system will perform well in all situations. The final testing is *site testing,* in which the system is placed in service with a small group of users to see what unexpected problems arise. This small group of users provides the "field testing" that can be obtained only in a day-to-day real-world setting. The problems encountered in the site testing phase are typically severe enough to warrant a second site test after the system has been revised in response to the results of the first site test.

maintenance The end of the software engineering team's job is not marked by the system passing its site tests and being released for general use. The software must be maintained and updated. In fact the cost of maintenance typically far exceeds the cost of producing the original system. A large system is likely to exhibit bugs for some time after it is released. These bugs must be diagnosed and fixed. As new hardware is introduced, the system may be modified to run in new environments. As users' needs change, it is less expensive and quicker to modify the existing system than to produce a totally new system. The major part of a system programmer's time is spent on maintenance, not on designing completely new systems.

obsolescence Perhaps the last step in the software life cycle should be called "death." However, while all systems eventually become obsolete, they often do not go away. A large system represents such a huge capital investment that it usually seems less expensive to modify the existing system rather than build a completely new system. Often this impression is correct. Large systems are designed to be modified. A system may be productively revised many times. However, even large programs eventually become out-of-date in their basic design. Unless a large program is well written and suitable for the task at hand, just as is the case with a small program, it is more efficient to write a new program than it is to fix the old one.

Summary of Terms

abstract data type (ADT) A data structure (or data structures) and a collection of operations on the data structure defined so as to separate the details a programmer using the data structure needs to know from the details of how the data structure and operations are implemented.

algorithm abstraction Certain details of virtually any algorithm, as well as certain details of the data manipulated by the algorithm, are needed to implement the algorithm as Ada code, but they are not needed to formulate the algorithm. Algorithm abstraction is the disregarding ("forgetting") of some or all of these details.

data abstraction Disregarding ("forgetting") those features of a data structure that are irrelevant to the problems, algorithms, or programs under consideration.

efficiency The efficiency of a program is measured by the amount of resources that the program consumes. The less resources it consumes, the more efficient it is. Time and storage are the resources that are usually considered.

fully exercise A technique for testing a piece of code (like a program or procedure). It consists of finding a set of test inputs such that running the program on the test inputs will cause each statement and substatement to be executed on at least one of the test runs and will cause each boolean expression that controls a loop to assume the value TRUE on at least one run and FALSE on at least one run.

logical error A program error that is due to an error in the algorithm or an error in translating the algorithm into the programming language. Normally logical errors produce no error messages.

portability A program is portable if it can be moved from one system to another with little or no change.

procedural abstraction Disregarding (''forgetting'') those features of a procedure that are irrelevant to the problems, algorithms, or programs under consideration.

run-time error (exception) A program error that is discovered by the computer system at the time that the program is run. See *syntax error.*

syntax error An error consisting of a violation of the syntax rules of a language. Syntax errors are discovered and reported by the compiler. See *run-time error.*

testing all paths A technique for testing a piece of code (like a program or procedure). It consists of finding a set of test inputs such that running the program on the test inputs will cause each possible combination of branch and loop behaviors to occur on at least one of the runs.

tracing Inserting PUT statements into a program so that the values of the variables will be written out as the program performs its calculations. Some systems have debugging facilities that do this automatically.

verification Verifying a program means proving that it meets the specifications for the task it is supposed to perform.

Exercises

Self-Test Exercises

1. The following piece of code is supposed to set SUM equal to the sum of the first 100 positive numbers. It contains a bug. What is it?

```
SUM := 0;
COUNT := 1;
loop
     SUM := SUM + COUNT;
     COUNT := COUNT + 1;
     exit when COUNT >= 100;
end loop;
```

If you cannot find the bug, then replace **100** by **3** and trace the computation, either with pencil and paper or by embedding the code and a PUT statement in a program.

2. Choose some input values to fully exercise the following piece of code (all the variables are of type INTEGER):

```
GET ( OMEGA ); GET ( BRAVO ); GET ( CHARLIE );
SKIP_LINE;
if OMEGA >= 5 then
     ALPHA := BRAVO;
else
     ALPHA := CHARLIE;
end if;
```

```
SUM := 0;
loop
    exit when OMEGA <= 0;
    SUM := SUM + OMEGA;
    OMEGA := OMEGA - 1;
end loop;
```

3. Choose some input values to test all paths in the code of Exercise 2.

4. What is wrong with the following program? (It correctly computes the average of 10 integers.)

```
with I_O; use I_O;
procedure  MAIN is
    subtype LIST_RANGE is INTEGER range 1 . . 10;
    type LIST is array( LIST_RANGE ) of INTEGER;
    AVERAGE : FLOAT;
    SUM : INTEGER := 0;
    VALUE : LIST;
begin -- Main
    PUT ( "Enter 10 integers:" ); NEW_LINE;
    for INDEX in LIST_RANGE
    loop
        GET ( VALUE( INDEX ) );
    end loop;
    for INDEX in LIST_RANGE
    loop
        SUM := SUM + VALUE( INDEX );
    end loop;
    AVERAGE := FLOAT ( SUM ) / 10.0;
    PUT ( "The average is: " );
    PUT ( AVERAGE );
    NEW_LINE;
end MAIN;
```

Interactive Exercises

5. Redesign the algorithm for computing average terminal session times that was given in the pseudocode in the section entitled "Testing and Debugging." As noted in the text, the pseudocode contains a logical error.

6. If you have access to more than one computer with Ada available, run some of your programs from previous exercises on two or more machines. Is it necessary to change the programs in any way?

Programming Exercises

7. Write a program to read in a list of 100 or fewer integers, and then do any of the following, as the user requests:

(a) Display the list in sorted order largest to smallest.
(b) Display the list in sorted order smallest to largest.
(c) Compute the average.
(d) Compute the mean.
(e) Compute percentiles (e.g., the tenth percentile is a score where 10% of the scores are equal to or below it.).
(f) List the scores in the order largest to smallest or smallest to largest showing how much each differs from the average and/or median.

Do this jointly with two or three other people. Each person should do separate subtasks and the code should be integrated into a single program.

8. (To do this one you and another group must have done Exercise 7.) The two groups exchange programs, and then each modifies the other's program as follows: The option of computing the standard deviation is added to the program (see Exercise 21 in Chapter 4 for definitions). The user is also given the option of listing the scores in order, either lowest to highest or highest to lowest, with an annotation indicating whether or not the score is within one standard deviation of the average.

9. A polynomial

$$a_n x^n + a_{n-1} x^{n-1} + \ldots + a_0$$

can be evaluated in a straightforward way by performing the indicated operations and using the exponentiation operator **. An alternative method is to factor the polynomial according to the following formula, known as Horner's rule:

$$(\ldots((a_n x + a_{n-1})x + \ldots + a_1)x + a_0$$

Write two procedures to evaluate polynomials by these two different methods. The procedures will read **n** as well as the coefficients a_n, a_{n-1}, and so forth from the keyboard. After completely debugging the procedures, insert extra code to count the number of additions and multiplications performed. (Remember that exponentiation is really repeated multiplication, that is, x ** 3 is really x * x * x.)

References for Further Reading

J. L. Bently, *Writing Efficient Programs* (Englewood Cliffs, NJ: Prentice-Hall, 1982). A good source for more information on writing efficient programs.

Grady Booch, *Software Engineering with Ada,* 2nd Edition (Redwood City, CA: The Benjamin/Cummings Publishing Co., 1986).

F. P. Brooks, *The Mythical Man-Month* (Reading, MA: Addison-Wesley, 1975). A good collection of essays to give you a feel for the problems involved in writing very large programs.

O. J. Dahl, E. W. Dijkstra, and C. A. R. Hoare, *Structured Programming* (New York: Academic Press, 1972). Good essays on programming techniques, data structures, and programming style.

E. W. Dijkstra, *A Discipline of Programming* (Englewood Cliffs, NJ: Prentice-Hall, 1976). A good series of essays on programming techniques and programming style.

D. Gries, *The Science of Programming* (New York: Springer-Verlag, 1981). A good source for more information on program verification.

John Guttag and Barbara Liskov, *Abstraction and Specification in Program Development* (Cambridge, MA: M.I.T. Press, 1986, and New York: McGraw-Hill, 1986).

Gerald M. Weinberg, *The Psychology of Computer Programming* (New York: Van Nostrand Reinhold, 1971). A collection of essays.

Edward Yourdon, *Classics in Software Engineering* (New York: Yourdon Press, 1979). A collection of famous essays on programming methodology.

C H A P T E R

13

TEXT FILES AND SECONDARY STORAGE

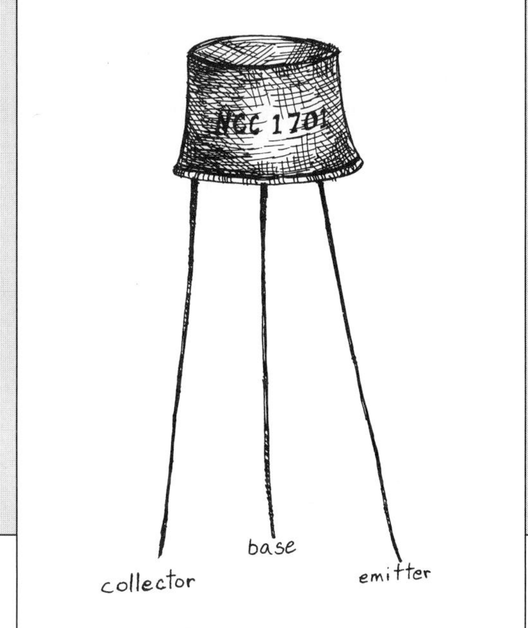

Transistor

Computers existed before the invention of the transistor, but they were extremely large (see ENIAC, in Chapter 9). Tom Watson (Chapter 11) was probably correct in thinking that the demand for this kind of computer was limited. Three men, William Shockley, Walter Brattain, and John Bardeen, working at Bell Laboratories, changed all of that with the invention of the transistor. The transistor is a solid-state device made using semiconductors. It replaced the vacuum tube because it required far less power, produced far less heat, and was far more reliable.

Chapter Contents

secondary storage

disks

Chapter 1 presented a description of the main components of a computer. That description emphasized what is called *main memory*. Virtually all computers have an additional form of memory called *secondary storage* or *external storage*. This secondary memory is typically some sort of disk device. One type, called a hard disk, has the disk mounted permanently or semipermanently. Another type, called a diskette or floppy disk drive, has disks that are easily removed and changed. Both types of disks are similar to phonograph records and compact music disks in that they store information on tracks of a disk and read the information via an arm that rests over the disk. However, their physical properties are closer to those of the magnetic tape commonly used to record music than they are to those of a phonograph record or compact disk. In any event, it is their characteristics as viewed by the programmer that are important to us. We will not need to know about the physics of how they work.

Main memory is often of the type called *volatile*, which means that when you shut off the computer, the data stored in memory goes away. In fact, for all practical purposes, the data goes away as soon as the program ends. Secondary storage is *nonvolatile*. It can be used to store data for as long as is needed.

In this chapter we will describe a method whereby an Ada program can store text data in secondary storage. We will also describe how another program can access that data.

PART I

Text Files

files

In Ada a *file* is a named collection of data in secondary storage. The important properties of a file are that a program can write data to it, it can remain in storage after the program has finished running, it has a name, and other programs can read it later. In Chapter 16 we will describe other types of files which are available in Ada. For now we will only discuss one special kind of file called a *text file*.

text files

A text file is a file that contains the same sort of data as displayed on the output screen. More precisely, a text file contains a stream of characters divided into units called *lines*. One way to think of a text file is as a very long sheet of paper that a program can write on and that the same or a different program can read later. These conceptual sheets of paper are divided into lines in the same way that output to the screen is divided into lines. However, unlike a screen and a sheet of paper, there is no limit to the size of a text file. There is no limit to the number of characters on a line in a text file and no limit to the number of lines (as long as the file does not use all of the computer's available secondary storage).

the type File_Type

Inside an Ada program, a text file is referred to by means of an Ada identifier that is declared as if it were a variable of a type called `FILE_TYPE`. It is part of package `TEXT_IO` and is available to any program that has **`with`** `TEXT_IO`. For example, the following declares `STUFF` to be of type `FILE_TYPE` and would occur in the variable declaration section of a program:

```
STUFF : TEXT_IO.FILE_TYPE;
```

file variables

Identifiers such as `STUFF` are called *file variables*. Although a file variable is a kind of variable, it is a very atypical kind of variable. It cannot appear in an assignment statement, nor can it be used in many of the other ways that the usual kinds of variables are used. It has special standard procedures and special syntax rules of its own. It is probably better simply to think of it as a name for a file and not think of it as a variable at all.

other names for files

Text files are used for many purposes that do not involve the Ada language. Any file that you create or read with the usual editor is a text file. Hence, a text file can exist and have a name before it is used by an Ada program. On some systems, this name might not even satisfy the Ada syntax for identifiers. To accommodate such file names, Ada provides a mechanism to associate a file variable name with a file and thus rename it for the duration of the Ada program. A file will have one name outside of the Ada program called the *external file name*. The file will be referred to by a file variable name within the Ada program called the *internal file name*. A text file is always referred to by its file variable name when reading or writing is performed by an Ada program. In our discussion and examples, we will usually refer to a file by its file variable name (i.e., its internal name).

Creating Text Files

The details of naming external files differ somewhat from one implementation to another. To accommodate these differences, the external file name always appears as a string. All other things are the same regardless of the system on which the program is run. In this section we will follow the naming method for external file names used for a typical PC running under MS_DOS.

A file must be *opened* before a program can get information from that text file. A file must be *created* before a program can put information to that file. Opening a file instructs the system to prepare the file for reading. Creating a file instructs the system to prepare the file for writing. A text file may be opened for reading or created for writing but not for both at the same time.

Create

A text file is created for writing with the procedure CREATE found in TEXT_IO. The procedure has three parameters: the file variable (internal file name), the file mode (OUT_FILE), and a character string (external file name). The purpose of this procedure is twofold: first, to tell the system the name of the external file name and second, to associate that external file name with the internal file name. You can think of the internal file name as an alias that the program uses for the external file name. By way of example, the following statement creates a file for writing, whose internal name is NEW_FILE and whose external name is **text_1.dat**:

```
CREATE ( NEW_FILE, OUT_FILE, "text_1.dat" );
```

The external file name is a character string that conforms to the file naming convention of the system on which the program is running. (It would appear that this ties the program to a particular system and thus has no portability to other systems, but not to worry; later we will add portability. For now we will stick with simplicity.)

The middle parameter, OUT_FILE, in the above CREATE statement is called the FILE_MODE. In CREATE we are marking the file as an output file; information will flow out of the program to the file. A file's mode indicates a direction of information flow. The name FILE_MODE is declared in TEXT_IO as

```
type FILE_MODE is ( IN_FILE, OUT_FILE );
```

Thus text files can only have a FILE_MODE of either IN_FILE or OUT_FILE. For text files, the FILE_MODE for CREATE should always be OUT_FILE.

After the CREATE statement above is executed, the program may use PUT or NEW_LINE statements with the file NEW_FILE. The CREATE procedure always gives a blank file, a "clean sheet of paper" so to speak. If the file **text_1.dat** existed prior to the execution of the CREATE, then that text is lost. It is as if the file were completely erased.

Put and New_Line

Data is written to text files in the same way that it is written to the screen; that is, by PUT and NEW_LINE statements. To write to a text file, the PUT and NEW_LINE statements must contain the file variable associated with the file; otherwise, the output will go to the screen. For example, to write the string **"Hello"** to the file NEW_FILE, the following statement will suffice:

```
PUT ( NEW_FILE, "Hello" );
NEW_LINE ( NEW_FILE );
```

specifying the file

Don't let the syntax confuse you; the PUT can output only one value. Recall that there are several PUT's in TEXT_IO. This is just one more case; the name is simply overloaded. The identifier NEW_FILE may look like a variable whose value is to be written out. It is not. It is the file variable name of the file that the output is being sent to. There is no way to determine this by looking only at the PUT statement. The only way that you, or the compiler, can figure this out is to look at the variable declaration section. If NEW_FILE is declared to be of type FILE_TYPE, then this first argument names the file that is to receive the output. If, on the other hand, we had declared NEW_FILE to be a variable of some type such as CHARACTER or INTEGER, then this statement would produce a syntax error.

When reading or writing files, the system handles numbers just as it handles them when reading from the keyboard or writing to the screen. The system automatically converts numbers to characters when it is writing numbers and automatically converts characters to numbers when it is reading into variables of type INTEGER or FLOAT. A text file can contain nothing but characters divided into lines. It cannot contain numbers, but because of the type conversion performed by the PUT procedure in INTEGER_IO, the following statement will cause no problems:

```
PUT ( NEW_FILE, 5 );
```

Just as with output to the screen, numbers are handled as you would hope. The procedure changes the number **5** to the character **'5'**, and it is the character **'5'** that is written into the text file.

Close

After a program has read from or written to the file and the program is ready to terminate, the file must be *closed.* To close a file means that the file is no longer available for reading or writing. The CLOSE procedure in TEXT_IO has one parameter, the internal file name. The CLOSE procedure is used to close a file that has been created for output or opened for input. The same procedure with the same syntax is used for input and output files. The LRM does not define what happens to a file if it is not closed when the program terminates. Failure to close a newly created file may cause the file to be lost. Even though some systems will close all active files automatically as the program terminates, it is always best to do it under program control; don't leave it to the compiler writer or the system to make that decision for you. The following is an example based on the CREATE procedure given on the previous page:

```
CLOSE ( NEW_FILE );
```

A complete example is given in Figure 13.1. That program writes the numbers **3** and **4** to the text file NEW_FILE. The numbers will be on two lines. If **Fig13_1.txt** did not exist before the program was run, the program will create it. If **Fig13_1.txt** was present before the program was run, then the previous contents of the file will be lost. After the program is run, the file will contain only the characters **3** and **4**. The first and last PUT and NEW_LINE do not contain the identifier NEW_FILE, so their output goes to the screen. If those two pairs of statements are omitted, the program will output nothing at all to the screen.

Program

```
with TEXT_IO;
use TEXT_IO;
procedure WRITER is
--                    INPUT  : None
--                    OUTPUT : Two numbers to a text file.
--                    DESCRIPTION : Writes the numbers 3 and 4 to
--                                  the text file new_file.
    NEW_FILE : FILE_TYPE;
    VALUE : INTEGER;
    package VALUE_IO is new INTEGER_IO ( INTEGER );
    use VALUE_IO;
begin -- Writer
    PUT ( "Start program" ); NEW_LINE;
    CREATE ( NEW_FILE, OUT_FILE, "Fig13_1.txt" );
    PUT ( NEW_FILE, 3 ); NEW_LINE ( NEW_FILE );
    VALUE := 4;
    PUT ( NEW_FILE, VALUE ); NEW_LINE ( NEW_FILE );
    CLOSE ( NEW_FILE );
    PUT ( "End of program" ); NEW_LINE;
end WRITER;
```

Output to the screen

```
Start program
End of program
```

Output to text file Fig13__1.txt

```
3
4
```

Figure 13.1 Program that writes to a text file.

Reading Text Files

Open Many of the details for reading from a text file are similar to what we have just described for writing to a text file. The file variable name must be declared to be of type `TEXT_IO.FILE_TYPE`, as shown previously. The file must be opened; the `TEXT_IO` procedure that opens a file for reading is called `OPEN`. For example, suppose the program in Figure 13.1 has been run and so has created the external file **`Fig13_1.txt`**. Another program can open that same text file for reading with the following statement:

```
OPEN ( OLD_FILE, IN_FILE, "Fig13_1.txt" );
```

After this statement is executed, the program may use GET or SKIP_LINE statements with the file OLD_FILE. A complete example of reading from a text file is given in Figure 13.2. That program will read from the text file created by the program in Figure 13.1.

Get and Skip_Line

Text files can be read by means of a GET statement and reset to the beginning of the next line with a SKIP_LINE statement. There are problems associated with mixing GET and PUT statements to the same text file. So for now we will assume that different programs are doing the reading and the writing. Suppose we used PUT, as described above, to write to a file. We can then write another program to read this same file. This other program contains the following declarations:

```
OLD_FILE : TEXT_IO.FILE_TYPE;
FIRST_LETTER, SECOND_LETTER : CHARACTER;
```

This other program can then prepare the same file for reading. In the previous program in which we wrote to the file, the file had the file variable name NEW_FILE; in the second program we will give it the file variable name OLD_FILE. Assume that the previous program wrote **"Hello"** to the file with a PUT, just as we described earlier. Our second program can read from the file by a GET statement such as the following:

```
GET ( OLD_FILE, FIRST_LETTER );
GET ( OLD_FILE, SECOND_LETTER );
```

This will set the value of FIRST_LETTER to **'H'** and the value of SECOND_LETTER to **'e'**. Reading starts with the first character of the first line of the file and proceeds through the file. The first GET statement reads the first character, the next GET executed reads the next character. There is no way to backspace.

The statements GET and SKIP_LINE behave the same for text files as they do for the sort of keyboard reading we have used so far. The only difference is that if a text file variable is given as the first argument, then the data is read from the indicated text file rather than from the keyboard. Just as with a PUT statement, this can be confusing syntax. The only way to tell that the first argument of a GET refers to a text file is to look at the declarations section to see if it is declared to be of type FILE_TYPE.

Program

```
with TEXT_IO;
use TEXT_IO;
procedure READER is
--                  INPUT  : Two numbers from a text file.
--                  OUTPUT : Two numbers to the screen.
--                  DESCRIPTION : Reads two numbers from
--                                the text file test_file.
   FIRST_VALUE : INTEGER;
   SECOND_VALUE : INTEGER;
   OLD_FILE : FILE_TYPE;
```

```
    package VALUE_IO is new INTEGER_IO ( INTEGER );
    use VALUE_IO;
begin -- Reader
    PUT ( "Start program" ); NEW_LINE;
    OPEN ( OLD_FILE, IN_FILE, "Fig13_1.txt" );
    GET ( OLD_FILE, FIRST_VALUE ); SKIP_LINE ( OLD_FILE );
    GET ( OLD_FILE, SECOND_VALUE ); SKIP_LINE ( OLD_FILE );
    CLOSE ( OLD_FILE );
    PUT ( FIRST_VALUE ); NEW_LINE;
    PUT ( SECOND_VALUE ); NEW_LINE;
    PUT ( "End of program" ); NEW_LINE;
end READER;
```

Output

(Assuming the program in Figure 13.1 was run first)

```
Start program
     3
     4
End of program
```

Figure 13.2 Program that reads from a text file.

Reset

There are occasions when a program is reading a file and it is necessary to go back to the beginning and start reading again. One way to accomplish this is to close the file and then open it again. The best and easiest way is to simply *reset* the file to the beginning. The RESET procedure will do exactly that. The syntax for RESET is

RESET (*internal_file_name*);

The first GET from the newly reset text file will read the first character in the file. Subsequent GETs will read the second and third characters, and so on.

Pitfall

Mixing Reading and Writing to a Text File

A program cannot simply intermix reading and writing to the same file. At any one time a text file that has been opened is available for either reading or writing but not both. To switch from writing to reading, the file must first be *closed* by a call to CLOSE and then opened. To switch from reading to writing, the file must first be closed and then created as a new file. This is a nontrivial restriction, since opening the file for writing completely erases the file. The typical sequence of actions is as follows: create the file with CREATE, write to it, and, when finished, CLOSE it. Then the same or a different program can open the file any number of times with OPEN and read the file contents; the next time it is created with CREATE, any previous file contents of the file with that external file name are lost.

One productive variation on this pattern of writing and reading is as follows: The file can be created or changed by a person using the editor to write in the file instead of having an Ada program do the writing. Text files are exactly the same kind of files as those used to hold Ada programs, shopping lists, and term papers, and they can be edited with the editor just as an Ada program can be edited.

Pitfall

The Silent Program

It is quite common to write a program so that all the data that is output is directed to a text file. If you do this, then the program will produce no output to the screen. This can be bewildering. If you write programs that way, the user may not even be able to tell when the program has finished. To let the user know what is going on, there should always be some output to the screen, even if it just says when the program starts and when it ends.

Exercises

Self-Test Exercise

1. Suppose the text file named by the file variable EX_1_FILE contains the following:

```
5     63    75
5     63    75
```

Suppose variables are declared as follows:

```
EX_1_FILE : FILE_TYPE;
LETTER_1, LETTER_2 : CHARACTER;
NUMBER : INTEGER;
```

What will be the output produced by the following, provided it is embedded in a complete program that opens EX_1_FILE and that declares variables as shown above?

```
GET ( EX_1_FILE, NUMBER ); PUT ( NUMBER );
GET ( EX_1_FILE, NUMBER ); PUT ( NUMBER );
SKIP_LINE ( EX_1_FILE ); NEW_LINE;
GET ( EX_1_FILE, LETTER_1 ); GET ( EX_1_FILE, LETTER_2 );
SKIP_LINE ( EX_1_FILE );
PUT ( LETTER_1 ); PUT ( LETTER_2 );
NEW_LINE;
```

Interactive Exercises

2. Write a program that writes your name to a text file. Look at the text file after the program is run. On most systems, programs are kept in text files and can be written and read using an editor program. Hence, if your system is typical, you already know how to look at a text file.

3. Create a text file using the editor (as you do when you write a program) and write three numbers in the text file. Write a program to read the three numbers and write them to the screen. After running the program once, go back and change the numbers. Then rerun the program.

4. Using the editor, change the text file from Exercise 3 so that the three numbers are two digits long, there is one space between them, and there are no spaces at the front of the line. For example, the text file might contain

```
25 36 47
```

Rerun the program from Exercise 3. Next write a slightly different program that reads three characters from the same text file into three variables of type CHARACTER and then outputs them to the screen. Run this new program on the same text file.

Part II

Writing and Reading Reexamined

It will give you a more precise notion of how the statements PUT, NEW_LINE, GET, and SKIP_LINE work when we associate it with a text file.

arrow

When a text file is opened or created, a location marker is placed at the beginning of the file. For purposes of explanation let us call this location marker an *arrow* (↑), and think of it as pointing to a file location that contains, or could contain, one character. This arrow tells where the next character to be read is or where the next character to be written will go. In the figures we will underscore the location pointed to by the arrow to make it more prominent.

writing

When a file is created with the CREATE procedure, the arrow is placed at the first location in the file as the only thing in the file. Every time the program writes a character, the character is written at the location of the arrow, and then the arrow is advanced to the next location. Some sample code and its effect on the text file TEST_FILE is shown in Figure 13.3. Notice that a second line is started when the NEW_LINE statement is executed. This is the only way that a new line is initiated. There is no limit to the length of a line in a text file.

Also notice that, in the example, the output to the file was written from the beginning of the file and continued on through the file. The arrow did not "back up." When using a text file, you cannot backspace and change a character. With text files, the moving arrow writes and then moves on. The only way to get the arrow back to a previous position is to call the OPEN, CREATE, or RESET procedure, and these do not allow the program to change a portion of the file. CREATE will, in effect, erase the entire contents of the file. OPEN will move the arrow all the way back to the first character in the file, but only if the file is closed. Also, OPEN will only allow the program to read from the file; it will not allow it to write to the file. RESET will move the arrow all the way back to the first character in the file without first closing the file.

lines

end-of-line marker

To fully understand text files, we need to examine the notion of a *line* more carefully. Figure 13.3 is the way we normally think of lines, and text files are implemented so as to reflect this intuition. However, there are no physical lines in a text file. Instead, a text file is one continuous stream of characters, rather like a ticker tape. The end of a line is indicated by inserting a special marker called the *line terminator.* This marker is a character of sorts, but it is not possible to see it on the screen. The computer can recognize it, though, and it is this character that indicates what we call an *end of a line.* In the diagram in Figure 13.4, the marker is denoted <eol>. The easiest and best way to insert an <eol> marker in a text file is with a NEW_LINE.

end-of-file marker

Secondary storage is divided into files. There has to be a marker to indicate where a given file ends. The end of a file is indicated by inserting a special marker. This special marker, called the *file terminator,* is similar to the marker used for the end of a line in that it is a character but a character that cannot be seen on the screen.

The file is TEST__FILE.

Program Action	File After the Action
`CREATE ( TEST_FILE, OUT_FILE, "Fig13_3.txt" );`	_ ↑
`PUT ( TEST_FILE, 'a' );`	a_ ↑
`PUT ( TEST_FILE, 'b' );`	ab_ ↑
`PUT ( TEST_FILE, 'c' );`	abc_ ↑
`PUT ( TEST_FILE, 'd' );`	abcd_ ↑
`NEW_LINE ( TEST_FILE );`	abcd _ ↑
`PUT ( TEST_FILE, 'e' );`	abcd e_ ↑
`PUT ( TEST_FILE, 'f' );`	abcd ef_ ↑

Figure 13.3 Writing to a text file, intuitive picture.

The computer can recognize it as the *end-of-file marker*. In the diagram in Figure 13.4, the end-of-file marker is shown as <eof>. The <eof> marker is inserted originally into the file when the file is created. The CREATE procedure creates the file and inserts the <eof> marker as the only thing in the file. Each time a character is writing to the file, it is writing over the <eof> character, and another <eof> is written immediately following the newly inserted character. In Figure 13.4 we have redone Figure 13.3, but this time we have indicated the end of a line by <eol> and the end of a file by <eof>.

reading

An existing file is opened for reading with the OPEN procedure. When a file is opened in this way, the arrow is placed at the first character of the first line of the file. Every time a character is read, the arrow is advanced to the next character. The situation is diagrammed in Figure 13.5. Notice that the `SKIP_LINE` procedure moves the arrow to the beginning of the next line, and all the remaining characters on the old line are thus ignored. If the program runs out of characters on one line, there can be problems. Usually, the programmer must ensure that the arrow is explicitly moved to the next line by means of a SKIP__LINE. An exception is made for numbers. If

The file is TEST_FILE

Program Action	File After the Action
`CREATE ( TEST_FILE, OUT_FILE, "Fig13_3.txt" );`	<eof> ↑
`PUT ( TEST_FILE, 'a' );`	a<eof> ↑
`PUT ( TEST_FILE, 'b' );`	ab<eof> ↑
`PUT ( TEST_FILE, 'c' );`	abc<eof> ↑
`PUT ( TEST_FILE, 'd' );`	abcd<eof> ↑
`NEW_LINE ( TEST_FILE );`	abcd<eol><eof> ↑
`PUT ( TEST_FILE, 'e' );`	abcd<eol>e<eof> ↑
`PUT ( TEST_FILE, 'f' );`	abcd<eol>ef<eof> ↑

Figure 13.4 Writing to a text file, the "real" picture.

Program Action	Value of BUFFER After Action	File After the Action
`OPEN ( TEST_FILE, IN_FILE, "Fig13_3.txt" );`	?	abcd<eol>ef<eof> ↑
`GET ( TEST_FILE, BUFFER );`	'a'	abcd<eol>ef<eof> ↑
`GET ( TEST_FILE, BUFFER );`	'b'	abcd<eol>ef<eof> ↑
`SKIP_LINE ( TEXT_FILE );`	'b'	abcd<eol>ef<eof> ↑
`GET ( TEST_FILE, BUFFER );`	'e'	abcd<eol>ef<eof> ↑

Figure 13.5 Reading from a text file.

the program is reading into a variable of type INTEGER or FLOAT and there is no more data on the current line, it will automatically go to the next line.

Using a Buffer

The word *buffer* is frequently used in discussions about files and has a semitechnical meaning. A buffer is a location where some data is held on its way from one place to another. That is why we chose BUFFER as the name of the character variable in the following loop example. The program reads a character from one file into BUFFER and then writes it from BUFFER into the other file. The variable serves as a temporary location for one character.

End_Of_File and End_Of_Line

End_Of_File

When reading from a text file, it is often helpful if a program can detect the end of the file. Ada provides a special boolean-valued function that does just that. The function END_OF_FILE is part of package TEXT_IO and is available to any program that has **with** TEXT_IO. It takes one argument, a file variable, and it returns TRUE if the program is at the end of that file. More specifically

END_OF_FILE (*file_variable*);

evaluates to TRUE if the arrow in the file indicated by *file_variable* is pointing to the <eof> marker in the file; otherwise, it evaluates to FALSE.

As an example, the program in Figure 13.6 reads a list of numbers from the file OLD_FILE, multiplies each number by two, and copies the result into a second (new) file, which it calls NEW_FILE. The function END_OF_FILE is used to detect when all the numbers in the file have been read. Suppose the file OLD_FILE contains the following when the program is run:

```
1
2
3
<eof>
```

The body of the loop in the program then will be executed three times. Each time one of the following three lines will be written to the file NEW_FILE:

```
2
4
6
<eof>
```

```
with TEXT_IO;
use TEXT_IO;
procedure DOUBLER is
    BUFFER : INTEGER;
    OLD_FILE : FILE_TYPE;
    NEW_FILE : FILE_TYPE;
    package BUFFER_IO is new INTEGER_IO ( INTEGER );
    use BUFFER_IO;
begin -- Doubler
    PUT ( "Program started." ); NEW_LINE;
    OPEN ( OLD_FILE, IN_FILE, "Fig13_1.txt" );
    CREATE ( NEW_FILE, OUT_FILE, "Fig13_6.txt" );
    loop
        exit when END_OF_FILE ( OLD_FILE );
        GET ( OLD_FILE, BUFFER ); SKIP_LINE ( OLD_FILE );
        BUFFER := BUFFER * 2;
        PUT ( NEW_FILE, BUFFER ); NEW_LINE ( NEW_FILE );
    end loop;
    CLOSE ( OLD_FILE );
    CLOSE ( NEW_FILE );
    PUT ( "Numbers in old_file doubled" ); NEW_LINE;
    PUT ( "and results copied to new_file." ); NEW_LINE;
end DOUBLER;
```

Figure 13.6 Program using End__Of__File.

The fourth time the program enters the loop, the arrow in the file OLD_FILE has moved beyond the third line to the <eof> marker. So END_OF_FILE (OLD_FILE) in the **exit when** statement evaluates to TRUE and the program will exit the loop.

End__Of__Line

The function END_OF_LINE (*file__variable*) performs the same as the END_OF_LINE that we have already used with input from the keyboard, but we will now see how to use it with text files as well. It is similar to END_OF_FILE except it tests for the end of a line rather than the end of the entire file. In terms of the arrow discussed above, END_OF_LINE can be explained as follows: When the arrow in the file specified by *file__variable* is pointing to the end-of-line marker (what we have been denoting by <eol> in the diagrams), then

END_OF_LINE (*file__variable*)

returns TRUE; otherwise, it returns FALSE.

As it turns out, END_OF_LINE will return TRUE if the arrow points to the <eol> marker or the <eof> marker. The function END_OF_FILE returns TRUE only if the arrow points to the <eof> marker.

To construct an example using END_OF_LINE, suppose that a program contains the following declarations:

```
BUFFER   : CHARACTER;
NEW_FILE : FILE_TYPE;
OLD_FILE : FILE_TYPE;
```

If both files are opened properly and the arrow is at the start of a line, then the following loop will copy one line of text from OLD_FILE into NEW_FILE:

```
loop
    exit when END_OF_LINE ( OLD_FILE );
    GET ( OLD_FILE, BUFFER );
    PUT ( NEW_FILE, BUFFER );
end loop;
```

The effect of this loop on some sample file contents is shown in Figure 13.7. After the two characters on the line have been read, the arrow in OLD_FILE is at the end-of-line marker. At this point the END_OF_LINE (OLD_FILE) in the **exit when** statement returns TRUE, and the program terminates the loop after the second iteration of the loop body. Typically this loop would be followed by

```
SKIP_LINE ( OLD_FILE );
NEW_LINE ( OLD_FILE );
```

This moves the arrow in each file to the beginning of the next line.

Recall that input from the keyboard is considered to be from a special file called STANDARD_INPUT. The TEXT_IO functions END_OF_FILE and END_OF_LINE also apply to STANDARD_INPUT. Indeed, we used END_OF_LINE with STANDARD_INPUT in Chapter 7. If no argument is given, then the file is assumed to be STANDARD_INPUT; that is, END_OF_FILE by itself is equivalent to END_OF_FILE (STANDARD_INPUT) and, as we saw in previous chapters, END_OF_LINE by itself is equivalent to END_OF_LINE (STANDARD_INPUT). The end-of-line marker at the keyboard is the return key. The end-of-file marker at the keyboard varies from system to system. Since the exact details vary from system to system, using END_OF_FILE with STANDARD_INPUT can be troublesome.

The files STANDARD_INPUT (keyboard) and STANDARD_OUTPUT (screen) cannot be used as file parameters in the procedures CREATE and OPEN found in package TEXT_IO.

Pitfall

Forgetting the File Variable in End_Of_Line and End_Of_File

There are a number of pitfalls associated with the special boolean functions END_OF_LINE and END_OF_FILE. The simplest one of all is forgetting to include the file variable as an argument. For example, if you are testing

```
OLD_FILE                NEW_FILE            BUFFER   END_OF_LINE(OLD_FILE)
ab<eol>cd<eol><eof>     <eof>                 ?              FALSE
↑                         ↑
After GET ( OLD_FILE, BUFFER );
ab<eol>cd<eol><eof>     <eof>                'a'             FALSE
 ↑                        ↑
After PUT ( NEW_FILE, BUFFER );
ab<eol>cd<eol><eof>     a<eof>               'a'             FALSE
 ↑                         ↑
After GET ( OLD_FILE, BUFFER );
ab<eol>cd<eol><eof>     a<eof>               'b'             TRUE
  ↑                        ↑
After PUT ( NEW_FILE, BUFFER );
ab<eol>cd<eol><eof>     ab<eof>              'b'             TRUE
  ↑                         ↑
After SKIP_LINE ( OLD_FILE );
ab<eol>cd<eol><eof>     ab<eof>              'b'             FALSE
       ↑                    ↑
After NEW_LINE ( NEW_FILE );
ab<eol>cd<eol><eof>     ab<eol><eof>         'b'             FALSE
       ↑                       ↑
```

Figure 13.7 Copying a line from one text file to another.

for the end of the file OLD_FILE, you must use END_OF_FILE (OLD_FILE). If you forget and instead use the unadorned END_OF_FILE, you are referring to the file STANDARD_INPUT and not the file OLD_FILE. This can be frustrating, since the program will compile without an error message. After all, the compiler has no way of knowing that you did not mean to refer to the file STANDARD_INPUT. However, problems will occur when the program is run. If your program is reading from the file OLD_FILE and instead of END_OF_FILE (OLD_FILE) you mistakenly use END_OF_FILE to terminate the reading, then your program is in trouble. It is essentially guaranteed that the unadorned END_OF_FILE will not be TRUE when your program reaches the end of the file OLD_FILE, so your program will attempt to read beyond the end of the file. The exception END_ERROR will be raised if you attempt to read beyond the end of a file.

Pitfall

Use of End_Of_Line and End_Of_File with Numeric Data

Text files are designed for holding characters. When reading or writing numbers, a type conversion is performed. The exact details of how a system handles numbers in text files will vary slightly from one installation to another. When dealing with numeric data, these details can cause the behavior of END_OF_LINE and END_OF_FILE to vary in what may appear to be an unpredictable way from one system to another. The easiest way to avoid any problems when using END_OF_FILE with numeric text data is to always use SKIP_LINE and to avoid using END_OF_LINE completely. If you write a program that reads numeric data from a text file and you do not use SKIP_LINE (*file_name*), you are asking for trouble. You may not always need SKIP_LINE, but using it *always* works. When processing data of type CHARACTER, there are no such problems. However, you should be aware that END_OF_LINE is TRUE if the next character is the end-of-line marker or the end-of-file marker.

Text Files as Parameters to Procedures

A text file may be a parameter to a procedure, just like things of other data types. There is, however, one qualification. Text file parameters may be **in** or **in out** parameters; they cannot be **out** parameters.

example copying a file

As an example we will design a program that has two text file parameters called OLD_FILE and NEW_FILE. These file parameters are passed to a procedure with parameters IN_FILE and OUT_FILE. The procedure will copy the contents of the file IN_FILE into the file OUT_FILE. A precise definition of the task to be accomplished is

```
procedure COPY ( IN_FILE, OUT_FILE : in FILE_TYPE ) is
--                 INPUT  : A text file.
--                 OUTPUT : A copy of the input file in an output file
--                 DESCRIPTION : The input file has been opened
--                               and the output file has been created
--                               prior to the call to this procedure.
--                               The contents of the input file
--                               are unchanged.
```

The basic outline of the COPY procedure is given as follows:

```
loop
    exit when END_OF_FILE ( IN_FILE );
    Copy a line from IN_FILE to OUT_FILE
    SKIP_LINE ( IN_FILE );
    NEW_LINE ( OUT_FILE );
end loop;
```

To convert that piece of pseudocode into Ada, all we need to do is design some Ada code for the informal instruction:

Copy a line from IN_FILE to OUT_FILE

That is exactly what we did in the section on END_OF_LINE. The Ada code we developed there is

```
loop
    exit when END_OF_LINE ( IN_FILE );
    GET ( IN_FILE, BUFFER );
    PUT ( OUT_FILE, BUFFER );
end loop;
```

If we now put together all the details, we obtain the procedure COPY shown in Figure 13.8.

```
with TEXT_IO;
use TEXT_IO;
procedure COPIER is
    OLD_FILE : FILE_TYPE;
    NEW_FILE : FILE_TYPE;
    procedure COPY ( IN_FILE, OUT_FILE : in FILE_TYPE ) is
        BUFFER : CHARACTER;
    begin -- Copy
        loop
            exit when END_OF_FILE ( IN_FILE );
            loop
                exit when END_OF_LINE ( IN_FILE );
                GET ( IN_FILE, BUFFER );
                PUT ( OUT_FILE, BUFFER );
            end loop;
            SKIP_LINE ( IN_FILE );
            NEW_LINE ( OUT_FILE );
        end loop;
    end COPY;
```

```
begin -- Copier
    OPEN ( OLD_FILE, IN_FILE, "Fig13_8.in" );
    CREATE ( NEW_FILE, OUT_FILE, "Fig13_8.out" );
    COPY ( OLD_FILE, NEW_FILE );
    CLOSE ( OLD_FILE );
    CLOSE ( NEW_FILE );
end COPIER;
```

Figure 13.8 A procedure with text file parameters.

Pitfall

Portability

If a program has the external file name as a character string literal, as in Figure 13.8 ("Fig13_8.in"), the program may not be portable to another system. The reason is that the naming conventions for external file names varies from system to system. For example, the underline may not be allowed, or there may be a prefix required (such as in "petersen*fig138.in"), or the extension **in** may not be permitted.

To avoid this problem and make them portable, the program could read in the file name. A dialogue in the main procedure could be used to replace the first two lines. This code, as shown below, assumes a declaration for FILENAME as

```
FILENAME : STRING( 1 . . 40 );
LAST : NATURAL;
```

```
PUT ( "Enter the input file name: " ); NEW_LINE;
GET_LINE ( FILENAME, LAST );
OPEN ( OLD_FILE, IN_FILE, FILENAME( 1 . . LAST) );
PUT ( "Now enter the output file name: " ); NEW_LINE;
GET_LINE ( FILENAME, LAST );
CREATE ( NEW_FILE, OUT_FILE, FILENAME( 1 . . LAST) );
```

slice

The GET_LINE procedure is used to read in any number of characters up to the maximum specified in the string declaration of the first parameter. In the case above, FILENAME has 40 characters. The second parameter reports how many characters were read in before the **return** was pressed. In the OPEN and CREATE procedures, we want to use only those characters that were entered, not all 40 characters of the string FILENAME. FILENAME (1 . . LAST) takes what is called a *slice* or portion of FILENAME. What is passed to OPEN and CREATE is a string made up of the characters 1 through **LAST** of FILENAME. This is exactly what was entered for the file's name and no more.

Is the program now totally portable? No, not really; for instance, the program could not be moved to batch mode environment since it is designed to work interactively. Another problem is the size of the string in the declaration of FILENAME; it might be too small. (Declaring FILENAME : STRING (1 . . 80); might be overkill, but it would undoubtedly cover almost all cases.) The point is, some rewriting may be necessary. To make this rewriting problem as easy as possible, all file handling should be isolated into self-contained procedures or at least easy-to-find, isolated code.

Basic Technique for Editing Text Files

As we have already noted, there is no way to change part of a text file. The only way to write to a text file is to create a new file or to completely erase an old file. However, there is a way to get the effect of changing a file. To change part of a text file, an Ada program must do something like the following:

1. Copy the entire contents from the given file into some temporary file, making changes as the copying is done.
2. Copy the entire contents of the temporary file back to the original file.

Internal Temporary Files

permanent versus temporary files

What we have been describing so far are called *permanent* text files. They exist before and/or after the program is run. In Ada there are also files that only exist for the duration of the program. These are called *temporary* text files. The name of a temporary file is local to a program and does not exist after the program terminates. In particular, if a program edits a text file in the manner outlined in the previous section, then it needs a temporary file.

It is very easy to make a file temporary for the life of a program. Simply omit the external file name from the CREATE procedure. A temporary file is manipulated in exactly the same way as a permanent file, but when the program ends, the file disappears. For example, suppose you want to write a program to edit a file called DATA_FILE, and your program uses a file called TEMP_FILE to temporarily hold some text. Both files are declared as type FILE_TYPE. The CREATE procedure for the temporary file should be

```
CREATE ( TEMP_FILE );
```

The system will provide it with a special external file name that will not conflict with any existing permanent or other temporary files.

A temporary file is like a local variable. It is perfectly correct to think of a temporary file variable as one that is local to the program. However, the way to make it temporary is to omit the external file name. Simply making it a local variable in some procedure will not make it a temporary file.

The reason one would want to create a temporary file is so the program could, at some point later in the program, read the information that is in the temporary file. CREATE makes the FILE_MODE OUT_FILE, but to read a file its FILE_MODE must be IN_FILE. To change the FILE_MODE of a file you use a RESET procedure. This form of RESET must include the file's internal name and also its new FILE_MODE. This RESET not only changes the FILE_MODE but it also sets the file location pointer back to the beginning of the file. The syntactical form for this RESET is

RESET (*internal_file_name* , *new_file_mode*);

An example of the use of RESET is given in the solution of the following "Case Study" (Figure 13.9).

RESET works only on previously opened or created files. It is possible to change a file from IN_FILE to OUT_FILE using RESET. Resetting a file from IN_FILE to OUT_FILE will cause all the information presently in the file to be lost. After being RESET, the file location pointer is back at the beginning and the file is now ready for its first bit of information.

Case Study

Editing Out Excess Blanks

Problem Definition

Suppose you want to write a program to edit excess blanks from a text file containing some ordinary English text. To be more precise, let us say that the program is to delete all initial blanks on a line and is to compress every other string of two or more blanks down to a single blank. So, for example, consider the following lines:

```
   The      Answer to the     question of Life,
the          Universe,              and    Everything is:
```

They should be edited to look like

```
The Answer to the question of Life,
the Universe and Everything is:
```

Discussion

We will use the basic technique for editing text files that we outlined two sections ago. Let us use DATA_FILE as the name of the file to be edited. We will need one temporary file, which we will call TEMP_FILE. The basic outline of the program is

1. Get the name of the external file to be edited.
2. OPEN DATA_FILE and CREATE TEMP_FILE.
3. (CLEAN_BLANKS:) Copy DATA_FILE into TEMP_FILE but delete excess blanks as this is done. That is, copy all characters except the unwanted blanks from DATA_FILE to TEMP_FILE.
4. Change TEMP_FILE's mode to an input file with a RESET; discard the old DATA_FILE and make a new one with a CREATE.
5. (COPY:) Copy the contents of TEMP_FILE into DATA_FILE.
6. Close both files.

Separate Compilation

We will implement steps 3 and 5 as separately compiled procedures named CLEAN_BLANKS and COPY. The Ada program without the separately compiled procedures is given in Figure 13.9. The procedure COPY is the one used in Figure 13.8, but this time it is a *separate* subunit of the program EDIT. The exact form of COPY is shown in Figure 13.10. The procedure CLEAN_BLANKS is also *separate* from the program EDIT, and it has yet to be designed. The completed procedure CLEAN_BLANKS is given in Figure 13.11.

One of the advantages of separately compiled procedures is that they allow us to complete the top-down design of the program, enter that program, and compile it without worrying about the details of the locally declared procedures. It is a lot like the use of stubbed procedures that was introduced in Chapter 5. The advantage is that once we compile the main program, we will never have to go back to it again unless we want to make changes in the top level of our design.

Note the use of the term **separate** in the declaration of procedure CLEAN_BLANKS and COPY. The complete subprogram specification for the subprograms is given, just like we did in package specifications. In a package specification, the subprogram specification is terminated with a semicolon. To mark the subprogram as a separately compiled unit from the main program, we mark the subprogram with **is separate**.

To tell the compiler that the procedure to be compiled is a separate part of a main program, the procedure must have a prefixed **separate** that specifies the name of the main program. Note that the procedure COPY shown in Figure 13.10 has as its first line **separate** (EDIT). (Also note the lack of a terminating semicolon on this line.) This line ties the procedure to the previously compiled main program named EDIT.

```
with TEXT_IO;
use TEXT_IO;
procedure EDIT is
--                INPUT  : A text file with excess blanks.
--                OUTPUT : The same file without excess blanks.
--                DESCRIPTION : Edits out excess blanks from
--                              the text file called data_file.
    DATA_FILE : FILE_TYPE;
    FILENAME : STRING( 1 . . 40 );
    LAST : NATURAL;
    TEMP_FILE : FILE_TYPE;
    procedure CLEAN_BLANKS ( DIRTY_FILE : in FILE_TYPE;
                             CLEAN_FILE : in out FILE_TYPE )
                             is separate;
    procedure COPY ( IN_FILE  : in FILE_TYPE;
                     OUT_FILE : in out FILE_TYPE )
                     is separate;
begin -- Edit
    PUT ( "Enter the name of the file to be edited:" ); NEW_LINE;
    GET_LINE ( FILENAME, LAST );
    PUT ( "Program is running" ); NEW_LINE;
    OPEN ( DATA_FILE, IN_FILE, FILENAME( 1 . . LAST ) );
    CREATE ( TEMP_FILE );
    CLEAN_BLANKS ( DATA_FILE, TEMP_FILE );
    CLOSE ( DATA_FILE );
    RESET ( TEMP_FILE, IN_FILE );
    CREATE ( DATA_FILE, OUT_FILE, FILENAME( 1 . . LAST ) );
    COPY ( TEMP_FILE, DATA_FILE );
    CLOSE ( DATA_FILE );
    CLOSE ( TEMP_FILE );
    PUT ( "End of program" ); NEW_LINE;
end EDIT;
```

Figure 13.9 Program that edits a text file.

You could think of the **is separate** in the main program as a promise of things to come and the **separate** (*main's_name*) as keeping that promise by providing the completed subprogram. The separate subprogram can reference or use the same identifiers that are outside of its own scope just as it would if it were physically in the main program. Its visibility to nonlocal references, including **with**ed packages, does not change. Notice that the COPY procedure below makes reference to several things that are in TEXT_IO, but it was the main program that **with**ed TEXT_IO, not COPY. The COPY procedure could have referenced any of the variables declared in the main program (i.e., DATA_FILE, FILENAME, LAST, TEMP_FILE). It could even make a call to the procedure CLEAN_BLANKS.

```
separate ( EDIT )
procedure COPY ( IN_FILE  : in FILE_TYPE;
                 OUT_FILE : in out FILE_TYPE ) is
--                 INPUT  : in_file has been opened
--                          out_file has been created
--                 OUTPUT : out_file is a copy of in_file
--                 DESCRIPTION : copies in_file into out_file
--                               in_file is unchanged
    BUFFER : CHARACTER;
begin -- Copy
    loop
        exit when END_OF_FILE ( IN_FILE );
        loop
            exit when END_OF_LINE ( IN_FILE );
            GET ( IN_FILE, BUFFER );
            PUT ( OUT_FILE, BUFFER );
        end loop;
        SKIP_LINE ( IN_FILE );
        NEW_LINE ( OUT_FILE );
    end loop;
end COPY;
```

Figure 13.10 A separately compiled procedure.

mixing reading and writing

Before designing the code for the procedure CLEAN_BLANKS, let us observe a few things about the program outline. Notice that the program in Figure 13.9 both reads from and writes to the same file. This is permitted as long as the reading and writing is not mixed. The program must first read from the file and then RESET it for the purpose of writing. It is also possible to write first and then read, but every change from reading to writing and every change from writing to reading requires that the file be RESET.

CleanBlanks

We next design the algorithm and code for the one unfinished procedure. The procedure heading indicates what the procedure needs to accomplish.

```
procedure CLEAN_BLANKS ( DIRTY_FILE : in FILE_TYPE;
                         CLEAN_FILE : in out FILE_TYPE ) is
--                  INPUT  : dirty_file has been opened
--                           clean_file has been created
--                  OUTPUT : clean_file without excess blanks
--                  DESCRIPTION : dirty_file is left unchanged.
--                                Removes excess blanks as it copies
--                                nonblanks from dirty_file
--                                to clean_file.
```

Algorithm

negative thinking

The procedure CLEAN_BLANKS can be very much like the procedure COPY. In fact, the only difference between CLEAN_BLANKS and COPY is that CLEAN_BLANKS will sometimes read a character and decide not to copy it to the second file. It sometimes pays to think about when things should not be done rather than about when it should be done. The algorithm is given in Figure 13.11.

```
loop
    exit when END_OF_FILE ( DIRTY_FILE );
    loop
        exit when END_OF_LINE ( DIRTY_FILE );
        GET ( DIRTY_FILE, SYMBOL );
        if SYMBOL is not an extra blank
            PUT ( CLEAN_FILE, SYMBOL );
        end if;
--      This is the end of a line from file dirty_file
    SKIP_LINE ( DIRTY_FILE );
    NEW_LINE ( CLEAN_FILE );
--      Both files are now at the beginning of the next line
```

We still need some way to tell when a character is an extra blank. For the moment let us ignore the problem of initial blanks and concentrate only on strings of blanks within a line. We want to compress every string of two or more blanks to a single blank. One solution is to copy only the first blank and to consider the other blanks as extra blanks to be skipped over. In this approach a blank is extra (*not* copied) provided

1. The character is a blank
2. The character that precedes it on the same line is also a blank

This test requires that the program remember two characters instead of just one. Hence, we will use two variables of type CHARACTER as buffer variables. One, called CURRENT, serves the same purpose as the variable SYMBOL in the pseudocode above. It will contain the current symbol, which either does or does not get copied to the second file. The other variable, called PREVIOUS, will contain the previous character on the line being copied from. So the value of PREVIOUS is just the previous value of CURRENT. The following algorithm refinement uses these two variables:

```
    loop
        exit when END_OF_FILE ( DIRTY_FILE );
--      initialize previous to something for the first iteration
        loop
            exit when END_OF_LINE ( DIRTY_FILE );
            GET ( DIRTY_FILE, CURRENT );
            if not ( PREVIOUS = BLANK and CURRENT = BLANK ) then
                PUT ( CLEAN_FILE, CURRENT );
            end if;
            PREVIOUS := CURRENT;
        end loop;
        SKIP_LINE ( DIRTY_FILE );
        NEW_LINE ( CLEAN_FILE );
    end loop;
```

force the special case

This is not yet a complete solution. It does not make sense for the first symbol of a line. To make it work for the first symbol of a line, recall that we want to copy the first symbol as long as it is not a blank. Hence, if we set PREVIOUS equal to the blank symbol before we start each line, then this test works for the first symbol of a line as well. The complete final code for the separately compiled procedure CLEAN_BLANKS is shown in Figure 13.11.

```
separate ( EDIT )
procedure CLEAN_BLANKS ( DIRTY_FILE : in FILE_TYPE;
                         CLEAN_FILE : in out FILE_TYPE ) is
--                  INPUT  : dirty_file has been opened
--                           clean_file has been created
--                  OUTPUT : clean_file without excess blanks
--                  DESCRIPTION : dirty_file is left unchanged.
--                                Removes excess blanks as it copies
--                                nonblanks from dirty_file
--                                to clean_file.
    BLANK : constant CHARACTER := ' ';
    CURRENT,
    PREVIOUS : CHARACTER;
begin -- Clean_Blanks
    loop
        exit when END_OF_FILE ( DIRTY_FILE );
        PREVIOUS := BLANK;
        loop
            exit when END_OF_LINE ( DIRTY_FILE );
            GET ( DIRTY_FILE, CURRENT );
            if not ( PREVIOUS = BLANK
                 and CURRENT = BLANK ) then
                PUT ( CLEAN_FILE, CURRENT );
            end if;
```

```
            PREVIOUS := CURRENT;
        end loop;
        SKIP_LINE ( DIRTY_FILE );
        NEW_LINE ( CLEAN_FILE );
    end loop;
end CLEAN_BLANKS;
```

Figure 13.11 Procedure to copy text with excess blanks omitted.

Text Editing as a Programming Aid

An Ada program is a piece of text and is stored in a text file. Hence, it can be edited by another program in the ways we have been describing. This can sometimes be a helpful programming aid. As an example, consider the task of tracing a program, which we discussed in Chapters 3 and 7. Tracing is a technique to aid in debugging programs. Specifically, it consists of inserting temporary PUT statements that output intermediate results. Once the program is debugged, we want to remove these extra PUT statements used for tracing. To aid us in finding and removing trace statements or for that matter any other sort of temporary lines, we suggested marking the previous line by a comment and to use all lowercase letters in a PUT statement, as in the following sample:

```
-- TEMPORARY OUTPUT
put ( sum ); new_line;
```

Suppose all our temporary statements are marked in the way we described. Then to remove the temporary statements, all we need to do is locate the line that begins with -- TEMPORARY OUTPUT, and then delete it and those temporary statements that follow it. This sort of tedious and uninteresting task is best left to the computer. In Exercise 16 you are asked to write a program to do this editing. After writing the program, it would be a good idea to actually use the program as a programming tool from then on. It is not just a "toy problem."

Summary of Problem Solving and Programming Techniques

- Text files are used for storing data that is to remain in secondary storage after a program terminates. The data is stored as strings of symbols, like the data displayed on the output screen.
- The text files that are manipulated by Ada programs can also be read and changed using the editor.

- Any location, be it a variable, a text file, or anything else, that holds data on its way from one place to another is called a *buffer*. Since it is not possible to move data directly from one file to another, a program that moves data between files must use a variable (or variables) as a buffer. The data is read from one file into the buffer and then written out from the buffer to the other file.
- A text file may not be opened for reading and writing at the same time. Hence, in a program that edits a text file, the usual technique is to use an additional temporary file. The contents of the text file are copied into the temporary file, and the editing changes are made in the process of copying. After that, the edited version of the text is recopied back into the original file.
- One application of text editing is to edit the temporary trace statements out of a debugged Ada program.
- The exact details of file handling will vary slightly from one installation to another. Hence, file handling should be isolated into procedures to make any needed changes easy to carry out.
- When designing conditions for some program or algorithm action, it is sometimes clearer to think in terms of when the action should not take place, rather than in terms of when it should take place.
- Once a general solution that applies to most cases has been found, it is often possible to force the solution to fit the remaining cases by setting some initial conditions or by making some other small changes.

Summary of Ada Constructs

type for text files

Syntax:

```
TEXT_IO.FILE_TYPE
```

The Ada type name for text files.

text file variables

Syntax:

```
file_variable : TEXT_IO.FILE_TYPE;
```

Example:

```
DATA_FILE : TEXT_IO.FILE_TYPE;
```

Declaration of a file variable of type `TEXT_IO.FILE_TYPE`. These file variables are used as names for text files within an Ada program.

Open

Syntax:

```
OPEN ( file_variable, IN_FILE, external_file_name );
```

Example:

```
OPEN ( FILE_1, IN_FILE, "c:\chap_13\summary.epl" );
```

Opens the text file specified by *external__file__name* for reading. *file__variable* is a variable of type TEXT_IO.FILE_TYPE. Reading starts at the first character of the first line of the text file and proceeds through the file.

Create

Syntax:

CREATE (*file__variable*, OUT_FILE, *external__file__name*);

Example:

```
CREATE ( FILE_2, OUT_FILE, "c:\chap_13\data.out" );
```

Opens the text file specified by *external__file__name* for writing. *file__variable* is a variable of type TEXT_IO.FILE_TYPE. This always produces a blank file. If no file exists with *file__variable* as its file variable name, then a blank one is created. If there already is a file associated with *file__variable*, then the information in that file is no longer available.

The CREATE procedure can also be used for temporary files. In the case of a temporary file, only the name of the temporary file is given in the parameter list. Example:

```
CREATE ( TEMP_FILE );
```

Reset procedure

Syntax:

RESET (*file__variable*);
RESET (*file__variable*, *file__mode*);

Examples:

```
RESET ( FILE_1 );
RESET ( FILE_2, IN_FILE );
```

The first form of RESET is used to move the arrow in a previously opened file back to the first character in the file. It allows the program to reread the information in the file. The second form can be used to change an output file that was previously created in the program into an input file. The arrow is moved back to the first character in the file. The *file__variable* must be of type TEXT_IO.FILE_TYPE.

Put procedure

Syntax:

PUT (*file__variable*, *output__item*);

Example:

```
PUT ( DATA_FILE, "Hello" );
```

Just like using PUT to write to the screen, but when done this way the *output__item* is written to the text file specified by *file__variable*. *file__variable* is a variable of type `TEXT_IO.FILE_TYPE`. The file specified by *file__variable* must have been opened with a call to `CREATE`. The *output__item* can be an object identifier, an expression, or a quoted string.

New__Line procedure

Syntax:

`NEW_LINE (` *file__variable* `);`

Example:

```
NEW_LINE ( FILE_2 );
```

The procedure inserts an end-of-line marker in the text file. In other words, it causes any subsequent output to *file__variable* to be written on the next line.

Get procedure

Syntax:

`GET (` *file__variable* `,` *input__variable* `);`

Example:

```
GET ( DATA_FILE, QUANTITY );
```

Just like using `GET` to read from the keyboard, but done this way the values are read from the text file specified by *file__variable*. *file__variable* is a variable of type `TEXT_IO.FILE_TYPE`. The file specified by *file__variable* must have been opened with a call to `OPEN`. The *input__variable* can be a variable identifier, an indexed variable, or a record component.

Skip__Line procedure

Syntax:

`SKIP_LINE (` *file__variable* `);`

Example:

```
SKIP_LINE ( DATA_FILE );
```

The procedure causes any subsequent read from the file to start at the beginning of the next line.

end__of__file function

Syntax:

`END_OF_FILE (` *file__variable* `)`

Example:

```
END_OF_FILE ( FILE_1 );
```

This is a boolean-valued function that returns TRUE if all of the text file specified by *file__variable* has been read. More precisely, it evaluates to TRUE if the arrow (described earlier in this chapter) is pointing at the end-of-file marker (also called the file terminator) which follows the last line in the file. *file__variable* is a variable of type TEXT_IO.FILE_TYPE.

end__of__line function

Syntax:

END_OF_LINE (*file__variable*)

Example:

```
END_OF_LINE ( DATA_FILE )
```

This is a boolean-valued function that returns TRUE if all of the data on the current line of the file specified by *file__variable* has been read. More precisely, it evaluates to TRUE if the arrow (described earlier in this chapter) is pointing to the end-of-line marker. *file__variable* is a variable of type TEXT_IO.FILE_TYPE.

Exercises

Self-Test Exercises

5. What will be the contents of the file "Lincoln.adr" after the following program is run with the following input from the keyboard?

```
with TEXT_IO; use TEXT_IO;
procedure EXERCISE_5 is
     EX_5_FILE : FILE_TYPE;
     NEXT : CHARACTER;
begin -- Exercise_5
     CREATE ( EX_5_FILE, OUT_FILE, "Lincoln.adr" );
     PUT ( "Start input" );
     loop
          exit when END_OF_LINE;
          GET ( NEXT );
          PUT ( EX_5_FILE, NEXT );
     end loop;
     SKIP_LINE;
     NEW_LINE ( EX_5_FILE );
     GET ( NEXT ); SKIP_LINE;
     PUT ( EX_5_FILE, NEXT ); NEW_LINE ( EX_5_FILE );
     GET ( NEXT ); SKIP_LINE;
     PUT ( EX_5_FILE, NEXT ); NEW_LINE ( EX_5_FILE );
     PUT ( EX_5_FILE, "The End." ); NEW_LINE ( EX_5_FILE );
     CLOSE ( EX_5_FILE);
end EXERCISE_5;
```

Input:

```
Four score and seven years ago,
our fathers brought forth upon
this continent a new nation,
conceived in liberty and
dedicated to the proposition that
all men are created equal.
```

6. Suppose the text file named by the file variable SALLY contains the following:

```
abcdef<eol>ghijk<eol>lmnop<eol><eof>
```

Suppose variables are declared as follows:

```
BUFFER : CHARACTER;
LETTER_1, LETTER_2 : CHARACTER;
EX_6_FILE : FILE_TYPE;
```

What will be the output produced by the following, provided it is embedded in a complete program that opens EX_6_FILE with OPEN and that declares variables as shown above?

```
GET ( EX_6_FILE, LETTER_1 );
GET ( EX_6_FILE, LETTER_2 );
SKIP_LINE ( EX_6_FILE );
PUT ( LETTER_1 );
PUT ( LETTER_2 );
NEW_LINE;
loop
     exit when END_OF_LINE ( EX_6_FILE );
     GET ( EX_6_FILE, BUFFER );
     PUT ( BUFFER );
end loop;
PUT ( "Hi" );
```

7. Write a program to write the numbers **1** through **10** to a text file, one per line. Run the program and then look at the text file.

8. Write a program that reads the list of numbers from the text file of Exercise 7, computes their sum, and outputs the sum to the screen. The program should use END_OF_FILE to detect the end of the file.

Interactive Exercises

9. It can be handy for a program to read a file name from the keyboard. Write a program that reads in a file name, creates a new file by that name, and writes to that file whatever is input from the keyboard.

10. Write a program to read a line of text from a text file and display it on the screen. Use END_OF_LINE. Use the editor or another program to create the text file.

Programming Exercises

11. Write a procedure that appends the contents of one text file to the end of a second text file. The contents of the first file should be unchanged after the procedure is called.

12. Write a program that creates a table telling how to give change using quarters, dimes, and pennies. It should show the coins for all amounts from 1 to 99 cents. There should be a heading for the table. The program should output the table to a text file.

13. Write a program that outputs a table for converting from Celsius (centigrade) temperatures to Fahrenheit temperatures. Show all temperatures from $-10°$ Celsius to $100°$ Celsius. A Celsius (centigrade) temperature (C) can be converted to an equivalent Fahrenheit temperature (F) according to the following formula:

$$F = (9/5)C + 32$$

The program should output the table to a text file.

14. Write a program that gives and takes advice on program writing. The program should open by writing a piece of advice to the screen. It should then ask the user to type in a different piece of advice. The next user of the program receives the advice typed in the last time the program was run. Be sure that the first person to run the program gets some advice.

15. The organization Ada Smut Suppressors has declared **'A'** and **'S'** to be dirty letters and has hired you to write a program to eliminate these letters from text files. Write a program that will replace all occurrences of the letters **'A'** and **'S'** in a text file with the letter **'X'**. The program should replace both upper- and lowercase letters, **'A'**, **'a'**, **'S'**, and **'s'**, with **'X'**.

16. Write a program to delete all temporary lines from a text file containing an Ada program. See the section entitled "Text Editing as a Programming Aid" for a discussion of this problem.

17. (This is an exploratory exercise for those who did Exercise 16.) In writing the program for Exercise 16, you may have added some temporary PUT and NEW_LINE statements. If you did not, then go back and add some. Now you have a copy of the program with lines that need to be deleted. Run this program on the text file containing the program; that is, "run the program on itself." The program will clean itself, so to speak. (Some systems may require that you have two copies of the program to do this, but most systems will let you do it with just one copy. In any event, you should have an extra copy of the program just in case some mistake causes the program to damage itself.)

18. Write a program that takes two lists of integers, each sorted from smallest to largest, and merges the numbers into a single larger list containing all of the numbers sorted from smallest to largest. The two lists are in two text files and the merged list is placed in a third text file.

19. Write a program to generate personalized junk mail. The program will work with a text file that contains a letter in which the location of the name of the recipient is indicated by some special string of characters, such as **"#name#"**. The program

will ask for the name from the keyboard, read it in and then make a copy of the letter with the name inserted where indicated. The letter with the name inserted should be written to another text file.

20. Write a program that computes the average number of characters per word and the average number of words per sentence for the text in some text file. The name of the text file should be read from the keyboard.

21. Write a program that produces a list of all the words used in a text file and the number of times each word is used. The list should be output to the screen as well as to another text file. The list should be in alphabetical order. Do not forget to consider punctuation marks, such as periods and commas, when determining the ends of words. The program should treat upper- and lowercase letters as being the same. For example, `"Word"` and `"word"` should be treated as the same word.

22. (This exercise uses information from the optional sections ''Random Number Generators'' and ''Using Pseudorandom Numbers'' in Chapter 8.) Write a program to generate pseudorandom test data for other programs. The data is written to a text file that contains NUMBER_OF_LINES lines of NUMBER_PER_LINE INTEGER values per line. The values of NUMBER_OF_LINES and NUMBER_PER_LINE as well as a range of possible integer values are to be read from the keyboard. If your system has a predefined pseudorandom number generator in a support library, then you may use it; otherwise, use the function RANDOM described in Chapter 8.

23. Books and newspapers contain text that is right-justified, that is, all lines are the same length. This is accomplished by copying as many words as possible onto one line and then adding extra blanks between the words so that the line is filled out to the prescribed line length. The line breaks in the original unjustified text are ignored in determining line lengths in the justified text. Write a program that produces right-justified text. The program will read from one file and write the right-justified text to another file. Use 80 characters, or whatever is convenient, as the line length.

24. (This exercise uses information from the optional sections ''Random Number Generators'' and ''Using Pseudorandom Numbers'' in Chapter 8.) Write a program to generate random English sentences. The program uses two text files, one containing a list of nouns and one containing a list of verbs, and it uses a random number generator to choose words from these files.

25. Enhance the program from Exercise 24 so it outputs a series of sentences that seem to be related. Do this by repeating the nouns and verbs used. Specifically, once a noun or verb is used, the program remembers it and uses it more often than the other words on the lists. To make the output seem even more reasonable, you might try grouping related words and have the program choose words related to those already chosen. Use your imagination in forming word groupings and the other details of the algorithm.

26. Since the rules of grammar are not as rigid for poetry as they are for prose, it is usually easier to write a poetry-writing program that produces humanlike output than it is to produce a reasonable prose-writing program. Use the techniques discussed in Exercises 24 and 25 to write a program that outputs free-verse poetry.

27. Design a version of Ada in a foreign language of your choice. To do this choose a fixed translation for each reserved word and standard identifier. Write a program that takes a text file containing an Ada program and translates it into the foreign language version by replacing each reserved word and standard identifier by its translation. Then enhance your program so it can also translate a foreign language program into English Ada.

References for Further Reading

N. E. Miller and C. G. Petersen, *File Structures with Ada* (Redwood City, CA: The Benjamin/Cummings Publishing Co., 1989).

CHAPTER

14

PROBLEM SOLVING USING RECURSION

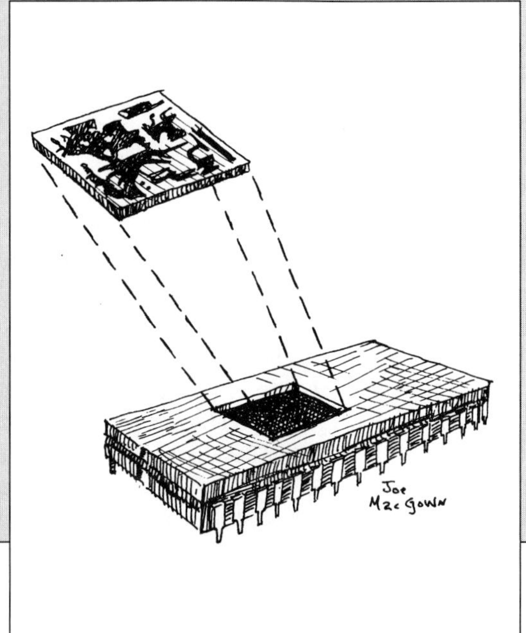

Integrated Circuit

Personal computers (PCs) as we know them today would not be possible without the integrated circuit. Discrete (individual) electronic components are combined and miniaturized into a single semiconductor chip called an integrated circuit. Jack Kilby, who developed the early hand-held calculator, introduced the integrated circuit at Texas Instruments in 1958. Robert Noyce of Fairfield Semiconductor developed a process in 1959 of interconnecting circuit components via photo-engraving on a silicon wafer.

Chapter Contents

recursive procedures and functions

We have encountered a few cases of circular definitions that worked out satisfactorily. The most prominent examples are the definitions of certain Ada statements. For example, the definition of a `loop` statement says that it must contain other statements. Since one possibility for these other statements is another `loop` statement, there is a kind of circularity in that definition. The definition of the `loop` statement, if written out in complete detail, will contain a reference to `loop` statements. In mathematics these kinds of circular definitions are called *recursive definitions.* In Ada a procedure or function may be defined in terms of itself in the same way. To put it more precisely, a procedure or function body may contain a call to itself. In such cases the procedure or function is said to be *recursive.* In this chapter we will discuss recursion in Ada, and more generally we will discuss recursion as a programming and problem solving technique. We will start with an example.

Case Study

A Recursive Function

Problem Definition

Back in Chapter 3 the Fly by Night Thrift was offering a high rate of interest for savings accounts at their institution. They have now decided to sweeten the deal a little more. Starting the beginning of next month, they will begin compounding the interest every month, and it will be retroactive to the beginning of the year or the date of deposit, whichever is latest. The top brass of the institution made this decision, and now they turn to us (their programmers) to write a new computer program to carry out this new plan. A program is needed to compute compound interest for a varying number of months, and since not all accounts pay the same, it must work for different interest rates.

Discussion

The main program for this problem is given in Figure 14.1. Note that, for the moment, the function to compute the compound interest is listed as **separate**. It was done this way because we have two programmers. One programmer was assigned to write the main procedure, and the other was assigned to write the COMPOUND_INTEREST function. Once the two programmers agreed upon a plan and decided what the interface between the main procedure and the COMPOUND_INTEREST function would be, they went to work separately on their individual computers. The interface consists of the subprogram specifications and the documentation. The subprogram specification consists of the subprogram type (in this case **function**), the subprogram name (COMPOUND_INTEREST), the following parameters (their names, order, modes, and types)

```
PRESENT_BALANCE : FLOAT;
INTEREST_RATE : FLOAT;
NUMBER_OF_MONTHS : NATURAL
```

and, since it is a function, the type of the value to be returned (FLOAT).

Algorithm

The algorithm for computing interest and updating the balance is quite simple.

```
INTEREST := PRESENT_BALANCE * INTEREST_RATE;
NEW_BALANCE := PRESENT_BALANCE + INTEREST;
```

To compound the interest, we set the present balance equal to the just-computed new balance, and another new balance is computed. The outline of our example is

Program

```
with TEXT_IO;
use TEXT_IO;
procedure INTEREST is
    ACTUAL_MONTHLY_RATE : FLOAT;
    PRESENT_BALANCE : FLOAT;
    INTEREST_RATE : FLOAT;
    NEW_BALANCE : FLOAT;
    NUMBER_OF_MONTHS : NATURAL;
    package MONEY_IO is new FLOAT_IO ( FLOAT );
    use MONEY_IO;
    package MONTH_IO is new INTEGER_IO ( NATURAL );
    use MONTH_IO;
    function COMPOUND_INTEREST ( BALANCE : FLOAT;
                                 INTEREST_RATE : FLOAT;
                                 NUMBER_OF_MONTHS : NATURAL )
                                 return FLOAT is separate;
--                  INPUT  : The account balance, the actual monthly
--                           interest rate, and the months for the
--                           compounding of the interest.
--                  OUTPUT : A new balance.
--                  DESCRIPTION : Compute a new balance based on
--                                monthly compound interest.
begin -- Interest
     PUT ( "Enter the present balance:" ); NEW_LINE;
     GET ( PRESENT_BALANCE ); SKIP_LINE;
     PUT ( "Enter annual interest rate in percent (i.e., 5.53):" );
     NEW_LINE;
     GET ( INTEREST_RATE ); SKIP_LINE;
     PUT ( "Enter the number of months:" ); NEW_LINE;
     GET ( NUMBER_OF_MONTHS ); SKIP_LINE;
     ACTUAL_MONTHLY_RATE := INTEREST_RATE / 100.0 / 12.0;
     NEW_BALANCE := COMPOUND_INTEREST ( PRESENT_BALANCE,
                                        ACTUAL_MONTHLY_RATE,
                                        NUMBER_OF_MONTHS );
     PUT ( "The new balance after " );
     PUT ( NUMBER_OF_MONTHS, 1 );
     PUT ( " months of compound interest is $" );
     PUT ( NEW_BALANCE, 1, 2, 0 );
end INTEREST;
```

Figure 14.1 Program to compute interest of savings accounts.

```
NEW__BALANCE := ORIGINAL__BALANCE;
Repeat
    INTEREST := NEW__BALANCE * INTEREST__RATE;
    NEW__BALANCE := NEW__BALANCE + INTEREST;
```

The new balance is first assigned the original balance, and the process is then repeated for each period of compounding. Figure 14.2 has the completed COMPOUND__INTEREST function.

```
separate ( INTEREST )
function COMPOUND_INTEREST ( BALANCE : FLOAT;
                             INTEREST_RATE : FLOAT;
                             NUMBER_OF_MONTHS : NATURAL )
                             return FLOAT is
--                   INPUT  : The account balance, the actual monthly
--                            interest rate, and the months for the
--                            compounding of the interest.
--                   OUTPUT : A new balance.
--                   DESCRIPTION : Compute a new balance based on
--                                 monthly compound interest.
    INTEREST : FLOAT;
    NEW_BALANCE : FLOAT := BALANCE;
begin -- Compound_Interest
    for MONTH in 1 . . NUMBER_OF_MONTHS
    loop
        INTEREST := NEW_BALANCE * INTEREST_RATE;
        NEW_BALANCE := NEW_BALANCE + INTEREST;
    end loop;
    return NEW_BALANCE;
end COMPOUND_INTEREST;
```

Figure 14.2 Nonrecursive function for compound interest.

Another way to look at the computation of compound interest is to say that the balance after zero months is the amount deposited originally. We can write it

```
b(0) = d
```

The balance after **1** month is (ir = interest rate)

```
b(1) = b(0) + b(0) * ir
```

The balance after **2** months is

```
b(2) = b(1) + b(1) * ir
```

The balance after **3** months is

```
b(3) = b(2) + b(2) * ir
```

In general the balance after **m** months (m > 0) is

```
b(m) = b(m-1) + b(m-1) * ir
```

Notice that we have a recursive definition; the balance after **m** months is defined in terms of the balance after **m − 1** months. A recursive function for compound interest could be written as

```
b(0) = d
b(1) = b(0) + b(0) * ir
b(m) = b(m-1) + b(m-1) * ir
```

or more simply as

```
b(0) = d
b(m) = b(m-1) + b(m-1) * ir
```

which may not be quite as intuitive but nevertheless works well to define the function.

recursive call

To write this as an Ada function, we would first test the month for zero and return the original deposit or present balance in the account.

```
if NUMBER_OF_MONTHS = 0 then
    return BALANCE;
```

If the money has been on deposit for one month, interest is added to the present balance.

```
elsif NUMBER_OF_MONTHS = 1 then
    return BALANCE + BALANCE * INTEREST_RATE;
```

Again, this could be left out, but nevertheless we include it to make a more illustrative example. Beyond the first month we will apply our general formula that requires a *recursive call* to the function that computes compound interest.

```
else
    NEW_BALANCE := COMPOUND_INTEREST ( BALANCE,
                                       INTEREST_RATE,
                                       NUMBER_OF_MONTHS - 1 );
    return NEW_BALANCE + NEW_BALANCE * INTEREST_RATE;
```

The function call is called recursive because the call to COMPOUND_INTEREST occurs inside the body of the function COMPOUND_INTEREST. The function is called again and again, each time passing it the previous month (NUMBER_OF_MONTHS − 1). Note that a local variable, NEW_BALANCE, is introduced so that the function does not have to be called twice to compute the same value (b(m−1)).

We can now put this all together to get a recursive body of COMPOUND_INTEREST that works for any number of months. The function is shown in Figure 14.3.

```
separate ( INTEREST )
function COMPOUND_INTEREST ( BALANCE : FLOAT;
                             INTEREST_RATE : FLOAT;
                             NUMBER_OF_MONTHS : NATURAL )
                             return FLOAT is
--                  INPUT  : The account balance, the actual monthly
--                           interest rate, and the months for the
--                           compounding of the interest.
--                  OUTPUT : A new balance.
--                  DESCRIPTION : Compute a new balance based on
--                                monthly compound interest.
    NEW_BALANCE : FLOAT;
begin -- Compound_Interest
    if NUMBER_OF_MONTHS = 0 then
        return BALANCE;
    elsif NUMBER_OF_MONTHS = 1 then
        return BALANCE + BALANCE * INTEREST_RATE;
    else
        NEW_BALANCE := COMPOUND_INTEREST ( BALANCE,
                                           INTEREST_RATE,
                                           NUMBER_OF_MONTHS - 1 );
        return NEW_BALANCE + NEW_BALANCE * INTEREST_RATE;
    end if;
end COMPOUND_INTEREST;
```

Figure 14.3 Recursive function for compound interest.

Let us see what happens when this function is called with some sample values. First let us consider the simple expression

```
COMPOUND_INTEREST ( 1000.00, 0.005, 1 )
```

When the function is called, the value of BALANCE is set equal to **1000.0**, the value of INTEREST_RATE is set equal to **0.005**, the value of NUMBER_OF_MONTHS is set equal to **1**, and the code is executed. (If 0.005 seems like a small interest rate, remember that is the monthly rate, not the annual rate. Anyway, our function will work for any interest rate.) Since **1** is greater than zero, it fails the first test and passes the second. So in this case it is easy to see that the value returned is **1005.0** (1000.0 + 1000.0 * 0.005).

Next let us try a set of parameters that exercise the recursive part of the function body. Let us determine the value of

example of a recursive call

```
COMPOUND_INTEREST ( 1000.0, 0.005, 2 )
```

We proceed just as before. When the function is called, the value of BALANCE is set equal to **1000.0**, the value of INTEREST_RATE is set equal to **0.005**, the value of NUMBER_OF_MONTHS is set equal to **2**, and the code is executed. Since **2** is greater than 1, the **else** part is executed. Consequently NEW_BALANCE is assigned to the value returned by a call to COMPOUND_INTEREST with parameters (1000.0, 0.005, 2−1). We know from our previous example that NEW_BALANCE will be assigned the value **1005.0**. Thus, the value returned by the original call to COMPOUND_INTEREST with parameters (1000.0, 0.005, 2) will be **1010.025** (1005.0 + 1005.0 * 0.005).

A Closer Look at Recursion

The body of the function COMPOUND_INTEREST uses recursion. Yet we did nothing new or different in evaluating the function call COMPOUND_INTEREST (1000.0, 0.005, 2). We treated it just like any of the function calls we saw in previous chapters. We simply substituted the actual parameters for the formal parameters and then executed the code. When we reached the recursive call COMPOUND_INTEREST (1000.0, 0.005, 1), we simply repeated this process one more time.

how recursion works

The computer keeps track of recursive calls in the following way: When a function is called, the computer plugs in the actual parameters for the formal parameters and begins to execute the code. If it should encounter a recursive call, then it temporarily stops its computation because it must know the result of the recursive call before it can proceed. It saves all the information it needs to continue the computation later on and proceeds to evaluate the recursive call. When the recursive call is completed, the computer returns to the outer computation and completes that outer computation. Figure 14.4 illustrates this for the example of the previous section. Notice that when a recursive call is encountered, the current computation is temporarily suspended, and a second copy of the function is used to evaluate the recursive call. When that is completed, the value returned by the recursive call is used to complete the suspended computation. In the example there are two levels of function calls. There may be several levels of recursive calls. The principle is the same no matter how many levels of recursive calls there are.

a highly recursive example

As a further example, let us write a recursive function for the second order Fibonacci sequence. The second order Fibonacci sequence starts with the values of 0 and 1, then each succeeding number is the sum of the previous two numbers in the sequence. (The term *second order* comes from the fact that two numbers are added. A third order adds three numbers, a fourth order adds four, etc.) With the first two numbers being 0 and 1, the next value in the sequence is 0 + 1 = 1. The next is 1 + 1 = 2, the next is 1 + 2 = 3, and so forth. The Fibonacci sequence is a growth rate that commonly occurs in nature. In an ideal population where each organism matures in one time unit and has one offspring every time unit after it matures, then the *n*th Fibonnacci number gives the size of the population after *n* time units. This analysis also makes the idealizing assumption that there are no deaths. Despite all this idealization, the sequence is still faithful enough to nature that it is used in modeling and can be seen in actual population figures. However, the biology need not concern us here. We will simply take the abstract definition and define a function to compute the values described.

The evaluating `COMPOUND_INTEREST ( 1000.0, 0.005, 2 )` requires evaluating code equivalent to

First

```
if 2 = 0 then
    return 1000.0
elsif 2 = 1 then
    return 1000.0 + 1000.0 * 0.005;
else
    NEW_BALANCE := COMPOUND_INTEREST ( 1000.0, 0.005, 1 );
    return NEW_BALANCE + NEW_BALANCE * 0.005;
end if;    -- 1005.0    +   1005.0    * 0.005
```

Fourth

1010.025 is the value finally returned

Second

Third
`COMPOUND_INTEREST ( 1000.0, 0.005, 1 )`
`returns 1005.0`

Computation stops to evaluate the recursive call

```
    if 1 = 0 then
        return 1000.0
    elsif 1 = 1 then
        return 1000.0 + 1000.0 * 0.005;
    else
        NEW_BALANCE := COMPOUND_INTEREST ( 1000.0, 0.005, 1 );
        return NEW_BALANCE + NEW_BALANCE * 0.005;
    end if;
```

Figure 14.4 Evaluation of a recursive function.

Algorithm

The second order Fibonacci sequence can be defined in terms of the position of a number in the sequence using the following algorithm:

If position = 0 Then --> 0
If position = 1 Then --> 1
If position > 1 Then --> Fibonacci (position − 2)
+ Fibonacci (position − 1)

Computing a value for a position greater than **1** requires two calls to the Fibonacci function. The Ada version of a recursive function that computes the second order Fibonacci sequence is given in Figure 14.5.

```
function FIBONACCI ( POSITION : NATURAL ) return NATURAL is
--                 INPUT  : A position in the Fibonacci sequence.
--                 OUTPUT : The Fibonacci value for a position.
--                 DESCRIPTION : Computes a Fibonacci value
--                               using a recursive algorithm.
begin -- Fibonacci
    if POSITION = 0 then
        return 0;
    elsif POSITION = 1 then
        return 1;
    else
        return FIBONACCI ( POSITION - 2 )
             + FIBONACCI ( POSITION - 1 );
    end if;
end FIBONACCI;
```

14.5 A highly recursive function.

Evaluation of a recursive function such as our example for FIBONACCI numbers can get fairly involved. Consider what happens when the following statement is executed:

```
VALUE := FIBONACCI ( 3 );
```

recursion within recursion

The computer starts to evaluate FIBONACCI (3) but must stop to compute FIBONACCI (1), which is **1**. It must stop again to compute FIBONACCI (2). While computing FIBONACCI (2), it must stop to compute FIBONACCI (0) and then again to compute FIBONACCI (1). It can easily compute FIBONACCI(0), which is **0**. The **0** is added to the value of FIBONACCI (1), which is **1**, to get **1**. It then returns and completes the computation by adding the **1**, which it got from completing the first call to FIBONACCI (1), to the **1**, which it got from completing the call to FIBONACCI (2). The **1** + **1** gives **2**, which is the value returned by FIBONACCI (3). The entire process is diagrammed in Figure 14.6.

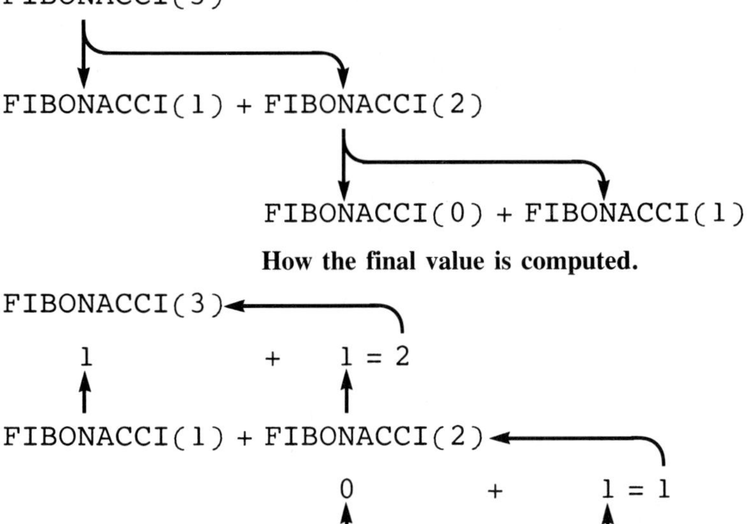

Figure 14.6 Evaluating the recursive function call FIBONACCI (3).

Pitfall

Infinite Recursion

how recursion terminates

Ada places no restrictions on how recursive calls are used in function and procedure bodies. However, for a recursive function to be useful it must be designed so that any call of the function must ultimately terminate with some piece of code that does not depend on recursion. The function may call itself, and that recursive call may call the function again. The process may be repeated any number of times. However, the process will not terminate unless eventually one of the recursive calls does not depend on recursion to return a value. The general outline of a recursive function is as follows:

- One or more cases in which the value returned is computed in terms of simpler cases of the same function (i.e., using recursive calls).
- One or more cases in which the value returned is computed without the use of any recursive calls. These cases, without any recursion, are called *base cases* or *stopping cases.*

Often an **if-then-else** statement or series of **if-then** statements determine which of the cases will be executed. A typical scenario is for the original function call to execute a case that includes a recursive call. That recursive call may in turn execute a case that requires another recursive call. For some number of times, each recursive call produces another recursive call, but eventually one of the stopping cases should apply. Every call of the function must eventually lead to a stopping case; otherwise, the function call will never end because of an infinite string of recursive calls. (In practice, a call that includes infinite recursion will terminate abnormally when the system raises the exception STORAGE_ERROR rather than actually running forever.)

The most common way to ensure that a stopping case is eventually reached is to write the function so that some numeric quantity is decreased on each recursive call and to provide a stopping case for some "small" value such as zero. This is how we designed the function COMPOUND_INTEREST in Figure 14.2 and the function FIBONACCI in Figure 14.5. Look back at Figure 14.5. To compute FIBONACCI (3) the function makes the following sequence of recursive calls: FIBONACCI (1), FIBONACCI (2), FIBONACCI (0), and FIBONACCI (1). The call to FIBONACCI (0) returns a value by executing a stopping case:

```
if POSITION = 0 then
    return 0;
```

Similarly the call to FIBONACCI (1) returns a value by executing a stopping case:

```
elsif POSITION = 1 then
    return 1;
```

Those two pieces of code include no recursive call. Hence, the code does eventually terminate; a value is returned for FIBONACCI (0) and FIBONACCI (1) and the process works its way back to the original call, which terminates and returns a value for FIBONACCI (3).

example of infinite recursion

Examples of infinite recursion are not hard to come by. The following is a syntactically correct Ada function body that might result from an attempt to declare an alternative version of the function FIBONACCI:

```
function FIBONACCI ( POSITION : INTEGER ) return INTEGER is
begin -- Fibonacci
    return FIBONACCI ( POSITION - 2 )
        + FIBONACCI ( POSITION - 1 );
end FIBONACCI;
```

If embedded in a program that calls this function, the compiler will translate it to machine code, and the machine code can be executed. Moreover, it even has a certain reasonableness to it. We said that the Fibonacci value was the sum of the previous two values in the sequence.

However, this function will produce an infinite sequence of recursive calls, assuming `INTEGER'FIRST` is minus infinity, which is mathematically correct. An attempt to evaluate `FIBONACCI ( 3 )` will stop to evaluate `FIBONACCI ( 1 )`. That evaluation will in turn stop to evaluate an expression equivalent to `FIBONACCI ( -1 )`. That in turn will attempt to compute `FIBONACCI ( -3 )`. The process will proceed deeper and deeper, ad infinitum. It never does get around to evaluating the second call to `FIBONACCI`, which would lead to another infinite sequence of calls.

Stacks

To keep track of recursion and a number of other things, most computer systems make use of a structure called a *stack*. A stack is a very specialized kind of memory structure that is analogous to a stack of paper sheets. In this analogy there is an inexhaustible supply of blank sheets. To place some information in the stack, it is written on one of these sheets of paper and placed on top of the stack of papers. To place more information in the stack, a clean sheet of paper is taken, the information is written on it, and this new sheet of paper is placed on the stack. In this straightforward way more and more information may be placed on the stack. (This is a very common memory structure; a large number of office desks are organized in this fashion.)

Getting information out of the stack is also accomplished by a very simple procedure. The top sheet of paper can be read, and when it is no longer needed, it can be thrown away. There is one complication: only the top sheet of paper is accessible. To read, say, the third sheet from the top, the top two sheets must be thrown away. For this reason a stack is sometimes called a *last-in/first-out* memory structure.

Let us be a bit more precise about which pieces of paper are available to read and/or write on. In this analogy only the top sheet of paper on the stack is accessible. We will also allow one other sheet to be available to work on. That extra sheet is not part of the stack, but it is still available. All sheets of paper in the stack other than the top one are not available. To access those sheets, some other sheets must be thrown away.

stacks and recursion

Using a stack, the computer can easily keep track of recursion. Whenever a function is called, a new sheet of paper is taken. The function is copied onto the sheet of paper, and the actual parameters are plugged in for the formal parameters. Then the computer starts to execute the function. When it encounters a recursive call, it stops the computation it is doing on that sheet to compute the value returned by the recursive call. But before computing the recursive call, it saves enough information so when it does finally determine the value returned by the recursive call, it can continue the stopped computation. This saved information is written on the sheet of paper and placed on the stack. A new sheet of paper is used for the recursive call. It writes a second copy of the function on this new sheet of paper, plugs in the actual parameters, and starts to execute the recursive call. When it gets to a recursive call within the recursively called copy, it repeats the process of saving information on the stack and using a new sheet of paper for the new recursive call.

This process continues until some recursive call is completed and returns a value. When that happens it takes the top sheet of paper off the stack. This sheet contains the partially completed computation that needs the value just returned. So it is possible to proceed with that computation. The process continues until the computation on the bottom sheet is completed. The value returned by that bottom computation is the value returned by the original function call. Depending on how many recursive calls are made and how the function body is written, the stack may grow and shrink in any fashion.

In Figure 14.7 we have redrawn the computation in Figure 14.6 to show how the stack behaves for this particular function call. Notice that the sheets in the stack can only be accessed in a last-in/first-out fashion, but that is exactly what is needed to keep track of recursive calls. The version currently being worked on is the one that was called by the version on top of the stack, and that is the one waiting for it to return a value.

Evaluating FIBONACCI(3)

	Stack
	is initially empty
The first frame is added to stack	**FIBONACCI (3) is FIBONACCI(1) + FIBONACCI(2)**
A new frame is added to stack top	**FIBONACCI (1) is 1**
The first frame is still there	FIBONACCI (3) is FIBONACCI(1) + FIBONACCI(2)
Top frame is removed leaving the original	**FIBONACCI (3) is 1 + FIBONACCI(2)**
A new frame is added to stack top	**FIBONACCI (2) is FIBONACCI(0) + FIBONACCI(1)**
The first frame is still there	FIBONACCI (3) is 1 + FIBONACCI(2)
A new frame is added to stack top	**FIBONACCI (0) is 0**
The second frame is still there	FIBONACCI (2) is FIBONACCI(0) + FIBONACCI(1)

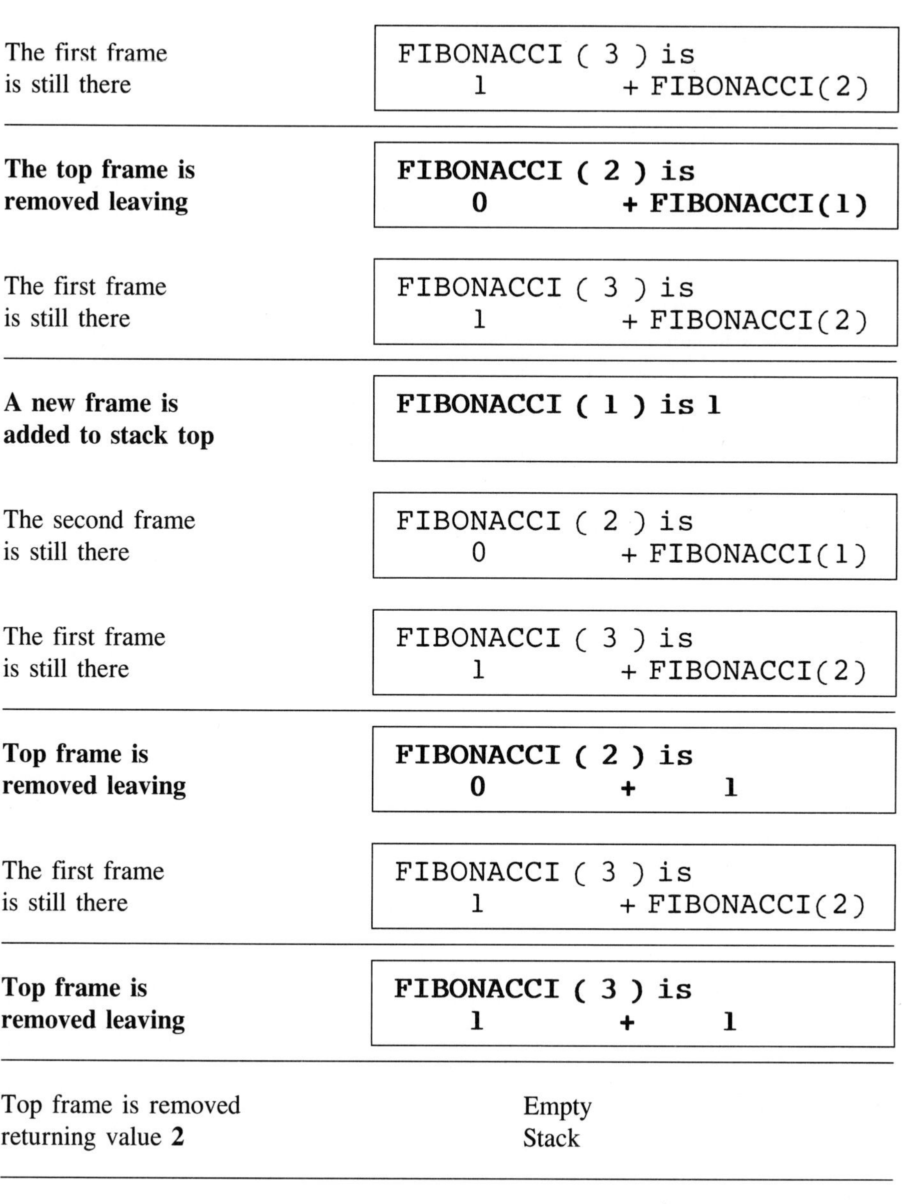
The first frame
is still there
FIBONACCI (3) is
1 + FIBONACCI(2)
The top frame is
removed leaving
FIBONACCI (2) is
0 + FIBONACCI(1)
The first frame
is still there
FIBONACCI (3) is
1 + FIBONACCI(2)
A new frame is
added to stack top
FIBONACCI (1) is 1
The second frame
is still there
FIBONACCI (2) is
0 + FIBONACCI(1)
The first frame
is still there
FIBONACCI (3) is
1 + FIBONACCI(2)
Top frame is
removed leaving
FIBONACCI (2) is
0 + 1
The first frame
is still there
FIBONACCI (3) is
1 + FIBONACCI(2)
Top frame is
removed leaving
FIBONACCI (3) is
1 + 1
Top frame is removed
returning value 2
Empty
Stack

Figure 14.7 Stack contents while evaluating a recursive function.

activation frames

Needless to say, computers do not have stacks of paper of this kind. This is just an analogy. The computer uses portions of memory rather than pieces of paper. The analogy is very exact, though. The content of one of these portions of memory is called an *activation frame*. These activation frames (just like the sheet of paper) are handled in this last-in/first-out manner, and the memory dedicated to holding these activation frames is called a *stack.*

stacks and local variables

Stacks are used for a number of things besides recursion. They are also used to keep track of local variables. Whenever any procedure calls another procedure, the computation of the calling procedure is suspended, and an activation frame (analogous to our sheet of paper) that shows where the procedure is in its computation is placed on the stack. Then a new activation frame is started for the procedure just called. If an identifier, say ZED, is local to the procedure just called, then there may be values for ZED in both the new and the old activation frames. These are two different ZEDs: one is local to the procedure just called, and one is local to some procedure with a wider scope. The computer knows they are different because they are in different activation frames. If you look back at Figure 5.11 you will see an illustration of how a stack can be used to keep track of the values of a variable identifier ZED when it is declared more than once. Although we did not call it a stack in Chapter 5, the illustrative boxes that contain the values of ZED show how a stack will change as the program is executed. The sequence of boxes shows the changes in stack contents. To simplify the figure we have assumed that this stack does nothing other than keep track of the values of ZED. This is the same kind of stack as the one used to keep track of recursive function calls. In fact often there is just one stack that contains all the information needed to keep track of all local identifiers as well as all recursive calls; at each call of a function or procedure, be it recursive or not, a new activation frame with all the required information is placed on the stack.

Pitfall

Stack Overflow

Many systems limit the size of the stack for various reasons. Suppose the stack is limited to 20 activation frames, suppose that the function FIBONACCI is declared as shown in Figure 14.5, and suppose that the following statement is executed:

```
VALUE := FIBONACCI ( 30 );
```

stack overflow

In that case the system will try to place approximately 30 activation frames on the stack. However, the stack is limited to 20 frames. The system cannot proceed within the constraints imposed. So the computation is aborted when the system raises STORAGE__ERROR and an error statement is output. Raising the exception STORAGE__ERROR simply means that the system tried to make the stack grow larger than what is permitted. One common cause of STORAGE__ERROR is infinite recursion. If a procedure or function is recursing infinitely (or even a large finite number of times), then it will eventually try to make the stack exceed any allowable stack size limit. Remember that the computer's memory is indeed finite in size.

Exercises

Self-Test Exercises

1. What is the output of the following program?

```
with TEXT_IO; use TEXT_IO;
procedure EXERCISE_1 is
    package MYSTERY_IO is new INTEGER_IO ( POSITIVE );
    use MYSTERY_IO;
    function MYSTERY ( NUMBER : POSITIVE )
             return POSITIVE is
    begin -- Mystery
        if NUMBER = 1 then
            return 1;
        else
            return NUMBER + MYSTERY ( NUMBER - 1 );
        end if;
    end MYSTERY;
begin -- Exercise_1
    PUT ( MYSTERY ( 3 ) );
    NEW_LINE;
end EXERCISE_1;
```

2. Suppose that the function call in Exercise 1 is changed to

```
PUT ( MYSTERY ( 0 ) );
```

What then will be the output of the program?

3. What is the output of the following program? What well-known mathematical function is ROSE?

```
with TEXT_IO; use TEXT_IO;
procedure EXERCISE_3 is
    package ROSE_IO is new INTEGER_IO ( NATURAL );
    use ROSE_IO;
    function ROSE ( NUMBER : NATURAL )
             return NATURAL is
    begin -- Rose
        if NUMBER <= 1 then
            return 1;
        else
            return NUMBER * ROSE ( NUMBER - 1 );
        end if;
    end ROSE;
```

```
begin -- Exercise_3
    PUT ( ROSE ( 4 ) );
    NEW_LINE;
end EXERCISE_3;
```

4. What is the output of the following program? CABIN is a fairly well-known mathematical function. You are likely to know of it or of a similar function.

```
with TEXT_IO; use TEXT_IO;
procedure EXERCISE_4 is
    package CABIN_IO is new INTEGER_IO ( NATURAL );
    use CABIN_IO;
    function CABIN ( NUMBER : POSITIVE )
                return NATURAL is
    begin -- Cabin
        if NUMBER = 1 then
            return 0;
        else
            return CABIN ( NUMBER / 2 ) + 1;
        end if;
    end CABIN;
begin -- Exercise_4
    PUT ( CABIN ( 8 ) );
    NEW_LINE;
end EXERCISE_4;
```

Proving Termination and Correctness for Recursive Functions
(Optional)

variant expression and threshold

Since a recursive function has the potential to go on without stopping, it is similar to a loop. As with a loop, the programmer has a responsibility to make certain that a function with a recursive call will terminate provided the precondition was satisfied. Fortunately, this can be done by the same technique that we used to demonstrate that loops terminate. To prove that a recursive function terminates, it is enough to find a *variant expression* and *threshold* with the following conditions:

0. Whenever the function is called, it will either terminate or make a recursive call.
1. There is some fixed amount such that, between one call of the function and any succeeding recursive call of that function, the value of the variant expression will decrease by at least that amount.
2. If the function is called and the value of the variant expression is less than or equal to the threshold, then the function will terminate without making any recursive calls.

Condition 0 is included to take account of factors other than recursion. For example, if the function body consists of a loop followed by a recursive call of thc function, then the loop must be shown to terminate by means of the techniques discussed in Chapter 7. That has nothing to do with recursion, but it can affect termination.

Conditions 1 and 2 have to do with recursion. To see that they, together with condition 0, guarantee termination, reason as follows: Suppose the three conditions hold. Since condition 0 is true, every call of the function will either terminate or produce a recursive call. Since condition 1 is true, every recursive call will decrease the variant expression. This means that either the function will terminate, which is fine, or else the variant expression will decrease until it reaches the threshold. But if condition 2 holds, then once the variant expression reaches the threshold, the function will terminate. That covers all the cases.

Interestingly enough, these conditions are themselves recursive. Conditions 0 and 2 include a test for termination, and it is termination for which we are testing. However, this is not a problem, since the conditions only discuss termination when there are no recursive calls of the function, and that kind of termination can be checked by the techniques we discussed in Chapter 7. A complete list of our conditions would also summarize those tests for termination.

As an example, consider the recursive function POWER in Figure 14.8. The variant expression can be taken to be

> **abs** EXPONENT + 1 *for negative values of EXPONENT* and
> EXPONENT *for nonnegative values of EXPONENT.*

With a threshold of zero, conditions 0 through 2 hold, so we know that any call of the function will eventually terminate and return a value.

Function

```
function POWER ( VALUE : FLOAT; EXPONENT : INTEGER )
        return FLOAT is
begin -- Power
    if EXPONENT = 0 then
        return 1.0;
    elsif EXPONENT > 0 then
        return VALUE * POWER ( VALUE, EXPONENT - 1 );
    else
        return 1.0 / POWER ( VALUE, -EXPONENT );
    end if;
end POWER;
```

Figure 14.8 Recursive function POWER.

induction

In addition to checking that a recursive function terminates, you should also check that it always returns the correct value. The usual technique for that is called *induction.* (If you have heard of mathematical induction, it may help to note that this is the same thing.) To show that a recursive function returns the correct value, the following conditions must be met:

3. If the function returns without making any recursive calls, then it returns the correct value. (This is sometimes called the *base case.*)
4. If the function is called and if all subsequent recursive calls return the correct value, then the original call will also return the correct value. (This is sometimes called the *inductive step.*)

By the *correct value* we mean whatever it is you want the function to return. That is part of the specification of the task of the function.

The conditions are numbered 3 and 4 to emphasize that they only ensure correctness if you know that the function calls always terminate. You must also ensure that conditions 0 through 2 hold to guarantee that a recursive function performs its task as desired.

Let us return to the function POWER defined above. To complete our demonstration that it performs as desired, we must show that conditions 3 and 4 hold.

It is easy to see that condition 3 holds. The only way that the function can terminate without a recursive call is if the value of EXPONENT is zero. In that case it returns **1**, which is the answer we said we wanted. Any number to the power **0** is **1** by definition. (There is a reason for that definition, but that is a topic in algebra, not program verification.)

To see that condition 4 holds, we need only recall the following algebraic identities:

$x^n = 1$, when **n** is zero
$x^n = x\ (\ x^{n-1}\ )$, when **n** is positive
$x^n = 1\ /\ x^{-n}$, when **n** is negative

Case Study

A Simple Example of a Recursive Procedure

Problem Definition

All our remarks about recursive functions apply equally well to recursive procedures. As a first example, consider the problem of writing an integer to the screen with its decimal digits reversed. For example, the number **1234** should be output as

```
4321
```

Discussion

It is easy to decide that the first digit output should be the last digit of the number; for example, if the number is **1234**, then the first digit output is **4**. Suppose we delete that last digit from the number being processed. In the example, that would delete **4** from **1234** leaving the smaller number **123**. The problem remaining is to then output the digits of this smaller number in the reverse order. Since this is a smaller version of the original problem it is natural to use recursion here. We will design a recursive algorithm based on this strategy. The solution outline is as follows:

Algorithm

```
if the number is one digit long then
     write that digit to the screen
else
     write the last digit;
     remove the last digit;
     write the rest to the screen backwards
end if;
```

recursive solution

In the example, **4** is the last digit and **123** is the rest. This algorithm is recursive because the last step is an instance of the same problem of writing a number backwards. It is routine to implement it as a recursive procedure. The implementation is shown in Figure 14.9, and execution for parameter **1234** is shown in Figure 14.10. The arithmetic is straightforward. The last digit is always the remainder from division by 10, that is,

the_number **rem** 10

For example, **1234 rem 10** is **4**. "The rest" is just the quotient when the number is divided by 10; that is,

the_number / 10

For example, **1234 / 10** is **123**.

Program

```
with TEXT_IO;
use TEXT_IO;
procedure REVERSE_THE_DIGITS is
--                    INPUT  : A nonnegative integer.
--                    OUTPUT : A nonnegative integer.
--                    DESCRIPTION : Reverses the digits of the
--                                  input value.
    NUMBER : NATURAL;
    package NUMBER_IO is new INTEGER_IO ( NATURAL );
    use NUMBER_IO;
    procedure WRITE_BACKWARDS ( NUMBER : in NATURAL ) is
--                    INPUT  : Any nonnegative integer.
--                    OUTPUT : None
--                    DESCRIPTION : Writes the digits of the
--                                  input value backwards.
```

```
    begin -- Write_Backwards
        if NUMBER < 10 then
            PUT ( NUMBER, 1 );
        else
--                output the right-most digit
            PUT ( NUMBER rem 10, 1 );
--                pass the rest of the digits
            WRITE_BACKWARDS ( NUMBER / 10 );
        end if;
    end WRITE_BACKWARDS;
begin -- Reverse_The_Digits
    PUT ( "Enter a nonnegative whole number:" ); NEW_LINE;
    GET ( NUMBER ); SKIP_LINE;
    PUT ( NUMBER ); PUT ( " written backwards is:" ); NEW_LINE;
    WRITE_BACKWARDS ( NUMBER );
    NEW_LINE;
end REVERSE_THE_DIGITS;
```

Sample Dialogue

```
Enter a nonnegative whole number:
1066
  1066 written backwards is:
6601
```

Figure 14.9 Program with a recursive procedure.

Technique for Designing Recursive Algorithms

To design a recursive procedure, the general technique is to divide the task into subproblems in such a way that some subproblem(s) are smaller instances of the same problem. These smaller instances of the same problem will be the recursive calls. The sense in which they are smaller is a bit vague and depends on the particular problem, but the idea is that on each successive recursive call the problem should become smaller and smaller until they have a simple solution that does not involve recursion. Hence, the algorithm and the final procedure body will include some cases that involve a recursive call and others that do not. As with recursive function bodies, the general outline of a recursive procedure body contains cases of two forms:

- One or more cases in which the procedure solves the problem in terms of simpler cases of the same problem (i.e., using recursive calls to itself).
- One or more cases in which the problem is solved without the use of any recursive calls. These cases without any recursion are called *base cases* or *stopping cases*.

```
if 1234 < 10 then
    PUT ( 1234, 1 );
else
    PUT ( 1234 rem 10, 1 );  ----------> Output a 4
    WRITE_BACKWARDS ( 1234 / 10 );
end if;
---------------------------------------
if 123 < 10 then
    PUT ( 123, 1 );
else
    PUT ( 123 rem 10, 1 );  -----------> Output a 3
    WRITE_BACKWARDS ( 123 / 10 );
end if;
---------------------------------------
if 12 < 10 then
    PUT ( 12, 1 );
else
    PUT ( 12 rem 10, 1 );  ------------> Output a 2
    WRITE_BACKWARDS ( 12 / 10 );
end if;
---------------------------------------
if 1 < 10 then
    PUT ( 1, 1 );  --------------------> Output a 1
else
    PUT ( 1 rem 10, 1 );
    WRITE_BACKWARDS ( 1 / 10 );
end if;
```

Figure 14.10 Execution of a recursive procedure.

As with recursive functions, every procedure call must ultimately lead to a stopping case, or else the procedure call will produce infinite recursion. In the previous "Case Study" involving reversing the digits in a number, the stopping case applied when the number was one digit long.

Case Study

Towers of Hanoi—An Example of Recursive Thinking

Recursion can be a very powerful programming tool. Sometimes a problem that appears to be difficult when tackled with any other programming technique can turn out to be very simple when thought of in terms of recursion. One dramatic example of this is provided by a children's game called Towers of Hanoi. As with any programming task, the first step is to understand the problem.

Problem Definition

The game consists of three pegs and a collection of rings that fit over the pegs, rather like phonograph records on a spindle. The rings are of different sizes. The initial configuration for a six-ring game is shown in Figure 14.11. Notice that the rings are stacked in decreasing order of their size. A move consists of transferring a single ring from the top of one peg to that of another. The object of the game is to move all the rings from the first peg to the second peg. The difficulty is that you are never allowed to place a ring on top of one with a smaller radius. You do have the one extra peg to temporarily hold rings, but the prohibition against placing a larger ring on a smaller ring applies to it as well as the other two pegs. A solution for the case of three rings is given in Figure 14.11.

This game apparently has an impressive and long history. Legend has it that it was invented by God at the dawn of time and was given to man as one of the major tasks of humanity. The problem of solving it eventually fell to the monks of a certain monastery in what was then an obscure eastern village called Hanoi. The legend goes on to say that when the game is completed, the last task assigned to humanity will have been accomplished and that will mark the end of the world. The version God presented to mankind had 64 rings, so do not worry about trying it with three or four rings.

Initial configuration for a six-ring game

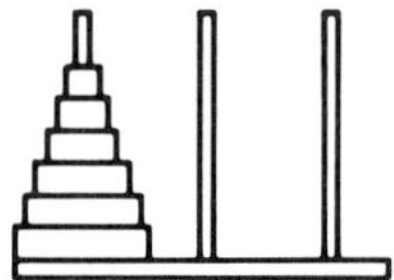

Solution for a three-ring game

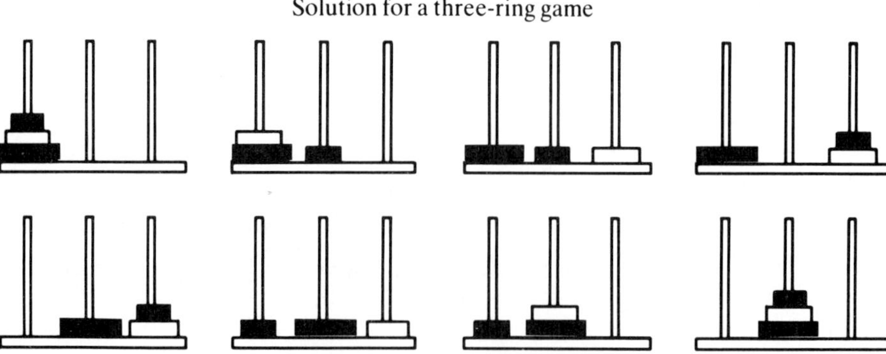

Figure 14.11 Towers of Hanoi.

(Besides, it cannot end the world unless the rings are made of gold, the pegs are made of diamonds, and it is played in Hanoi.)

parameters and output (first try)

We want a procedure that solves the problem for any number of rings. Hence, there will be one parameter, `NUMBER_OF_RINGS`, which specifies the number of rings. The procedure cannot actually move rings, so instead it will output instructions of the form "move a ring from *one_peg* to *another_peg*." The list of instructions output will be instructions for solving the puzzle.

Discussion

The game sounds simple enough, but a solution has not been easy to derive, at least not until very recently. It is easy to solve it for the case of three rings, but even four can take some thought. Ten rings boggle the mind. Sixty-four is almost unimaginable. To get the feel of it, try to solve it for the case of four rings. If you succeed, then try the six-ring case.

thinking recursively

Although it is very difficult to solve by other means, the solution is almost trivial if you think recursively. The trick is to reduce the problem to a smaller one of the same type. This trick is illustrated in Figure 14.12. First we move all but one ring onto the spare peg. We do that by a recursive call that uses peg 3 rather than peg 2 as the goal peg. Then we move the last ring to where it belongs. After that we move the rings from the spare peg to peg 2 (the ultimate goal peg) by another recursive call.

All the pegs are identical, so we can mix up their roles like this: Sometimes we make peg 3 the goal peg for a recursive call, even though our ultimate goal is to move the rings to peg 2. Moving the rings from the first peg to the second using the third as a spare is exactly the same problem as moving them from, say, the first to the third using the second as a spare.

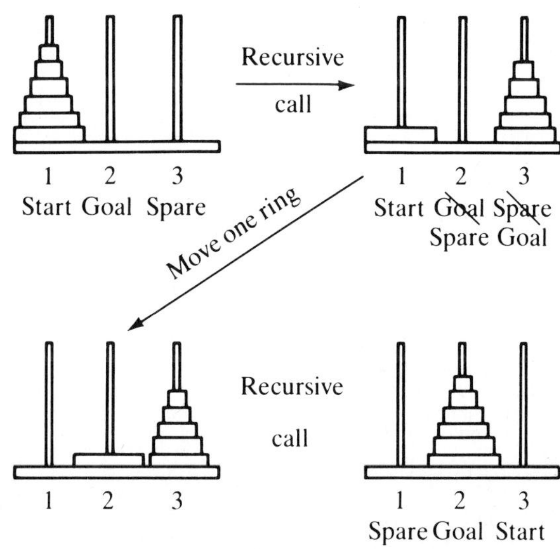

Figure 14.12 Idea of a recursive solution.

parameters (final form)

Our analysis required that we change the roles of the various pegs. We want to move the rings to peg 2, but for the recursive calls we sometimes want to change the roles of the various pegs using, for example, peg 3 in the role of peg 2 and thus moving some of the rings to peg 3. To allow this, we will use three more parameters, in addition to the parameter specifying the number of rings. The parameters will tell us which peg is the start peg, which is the goal peg, and which is left over as a spare. For each call, these three parameters will be given values chosen from the integers `1`, `2`, and `3`. The complete procedure specification will be the following, where the type PEG_NUMBER has been defined to be the subtype `1 .. 3`:

```
procedure WRITE_MOVES ( NUMBER_OF_RINGS : in POSITIVE;
                        START, GOAL, SPARE : in PEG_NUMBER )
--             INPUT  : The number of rings and the peg alignment
--             OUTPUT : None
--             DESCRIPTION : Write out the moves needed to move
--                           the rings from the start peg to the
--                           goal peg. Spare is the extra peg.
```

For example, if we want to move rings from peg 3 to peg 1 using peg 2 as the spare, then we call the procedure with `START` set equal to `3`, `GOAL` set equal to `1`, and `SPARE` set equal to `2`.

Algorithm

The algorithm is now easy to express:

if there is just one ring **then**
  instruct the user to move it from START to GOAL
else
  Output instructions for moving **n-1** rings from START to SPARE;
  instruct the user to move one ring from START to GOAL;
  output instructions for moving **n-1** rings from SPARE to GOAL;

A program with a complete recursive procedure to write out the moves is given in Figure 14.13. Figure 14.14 diagrams the sequence of recursive calls for the case of three rings.

Program

```
with TEXT_IO;
use TEXT_IO;
procedure HANOI is
--                INPUT  : The number of rings.
--                OUTPUT : A list of move instructions.
--                DESCRIPTION : Gives instructions to play the
--                              Towers of Hanoi.
   subtype PEG_NUMBER is INTEGER range 1 .. 3;
   NUMBER_OF_RINGS : POSITIVE;
   package RING_IO is new INTEGER_IO ( POSITIVE );
   use RING_IO;
   procedure WRITE_MOVES ( NUMBER_OF_RINGS : in POSITIVE;
                           START, GOAL, SPARE : in PEG_NUMBER ) is
```

```
--                  INPUT  : The number of rings and the peg alignment
--                  OUTPUT : None
--                  DESCRIPTION : Write out the moves needed to move
--                                the rings from the start peg to the
--                                goal peg. Spare is the extra peg.
    begin -- Write_Moves
        if NUMBER_OF_RINGS = 1 then
            PUT ( "Move a ring from " );
            PUT ( START, 1 );
            PUT ( " to " );
            PUT ( GOAL, 1 );
            NEW_LINE;
        else
--                  The spare peg becomes the goal
            WRITE_MOVES ( NUMBER_OF_RINGS - 1, START, SPARE, GOAL );
            PUT ( "Move a ring from " );
            PUT ( START, 1 );
            PUT ( " to " );
            PUT ( GOAL, 1 );
            NEW_LINE;
--                  The spare peg becomes the start peg
            WRITE_MOVES ( NUMBER_OF_RINGS - 1, SPARE, GOAL, START );
        end if;
    end WRITE_MOVES;
begin -- Hanoi
    PUT ( "Enter the number of rings and" ); NEW_LINE;
    PUT ( "I'll explain how to play Towers of Hanoi." ); NEW_LINE;
    GET ( NUMBER_OF_RINGS ); SKIP_LINE;
    PUT ( "To move " ); PUT ( NUMBER_OF_RINGS, 1 ); PUT ( " rings" );
    NEW_LINE;
    PUT ( "from peg 1 to peg 2, proceed as follows:" ); NEW_LINE;
    WRITE_MOVES ( NUMBER_OF_RINGS, 1, 2, 3 );
    PUT ( "That does it." ); NEW_LINE;
end HANOI;
```

Sample Dialogue

```
Enter the number of rings and
I'll explain how to play Towers of Hanoi.
3
To move 3 rings
from peg 1 to peg 2, proceed as follows:
Move a ring from 1 to 2
Move a ring from 1 to 3
Move a ring from 2 to 3
Move a ring from 1 to 2
```

```
Move a ring from 3 to 1
Move a ring from 3 to 2
Move a ring from 1 to 2
That does it.
```

Figure 14.13 A program to play Towers of Hanoi.

```
WRITE_MOVES ( NUMBER_OF_RINGS, 1, 2, 3 );
        |
        v
     Frame 1
---------------------------------------------------------------------------------
NUMBER_OF_RINGS = 3
START = 1
GOAL = 2
SPARE = 3

WRITE_MOVES ( NUMBER_OF_RINGS - 1, START, SPARE, GOAL );  ------> To Frame 2
PUT ( "Move a ring from " );  --
PUT ( START, 1 );               |
PUT ( " to " );                 |---> Fourth Output <------------ From Frame 2
PUT ( GOAL, 1 );                |
NEW_LINE;                     --
WRITE_MOVES ( NUMBER_OF_RINGS - 1, SPARE, GOAL, START );  ------> To Frame 5
        |
        v
Program Terminates

     Frame 2
---------------------------------------------------------------------------------
NUMBER_OF_RINGS = 2
START = 1
GOAL =  3     -- SPARE of calling procedure
SPARE = 2     -- GOAL of calling procedure

WRITE_MOVES ( NUMBER_OF_RINGS - 1, START, SPARE, GOAL );  ------> To Frame 3
PUT ( "Move a ring from " );  --
PUT ( START, 1 );               |
PUT ( " to " );                 |---> Second Output <------------ From Frame 3
PUT ( GOAL, 1 );                |
NEW_LINE;                     --
WRITE_MOVES ( NUMBER_OF_RINGS - 1, SPARE, GOAL, START );  ------> To Frame 4
        |
        v
Return to Frame 1
```

Frame 3

```
NUMBER_OF_RINGS = 1
START = 1
GOAL =  2     --SPARE of calling procedure
SPARE = 3     --GOAL of calling procedure

if NUMBER_OF_RINGS = 1 then
     PUT ( "Move a ring from " );   ┐
     PUT ( START, 1 );              │
     PUT ( " to " );                ├──► First Output
     PUT ( GOAL, 1 );               │
     NEW_LINE;                      ┘
          │
          ▼
     Return to Frame 2
```

Frame 4

```
NUMBER_OF_RINGS = 1
START = 2      --SPARE of calling procedure
GOAL =  3
SPARE = 1      --START of calling procedure

if NUMBER_OF_RINGS = 1 then
     PUT ( "Move a ring from " );   ┐
     PUT ( START, 1 );              │
     PUT ( " to " );                ├──► Third Output
     PUT ( GOAL, 1 );               │
     NEW_LINE;                      ┘
          │
          ▼
     Return to Frame 2
```

Frame 5

```
NUMBER_OF_RINGS = 2
START = 3       --START of calling procedure
GOAL =  2
SPARE = 1       --GOAL of calling procedure
WRITE_MOVES ( NUMBER_OF_RINGS - 1, START, SPARE, GOAL ); ──► To Frame 6
PUT ( "Move a ring from " );   ┐
PUT ( START, 1 );              │
PUT ( " to " );                ├──► Sixth Output ◄────── From Frame 6
PUT ( GOAL, 1 );               │
NEW_LINE;                      ┘
WRITE_MOVES ( NUMBER_OF_RINGS - 1, SPARE, GOAL, START ); ──► To Frame 7
     │
     ▼
Return to Frame 1
```

Frame 6

```
NUMBER_OF_RINGS = 1
START = 3
GOAL =  1      --SPARE of calling procedure
SPARE = 2      --GOAL of calling procedure

if NUMBER_OF_RINGS = 1 then
     PUT ( "Move a ring from " );  ┐
     PUT ( START, 1 );             │
     PUT ( " to " );               ├──► Fifth Output
     PUT ( GOAL, 1 );              │
     NEW_LINE;                     ┘
          │
          ▼
     Return to Frame 5
```

Frame 7

```
NUMBER_OF_RINGS = 1
START = 1      --SPARE of calling procedure
GOAL =  2
SPARE = 3      --START of calling procedure

if NUMBER_OF_RINGS = 1 then
     PUT ( "Move a ring from " );  ┐
     PUT ( START, 1 );             │
     PUT ( " to " );               ├──► Seventh Output
     PUT ( GOAL, 1 );              │
     NEW_LINE;                     ┘
          │
          ▼
     Return to Frame 5
```

Figure 14.14 Execution of Towers of Hanoi procedure.

Recursive Versus Iterative Subprograms

iterative version

Recursion is not absolutely necessary. In fact many programming languages do not allow it. Any solution that can be accomplished using recursion can also be done in some other way without using recursion. For example, Figure 14.5 contains a recursive function body. A nonrecursive version of that function is given in Figure 14.15. In such cases the nonrecursive version typically uses a loop of some sort in place of recursion. For that reason the nonrecursive version is usually referred to as an *iterative* version.

```
function FIBONACCI ( POSITION : NATURAL ) return NATURAL is
--              INPUT  : A position in the Fibonacci sequence.
--              OUTPUT : The Fibonacci value for a position.
--              DESCRIPTION : Computes a Fibonacci value
--                            using an iterative algorithm.
    PREVIOUS_VALUE : NATURAL := 1;
    SECOND_VALUE_BACK : NATURAL := 0;
    SUM : NATURAL;
begin -- Fibonacci
    if POSITION = 0 then
        return 0;
    elsif POSITION = 1 then
        return 1;
    else
        SUM := SECOND_VALUE_BACK + PREVIOUS_VALUE;
        for COUNT in 3 . . POSITION
        loop
            SECOND_VALUE_BACK := PREVIOUS_VALUE;
            PREVIOUS_VALUE := SUM;
            SUM := SECOND_VALUE_BACK + PREVIOUS_VALUE;
        end loop;
        return SUM;
    end if;
end FIBONACCI;
```

Figure 14.15 Iterative version of the function in Figure 14.5.

inefficiency of recursion

On many computer systems the recursive version of FIBONACCI given in Figure 14.5 runs slower and uses more storage than the iterative version given in Figure 14.15. The reason is that the recursive version uses a significant amount of time and storage to keep track of the recursive calls. Recall our discussion of how recursion is implemented using a stack. Suppose the recursive version is called to evaluate

```
FIBONACCI ( 10 )
```

The computer creates more than 100 stack frames in the process of evaluating this function call, even though no more than 10 frames will be on the stack at any point in time. This consumes an extra amount of time and memory. On the other hand, the iterative version does not do all this extra manipulating of the stack. It just performs nine simple additions and returns the answer.

The FIBONACCI example is typical. A recursively written function usually runs slower and uses more storage than an equivalent iterative version. The difference in efficiency depends on how large the stack grows when the recursive version is used, that is, on how long the string of recursive calls is.

If efficiency is an important issue, then it may make sense to avoid recursion. However, the efficiency issue is a subtle one. First of all, not all recursive subprograms are equally inefficient. The inefficiency introduced by the recursive call in the function COMPOUND_INTEREST of Figure 14.2 is negligible, because the number of arithmetic operations are about the same whether it is done iteratively or recursively. The only overhead is that of maintaining the run-time stack. Moreover, the recursion makes the code easier to read, since it reflects our normal manner of thinking about this computation. Also, recursion can sometimes make a procedure or function so much easier to understand that it would be foolish to avoid it. Consider the Towers of Hanoi procedure. If we had not thought recursively, we might not have produced a solution at all. If we convert that procedure to an iterative procedure, it will be much more complicated, and as a result it will most likely contain bugs. No procedure can be considered efficient unless it gives the correct answers.

Many recursive algorithms require stacks, even if they are written iteratively. In the iterative case it means that we implement a stack within the program. In the recursive case it means that we can rely on the system run-time stack. Do we use our own stack or the system stack? It is hard to tell which is better. However, generally speaking, the recursive algorithm is often much smaller than the iterative version.

Case Study

Binary Search

In this section we will develop a recursive procedure that searches an array to find out if a given value is in the array. For example, the array may contain a list of the numbers for credit cards that are no longer valid, perhaps because the cards have been stolen. A store clerk will need to search the list to see if a customer's card is still valid. In Chapter 10 (Figure 10.10) we discussed a simple method for searching an array by simply checking every array element. In Chapter 11 (Figure 11.13) we showed how the search could be made more efficient if the array is first sorted. In this section we will develop a method for searching a sorted array that is much faster than either of those two algorithms.

Let us call the array LIST. The indexes of the array LIST are LOWER_BOUND through UPPER_BOUND. LOWER_BOUND and UPPER_BOUND are some specified integers, but their values are not relevant to the discussion. To make the problem of searching the array easier, we will assume that the array is sorted. So if the array is LIST, then

LIST(LOWER_BOUND) <= LIST(LOWER_BOUND+1) . . . <= LIST(UPPER_BOUND)

When searching an array, we are likely to want to know both whether the value is in the list and (if it is) where it is in the list. For example, if we are searching for a credit card number, then the array index may serve as a record number. Another array indexed by these same indexes may hold a phone number or other information to use for reporting the suspicious card.

Problem Definition

We will design the procedure to have an **out** parameter to return the location of the searched-for value. If the value is not in the array, the procedure will raise an exception called KEY_NOT_FOUND. If value is found, the **out** parameter, called LOCATION, will be set to the index of the value found. If we use KEY to denote the value being searched for, the job to be accomplished can be formulated precisely as follows:

Precondition: The list is sorted into increasing order.

Postcondition: If KEY is one of the values in LIST then
LIST(LOCATION) = KEY;
otherwise
KEY_NOT_FOUND is raised.

Discussion

Now let us proceed to produce an algorithm to solve this problem. To do so it will help to visualize the problem in very concrete terms. Suppose the list of numbers is so long that it takes a book to list them all. This is in fact how invalid credit card numbers are distributed to stores that do not have access to a computer. If you are a clerk and are handed a credit card, you must check to see if it is on the list and hence invalid. How would you proceed? Open the book to the middle and see if it is there; if not and it is smaller than the middle number, then you work backwards towards the beginning of the book; if it is larger than the middle number, you work your way towards the back of the book. This idea produces our first draft of an algorithm:

```
MIDPOINT := approximate midpoint of the list
if KEY = LIST( MIDPOINT ) then -- key is in the list
   LOCATION := MIDPOINT;
   return;
elsif KEY < LIST( MIDPOINT ) then
   search the lower part of the list
elsif KEY > LIST( MIDPOINT )
   search the upper part of the list
```

Algorithm (first version)

Since searching the shorter list is a smaller version of the very task that we are designing the algorithm to perform, it naturally lends itself to the use of recursion. The smaller lists can be searched with a recursive call to the algorithm.

Our pseudocode is a bit too imprecise to be easily translated into Ada. The problem has to do with the recursive calls. There are two recursive calls shown:

```
Search the lower part of the list
Search the upper part of the list
```

slice

To implement that recursive call, we need to pass only part of the list. As you may recall from previous chapters, a smaller part of a list is called a *slice* of the original list. As a quick review, recall that the syntax for the slice is

array_variable (*slice_low_index* . . *slice_high_index*)

The recursive call specifies that a slice of the array is to be searched. In one case it is the elements indexed by `LIST'FIRST`, the lower bound for the list, through `MIDPOINT - 1`. In the other case it is the elements `MIDPOINT + 1` through `LIST'LAST`, the upper bound of the list. There is no need for additional parameters, for once inside any of the recursive calls, the bounds of the smaller list are defined by `LIST'FIRST` (the lower bound) and `LIST'LAST` (the upper bound). Using the attributes `FIRST` and `LAST`, we can express the pseudocode more precisely as follows:

Algorithm (first refinement)

To search any portion of the list, do the following:

MIDPOINT := approximate midpoint between
                    LIST'FIRST **and** LIST'LAST;
if KEY = LIST(MIDPOINT) **then** -- key found
    LOCATION := MIDPOINT;
    return;
elsif KEY < LIST(MIDPOINT) **then**
    search LIST(LIST'FIRST . . MIDPOINT − 1)
elsif KEY > LIST(MIDPOINT)
    search LIST(MIDPOINT + 1 . . LIST'LAST)

To search the entire array, the algorithm would be executed by simply passing the array name, which is the entire array. The recursive calls will use slices of the entire original array. For example, if the first recursive call is made, it will pass a slice of the `LIST` with indexes starting at `LIST'FIRST` and ending at the calculated value `MIDPOINT - 1`.

Algorithm (final version)

termination

As with any recursive algorithm, we must ensure that our algorithm ends and does not produce an infinite recursion. If the number is found on the list, then there is no recursive call and the process terminates, but we need some way to detect when the number is not on the list. On each recursive call, the lower bound of the slice is increased or the upper bound of the slice is decreased. If they ever attempt to pass one another, that is, try to make the lower bound of the slice larger than the upper bound, the predefined exception CONSTRAINT_ERROR will be raised. If that happens, we will know that there are no more indexes left to check and that the number is not in the array. When we add an exception handler to our pseudocode, we obtain a complete solution, as shown in Figures 14.16 and 14.17.

unconstrained array

The main procedure is in Figure 14.16. Note in particular the declaration for LIST_ARRAY and LIST:

```
subtype INDEX is INTEGER range LOWER_BOUND . . UPPER_BOUND;
type LIST_ARRAY is array( INDEX range <> ) of INTEGER;
LIST : LIST_ARRAY( INDEX );
```

LIST_ARRAY is an *unconstrained array*; the bounds for the indexes are simply marked as some INDEX **range**. (The values of LOWER_BOUND and UPPER_BOUND are not important to the discussion.) When the object LIST is declared, the array is *constrained* by giving the range of indexes. In this case the INDEX **range** is the entire range of type INDEX. The advantage of this is that the type name LIST_ARRAY can be used in a subprogram parameter list. Since LIST_ARRAY has unconstrained indexes, it will work for any array whose index is within the bounds of the type INDEX. This is the mechanism that allows us to pass a slice of an array as a parameter.

Now we can routinely translate the pseudocode into Ada. The procedure SEARCH is an implementation of the above recursive algorithm. The resulting SEARCH procedure is shown in Figure 14.17 as a **separate** from the main procedure.

The term *separate subprogram* means just what it says. As a quick review, recall that the subprogram is compiled separately from the main program. The complete subprogram specification is given in the main program and is followed by the reserved words **is separate**. The first line of the separately compiled subprogram is marked with **separate**, followed by its ancestors enclosed in parentheses. As far as the scope of identifiers is concerned, a **separate** is treated as if the entire subprogram body is in the main procedure at the spot of the separate declaration. The major advantage is that once the main procedure is written and compiled, the programmer or the

```
with TEXT_IO;
use TEXT_IO;
procedure BINARY_SEARCH is
    LOWER_BOUND : constant INTEGER := 1;
    UPPER_BOUND : constant INTEGER := 10;
```

```
    subtype INDEX is INTEGER range LOWER_BOUND . . UPPER_BOUND;
    type LIST_ARRAY is array( INDEX range <> ) of INTEGER;
    ANSWER : CHARACTER;
    KEY : INTEGER;
    LIST : LIST_ARRAY( INDEX );
    LOCATION : INDEX;
    KEY_NOT_FOUND : exception;
    package SEARCH_IO is new INTEGER_IO ( INTEGER );
    use SEARCH_IO;
    procedure SEARCH ( LIST : LIST_ARRAY;
                       KEY  : INTEGER;
                       LOCATION : out INDEX ) is separate;
begin -- Binary_Search
    PUT ( "Insert 10 integer values in ascending order" );
    NEW_LINE;
    for COUNT in LIST'range
    loop
        GET ( LIST( COUNT ) );
    end loop;
    SKIP_LINE;
    loop
        PUT ( "Enter number to be located:" ); NEW_LINE;
        GET ( KEY ); SKIP_LINE;
        begin
            SEARCH ( LIST, KEY, LOCATION );
            PUT ( KEY );
            PUT ( " is in location " );
            PUT ( LOCATION );
            NEW_LINE;
        exception
            when KEY_NOT_FOUND => PUT ( KEY );
                                  PUT ( " is not in the list" );
                                  NEW_LINE;
        end;
        PUT ( "Do you want to search for another value? (y/n)" );
        NEW_LINE;
        GET ( ANSWER ); SKIP_LINE;
        exit when ANSWER = 'n'
          or else ANSWER = 'N';
    end loop;
end BINARY_SEARCH;
```

Figure 14.16 Program with a procedure for binary search.

```
separate ( BINARY_SEARCH )
procedure SEARCH ( LIST : LIST_ARRAY;
                   KEY : INTEGER;
                   LOCATION : out INDEX ) is
    MIDPOINT : INDEX := ( LIST'FIRST + LIST'LAST ) / 2;
begin -- Search
    if KEY = LIST( MIDPOINT ) then
        LOCATION := MIDPOINT;
        return;
    elsif KEY < LIST( MIDPOINT ) then
        SEARCH ( LIST( LIST'FIRST . . MIDPOINT - 1 ), KEY, LOCATION );
    else -- key > list( midpoint )
        SEARCH ( LIST( MIDPOINT + 1 . . LIST'LAST ), KEY, LOCATION );
    end if;
exception
    when CONSTRAINT_ERROR => raise KEY_NOT_FOUND;
end SEARCH;
```

Figure 14.17 Recursive version of the binary search.

programmer's helper or the programmer's teammate need only concentrate on the separate subprogram. The main procedure need not be compiled again, no matter how many times the separate subunit is compiled. The system will link the main procedure and any **separates** together before the program is run.

A diagram of how the SEARCH procedure performs on a sample array is given in Figure 14.18.

solve a more general problem

Notice that the procedure SEARCH solves a more general problem than the original problems. Our goal was to design a procedure to search an entire array of type LIST. Yet the procedure will let us search any slice of the array by specifying the index bounds of the slice when SEARCH is called. This is a common phenomenon when designing recursive procedures. Frequently we must solve a more general problem in order to express the recursive algorithm.

efficiency

The binary search algorithm is extremely fast compared to an algorithm that simply tries all array elements in order. In the binary search we eliminate about half the array from consideration right at the start. We then eliminate a quarter and then an eighth of the array and so forth. These savings add up to a dramatically fast algorithm. For an array of 100 elements, the binary search will never need to compare more than 7 elements to the key. We have presented two simple search algorithms, Figures 9.8 and 10.3. Either of these could require as many as 100 and on the average will require 50 comparisons to locate a key that is in the array. Moreover, the larger the array is the more dramatic the savings will be. On an array with 1000 elements, the binary

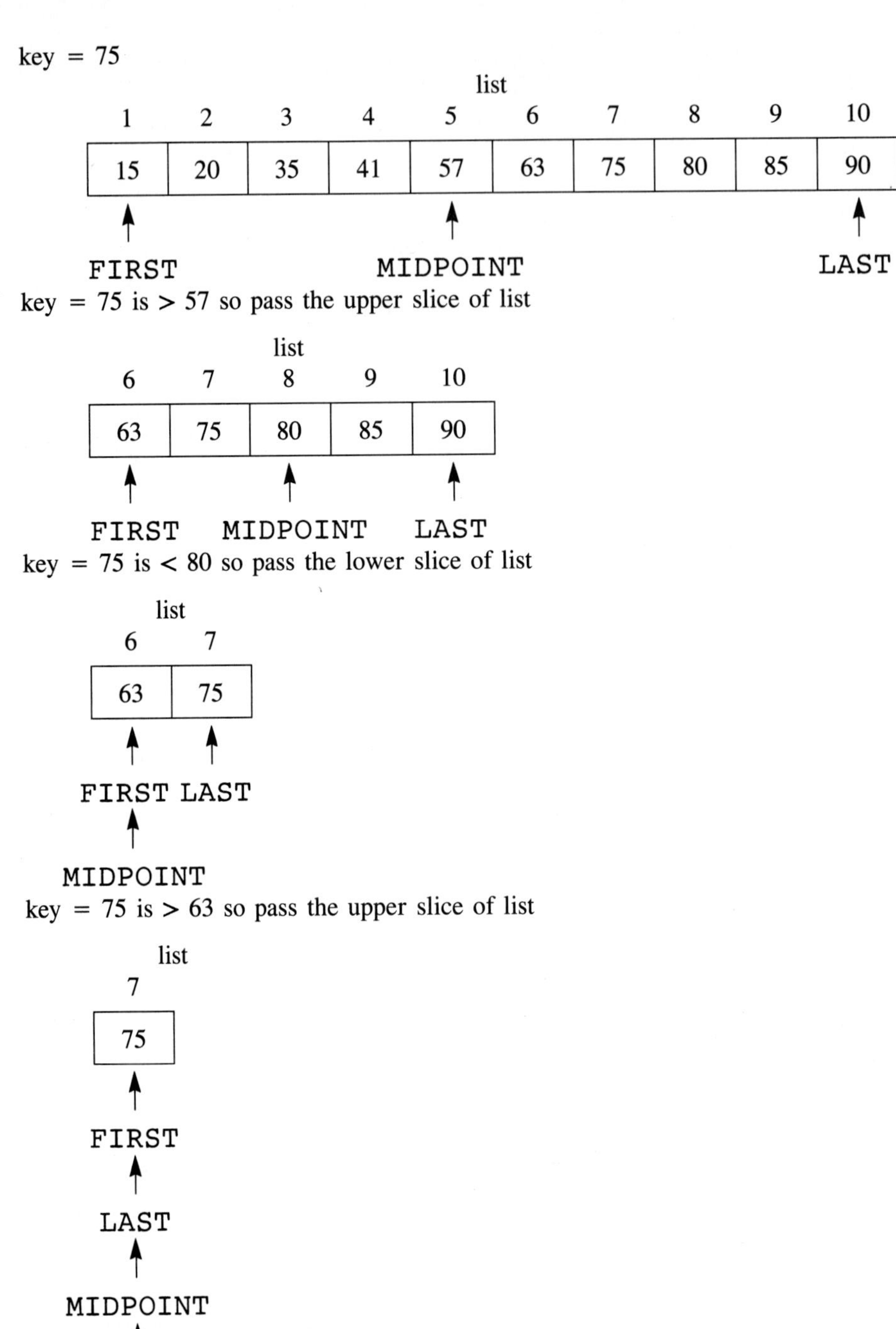

Figure 14.18 Execution of the procedure Search.

search will use at most 11 comparisons compared to an average of 500 for the simple search algorithms. There are some cases for which the search algorithm in Figure 14.5 is faster in determining that a key is not in the array. However, these cases are not the most commonly occurring ones, and in other cases the binary search algorithm is dramatically faster.

iterative version

Any recursive procedure can be replaced by an iterative procedure that accomplishes the same task. In some cases the iterative procedure may be more efficient, and if efficiency is a major issue, you may want to convert a recursive procedure to an iterative one. An iterative version of the binary search algorithm is given in Figure 14.19. On some systems it may run more efficiently than the recursive version. The algorithm for the iterative version was derived by mirroring the recursive version. In the iterative version the local variables LOW and HIGH mirror the roles of the bounds for the slice in the recursive version. As this example illustrates, it often makes sense to derive a recursive algorithm even if you expect to later convert it to an iterative algorithm.

```
separate ( BINARY_SEARCH )
procedure SEARCH ( LIST : LIST_ARRAY;
                   KEY  : INTEGER;
                   LOCATION : out INDEX ) is
    HIGH : INDEX := LIST'LAST;
    LOW  : INDEX := LIST'FIRST;
    MIDPOINT : INDEX;
begin -- Search
    loop
        MIDPOINT := ( LOW + HIGH ) / 2;
        if KEY = LIST( MIDPOINT ) then
            LOCATION := MIDPOINT;
            return;
        elsif KEY < LIST( MIDPOINT ) then
            HIGH := MIDPOINT - 1;
        else -- KEY > LIST( MIDPOINT )
            LOW := MIDPOINT + 1;
        end if;
        if LOW > HIGH then
            raise KEY_NOT_FOUND;
        end if;
    end loop;
end SEARCH;
```

Figure 14.19 Iterative version of binary search.

Use of Subprogram Declarations
(Optional)

Normally you declare a subprogram body before the place where it is first called. However, there is a way around this rule. You can declare a subprogram body after the declaration of some other subprogram bodies that use it, provided you advise the compiler by including a *subprogram declaration* before the location of the first subprogram call. A subprogram declaration consists of the subprogram specification terminated by a semicolon, just like it is done in a package specification, as in

```
procedure REJECT ( ANSWER : in out CHARACTER );
```

The subprogram body can then be placed anywhere after the subprogram declaration. Although the formal parameter list is given in the subprogram declaration, it is given again when the subprogram body is declared. In fact a subprogram specification in a subprogram declaration must be exactly the same as the one given in the subprogram body.

mutual recursion

The program in Figure 14.20 requires a subprogram declaration. In that program the procedures GET and REJECT each include a call to the other. Such a phenomenon is called *mutual recursion.* Subprogram declarations also can be used for less essential reasons, such as for putting all the most important subprograms together in one place. We had seen subprogram declarations before in package specifications.

```
with TEXT_IO;
procedure MUTUALLY_RECURSIVE is
    ANSWER : CHARACTER;
    procedure REJECT ( ANSWER : in out CHARACTER );
    procedure GET ( ANSWER : in out CHARACTER ) is
    begin
        TEXT_IO.PUT ( "Answer cap Y for Yes or cap N for No:" );
        TEXT_IO.NEW_LINE;
        TEXT_IO.GET ( ANSWER );
        TEXT_IO.SKIP_LINE;
        if ANSWER = 'Y'
        or else ANSWER = 'N' then
            return;
        else
            REJECT ( ANSWER );
        end if;
    end GET;
    procedure REJECT ( ANSWER : in out CHARACTER ) is
    begin
        TEXT_IO.PUT ( ANSWER );
        TEXT_IO.PUT ( " is not an acceptable response." );
        TEXT_IO.NEW_LINE;
        GET ( ANSWER );
    end REJECT;
```

```
begin -- Mutually_Recursive
    TEXT_IO.PUT ( "This is a test." );
    TEXT_IO.NEW_LINE;
    GET ( ANSWER );
    TEXT_IO.PUT ( "The value of answer is " );
    TEXT_IO.PUT ( ANSWER );
    TEXT_IO.NEW_LINE;
    TEXT_IO.PUT ( "That ends the test." );
    TEXT_IO.NEW_LINE;
end MUTUALLY_RECURSIVE;
```

Figure 14.20 Example of a subprogram declaration.

Another point is made in this example. Note the use of the procedure named GET. GET is not a reserved word in Ada. None of the input/output subprogram names are reserved words. We are free to use those names whenever it is convenient and appropriate to do so. When we want the GET in TEXT_IO, we simply add the prefix TEXT_IO to the procedure call, and then the system knows which we want. Without the prefix, the system uses the local GET just as it would with another local identifier.

Case Study

Quicksort—An Example of Slicing
(Optional)

Problem Definition

In this "Case Study," we will describe an efficient method for sorting an array of integers. The algorithm for *quicksort* has some similarity to the binary search algorithm of the previous "Case Study." We will develop the algorithm into a procedure for sorting an array of integers of the same type as we used in the binary search algorithm.

Discussion

In the binary search algorithm, we divided a sorted array at its midpoint and then compared the sought-after value to the midpoint value to determinc which half of the array could possibly contain the sought-after value. We can apply this same general idea of dividing the array in half and comparing values to an approximate midpoint value to obtain an efficient algorithm for sorting an array. The basic idea is simple. Suppose you know the value that belongs in the middle of the array, or at least the approximate middle of the array. We will call this value the *splitting value*. When the array is correctly sorted, this splitting value will have some particular index giving its array location. Suppose we somehow put this splitting value into its correct location in the array. We then put all the values less than or equal to it in array positions before the splitting value, and we put all the values greater than the splitting value in array positions after the splitting value. We do not sort the values less than the splitting value; we simply place them, in any order, in array positions before the splitting value. Similarly we do not sort the values greater than the splitting value; we simply place them, in any order, in array positions after the splitting value. After this initial moving of array elements, we have moved the array closer to being sorted. We know that the splitting value of the array is in the correct position. We also know that all other values are in the correct slice of the array, either the slice before the splitting value or the slice after the splitting value. However, although we know they are in the correct slice, those slices are still not sorted. One way to proceed is to sort the two slices separately. This works because we know that all values in the first slice are less than all values in the second slice, so no value ever needs to move from one slice to the other. How do we sort the two slices? These are smaller versions of the original sorting problem, so we can sort the two smaller array portions by recursive calls.

stopping case

How do we know our recursive procedure will stop? If we continue to divide the array into smaller portions in the way we outlined, we will eventually get down to array segments of size one, and we can use that as a stopping case. An array segment with just one element is always sorted. Hence, for array segments of size one, our procedure can return without making any recursive calls.

The above idea is sound except for one problem. How do we find a splitting value and its correct final position in the sorted array? There is no obvious way to quickly find the midpoint value until the array is sorted. Our solution will be to take an arbitrary array value and use it as the splitting value. As a result, we may not be dividing the array exactly in half, but as long as we do divide it into smaller pieces, our algorithm will still eventually sort the array. We perform the subproblem of dividing the array elements with a procedure called PARTITION. The procedure specification is as follows:

```
procedure PARTITION ( LIST : in out LIST_ARRAY;
                      SPLIT_INDEX : out INDEX )
--                  INPUT  : A list to be partitioned
--                  OUTPUT : An index used to split the list
--                  DESCRIPTION : Chooses a splitting value,
--                                rearranges the list, and
--                                sets the output such that
--                                list( split_index ) = split_value and
--                                list(i) <= split_value,
--                                for all i < split_index and
--                                list(i) > split_value,
--                                for all i > split_index.
```

The procedure PARTITION chooses some arbitrary splitting value, positions it at the correct index position, and divides the remaining array elements as we have described. The procedure will not necessarily do those three things in that order, but it will do them all. Because the procedure will be used on subportions of the array when we make recursive calls, we will again use slices of the array for the array portion being partitioned.

We will formulate our sorting algorithm as a recursive procedure called QUICK_SORT, which makes a call to the procedure PARTITION. The procedure QUICK_SORT will need one **in out** parameter for the array. When it is called recursively, the procedure will be called on to sort slices of the array. The complete procedure QUICK_SORT is given in Figure 14.22 as a **separate** from the SORT procedure shown in Figure 14.21. At this point you need not worry about the code for the procedure PARTITION. We will discuss it in the next few paragraphs. For now, simply look at the body for the procedure QUICK_SORT and convince yourself that it works correctly, assuming that the procedure PARTITION does what it is supposed to do. The code for QUICK_SORT is straightforward. However, we still need to show how the code for the procedure PARTITION was developed.

Algorithm for PARTITION

splitting value

Since we have no information about the values in the array, all values are equally likely to be the value that belongs in the middle of the array. Moreover, we know that the algorithm will work no matter what value we use for the splitting value. Hence, we arbitrarily choose the first array element to use as the splitting value.

The procedure PARTITION will move all the values that are less than or equal to this splitting value toward the beginning of the array and all values that are greater than this splitting value toward the tail end of the array. Because the splitting value is not necessarily the value that belongs at the midpoint position of the array, we do not know where the dividing line between the two array portions belongs. Hence, we do not know how far forward we need to move elements less than or equal to the splitting value, nor do we know how far toward the end of the array we must move elements that are greater than the splitting value. We solve this dilemma by working inward from the two ends of the array. We move smaller elements to the beginning of the array and we move larger elements to the tail end of the array. In this way we obtain two segments, one segment of smaller elements growing inward from the front of the array and one segment of larger elements growing inward from the tail end of the array. When these two segments meet, we have correctly partitioned the array. The correct location for the splitting value is at the boundary of these two segments. Starting at the front of the array, the algorithm passes over smaller elements at the front of the array until it encounters a larger element. This larger element is not in the correct segment and must somehow move to the tail-end segment. Starting at the tail end of the array, the algorithm passes over larger elements at that end of the array until it encounters a smaller element. This smaller element is not in the correct segment and must somehow move to the front segment. At this point we know that the elements in the two segments up to, but not including, these out-of-place elements are in the correct segment of the array. If we switch these two out-of-place elements, then we will know that they also are in the correct portion of the array. Using this technique of locating and switching elements at incorrect ends of the array, our algorithm proceeds to continually expand the segment at the front end of the array and the segment at the tail end of the array until these two segments meet.

For example, suppose the following represents our array value:

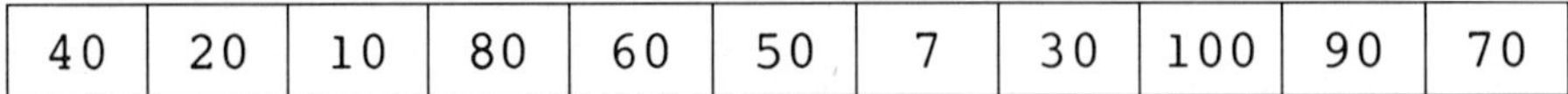

We choose the first value, **40**, as our splitting value. Starting at the beginning we look for the first element that is greater than the splitting value. That is **80**. Starting from the other end we look for the first value that is less than or equal to the splitting value. That is **30**. We use two variables called UP and DOWN to hold the indexes of these two array elements. The array can be represented as follows:

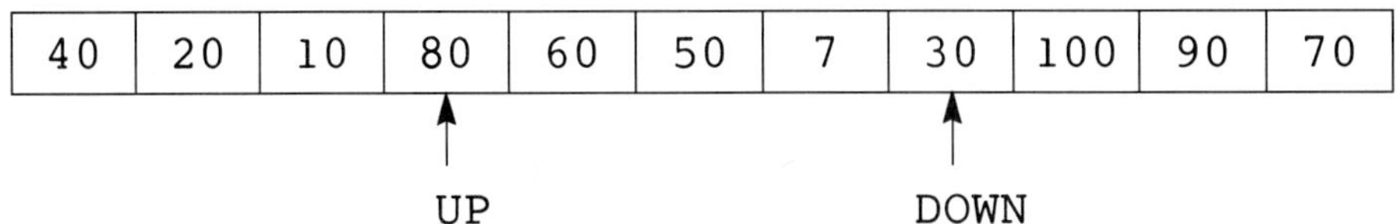

We have just located two elements in incorrect segments of the array. If we interchange them, the array will be closer to being divided correctly. After the exchange the array will contain

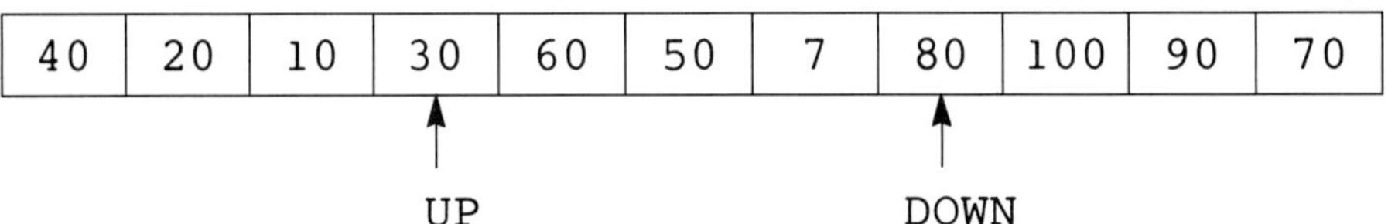

We now repeat the process. Continuing from the places we left off, we increment UP until we find an element larger than the splitting value and decrement DOWN until we find an element less than or equal to the splitting value. That changes the values of UP and DOWN so that we obtain the following situation:

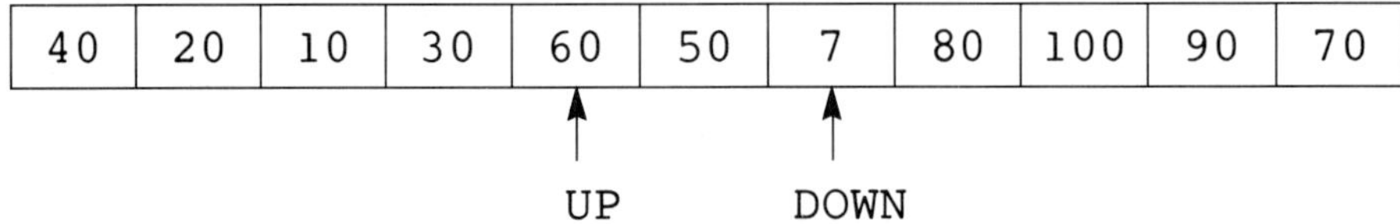

Exchanging these two elements places them in the correct array portions and yields the following array value:

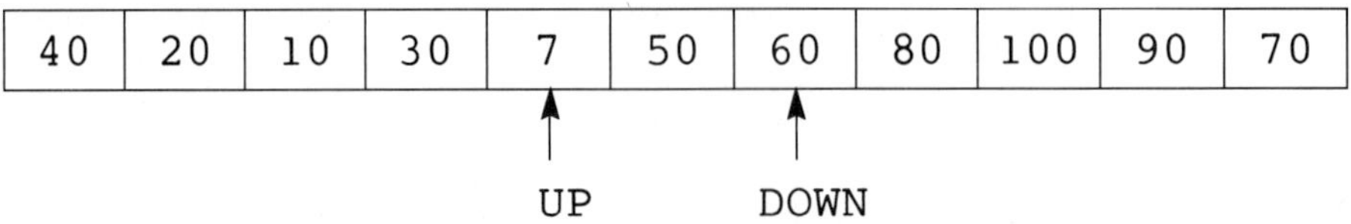

If we continue to look for elements to exchange, we will increment UP until it reaches the element **50**, and we will decrement DOWN past the element **50** to the index of the element **7**. At this point the indexes UP and DOWN have passed each other so the situation is as follows:

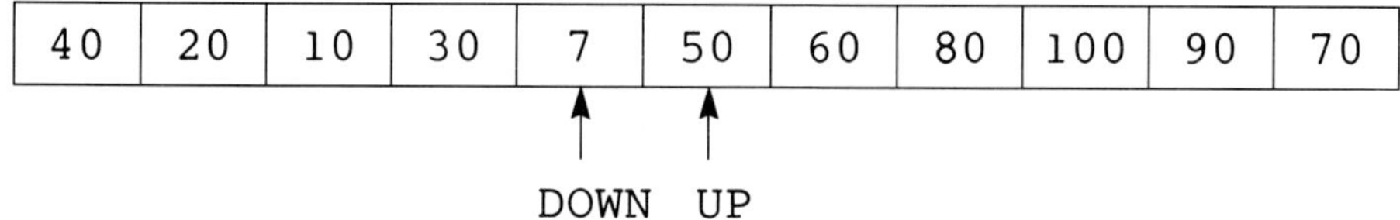

Once the indexes UP and DOWN pass each other, we have partitioned the array. All elements less than or equal to the splitting value of **40** are in the first five positions. All elements greater than the splitting value of **40** are in the last six positions. However, the splitting value is not yet at the dividing point between the two parts of the array. To complete the algorithm, we move the splitting value, **40**, to the last position in the first of the two array segments. Because we know that the index DOWN is one beyond (i.e., one less than) the segment of larger elements at the tail end of the array, we know that it is the last index in the segment of smaller elements at the front of the array. Hence, `LIST( DOWN )` is where the splitting value **40** belongs. After moving the splitting value, the array configuration is as follows:

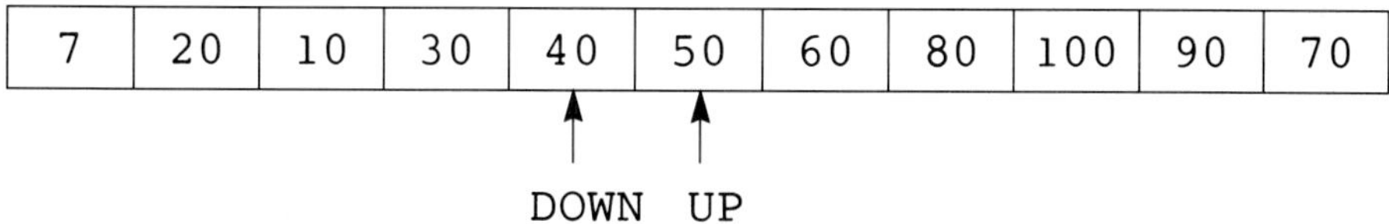

The pseudocode for our algorithm is given below. The splitting value is stored in the variable `SPLIT_VALUE`. The complete code for the `PARTITION` procedure is given in Figure 14.23 as a **`separate`** from procedure `QUICK_SORT`, which is a **`separate`** from procedure `SORT`. Note the first line in Figure 14.23 lists all of `PARTITION`'s ancestors.

1. Initialize values:

   DOWN := LIST'LAST;
   SPLIT_VALUE := LIST(LIST'FIRST);
   UP := LIST'FIRST;

2. Repeat the following until `UP` and `DOWN` pass each other:
   2a. Increase UP until `LIST( UP ) > SPLIT_VALUE`.
   2b. Decrease DOWN until `LIST( DOWN ) <= SPLIT_VALUE`.
   2c. If UP < DOWN, then there is still room for both end portions to grow so interchange the values of `LIST( UP )` and `LIST( DOWN )`.
3. Set SPLIT_INDEX and position the splitting value:
   3a. SPLIT_INDEX := DOWN;
   3b. Interchange LIST(LIST'FIRST), which still contains the splitting value, and `LIST( SPLIT_INDEX )`.

efficiency

If the two slices produced by the procedure PARTITION are of approximately equal size, then the number of levels of recursion will be relatively small. If we are unlucky and one slice always contains almost the entire array, then the number of levels of recursion will be relatively large, and the procedure will take longer to sort the array. Ironically this means that our procedure will run slowest when the array is already sorted. If the array elements are in random order, then the splitting value will be close enough to the midpoint value most of the time, and the procedure will run much faster than the sorting algorithm we developed in Chapter 10. If you plan to use this procedure on arrays that are already sorted or almost sorted, then it may pay you to use a different splitting value, such as the middle value of the array. However, our procedure, without any changes, will sort any array. Only the efficiency of the procedure is affected by the choice of a splitting value.

Figure 14.21 is a program that uses the QUICK_SORT to sort an array of integer values.

Program

```
with TEXT_IO;
use TEXT_IO;
procedure SORT is
    LOWER_BOUND : constant INTEGER := 1;
    UPPER_BOUND : constant INTEGER := 11;
    subtype INDEX is INTEGER range LOWER_BOUND . . UPPER_BOUND;
    type LIST_ARRAY is array( INDEX range <> ) of INTEGER;
    LIST : LIST_ARRAY( INDEX );
    package SORT_IO is new INTEGER_IO ( INTEGER );
    use SORT_IO;
    procedure QUICK_SORT ( LIST : in out LIST_ARRAY ) is separate;
begin -- Sort
    PUT ( "Enter the list to be sorted:" ); NEW_LINE;
    for COUNT in LIST'range
    loop
        GET ( LIST( COUNT ) );
    end loop;
    SKIP_LINE;
    QUICK_SORT ( LIST );
    PUT ( "The sorted list" ); NEW_LINE;
    for COUNT in LIST'range
    loop
        PUT ( LIST( COUNT ) );
    end loop;
    NEW_LINE;
end SORT;
```

Figure 14.21 Program that sorts using QUICK_SORT.

Procedure

```
separate ( SORT )
procedure QUICK_SORT ( LIST : in out LIST_ARRAY ) is
--                    INPUT  : An unsorted slice of the list.
--                    OUTPUT : A sorted slice of the list.
--                    DESCRIPTION : Uses split_index to divide the list
--                                  into two slices for recursive calls to
--                                  itself. If a slice is only one
--                                  element of the list, that portion is
--                                  sorted.
    SPLIT_INDEX : INDEX;
    procedure PARTITION ( LIST : in out LIST_ARRAY;
                          SPLIT_INDEX : out INDEX ) is separate;
begin -- Quick_Sort
    PARTITION ( LIST, SPLIT_INDEX );
    if SPLIT_INDEX > LIST'FIRST + 1 then
        QUICK_SORT ( LIST( LIST'FIRST . . SPLIT_INDEX - 1 ) );
    end if;
    if SPLIT_INDEX < LIST'LAST - 1 then
        QUICK_SORT ( LIST( SPLIT_INDEX + 1 . . LIST'LAST ) );
    end if;
end QUICK_SORT;
```

Figure 14.22 The recursive QUICK__SORT procedure.

Procedure

```
separate ( SORT.QUICK_SORT )
procedure PARTITION ( LIST : in out LIST_ARRAY;
                      SPLIT_INDEX : out INDEX ) is
--                    INPUT  : A list to be partitioned
--                    OUTPUT : An index used to split the list
--                    DESCRIPTION : Chooses a splitting value,
--                                  rearranges the list, and
--                                  sets the output such that
--                                  list( split_index ) = split_value and
--                                  list(i) <= split_value,
--                                  for all i < split_index and
--                                  list(i) > split_value,
--                                  for all i > split_index.
    DOWN : INDEX := LIST'LAST;
    SPLIT_VALUE : INTEGER := LIST( LIST'FIRST );
    UP : INDEX := LIST'FIRST;
```

```
    procedure EXCHANGE ( FIRST_VALUE,
                         SECOND_VALUE : in out INTEGER ) is
        TEMPORARY : INTEGER := FIRST_VALUE;
    begin -- Exchange
        FIRST_VALUE := SECOND_VALUE;
        SECOND_VALUE := TEMPORARY;
    end EXCHANGE;
begin -- Partition
    loop
        loop
            exit when LIST( UP ) > SPLIT_VALUE;
            UP := UP + 1;
            exit when UP = LIST'LAST;
        end loop;
        loop
            exit when LIST( DOWN ) <= SPLIT_VALUE;
            DOWN := DOWN - 1;
            exit when DOWN = LIST'FIRST;
        end loop;
        if UP < DOWN then
            EXCHANGE ( LIST( UP ), LIST( DOWN ) );
        end if;
        exit when UP >= DOWN;
    end loop;
    SPLIT_INDEX := DOWN;
    EXCHANGE ( LIST( LIST'FIRST ), LIST( DOWN ) );
end PARTITION;
```

Figure 14.23 The procedure to partition a list for QUICK_SORT.

Summary of Problem Solving and Programming Techniques

- If a problem can be reduced to smaller instances of the same problem, then a recursive solution is likely to be easy to find and implement.
- A recursive algorithm for a function or procedure normally contains two kinds of cases: one or more cases that include a recursive call and one or more *stopping* cases in which the problem is solved without the use of any recursive calls.
- When writing recursive procedures or functions, always check to see that the procedure will not produce infinite recursion.
- When designing a recursive procedure to solve a task, it is often necessary to solve a more general problem than the given task. This may be required to allow for the proper recursive calls since the smaller problems may not be exactly the same type of problem as the given task. For example, in the binary search problem, the task was to search an entire array, but the recursive solution is an algorithm to search any portion of the array (either all of it or a part of it).

Exercises

Self-Test Exercises

5. What is the output of the following program?

```
with TEXT_IO; use TEXT_IO;
procedure TEST_2 is
    procedure CHEERS ( NUMBER : in INTEGER ) is
    begin -- Cheers
        if NUMBER = 1 then
            PUT ( "Hurray" ); NEW_LINE;
        else
            CHEERS ( NUMBER - 1 );
            PUT ( "Hip" );
        end if;
    end CHEERS;
begin -- Test_2
    CHEERS ( 3 );
end TEST_2;
```

6. Write an iterative version of the function MYSTERY declared in Exercise 1.

7. Write an iterative version of the function ROSE declared in Exercise 3.

8. Write a recursive procedure that has one parameter that is a positive integer and that writes out that number of asterisks '*' to the screen.

Interactive Exercises

9. Take a pad of paper to use as the inexhaustible supply of paper for a stack. Simulate the following procedure call using a stack of real paper. First, use the one word sentence *Hi.* Next, use a sentence of your own choice, which is about 10 characters long. After that, type up the program and run it.

```
with TEXT_IO; use TEXT_IO;
procedure REVERSE_INPUT is
    procedure READ_WRITE is
        PERIOD : constant CHARACTER := '.';
        LETTER : CHARACTER;
    begin -- Read_Write
        GET ( LETTER );
        if LETTER /= PERIOD then
            READ_WRITE;
        end if;
        PUT ( LETTER );
    end READ_WRITE;
```

```
begin -- Reverse_Input
    PUT ( "Type in a sentence ending with a period." );
    NEW_LINE;
    READ_WRITE;
    NEW_LINE;
end REVERSE_INPUT;
```

10. Get hold of a real Towers of Hanoi game. Run the program in Figure 14.13 and follow its instructions for playing the game. Also simulate the program using a stack of paper, as in Exercise 9. The stack simulation is worth doing even if you do not have the game available.

Programming Exercises

11. The formula for computing the number of ways of choosing *r* different things from a set of *n* things is the following:

$$C(n, r) = \frac{n!}{r!\,(n - r)!}$$

n! is the factorial function ($n! = n*(n-1)*(n-2)* \ldots *1$). Discover a recursive version of the above formula and write an Ada function that computes the value of the formula.

12. Write a recursive procedure that has an argument that is a slice of an array of characters. The procedure should reverse the order of those entries in the array slice. For example, if the array is

```
a(1) = 'A' a(2) = 'B' a(3) = 'C' a(4) = 'D' a(5) = 'E'
```

and the slice is `a( 2 .. 5 )`, then after the procedure is run the array elements should be

```
a(1) = 'A' a(2) = 'E' a(3) = 'D' a(4) = 'C' a(5) = 'B'
```

Embed the procedure in a program and test it.

13. Write an iterative version of the procedure in Exercise 12. Embed it in a program and test it.

14. Write a recursive procedure to sort an array of integers into ascending order using the following idea: First place the smallest element in the first position, then sort the rest of the array by a recursive call. (This is a recursive version of the selection sort algorithm discussed in Chapter 10.)

15. Write a procedure that takes two parameters that are arrays of integers of the same size and one array parameter that is an array of integers of twice that size. The procedure assumes that the two smaller arrays are sorted and copies their contents into the larger array. It does so in such a way that the integers in the larger array are also sorted. Embed the procedure in a program to test it.

16. Use the ideas of Exercise 15 to design a recursive sorting procedure that works along the following general lines: The array is divided in half. Each half is sorted by a recursive call, and then the two halves are merged into a single sorted array. Embed the procedure in a program and test it.

17. Write an iterative version of the procedure in Exercise 16.

18. Write an iterative version of the procedure WRITE_MOVES from the Towers of Hanoi program (Figure 14.13).

19. Write a set of procedures for using an array of characters as a stack. There should be one procedure to add a character to the stack, one to remove a character, and one to read the "top" character on the stack.

20. Write a recursive procedure that takes as input a slice of an array of characters and outputs all permutations of the characters in the array. The array can hold a maximum of five characters, but it need not be full.

21. Find a formula for the number of times a disk is transferred from one peg to another in the Towers of Hanoi game with n rings. Compute the value for n equal to 5, 10, and 20.

22. Rewrite the Towers of Hanoi procedure so that it draws a stylized picture of the game being played. The output should be a series of pictures showing the game configuration after each ring is moved.

23. A *pretty print* program takes a program, which may not be indented in any particular way, and produces a copy with the same program indented so that **begin/end** pairs line up with inner pairs indented more than outer pairs, **if-then-else** statements are indented with the **if**, **else**, and **end if** lined up, comments are lined up, and so forth. Write a program that reads an Ada program from one text file and produces a "pretty print" version of the program in a second text file. To make it easier, simply do this for the block of the program, ignoring the declarations, and assume that all substatements of complex statements are indented as if they were in pairs, like **if/end if** and **loop/end loop**. To make it harder add any or all of the features omitted from the easy version.

References for Further Reading

P. Helman and R. Veroff, *Intermediate Problem solving and Data Structures,* Chapters 4 and 5 (Redwood City, CA: The Benjamin/Cummings Publishing Co., 1986).

E. S. Roberts, *Thinking Recursively* (New York: John Wiley & Sons Inc., 1986).

CHAPTER

15

SOLVING NUMERIC PROBLEMS

Niklaus Wirth

Wirth was associated with the early development of programming languages, such as ALGOL 60 (see Chapter 12) and ALGOL W. He is most famous for the development of the Pascal programming language. Pascal was developed by Wirth at the Eidgenossische Technische Hochschule in Zurich, Switzerland, during the late 1960s and early 1970s. Wirth designed Pascal to be a good first language for people learning to program.

Chapter Contents

Most of the computing done by scientists and engineers involves numbers, and more often than not with fractional numbers rather than integers. The general program design rules we have presented throughout this book apply to numeric calculations. There are also some additional considerations that apply specifically to numeric calculations. These considerations arise because of a very important but perhaps not obvious principle. To illustrate the principle, consider the following very simple piece of code and predict its output:

```
SUM := 1.0 / 3.0 + 1.0 / 3.0 + 1.0 / 3.0;
PUT ( SUM ); NEW_LINE;
```

The calculation hardly needs a computer. The expected output is 1. Yet many computers will give an output such as

```
0.9999
```

One need not be Sherlock Holmes to observe that the computer's performance is either incorrect or more subtle than our simple mental model of arithmetic. As it turns out, the second alternative is the better explanation. The numbers inside a computer are unlike the numbers you have learned about in mathematics classes from grade chool through calculus. Consequently, you must learn to think quite differently when performing involved numeric calculations on a computer. A detailed treatment of umeric programming techniques is beyond the scope of this book, but in this chapter we will describe some of the basic principles involved.

A Hypothetical Decimal Computer

Most computers work in binary notation, and some of the problems that arise when doing numeric calculations are due to the differences between binary and decimal notation. However, the difference between the two ways of writing numerals is small, and the problems caused by this difference are typically small. We will discuss numeric calculations in terms of a fictitious computer that works in decimal (base 10) rather than in binary (base 2) notation. Since we normally think in base 10, this will make the entire process easier to understand. Aside from the fact that it works in base 10, our hypothetical computer handles numbers in a very typical way.

word size

In Chapter 1 we observed that most computers have their main memory divided into a series of locations called *words*. Numeric values are usually stored one value per word. The size of a word will vary from machine to machine, but usually all words in any one machine are of the same size. One word of our hypothetical computer has room for eight symbols, and each symbol is either a sign or a decimal digit. So a word may be diagrammed as follows:

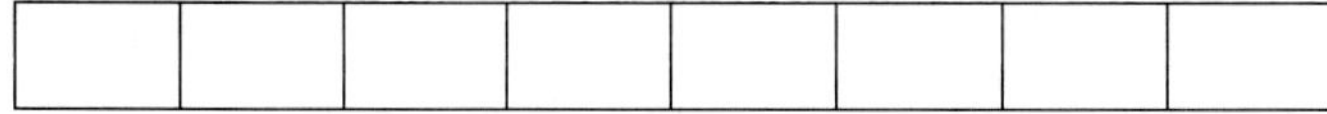

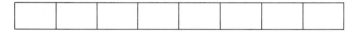

Each of the small boxes within a word can hold any one of the following 12 symbols: 0, 1, 2, 3, 4, 5, 6, 7, 8, 9, +, −.

storing integers

In our hypothetical computer, values of type INTEGER are stored as their usual base 10 numeral preceded by a sign. For example, the number 2957 would be stored as

+	0	0	0	2	9	5	7

The number −67543 would be stored as

−	0	0	6	7	5	4	3

The largest integer that can be stored in our computer is thus

+	9	9	9	9	9	9	9

Integer'Last

which is one less than ten million. With Ada implemented on our computer in this way, the value of INTEGER'LAST is 9999999. Similarly, the value INTEGER'FIRST is minus this amount.

floating point (Float) numbers

On our computer, values of type FLOAT are stored in what is called *floating point* notation. This is a variation on the **E** notation used to write FLOAT constants in Ada. The computer word is divided into two parts. On our hypothetical computer one part consists of five boxes and the other part consists of three boxes. The value of each floating point number is first converted to a form consisting of a decimal fraction multiplied by a power of 10. For example, the value **123.4** would be converted to the equivalent form:

$+0.1234 \times 10^3$

fractional part

The number with the decimal point in it is called the *fractional part* (or *mantissa*.) The fractional part (including the sign) is stored in the first five boxes, and the exponent of 10 (including its sign) is stored in the last three boxes. So **123.4** is stored as

+	1	2	3	4	+	0	3

exponent part

The position of the decimal point is assumed to be before the first digit. It is not marked in any way in the computer word. The division between the exponent part and the fractional part is also fixed and understood by the computer. It is not marked in any way. (In our hypothetical computer the boundary can be inferred by the presence of a plus or minus sign. However, in a typical computer, plus and minus would be represented by two digits such as 0 and 1.)

significant digits

Other examples of storing values of type `FLOAT` are given in Figure 15.1. Notice that all numbers are *normalized* so that the fractional part has the decimal point immediately in front of the first nonzero digit. This is an attempt to preserve the maximum number of significant digits. Consider the number **0.01234.** If the computer merely stores the first four digits after the decimal point, then the final digit **4** would be lost. However, because the computer normalizes the position of the decimal point, this number is stored as follows:

$+0.1234 \times 10^{-1}$

The normalization has saved that last digit. This moving of the decimal point is the origin of the term *floating point* and thus the name of the type FLOAT.

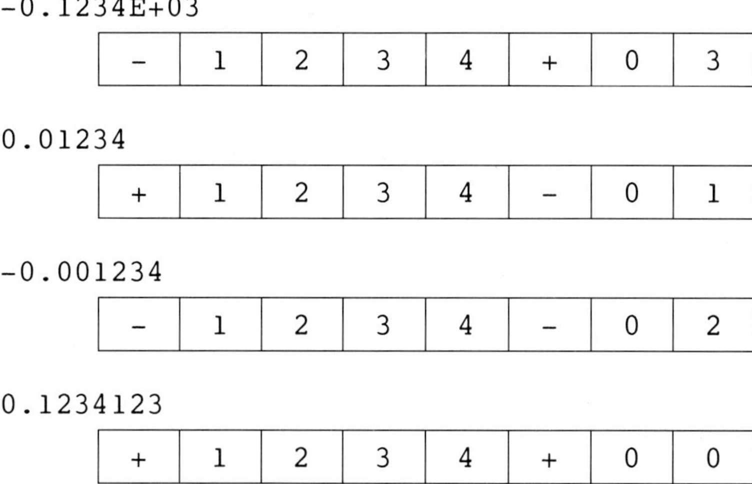

Figure 15.1 Storing floating point values.

There is only room for four decimal digits in our computer. For this reason the value stored is sometimes only an approximation of the value we might expect an Ada expression to represent. For example, **0.1234123** and **0.12340** have the same representation in our computer. Hence, on our hypothetical computer the following boolean expression evaluates to TRUE: *equality of floats*

```
0.1234123 = 0.12340
```

As this example indicates, testing for equality between two values of type FLOAT is pointless and even dangerous.

Our computer rounds numbers when they have too many digits to fit in a word. So **765.46** is rounded to **765.5**. Some systems truncate (i.e., discard the extra digits) instead. If our computer were to truncate instead of round, then the number **765.46** would be stored as **765.4** instead of **765.5**.

On our computer the largest positive value of type `FLOAT` that we can store would look as follows in memory: *largest floating point number*

+	9	9	9	9	+	9	9

Expressed more conventionally, this is the value

0.9999×10^{99}

Hence, the largest possible value of type `FLOAT` is about 10^{99}. By contrast, the largest possible value of type INTEGER is only **9999999** or about 10^7.

When a program attempts to compute a value of type FLOAT whose exponent is too large to fit into the space allocated for one exponent, that is called *floating point overflow*. Similarly, when a program attempts to compute a value of type `INTEGER` that is larger than `INTEGER'LAST` or smaller than the smallest integer that can be held in one word, that is called *integer overflow*. (Remember small negative numbers are large in absolute value. For example, $-9999999 < -1$. Hence, an equivalent way to describe overflow is to say that it occurs when the computer attempts to produce numbers that are too large in magnitude, that is, too large in absolute value.) Whenever any sort of overflow occurs, the exception `NUMERIC_ERROR` is raised. If there is no exception handler for `NUMERIC_ERROR`, the program will terminate. Even if there is an exception handler for `NUMERIC_ERROR`, the system is stopped from producing some meaningless value and making the entire computation meaningless. *overflow*

In addition to a largest magnitude that can be stored as a value of type `FLOAT`, there is also a smallest possible magnitude. The smallest positive number of type `FLOAT` that can be stored in our machine will be produced by the following word configuration: *smallest fraction*

+	1	0	0	0	−	9	9

That is the number

0.1000×10^{-99}

underflow

which is a decimal point followed by 99 zeros and then the number 1—certainly a very small number. However, calculations involving such small quantities do occur. When the computer attempts to produce a nonzero number whose absolute value is smaller than this quantity, that is called *floating point underflow*. When floating point underflow occurs, the exception NUMERIC_ERROR is raised. Underflow generally produces fewer problems than overflow. The situation with respect to overflow and underflow is diagrammed in Figure 15.2.

As you can see from the preceding discussion, the types INTEGER and FLOAT are implemented in different ways. As an illustration, consider the difference between the constants **123412** and **123412.0**. The first is of type INTEGER and is stored exactly as

+	0	1	2	3	4	1	2

The second is of type FLOAT and is stored only as the approximate value:

+	1	2	3	4	+	0	6

Most problems peculiar to numeric calculations arise because of the approximate nature of FLOAT values. When studying mathematics we frequently think in terms of an ideal world where quantities are represented as exact values called *real numbers*. These exact numbers are not available on a computer. If the quantity we need to write down requires more than four decimal digits after the decimal point, then it will not be represented exactly in our computer. If it consists of a decimal point followed by five or six nonzero digits, then we could use a computer with a larger word size. However, some quantities, such as the number *pi* used in geometry, cannot be represented exactly by any finite string of digits. For these real numbers, even a computer with a word size of one million digits could only store an approximation to the quantities they represent. Many of the real numbers of classical mathematics are simply not available on computers. Moreover, the missing numbers are not always very exotic ones. Recall the example that opened this chapter. It performs the following calculation:

```
SUM := 1.0 / 3.0 + 1.0 / 3.0 + 1.0 / 3.0
```

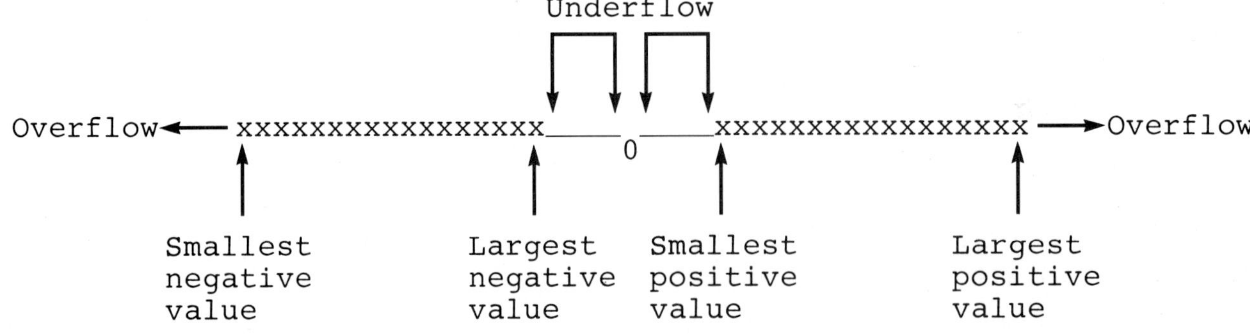

Figure 15.2 Range of available floating point values.

The number 1/3 has no representation as a finite string of decimal digits. Our computer will represent **1.0 / 3.0** as

$$0.3333 \times 10^0$$

When three of these are added together, the result is

$$0.9999 \times 10^0$$

rather than the value **1.0** that is predicted by the usual idealized model of arithmetic.

Binary Numerals
(Optional)

Most computers represent numbers in *binary notation* rather than in the more familiar base 10 notation. On occasion this can have a significant effect on the outcome of a numeric calculation. The basic idea of binary notation is quite simple. It is just like the base 10 notation we normally use, except that the role of 10 is replaced by the number 2. Base 10 notation uses 10 digits, 0 through 9. Base 2 notation uses only 2 digits, 0 and 1. In base 10 each change in position, from the rightmost to the leftmost digit, represents multiplication by 10. In base 2 each change in position, from the rightmost to the leftmost digit, represents multiplication by 2.

For example, consider the ordinary base 10 numeral 3019. It satisfies the following equality:

$$\begin{aligned} 3019 &= 3 \times 10^3 + 0 \times 10^2 + 1 \times 10^1 + 9 \times 10^0 \\ &= 3 \times 1000 + 0 \times 100 + 1 \times 10 + 9 \times 1 \\ &= 3000 + 000 + 10 + 9 \end{aligned}$$

The meaning of any base 10 numeral is decomposed in a similar way.

example

Next consider an example of a binary numeral, such as 100101. The situation is the same except that now each digit position represents some power of 2. For example, consider the following base 2 number:

$$100101_2$$

(The base of the number is represented as a subscript, that is, 101_2 is a base 2 number.) Written as a base 10 expression this number is

$$\begin{aligned} &= 1 \times 2^5 + 0 \times 2^4 + 0 \times 2^3 + 1 \times 2^2 + 0 \times 2^1 + 1 \times 2^0 \\ &= 1 \times 32 + 0 \times 16 + 0 \times 8 + 1 \times 4 + 0 \times 2 + 1 \times 1 \\ &= 32 + 4 + 1 = 37_{10} \end{aligned}$$

whole numbers

In binary notation the rightmost digit represents that digit multiplied by $2^0 = 1$, the next digit to the left represents that digit multiplied by $2^1 = 2$, the next multiplied by $2^2 = 4$, the next multiplied by $2^3 = 8$, and so forth. Any integer can be represented in this binary notation.

fractions

The treatment of fractions in binary notation is similar to that of decimal fractions. In decimal fractions the digit positions after the decimal point represent smaller and smaller fractions. Each shift to the right represents division by 10. For example

$$\begin{aligned} 0.103_{10} &= 1 \times 10^{-1} + 0 \times 10^{-2} + 3 \times 10^{-3} \\ &= 1 / 10 \quad + 0 / 10^2 \quad + 3 / 10^3 \\ &= 1 / 10 \quad + 0 / 100 \quad + 3 / 1000 \end{aligned}$$

Fractions in binary notation follow the same principle, but with 10 replaced by 2. For example

$$0.1101_2 = 1 \times 2^{-1} + 1 \times 2^{-2} + 0 \times 2^{-3} + 1 \times 2^{-3}$$

written as a base 10 expression is

$$\begin{aligned} &= 1 / 2 + 1 / 4 + 0 / 8 + 1 / 16 \\ &= 0.8125_{10} \end{aligned}$$

In binary notation the "point" is called a *binary point*, rather than a decimal point (in general the "point" is called the *radix point*). The first digit after the binary point represents that number divided by $2^1 = 2$, the next digit after the binary point represents that digit divided by $2^2 = 4$, the next digit represents the digit divided by $2^3 = 8$, and so forth.

In both decimal and binary notation, any quantity between zero and 1 can be represented by a point followed by a string of digits. In both binary and decimal notation, this may require an infinite string of digits, as in this base 10 number:

$$1/3 = 0.3333333333333333\ldots$$

As we add more **3**s we get a better approximation to 1/3, but no finite number of digits after the decimal point will yield a number exactly equal to 1/3.

A similar phenomena occurs in binary notation. In binary notation, the fraction 1/4, for example, can be expressed as the finite string 0.01, but the exact representation of 1/5 requires an infinite string of binary digits after the binary point.

$$1/5 = 0.00110011001100110011\ldots_2$$

Any finite string of binary digits can only approximate the value 1/5. In decimal notation 1/5 can be represented exactly as 0.2. As this example indicates, some quantities that we express exactly in decimal notation can become approximate quantities when stored in a binary computer.

In both binary and decimal notation you can combine the notation for whole numbers and that for fractions. In base 10, 12.34 means 12 plus 0.34. In base 2, 10.101_2 means 10_2 plus 0.101_2.

binary arithmetic

Arithmetic on binary numerals is very similar to arithmetic on base 10 numerals. In particular, shifting the binary point is similar to shifting the decimal point in base 10. In base 10, shifting the point to the right one position is the same as multiplying by 10. In base 2 it is the same as multiplying by 2. For example, in base 2, 1.011 multiplied by 2 is 10.11 and 1.011 multiplied by 4 is 101.1.

Machine Representation of Numbers in Binary
(Optional)

bits

Like our hypothetical decimal computer, most real computers have a memory that is divided into locations called *words*. However, these words usually store strings of zeros and ones rather than strings of decimal digits. Recall that a digit that must always be either zero or one is called a *bit*. Computer word sizes are usually described as being some number of bits. Some typical word sizes are 16, 32, and 64 bits. When people refer to ''16-bit machine,'' they mean that each word of the machine holds 16 binary digits. (They do not mean that the computer costs \$2.)

Since computer words usually hold bits, most computers store numbers in binary notation. Aside from the fact that the numbers are expressed in binary notation, the method of representing numbers is the same as we described for our hypothetical decimal machine.

integers

Numbers of type `INTEGER` are stored as binary numerals, either in the exact form we described in the previous section or in some variant of that notation. Each value of type `INTEGER` is stored in one word. For example, the number 5 has the binary representation 101 and, in a 16-bit word, it might be stored as

+	0	0	0	0	0	0	0	0	0	0	0	0	1	0	1

A word holds only zeros and ones. What we have written as the sign + must be represented as a zero or one. If we take 0 to stand for plus and 1 to stand for minus, then in this 16-bit computer, the preceding word contents is an abbreviation for

0	0	0	0	0	0	0	0	0	0	0	0	0	1	0	1

We will always use the plus and minus sign rather than 0 and 1 to denote the sign of a number in storage. It helps avoid confusion.

largest integer

Since one bit is occupied by the sign, the largest integer that can be stored in a 16-bit computer is the number with binary representation consisting of 15 ones. In base 10 that number is written 32767. You can compute this base 10 numeral by evaluating the following sum:

$$1 \times 2^{14} + 1 \times 2^{13} + 1 \times 2^{12} + \ldots + 1 \times 2^{1} + 1 \times 2^{0}$$

(If you understand a bit of binary arithmetic, you can calculate it more quickly as follows:

$$\begin{aligned} &111111111111111_2 \\ &= 1000000000000000_2 - 1 \\ &= 2^{15} - 1 \\ &= 32768_{10} - 1 \\ &= 32767_{10} \end{aligned}$$

However, if you are uncomfortable with binary arithmetic, simply do it the long way.)

If you are working on a 16-bit machine, you can expect the value of INTEGER'LAST to be 32767. The smallest negative number (INTEGER'FIRST) your 16-bit machine can hold will probably be about −32768. This is not part of the definition of the Ada language. The exact way that numbers are represented is left up to the implementors. So the value of INTEGER'LAST and the value of the smallest negative integer in your machine might vary somewhat from these figures. However, these values will be approximately correct for most 16-bit machines.

floating point numbers

Aside from the fact that binary notation is used, numbers of type FLOAT are stored in the same way as we described for our decimal computer. For example, a 16-bit word might be divided to allow 4 digits to express the exponent and 12 digits to express the fractional part. On a binary machine the exponent represents a power of 2 rather than a power of 10. For example, consider the following word configuration for such a machine:

+	1	0	1	1	0	0	0	0	0	0	0	+	1	0	1

It represents the number

$$0.1011_2 \times 2^{101}$$

which is written as a base 10 expression as

$$(1 / 2 + 0 / 4 + 1 / 8 + 1 / 16) \times (2^5)$$

We have taken the liberty of using the digit **2** in our binary expression. This mixed notation is sometimes easier to understand than absolutely pure binary notation.

Although numbers are invariably stored in binary notation, that notation normally has little, if any, effect on the outcome of a numeric computation. So we will end our discussion of binary arithmetic here and return to using our hypothetical decimal computer.

Extra Precision
(Optional)

Some computer installations have facilities to store numbers in more than one word and so obtain a more accurate representation for values of type FLOAT. Extra precision for floating point values is not a required part of the definition of Package Standard in Ada, but is available on most Ada systems.

double precision

One common method for obtaining extra accuracy when storing floating point values is called *double precision* (Package STANDARD, see Appendix C, recommends that these types be given names ending with FLOAT, such as LONG_FLOAT). In double precision each LONG_FLOAT number is stored in two words. This yields more than double the number of meaningful digits, because all the extra digits of the second word normally go into the fractional part. Our hypothetical decimal computer had an eight-decimal digit word size. On that computer a typical double precision implementation would store one LONG_FLOAT value in two words as illustrated by the example in Figure 15.3. In our hypothetical decimal computer, this accurately represents the decimal number

```
12.3456789012
```

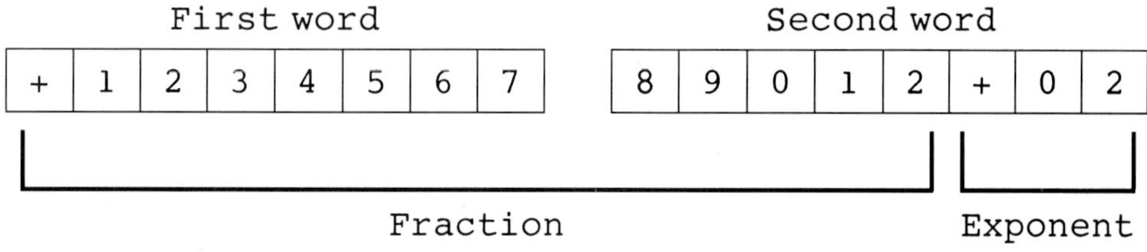

Figure 15.3 Example of a double precision number.

With this sort of double precision, the largest possible LONG_FLOAT value that can be stored is about the same as it is for the normal one-word representation. However, a full 12 decimal digits of accuracy can be represented. The ordinary one-word representation only allowed for four decimal digits of accuracy.

The disadvantages of double precision are that it uses more storage and that it usually causes programs to run more slowly.

There is no standard Ada name for double precision numbers; however, LONG_FLOAT is the recommended type name. You will have to consult the documentation for your particular Ada compiler system to see if it is available and, if available, to see how to use it in an Ada program.

Exercises

Self-Test Exercises

1. Describe how each of the following INTEGER and FLOAT constants are represented in our hypothetical decimal computer:

123456	−123456
123.456	−123.456
0.00123123	−0.00123123
3.14159265358979323846	

2. Our hypothetical decimal computer had a word size of eight. To store values of type FLOAT, it used five digit positions for the fractional part and three digit positions for the exponent part. Suppose that we instead used other combinations. At what value would FLOAT overflow occur if instead we used the following combinations?

(a) Fractional part uses four digit positions and exponent part uses four
(b) Fractional part uses three digit positions and exponent part uses five
(c) Fractional part uses six digit positions and exponent part uses two

3. (Applies to the optional section "Binary Numerals.") Convert the following binary numerals into equivalent decimal numerals: 111, 101, 100, 11011, 010110, 0.1, 0.01, 0.001, 0.101, 1.001, 101.101

4. (Applies to the optional section "Machine Representation of Numbers in Binary.") What would you expect as the value of INTEGER'LAST in a 32-bit machine? Assume that numbers are stored as described in this chapter. What about a 64-bit machine?

Pitfall

Sources of Error in Real Arithmetic

When you are computing with values of type FLOAT, you may have errors arise because numbers are stored as approximate values. These approximations are sometimes accurate enough and other times very inaccurate. In this and the next section we will discuss some common sources of inaccuracy in programs that compute values of type FLOAT.

overflow

As you will recall, overflow results when the computer tries to compute a number larger than it can hold in memory. The problem of integer overflow can sometimes be avoided by using variables of type FLOAT to do calculations involving large numbers, even if the quantities involved are whole numbers. The computer can store much larger values of type FLOAT than it can values of type INTEGER. There is a certain loss of accuracy in doing this, but often this loss of accuracy is tolerable.

underflow

Recall that floating point underflow occurs when the computer attempts to produce a nonzero value of type FLOAT that is too small in absolute value, that is, too close to zero. These values cannot be represented in memory, and Ada raises NUMERIC_ERROR. The exception NUMERIC_ERROR is raised by the system wherever the result of a numeric operation (i.e., +, *, −, etc.) produces a result that cannot be represented. Just because a value may be close to zero, it is never rounded to zero.

multiplication and division

When a multiplication or division is performed, the answer usually has more digits than either of the two numbers being combined. Frequently these extra digits cannot be represented in memory and so are lost, along with a little bit of accuracy. For example, consider the following code. (Here and in the examples that follow, we will set the values of variables by means of assignment statements. This is to keep the examples small. In practice those values might be read from the keyboard or might be the results of other calculations.)

```
BIGGER := 912.0;
SMALLER := 0.11;
PRODUCT := BIGGER * SMALLER;
```

The value that should be stored in PRODUCT is

$$912.0 \times 0.11 = 100.32$$

However, our hypothetical decimal computer only stores four digits in the fractional part of a FLOAT value. Hence, it will store the value of PRODUCT as

+	1	0	0	3	+	0	3

which represents the value

$$0.1003 \times 10^3$$

That means that the last digit is lost, and the value of PRODUCT becomes **100.30.** Even if the values of BIGGER and SMALLER were completely accurate, the value of PRODUCT has lost one digit of accuracy as the result of a simple multiplication. In all the examples of this section and the next section, we will use our hypothetical decimal computer; so we are allowed only four digits after the decimal point.

simple addition

Even a very simple addition or subtraction can produce a slightly inaccurate result. If the computer adds the number **9.222** to itself, the result should be

```
9.222 + 9.222 = 18.444
```

However, our computer only retains four digits and so will store the answer as

$$0.1844 \times 10^2$$

This means that **18.444** was rounded to **18.440,** and one digit of the answer was lost.

Under some circumstances the loss of accuracy in addition can be dramatic. Consider the following piece of code:

```
BIG := 2000.0;
SMALL := 0.4;
BIG := BIG + SMALL;
```

The values of BIG and SMALL are stored as

$$0.2000 \times 10^4$$

$$0.4000 \times 10^0$$

Like most computers, our hypothetical decimal machine cannot add two numbers unless they have the same exponent part. Hence, it must change one of the two numbers. On our machine the second number is changed to

$$0.00004 \times 10^4$$

Then the following addition is performed:

$$\begin{array}{r} 0.2000 \times 10^4 \\ +\ 0.00004 \times 10^4 \\ \hline 0.20004 \times 10^4 \end{array}$$

This answer is what we might expect as the value of BIG, but unfortunately that is not the value stored. Since our computer only stores four digits after the decimal point, the computer stores the following as the value of BIG:

$$0.2000 \times 10^4$$

The adding in of SMALL had absolutely no effect on the value of BIG.

adding large and small numbers

Situations like the preceding example are common. To avoid this sort of problem, you must somehow avoid adding or subtracting two values of very different size. Sometimes this can be done by rearranging the order in which numbers are combined. As an example, consider the following code:

```
TOTAL := 2000.0;
FIRST := 0.4;
SECOND := 0.3;
THIRD := 0.4;
TOTAL := TOTAL + FIRST;
TOTAL := TOTAL + SECOND;
TOTAL := TOTAL + THIRD;
```

As we have just seen, adding FIRST has no effect on the value of TOTAL. Similarly, adding SECOND and adding THIRD each have no effect. This calculation leaves the value of TOTAL unchanged at

$$0.2000 \times 10^4$$

However, if we first combine FIRST, SECOND, and THIRD to obtain a larger number and then combine this larger number with TOTAL, then the resultant value of TOTAL will be close to the value we expect. Consider the following slightly different code for the same computation:

```
TOTAL := 2000.0;
FIRST := 0.4;
SECOND := 0.3;
THIRD := 0.4;
BIGGER := FIRST + SECOND + THIRD;
TOTAL := TOTAL + BIGGER;
```

The value of BIGGER is obtained by first adding the values of FIRST and SECOND and then combining that sum with the value of THIRD, as shown below:

$$\begin{array}{r} 0.4000 \times 10^0 \\ +\ 0.3000 \times 10^0 \\ \hline 0.7000 \times 10^0 \end{array}$$

$$\begin{array}{r} 0.7000 \times 10^0 \\ +\ 0.4000 \times 10^0 \\ \hline 1.1000 \times 10^0 \end{array} = 0.1100 \times 10^1$$

This value is then added to the value of TOTAL as follows:

$$\begin{array}{r} 0.2000 \quad \times 10^4 \\ +\ 0.00011 \times 10^4 \\ \hline 0.20011 \times 10^4 \end{array}$$

The final value of TOTAL is stored as

$$0.2001 \times 10^4$$

By rearranging the order of the additions, we have added one digit of accuracy to the answer. This is a standard trick. If the small numbers are first added together, then that will produce a somewhat larger value. This larger value can then be combined with other large values. In this way the numbers being combined are more nearly equal, and the results of their addition will be more accurate.

Pitfall

Error Propagation

Each individual operation on a value of type FLOAT is likely to introduce only a very small error. However, after a number of operations, these small errors may be compounded to produce a very large inaccuracy. Once again we illustrate the pitfall with a piece of code:

```
. . .
MINUEND := 0.1232;
DIFFERENCE := SUBTRAHEND - MINUEND;
MULTIPLIER := 10000.0;
PRODUCT := DIFFERENCE * MULTIPLIER;
```

The three dots represent some computation that sets the value of SUBTRAHEND. Let us say that SUBTRAHEND gets set to **0.1234,** a value very close to that of MINUEND. The value of DIFFERENCE gets set by the following calculation:

$$\begin{array}{r} 0.1234 \times 10^0 \\ -\ 0.1232 \times 10^0 \\ \hline 0.0002 \times 10^0 \end{array} = 0.2000 \times 10^{-3}$$

The value of PRODUCT is then computed by multiplying that value by 10,000 to obtain

$$0.2000 \times 10^1$$

So far things look fine. The answer appears to be **2.0**. However, as we have already seen, it is easy for a program to calculate a value that is slightly in error. Suppose that the value of SUBTRAHEND was slightly in error. Specifically, suppose the correct value of SUBTRAHEND is **0.1233**. Then the correct answer is

$$(0.1233 - 0.1232) \times 10{,}000 = 1$$

The correct answer is **1.0**, but our code computed it as **2**. A slight mistake has been compounded, and our answer is now wrong by a factor of two.

subtracting almost equal numbers

The problem is that when subtraction is performed on two nearly equal numbers, the answer is the difference between the end digits of the two numbers. After the subtraction, only the last digits of the two almost-equal numbers have any effect on the rest of the computation. But these are exactly the digits that are likely to be incorrect. Hence a program should somehow avoid subtracting two almost equal numbers of type FLOAT.

All the examples in this and the previous section are unrealistic in the sense that most computers represent FLOAT values with an accuracy equivalent to more than four decimal digits. In all other respects they are real pitfalls. Realistic examples can be manufactured by simply adding a few more digits to the initial values and leaving the rest of the code unchanged.

Case Study

Series Evaluation

Problem Definition

One common numeric task is to sum a series. For example, consider the following series:

$$1 / 2 + 2 / 2^2 + 3 / 2^3 + \ldots + \text{LAST\_TERM} / 2^{\text{LAST\_TERM}}$$

Our job is to compute the value of the sum given the value of LAST_TERM.

Discussion

For the sake of concreteness suppose the value of LAST_TERM is 100. The most obvious way to calculate the sum is as follows:

```
LAST_TERM := 100;
SUM := 0.0;
for INDEX in 1 .. LAST_TERM
loop
    SUM := SUM + FLOAT ( INDEX ) / ( 2.0 ** INDEX );
end loop;
```

If the calculation is carried out with complete accuracy, this will set the value of SUM to the desired value. However, the operations are not carried out with complete accuracy. Moreover, the values of the successive terms rapidly become very small, while in comparison the value of SUM remains moderately large. Hence, after the first few iterations, the loop is adding two numbers of very different sizes. As we have seen, this can lead to inaccuracies in the answer.

order of summation

We can avoid adding numbers of such greatly differing sizes by summing the series in the other direction as follows:

```
LAST_TERM := 100;
SUM := 0.0;
for INDEX in reverse 1 . . LAST_TERM
loop
     SUM := SUM + FLOAT ( INDEX ) / ( 2.0 ** INDEX );
end loop;
```

The numbers being combined will then be more nearly equal; hence, the results of the additions are likely to be more accurate.

Algorithm

The general algorithm is the same.

```
SUM := 0;
for INDEX in reverse 1 . . LAST_TERM
loop
     SUM := SUM + FLOAT ( INDEX ) / ( 2.0 ** INDEX );
end loop;
```

Case Study

Finding the Root of a Function

A common numeric programming problem is to solve an equation. For example, consider the following equation:

$$x^3 + 2x = 33$$

One solution is 3, since

$$3^3 + 2 \times 3 = 33$$

By rearranging the equation, we can always get it into the form

```
F(x) = 0
```

where **F(x)** is some expression that can be made into an Ada function having one argument of type FLOAT and returning a value of type FLOAT. For example, the equation

$$3^3 + 2 \times 3 = 33$$

can be rearranged to the following equivalent equation:

$$3^3 + 2 \times 3 - 33 = 0$$

The expression on the left-hand side is computed by the Ada function declared as follows:

```
function F ( X : FLOAT ) return FLOAT is
begin -- F
    return X ** 3 + 2.0 * X - 33.0;
end F;
```

roots

Viewed this way, solving equations of this form is equivalent to finding a value **x** such that the expression **F(x)** on the left side of the rearranged equation is made equal to zero. Such a value **x** is called the *root* of the function **F(x)**.

Problem Definition

In this section we will design a program to find the root of the function **F**. The function **F** is given as an Ada function that we will incorporate into our final program. The user will provide two values, $\mathbf{x_1}$ and $\mathbf{x_2}$, such that there is exactly one root between $\mathbf{x_1}$ and $\mathbf{x_2}$. We will design a program that finds the approximate value of the root of the function **F**. The method works for a wide range of different functions **F**. We need only assume that the graph of the function can be drawn on paper as a smooth line. (The technically precise condition is that the function must be *continuous*. However, we will not stop to define that term. The informal notion of ''easy to draw as a smooth line'' will do here.)

Discussion

bisection method

Our goal is to find a value *midpoint* such that *F(midpoint)* is approximately equal to zero. The method we will use is called the *bisection method*. (The technique is similar to that of the binary search algorithm we discussed in Chapter 14, but you need not have read that section to understand this method.) The idea of the bisection method is diagrammed in Figure 15.4. The graph represents the function **F**. Two values, **low** and **high**, are chosen so that exactly one root lies between these two values. We therefore know that the following relation holds:

```
low < root < high
```

The MIDPOINT between the two values LOW and HIGH is then computed. In Figure 15.4 this MIDPOINT is denoted **M**. The root is either between LOW and MIDPOINT or else it is between MIDPOINT and HIGH. For now assume we can tell which of these two intervals contains the root; later we will return and figure out a way to do so. In the figure the root is between MIDPOINT and HIGH. This

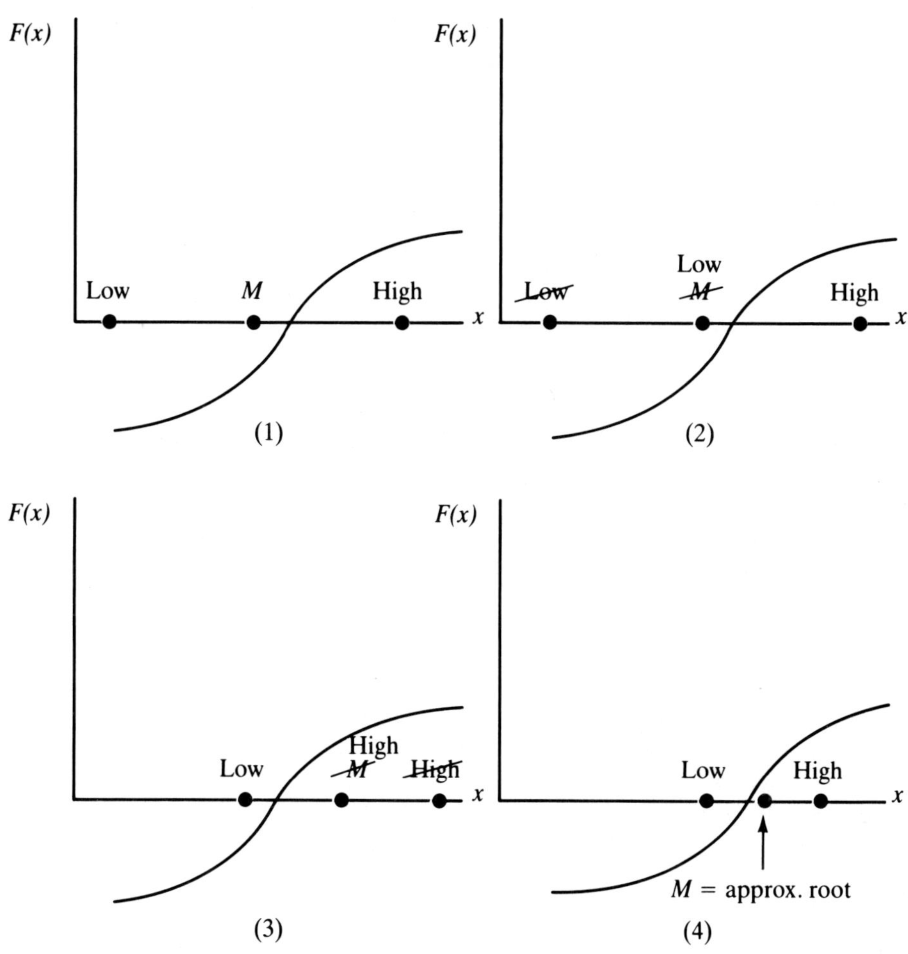

Figure 15.4 One way to find a root.

process has managed to narrow down the location of the root. Originally we knew it was between LOW and HIGH. Now we know that it is in the smaller interval between MIDPOINT and HIGH (in other cases it could be between LOW and MIDPOINT). Next we change the values LOW and HIGH to these new end point values; in the figure, MIDPOINT becomes the new value of LOW and the value of HIGH is unchanged. If we keep repeating this process, we eventually get a very small interval that contains the root. This gives us an approximation to the value of the root. The method is outlined in the following pseudocode:

Algorithm

Request values for LOW and HIGH such that:

```
    LOW < ROOT < HIGH
loop
    MIDPOINT := ( LOW + HIGH ) / 2.0
    if F ( MIDPOINT ) is approximately equal to 0 then
        return MIDPOINT
    elsif the ROOT is between LOW and MIDPOINT then
        HIGH := MIDPOINT
    else
        LOW := MIDPOINT
    end if
end loop
```

Algorithm Refinement

We still must design a subalgorithm to decide whether the root is between LOW and MIDPOINT or between MIDPOINT and HIGH. The interval containing the root can be determined from the signs of the values: F (LOW), F (MIDPOINT), and F (HIGH). Of the two values F (LOW) and F (HIGH), one will be positive and one will be negative. If the sign of F (MIDPOINT) matches F (HIGH), then HIGH gets its value changed to MIDPOINT. If the match is with LOW, then LOW gets changed. So the pseudocode for the **if** statement can be refined to

```
if F ( MIDPOINT ) approximately equal 0.0 then
    return MIDPOINT
elsif SAME_SIGN ( F ( HIGH ), F ( MIDPOINT ) ) then
    HIGH := MIDPOINT
elsif SAME_SIGN ( F ( LOW ), F ( MIDPOINT ) ) then
    LOW := MIDPOINT
else
    something is wrong
end if
```

where SAME_SIGN is a boolean-valued function that tests two values to see if they have the same sign.

additional input needed

The test for approximate zero will depend on a constant called THRESHOLD. As long as a number is less than THRESHOLD in absolute value, it will be considered close enough to zero. The value of THRESHOLD will depend on the accuracy of the computer and the accuracy needed for the particular application. Hence we will ask the user to supply the value. The test for approximately zero can then be expressed as

```
abs F ( MIDPOINT ) <= THRESHOLD
```

The final program is in Figure 15.5. The function body for **F** has

```
return X ** 3 + 2.0 * X - 33.0;
```

but it could be filled in with any function definition that satisfies the assumptions we made.

additional error checks

If incorrect initial values are used, the algorithm expressed in our pseudocode can go into an infinite loop. Hence, in the final program we have placed a limit on the number of loop iterations allowed. When that limit is exceeded, an exception is raised and the program halts and reports that something is likely to be amiss. As an additional check on faulty data, we have added a statement at the end of the **if** statement to raise an exception. If the data and function are as they should be, the **raise** statement will not be executed. However, incorrect data could cause all of the boolean expressions to be false. The **else** clause will catch this situation immediately.

Program

```
with TEXT_IO;
use TEXT_IO;
procedure ROOT is
    BAD_DATA : exception;
    HIGH : FLOAT;
    LOW : FLOAT;
    THRESHOLD : FLOAT;
    TOO_MANY_ITERATIONS : exception;
    package ROOT_IO is new FLOAT_IO ( FLOAT );
    use ROOT_IO;
    function F ( X : FLOAT ) return FLOAT is
    begin -- F
        return X ** 3 + 2.0 * X - 33.0;
    end F;
    function SAME_SIGN ( VALUE_1, VALUE_2 : FLOAT ) return BOOLEAN is
    begin -- Same_Sign
        return ( VALUE_1 >= 0.0 and then VALUE_2 >= 0.0 )
            or else ( VALUE_1 <= 0.0 and then VALUE_2 <= 0.0 );
    end SAME_SIGN;
    procedure READ_INTERVAL ( LOW, HIGH : in out FLOAT ) is
    begin -- Read_Interval
        loop
            PUT ( "Enter two floating point values," ); NEW_LINE;
            PUT ( "the first less than the root," ); NEW_LINE;
            PUT ( "the second less than the root." ); NEW_LINE;
            PUT ( "Be sure there is" ); NEW_LINE;
            PUT ( "exactly one root between them." ); NEW_LINE;
            begin
                GET ( LOW );
                GET ( HIGH );
```

```
                if SAME_SIGN ( F ( LOW ), F ( HIGH ) ) then
                    raise BAD_DATA;
                end if;
                SKIP_LINE;
                exit;
            exception
                when DATA_ERROR | BAD_DATA =>
                    SKIP_LINE;
                    PUT ( "Those can't be right." ); NEW_LINE;
                    PUT ( "Try again." ); NEW_LINE ( 2 );
            end;
        end loop;
    end READ_INTERVAL;
    function FIND_ROOT ( LOW_POINT, HIGH_POINT, THRESHOLD : FLOAT )
            return FLOAT is
        COUNT : NATURAL := 0;
        HIGH : FLOAT := HIGH_POINT;
        LOW : FLOAT := LOW_POINT;
        MAXIMUM_ITERATIONS : constant NATURAL := 1000;
        MIDPOINT : FLOAT;
    begin -- Find_Root
        loop
            MIDPOINT := ( LOW + HIGH ) / 2.0;
            if abs F ( MIDPOINT ) = THRESHOLD then
                return MIDPOINT;
            elsif SAME_SIGN ( F ( HIGH ), F ( MIDPOINT ) ) then
                HIGH := MIDPOINT;
            elsif SAME_SIGN ( F ( LOW ), F ( MIDPOINT ) ) then
                LOW := MIDPOINT;
            else
                raise BAD_DATA;
            end if;
            COUNT := COUNT + 1;
            if COUNT >= MAXIMUM_ITERATIONS then
                raise TOO_MANY_ITERATIONS;
            end if;
        end loop;
    end FIND_ROOT;
    begin -- Root
        READ_INTERVAL ( LOW, HIGH );
        PUT ( "Enter the accuracy desired." ); NEW_LINE;
        GET ( THRESHOLD ); SKIP_LINE;
        PUT ( "The root is approximately " );
        PUT ( FIND_ROOT ( LOW, HIGH, THRESHOLD ), 1, 4, 0 );
        NEW_LINE;
```

```
exception
    when BAD_DATA =>
        PUT ( "Something is wrong." ); NEW_LINE;
    when TOO_MANY_ITERATIONS =>
        PUT ( "Exceeded iteration limit." ); NEW_LINE;
end ROOT;
```

Figure 15.5 Program to find the root of a function.

Summary of Problem Solving and Programming Techniques

- The largest value of type FLOAT that an installation can accommodate is always much larger than the largest value of type INTEGER it can handle. Hence, one way to avoid INTEGER overflow is to represent quantities as values of type FLOAT, even though they are whole numbers.
- Values of type FLOAT are stored as approximate quantities. Hence, computations involving these numbers yield only approximations of the desired results. Unless particular care is taken to minimize errors, these approximations often can be very inaccurate.
- Since FLOAT values are stored as approximate quantities, any test of two floating point values for exact equality yields a meaningless result.
- A common source of error in programs involving the type FLOAT is round-off error in any arithmetic operation, such as addition or multiplication, but especially in certain combinations, such as adding two numbers of very different sizes or subtracting two numbers of almost equal size.

Summary of Terms

floating point numbers In Ada, numbers of type FLOAT.

overflow The condition that results when a program attempts to compute a numeric value whose magnitude is too large. More precisely it is the condition that results when a program attempts to compute a numeric value larger than the largest value of that type that the computer can represent in memory, or a value smaller than the smallest value of that type that the computer can represent in memory.

underflow The condition that results when a program attempts to compute a value of type FLOAT such that the value is smaller in absolute value than the smallest positive FLOAT value that the system can represent in memory. In other words, the condition that results when a program attempts to compute a nonzero value that is too close to zero to be represented in memory (except possibly by the approximately equal value of zero).

Exercises

Self-Test Exercises

5. Assume that Ada arithmetic is implemented as we described for our hypothetical decimal computer. What is the output of the following when embedded in a complete program with the variables declared to be of type FLOAT?

```
ADDEND := 300.00;
AUGEND := 0.12345678;
PUT ( ADDEND + AUGEND );
NEW_LINE;
```

6. Assume that Ada arithmetic is implemented as we described for our hypothetical decimal computer. What is the output of the following when embedded in a complete program with the variables declared to be of type FLOAT?

```
ABLE := 0.1000E-90;
BAKER := 0.1000E-25;
CHARLIE := 0.1000E+25;
PUT ( ABLE * BAKER * CHARLIE );
PUT ( ABLE * CHARLIE * BAKER );
NEW_LINE;
```

Remember that multiplications are performed in left to right order and our hypothetical computer rounds to zero on floating point underflow.

Interactive Exercises

7. Find (approximately) the largest value for the constant EPSILON that will cause the following PUT_LINE to be executed on your system:

```
VALUE := 1.0 + EPSILON;
if VALUE = 1.0 then
    PUT_LINE ( "It's really nothing" );
end if;
```

8. Type up and run the program in Figure 15.5. Use the following body for **F**:

```
function F ( X : FLOAT ) return FLOAT is
begin -- F
    return X ** 2 - 4;
end F;
```

The exact root is thus 2.0. The program will approximate that root.

Programming Exercises

9. Write a function body for a function called `DIGIT` that returns the value of the *n*th digit from the right of an `INTEGER` argument. The value of *n* should be a second argument. For example, `DIGIT ( 9635, 1 )` returns **5** and `DIGIT ( 9635, 3 )` returns **6**.

10. If **e** denotes the base of the natural logarithm, then the value $\mathbf{e}^{\mathbf{x}}$ can be calculated by the series

$$e^x = 1 + x + x^2 / 2! + x^3 / 3! + x^4 / 4! \ldots$$

Write a program that computes an approximate value of **e** by summing that series for *n* terms, with **x** equal to **1**. Have the program compute the series from left to right and from right to left and output both results. The value of **e** is approximately **2.71828. . . .** Compare your result. Embed the calculations in a loop that repeats the calculation for values of *n* from **1** to **100**. To avoid integer overflow, store the factorials as values of type `FLOAT` (or avoid using factorials at all).

11. Write a program that sums the following series from left to right until a term of absolute value less than **0.00001** is encountered and then outputs the answer

$$4 - 4 / 3 + 4 / 5 - 4 / 7 + 4 / 9 \ldots$$

(The denominators are the positive odd numbers 1, 3, 5, 7, 9, 11, and so on.) Have the program then recalculate the sum from right to left using the same number of terms and output that value as well. Compare the two results.

12. (Applies to the optional section "Binary Numerals.") Write a program that takes a base 2 numeral (for a whole number) as input and outputs the equivalent base 10 numeral.

13. (Applies to the optional section "Binary Numerals.") Write a program that takes a base 10 numeral (for a whole number) as input and outputs the equivalent base two numeral.

14. (Applies to the optional section "Binary Numerals.") A *hexadecimal numeral* is a numeral written in base 16. Write a program that takes a hexadecimal numeral (for a whole number) as input and outputs the equivalent base 10 numeral. Use the first six letters of the alphabet for the digits "ten" through "fifteen."

15. (Applies to the optional section "Binary Numerals.") Write a program that takes a base 10 numeral (for a whole number) as input and outputs the equivalent hexadecimal numeral. (See Exercise 14 for a definition of hexadecimal numerals.)

16. One way to obtain extra digits is to store numbers as arrays of digits. Write a program that will read in two whole numbers with up to 20 digits each and store their digits in arrays of the following type:

```
array( 0 . . 19 ) of NATURAL
```

The program computes the sum of the two numbers, stores the result in an array of the same type, and then outputs the result to the screen. Use the ordinary addition algorithm that you learned in grade school. Be sure to issue an "overflow" message if the result is more than 20 digits long.

17. It is wasteful to store just one digit in an array location that can hold about the number of digits in `INTEGER'LAST`. Redo Exercise 16, but this time store **width** digits in each array variable, where **width** is one less than `INTEGER'WIDTH` written in base 10. (`'WIDTH` is a predefined attribute that returns the maximum length of its prefix, where maximum length is the number of characters needed to represent the largest value of the prefix type. For more information, see Appendix A of the LRM.) You will need to modify the addition algorithm slightly, but the idea is still the same. Use **0..4** as the array index type.

18. Do Exercise 17 for multiplication instead of addition.

19. Use the ideas in Exercise 18 to design a program that can do multiplication of real numbers that yields at least twice as many significant digits as your system's ordinary Ada FLOAT multiplication does.

20. (Assumes that you know what a derivative is.) If x is a maximum or minimum of a function F, and F has a derivative at x, then the derivative of F is zero at x. Use this idea to design a program to find local minima and maxima of polynomials of degree two. Use any input format that is convenient.

21. Redo Exercise 20, but allow polynomials of arbitrary degree and use the bisection method to find the roots of the derivatives.

References for Further Reading

B. W. Kernighan and P. J. Plauger, *The Elements of Programming Style,* (New York: McGraw-Hill, 1978). Includes material on pitfalls in both numeric and nonnumeric programming. The examples are in Fortran and PL/I, not in Ada.

D. E. Knuth, *The Art of Computer Programming, Volume 2, Seminumerical Algorithms,* 2nd ed. (MA: Addison-Wesley, 1981). Also does not use Ada, but the text can be read without reading the programs.

T. Stoer and R. Bulirsch, *Introduction to Numerical Analysis* (New York: Springer-Verlag, 1980). Uses ALGOL, an ancestor language of Ada.

C H A P T E R

16

MORE FILE TYPES

Edsger Dijkstra

In 1952, Dijkstra accepted a job as a programmer at the Mathematical Center in Amsterdam. In 1960, after the successful implementation of the new programming language ALGOL 60, he considered himself a professional programmer. Dijkstra has been researching and writing on the subject of programming ever since. He is perhaps most famous for his many commentaries on ''go-to-less'' programming.

Chapter Contents

Text files, which we have already used, are a special case of the more general construct known as *files*. In this chapter we describe Ada files in complete generality and also present programming and problem solving techniques that use files of types *other than text*. We will call these files *nontext files*.

The General Notion of a File

Files are used for holding data in secondary storage so that the data may remain after the program has run to completion. At some later time the same, or another, program may access the data in the file. A file is a named collection of data in secondary storage. In any kind of file, all the data must be of the same type. A text file is a special kind of file in which the data is all characters. In general, the data in a file may be of almost any Ada data type. All types of files are similar in nature, but text files have some additional properties that are not shared by other file types. Files of type TEXT_IO.FILE_TYPE can be read by using an editor and so are accessible by means other than an Ada program. Other types of files cannot normally be accessed by an editor; they can only be used as input and/or output data for Ada programs, because data is represented differently in text files and in nontext files. With text files all data is converted into characters and so can be read by the editor. In nontext files data is stored using the same binary encoding that is used in main memory to encode variable values of that data type. Since the data is not converted into characters, these files cannot be read using the editor. Because they use these binary encodings, files of types other than TEXT_IO.FILE_TYPE are often referred to as *binary files.* This term is somewhat misleading since all files, even text files, are stored in some binary format. Hence, we will simply call them *nontext files.*

element type

A *file* consists of a sequence of items called *elements,* all of which are values of some one type known as the *element type.* The element type of a file can be any of the data types we have seen. The element type may be a simple type, such as INTEGER or CHARACTER. It might be an array type, such as an array of integers. It very frequently is a record type. The only data types that are not allowed are file types and structured types that involve files, such as an array of files. In particular, you cannot have a file of files.

comparison to arrays

This description makes a file sound very much like an array, and indeed, a file is conceptually very much like a one-dimensional array. There are, however, three important conceptual differences between a file and an array. First, the size of an array must be declared in advance of using it, so it is bounded by some fixed number. On the other hand, there is no limit to the size of a file. The number of elements that are placed in a file is not declared anywhere in the program, and there is no limit to the number of such elements. Any particular implementation will impose an upper bound on the size of a file, but the upper bound typically is so large that, for most purposes, the file can be considered unbounded. Second, files are kept in secondary storage, so they can remain in storage after the program has run to completion. Finally, files are usually accessed sequentially. For example, to get to the tenth element of a file, a program steps through the first nine elements before it reaches the tenth element. With an array, a program can go directly to any element of the array by naming an index. (An indexing scheme is available for files with the package DIRECT_IO. We briefly discuss package DIRECT_IO later in this chapter. For more information on DIRECT_IO see ''References for Further Reading'' at the end of this chapter.)

Sequential_IO Package

syntax for type definitions

The abstract data type for sequential nontext files is described in the generic package SEQUENTIAL_IO. Like the other generic I/O packages that we have used, INTEGER_IO, FLOAT_IO, and ENUMERATION_IO, SEQUENTIAL_IO must be instantiated before a program can **use** it. SEQUENTIAL_IO is instantiated with the element type of the file elements. The general form for instantiating SEQUENTIAL_IO is

package *package_name* **is new** SEQUENTIAL_IO (*element_type*);

where *package_name* is any identifier, and *element_type* is some previously declared type name.

For example, if the element type is INTEGER, then the instantiation would look like the following:

```
package NUMBER_IO is new SEQUENTIAL_IO ( INTEGER );
```

An object declaration for a sequential nontext file consists of two names separated by a period (i.e., *package_name*.FILE_TYPE). For example, if you want INTEGER_FILE to be the name of a file consisting of integers instantiated as above, then the file variable declaration is as follows:

```
INTEGER_FILE : NUMBER_IO.FILE_TYPE;
```

Below are sample type declarations followed by the necessary instantiations of package SEQUENTIAL_IO and declarations of file variables:

```
type LIST is array( 0 . . 10 ) of INTEGER;
type ITEM is record
                   NAME   : STRING( 1 . . 20 );
                   NUMBER : INTEGER;
                   PRICE  : FLOAT;
               end record;
package LIST_IO is SEQUENTIAL_IO ( LIST );
package ITEM_IO is SEQUENTIAL_IO ( ITEM );
package REAL_IO is SEQUENTIAL_IO ( FLOAT );
LIST_FILE : LIST_IO.FILE_TYPE;
ITEM_FILE : ITEM_IO.FILE_TYPE;
REAL_FILE : REAL_IO.FILE_TYPE;
```

text files

A text file is almost the same thing as

```
package CHARACTER_IO is SEQUENTIAL_IO ( CHARACTER );
CHARACTER_FILE : CHARACTER_IO.FILE_TYPE;
```

The only difference is that a text file is divided into lines and CHARACTER_FILE is not. Despite their similarities, text files and other types of files are usually thought of as two different categories of files. Moreover, text files and nontext files have different procedures for reading from and writing to files. Because of these differences, text files are treated as a special category of files. To avoid problems, use the descriptions presented in this chapter for nontext files, and use the descriptions presented in Chapter 13 for text files.

The details for declaring file variables and for creating, opening, and closing nontext files are the same as those for text files, so we can be brief in presenting the details.

File Variables

Variables of file types are declared in the same way as other variables. Note the examples above. Within an Ada program, file variable names are used to refer to files when retrieving input from the file or producing output to the file.

The details of naming external files differ somewhat from one implementation to another, but within any one system it is the same for all file types. If you have already discovered the idiosyncrasies of how your system names external text files, you can apply that same naming technique to other files and be reasonably confident that it will work.

Creating, Opening, and Closing Files

create
open

All types of files must be created or opened before a program can access them. The CREATE and OPEN procedures in SEQUENTIAL_IO have the same format as those in TEXT_IO. As a quick review, note the general format that follows:

CREATE (*internal_file_name*, OUT_FILE, *external_file_name*);
OPEN (*internal_file_name*, IN_FILE, *external_file_name*);

A file is created for writing with the procedure CREATE and is opened for reading with the procedure OPEN. The *internal_file_name* is the name of a file variable of type *package_name*.FILE_TYPE. The *external_file_name* is a character string that represents the name of a file on the system on which the program is run.

close

When a program is finished with a file it must be closed. The general format for the CLOSE procedure is the same as we used for files in TEXT_IO.

CLOSE (*internal_file_name*);

read
write

The WRITE procedure is used to put items of the element type into a nontext file. A call to the WRITE procedure may be used with any file that has been created with the procedure CREATE. The READ procedure is used to get items of element type from a nontext file. A READ statement may be used with any file that has been opened with the procedure OPEN. The general format for WRITE and READ are as follows:

WRITE (*internal_file_name*, *item_of_element_type*);
READ (*internal_file_name*, *item_of_element_type*);

Note that the names of these input and output procedures are different than the ones that we used for TEXT_IO. Package SEQUENTIAL_IO uses READ and WRITE, not GET and PUT.

external and internal file names

Any type of file may be either external or internal. External files are stored permanently on a secondary storage device. Internal files, often called *temporary files,* exist only during the execution of the program; all information in the file is lost when the program terminates. If the file is external, then its external file name is given as the third parameter in the call to the procedure CREATE. If the file is to be a temporary file, the second and third parameters are not included in the call to the CREATE procedure. Thus the form for creating a temporary file is

CREATE (*internal_file_name*);

reset

A temporary file may be changed from an output file to an input file by a call to the procedure RESET. The general form used to make this change is

RESET (*internal_file_name*, IN_FILE);

This same procedure can be used to change a temporary input file to an output file also. The second parameter simply specifies OUT_FILE.

RESET (*internal_file_name*, OUT_FILE);

Another form of the RESET procedure allows a file that has been opened and either partially or completely read to begin at the beginning again. This allows a file to be read from the beginning as many times as is needed by the program. The general form has but one parameter, the internal file name.

RESET (*internal_file_name*);

Arrow

Before we go on to discuss ways of reading from and writing to nontext files, we must first explain one preliminary concept, namely, the notion of a file location indicator that in Chapter 13 we called an *arrow.* As we already said, a file is a sequence of elements, all of the same type. Every file has an arrow that is positioned at exactly one of these elements. If these elements are integers, then the arrow is positioned at one integer. If the file is composed of records, then the arrow is positioned at one record. As the term *arrow* indicates, the program has access to (points to) only one element in the file, namely, the element at which the arrow is positioned. To read things in a file, the program must somehow move the arrow to the position of the element to be read. Similarly when writing to a file, the program can only write at the current position of the arrow. That means that files can only be accessed one element (integer or record or whatever) at a time.

Reading and Writing

In Ada the procedure WRITE may be used only with nontext files. It cannot be used with text files. For example, suppose that FILE_1 and FILE_2 are declared as follows:

```
type REAL_ARRAY is array( 1 . . 100 ) of FLOAT;
package REAL_IO is new SEQUENTIAL_IO ( REAL_ARRAY );
package INTEGER_IO is new SEQUENTIAL_IO ( INTEGER );
FILE_1 : REAL_IO.FILE_TYPE;
FILE_2 : INTEGER_IO.FILE_TYPE;
```

Suppose further that the files FILE_1 and FILE_2 have been created with calls to CREATE. Now suppose that we wish to write some new elements to FILE_2. Specifically, suppose we wish to write the three values **5, 4,** and the value of the INTEGER variable NUMBER. The following statements will accomplish the writing:

```
INTEGER_IO.WRITE ( FILE_2, 5 );
INTEGER_IO.WRITE ( FILE_2, 4 );
INTEGER_IO.WRITE ( FILE_2, NUMBER );
```

If ONE_ARRAY and ANOTHER_ARRAY are array variables of type REAL_ARRAY, then their values can be written to the file FILE_1 by the following two statements:

```
REAL_IO.WRITE ( FILE_1, ONE_ARRAY );
REAL_IO.WRITE ( FILE_1, ANOTHER_ARRAY );
```

As with text files, the first argument to WRITE is the file variable name of the file. The other argument must be an expression that evaluates to a value of the element type. If the element type is INTEGER, then the values written must all be of type INTEGER. If the element type is an array type, then the values written must all be of that array type.

The procedure READ is used to ''get'' or read information from any nontext files. The first argument to READ is a file variable name, and the second argument is a variable of the element type of the file. The call will set the value of the variable equal to the value at the arrow in the file. After each value is read from the file, the file arrow is advanced to the next element. Reading is performed sequentially from the first component to the second and so forth. The READ for nontext files is similar to the GET used for text files, except that for nontext files, all variables must be of the element type of the file.

The procedures NEW_LINE and SKIP_LINE do not work for nontext files. In fact they make no sense for files of any type other than text files, since nontext files are not divided into lines.

Case Study

Processing a File of Numeric Data

Problem Definition

As a simple example of the use of files, we will design a program that reads numbers from a file of floating point values, multiplies each number by **2.0,** and then copies the result to a second file of floating point values. The file is declared as follows:

```
package NUMBER_IO is new SEQUENTIAL_IO ( FLOAT );
NEW_FILE : NUMBER_IO.FILE_TYPE;
OLD_FILE : NUMBER_IO.FILE_TYPE;
```

The file variable name for the file being read is OLD_FILE, and the file variable name for the file being written to is NEW_FILE. Suppose that before the program is run the file NEW_FILE does not exist and the file OLD_FILE contains the elements

```
1.1 2.2 3.3 4.4 5.5
```

Then after the program is run, the file OLD_FILE will be unchanged, the file NEW_FILE will have been created, and NEW_FILE will contain the elements

```
2.2 4.4 6.6 8.8 11.0
```

(Although the above displays might make you think you could read the numbers in the file using the editor, you cannot. The numbers are coded in machine-readable form and can be read only by an Ada program.)

Discussion

In order to copy a number from one file to another, an Ada program must first read the number into a variable and then write the value of the variable to another file. Such a variable is usually called a *buffer variable.* If the buffer variable is named BUFFER, the basic way to copy a number from OLD_FILE to NEW_FILE is as follows:

```
READ ( OLD_FILE, BUFFER );
WRITE ( NEW_FILE, BUFFER );
```

If we want to double the numbers, we simply double the value in BUFFER, before we have the program write it to the second file. So the basic outline of our algorithm is

Algorithm

open OLD__FILE with OPEN
create NEW__FILE with CREATE
for each number in OLD__FILE do the following:
    READ (OLD__FILE, BUFFER);
    BUFFER := 2.0 * BUFFER;
    WRITE (NEW__FILE, BUFFER);

Just as we did with text files, we can use the boolean function `END_OF_FILE` to detect the end of the file being read from. So the loop in our algorithm can be implemented with a **`loop`** that uses the boolean function `END_OF_FILE ( OLD_FILE )`. The complete program is given in Figure 16.1.

end of file

```
with TEXT_IO;
with SEQUENTIAL_IO;
procedure DOUBLE is
--                    INPUT  : The name of the input and output
--                             nontext files and floating point values
--                             from the nontext input file
--                    OUTPUT : Floating point values to a nontext file
--                    DESCRIPTION : Reads in the name of the input
--                                  and output nontext files.
--                                  Doubles the values read from
--                                  the input nontext file and writes
--                                  them to the output nontext file.
    package NUMBER_IO is new SEQUENTIAL_IO ( FLOAT );
    BUFFER   : FLOAT;
    FILENAME : STRING( 1 . . 80 );
    LAST     : NATURAL;
    NEW_FILE : NUMBER_IO.FILE_TYPE;
    OLD_FILE : NUMBER_IO.FILE_TYPE;
begin -- Double
    TEXT_IO.PUT ( "Enter the name of the input file:" );
    TEXT_IO.NEW_LINE;
    TEXT_IO.GET_LINE ( FILENAME, LAST );
    NUMBER_IO.OPEN ( OLD_FILE,
                     NUMBER_IO.IN_FILE,
                     FILENAME( 1 . . LAST ) );
    TEXT_IO.PUT ( "Enter the name of the output file:" );
    TEXT_IO.NEW_LINE;
    TEXT_IO.GET_LINE ( FILENAME, LAST );
    NUMBER_IO.CREATE ( NEW_FILE,
                       NUMBER_IO.OUT_FILE,
                       FILENAME( 1 . . LAST ) );
```

```
    loop
        exit when NUMBER_IO.END_OF_FILE ( OLD_FILE );
        NUMBER_IO.READ ( OLD_FILE, BUFFER );
        BUFFER := 2.0 * BUFFER;
        NUMBER_IO.WRITE ( NEW_FILE, BUFFER );
    end loop;
    NUMBER_IO.CLOSE ( OLD_FILE );
    NUMBER_IO.CLOSE ( NEW_FILE );
    TEXT_IO.PUT ( "Files closed, end of program" );
    TEXT_IO.NEW_LINE;
end DOUBLE;
```

Figure 16.1 Program using nontext files.

Pitfall

Unexpected End of File

If a program is reading from the keyboard, it can ask the user whether there is more data or not. If it is reading from a file, there is no user to ask, so the program must know when to stop reading data. If your program is not written so that it stops reading when the end of a file is reached, then the program will raise END_ERROR if you attempt to READ beyond the end of the file. Fortunately, the boolean function END_OF_FILE can be used to detect the end of a nontext file. The boolean function END_OF_FILE in package SEQUENTIAL_IO is used in the same way for nontext files as it is for text files. Its use is illustrated in Figure 16.1.

Exercises

Self-Test Exercises

1. Give suitable declarations and an instantiation for a sequential nontext file that is to hold student records, where each record consists of a name, final exam score in the range 0 to 100, and a letter grade.

2. Write a program to create a nontext file of integers and to write the numbers 1 through 10 to the file.

3. Write a program that displays to the screen the contents of a file of the type used in the program of Exercise 2.

4. Write a program to search a file of integers to see if it contains a particular integer. The particular integer should be read in from the keyboard.

Files and Parameters to Procedures

Procedures may have parameters of any file type, but they must be **in** or **in out** parameters; they cannot be **out** parameters. The situation for other types of files is the same as it is for text files. The next "Case Study" illustrates the use of file variable parameters.

Case Study

Changing a File of Records

Problem Definition

In this section we will design a program that modifies a file of records so that one field of each record is changed. For this "Case Study" we assume that a file named PAY_FILE contains employee records, each consisting of an employee's number, name, and rate of pay. We will design a program that increases the rate of pay field for each record by 10%. In other words, we want to write a program that will give every employee a raise of 10%. Package SEQUENTIAL_IO is instantiated for EMPLOYEE records, and PAY_FILE is declared as follows:

```
NAME_LENGTH : constant POSITIVE := 30;
type EMPLOYEE is record
                       NUMBER   : POSITIVE;
                       NAME     : STRING( 1 . . NAME_LENGTH );
                       PAY_RATE : FLOAT;
                 end record;
package EMPLOYEE_IO is new SEQUENTIAL_IO ( EMPLOYEE );
PAY_FILE : EMPLOYEE_IO.FILE_TYPE;
```

Discussion

The only way to modify a sequential nontext file by an Ada program is to use the same basic technique that we used for modifying a text file: The program copies the file records into a temporary file, making the desired changes as it performs the copying. After that, the contents are copied back to the original file. (A slight variation that we will not use but that also works is to first copy to a temporary file without making any changes and then to copy back to the original file, making the changes as part of the second copy operation.)

Algorithm

The basic outline of this technique for modifying the file is shown in Figure 16.2. The extra file is called TEMPORARY_FILE. The variable ONE_RECORD is used as a buffer variable to hold one record.

```
open PAY__FILE;
create TEMPORARY__FILE;
loop
    exit when end of PAY__FILE;
    READ ( PAY__FILE, ONE__RECORD );
    change the value of the record variable ONE__RECORD;
    WRITE ( TEMPORARY__FILE, ONE__RECORD );
end loop;
reset TEMPORARY__FILE for input;
create PAY__FILE;
copy the contents of TEMPORARY__FILE into PAY__FILE;
close both files;
```

Figure 16.2 Technique for modifying the data file PAY__FILE.

The complete program is given in Figure 16.3. The pay raises are computed in procedure COMPUTE_RAISE, with the original PAY_FILE being passed as the source file and the TEMPORARY_FILE being passed as the destination file. After the files have been reset to the opposite FILE_MODE, the procedure COPY is called. The copying is performed by the procedure COPY, where the TEMPORARY_FILE is passed as the source file and the original file, PAY_FILE, is passed as the destination file. Notice that the file TEMPORARY_FILE is an internal file. Any temporary file like this should be an internal file. Notice that the program closes and then creates the PAY_FILE, while the TEMPORARY_FILE is simply RESET from OUT_FILE mode to IN_FILE. The LRM (*Language Reference Manual*) states that some environments may not allow external files to be reset. Closing and recreating the original PAY_FILE helps ensure portability.

```
with TEXT_IO;
with SEQUENTIAL_IO;
procedure GIVE_RAISE is
    NAME_LENGTH : constant POSITIVE := 30;
    RAISE_FACTOR : constant FLOAT := 0.1;
```

```
    type EMPLOYEE is record
                        NUMBER   : POSITIVE;
                        NAME     : STRING( 1 .. NAME_LENGTH );
                        PAY_RATE : FLOAT;
                    end record;
    package EMPLOYEE_IO is new SEQUENTIAL_IO ( EMPLOYEE );
    use EMPLOYEE_IO;
    FILENAME : STRING( 1 .. 80 );
    LAST     : NATURAL;
    PAY_FILE : EMPLOYEE_IO.FILE_TYPE;
    TEMPORARY_FILE : EMPLOYEE_IO.FILE_TYPE;
    procedure COMPUTE_RAISE ( SOURCE, DESTINATION :
                              in EMPLOYEE_IO.FILE_TYPE ) is
        ONE_EMPLOYEE : EMPLOYEE;
    begin -- Compute_Raise
        loop
            exit when EMPLOYEE_IO.END_OF_FILE ( SOURCE );
            EMPLOYEE_IO.READ ( SOURCE, ONE_EMPLOYEE );
            declare
                PAY : FLOAT renames ONE_EMPLOYEE.PAY_RATE;
            begin
                PAY := PAY * ( 1.0 + RAISE_FACTOR );
            end;
            EMPLOYEE_IO.WRITE ( DESTINATION, ONE_EMPLOYEE );
        end loop;
    end COMPUTE_RAISE;
    procedure COPY ( SOURCE, DESTINATION :
                    in EMPLOYEE_IO.FILE_TYPE ) is
        ONE_EMPLOYEE : EMPLOYEE;
    begin -- Copy
        loop
            exit when EMPLOYEE_IO.END_OF_FILE ( SOURCE );
            READ ( SOURCE, ONE_EMPLOYEE );
            WRITE ( DESTINATION, ONE_EMPLOYEE );
        end loop;
    end COPY;
begin -- Give_Raise
    TEXT_IO.PUT ( "I'm going to give everyone a raise." );
    TEXT_IO.NEW_LINE;
    TEXT_IO.PUT ( "Enter the name of the employee pay file:" );
    TEXT_IO.NEW_LINE;
    TEXT_IO.GET_LINE ( FILENAME, LAST );
    EMPLOYEE_IO.OPEN ( PAY_FILE,
                       EMPLOYEE_IO.IN_FILE,
                       FILENAME( 1 .. LAST ) );
    EMPLOYEE_IO.CREATE ( TEMPORARY_FILE );
    COMPUTE_RAISE ( PAY_FILE, TEMPORARY_FILE );
```

```
    EMPLOYEE_IO.CLOSE ( PAY_FILE );
    EMPLOYEE_IO.RESET ( TEMPORARY_FILE, EMPLOYEE_IO.IN_FILE );
    EMPLOYEE_IO.CREATE ( PAY_FILE,
                         EMPLOYEE_IO.OUT_FILE,
                         FILENAME( 1 . . LAST ) );
    COPY ( TEMPORARY_FILE, PAY_FILE );
    EMPLOYEE_IO.CLOSE ( PAY_FILE );
    EMPLOYEE_IO.CLOSE ( TEMPORARY_FILE );
    TEXT_IO.PUT ( "Files closed, end of program" );
    TEXT_IO.NEW_LINE;
    TEXT_IO.PUT ( "Is everybody happy?" );
    TEXT_IO.NEW_LINE;
end GIVE_RAISE;
```

Figure 16.3 Program to modify a file of records.

Deciding What Type of File to Use

Since INTEGER and FLOAT values can be stored in text files, there may seem to be no need for sequential nontext files for these two types. This is not quite true. When storing numbers in a file of TEXT_IO.FILE_TYPE, a type conversion from character to internal numeric form is performed whenever a number is read from a text file. The opposite type conversion from internal numeric form to character is made when values are written to the file. With nontext files no type conversion is needed. Hence, if all the data in a file is of type INTEGER, then a program will run more efficiently if nontext files are used rather than text files. In the case of the type FLOAT, accuracy is also an issue. With a text file, each reading or writing of a value of type FLOAT can introduce inaccuracies in the value stored. This loss of accuracy is a result of the type conversion calculation. By using a nontext file, you avoid these type conversions and the inaccuracies they produce.

When choosing a file type, remember that the elements of a file can be of a structured type. If your program needs to place an array of FLOAT values in secondary storage, then a simple instantiation of SEQUENTIAL_IO for FLOAT will work acceptably. However, a much simpler program can be written using a file with an array element type. For example, consider the following declarations:

```
type ARRAY_TYPE is array( 1 . . 100 ) of FLOAT;
package ARRAY_IO is new SEQUENTIAL_IO ( ARRAY_TYPE );
DISK_FILE : ARRAY_IO.FILE_TYPE;
LIST : ARRAY_TYPE;
```

Once the file has been opened, the array can be placed in secondary storage with the following WRITE statement:

```
WRITE ( DISK_FILE, LIST );
```

This is much simpler and easier to read than a **for** loop that separately copies each value from the array to a nontext file of FLOATs.

Case Study

Merging Two Files

Problem Definition

Data is often provided in the form of files that need to be processed at some central location. As a simple example, let us suppose that a company has two plants that keep employee pay records of the form used in Figure 16.3. The files are sent from the plants to corporate headquarters, where they need to be merged into a single file containing all the records from the two files. In this section we will design a procedure to merge two such files into a third master file. We assume that both files are sorted by employee number from lowest to highest and that each file has a sentinel record that marks the end of the file. This sentinel record is assumed to have an employee number field that is larger than any actual employee number.

Discussion

The procedure that performs the merging must read the records in each file in the order that they occur, which is assumed to be from lowest to highest employee number, and it must write them to the master file one at a time in order from lowest to highest number. Things seem to be ordered in a fortuitous way. If the procedure reads the first record from each of the smaller files into two buffer variables, then we can be certain that one of the two buffer variables contains the lowest numbered record of all the records in the two files. Therefore, the procedure can write this record to the master file and then replace the just-written record with the next smallest record from the same file. At this point the two records in buffer variables include the next lowest number, and the process can repeat. The process is illustrated in Figure 16.4. Since each file is terminated with a sentinel record that contains a very large number, we know that neither file will run out of records until the procedure empties both files and needs to compare the two sentinel values. At this point we can have the procedure end the process and then arbitrarily write either of the sentinel records at the end of the master file.

variables

Let us use FILE_1 and FILE_2 as the file variables for the two files being merged and MASTER_FILE as the file variable for the file to receive the merged list. The two buffer variables to hold one record from each file will be called BUFFER_1 and BUFFER_2. The files FILE_1 and FILE_2 are opened, the master file is created, and then the following algorithm is executed to perform the merge:

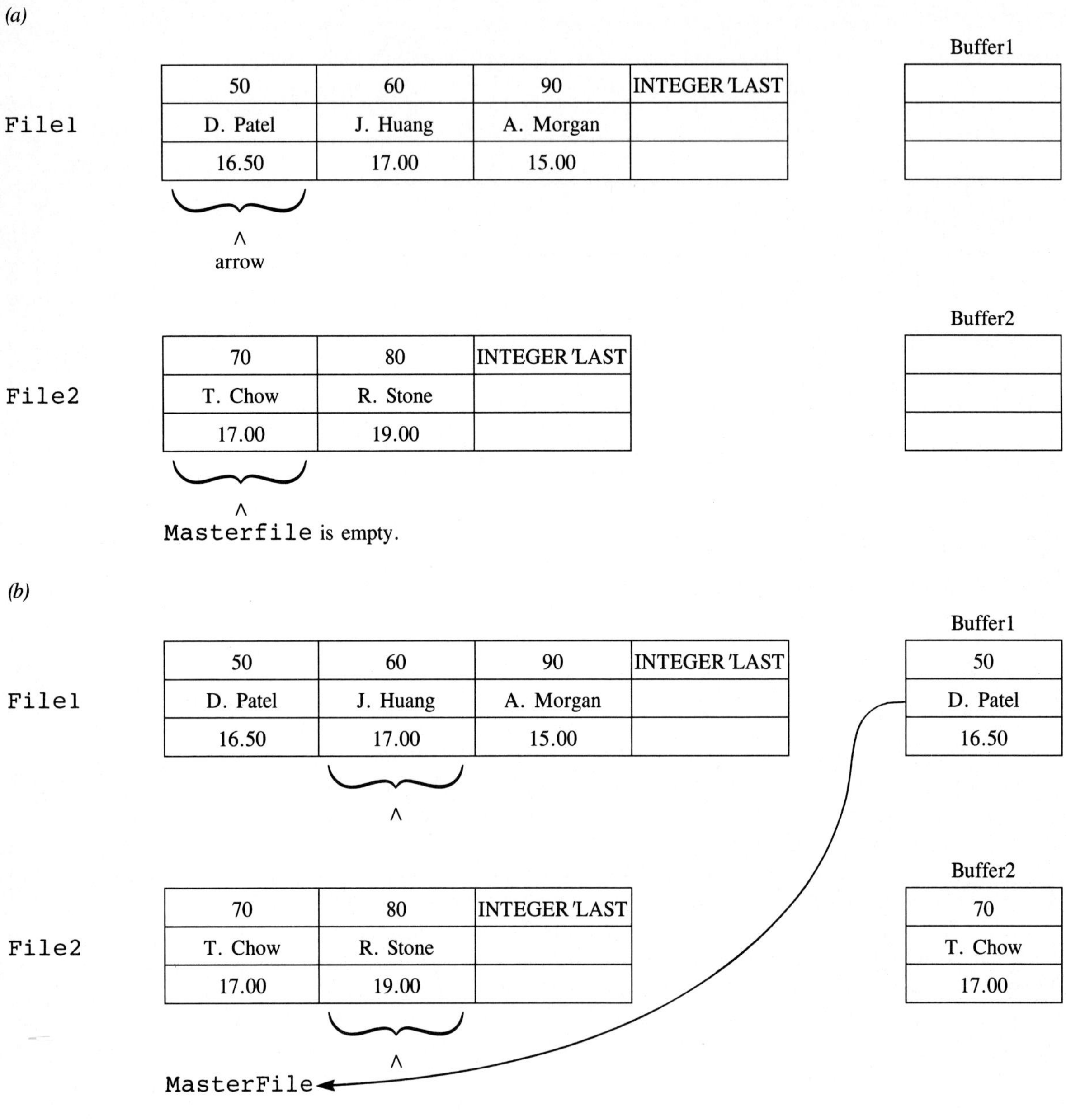

(a)

File1

50	60	90	INTEGER'LAST
D. Patel	J. Huang	A. Morgan	
16.50	17.00	15.00	

^
arrow

Buffer1

File2

70	80	INTEGER'LAST
T. Chow	R. Stone	
17.00	19.00	

^
`Masterfile` is empty.

Buffer2

(b)

File1

50	60	90	INTEGER'LAST
D. Patel	J. Huang	A. Morgan	
16.50	17.00	15.00	

^

Buffer1

50
D. Patel
16.50

File2

70	80	INTEGER'LAST
T. Chow	R. Stone	
17.00	19.00	

^

Buffer2

70
T. Chow
17.00

`MasterFile`

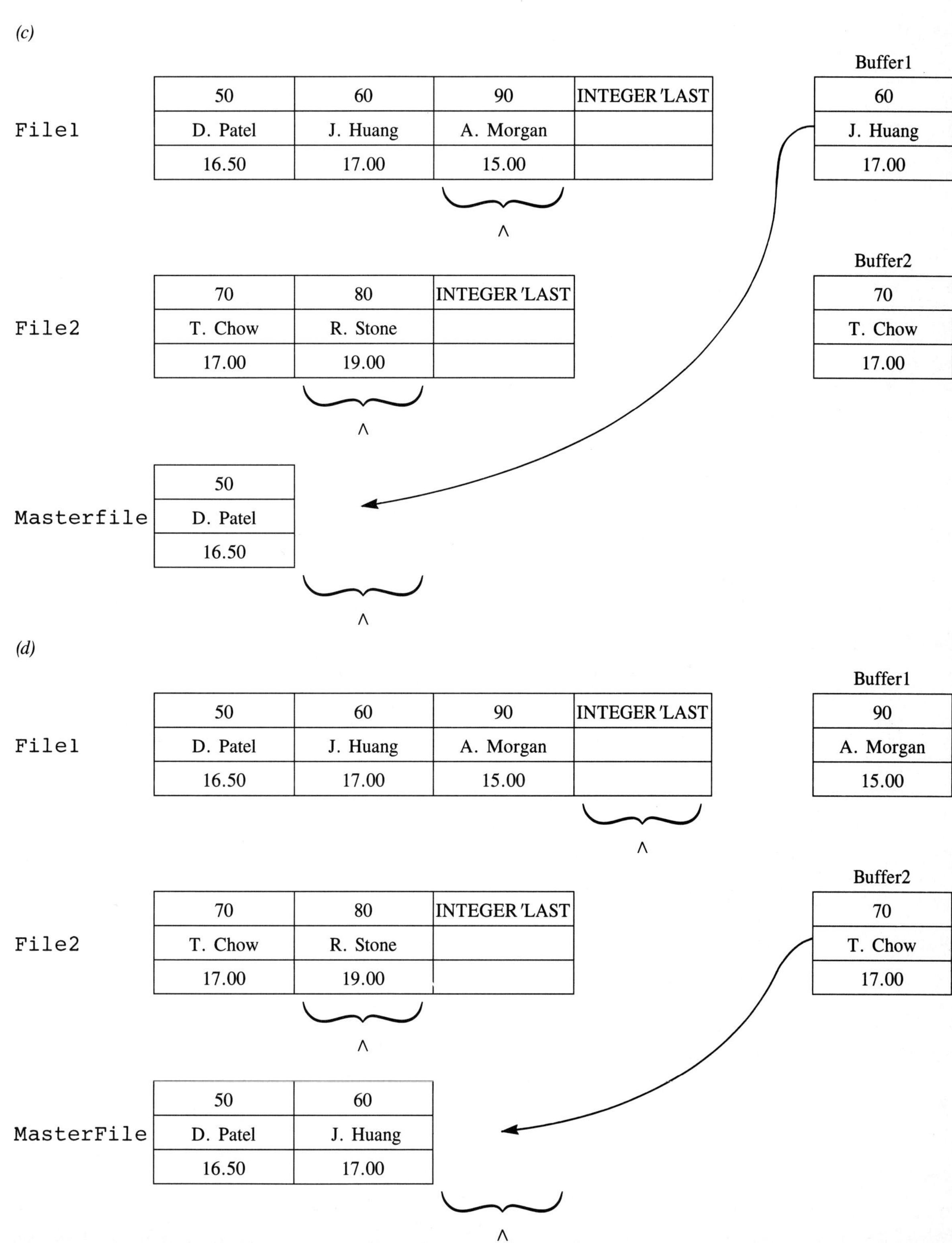
(c)
Buffer1
50
60
90
INTEGER'LAST
60
File1
D. Patel
J. Huang
A. Morgan
J. Huang
16.50
17.00
15.00
17.00
Buffer2
70
80
INTEGER'LAST
70
File2
T. Chow
R. Stone
T. Chow
17.00
19.00
17.00
50
Masterfile
D. Patel
16.50
(d)
Buffer1
50
60
90
INTEGER'LAST
90
File1
D. Patel
J. Huang
A. Morgan
A. Morgan
16.50
17.00
15.00
15.00
Buffer2
70
80
INTEGER'LAST
70
File2
T. Chow
R. Stone
T. Chow
17.00
19.00
17.00
50
60
MasterFile
D. Patel
J. Huang
16.50
17.00

(e)

File1

50	60	90	INTEGER'LAST
D. Patel	J. Huang	A. Morgan	
16.50	17.00	15.00	

Buffer1

90
A. Morgan
15.00

File2

70	80	INTEGER'LAST
T. Chow	R. Stone	
17.00	19.00	

Buffer2

80
R. Stone
19.00

MasterFile

50	60	70
D. Patel	J. Huang	T. Chow
16.50	17.00	17.00

(f)

File1

50	60	90	INTEGER'LAST
D. Patel	J. Huang	A. Morgan	
16.50	17.00	15.00	

Buffer1

90
A. Morgan
15.00

File2

70	80	INTEGER'LAST
T. Chow	R. Stone	
17.00	19.00	

End of file

Buffer2

INTEGER'LAST

MasterFile

50	60	70	80
D. Patel	J. Huang	T. Chow	R. Stone
16.50	17.00	17.00	19.00

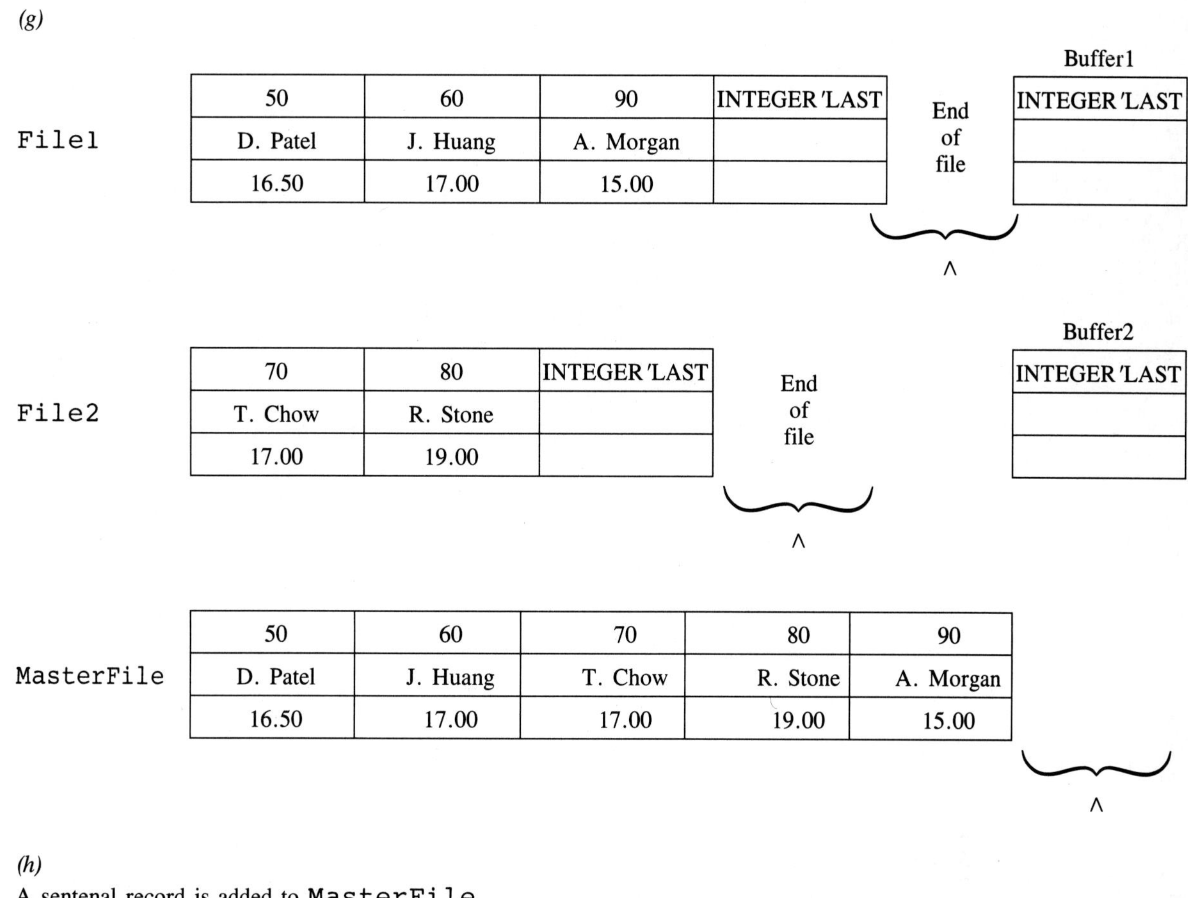

(h)

A sentenal record is added to `MasterFile`.

MasterFile						
	50	60	70	80	90	INTEGER'LAST
	D. Patel	J. Huang	T. Chow	R. Stone	A. Morgan	
	16.50	17.00	17.00	19.00	15.00	

Figure 16.4 Merging two files.

Algorithm

```
READ ( FILE_1, BUFFER_1 );
READ ( FILE_2, BUFFER_2 );
loop
    exit when end of FILE_1
     and then end of FILE_2;
    Find out which of BUFFER_1 or BUFFER_2
    has the smaller number and write that record to MASTER_FILE
    Replace the record written with one from the same file.
end loop;
WRITE ( MASTER_FILE, BUFFER_1 ); -- the sentinel record
```

The final program is shown in Figure 16.5. The body of the loop above is implemented as the procedure COPY_SMALLER. Note the use of the following declaration:

```
subtype EMPLOYEE_FILE is EMPLOYEE_IO.FILE_TYPE;
```

This declaration is necessary to provide a type name for the file parameters in the specification for the MERGE procedure.

Program

```
with TEXT_IO;
with SEQUENTIAL_IO;
procedure FILE_MERGE is
    NAME_LENGTH : constant POSITIVE := 30;
    type EMPLOYEE is record
                        NUMBER   : POSITIVE;
                        NAME     : STRING( 1 . . NAME_LENGTH );
                        PAY_RATE : FLOAT;
                    end record;
    package EMPLOYEE_IO is new SEQUENTIAL_IO ( EMPLOYEE );
    use EMPLOYEE_IO;
    subtype EMPLOYEE_FILE is EMPLOYEE_IO.FILE_TYPE;
    FILENAME : STRING( 1 . . 80 );
    FILE_1 : EMPLOYEE_FILE;
    FILE_2 : EMPLOYEE_FILE;
    LAST   : NATURAL;
    MASTER_FILE : EMPLOYEE_FILE;
```

```
    procedure MERGE ( FILE_1,
                      FILE_2,
                      MASTER_FILE : in EMPLOYEE_FILE ) is
        BUFFER_1,
        BUFFER_2 : EMPLOYEE;
        procedure COPY_SMALLER ( BUFFER_1,
                                 BUFFER_2 : in out EMPLOYEE;
                                 FILE_1,
                                 FILE_2,
                                 MASTER_FILE : in EMPLOYEE_FILE ) is
        begin -- Copy_Smaller
            if BUFFER_1.NUMBER < BUFFER_2.NUMBER then
                WRITE ( MASTER_FILE, BUFFER_1 );
                READ ( FILE_1, BUFFER_1 );
            else
                WRITE ( MASTER_FILE, BUFFER_2 );
                READ ( FILE_2, BUFFER_2 );
            end if;
        end COPY_SMALLER;
    begin -- Merge
        TEXT_IO.PUT ( "Merging started." );
        TEXT_IO.NEW_LINE;
        READ ( FILE_1, BUFFER_1 );
        READ ( FILE_2, BUFFER_2 );
        loop
            exit when END_OF_FILE ( FILE_1 )
             and then END_OF_FILE ( FILE_2 );
            COPY_SMALLER ( BUFFER_1, BUFFER_2,
                           FILE_1, FILE_2, MASTER_FILE );
        end loop;
        WRITE ( MASTER_FILE, BUFFER_1 );
        TEXT_IO.PUT ( "Merging completed." );
        TEXT_IO.NEW_LINE;
    end MERGE;
begin -- File_Merge
    TEXT_IO.PUT ( "Enter the name of the first file:" );
    TEXT_IO.NEW_LINE;
    TEXT_IO.GET_LINE ( FILENAME, LAST );
    EMPLOYEE_IO.OPEN ( FILE_1,
                       IN_FILE,
                       FILENAME( 1 . . LAST ) );
    TEXT_IO.PUT ( "Enter the name of the second file:" );
    TEXT_IO.NEW_LINE;
    TEXT_IO.GET_LINE ( FILENAME, LAST );
```

```
    EMPLOYEE_IO.OPEN ( FILE_2,
                       IN_FILE,
                       FILENAME( 1 . . LAST ) );
    TEXT_IO.PUT ( "Enter the name of the master file:" );
    TEXT_IO.NEW_LINE;
    TEXT_IO.GET_LINE ( FILENAME, LAST );
    EMPLOYEE_IO.CREATE ( MASTER_FILE,
                         OUT_FILE,
                         FILENAME( 1 . . LAST ) );
    MERGE ( FILE_1, FILE_2, MASTER_FILE );
    EMPLOYEE_IO.CLOSE ( FILE_1 );
    EMPLOYEE_IO.CLOSE ( FILE_2 );
    EMPLOYEE_IO.CLOSE ( MASTER_FILE );
    TEXT_IO.PUT ( "Files closed, end of program" );
    TEXT_IO.NEW_LINE;
end FILE_MERGE;
```

Figure 16.5 A program to merge two files.

efficiency

The procedure MERGE can be quite inefficient for some files. If the records in one file are all copied before the other file is emptied, then the procedure will compare all the remaining records to the sentinel record. If the number of records remaining is large, this can be very time consuming. A more efficient procedure would detect when it has reached the end of one of the files and at that point simply copy the records remaining in the other file onto the master file. We leave the design and coding of such an efficient procedure as an exercise (see Exercise 10).

Random Access Files in Ada (Direct_IO)
(Optional)

Random access files in Ada are those files used for random (or direct) access. The file is viewed as a set of elements occupying consecutive positions in linear order. Data can be transferred to or from an element of the file at any selected position. The position of an element is specified by its *index,* which is a number of subtype POSITIVE_COUNT, defined in the package DIRECT_IO, that is, in the range of 1 . . COUNT'LAST. COUNT is also defined in DIRECT_IO and is 1 . . *implementation_defined*. Neither of these types are compatible with POSITIVE or NATURAL, respectively. There are no operations defined for COUNT and subsequently none for POSITIVE_COUNT. Therefore, random access files in Ada (termed *direct* files in Ada) are organized as relative files, in which the relative record number (termed the *index* in Ada) of the first element is 1. The index of the last element of a direct file is called the CURRENT_SIZE; the current size is zero if there are no elements. The current size is a property of the external file. An open direct file in Ada has a CURRENT_INDEX, much like the location indicator used for sequential files. The current index is the index that is used by the next read or write operation to indicate the position in the file for access. When a direct file is opened, the current index is set to 1. The current index of a direct file is a property of a file object, not of an external file.

A direct file in Ada is defined by means of the generic package DIRECT_IO. A skeleton of the specification part of this package is given below:

```
with IO_EXCEPTIONS;
generic
    type ELEMENT_TYPE is private;
package DIRECT_IO is
    type FILE_TYPE is limited private;
    type FILE_MODE is ( IN_FILE,INOUT_FILE, OUT_FILE );
    type COUNT is range 0 . . implementation_defined;
    subtype POSITIVE_COUNT is COUNT range 1 . . COUNT'LAST.

    procedure READ ( FILE : FILE_TYPE;
                     ITEM : out ELEMENT_TYPE );
    procedure READ ( FILE : FILE_TYPE;
                     ITEM : out ELEMENT_TYPE;
                     FROM : POSITIVE_COUNT );
    procedure WRITE ( FILE : in FILE_TYPE;
                      ITEM : ELEMENT_TYPE );
    procedure WRITE ( FILE : in FILE_TYPE;
                      ITEM : ELEMENT_TYPE;
                      TO   : POSITIVE_COUNT );

    procedure SET_INDEX ( FILE : in FILE_TYPE;
                          TO   : in POSITIVE_COUNT );
    function INDEX ( FILE : FILE_TYPE ) return POSITIVE_COUNT;
    function SIZE ( FILE  : FILE_TYPE ) return COUNT;
end DIRECT_IO;
```

The declaration of a direct file requires an instantiation of this generic package, with a given type as an actual parameter. The resulting package contains the declaration of a file type (called FILE_TYPE) for files of such elements, as well as I/O operations for these files, such as OPEN, READ, WRITE, SET_INDEX, and INDEX subprograms.

The following code creates the package KEY_IO that is an instance of the generic package DIRECT_IO:

```
with DIRECT_IO;
procedure SKELETON is
    type RELATIVE_RECORD_TYPE is
        record
            KEY         : INTEGER;
            INFORMATION : STRING ( 1 . . 20 );
        end record;
```

```
package KEY_IO is new DIRECT_IO (RELATIVE_RECORD_TYPE );
RELATIVE_FILE : KEY_IO.FILE_TYPE;
```

The element type is the record RELATIVE_RECORD_TYPE, and the I/O operations are instantiated for this particular FILE_TYPE. The internal file name, RELATIVE_FILE, is declared to be a file of this FILE_TYPE, where one element or component of the file is a record containing an integer KEY component and an INFORMATION component. Such a file is stored on secondary storage devices; the declaration does not specify length as the declaration of an array does. In a file declaration only the type of each component is specified.

The operations described in Chapter 13 for text files (CREATE, OPEN, and CLOSE) are the same for nontext files whether they are accessed sequentially or randomly. The default access mode for the procedure CREATE is the mode INOUT_FILE for DIRECT_IO. The physical size of the created direct file is implementation-dependent. The six operations available for direct input and output are described in this section.

Output to a direct file involves the Ada output procedure WRITE, of which there are two forms:

```
procedure WRITE ( FILE : in FILE_TYPE;
                  ITEM : ELEMENT_TYPE );

procedure WRITE ( FILE : in FILE_TYPE;
                  ITEM : ELEMENT_TYPE;
                  TO   : POSITIVE_COUNT );
```

The second form sets the current index of the given file to the index value specified by the parameter TO. Then, for both forms of the WRITE, the value of ITEM is written to the file named into the position specified by the CURRENT_INDEX. Finally, the CURRENT_INDEX is increased by one. The first form of the WRITE is the same as for sequential nontext files. The second form allows the current index to be modified before the contents of ITEM are output. The exception MODE_ERROR is raised if the mode is IN_FILE. The exception USE_ERROR is raised if the capacity of the external file is exceeded. The exception STATUS_ERROR is raised if the file is not open.

Input from a direct file in Ada involves the procedure READ, of which there are two forms:

```
procedure READ ( FILE : FILE_TYPE;
                 ITEM : out ELEMENT_TYPE );

procedure READ ( FILE : FILE_TYPE;
                 ITEM : out ELEMENT_TYPE;
                 FROM : POSITIVE_COUNT );
```

The second form sets the current index of the given file to the index value specified by the parameter FROM. Then, for both forms of READ, the procedure inputs the element from the file in the position specified by CURRENT_INDEX and returns the data in ITEM. Finally CURRENT_INDEX is increased by one. The first form of READ is the same as for sequential nontext files. The second form allows the CURRENT_INDEX to be modified before the element in position CURRENT_INDEX is input. The exception MODE_ERROR is raised if the mode is OUT_FILE. The exception END_ERROR is raised if the index to be used exceeds the size of the external file. The exception DATA_ERROR is raised if the element read cannot be interpreted as a value of the type ELEMENT_TYPE; however, an implementation is allowed to omit this check if performing the check is too complex. The exception STATUS_ERROR is raised if the file is not open.

The CURRENT_INDEX of a direct file can be set by the procedure SET_INDEX.

```
procedure SET_INDEX ( FILE : in FILE_TYPE;
                      TO : in POSITIVE_COUNT );
```

SET_INDEX operates on a file of any mode, and it sets the CURRENT_INDEX of the given file to the index value specified by the parameter TO (which may exceed the CURRENT_SIZE of the file). The exception STATUS_ERROR is raised if the file is not open.

The function INDEX interrogates the value of CURRENT_INDEX.

```
function INDEX ( FILE : in FILE_TYPE ) return POSITIVE_COUNT;
```

INDEX operates on a file of any mode, and it returns the CURRENT_INDEX of the file named in the parameter FILE. The exception STATUS_ERROR is raised if the file is not open.

The function SIZE interrogates the value of CURRENT_SIZE.

```
function SIZE ( FILE : in FILE_TYPE ) return COUNT;
```

SIZE operates on a file of any mode, and it returns the CURRENT_SIZE of the file named in the parameter FILE. The exception STATUS_ERROR is raised if the file is not open.

A program that is reading a direct file in a sequential fashion (using the first form of READ) needs to be able to detect when the end of the file has been reached. The function END_OF_FILE checks the CURRENT_INDEX of a file.

```
function END_OF_FILE ( FILE : in FILE_TYPE ) return BOOLEAN;
```

END_OF_FILE operates on a file of mode IN_FILE or INOUT_FILE. If the CURRENT_INDEX of the file named in the parameter FILE exceeds the size of the external file, the function returns TRUE; otherwise, the function returns FALSE. The exception STATUS_ERROR is raised if the file is not open.

A direct file may be created using sequential access or random access. With sequential access the records of data are written to the direct file in a sequential order: the first record is stored in position 1, the second record is stored in position 2, the third record is stored in position 3, and so on. This scheme for creating a file is often used when a directory is to accompany the file to provide indirect access.

When a direct file is built using random access, the key of the record is hashed to a random position; records can be inserted in random order. However, for hashed files the direct file must first be skeletonized with dummy records; this is usually done in a sequential fashion. The key component of the record is hashed using a function similar to the ones used in Chapter 11. The skeletonization of the direct file with dummy records involves initializing the record with dummy information. For example, character components might be filled with spaces, numeric components and link components for chaining synonyms might be filled with zeros. The dummy record is written to each record position in the file of *n* record positions. The skeletonization ensures that the empty record positions can be recognized because the fields in the record have spaces and zeros. Once the file has been skeletonized, records can be stored randomly into the file.

Summary of Problem Solving and Programming Techniques

- Data of almost any type, including record types, may be kept in secondary storage by using a file with that particular element type.
- Although numeric data can be stored in a text file, it is usually more efficient and clearer to store it in a file whose element type matches the type of the data.
- Nontext files are opened and named in the same way as text files.
- The procedures NEW_LINE and SKIP_LINE and the boolean function END_OF_LINE do not make sense for and so cannot be used with nontext files. The procedures READ and WRITE are used with nontext files instead of GET and PUT, which are used for text files. The boolean function END_OF_FILE can be used with other files in basically the same way it is used with text files.
- Data in a file is accessed one component at a time.
- To change a file, a program must use a temporary file. The data is copied into the temporary file and changed as part of the copying. The contents are then copied back to the original file. The temporary file should be an internal file.

Summary of Ada Constructs

instantiation of Sequential_IO

Syntax:

```
package new_package is new SEQUENTIAL_IO ( element_type );
```

Example:

```
type ITEM is record
                FIELD_1 : INTEGER;
                FIELD_2 : FLOAT;
             end record;
package ITEM_IO is new SEQUENTIAL_IO ( ITEM );
```

The generic parameter is of *element_type* (the type ITEM in the example). The *new_package* is called ITEM_IO.

file variable declaration

Syntax:

file__name : *new__package*.FILE_TYPE;

Example:

```
DISK_FILE : ITEM_IO.FILE_TYPE;
```

A file to hold components of type *element__type*. The *element__type* may be any type that does not involve a file type.

open

Syntax:

OPEN (*internal__file__name*, IN_FILE, *external__file__name*);

Example:

```
OPEN ( DISK_FILE, IN_FILE, "summary.exp" );
```

Opens the file named by the file variable *internal__file__name* for reading and positions the arrow to the first element in the file. The system name for the file is represented as a character string.

create

Syntax:

CREATE (*internal__file__name*, OUT_FILE, *external__file__name*);

Example:

```
CREATE ( DISK_FILE, OUT_FILE, "file.new" );
```

Creates a new file named by the file variable *internal__file__name*, opens the file for writing, and positions the arrow to receive the first element. If there already is a file whose file variable name is *internal__file__name*, then the contents of the old file are lost.

reset

Syntax:

RESET (*internal__file__name*, *new__mode*);

or

RESET (*internal__file__name*);

Example:

```
RESET ( TEMPORARY_FILE, IN_FILE );
```

or

```
RESET ( REPEAT_FILE );
```

The RESET procedure has two formats. The first is used to change (reset) the file mode of a temporary file to IN_FILE and thus prepare it for reading. The second simply moves the arrow from wherever it is back to the first element in the file. With this a file can be read over and over again.

read

Syntax:

READ (*internal_file_name*, *element_type_variable*);

Example:

```
READ ( FILE_1, NEXT_ELEMENT );
```

The SEQUENTIAL_IO procedure READ is used with a nontext file. The *internal_file_name* is the file variable name of the file, and *element_type_variable* is a variable of the element type of the file. There may be any number of variables. The value of *element_type_variable* is set equal to the value of the element at the arrow, and the arrow is advanced to the next component.

write

Syntax:

WRITE (*internal_file_name*, *item_of_element_type*);

Example:

```
WRITE ( OUT_FILE, PINS + 9 );
```

The SEQUENTIAL_IO procedure WRITE is used with a nontext file. The *internal_file_name* is the file variable name of the file, and *item_of_element_type* is an element with a value of the element type of the file. The value of the file element at the arrow is set equal to the value of the *item_of_element_type*, and the arrow is advanced to the next element.

end_of_file

Syntax:

END_OF_FILE (*internal_file_name*)

Example:

```
END_OF_FILE ( FILE_1 )
```

A boolean function that returns TRUE if the arrow in the file named by the file variable *internal_file_name* is beyond the last component and FALSE when a file element is at the arrow.

Exercises

Self-Test Exercises

5. Write a boolean-valued function with two arguments: PAY_FILE, a file of type PAY_IO, and KEY, an integer. The PAY_IO is defined in Figure 16.3. The function should return TRUE if the file contains a record for employee number KEY and should return FALSE if the file contains no such record.

Interactive Exercises

6. Write a program that fills an array with 10 integers read from the keyboard and then stores the array value in a nontext file defined as follows:

```
type LIST is array( 1 .. 10 ) of INTEGER;
package LIST_IO is new SEQUENTIAL_IO ( LIST );
A_FILE : LIST_IO.FILE_TYPE;
```

7. Write a program that fills an array from the file created by the program of Exercise 6 and then displays the array values to the screen.

Programming Exercises

8. Write a program to search an existing nontext file of integers and find both the largest and the smallest integers in the file.

9. Write a program that fills a file of the type used in Figure 16.3 with data read from the keyboard.

10. Rewrite the procedure MERGE from Figure 16.5 so it is more efficient, in the manner described in the chapter. The sentinel records are not essential in this approach, so your program should be designed to work with files that do not contain a sentinel record at the end.

11. Write a program that reads 10 INTEGER values from a nontext file of integer into an array, sorts the array, and then writes the sorted list back into the same file, so the effect is to sort the numbers in the file.

12. Write a program that sorts a nontext file of INTEGER values so that the numbers appear in numeric order from the smallest to the largest. The final sorted list should be in the same file as the one originally containing the integers. The program should work for any size file, and the program should not read the numbers into an array as it did in Exercise 11. (One simple way to do this is to use a second file; the smallest number is copied to the file, then the next smallest, and so forth. Then the sorted file is copied back into the original file. There are also more efficient ways to do the sorting.)

13. A record for describing a person is to consist of the following items: last name, initial of first name, sex, age, height, weight, and telephone number. The records are to be stored in an array indexed by integers in the range one to LIMIT. LIMIT is

to be declared as a constant. Write a program that reads in up to `LIMIT` records from the keyboard, stores them in an array, writes them out to the screen, and then writes them to a file. The file should be a file of records, not a text file or a file of arrays. Your program should allow the possibility of fewer than `LIMIT` records being read in.

14. Write a program that reads the file created in Exercise 13, places the components into an array, sorts the records in the array according to the alphabetical order of the last names, writes the sorted records to the screen, and then copies the records back to the file in alphabetical order.

15. Modify your program from Exercise 14 so that the second and succeeding times that it is run, the contents of the file are copied into an array, and then the user has the option of either clearing all records and starting over or adding more records to those already in the array. Modify your program further to allow the user to delete individual records by specifying the last name for the record to be deleted. The user should also have the option of clearing all records without having to specify every name. Modify your program further to allow the user to see all records of a given category (such as all records for individuals between two specified ages) on the screen. All manipulations should be done with the array. When the user is finished, the program should copy the modified collection of records back to the file so that the file then contains the same records as the array.

16. Redo Exercise 15, but this time have your program deal directly with the file; do not use an array.

17. Write a program for a computerized dating service. The information on individuals should be kept in a file of records and should include all the information described in Exercise 13, plus other information such as a hobbies, favorite color, etc. A user should be able to request a list of all dates that satisfy the user's specifications. Include a "best match" option that finds the date that is best suited to the user based only on the user's own record. Use a nontext file of records.

18. Write a program to sort a file of records of the type described in Exercise 13. The files are to be arranged into alphabetical order according to last names. (One simple way to do this is to use a second file; the alphabetically first record is copied to the file, then the alphabetically next, and so forth. There are also more efficient ways to do the sorting.)

19. Write a program to keep track of airline flight reservations and seat reservations. Allow any number of flights. Display seating plans as described in Exercise 17 of Chapter 10. The program should be able to add or delete flights. It should keep track of who is in what seat, as well as which seats are reserved. Keep the information in a file so the program can be rerun and the information is as it was left the last time the program was run. Use a nontext file.

20. Write a program that fills a two-dimensional array of characters with a pattern typed in from the keyboard and then echoes back the pattern on the screen. Next write a program that uses a file whose element type is the type of the two-dimensional array. This program should store one array for each letter of the alphabet. When displayed, the array for each letter should display that letter as a large block letter. Finally,

write a program that uses this file of arrays to read a word from the keyboard and to echo it back to the screen in block letters, one letter at a time.

21. If you are enrolled in a programming (or other) course, write a program that serves as a recordkeeper for grades in your course. The program should allow the user to enter, display, and change any particular grade, such as a particular quiz or exam. If there is a formula for the final numeric grade, the program should calculate it. The program should allow the user to ask the class average for any particular grade, such as a quiz or exam grade. Use a nontext file of records.

References for Further Reading

N. E. Miller and C. G. Petersen, *File Structures with Ada* (Redwood City, CA: The Benjamin/Cummings Publishing Co., 1990).

C H A P T E R

17

DYNAMIC DATA STRUCTURES

Apple Computer

The Apple Computer was one of many microcomputers developed for personal use in the home, school, and office. The cofounders of Apple Computer, Inc., Steve Jobs and Stephen Wozniak, were instrumental in bringing the power of computing to the layman. Their development of the Macintosh computer revolutionized the way people interact with the computer. The incorporation of a mouse and icons has eliminated the need for esoteric operating system commands.

Chapter Contents

A *static data structure* is one whose structure is completely specified at the time the program is written and cannot be changed by the program. Most of the data structures we have seen thus far, such as constrained arrays and simple records, are static data structures. The values of the various components in these structures may change, but the structures themselves do not change. A program cannot change the size of a constrained array or the number of indexes for the array. The structure is fixed.

Dynamic data structures may have their structure changed by the program. They may expand and contract in size as the program is executed, and as we will see in this chapter, the program can even change the manner in which the data is organized. In this chapter we will introduce a construct called an *access type* and show how access types can be used to construct a wide variety of dynamic data structures, including *lists, stacks,* and a new data structure called a *tree. Access value* is the official Ada term for what most programming languages call a *pointer*; soon we will drop the pointer term and use Ada terminology.

The Notion of a Pointer

nodes

A *pointer* is, quite plainly and simply, something that points. That definition is very abstract. To make it concrete, we will give it a geometric interpretation in terms of figures drawn on paper. These figures will always be configurations of boxes connected by arrows. In these figures a pointer is represented by an arrow. Each of these arrows, or pointers, usually points to an object called a *node*. In these drawings a node is represented by a box, of any shape, in which things may be written or, more abstractly, in which data may be stored. For example, a list of records might be represented as nodes and pointers in the manner of Figure 17.1. In this case each record contains a number and a letter, so the records might be student numbers and final course grades.

The meaning of HEAD and **null** and the details of how such a list can be constructed will be explained as we go along. For now, think of HEAD as designating, or pointing to, the first node in the list and **null** as marking the last node in the list. Before we present any more discussion of dynamic data structures, we will first discuss the Ada syntax for access objects and nodes.

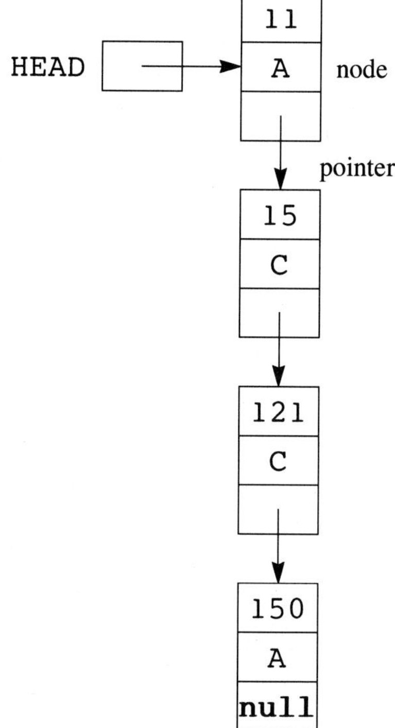

Figure 17.1 A data structure containing pointers.

Ada Access Objects and Dynamic Objects

dynamic objects

In Ada there is a special class of objects that we will refer to as *dynamic objects.* These dynamic objects are designed to be used as the nodes in dynamic data structures such as the list in Figure 17.1. In many ways dynamic objects are like the ordinary variables we have been using until now. Like other objects, dynamic objects have a type. Dynamic objects may be of any type. Dynamic objects can be assigned a value by means of an assignment operator, or a GET statement, or by any other means that the value of an ordinary variable can be set. Similarly the value in a dynamic object can be accessed in any of the ways that the value of an ordinary object can be accessed: by a PUT statement, by being an actual parameter to a subprogram, or by any other means that the value of an ordinary object may be accessed.

Dynamic objects differ from ordinary objects in only two ways. First, they may be created and destroyed by the program, so the number of such dynamic objects need not, indeed cannot, be determined at the time the program is written. Second, dynamic objects have no names in Ada; there are no identifiers that name them in the way that ordinary variables are named by identifiers. For these two reasons, dynamic objects are not declared.

access object

To refer to a dynamic object, Ada uses another type of variable called an *access object* (in other languages they are called a *pointer variable* or a *reference variable*). Access objects are declared and do have identifiers associated with them. (HEAD, in Figure 17.1, is an example of an access object.) Access objects also have a type associated with them, and this type specifies the type of the dynamic objects with which they can be used. The value of an access object is often called a *pointer* or *access value,* and an access value may point to or reference any dynamic object of the appropriate type. In this way a dynamic object may be referred to indirectly by giving an access object that points to the dynamic object. Typically this is done by giving an access object a value that *designates* or *points to* the dynamic object. From here on we will use the word *designate* instead of *point.*

As an example, suppose we have the following record type declared in a program:

```
type STUDENT_RECORD is record
                            NUMBER : POSITIVE;
                            GRADE  : CHARACTER;
                       end record;
```

The program can have dynamic objects of type STUDENT_RECORD, but these dynamic objects are not declared. An access object holds a value that designates a dynamic object, and all access objects must be declared. The following declares the access type STUDENT_ACCESS, and the variable STUDENT is declared to be an access variable whose value designates a dynamic object of type STUDENT_RECORD:

```
type STUDENT_ACCESS is access STUDENT_RECORD;
STUDENT : STUDENT_ACCESS;
```

The type of a dynamic object, such as STUDENT_RECORD in this example, is called the *designated type* of the access object. The variable STUDENT can only contain values that designate dynamic objects of type STUDENT_RECORD. To hold an access value that designates a dynamic object of some other type, for instance FLOAT, requires a different access object of the type, say FLOAT_ACCESS. Dynamic objects and access objects both have types and, in order to hold a designater of a dynamic object, the type of the access object must match that of the dynamic object.

designated type

Of course, an access object is of no use unless there is something for it to designate or access. To create a dynamic object, the operator **new** is used. This **new** operator is called an *allocator* because it allocates space for, or creates, a dynamic object. For example, suppose that STUDENT is as previously declared and consider the following statement:

new

```
STUDENT := new STUDENT_RECORD;
```

This will create a new dynamic object of type STUDENT_RECORD and set the value of STUDENT equal to an access object that designates this new dynamic object. This dynamic object can then be referred to as ''the thing designated by STUDENT.'' To set the value of the component NUMBER in this new dynamic variable, we can use an assignment statement as follows:

```
STUDENT.NUMBER := 5;
```

The notation is the same as it would be if STUDENT were a variable of type STUDENT_RECORD. In reality the only difference is that an object of type STUDENT_RECORD is allocated by the system and is static, whereas an access to an object of type STUDENT_RECORD is allocated by the program and is dynamic.

The Access Value null

There is one last Ada construct that we need to describe before going on to discuss the applications of access objects. That is the access value **null**. You could think of **null** as a predefined literal. It is a predefined literal, just like the boolean literals TRUE and FALSE, although **null** is of a different type than these. The literal **null** is used to give a value to access objects which do not designate anything. The LRM (*Language Reference Manual*) states it this way, ''For each access type, there is a literal **null** which has a null access value designating no object at all.'' As such it can be used as a kind of end marker. For example, in the data structure shown in Figure 17.1, we show the last component of the last node as **null**. A program can test for the end of the list by checking to see if that component equals **null**. The usage of **null** as an end marker is illustrated in several other examples in this chapter.

The predefined literal **null** is a bit peculiar in that it can denote the value of an access object of any access type. However, since it never can actually designate any object, this produces no conflict. It is only used as an endmarker. The LRM says that all access objects must designate something, but in the case of **null**, that something is nothing at all.

type of **null**

Manipulating Access Objects

The process of allocating and assigning values to dynamic objects is illustrated in Figure 17.2. As shown there, the GRADE component can be set in a similar way.

The values of the component of this dynamic object can be written to the screen in the usual way:

```
PUT ( STUDENT.NUMBER );
PUT ( STUDENT.GRADE );
NEW_LINE;
```

Similarly STUDENT can be used generally wherever it is appropriate to use a record variable of type STUDENT_RECORD.

Before going any further, we had best stop and clarify the common English syntax used by programmers when discussing access objects, access values, and designaters. In the preceding example, STUDENT is an access object. Technically speaking it does not designate anything. It has value, called an access value, that is a designater, and

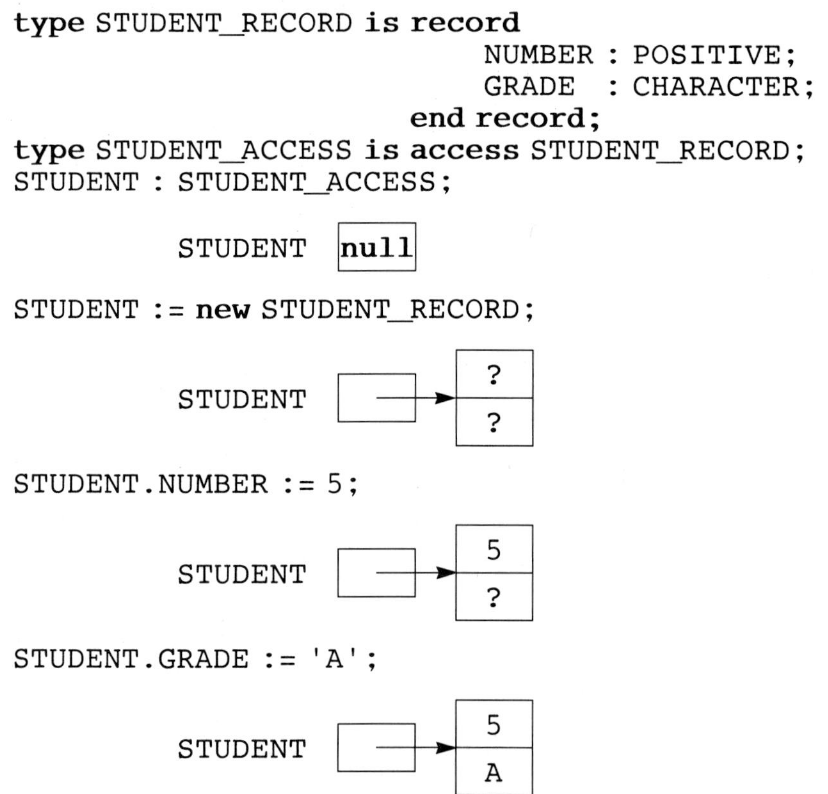
type STUDENT_RECORD is record
NUMBER : POSITIVE;
GRADE : CHARACTER;
end record;
type STUDENT_ACCESS is access STUDENT_RECORD;
STUDENT : STUDENT_ACCESS;
STUDENT
null
STUDENT := new STUDENT_RECORD;
STUDENT
?
?
STUDENT.NUMBER := 5;
STUDENT
5
?
STUDENT.GRADE := 'A';
STUDENT
5
A

Figure 17.2 Use of access objects and dynamic objects.

these access values designate dynamic objects. It may help to think of the designater as an arrow and the access object as something or somebody that can hold one designater arrow at a time. This distinction between a designater and an access object is sometimes important. However, we will follow common usage and usually blur this distinction. We will usually write, for example, "STUDENT designates a dynamic object" when we really mean "the value of STUDENT designates a dynamic object."

:= and access values

Dynamic objects may have more than one access object that designates it. Also, access values may be changed so that they designate different dynamic objects at different times. These changes are accomplished with the assignment operator **:=**. Technically speaking there is nothing new involved. The assignment operator works in exactly the same way with access objects as it does with the other types of variables we have seen. However, interpreting the result can be a bit subtle. A sample program will help to illustrate the concepts. The workings of the program in Figure 17.3 are illustrated in Figure 17.4.

A new syntactical form (**.all**) is also introduced in these figures. Recall that all objects in a record can be assigned via an aggregate. However, that is a bit awkward for a dynamic record object since the only reference to it is via an access object. To distinguish between the access object itself and the thing it designates, we use the **.all** suffix when we want the entire dynamic object referenced by a particular access object. Note the assignment

```
STUDENT_2.all := ( 2, 'B' );
```

used in both Figures 17.3 and 17.4.

```
with TEXT_IO;
use TEXT_IO;
procedure TEST_ACCESS is
    type STUDENT_RECORD is record
                              NUMBER : INTEGER;
                              GRADE  : CHARACTER;
                          end record;
    type STUDENT_ACCESS is access STUDENT_RECORD;
    STUDENT_1,
    STUDENT_2 : STUDENT_ACCESS;
    package NUMBER_IO is new INTEGER_IO ( INTEGER );
    use NUMBER_IO;
begin -- Test_Access
    STUDENT_1 := new STUDENT_RECORD;
    STUDENT_1.NUMBER := 1;
    STUDENT_1.GRADE := 'A';
    PUT ( STUDENT_1.NUMBER ); PUT ( STUDENT_1.GRADE ); NEW_LINE;
    STUDENT_2 := new STUDENT_RECORD;
    STUDENT_2.all := ( 2, 'B' );
    PUT ( STUDENT_2.NUMBER ); PUT ( STUDENT_2.GRADE ); NEW_LINE;
    STUDENT_1 := STUDENT_2;
    STUDENT_2.NUMBER := 3;
    STUDENT_1.GRADE := 'C';
```

```
   PUT ( STUDENT_1.NUMBER ); PUT ( STUDENT_1.GRADE );
   PUT ( STUDENT_2.NUMBER ); PUT ( STUDENT_2.GRADE ); NEW_LINE;
end TEST_ACCESS;
```

Figure 17.3 Program that illustrates access objects.

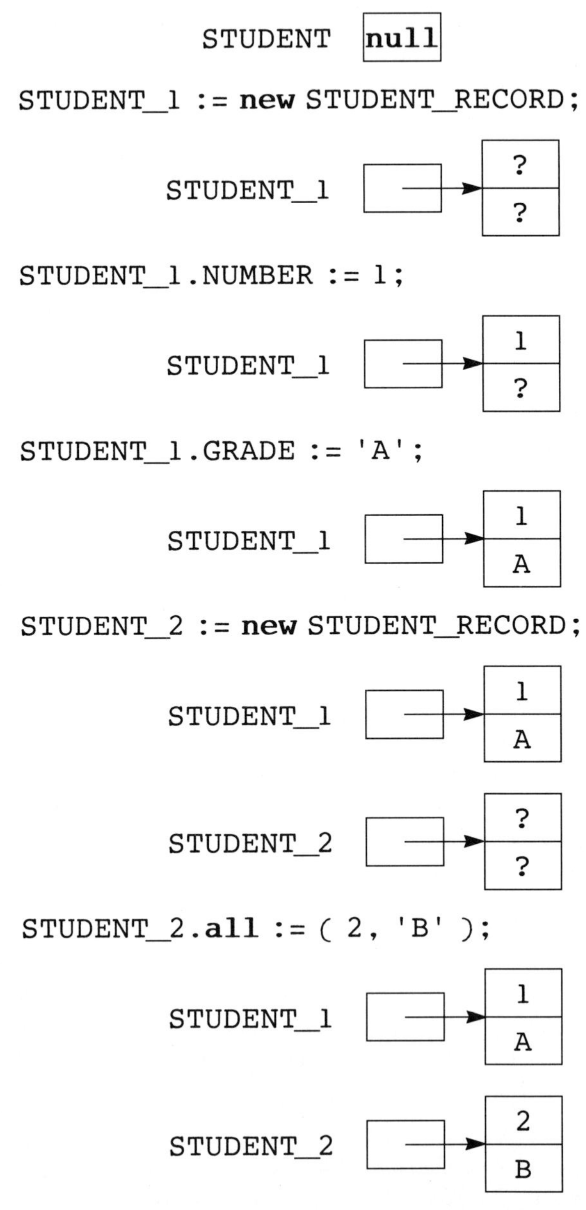

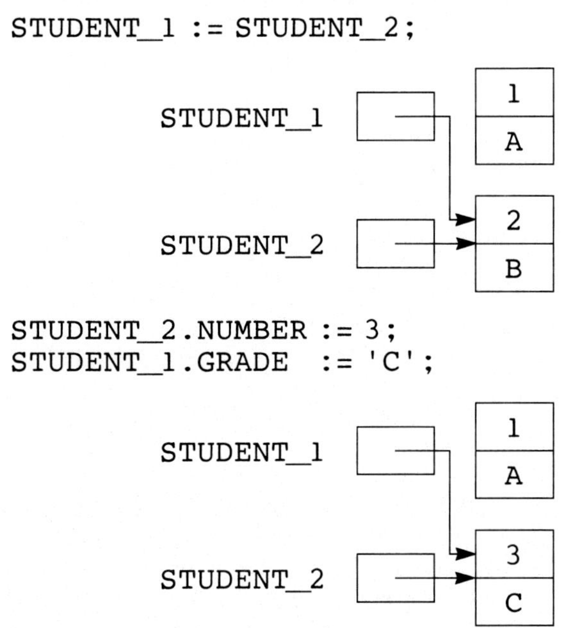

Figure 17.4 Explanation of Figure 17.3.

Nodes

type declaration

The program in the previous section is a toy program. Nobody would use it for anything other than a learning aid. In fact dynamic variables of type STUDENT_RECORD have almost no use. Like the type STUDENT_RECORD, the type of a dynamic variable is usually some sort of record type. However, the record type of a dynamic object normally contains at least one component that is of an access type. By way of example, consider the data structure in Figure 17.1. The nodes in that data structure would be represented by records with three components, two are of the types INTEGER and CHARACTER, the same as the type STUDENT_RECORD, but there is also one more component of an access type that can designate such nodes. The Ada type declarations as well as the declaration of the access object HEAD are shown in the next paragraph. The identifier NODE can be replaced by any other identifier, but since the record represents a node, there is a tendency to call the type NODE.

incomplete type specification

To declare a record like the one in this paragraph, Ada requires the use of what is called an *incomplete type specification.* An incomplete type specification can be thought of as a promise to the system that if it will accept this identifier as a **type**, you will in short order complete the specification. The syntax for an incomplete type specification is simply the reserved word **type** followed by the *type_name* followed by a semicolon. The first line below is an example of an incomplete type specification:

```
type NODE;
type NODE_POINTER is access NODE;
type NODE is record
                   NUMBER : INTEGER;
                   GRADE  : CHARACTER;
                   LINK   : NODE_POINTER;
              end record;
HEAD : NODE_POINTER;
```

This declaration is blatantly circular. NODE_POINTER is defined in terms of NODE, and NODE is defined in terms of NODE_POINTER. As it turns out, there is nothing wrong with this circularity, and it is allowed in Ada. One indication that this definition is not logically inconsistent is the fact that we can draw pictures representing such structures. Figure 17.1 is one such picture. This is fortunate because we must use some sort of circularity if we are to have data structures of this kind. After all, we want each node to contain a designater of other nodes of the same type. If this is to be the situation, then the straightforward definition of the node type must contain an access object, and the straightforward definition of the access type must contain a reference to a node type. This is yet another example of how circular definitions can be meaningful and also extremely useful in computer programming. (In an attempt to avoid circularity, one clever programmer suggested defining *access values* as an arrow that designates *anything*. But alas, the programmer's definition of *anything* referred to nodes, and the definition of *nodes* referred to access objects.)

Ada does require that the incomplete type definition precede the associated access type definition, so the definitions of the types NODE_POINTER and NODE must be in the order shown.

We now have access objects inside of records, and these access objects can designate records that contain access objects, and so forth. In these situations the syntax can sometimes get involved, but in all cases the syntax follows those few rules we have described for access objects and records. As an illustration, suppose the declarations are as above, the situation is as diagrammed in Figure 17.1, and we want to change the value of the NUMBER component of the second node to **23**; in other words, we want to change the **15** to a **23**. One way to accomplish this is with the following statement:

```
HEAD.LINK.NUMBER := 23;
```

To understand the expression on the left-hand side of the assignment operator, read it carefully and look at it from left to right. The node, referred to by HEAD, is a record, and the component of this record, which contains an access object, is called LINK. Hence, HEAD.LINK is the name of an access object that designates the node containing **15**. Since HEAD.LINK is the name of an access object that designates the node containing 15, HEAD.LINK is a name for the node itself. Finally, HEAD.LINK.NUMBER is a name for the NUMBER component of the node containing 15, and the assignment statement changes its value to 23. One can usually avoid such long expressions involving access objects, but occasionally they are useful, and they are a good test of whether or not you understand the syntax and semantics of access objects.

Linked Lists—An Example of Access Object Use

head

Structures like those in Figure 17.1 are called *linked lists.* The access object HEAD (in either Figure 17.3 or 17.4) is not part of the linked list but is inevitably present when a linked list is manipulated. A linked list consists of nodes, each of which has one access object component. The access objects are set so that they order the nodes into a list. There is always one node called the *head* such that if you follow the arrows starting from that node, you will pass through each node exactly once. To put it less formally, the head is the first node in the list. The access object, called HEAD in these figures, designates the head of the linked list given in each figure. (Do not confuse the access object called HEAD with the head of the list. The first node in the list is called the head. The access object is named HEAD, *not* because it *is* the head, but because it *designates* the head.)

Linked lists are used for many of the same things that arrays are used for, namely, for storing lists of data. As we will see, a program can change the size of a linked list. Also, it is easy to insert or delete nodes in a linked list. For these reasons, linked lists are preferable to arrays for some applications.

Case Study

Building a Linked List

As a warm-up exercise, let us consider how we might construct the start of a linked list, that is, how we might make a short linked list consisting of one node. We will use nodes of the same type as we have been discussing, but with a slightly different declaration. Think of the node in a linked list as an abstract data type (ADT). An ADT is made up of three parts: declaration, operations, and encapsulation. First, the declaration below is done to divorce the type of the node elements from the node itself. The usefulness of this is that we will be able to write operations (the second part of an ADT) on linked lists that will be totally generic; the operations make no reference to the kind of information that is in the linked list. Eventually we will have a collection of such operations and encapsulate them in a generic package (the third part of an ADT).

```
type DATA_ITEM is record
                        NUMBER : INTEGER;
                        GRADE  : CHARACTER;
                  end record;
type NODE;
type NODE_POINTER is access NODE;
type NODE is record
                  NODE_DATA : DATA_ITEM;
                  LINK : NODE_POINTER;
             end record;
HEAD : NODE_POINTER;
NEW_DATA : DATA_ITEM;
```

First the information is assigned; in this case a record aggregate is used. To create a node we use the operator **new**, set the two data components, and then, since this is the last node as well as the first node, we set the LINK component equal to **null** to mark the end of the list. The following code will accomplish our goal and produce the short one-node list displayed:

```
NEW_DATA := ( 150, 'A' );
HEAD := new NODE;
HEAD.NODE_DATA := NEW_DATA;
HEAD.LINK := null;
```

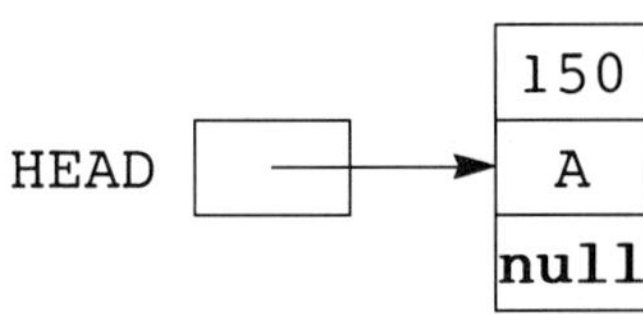

We included the assignment below to emphasize what is happening:

```
HEAD.LINK := null;
```

In reality it is not necessary because all access types are initialized to **null** by the run-time system when they are created. In the future we will omit such redundant code.

adding nodes

Our one-node list was built in a purely ad hoc way. To have a large linked list, a program must be able to add nodes to the linked list in a systematic way. We next describe one simple way to insert nodes in a link list. It will turn out that the procedure will work even if we start with an empty list. However, the process is clearer if we first assume that the list already has at least one node in it.

Problem Definition

We want a procedure that will insert new data in a linked list of the type shown in Figure 17.5(a). The linked list will be given by an access object HEAD that designates the head of the list. The data will be given by a record variable called NEW_DATA of the type DATA_ITEM, as defined above.

The procedure will change the list so a new node with the given data is inserted and will redirect HEAD to designate the head of the modified list. For this problem we will not require that the list be in any particular order, so the new node may be inserted anyplace in the list that is convenient. The job to be accomplished can be summarized as follows:

Precondition: HEAD designates the head of a linked list and NEW_DATA contains data for a new node.
Postcondition: A node, containing the data in NEW_DATA, has been added someplace in the linked list; HEAD designates the head of this enlarged list.

Discussion

To insert the data into the linked list, the procedure will need to use **new** to create a new node. The data is then copied into the new node, and the new node is inserted at the head of the list. Since dynamic objects have no names, we must use a local access object to designate this node. If we call the local access object NEW_POINTER, then the new node can be referred to using that name. The complete process can be summarized as follows:

Algorithm

1. Create a dynamic object designated by NEW__POINTER;
2. Place the data in this dynamic object (which can be referred to as NEW__POINTER.NODE__DATA);
3. Make NEW__POINTER.LINK designate the head (first node) of the original linked list;
4. Make HEAD the same as NEW__POINTER (i.e., the new dynamic variable).

Figure 17.5 gives the algorithm in diagrammatic form. Steps 3 and 4 can be expressed by the following two Ada assignment statements:

```
NEW_POINTER.LINK := HEAD;
HEAD := NEW_POINTER;
```

(a)

```
NEW_DATA := ( 110, 'B' );
```

110
B

HEAD

11
A

15
C

121
C

11
A
null

(b)

```
NEW_POINTER := new NODE;
NEW_POINTER.NODE_DATA := NEW_DATA;
```

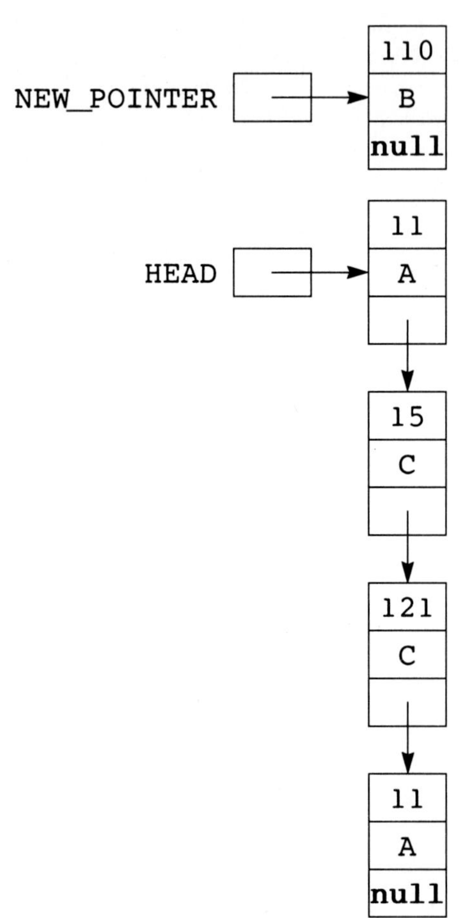

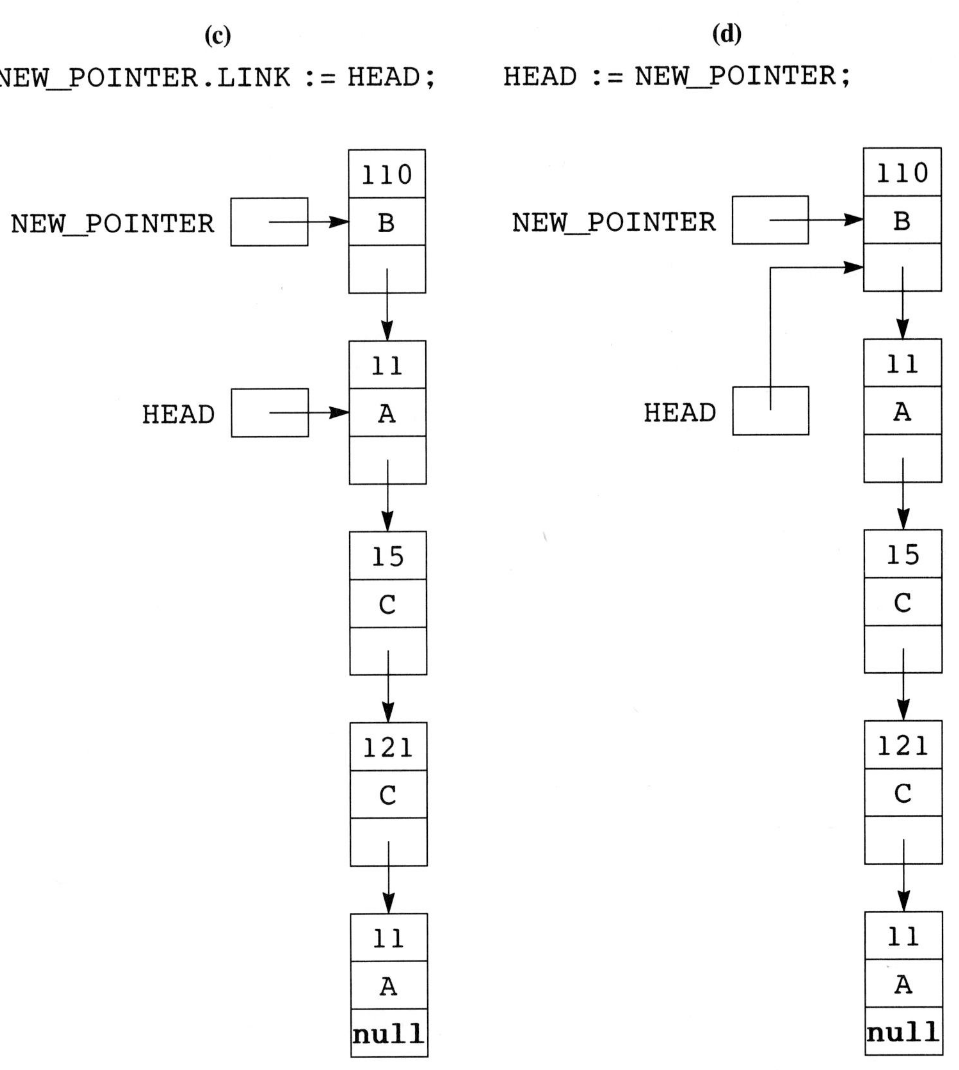

Figure 17.5 Inserting a node at the front of a list.

The alternate form for the allocator **new** shown below includes an aggregate:

allocator

aggregate

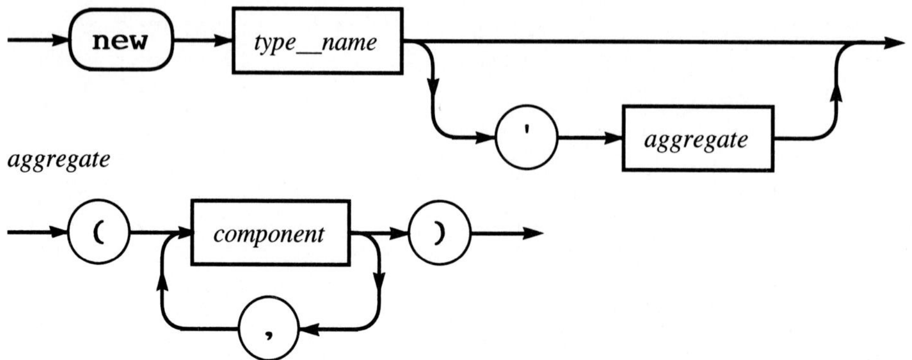

Using this alternate form for the allocator, we can accomplish the creation of a new node and the assignment of the NODE_DATA and LINK components all in one statement, as follows:

```
HEAD := new NODE'( NEW_DATA, HEAD );
```

This more complex statement eliminates the need for NEW_POINTER and does exactly what the following four statements do, in exactly the same order:

```
NEW_POINTER := new NODE;
NEW_POINTER.NODE_DATA := NEW_DATA;
NEW_POINTER.LINK := HEAD;
HEAD := NEW_POINTER;
```

It may be more clear if we use named association in a record aggregate, as we did in Chapter 12.

```
HEAD := new NODE'( NODE_DATA => NEW_DATA, LINK => HEAD );
```

A record aggregate is used in the complete procedure ADD_TO_FRONT, which is given in Figure 17.6.

```
procedure ADD_TO_FRONT ( NEW_DATA : in DATA_ITEM;
                         HEAD : in out NODE_POINTER ) is
begin -- Add_To_Front
   HEAD := new NODE'( NEW_DATA, HEAD );
end ADD_TO_FRONT;
```

Figure 17.6 Procedure to add a node to a linked list.

The Empty List

A linked list is established by naming an access object that designates the head of the list. To specify an empty list, the normal thing to do is to set this access object equal to **null**:

```
HEAD := null;
```

Whenever you design a subprogram for manipulating a linked list, you should always check to see if it works on the empty list. If it does not, then it may be possible to add a special case for the empty list. If you cannot design the subprogram to apply to the empty list, then the program must be designed to handle empty lists some other way or to avoid them completely.

Fortunately the empty list can often be treated just like any other list. For example, the procedure ADD_TO_FRONT in Figure 17.6 was designed with nonempty lists as the model, but a check will show that it works for the empty list as well.

In addition, also check the algorithm for lists that contain one and two nodes. If the algorithm works in these cases and the empty case, it probably will work for all cases.

Pitfall

Losing Nodes

You might be tempted to write the procedure ADD_TO_FRONT using the access object HEAD directly instead of the local access object NEW_POINTER to construct a new node. If we were to try, we might start the procedure as follows:

```
HEAD := new NODE;
HEAD.NODE_DATA := NEW_DATA;
```

At this point the new node is constructed, contains the correct data, and is designated by the access object HEAD; all as it is supposed to be. All that is left to do is to attach the rest of the list to this node by setting the access object component HEAD.LINK so that it designates what was formerly the first node of the list. Figure 17.7 shows the situation where the new data values are **110** and **'B'**. The diagram reveals the problem. If we proceed in this way, unfortunately there would be nothing designating the node containing **11**. Since there is no named access object that designates it or any of the nodes below it, all those nodes are lost. There is no way that the program can reference them. It cannot make an access object designate any of the nodes, nor can it access the data in those nodes, nor can it do anything else to the nodes. It simply has no way to refer to these nodes. To avoid such lost nodes, the program must always keep some access object designating the head of the list, usually the designater is an access object like HEAD.

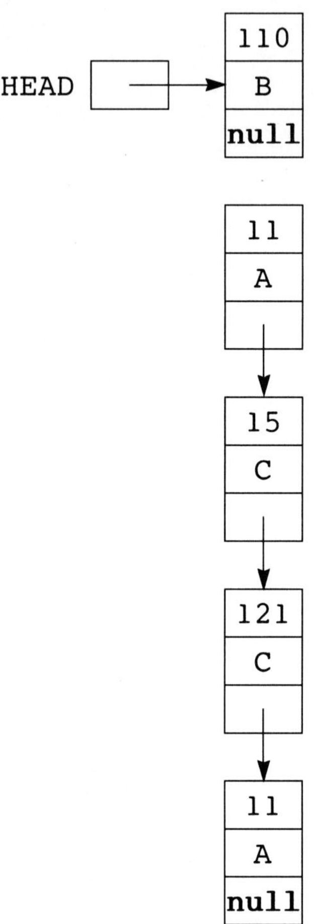

Figure 17.7 Lost nodes.

Case Study

A Generic Linked List Package

In this section we will design a set of procedures to perform some basic manipulations on linked lists of some type called DATA_ITEM. We will write these operations so we can use them without knowing the details in the definition of DATA_ITEM. We want to use a more versatile procedure to add a node to the list. The procedure ADD_TO_FRONT inserted a node at the head of a list. We will design a procedure that can insert a node at any location in an existing list, not just at the head of the list. We also need a way to delete a node from the list.

The generic linked list package is designed to alleviate the user from the chore of manipulating access values in the linked list. The intent is to help avoid lost nodes. The package also gives us a piece of reusable software that will work for any linked list of the kind we have been dealing with up to this point.

To provide this capability, the package will have an operation that, when given an access object that designates a node in the linked list, returns an access value that designates the next node in the list. This is particularly helpful when we attempt to search a list for a particular node. For example, if the linked list contains a list of student numbers and grades, then one procedure will find a student's record given the student's number. We will also need an operation that will allow us to extract or copy the data information out of a specific node. We will show how to use this package to search for a node with a particular number.

generic package

Figure 17.8 has the package specification for a generic linked list package that includes all of the functions mentioned above. The ADT in this case is a type called NODE. The complete type definition for NODE is given in the **private** section that hides the details from the user program. The operations available on this data type are listed, along with their interface (parameters). The implementation of the operations is hidden from the user program. The data description and the operations are encapsulated in the package specification.

```
generic
    type DATA_ITEM is private;
package LINKLIST is
    type NODE is private;
    type NODE_POINTER is access NODE;
    procedure ADD_TO_FRONT ( NEW_DATA : in DATA_ITEM;
                             HEAD : in out NODE_POINTER );
    procedure INSERT ( NEW_DATA : in DATA_ITEM;
                       AFTER : in NODE_POINTER );
    procedure DELETE ( DISCARD : in NODE_POINTER;
                       HEAD : in out NODE_POINTER );
```

```
    function SUCCESSOR ( OF_THIS : NODE_POINTER )
                         return NODE_POINTER;
    function DATA_PART ( FROM_THIS : NODE_POINTER )
                         return DATA_ITEM;
private
    type NODE is record
                   NODE_DATA : DATA_ITEM;
                   LINK : NODE_POINTER;
                 end record;
end LINKLIST;
```

Figure 17.8 Generic linked list package specifications.

building a list

We can use the generic package LINKLIST given in Figure 17.8 to manipulate linked lists in a variety of ways. For example, suppose we wish to build a linked list like the one shown in Figure 17.5. The procedure BUILD_LIST, shown in Figure 17.9, builds such lists using the package LINKLIST. To use this procedure a program must instantiate the package LINKLIST as well as include the procedure. The following shows the declarations needed in such a program:

```
with TEXT_IO;
use TEXT_IO;
with LINKLIST;
procedure TEST_LINK_LIST is
    type STUDENT_RECORD is record
                              NUMBER : INTEGER;
                              GRADE  : CHARACTER;
                           end record;
    package STUDENT_LIST is new LINKLIST ( STUDENT_RECORD );
    use STUDENT_LIST;
    package NUMBER_IO is new INTEGER_IO ( INTEGER );
    use NUMBER_IO;
    STUDENT : NODE_POINTER;
```

First, a record to hold the information about a student is declared (STUDENT_RECORD). Second, the generic package LINKLIST is instantiated for STUDENT_RECORD's and called STUDENT_LIST. Third, an access object is declared that will serve as the head of the list of students (STUDENT). The main program calls the BUILD_LIST procedure, passing it the access object STUDENT as follows:

```
BUILD_LIST ( STUDENT );
```

The BUILD_LIST procedure uses the procedure ADD_TO_FRONT found in the linked list package to construct a list like the one in Figure 17.6. The procedure that builds the list does not have to manipulate any access values; it relies on the linked list package to do this for it. There is no way to make a mess out of the list and possibly lose nodes.

```
procedure BUILD_LIST ( HEAD : in out NODE_POINTER ) is
    ANSWER : CHARACTER;
    STUDENT : STUDENT_RECORD;
begin -- Build_List
    loop
        PUT ( "Enter student number:" ); NEW_LINE;
        GET ( STUDENT.NUMBER ); SKIP_LINE;
        PUT ( "Enter student grade:" ); NEW_LINE;
        GET ( STUDENT.GRADE ); SKIP_LINE;
        ADD_TO_FRONT ( STUDENT, HEAD );
        PUT ( "More students? (y/n)" ); NEW_LINE;
        GET ( ANSWER ); SKIP_LINE;
        exit when ANSWER = 'n'
          or else ANSWER = 'N';
    end loop;
end BUILD_LIST;
```

Figure 17.9 Procedure to build a list of student records.

Problem Definition

searching a list

We will first consider the problem of locating a node. We want to design a function that locates a node in a linked list made up of nodes of STUDENT_RECORDS. More precisely, the function has two parameters: KEY of type INTEGER and HEAD of type NODE_POINTER. If the function cannot find a node in the list whose NUMBER component is KEY, the function raises an exception called KEY_NOT_FOUND. If the KEY is found in the list, the function returns an access value of type NODE_POINTER. This access object designates the node where KEY is found.

We assume that the head (first) node is designated by an access object called HEAD and that the end of the list is marked with **null**. If the list is empty, then the value of HEAD is **null**. The situation is diagrammed in Figure 17.10(a). Our assumptions can be summarized by the following precondition:

Precondition: HEAD designates a linked list of nodes of type STUDENT_RECORD; the end of the list is marked by **null**; if the list is empty, then HEAD = **null**.

The goal of a search can be expressed precisely by the following postcondition:

Postcondition: If there is a node that contains the integer KEY, then HERE designates the first such node, and the function returns that access value. If no node contains KEY, then KEY_NOT_FOUND is raised.

The process of searching a list is demonstrated for a sample situation by Figure 17.10.

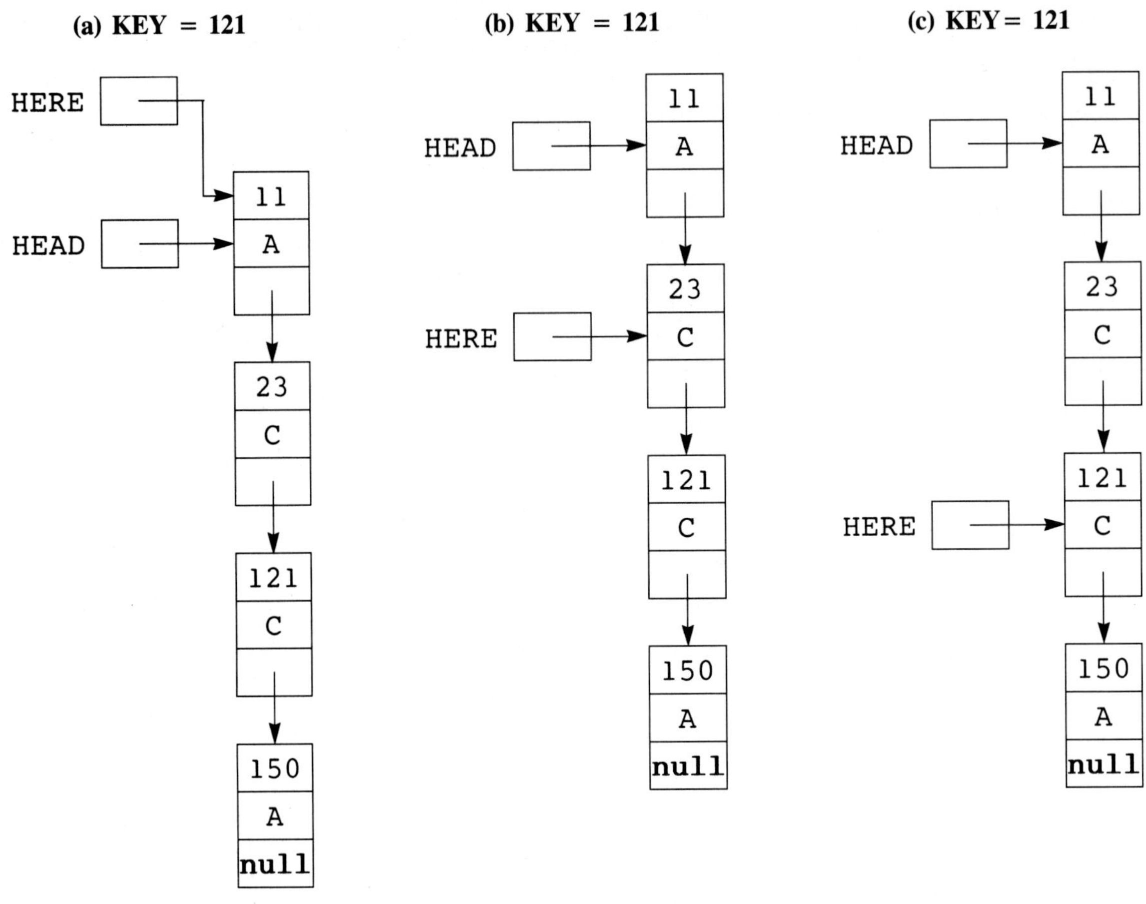

Figure 17.10 How the function SEARCH works.

Discussion

The only way to move around a linked list, or any other data structure made up of nodes and access objects, is to follow the access values in Ada code, which are the arrows in the figures. So we will place the access object HERE at the first node and then move it from node to node using the LINKLIST package's function SUCCESSOR. We will follow the access values until we find a node containing the integer KEY or until we encounter the end of the linked list. To inspect the data in a node of the linked list, we must use the LINKLIST package's function DATA_PART. The code for these two linked list operations is given below:

```
function SUCCESSOR ( OF_THIS : NODE_POINTER )
                          return NODE_POINTER is
begin -- Successor
    return OF_THIS.LINK;
end SUCCESSOR;
```

```
function DATA_PART ( FROM_THIS : NODE_POINTER )
                         return DATA_ITEM is
begin -- Data_Part
    return FROM_THIS.NODE_DATA;
end DATA_PART;
```

Algorithm

Make HERE designate the HEAD (first node) in the list;
Go into a **loop**

if HERE is **null** (the link component of the last node), the KEY is not in the list, **raise** KEY_NOT_FOUND. Use the function DATA_PART to see if HERE is designating a node containing KEY. If so, the KEY is in the list, return HERE (an access object to that node). Otherwise, make HERE designate the next node in the list using the SUCCESSOR function.

We can now translate this algorithm into Ada code. Since the access object HEAD designates the first node, the following will declare HERE and leave it designating the first node:

```
HERE : NODE_POINTER := HEAD;
```

The first test in our algorithm and its result are quite simple. It is accomplished by the following:

```
if HERE = null then
    raise KEY_NOT_FOUND;
```

The algorithm's second test is a little more complex. We want to see if the value of KEY is in the node designated by HERE. In order to do this, we must first extract the information from the node. The LINKLIST package's function DATA_PART will do that for us. The KEY is then compared to the component NUMBER. If KEY equals NUMBER, then KEY is found at the node designated by HERE, so HERE is returned as follows:

```
elsif KEY = DATA_PART ( HERE ).NUMBER then
    return HERE;
```

To move the access object HERE to the next node, we must think in terms of the operations we have available to us via the LINKLIST package. The SUCCESSOR function returns a designater to the next node in the list after its input parameter. In order to move HERE to the next node, we simply write

```
HERE := SUCCESSOR ( HERE );
```

empty list

When we check the above algorithm, we find that there is no problem with the empty list. If the list is empty, then HERE is equal to **null**, which is the first thing we test for inside the loop. Hence, there is no need to make a special case for the empty list. The complete function is given in Figure 17.11.

```
function SEARCH ( KEY : in INTEGER;
                  HEAD : in NODE_POINTER )
                  return NODE_POINTER is
    HERE : NODE_POINTER := HEAD;
begin -- Search
    loop
        if HERE = null then
            raise KEY_NOT_FOUND;
        elsif KEY = DATA_PART ( HERE ).NUMBER then
            return HERE;
        else
            HERE := SUCCESSOR ( HERE );
        end if;
    end loop;
end SEARCH;
```

Figures 17.11 Function to locate a node in a linked list.

inserting nodes

Problem Definition

We next will design the linked list package procedure to insert a node at a specified place in a linked list. Since we may want the nodes in some particular order, such as numeric order, we cannot simply insert the node at the beginning (head) of the list, using ADD_TO_FRONT, nor at the end of the list. We will therefore design the procedure to insert a node between two specified nodes in a linked list. We assume that some other procedure or program part has placed two access objects called BEFORE and AFTER to designate two nodes in the list, as shown in Figure 17.12(b). We wish to insert a new node with new data after one access object and before another, as shown in Figure 17.12(c). The data for the new node will be of the type DATA_ITEM, as defined in Figure 17.6. The procedure will create a new node, copy the data into the new node, and insert the node in the linked list. (The access object BEFORE is not absolutely necessary, and later we will eliminate it, but to start with it does simplify our reasoning.)

Discussion

A new node is set up in the same way that we did in the original procedure ADD_TO_FRONT, as follows:

```
NEW_POINTER := new NODE;
NEW_POINTER.NODE_DATA := NEW_DATA;
```

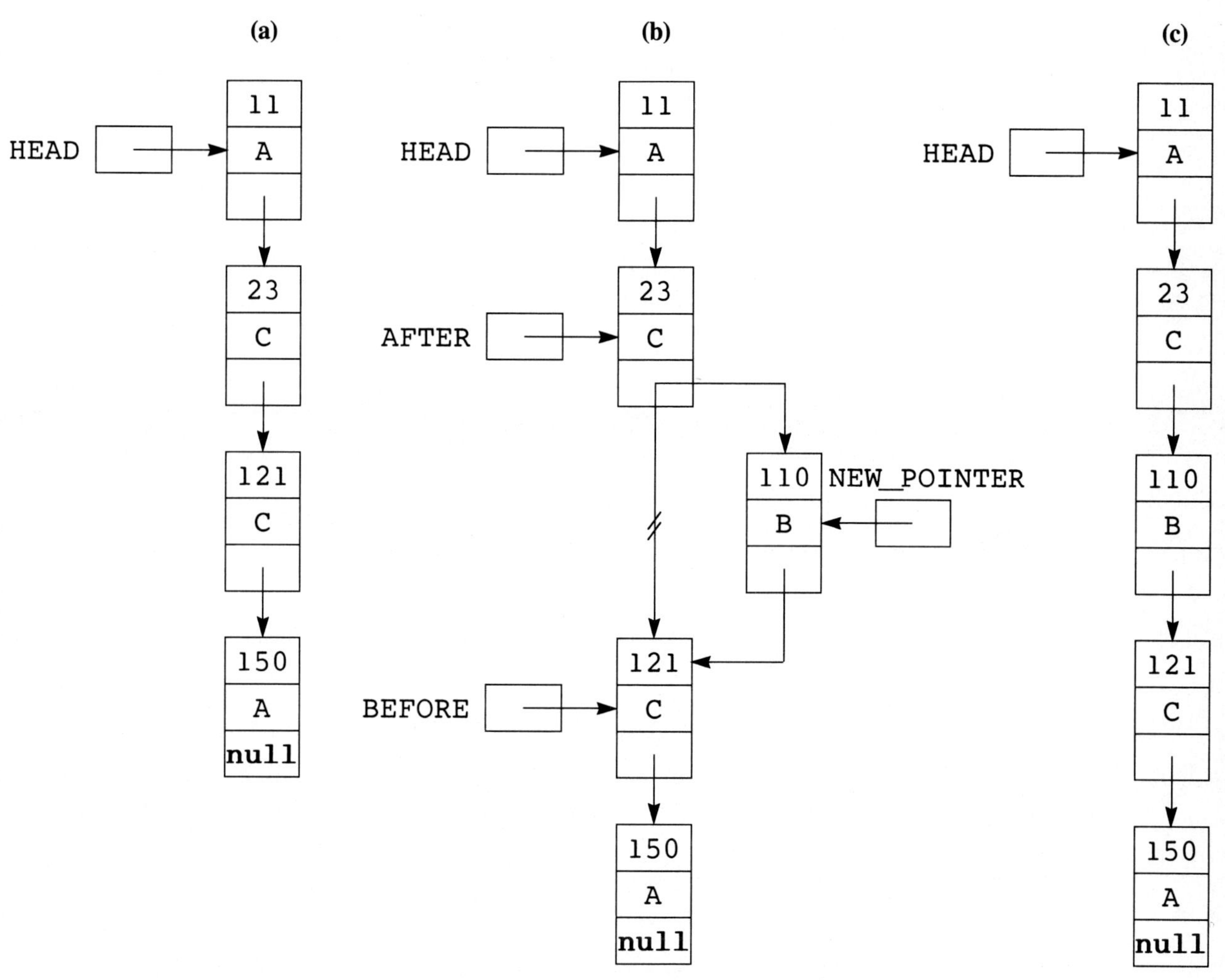

Figure 17.12 Inserting a node in the middle of a linked list.

The difference between this procedure and that one is that we now wish to insert the node not at the head of the list but in some location inside the list. The method of inserting the node is shown in Figure 17.12(b). The way to express the indicated resetting of the access objects is given below:

Algorithm

```
NEW_POINTER.LINK := BEFORE; --Tie the new node to the list
AFTER.LINK := NEW_POINTER; --Redirect a link to the new node
```

As we saw before, with the use of an aggregate on the allocator **new**, we can eliminate the need for NEW_POINTER altogether. Thus the code becomes

```
AFTER.LINK := new NODE'( NEW_DATA, BEFORE );
```

By looking carefully at Figure 17.12(b), we discover that originally the access object BEFORE designates the same node as does AFTER's LINK component. So AFTER.LINK can be substituted for the BEFORE access object, and we have the complete procedure as given in Figure 17.13.

```
procedure INSERT ( NEW_DATA : in DATA_ITEM;
                   AFTER : in NODE_POINTER ) is
begin -- Insert
   AFTER.LINK := new NODE'( NEW_DATA, AFTER.LINK );
end INSERT;
```

Figure 17.13 Procedure to insert a node in a linked list.

insertion at the ends

The procedure INSERT will not work for inserting a node at the beginning of a list, because the function INSERT assumes that AFTER designates some node in the list. AFTER would not designate anything if we wish to add to the front of the list. However, by eliminating the BEFORE access object, as we have done in Figure 17.13, INSERT does work to add to the end of a linked list. The procedure ADD_TO_FRONT in Figure 17.6 can be used to insert a node at the head of the list.

comparison to arrays

By using the procedure INSERT, we can maintain the linked list in numerical order without rewriting existing nodes. We could "squeeze" a new node into the correct position by simply adjusting two access objects. Furthermore, this is true no matter how long the linked list is or where in the list we want the new record to go. If we had instead used an array of records, then much, and in extreme cases all, of the array would have to be copied over in order to make room for a new record in the correct spot. In spite of the overhead involved in positioning the access objects, inserting into a linked list is frequently more efficient than inserting into an array.

Deleting a node from a linked list is also quite easy. Figure 17.14 illustrates the method. Once the access objects BEFORE and DISCARD have been positioned, all that is required to delete the node is the following Ada statement:

deleting nodes

```
BEFORE.LINK := DISCARD.LINK;
```

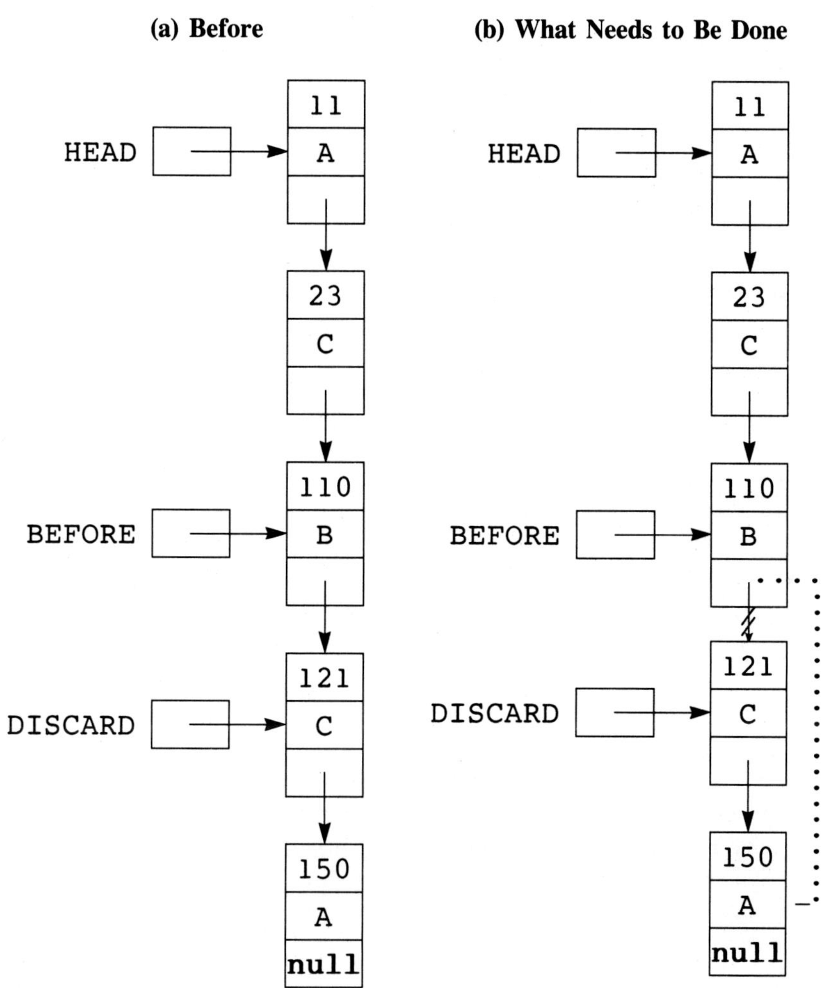

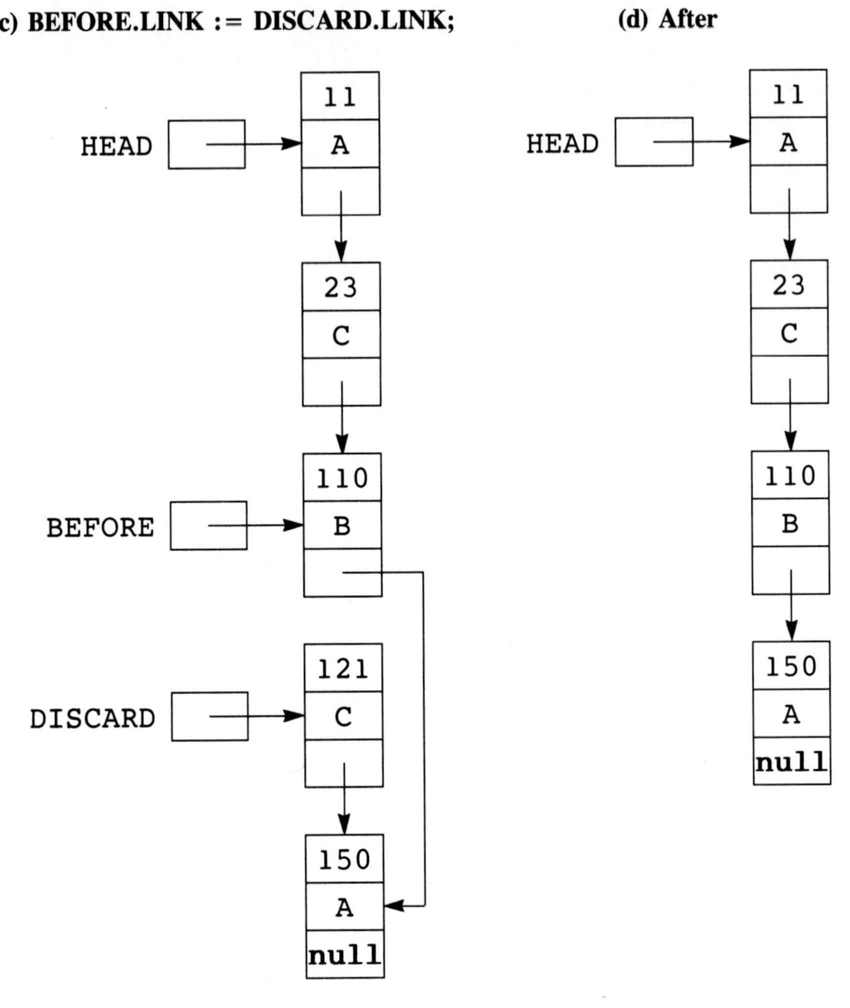

Figure 17.14 Deleting a node from a linked list.

If, however, the node you wish to discard is the head node of a list, the BEFORE access object is meaningless. A test for this condition extends the algorithm to the following:

```
if DISCARD = HEAD then
     HEAD := HEAD.LINK;
else
     BEFORE.LINK := DISCARD.LINK;
end if;
DISCARD.LINK := null;
```

The last line above may not seem necessary, and it may not be in most cases, but it does ensure that the node being discarded cannot serve as an additional head node. Without that last line the list is now a two-headed monster that could come back to get you. This little clean-up statement helps ensure the integrity of the linked list.

A more general form of the delete algorithm begins with a linked list designated by a head access object and a designater to the node that we wish to delete from the list. A temporary access object (BEFORE) starts at the head of the list and works its way down the list until its link (BEFORE.LINK) designates the node we wish to delete (DISCARD). This is accomplished as follows:

```
loop
     if BEFORE.LINK = DISCARD then
          BEFORE.LINK := DISCARD.LINK;
          DISCARD.LINK := null;
          return;
     else
          BEFORE := BEFORE.LINK;
     end if;
end loop;
```

The complete delete procedure that incorporates all of these refinements is shown in Figure 17.15 as part of the entire LINKLIST package body. Note that the code in the package takes advantage of the SUCCESSOR function whenever possible.

```
package body LINKLIST is
     procedure ADD_TO_FRONT ( NEW_DATA : in DATA_ITEM;
                              HEAD : in out NODE_POINTER ) is
     begin -- Add_To_Front
          HEAD := new NODE'( NEW_DATA, HEAD );
     end ADD_TO_FRONT;
     procedure INSERT ( NEW_DATA : in DATA_ITEM;
                        AFTER : in NODE_POINTER ) is
     begin -- Insert
          AFTER.LINK := new NODE'( NEW_DATA, AFTER.LINK );
     end INSERT;
```

```
    procedure DELETE ( DISCARD : in NODE_POINTER;
                       HEAD : in out NODE_POINTER ) is
        BEFORE : NODE_POINTER := HEAD;
    begin -- Delete
        if DISCARD = HEAD then
            HEAD := SUCCESSOR ( HEAD );
            DISCARD.LINK := null;
            return;
        else
            loop
                if SUCCESSOR ( BEFORE ) = DISCARD then
                    BEFORE.LINK := SUCCESSOR ( DISCARD );
                    DISCARD.LINK := null;
                    return;
                else
                    BEFORE := SUCCESSOR ( BEFORE );
                end if;
            end loop;
        end if;
    end DELETE;
    function SUCCESSOR ( OF_THIS : NODE_POINTER )
                         return NODE_POINTER is
    begin -- Successor
        return OF_THIS.LINK;
    end SUCCESSOR;
    function DATA_PART ( FROM_THIS : NODE_POINTER )
                         return DATA_ITEM is
    begin -- Data_Part
        return FROM_THIS.NODE_DATA;
    end DATA_PART;
end LINKLIST;
```

Figure 17.15 LinkList package body.

Exercises

Self-Test Exercises

1. What is the output produced by the following code?

```
with I_O; use I_O;
procedure MAIN is
    type POINTER is access INTEGER;
```

```
    P1, P2 : POINTER;
begin -- Main
    P1 := new INTEGER'( 10 );
    P2 := new INTEGER'( 20 );
    PUT ( P1.all ); PUT ( P2.all ) ; NEW_LINE;
    P1 := P2;
    PUT ( P1.all ); PUT ( P2.all ) ; NEW_LINE;
    P1.all := 30;
    PUT ( P1.all ); PUT ( P2.all ) ; NEW_LINE;
    P2.all := 40;
    PUT ( P1.all ); PUT ( P2.all ) ; NEW_LINE;
end MAIN;
```

2. What is the output produced by the following code?

```
with I_O; use I_O;
procedure MAIN is
    type POINTER is access INTEGER;
    P1, P2 : POINTER;
begin -- Main
    P1 := new INTEGER'( 10 );
    P2 := new INTEGER'( 20 );
    PUT ( P1.all ); PUT ( P2.all ) ; NEW_LINE;
    P1.all := P2.all;
    PUT ( P1.all ); PUT ( P2.all ) ; NEW_LINE;
    P1.all := 30;
    PUT ( P1.all ); PUT ( P2.all ) ; NEW_LINE;
    P2.all := 40;
    PUT ( P1.all ); PUT ( P2.all ) ; NEW_LINE;
end MAIN;
```

3. How would the output of the program in Figure 17.3 change if the lines

```
STUDENT_2.NUMBER := 3;
STUDENT_2.NUMBER := 'C';
```

were replaced by the following lines:

```
STUDENT_1.NUMBER := 3;
STUDENT_1.GRADE := 'C';
```

4. Given the situation shown below, what is the effect of the assignment statement shown? The access objects and nodes are of the types given in Figure 17.12. (The slash (/) indicates a **null** value.)

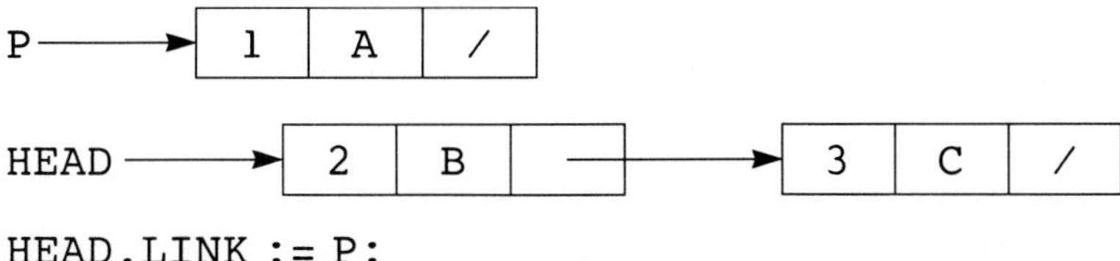


```
HEAD.LINK := P;
```

5. Write a procedure to fill a linked list with the integers one through **n**, where **n** is a parameter.

6. Write a procedure to display to the screen all the integers in a linked list of some general kind, as you used in Exercise 5. (The list may be of a different length and may contain numbers other than the ones that would be placed there by the procedure of Exercise 5.)

Recursive Access Function

In the previous section we wrote a function to search a linked list (Figure 17.11). We could redesign that function to use a recursive algorithm. Linked lists and other data structures made using access objects lend themselves to recursive algorithms because the structure is repeated. The access object HEAD designates a linked list. The access object coming out of the first node (HEAD.LINK or SUCCESSOR (HEAD)) designates another, shorter linked list; namely, the one starting with the second node of the longer list. This repeated structure allows us to state very simple recursive algorithms.

```
if head = null then
     key is not on the list
elsif head.number = key then
     key is the node designated by head
else
     search the linked list designated by head.link
end if
```

A complete function declaration is displayed in Figure 17.16. The recursive SEARCH function in the figure uses the LINKLIST package. NODE_POINTER, DATA_PART, and SUCCESSOR are all defined as part of the LINKLIST package.

```
function SEARCH ( KEY : in INTEGER;
                  HEAD : in NODE_POINTER )
                  return NODE_POINTER is
begin -- Search
    if HEAD = null then
            raise KEY_NOT_FOUND;
    elsif KEY = DATA_PART ( HEAD ).NUMBER then
            return HEAD;
    else
        SEARCH ( KEY, SUCCESSOR ( HEAD ) );
    end if;
end SEARCH;
```

Figure 17.16 A recursive search procedure.

Pitfall

Testing for the Empty List

The stopping case in recursive algorithms is typically the empty list, which is represented by the access value **null**. Hence, even if you know that the linked list or other structure in your program will not be empty, you may still need to include a test for the empty list. For example, the function SEARCH in Figure 17.16 can terminate when the value of the parameter HEAD is equal to **null**, so a series of recursive calls starting with a nonempty list can end with this case.

When dealing with the access value **null**, remember that it does not designate anything, so any reference to a node that it designates is undefined. For example, again consider the function SEARCH in Figure 17.16. The test for **null** must be the first case in the **if** statement. The reason is that if the value of HEAD is **null**, any reference to DATA_PART (HEAD) .NUMBER is undefined.

Case Study

Using the Linked List Package to Sort a File

Problem Definition

If we wish to sort a file of records, then we must read the records into some other location as we sort them. A linked list is a convenient intermediate data structure to use for this purpose. As an example, we will design a program to sort a file of records of the type declared below:

```
type STUDENT_RECORD is record
                          NUMBER : INTEGER;
                          GRADE  : CHARACTER;
                       end record;
```

We assume that the file is called GRADE_FILE and that the records might be in any order. We want the program to change the file so that it contains the same records, but they will be sorted smallest to largest according to the NUMBER component.

Discussion

Since we cannot open a file for both reading and writing at the same time, the only way to sort a file is to copy the data into some other location for sorting. One possible way to proceed is to copy the data into a linked list inserting each piece of data in the correct place so as to keep the list sorted. After that the program can simply copy the sorted list back into the file. (Even though Ada allows a program random access to a DIRECT_IO file, this might be an easy and relatively efficient way to accomplish the sort.)

Algorithm

One breakdown of the problem into subproblems yields the following algorithm outline:

I. BUILD_LIST: for each record in the file:
   1. Read the record.
   2. FIND_SLOT: Find the correct place to insert the record data in the list.
   3. INSERT: Insert a new node with the record data in the list.

II. COPY_TO_FILE: Copy the linked list back into the file.

The procedure FIND_SLOT positions the two access objects BEFORE and AFTER so that they designate two adjacent nodes such that the new node belongs between these two nodes. Expressed more precisely, that means that the following must hold after the procedure FIND_SLOT has completed:

BEFORE.NUMBER<=*(the number in the node to be inserted)*<=AFTER.NUMBER

sentinel node

If the list is empty, as it is at the start, or if the node to be inserted belongs at the start or end of the list, then there will not be two nodes with these properties. Rather than make special cases for empty lists, we will instead add a sentinel node as the first element of the list. The sentinel node will contain a number smaller than all the numbers in the file. Since the list will initially contain this node, the case of the empty list is eliminated. Since the INSERT procedure in the LINKLIST package does not care if it is inserting at the end of a list, there is no need to mark the other end of the list with a very large sentinel. The procedure FIND_SLOT is written with just two tests: One catches the end of the list, in the case where the value to be inserted is the largest value in the list, as shown below:

```
if AFTER = null then
    return BEFORE;
```

The other stops when the correct position for the number to be inserted has been found, as shown below:

```
elsif NEW_DATA.NUMBER < DATA_PART ( AFTER ).NUMBER then
    return BEFORE;
```

The complete program, including the procedure FIND_SLOT, is given in Figure 17.17.

```
with TEXT_IO;
use TEXT_IO;
with LINKLIST;
with SEQUENTIAL_IO;
procedure SORT_FILE is
    type STUDENT_RECORD is record
                              NUMBER : INTEGER;
                              GRADE  : CHARACTER;
                          end record;
    package STUDENT_LIST is new LINKLIST ( STUDENT_RECORD );
    use STUDENT_LIST;
    package STUDENT_IO is new SEQUENTIAL_IO ( STUDENT_RECORD );
    use STUDENT_IO;
    GRADE_FILE : STUDENT_IO.FILE_TYPE;
    LAST : NATURAL;
    LIST : NODE_POINTER := null;
    FILENAME : STRING( 1 . . 80 );
    STUDENT : STUDENT_RECORD;
    procedure BUILD_LIST ( GRADE_FILE : in STUDENT_IO.FILE_TYPE;
                           HEAD : in out NODE_POINTER ) is
        STUDENT : STUDENT_RECORD;
        function FIND_SLOT ( NEW_DATA : STUDENT_RECORD;
                             HEAD : NODE_POINTER )
                             return NODE_POINTER is
            BEFORE : NODE_POINTER := HEAD;
            AFTER : NODE_POINTER;
        begin -- Find_Slot
            loop
                AFTER := SUCCESSOR ( BEFORE );
                if AFTER = null then
                    return BEFORE;
                elsif NEW_DATA.NUMBER
                    < DATA_PART ( AFTER ).NUMBER then
                    return BEFORE;
                else
                    BEFORE := AFTER;
                end if;
            end loop;
        end FIND_SLOT;
    begin -- Build_List
        STUDENT := ( INTEGER'FIRST, 'A' );
        HEAD := MAKE_NODE ( STUDENT );
        loop
            exit when END_OF_FILE ( GRADE_FILE );
            READ ( GRADE_FILE, STUDENT );
            INSERT ( STUDENT , FIND_SLOT ( STUDENT, HEAD ) );
        end loop;
```

```
    end BUILD_LIST;
    procedure COPY_TO_FILE ( HEAD : in NODE_POINTER;
                             GRADE_FILE : STUDENT_IO.FILE_TYPE ) is
        TEMPORARY : NODE_POINTER := HEAD;
    begin -- Copy_To_File
        loop
            exit when TEMPORARY = null;
            WRITE ( GRADE_FILE, DATA_PART ( TEMPORARY ) );
            TEMPORARY := SUCCESSOR ( TEMPORARY );
        end loop;
    end COPY_TO_FILE;
begin -- Sort_File
    PUT_LINE ( "Enter the name of the student file:" );
    GET_LINE ( FILENAME, LAST );
    OPEN ( GRADE_FILE, IN_FILE, FILENAME( 1 . . LAST ) );
    PUT_LINE ( "Reading "
               & FILENAME( 1 . . LAST )
               & " into a sorted list." );
    BUILD_LIST ( GRADE_FILE, LIST );
    CLOSE ( GRADE_FILE );
    CREATE ( GRADE_FILE, OUT_FILE, FILENAME( 1 . . LAST ) );
    PUT_LINE ( "Copying sorted list back into "
               & FILENAME( 1 . . LAST ) );
    COPY_TO_FILE ( LIST, GRADE_FILE );
    CLOSE ( GRADE_FILE );
    PUT_LINE ( FILENAME( 1 . . LAST ) & " is sorted." );
end SORT_FILE;
```

Figure 17.17 Sorting with a linked list.

A Generic Stack Package

push and pop

We introduced the notion of a stack in Chapter 15 and showed how it could be used to keep track of recursive procedure calls and local variables. One way to implement a stack is by means of a linked list. In this implementation a stack is nothing but a linked list that is used in a restricted way; namely, nodes are only added at the head of the list and are only deleted from the head of the list. With stacks, adding a node is usually called a *push* operation, and deleting a node is called a *pop* operation. These operations and their implementations on linked lists are illustrated in Figure 17.18.

This terminology will explain the procedure names used in Figure 17.19, where the abstract data type for a stack is given as a generic package. A program (Figure 17.20) instantiates the stack package to create a stack of characters, reads in a line of text, and outputs it in reverse order. The procedure PUSH is essentially the same as the procedure ADD_TO_FRONT we designed earlier. The procedure POP simply moves the designater at the head of the list in the manner shown in Figure 17.18.

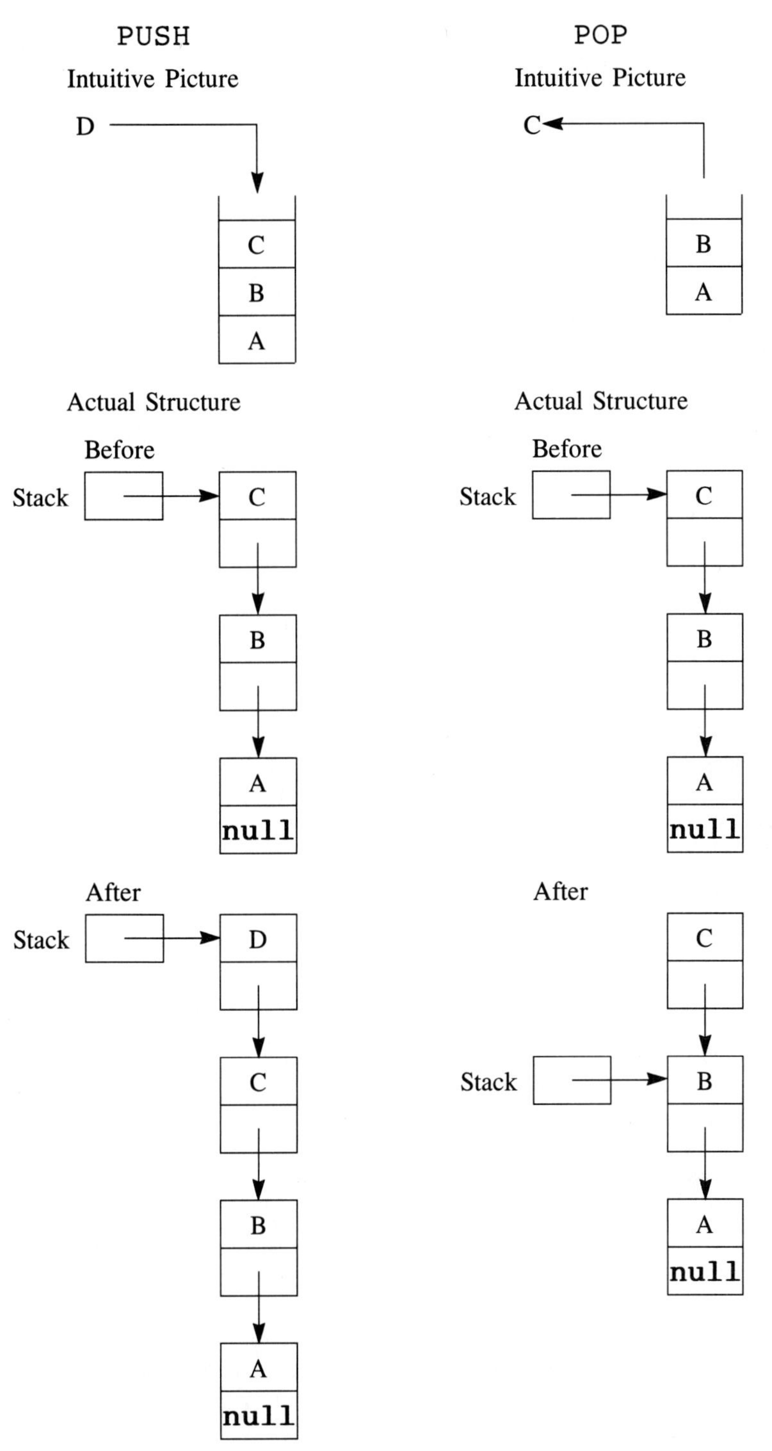

Figure 17.18 Stack operations.

```
generic
    type INFO_TYPE is private;
package STACK_PACKAGE is
    type STACK_TYPE is private;
    STACK_UNDERFLOW : exception;
    procedure PUSH ( NEW_DATA : in INFO_TYPE;
                     STACK : in out STACK_TYPE );
    procedure POP  ( TOP_DATA : out INFO_TYPE;
                     STACK : in out STACK_TYPE );
    function EMPTY ( STACK : STACK_TYPE ) return BOOLEAN;
private
    type STACK_NODE is record
                           DATA : INFO_TYPE;
                           LINK : STACK_TYPE;
                       end record;
    type STACK_TYPE is access STACK_NODE;
end STACK_PACKAGE;
package body STACK_PACKAGE is
    procedure PUSH ( NEW_DATA : in INFO_TYPE;
                     STACK : in out STACK_TYPE ) is
    begin -- Push
        STACK := new STACK_NODE'( NEW_DATA, STACK );
    end PUSH;
    procedure POP  ( TOP_DATA : out INFO_TYPE;
                     STACK : in out STACK_TYPE ) is
    begin -- Pop
        if EMPTY ( STACK ) then
            raise STACK_UNDERFLOW;
        else
            TOP_DATA := STACK.DATA;
            STACK := STACK.LINK;
        end if;
    end POP;
    function EMPTY ( STACK : STACK_TYPE ) return BOOLEAN is
    begin -- Empty
        return STACK = null;
    end EMPTY;
end STACK_PACKAGE;
```

Figure 17.19 A generic stack package.

Program

```
with STACK_PACKAGE;
with TEXT_IO;
use TEXT_IO;
procedure BACKWARDS is
    SYMBOL : CHARACTER;
    package SYMBOL_STACK is new STACK_PACKAGE ( CHARACTER );
    use SYMBOL_STACK;
    LINE : STACK_TYPE;
begin -- Backwards
    PUT_LINE ( "Enter a line of text." );
    loop
        exit when END_OF_LINE;
        GET ( SYMBOL );
        PUSH ( SYMBOL, LINE );
    end loop;
    SKIP_LINE;
    loop
        exit when EMPTY ( LINE );
        POP ( SYMBOL, LINE );
        PUT ( SYMBOL );
    end loop;
    NEW_LINE;
    PUT_LINE ( "That's it, forwards and backwards!" );
end BACKWARDS;
```

Sample Dialogue

```
Enter a line of text.
Able was I ere I saw Elba. Cute?
?etuC .ablE was I ere I saw elbA
That's it, forwards and backwards!
```

Figure 17.20 Program using a stack.

Unchecked_Deallocation

Look again at Figure 17.18. The node that is popped off the stack is no longer on the stack (linked list) and it cannot be referenced by the program. It is a lost node, but it has not been destroyed. Unless the program explicitly eliminates the node, it will remain in storage and will waste storage. The generic procedure UNCHECKED_DEALLOCATION can be used to eliminate useless dynamic variables. It marks the space taken by the dynamic variable as no longer being used and thus frees some storage for other purposes. The generic procedure UNCHECKED_DEALLOCATION is described in the LRM and is provided as part of the Ada implementation.

For example, the following will instantiate both the generic procedure UNCHECKED_DEALLOCATION for a node of type NODE and its access type (NODE_POINTER). The new procedure is called FREE, and it has one parameter, an access object to the dynamic object that we wish to eliminate.

```
procedure FREE is new UNCHECKED_DEALLOCATION ( NODE,
                                               NODE_POINTER );
```

If DISCARD designates the node we wish to eliminate, then we call FREE as follows:

```
FREE ( DISCARD );
```

In Figure 17.21 we have modified the stack package and rewritten the procedure POP from Figure 17.19 so it uses UNCHECKED_DEALLOCATION and thus does not waste storage. For the program in Figure 17.20, it makes little difference which version of POP we use. However, if we were to enclose the body of the program in a loop that repeated reading and writing a large number of times, then the one without UNCHECKED_DEALLOCATION will generate extra lost nodes on every iteration of the loop. These lost nodes will remain in storage and so consume storage. If the loop iterates enough times, the lost nodes could even cause the program to terminate because of lack of storage. The version with UNCHECKED_DEALLOCATION will need only enough storage for one line of text.

```
with UNCHECKED_DEALLOCATION;
package body STACK_PACKAGE is
    procedure FREE is new UNCHECKED_DEALLOCATION ( STACK_NODE,
                                                   STACK_TYPE );
    procedure POP ( TOP_DATA : out INFO_TYPE;
                    STACK : in out STACK_TYPE ) is
        TOP : STACK_TYPE := STACK;
    begin -- Pop
        if EMPTY ( STACK ) then
            raise STACK_UNDERFLOW;
        else
            TOP_DATA := STACK.DATA;
            STACK := STACK.LINK;
            TOP.LINK := null;
            FREE ( TOP );
        end if;
    end POP;
      .
      .
      .
end STACK_PACKAGE;
```

Figure 17.21 Procedure using UNCHECKED_DEALLOCATION.

Case Study

Implementing a Generic Queue Package

Problem Definition

queue

A stack is a last-in/first-out data structure; that is, if you fill a stack and then empty it, the elements are removed from the stack in the reverse of the order in which they were placed in the stack. In this section we will discuss a data structure known as a *queue.* A queue is a first-in/first-out data structure for storing and retrieving data; that is, if you fill a queue and then empty it, the elements are removed from the queue in the same order in which they were placed in the queue. A queue works on the same principle as a waiting line at a bank or post office. Customers in a line are served in the order in which they enter that line. Data in a queue is removed from the queue in the same order in which it was stored.

For example, consider a queue for storing integers. If the numbers 8, 9, 2, and 7 are placed in the queue in that order, then they must be retrieved in exactly that order. If your program wants the 2, it must first remove the 8 and the 9. Those two numbers are then no longer in the queue. As far as the queue is concerned, they were thrown away. The first column of Figure 17.22 shows a diagrammatic representation of a queue of integers and the basic operations of adding an integer and retrieving the next integer in the queue.

A queue such as this might be used to keep track of the students waiting to see an instructor on a day when office hours are particularly crowded. When a student arrives, the student places his or her student number in the queue. When the instructor has finished talking with one student and is ready to talk to another student, the instructor takes the next available number from the queue and announces that that student is next.

In this ''Case Study'' we will leave the data type for the elements in a queue unspecified. We will design a data type for a queue that stores elements of a type called `ELEMENT_TYPE`. If our application requires storing integers, then we can define `ELEMENT_TYPE` to be the type `INTEGER`. If some other application requires storing data of some other type, we can define `ELEMENT_TYPE` to be that type. The way to implement this operation for a variety of element types is to write a generic queue package in which `ELEMENT_TYPE` is the generic parameter.

We will need to design a way to represent a queue. We will also need to design operations for adding an element to the queue and for removing an element from the queue. Since we will want to know if the queue contains any elements at all before we try to remove an element, we will also need to design a test to see if the queue is empty.

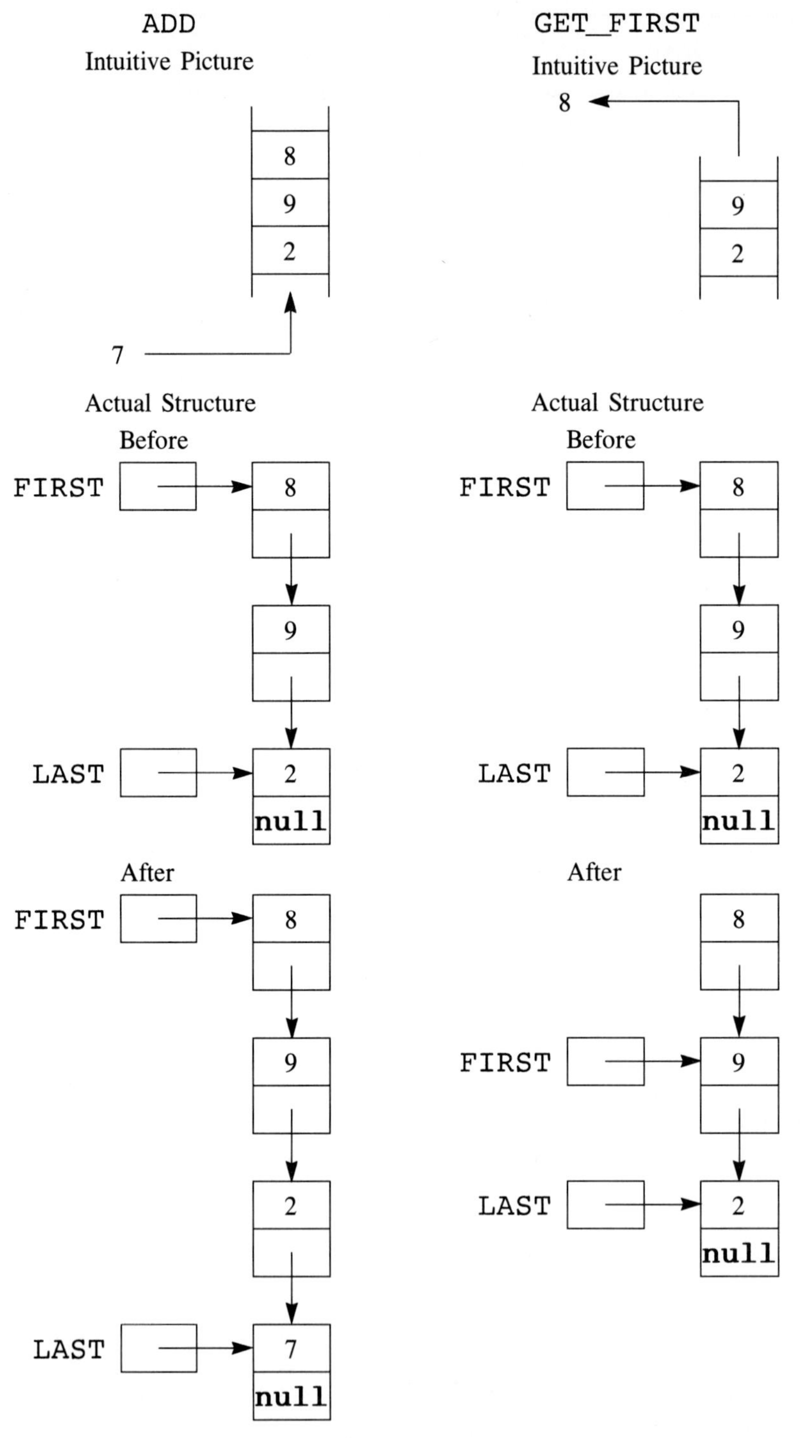

Figure 17.22 Queue operations.

Discussion

We will implement a queue as a linked list of the kind diagrammed in Figure 17.22. In that figure the elements stored in the queue are integers, but the idea is the same for queues with elements of any other type. Elements will be added at one end of the linked list and removed from the other end. Because we must keep track of both ends of the linked list, we will use two access objects to access this linked list. One access object will be called FIRST, and it will designate the element (node) to be removed first. The other access object will be called LAST, and will designate the element (node) at the other end of the linked list. To help keep the terminology straight, think of the queue as a line in a bank and think of FIRST and LAST as standing for "first in line" and "last in line." The queue itself will be a record with the two access object components FIRST and LAST:

```
type QUEUE_TYPE is record
                       FIRST : NODE_POINTER;
                       LAST : NODE_POINTER;
                   end record;
```

Each node in the queue is represented by

```
type NODE;
type NODE_POINTER is access NODE;
type NODE is record
                 ELEMENT : ELEMENT_TYPE;
                 NEXT : NODE_POINTER;
             end record;
```

Since the last node in our linked list is designated by the access object LAST, we could get by without marking it in any other way. However, it seems neater and will prove to be useful to mark the last node in the list by setting its access object component equal to **null**, as is customary with linked lists.

The operations of adding and removing an element from a queue of integers is diagrammed in Figure 17.22. These operations will be implemented by two procedures called ADD and GET_FIRST. The queue will be passed to the procedures as a parameter called QUEUE. QUEUE.FIRST will designate the first element in the queue; QUEUE.LAST will designate the last element in the queue.

The empty queue will be indicated by setting the access object FIRST equal to **null**. When the queue is empty, the value of LAST is irrelevant. *empty queue*

The final implementation of our queue along with operations on the queue are given in Figure 17.23. Notice that the procedure GET_FIRST works correctly even when removing the last element, because we have set the access object component of the last node in our linked list equal to **null**. So the assignment

```
QUEUE.FIRST := QUEUE.FIRST.NEXT;
```

sets FIRST equal to **null** when FIRST is designating the only, and hence the last, node in a list with only one node.

```
generic
    type ELEMENT_TYPE is private;
package QUEUE_PACKAGE is
    type QUEUE_TYPE is private;
    procedure ADD ( NEW_ENTRY : in ELEMENT_TYPE;
                    QUEUE : in out QUEUE_TYPE );
    procedure GET_FIRST ( RECEIVER : out ELEMENT_TYPE;
                          QUEUE : in out QUEUE_TYPE );
    function EMPTY ( QUEUE : QUEUE_TYPE ) return BOOLEAN;
private
    type NODE;
    type NODE_POINTER is access NODE;
    type NODE is record
                     ELEMENT : ELEMENT_TYPE;
                     NEXT : NODE_POINTER;
                 end record;
    type QUEUE_TYPE is record
                           FIRST : NODE_POINTER;
                           LAST  : NODE_POINTER;
                       end record;
end QUEUE_PACKAGE;

with UNCHECKED_DEALLOCATION;
package body QUEUE_PACKAGE is
    procedure FREE is new UNCHECKED_DEALLOCATION ( NODE,
                                                   NODE_POINTER );
    procedure ADD ( NEW_ENTRY : in ELEMENT_TYPE;
                    QUEUE : in out QUEUE_TYPE ) is
    begin -- Add
        if EMPTY ( QUEUE ) then
            QUEUE.FIRST := new NODE;
            QUEUE.LAST  := QUEUE.FIRST;
        else
            QUEUE.LAST.NEXT := new NODE;
            QUEUE.LAST := QUEUE.LAST.NEXT;
        end if;
        QUEUE.LAST.all := ( NEW_ENTRY, null );
    end ADD;
    procedure GET_FIRST ( RECEIVER : out ELEMENT_TYPE;
                          QUEUE : in out QUEUE_TYPE ) is
        TEMPORARY : NODE_POINTER := QUEUE.FIRST;
    begin -- Get_First
        RECEIVER := QUEUE.FIRST.ELEMENT;
        QUEUE.FIRST := QUEUE.FIRST.NEXT;
        TEMPORARY.NEXT := null;
        FREE ( TEMPORARY );
    end GET_FIRST;
```

```
    function EMPTY ( QUEUE : QUEUE_TYPE ) return BOOLEAN is
    begin -- Empty
        return QUEUE.FIRST = null;
    end EMPTY;
end QUEUE_PACKAGE;
```

Figure 17.23 A generic queue package.

Doubly Linked Lists—A Variation on Simple Linked Lists

A *doubly linked list* is like a simple linked list, except that a doubly linked list includes access objects that designate a backward direction as well as a forward direction. Figure 17.24 is a diagram for the general structure of a doubly linked list.

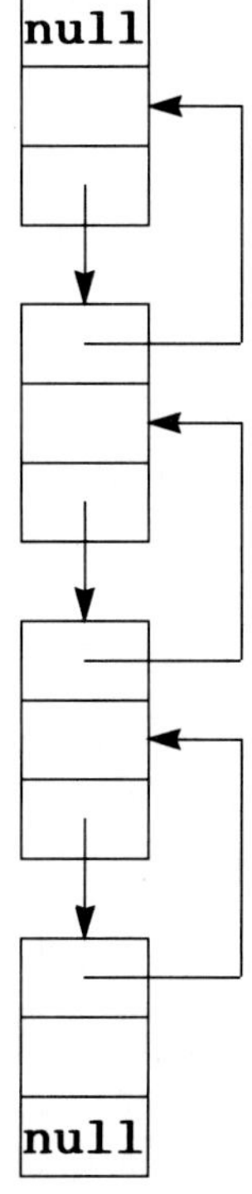

Figure 17.24 A doubly linked list.

Doubly linked lists illustrate the point that a node may contain more than one access object. Doubly linked lists are handled very much like ordinary linked lists, except they allow the program to move along the list in either direction. This can sometimes be useful. Our handling of linked lists would have been easier if they were doubly linked; we usually would not need trailer designaters such as the access object BEFORE in Figure 17.14. Doubly linked lists do, however, require more storage than ordinary linked lists because of the extra access object in each node.

The following is a possible set of type declarations for a doubly linked list:

```
subtype STYLE_RANGE is INTEGER range 1 . . 8;
type INFORMATION is record
                              NUMBER : INTEGER;
                              PRICE  : FLOAT;
                              STYLE  : STYLE_RANGE;
                          end record;
type NODE;
type LINK is access NODE;
type NODE is record
                  BACKWARD : LINK;
                  DATA : INFORMATION;
                  FORWARD : LINK;
              end record;
```

Notice that in the preceding type declarations, nodes have three components, one of which is itself a record. A node can be almost any sort of record. A hierarchical arrangement, such as that shown above, is often convenient.

Implementation
(Optional)

To program in a high-level language such as Ada, you do not need to know how the language is implemented, any more than you need to understand the workings of the human larynx or the human brain to use the English language. Ada programs are implemented as the machine code produced by the Ada compiler, and all you need to know is that the machine code makes the input and output behave as we have described for the language Ada. Still it is sometimes helpful, and invariably interesting, to know some details of the implementation. This is particularly true of access objects and dynamic objects. Since the description of their implementation is very much more concrete than the high-level description of Ada access objects, many people find it easier to understand access objects in terms of their implementation. Additionally it gives you a good idea of how the notion of access objects can be implemented in other programming languages, including many high-level programming languages that do not have access objects as a basic predefined construction.

To describe a typical implementation for Ada access objects and dynamic objects, we need to recall our discussion of the internal structure of computers. Recall that a computer's main memory consists of a very long sequence of numbered memory locations, and each memory location can hold one string of binary digits, which we can interpret as a data value of some simple type such as an integer or a character. The locations are frequently called *words,* and the number of a location is frequently called its *address.* As this discussion indicates, a computer memory is structured much like a very large one-dimensional array.

address

To be concrete, let us say we want to implement a linked list of the type shown in Figure 17.12(a). Each node will contain an integer component and a component of type CHARACTER in addition to the one access object component. One way to do this is to allocate three adjacent memory locations for each dynamic variable that is to serve as a node in the linked list. One of the three locations will hold the integer in the node, one will hold the character, and the third location will hold some integer that can be interpreted as a designater to a node.

What can be interpreted as a designater to one of these dynamic variables? These dynamic variables are implemented as three adjacent memory locations. Hence, one way to name one of these dynamic variables is to name the three addresses of these locations. That is exactly what we will do; however, we will use only the first address since the other two are trivial to compute from the first one. In our implementation a dynamic variable of the type under discussion is just three adjacent memory locations: the first two hold the integer and character values and the third holds the access object. In this implementation the access value is realized as the address of the first of the three memory locations that represent the dynamic variable that is designated.

By way of example, consider Figure 17.25. It shows a possible implementation of the linked list shown in Figure 17.12(a). The **null** access value is indicated by the number -1. We use -1 for **null** because we know there is no location with that address. Any other negative number would do as well. The right-hand figure is an abstraction that ignores the particular address numbers used. Since the particular address numbers used are not important to the realization, that right-hand figure is easier to deal with.

adding nodes

As a program proceeds to add and delete nodes from a linked list, the picture of memory becomes a good deal more intricate. Suppose we wish to add a node containing the integer **110** and the character '**B**' in a position that will keep the nodes in the linked list in numeric order; the result should be as shown in Figure 17.12(c). Figure 17.26 shows the configuration of memory after the dynamic object has been added. Note that the dynamic variable for this node was implemented with the next three available memory locations. In a linked list it is as if the new node were squeezed in. However, in this implementation all the old nodes stay where they are. Only the values of the designater locations change.

deleting nodes

Figure 17.27 shows the implementation of the same linked list after both adding the node containing **110** and '**B**' as just described and then deleting the node containing the **121** and '**C**'.

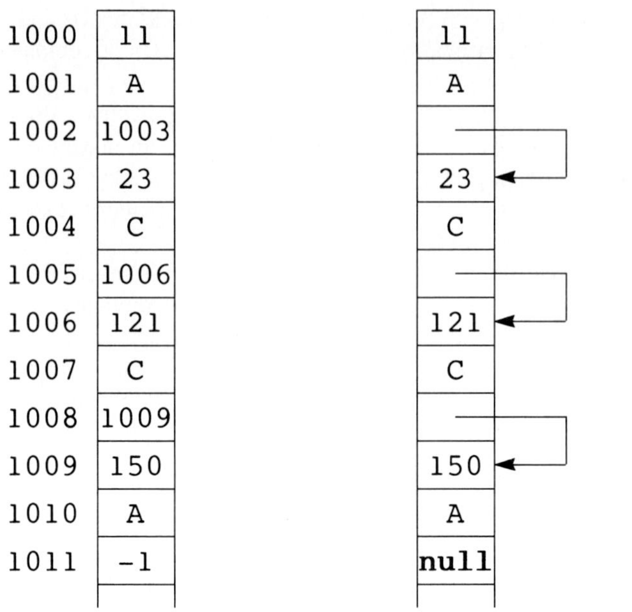

Figure 17.25 Implementation of a linked list.

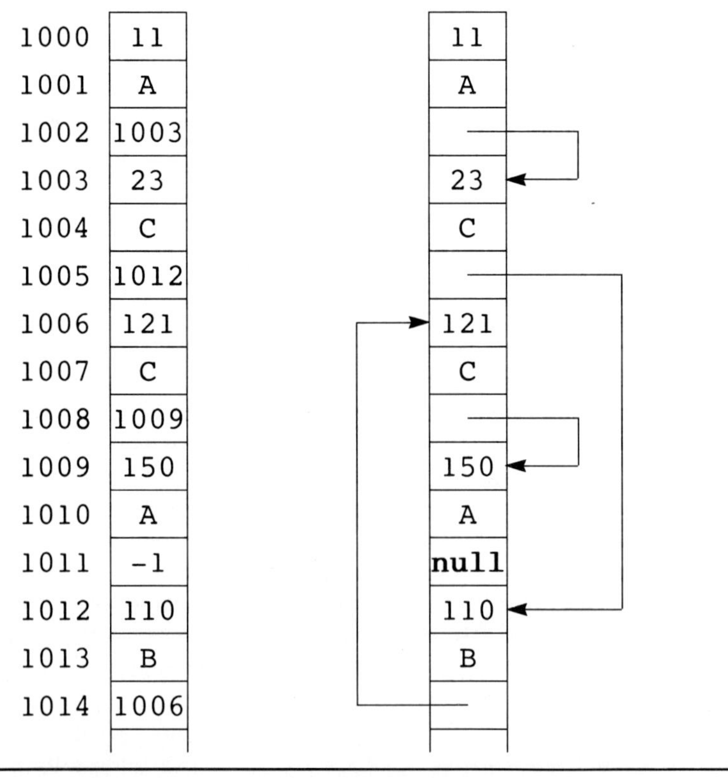

Figure 17.26 Implementation of a linked list with added node.

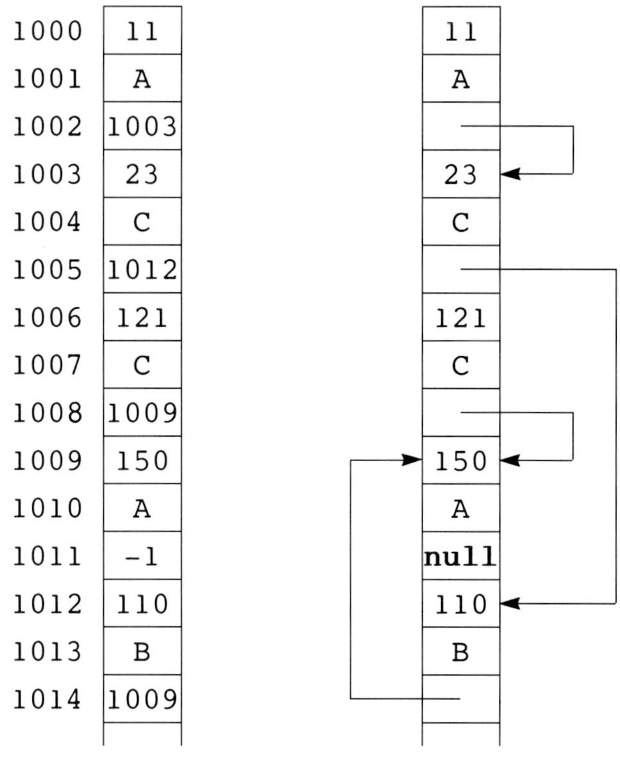

Figure 17.27 Implementation of a linked list with deleted node.

garbage collection

Notice that as we add and delete nodes, the pattern of arrows gets to be rather messy, but that need not concern us. Ordinarily we need not be concerned with the actual memory addresses when we use access objects and dynamic objects. We need only think in terms of an abstraction of the data structure that ignores the actual location of the dynamic objects. If we have enough memory, we can get away with thinking only on an abstract level and so ignore all the details of the particular memory addresses used. Unfortunately there is some danger of wasting memory if we think exclusively on this abstract level. Look again at the memory configuration shown in Figure 17.27. Notice that each dynamic object in locations 1006, 1007, and 1008 still has an integer, a letter, and an access object in it. Yet the node represented by that dynamic object is no longer on the linked list. The program will never be able to use the dynamic object stored in locations 1006 through 1008, and so those memory locations should be made available for other uses. Yet if we continue to add dynamic variables at the bottom of memory, then locations 1006 through 1008 will never be reused. Locations like 1006, 1007, and 1008 are frequently referred to by the technical term *garbage*—not a very dignified word but a descriptive one and the one that is generally used. A perfect implementation would keep track of these garbage memory locations and reuse them. Locating such garbage memory locations so they can be reused is called, appropriately enough, *garbage collection.*

Most implementations of Ada, and most other languages, do not have garbage collection. Any system that does garbage collection must, however, be given some help to do the garbage collection. Specifically, the system must be told which dynamic variables are garbage. This is what UNCHECKED_DEALLOCATION is used for.

The idea of this implementation can be used in high-level languages as well. If Ada did not have access objects as a built-in feature, we could still implement something like access objects by using an array of records in the same way that we used the computer's main memory in the implementation just described.

Trees

binary trees

A useful kind of data structure that is significantly different from the linked list structure is the *binary tree.* A sample binary tree together with possible type declarations for the access objects and nodes of the tree are shown in Figure 17.28. That tree stores names and hours worked for the employees of a small firm. (Any reasonable type definition for CHARACTER_STRING would be acceptable, such as an array of characters or the more complex record type defined in Chapter 12.) To understand why structures such as this are called trees, turn the page upside down. The resulting branching structure should, with a little bit of help from your imagination, look like the branching structure of a tree.

```
subtype CHARACTER_STRING is STRING ( 1 . . 10 );
type NODE;
type BRANCH is access NODE;
type NODE is record
                LEFT   : BRANCH;
                NAME   : CHARACTER_STRING;
                HOURS  : FLOAT;
                RIGHT  : BRANCH;
            end record;
ROOT : BRANCH;
```

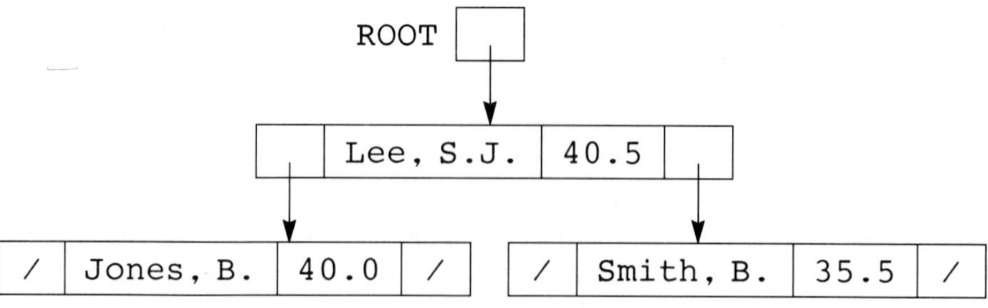

Figure 17.28 A binary tree (/ represents null).

To simplify the notation in our discussion of trees, we will use a simpler node that stores only a single integer plus the two access objects. However, the techniques we develop will apply to other node types as well. The type declarations we will use and a sample tree with nodes of this type are shown in Figure 17.29.

root node

The access objects called ROOT in Figures 17.28 and 17.29 each designate a special node called the *root* node. The name comes from the fact that if you turn the picture upside down, then that node is located where the root of the tree would start. The root node is the only node from which every other node can be reached by following the access objects. It serves a function similar to that of the head node in a linked list.

```
type TREE_NODE;
type TREE_TYPE is access TREE_NODE;
type TREE_NODE is record
                     LEFT  : TREE_TYPE;
                     DATA  : INTEGER;
                     RIGHT : TREE_TYPE;
                  end record;
```

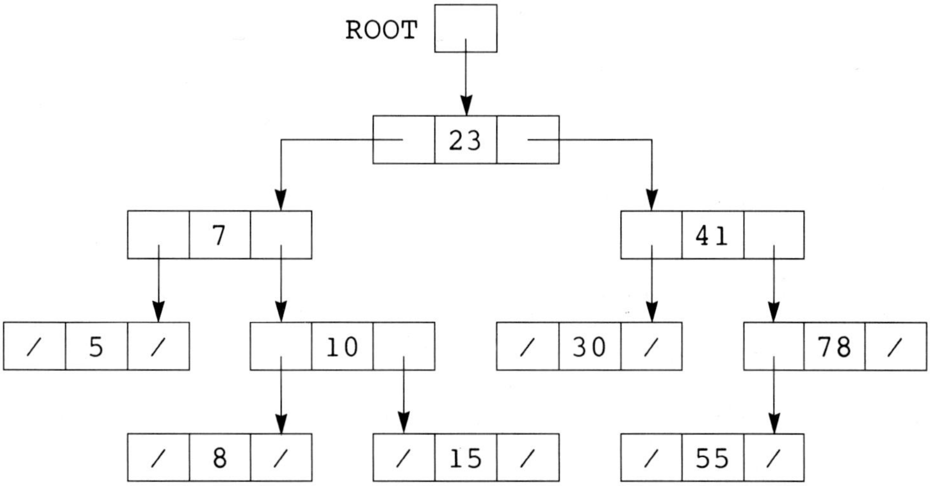

Figure 17.29 A binary tree of the type used in the text examples.

traversing a tree

A program that visits every node of a tree is said to *traverse* the tree. If we want to list the data in a tree, we must design our program to traverse the nodes in some order and write out the contents of each node. Algorithms for traversing a tree are expressed most easily in their recursive form.

recursion on trees

Figure 17.30 will help explain why it is convenient to express tree algorithms recursively. Notice that each arrow emanating from the root node designates a smaller binary tree. In the figure these subtrees are labeled *Left subtree* and *Right subtree*. Hence, algorithms can be stated very neatly in the form "do something to the root and apply the algorithm recursively, once to the left subtree and once to the right subtrees." As an example, the following traversal algorithm is called *inorder traversal*:

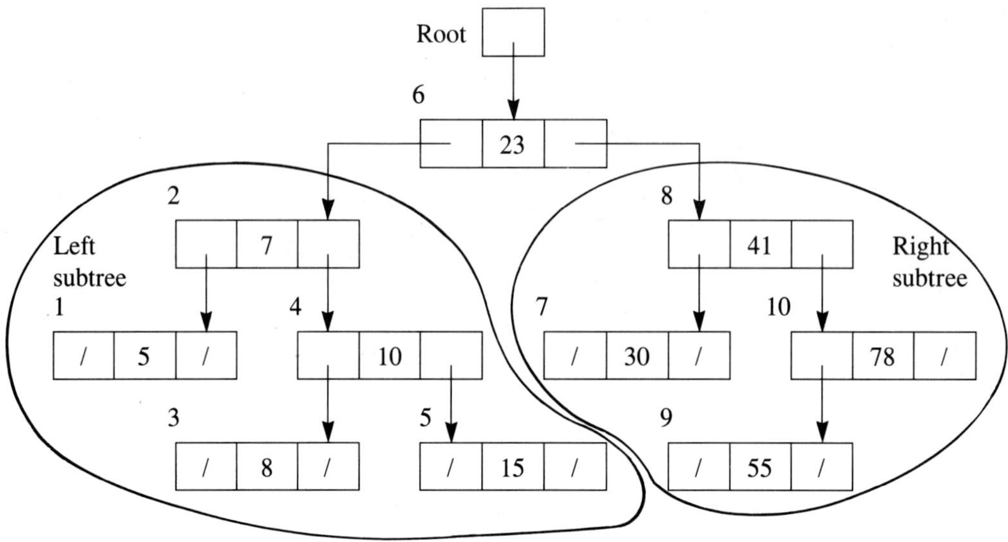

Figure 17.30 Inorder traversal of a tree.

Algorithm

inorder traversal

1. Traverse the left subtree.
2. Visit the root node (for example, to write out its contents).
3. Traverse the right subtree.

empty tree

The above algorithm assumes that the tree is nonempty, and it does not specify what should be done with an empty tree. Yet a recursive search of left and right subtrees will produce smaller and smaller subtrees, until the algorithm is applied recursively to the empty tree, indicated by **null**. At this point the algorithm should stop; to output the empty tree the instruction is ''do nothing.'' Hence, the complete procedure will execute the above algorithm only if the tree is nonempty. If the tree is empty, then after testing for and finding **null**, the algorithm literally does nothing. Figure 17.31 shows the complete algorithm implemented as a procedure.

The numbers outside each node in Figure 17.30 indicate the order in which the nodes are processed by the inorder traversal procedure. Notice that the numbers are output in numeric order. We will come back to discuss this interesting observation shortly.

Two other common methods for traversing a tree are similar and correspond to permuting the three instructions in the recursive algorithm. If the root node is visited first, the algorithm is called *preorder* traversal. If the root is visited last, the algorithm is called *postorder* traversal. However, we will not discuss these alternative algorithms here, except to note that they would traverse the nodes in a different order from the inorder traversal we coded in Figure 17.31.

```
procedure OUTPUT ( ROOT : TREE_TYPE ) is
begin -- Output
    if ROOT = null then
        return;
    else
        OUTPUT ( ROOT.LEFT );
        PUT ( ROOT.DATA ); NEW_LINE;
        OUTPUT ( ROOT.RIGHT );
    end if;
end OUTPUT;
```

Figure 17.31 Procedure for inorder traversal of a tree.

binary search trees

Let us return to our inorder traversal procedure for outputting the node contents and analyze why the nodes are output in numeric order. The reason is that we have stored the numbers in the tree in a special way that can also be expressed recursively as the following *Binary Search Tree Storage Rule:*

- All the numbers that are less than the number in the root node are in the left subtree.
- All the numbers that are greater than the number in the root node are in the right subtree.
- This rule applies recursively to the right and left subtrees.

binary search trees

As long as the numbers are stored in this way and we use the inorder traversal algorithm, then the root node number will always be output after all smaller numbers and before all larger numbers. The root node number thus is output in its correct location. Moreover, this applies to the root nodes of the subtrees and their subtrees and so on, until all nodes are accounted for and seen to be output in their correct position. The name *binary search tree* is not derived from the fact that they can be output in this convenient way, but from another useful property they have; namely, they lend themselves readily to a binary search algorithm similar to the binary search algorithm we described for arrays in Chapter 14. The version for binary trees is given by the function in Figure 17.32. The algorithm in outline form is

Algorithm

```
if root = null then
        the tree is empty and the number is not in the tree
elsif the number is in the root node then
        the number is found
elsif the number sought is < the number in the root node then
        search the left subtree
elsif the number sought is > the number in the root node then
        search the right subtree
```

This same basic method applies to retrieving any ordered data, such as names stored alphabetically, military personnel ordered by rank, and employees ordered by date of employment.

```
function SEARCH ( QUERY : INTEGER;
                  ROOT : TREE_TYPE ) return BOOLEAN is
begin -- Search
    if ROOT = null then
        return FALSE;
    elsif QUERY = ROOT.DATA then
        return TRUE;
    elsif QUERY < ROOT.DATA then
        return SEARCH ( QUERY, ROOT.LEFT );
    else -- query > root.data
        return SEARCH ( QUERY, ROOT.RIGHT );
    end if;
end SEARCH;
```

Figure 17.32 Function that searches a binary tree looking for a node.

The advantage of the binary search algorithm for a tree is the same as it is for the binary search algorithm for an array: It is faster than other methods, such as searching a linked list or serially searching an array. One advantage of using trees rather than arrays is that trees may be of any size and may even change size during program execution, while an array is of a fixed size declared when the program is written.

Case Study

A Binary Search Tree Package

Problem Definition

We wish to design a binary search tree that stores numbers according to the recursive rule we gave in the last section so that we can later use the function SEARCH (Figure 17.32) to search for numbers in the tree. For example, the numbers might be invalid credit card numbers that are read from a file or entered from the keyboard and then placed in a binary tree. For this problem we will assume they are read from a file of integers called DATA_FILE. The function SEARCH can then be used to see if a given credit card is invalid. Since two cancellations of a credit card are the same as one cancellation, we will discard any repetitions and enter each number only once. Our goal can be summarized as follows:

Postcondition: Root is designating the root node of a tree that contains all the numbers in the file DATA_FILE, contains no repetitions of numbers, and satisfies the Binary Search Tree Storage Rule.

Discussion

Searching a binary search tree is easy. Building one for a given collection of data is slightly more complicated but not too difficult. The idea of the algorithm is the same as that of the binary search algorithm implemented in Figure 17.32. Given a number to search for, that algorithm either finds the number or else it finds a **null** access value at the point where it expects to find a node that contains the number. Hence, if we already have a binary search tree and want to add a number, we can apply the same algorithm but end it slightly differently. If the number is found, the algorithm does nothing since the number is already in the tree. If the number is not found, the algorithm replaces the **null** access value by an access object that designates a new node containing the number. The algorithm follows this paragraph. To build a binary tree from a list of numbers, this algorithm can be used to add one node at a time, starting with the empty tree.

Algorithm

inserting a node

Input: An access object ROOT and a NUMBER to be inserted

```
if ROOT is null then
        insert a new node containing NUMBER
elsif NUMBER is in the node designated by ROOT then
        NUMBER is already in the tree and so do nothing
elsif NUMBER is < the number in the node designated by ROOT then
        insert NUMBER in the left subtree by a recursive call
elsif NUMBER is > the number in the node designated by ROOT then
        insert NUMBER in the right subtree by a recursive call
```

An Ada procedure for building a binary search tree from a file of numbers is given in Figure 17.35. That procedure includes a call to the recursive procedure INSERT, which implements the above algorithm. The procedure INSERT, shown in Figure 17.33, along with the previously developed SEARCH (Figure 17.32) and OUTPUT (Figure 17.31), are encapsulated in a package called TREE_PACKAGE. The specification for the TREE_PACKAGE is shown in Figure 17.34.

TREE_PACKAGE is another example of an ADT. The data type is an abstraction for a tree structure. The detailed description of TREE_TYPE is hidden from the user program in the private section of the package specification. The package specification lists the operations that can be made on this data abstraction of a tree. The package encapsulates the ADT, and the package body hides the implementation of the operations.

The purpose of all of this hiding of information is not that it is some deep, dark secret that needs protecting. Rather, its purpose is two fold. First, it relieves the user from the sometimes messy detail of access value manipulation. Second, it protects the integrity of the tree structure itself from any unintentional, inadvertent access value manipulation. It does not ensure that the tree will always be built properly (the package has no control over the order in which thing are inserted into the tree). It does ensure that, no matter which operations are used or in what order they are used, the structure will always be a tree structure and there will be no unattended lost dynamic objects.

```
procedure INSERT ( VALUE : in INTEGER;
                   ROOT : in out TREE_TYPE ) is
begin -- Insert
    if ROOT = null then
        ROOT := new TREE_NODE'( null, VALUE, null );
    elsif VALUE < ROOT.DATA then
        INSERT ( VALUE, ROOT.LEFT );
    elsif VALUE > ROOT.DATA then
        INSERT ( VALUE, ROOT.RIGHT );
--  Else value = root.data
--      Do nothing, the value is already in the tree
    end if;
end INSERT;
```

Figure 17.33 Procedure to insert into a binary search tree.

```
package TREE_PACKAGE is
    type TREE_TYPE is private;
    procedure INSERT ( VALUE : in INTEGER;
                       ROOT : in out TREE_TYPE );
    function SEARCH ( QUERY : INTEGER;
                      ROOT : TREE_TYPE ) return BOOLEAN;
    procedure OUTPUT ( ROOT : TREE_TYPE );
private
    type TREE_NODE;
    type TREE_TYPE is access TREE_NODE;
    type TREE_NODE is record
                          LEFT  : TREE_TYPE;
                          DATA  : INTEGER;
                          RIGHT : TREE_TYPE;
                      end record;
end TREE_PACKAGE;
```

Figure 17.34 Specification for Tree_Package.

```
with TEXT_IO;
use TEXT_IO;
with TREE_PACKAGE;
use TREE_PACKAGE;
procedure TREE_EXAMPLE is
    DATA_FILE : FILE_TYPE;
    FILENAME : STRING( 1 . . 80 );
    LAST : NATURAL;
    ROOT : TREE_TYPE;
    procedure TREE_BUILD  ( DATA_FILE : in FILE_TYPE;
                            ROOT : in out TREE_TYPE ) is
        NEXT : INTEGER;
        package NUMBER_IO is new INTEGER_IO ( INTEGER );
        use NUMBER_IO;
    begin -- Tree_Build
        loop
            exit when END_OF_FILE ( DATA_FILE );
            GET ( DATA_FILE, NEXT );
            SKIP_LINE ( DATA_FILE );
            INSERT ( NEXT, ROOT );
        end loop;
    end TREE_BUILD;
begin -- Tree_Example
    PUT_LINE ( "Enter the file name:" );
    GET_LINE ( FILENAME, LAST );
    OPEN ( DATA_FILE, IN_FILE, FILENAME( 1 . . LAST ) );
    TREE_BUILD ( DATA_FILE, ROOT );
    CLOSE ( DATA_FILE );
    OUTPUT ( ROOT );
end TREE_EXAMPLE;
```

Figure 17.35 Procedure to build a binary search tree.

empty tree

The empty tree is represented by setting ROOT equal to **null**, so the first clause of the algorithm serves to start things off. However, it applies more often as the result of a recursive call, when the search finds its way down to a **null** that marks an empty position in which to insert the node. Some people find the algorithm more intuitive if the clauses are read backwards. This is fine for intuition but in fact is not correct since, if the designater is **null**, it makes no sense to talk of left and right subtrees.

balanced trees

The tree-building procedure in Figure 17.35 will always produce a binary search tree, and if the list of numbers is in random order, then it may produce a balanced tree. A *balanced tree* is one in which all paths from the root node to the ends (the **null**s) are of the same or almost the same length. To get all the speed advantage of the binary search algorithm, the tree must be balanced, or almost balanced. If the data arrives in an unfortunate sequence, then the tree will not be balanced and the search will be slower. Techniques for making the tree balanced are quite complicated and are discussed in the references at the end of this chapter. In any event, the only issue is efficiency. The algorithm works for any sequence of integers.

Summary of Problem Solving and Programming Techniques

- Access objects provide a means for designing a wide variety of dynamic data structures, such as linked lists, stacks, and trees.
- As one check to see that you have an access expression correct, check the type to see if it is an access type or a node type.
- The advantages of a linked list over an array are that the linked list can grow and shrink and it is easy to insert or delete a value (node) in the middle of a linked list.
- A node (dynamic object) can only be referenced by naming an access object that designates the node. Unless a named access object designates some key node(s) of a structure, the nodes in that structure can be lost to the program because the program has no way to refer to the nodes.
- The literal **null** is used to mark end points, such as the end of a linked list, and to denote empty structures, such as an empty linked list or empty tree.
- Remember that **null** is an access value and not a node.
- Always check to see whether procedures to manipulate dynamic data structures, such as linked lists and trees, work correctly for the empty structure. Recursive procedures often terminate only when a series of recursive calls leads to an empty structure.
- Binary search trees can be used to store ordered data for rapid retrieval. Like a linked list, a binary search tree can grow and shrink in size. A binary search algorithm can be used with a tree, as it can with an array. Hence, in many situations the tree combines the advantages of both arrays and linked lists.
- Research on trees in particular and dynamic data structures in general has produced a large number of nonobvious techniques for building and maintaining dynamic data structures. The references at the end of this chapter include much more material on the subject.

Summary of Ada Constructs

access types

Syntax:

```
type access_type is access domain_type;
```

Example:

```
type NODE;
type ARROW is access NODE;
type NODE is record
                 DATA : INTEGER;
                 LINK : ARROW;
             end record;
POINTER : ARROW;
```

The type for access objects that designate dynamic objects (nodes). In the example the variable POINTER is declared so it can contain an access value to dynamic objects of type NODE.

referencing a dynamic object
Syntax:

access_object.all

Example:

```
POINTER.all
```

One way to reference the dynamic object designated by *access_object.*

referencing parts of a dynamic object
Syntax:

access_object.*component_name*

Example:

```
POINTER.DATA_OBJECT
```

Via this reference, a component in the dynamic object can be inspected or assigned a new value.

new
Syntax:

access_object := new *domain_type*;

or

access_object := new *domain_type*'(*aggregate*);

Example:

```
POINTER := new NODE;
```

or

```
POINTER := new NODE'( 5, null );
```

The first option creates a new dynamic object of the domain type of the *access_object* and leaves the value of the *access_object* designating this new dynamic object. The second option does the same thing as the first option, plus it assigns initial values to the components of the dynamic object.

access variables in assignment statements

Syntax:

access_variable_1 := *access_variable_2*

Example:

```
POINTER_1 := POINTER_2;
```

Makes the value of *access_variable_1* designate the same thing as the value of *access_variable_2*.

null

Syntax:

```
null
```

Predefined literal of a type that is compatible with access objects to any type of dynamic object. **null** does not designate any dynamic variable but is used to give a value to access objects which do not point to any dynamic object.

Exercises

Self-Test Exercises

7. What is the difference between the kind of node used in a binary tree and the kind used in a doubly linked list?

8. Modify the type declaration in Figure 17.34 so that each node of the tree can have one more access object that designates the node above it. The node above is often called the *parent* node, so call the new component PARENT.

Interactive Exercises

9. Using pencil and paper, simulate the procedure OUTPUT (Figure 17.31) on the tree in Figure 17.30.

Programming Exercises

10. Write a procedure that takes as parameters a linked list of integers (literally the parameter will be a pointer to the head of the list) and two integers LOWER_BOUND and UPPER_BOUND such that LOWER_BOUND is less than UPPER_BOUND. The procedure should write to the screen all integers in the list that are between LOWER_BOUND and UPPER_BOUND. The list need not be sorted.

11. Write a procedure that takes a (singly) linked list and reverses the order of the nodes in the linked list. For concreteness, make it a linked list of characters.

12. Redo Exercise 16 in Chapter 16, but this time use linked lists rather than arrays. With linked lists there is no limit to the number of digits in the two numbers being added.

13. Redo Exercise 19 in Chapter 16, but this time use linked lists rather than arrays. With linked lists there is no limit to the number of digits after the decimal point, which gives unlimited accuracy.

14. Write procedures to insert, find, and delete nodes in a doubly linked list. For simplicity, suppose the nodes store integers.

15. A binary tree can be used to classify items according to a series of yes/no questions. Write a program that builds a tree to classify animals according to yes/no questions. The questions are stored in the nodes in the tree, and the answers determine which direction to follow. Each leaf (end) node of the tree contains the name of an animal for which the yes/no answers are correct. For example: ''Is it very big?'' ''Does it eat meat?'' ''Does it have big ears?'' The answers ''yes,'' ''no,'' and ''yes,'' respectively, might lead to the name ''elephant.'' The program first constructs a tree with three levels of questions. It asks the user to input seven yes/no questions about animals. It then uses these seven questions as the questions in the tree. Each series consists of three questions, and there are eight possible sets of yes/no answers leading to animal names. The program displays each of the eight yes/no question sequences along with their answers, and it then asks the user for an appropriate animal to enter. At this point the program offers to guess animals that the user is thinking of. It tells the user to think of an animal and then asks the questions. The user thinks of an animal and answers questions. The program works its way to an end node and then ''guesses'' the animal named in that node.

16. Redo Exercise 15, but this time have the program start with a very small tree with just one question, like ''Is it big?'' and with two animals, like a mouse and an elephant. It then plays the game with the user, but whenever it guesses wrong (for example, if it guesses an elephant and the user says he/she was thinking of a dinosaur) it asks for a new question. For the two animals in this example, it would ask ''Please give me a question that will distinguish between an elephant and a dinosaur.'' The user might give the question ''Is it extinct?'' The program then adds a new node with that question and adds the two animals below that node. In this way the tree gets larger as the game is played.

17. Write a recursive procedure that takes a linked list of integers, already sorted into ascending order, and produces a binary search tree that contains the same integers, stored according to the Binary Search Tree Storage Rule. The tree should be balanced. A tree is balanced if, for each node, the two subtrees led to by its two access object components contain the same number of nodes (plus or minus one node).

18. Write a procedure that takes a binary search tree with integers stored according to the Binary Search Tree Storage Rule and copies them to a second tree that also

satisfies this rule. The second tree should be as close to balanced as possible. The first tree may not have been balanced, so this is a way to obtain a balanced search tree. A tree is balanced if for each node, the two subtrees led to by its two access object components contain the same number of nodes (plus or minus one node).

References for Further Reading

A. V. Aho, J. E. Hopcroft, and J. D. Ullman, *Data Structures and Algorithms* (Reading, MA: Addison-Wesley, 1983). Covers more advanced topics.

R. J. Baron and L. G. Shapiro, *Data Structures and Their Implementation* (New York: van Nostrand Reinhold, 1980).

G. Booch, *Software Components with Ada, Structures, Tools, and Subsystems* (Redwood City, CA: The Benjamin/Cummings Publishing Co., 1987).

P. Helman and R. Veroff, *Intermediate Problem Solving and Data Structures* (Redwood City, CA: The Benjamin/Cummings Publishing Co., 1986).

A. M. Tanenbaum and M. J. Augenstein, *Data Structures Using Pascal,* Second Edition (Englewood Cliffs, NJ: Prentice-Hall, 1986).

M. B. Feldman, *Data Structures with Ada* (Reston, VA: Reston Publishing Co., Inc., 1985).

APPENDIX A
RESERVED WORDS

abort
abs
accept
access
all
and
array
at

begin
body

case
constant

declare
delay
delta
digits
do

else
elsif
end
entry
exception
exit

for
function

generic
goto

if
in
is

limited
loop

mod

new
not
null

of
or
others
out

package
pragma
private
procedure

raise
range
record
rem
renames
return
reverse

select
separate
subtype

task
terminate
then
type

use

when
while
with

xor

APPENDIX B
SYNTAX DIAGRAMS

These syntax diagrams are a collection of those found in the text and are not intended to represent the entire Ada language. For a complete definition of the Ada language, see the LRM.

object__declarations

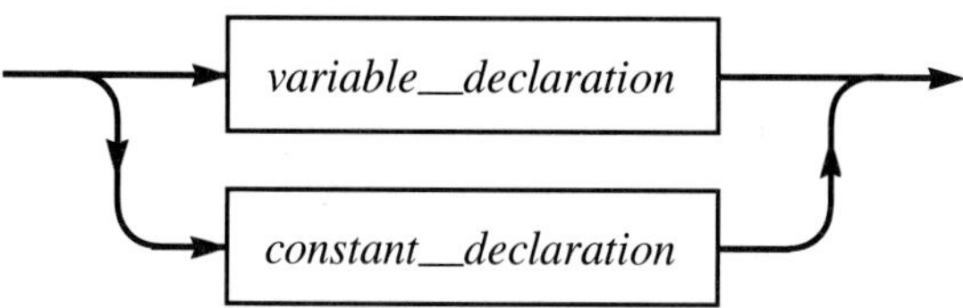

variable declaration

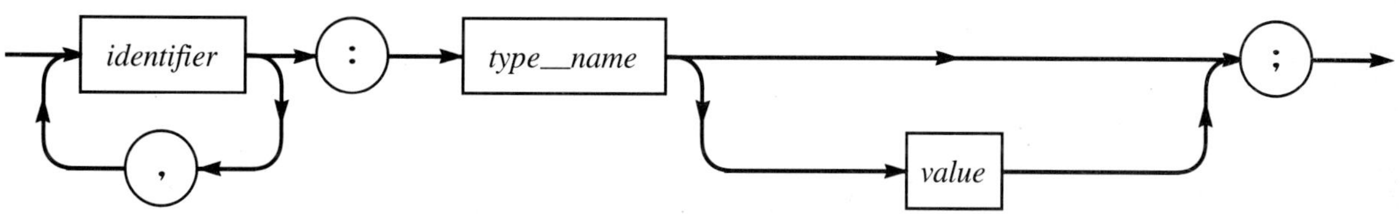

value

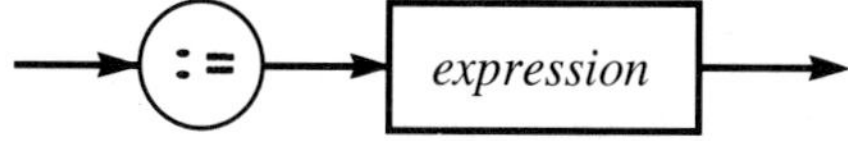

constant__declaration

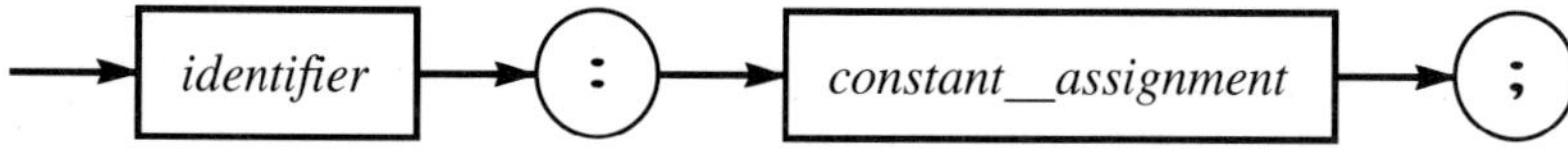

constant__assignment

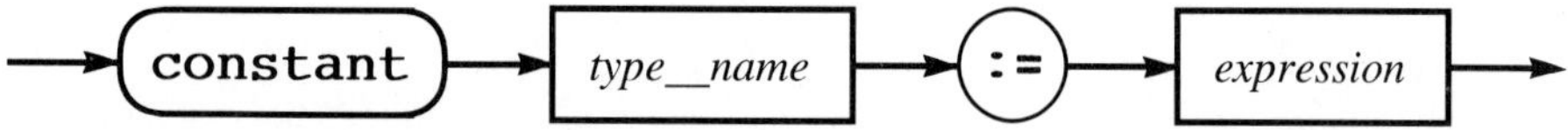

sequence of statements — statements

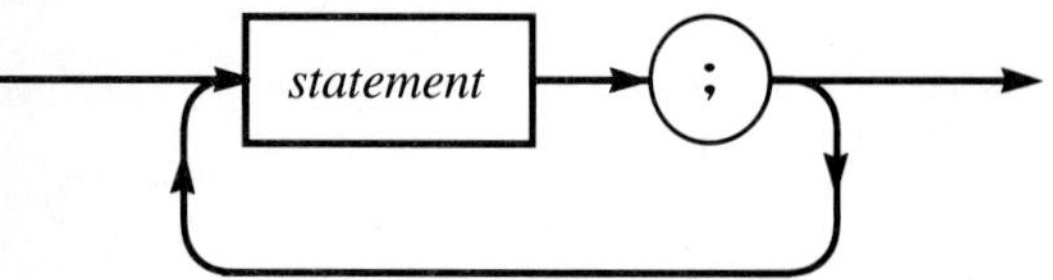

statement

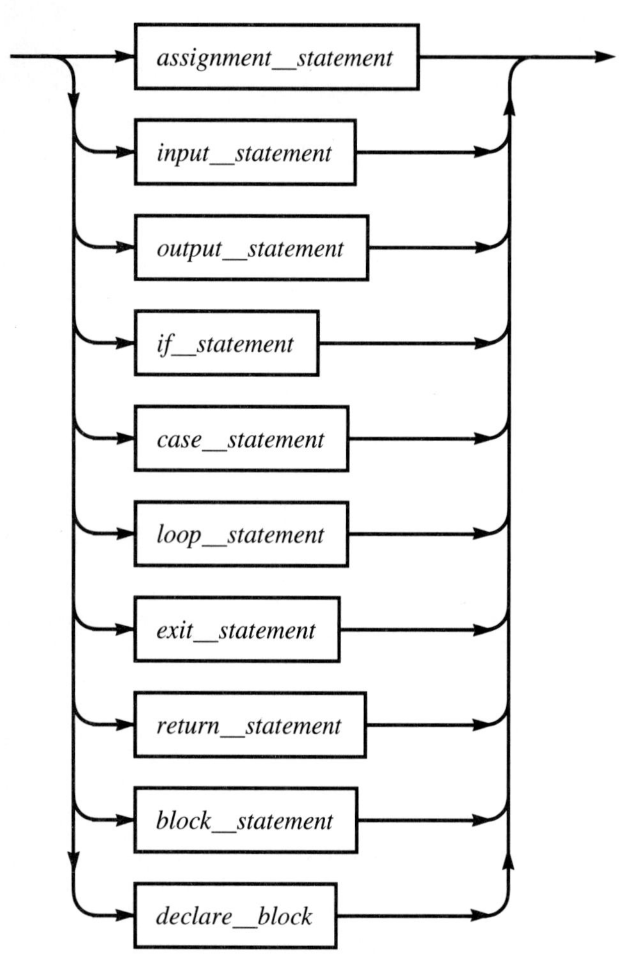

assignment__statement

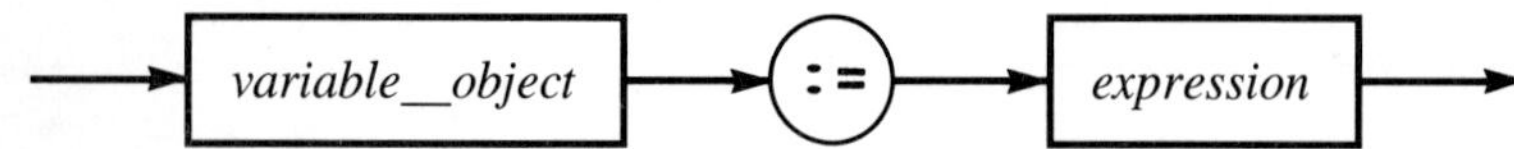

input__statement

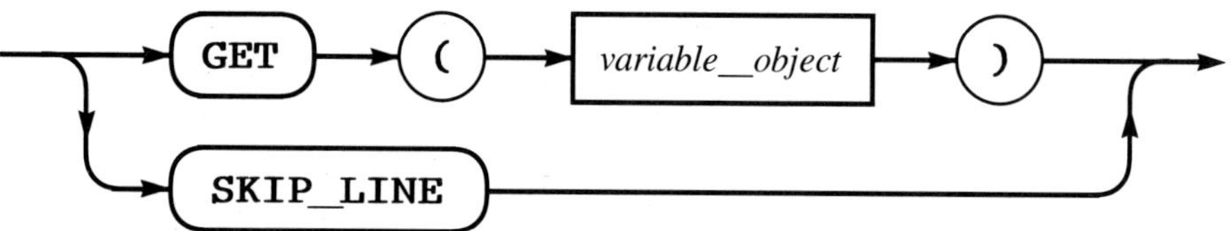

output__statement

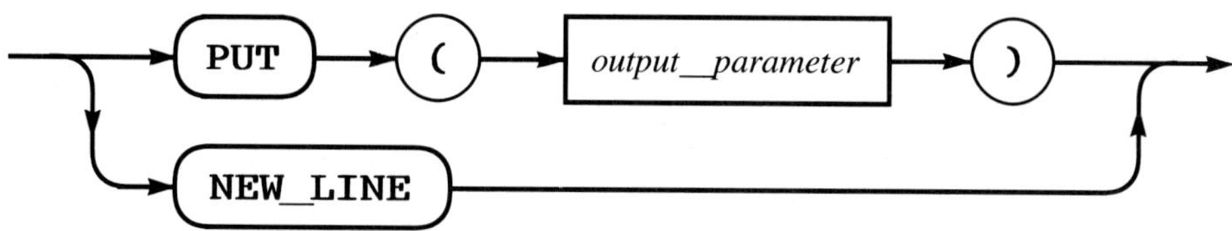

output__parameter

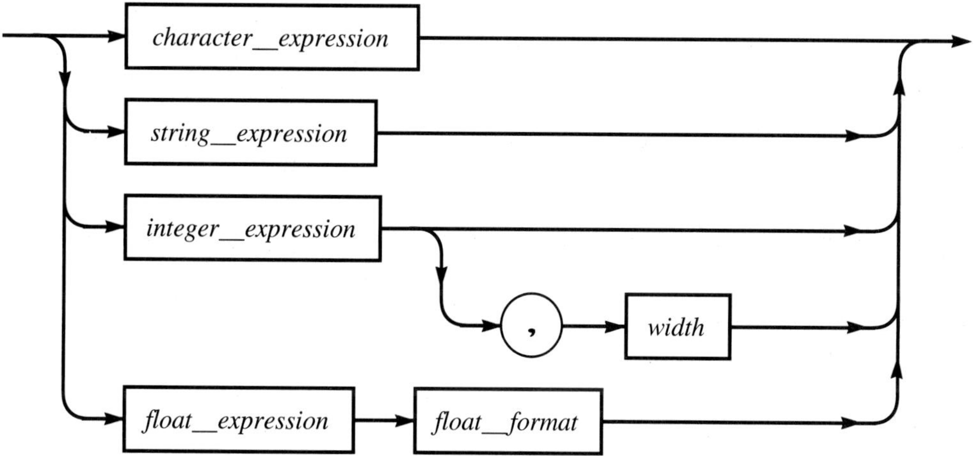

float__format

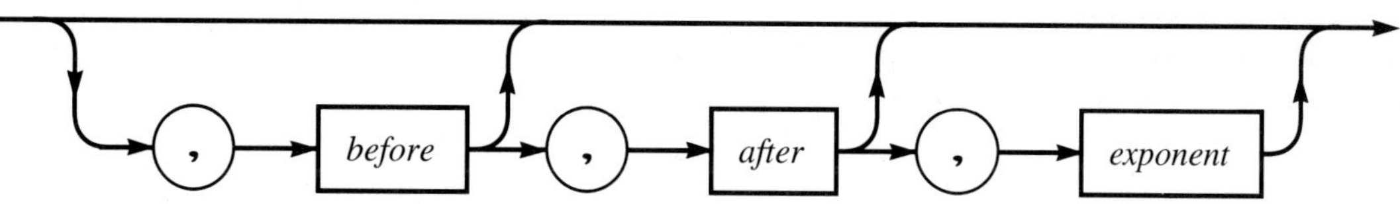

width, before, after, exponent

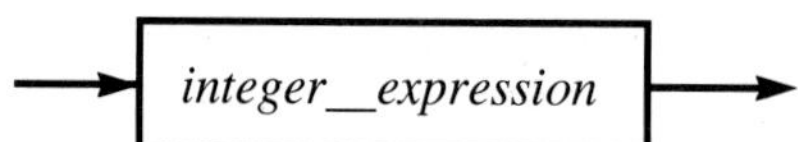

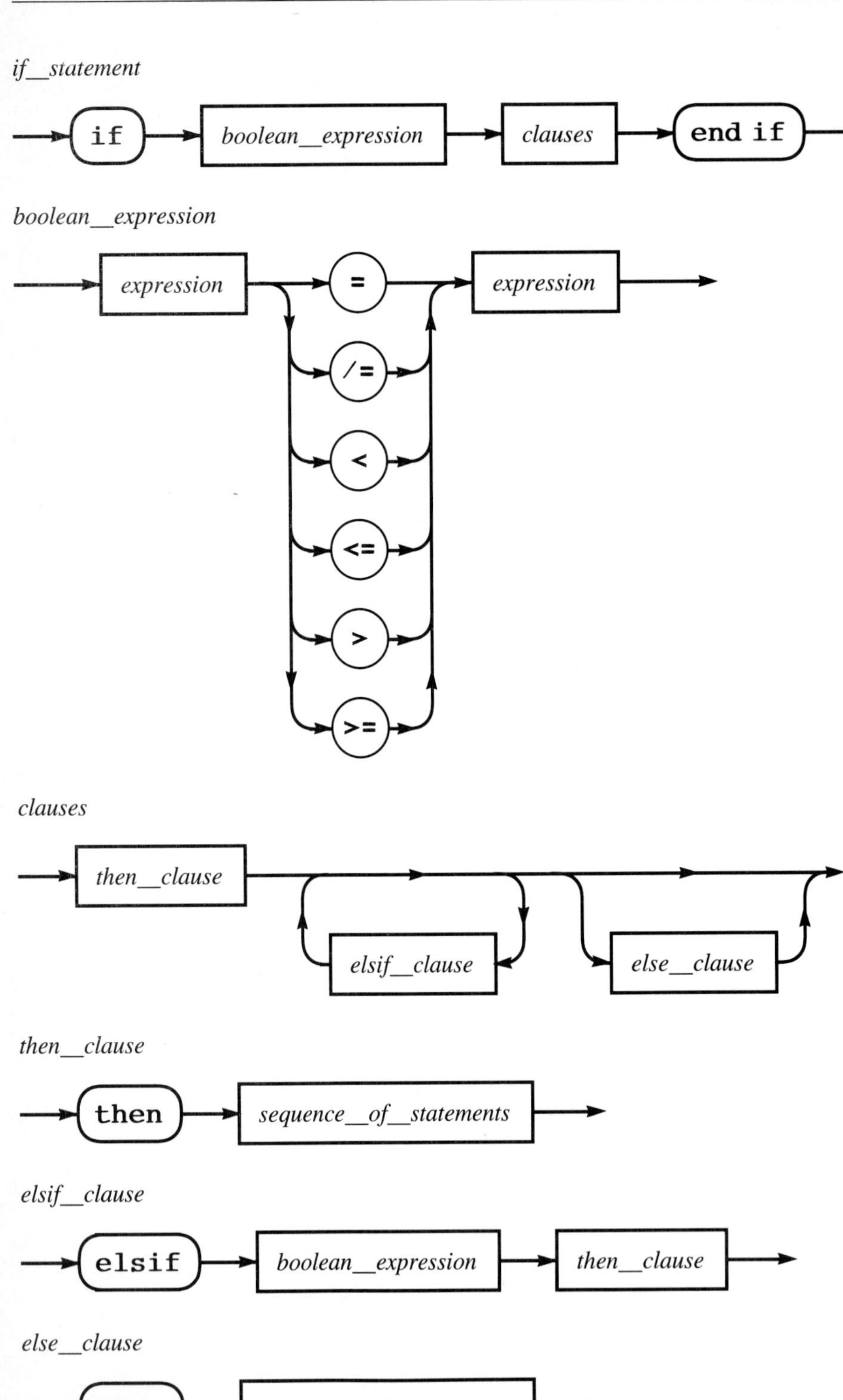
if_statement
if
boolean_expression
clauses
end if
boolean_expression
expression
=
/=
<
<=
>
>=
expression
clauses
then_clause
elsif_clause
else_clause
then_clause
then
sequence_of_statements
elsif_clause
elsif
boolean_expression
then_clause
else_clause
else
sequence_of_statements

procedure__specification

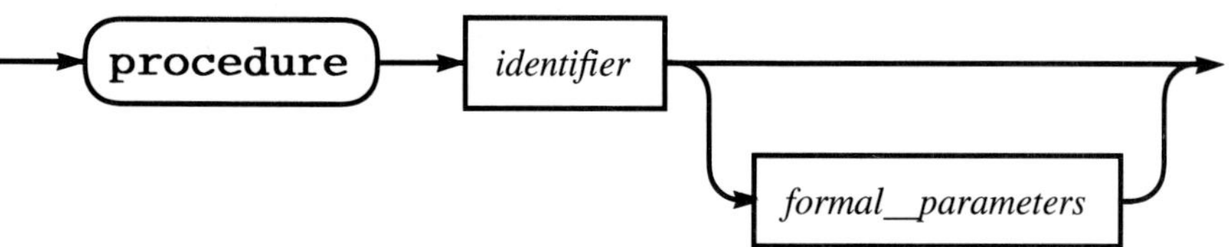

formal__parameters

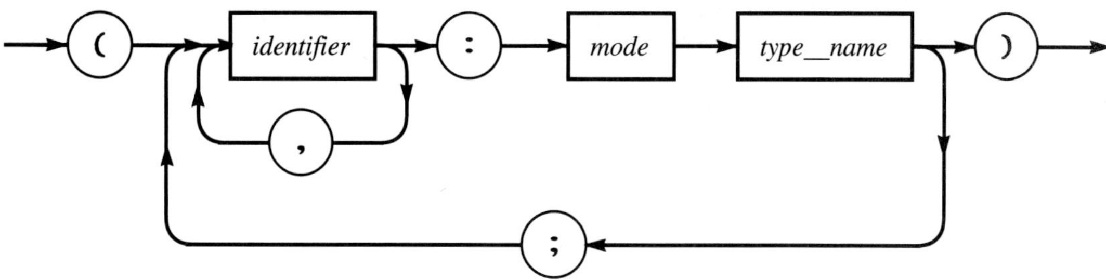

mode

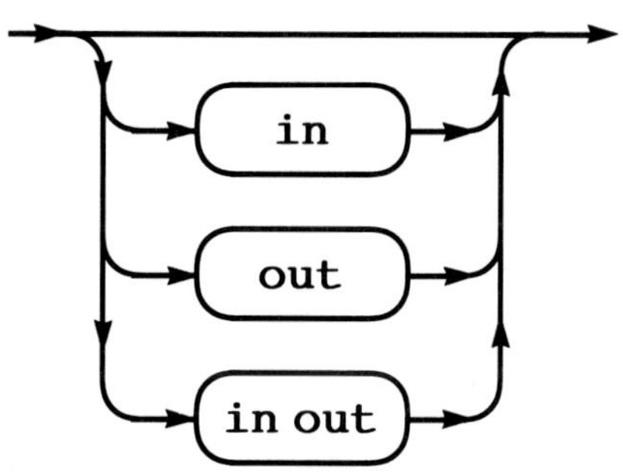

function__specification

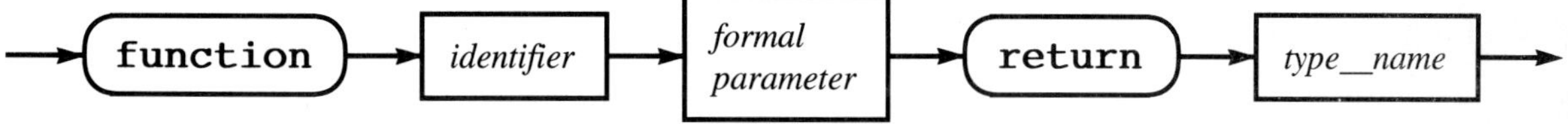

return__statement

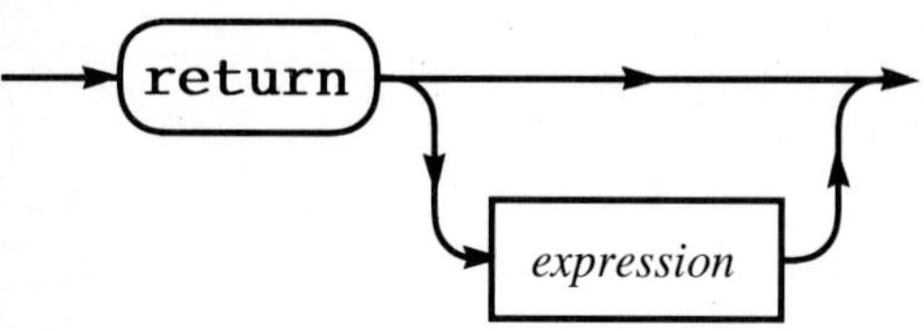

case__statement

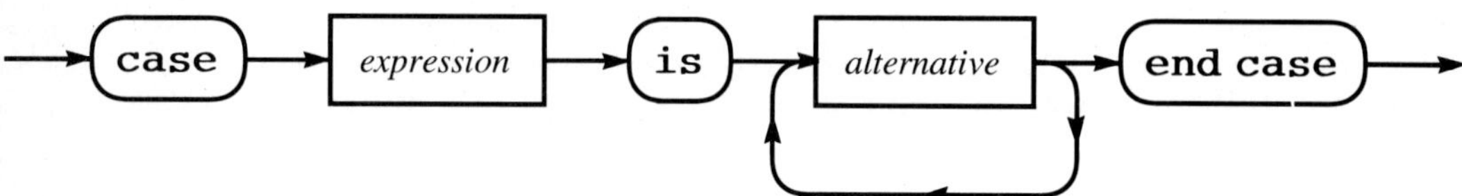

alternative

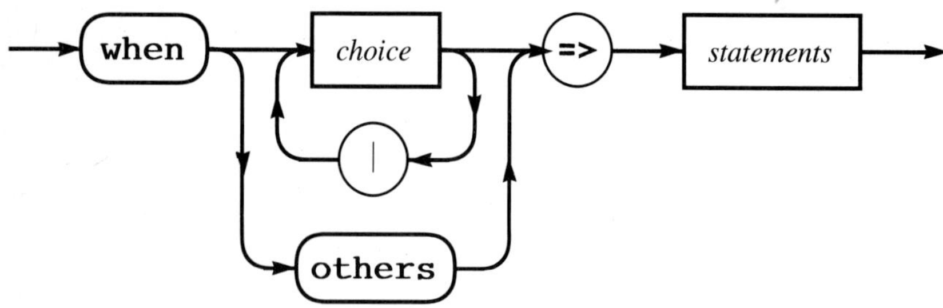

choice

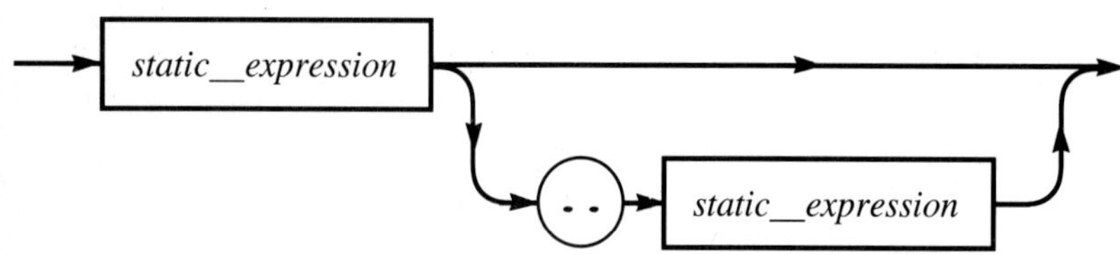

exception__handler

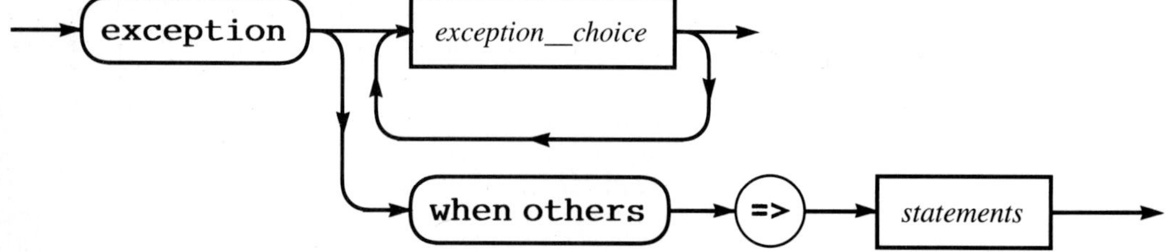

exception__choice

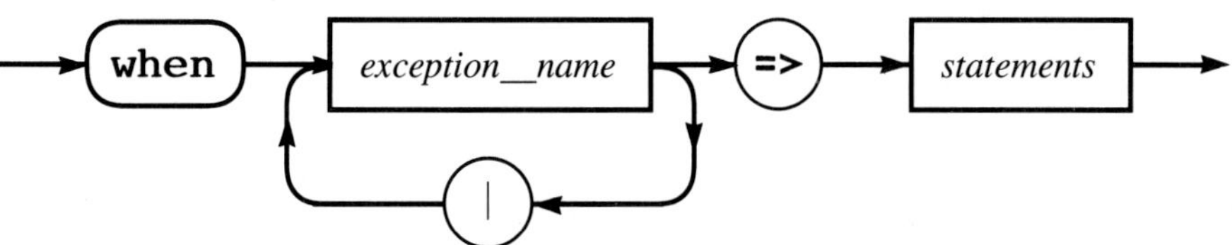

block__statement

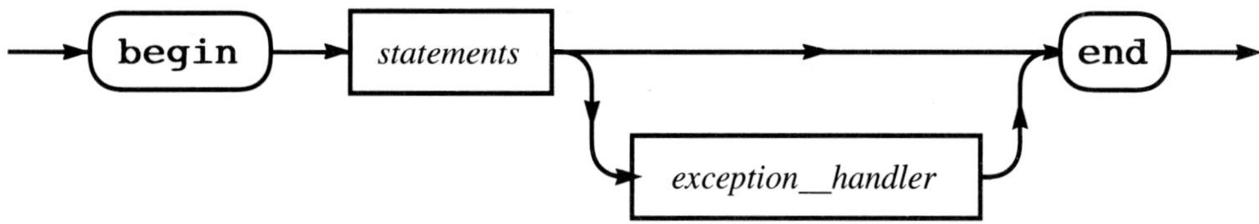

loop__statement

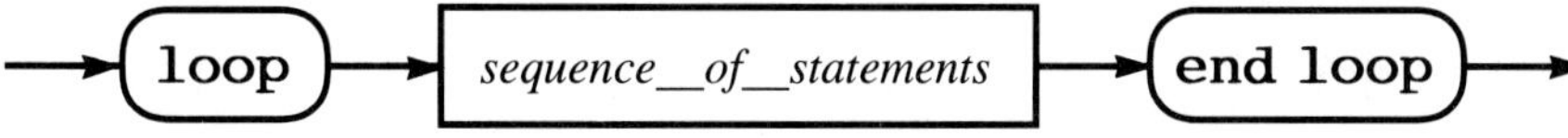

exit__statement

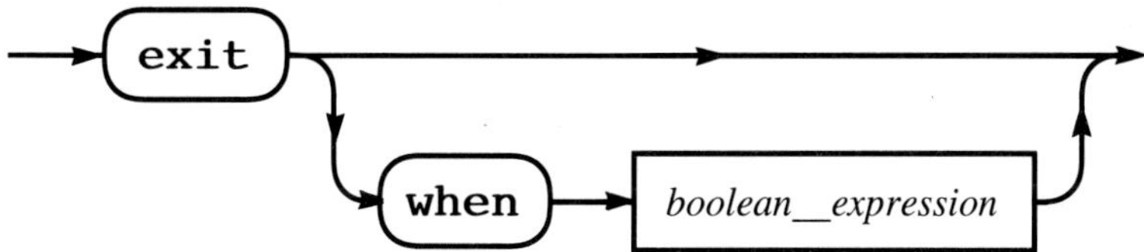

while__prefix

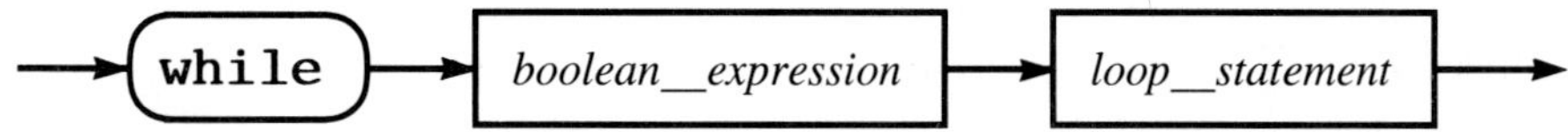

for__prefix

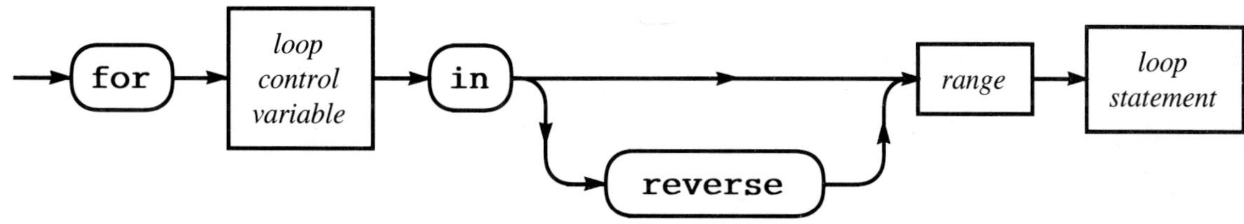

range

type_declaration

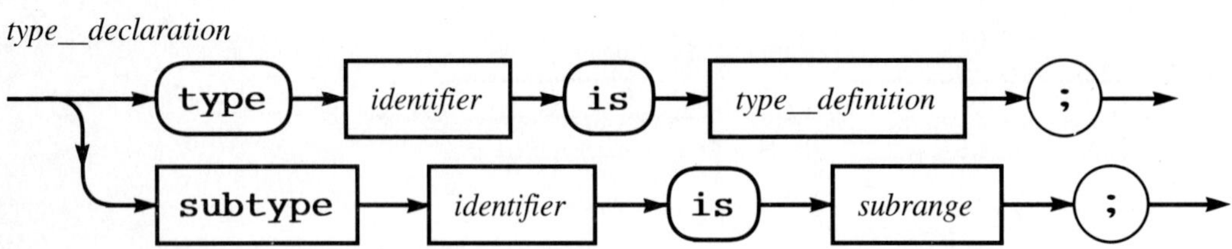

type_definition

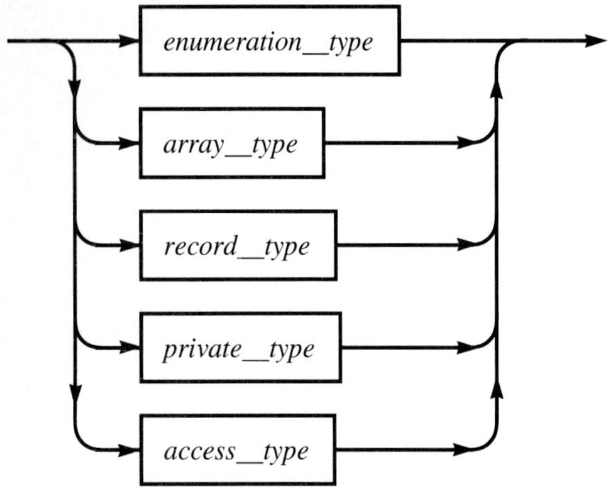

subrange

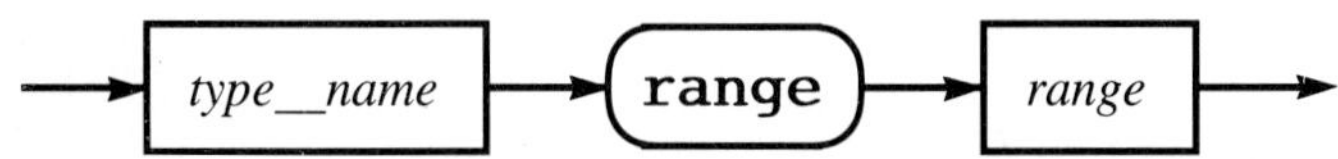

enumeration_type

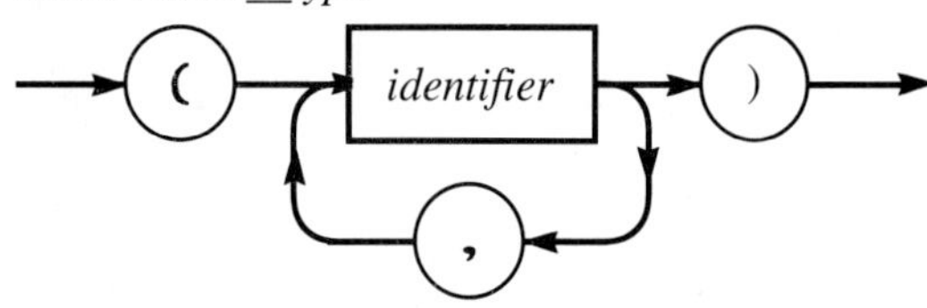

array_type

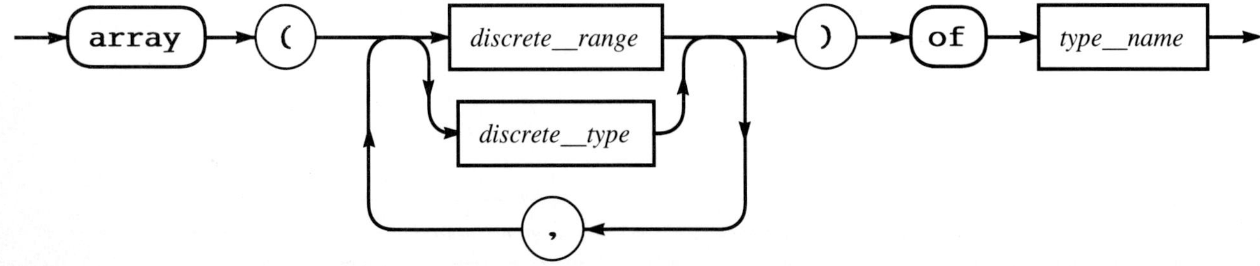

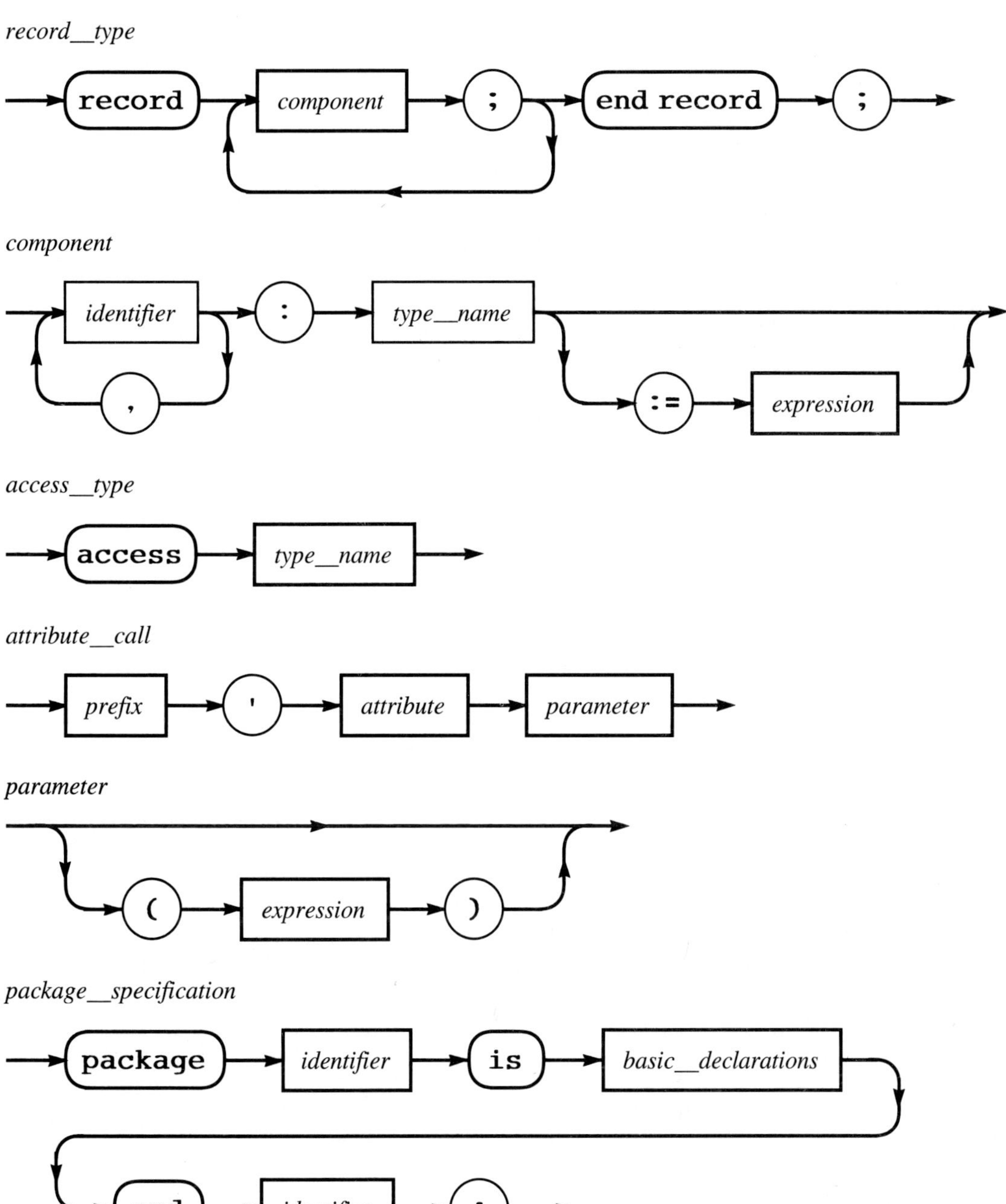
record__type
record
component
;
end record
;
component
identifier
,
:
type__name
:=
expression
access__type
access
type__name
attribute__call
prefix
'
attribute
parameter
parameter
(
expression
)
package__specification
package
identifier
is
basic__declarations
end
identifier
;

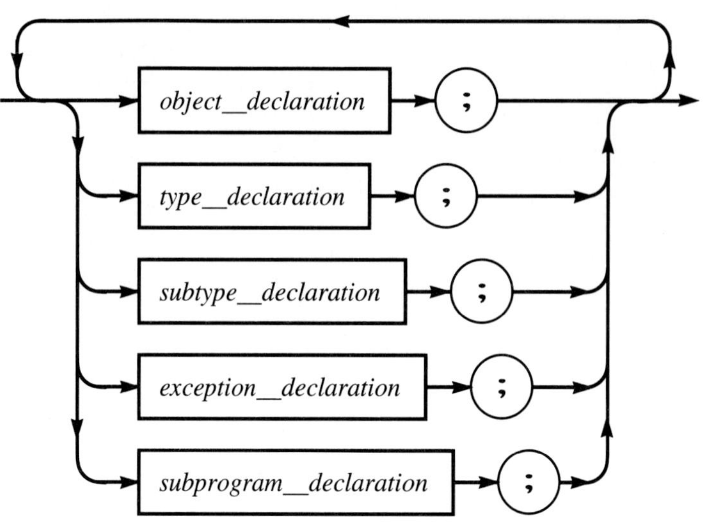

subprogram__specification

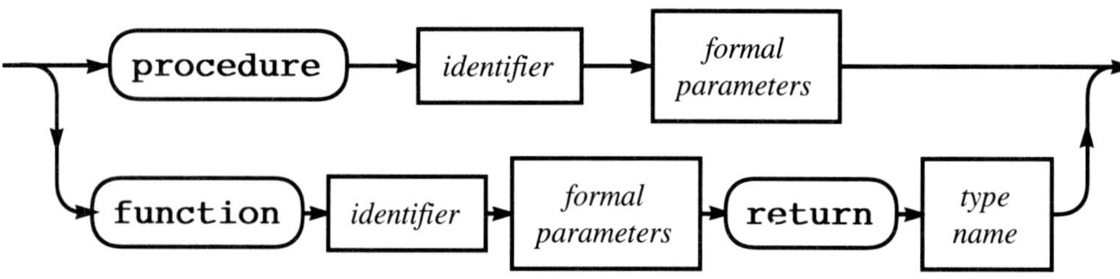

package body

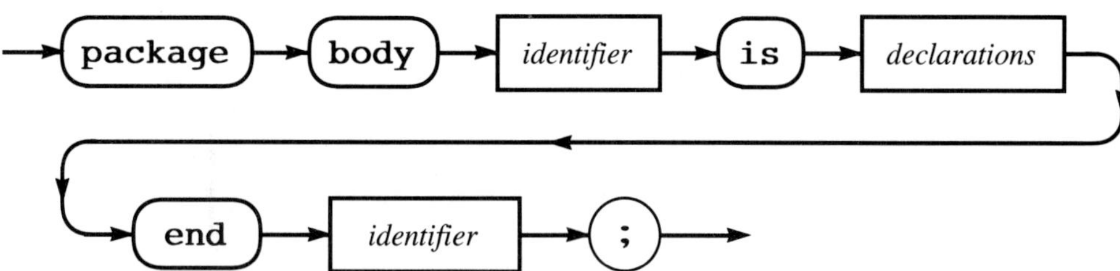

subprogram__body

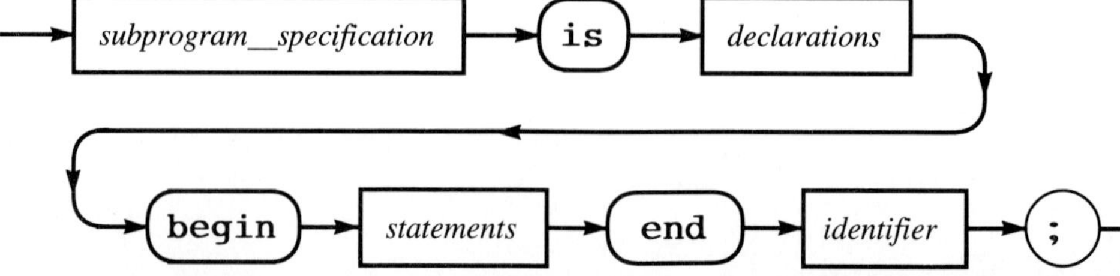

declarations

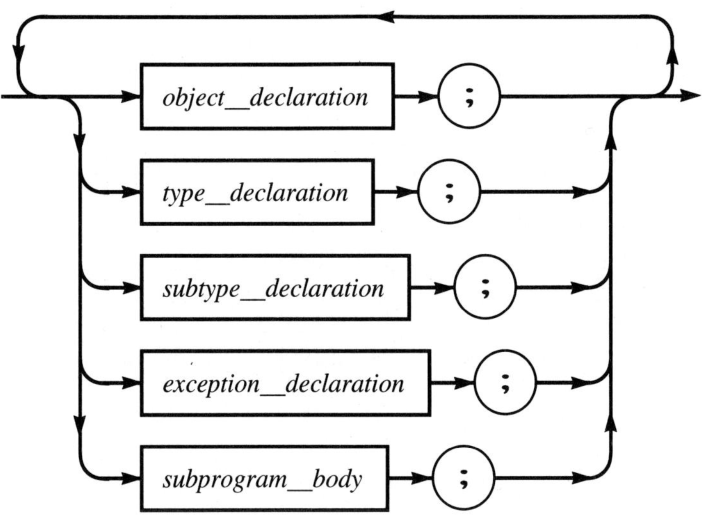

declare__block

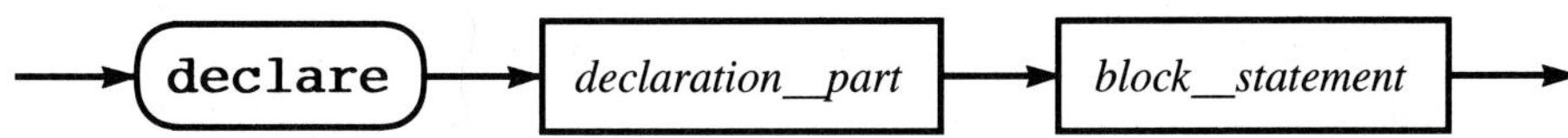

declaration__part

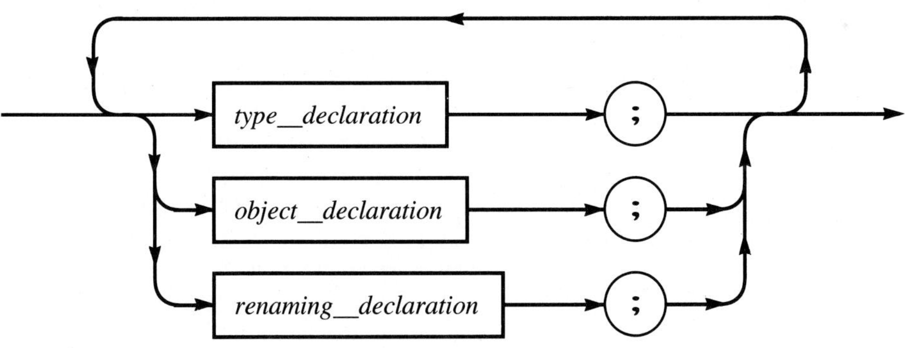

renaming__declaration

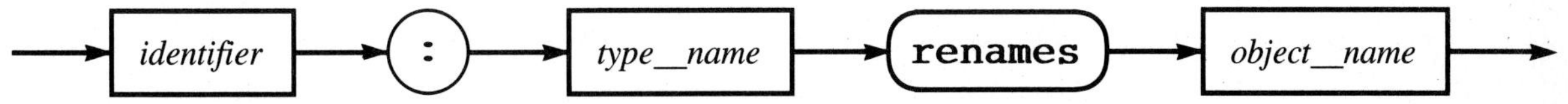

private__type

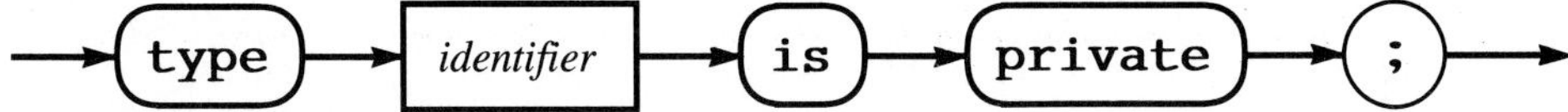

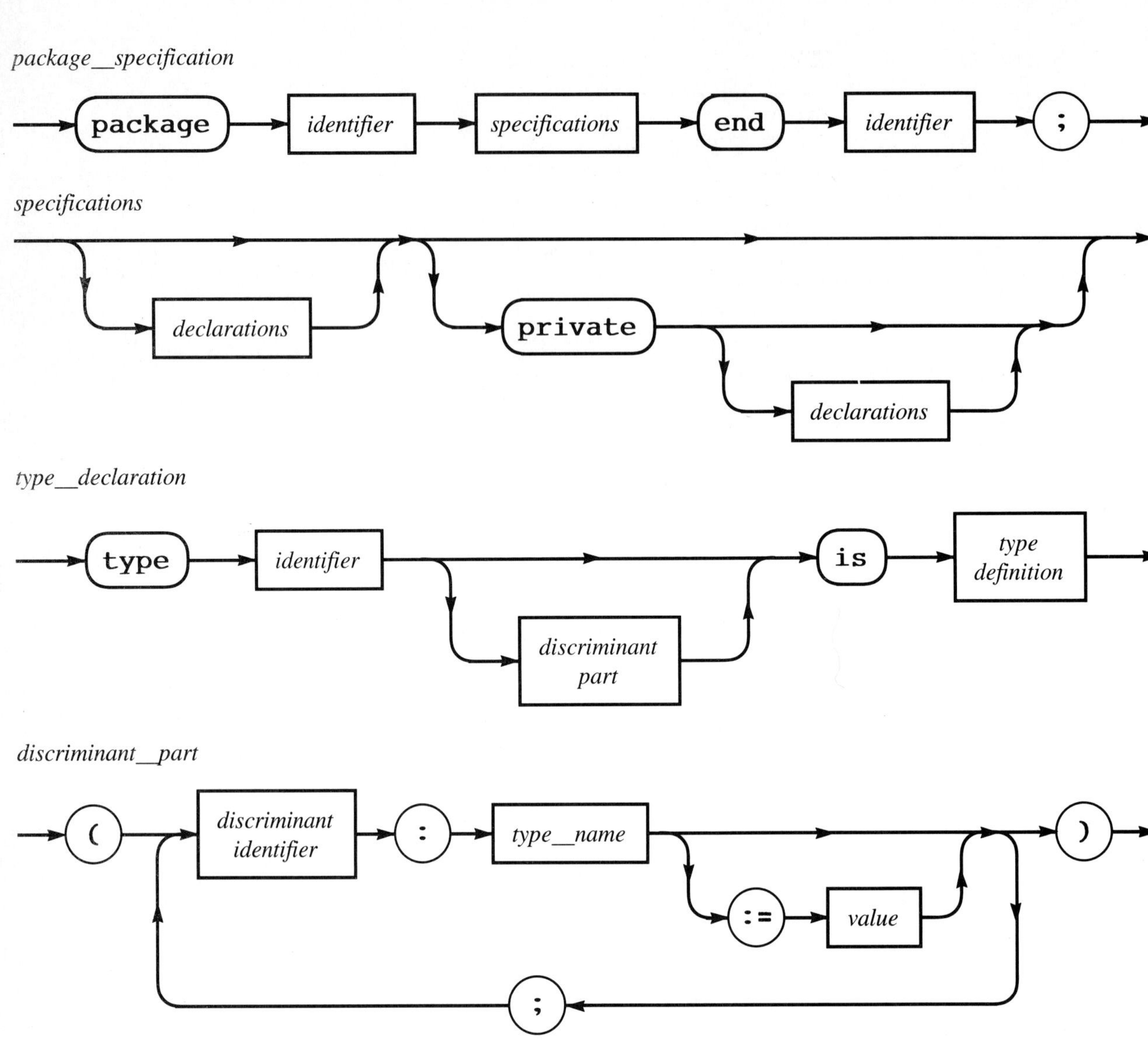

record__type

record → *component__list* → end → record → ;

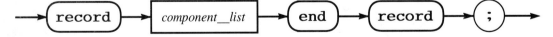

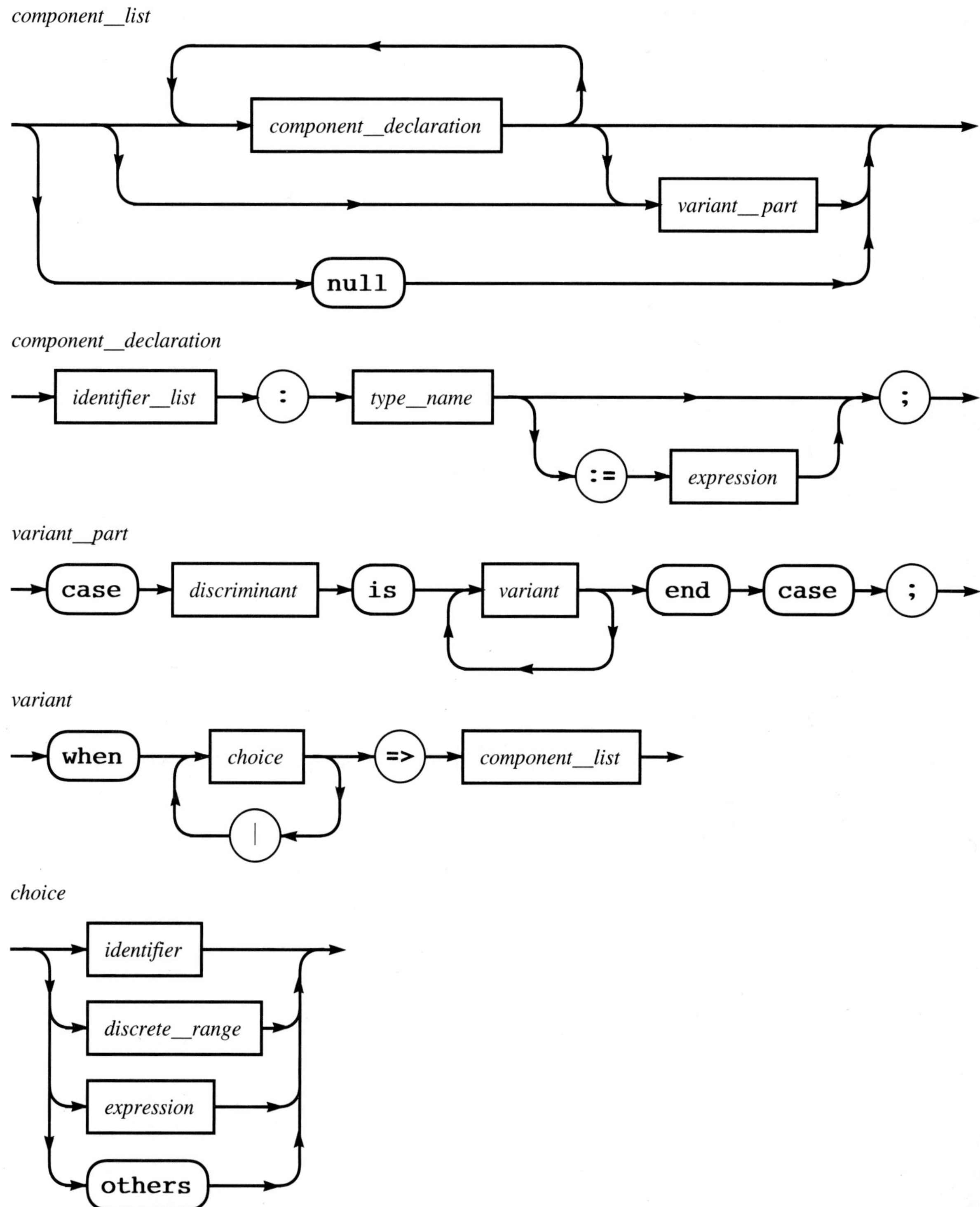
component__list
component__declaration
variant__part
null
component__declaration
identifier__list
:
type__name
:=
expression
;
variant__part
case
discriminant
is
variant
end
case
;
variant
when
choice
|
=>
component__list
choice
identifier
discrete__range
expression
others

APPENDIX C
PREDEFINED LANGUAGE ENVIRONMENT

This appendix outlines the specification of the **package** STANDARD containing all predefined identifiers in the language. The corresponding package body is implementation-defined and is not shown.

The operators that are predefined for the types declared in the **package** STANDARD are given in comments since they are implicitly declared. Italics are used for pseudonames of anonymous types (such as *universal_real*) and for undefined information (such as *implementation_defined* and *any_fixed_point_type*).

```
package STANDARD is

   type BOOLEAN is (FALSE, TRUE);

   --   The predefined relational operators for this type are as
   --   follows:

   --   function "="  (LEFT, RIGHT : BOOLEAN) return BOOLEAN;
   --   function "/=" (LEFT, RIGHT : BOOLEAN) return BOOLEAN;
   --   function "<"  (LEFT, RIGHT : BOOLEAN) return BOOLEAN;
   --   function "<=" (LEFT, RIGHT : BOOLEAN) return BOOLEAN;
   --   function ">"  (LEFT, RIGHT : BOOLEAN) return BOOLEAN;
   --   function ">=" (LEFT, RIGHT : BOOLEAN) return BOOLEAN;

   --   The predefined logical operators and the predefined logical
   --   negation operators are as follows:

   --   function "and" (LEFT, RIGHT : BOOLEAN) return BOOLEAN;
   --   function "or"  (LEFT, RIGHT : BOOLEAN) return BOOLEAN;
   --   function "xor" (LEFT, RIGHT : BOOLEAN) return BOOLEAN;

   --   function "not" (RIGHT       : BOOLEAN) return BOOLEAN;

   --   The universal type universal_integer is predefined.

   type INTEGER is implementation_defined;
```

```
--  The predefined operators for this type are as follows:

--  function "="  (LEFT, RIGHT : INTEGER) return BOOLEAN;
--  function "/=" (LEFT, RIGHT : INTEGER) return BOOLEAN;
--  function "<"  (LEFT, RIGHT : INTEGER) return BOOLEAN;
--  function "<=" (LEFT, RIGHT : INTEGER) return BOOLEAN;
--  function ">"  (LEFT, RIGHT : INTEGER) return BOOLEAN;
--  function ">=" (LEFT, RIGHT : INTEGER) return BOOLEAN;

--  function "+"   (RIGHT : INTEGER) return INTEGER;
--  function "-"   (RIGHT : INTEGER) return INTEGER;
--  function "abs" (RIGHT : INTEGER) return INTEGER;

--  function "+"   (LEFT, RIGHT : INTEGER) return INTEGER;
--  function "-"   (LEFT, RIGHT : INTEGER) return INTEGER;
--  function "*"   (LEFT, RIGHT : INTEGER) return INTEGER;
--  function "/"   (LEFT, RIGHT : INTEGER) return INTEGER;
--  function "rem" (LEFT, RIGHT : INTEGER) return INTEGER;
--  function "mod" (LEFT, RIGHT : INTEGER) return INTEGER;

--  function "**"  (LEFT : INTEGER; RIGHT : INTEGER) return INTEGER;

--  An implementation may provide additional integer types. It
--  is recommended that the names of such additional types end
--  with INTEGER as in SHORT_INTEGER or LONG_INTEGER. The
--  specification of each operator for the type
--  universal_integer, or for any additional predefined integer
--  type, is obtained by replacing INTEGER by the name of the
--  type in the specification of the corresponding operator of
--  the type INTEGER, except for the right operand of the
--  exponentiating operator.

--  The universal type universal_real is predefined.

type FLOAT is implementation_defined;

--  The predefined operators for this type are as follows:

--  function "="  (LEFT, RIGHT : FLOAT) return BOOLEAN;
--  function "/=" (LEFT, RIGHT : FLOAT) return BOOLEAN;
--  function "<"  (LEFT, RIGHT : FLOAT) return BOOLEAN;
--  function "<=" (LEFT, RIGHT : FLOAT) return BOOLEAN;
--  function ">"  (LEFT, RIGHT : FLOAT) return BOOLEAN;
--  function ">=" (LEFT, RIGHT : FLOAT) return BOOLEAN;

--  function "+"   (RIGHT : FLOAT) return FLOAT;
--  function "-"   (RIGHT : FLOAT) return FLOAT;
--  function "abs" (RIGHT : FLOAT) return FLOAT;
```

```
--   function "+" (LEFT, RIGHT : FLOAT) return FLOAT;
--   function "-" (LEFT, RIGHT : FLOAT) return FLOAT;
--   function "*" (LEFT, RIGHT : FLOAT) return FLOAT;
--   function "/" (LEFT, RIGHT : FLOAT) return FLOAT;

--   function "**" (LEFT : FLOAT; RIGHT : INTEGER) return FLOAT;

--   An implementation may provide additional floating point
--   types. It is recommended that the names of such additional
--   types end with FLOAT as in SHORT_FLOAT or LONG_FLOAT. The
--   specification of each operator for the type universal_real,
--   or for any additional predefined floating point type, is
--   obtained by replacing FLOAT by the name of the type in the
--   specification of the corresponding operator of the type
--   FLOAT.
--   In addition, the following operators are predefined for
--   universal types:
--   function "*" (LEFT  : universal_integer;
--                 RIGHT : universal_real)     return universal_real;
--   function "*" (LEFT  : universal_real;
--                 RIGHT : universal_integer)  return universal_real;
--   function "/" (LEFT  : universal_real;
--                 RIGHT : universal_integer)  return universal_real;

--   The type universal_fixed is predefined. The only operators
--   declared for this type are as follows:

--   function "*" (LEFT  : any_fixed_point_type;
--                 RIGHT : any_fixed_point_type)
--                 return universal_fixed:
--   function "/" (LEFT  : any_fixed_point_type;
--                 RIGHT : any_fixed_point_type)
--                 return universal_fixed:

--   The following characters form the standard ASCII character
--   set. Character literals corresponding to control characters
--   are identifiers; they are indicated in italics in this
--   definition.

type CHARACTER is ( nul,  soh,  stx,  etx,    eot,  enq,  ack,  bel,
                    bs,   ht,   lf,   vt,     ff,   cr,   so,   si,
                    dle,  dc1,  dc2,  dc3,    dc4,  nak,  syn,  etb,
                    can,  em,   sub,  esc,    fs,   gs,   rs,   us,

                    ' ',  '!',  '"',  '#',    '$',  '%',  '&',  ''',
                    '(',  ')',  '*',  '+',    ',',  '-',  '.',  '/',
                    '0',  '1',  '2',  '3',    '4',  '5',  '6',  '7',
                    '8',  '9',  ':',  ';',    '<',  '=',  '>',  '?',

                    '@',  'A',  'B',  'C',    'D',  'E',  'F',  'G',
                    'H',  'I',  'J',  'K',    'L',  'M',  'N',  'O',
```

```
'P', 'Q', 'R', 'S',    'T', 'U', 'V', 'W',
'X', 'Y', 'Z', '[',    '\', ']', '^', '_',

'`', 'a', 'b', 'c',    'd', 'e', 'f', 'g',
'h', 'i', 'j', 'k',    'l', 'm', 'n', 'o',
'p', 'q', 'r', 's',    't', 'u', 'v', 'w',
'x', 'y', 'z', '{',    '|', '}', '~', del  );

for CHARACTER use -- 128 ASCII character set without holes
      (0, 1, 2, 3, 4, 5, . . . , 125, 126, 127);

-- The predefined operators for the type CHARACTER are the same
-- as for any enumeration type.


package ASCII is

   -- Control characters

   NUL : constant CHARACTER := nul;
   SOH : constant CHARACTER := soh;
   STX : constant CHARACTER := stx;
   ETX : constant CHARACTER := etx;
   EOT : constant CHARACTER := eot;
   ENQ : constant CHARACTER := enq;
   ACK : constant CHARACTER := ack;
   BEL : constant CHARACTER := bel;
   BS  : constant CHARACTER := bs;
   HT  : constant CHARACTER := ht;
   LF  : constant CHARACTER := lf;
   VT  : constant CHARACTER := vt;
   FF  : constant CHARACTER := ff;
   CR  : constant CHARACTER := cr;
   SO  : constant CHARACTER := so;
   SI  : constant CHARACTER := si;
   DLE : constant CHARACTER := dle;
   DC1 : constant CHARACTER := dc1;
   DC2 : constant CHARACTER := dc2;
   DC3 : constant CHARACTER := dc3;
   DC4 : constant CHARACTER := dc4;
   NAK : constant CHARACTER := nak;
   SYN : constant CHARACTER := syn;
   ETB : constant CHARACTER := etb;
   CAN : constant CHARACTER := can;
   EM  : constant CHARACTER := em;
   SUB : constant CHARACTER := sub;
   ESC : constant CHARACTER := esc;
   FS  : constant CHARACTER := fs;
   GS  : constant CHARACTER := gs;
```

```
    RS  : constant CHARACTER := rs;
    US  : constant CHARACTER := us;
    DEL : constant CHARACTER := del;

    -- Other characters:

    EXCLAM     : constant CHARACTER := '!';
    QUOTATION  : constant CHARACTER := '"';
    SHARP      : constant CHARACTER := '#';
    DOLLAR     : constant CHARACTER := '$';
    PERCENT    : constant CHARACTER := '%';
    AMPERSAND  : constant CHARACTER := '&';
    COLON      : constant CHARACTER := ':';
    SEMICOLON  : constant CHARACTER := ';';
    QUERY      : constant CHARACTER := '?';
    AT_SIGN    : constant CHARACTER := '@';
    L_BRACKET  : constant CHARACTER := '[';
    BACK_SLASH : constant CHARACTER := '\';
    R_BRACKET  : constant CHARACTER := ']';
    CIRCUMFLEX : constant CHARACTER := '^';
    UNDERLINE  : constant CHARACTER := '_';
    GRAVE      : constant CHARACTER := '`';
    L_BRACE    : constant CHARACTER := '{';
    BAR        : constant CHARACTER := '|';
    R_BRACE    : constant CHARACTER := '}';
    TILDE      : constant CHARACTER := '~';

    -- Lowercase letters:

    LC_A : constant CHARACTER := 'a';
    . . .
    LC_Z : constant CHARACTER := 'z';

end ASCII;

-- Predefined subtypes:

subtype NATURAL  is INTEGER range 0 .. INTEGER'LAST;
subtype POSITIVE is INTEGER range 1 .. INTEGER'LAST;

-- Predefined string type:

type STRING is array(POSITIVE range <>) of CHARACTER;

pragma PACK(STRING);

-- The predefined operators for this type are as follows:

-- function "="  (LEFT, RIGHT : STRING) return BOOLEAN;
-- function "/=" (LEFT, RIGHT : STRING) return BOOLEAN;
-- function "<"  (LEFT, RIGHT : STRING) return BOOLEAN;
-- function "<=" (LEFT, RIGHT : STRING) return BOOLEAN;
-- function ">"  (LEFT, RIGHT : STRING) return BOOLEAN;
```

```
    -- function ">=" (LEFT, RIGHT : STRING) return BOOLEAN;

    -- function "&"  (LEFT  : STRING;
    --                RIGHT : STRING) return STRING;
    -- function "&"  (LEFT  : CHARACTER;
    --                RIGHT : STRING) return STRING;
    -- function "&"  (LEFT  : STRING;
    --                RIGHT : CHARACTER) return STRING;
    -- function "&"  (LEFT  : CHARACTER;
    --                RIGHT : CHARACTER) return STRING;

    type DURATION is delta implementation_defined
                     range implementation_defined;

    -- The predefined operators for the type DURATION are the same
    -- as for any fixed point type.

    -- The predefined exceptions:

    CONSTRAINT_ERROR : exception;
    NUMERIC_ERROR    : exception;
    PROGRAM_ERROR    : exception;
    STORAGE_ERROR    : exception;
    TASKING_ERROR    : exception;

end STANDARD;
```

Certain aspects of the predefined entries cannot be completely described in the language itself. For example, although the enumeration type BOOLEAN can be written showing the two enumeration literals FALSE and TRUE, the short-circuit control forms cannot be expressed in the language.

Note: The language definition predefines the following library units:

--	The package CALENDAR	(see LRM 9.6)
--	The package SYSTEM	(see LRM 13.7)
--	The package MACHINE_CODE (if provided)	(see LRM 13.8)
--	The generic procedure UNCHECKED_DEALLOCATION	(see LRM 13.10.1)
--	The generic function UNCHECKER_CONVERSION	(see LRM 13.10.2)
--	The generic package SEQUENTIAL_IO	(see LRM 14.2.3)
--	The generic package DIRECT_IO	(see LRM 14.2.5)
--	The package TEXT_IO	(see LRM 14.3.10)
--	The package IO_EXCEPTIONS	(see LRM 14.5)
--	The package LOW_LEVEL_IO	(see LRM 14.6)

APPENDIX D
OPERATORS AND EXPRESSION EVALUATION

The language defines the following six classes of operators. The corresponding operator symbols (except /=), and only those, can be used as designators in declarations of functions for user-defined operators. They are given in the order of increasing precedence.

- *logical_operator* **and** | **or** | **xor**
- *relational_operator* = | /= | < | <= | > | >=
- *binary_adding_operator* + | - | &
- *unary_adding_operator* + | -
- *multiplying_operator* * | / | **mod** | **rem**
- *highest_precedence_operator* ** | **abs** | **not**

The short-circuit control forms **and then** and **or else** have the same precedence as logical operators. The membership tests **in** and **not in** have the same precedence as relational operators.

For a term, simple expression, relation, or expression, operators of higher precedence are associated with their operands before operators of lower precedence. In this case, for a sequence of operators of the same precedence level, the operators are associated in textual order from left to right; parentheses can be used to impose specific associations.

The operands of a factor, of a term, of a simple expression, or of a relation, and the operands of an expression that does not contain a short-circuit control form, are evaluated in some order that is not defined by the language (but before application of the corresponding operator). The right operand of a short-circuit control form is evaluated if and only if the left operand has a certain value (see LRM 4.5.1).

APPENDIX E
PACKAGE TEXT_IO

```
with IO_EXCEPTIONS;
package TEXT_IO is

     type FILE_TYPE is limited private;
     type FILE_MODE is ( IN_FILE, OUT_FILE );
     type COUNT is range 0 . . implementation_defined;
     subtype POSITIVE_COUNT is COUNT range 1 . . COUNT'LAST;

     UNBOUNDED : constant COUNT := 0; -- line and page length

     subtype FIELD        is INTEGER range 0 . . implementation_defined;
     subtype NUMBER_BASE is INTEGER range 2 . . 16;

     type TYPE_SET is ( LOWER_CASE, UPPER_CASE );

--                   File management

     procedure CREATE ( FILE : in out FILE_TYPE;
                        MODE : in FILE_MODE := OUT_FILE;
                        NAME : in STRING := "";
                        FORM : in STRING := "");

     procedure OPEN   ( FILE : in out FILE_TYPE;
                        MODE : in FILE_MODE;
                        NAME : in STRING;
                        FORM : in STRING := "");

     procedure CLOSE  ( FILE : in out FILE_TYPE );
     procedure DELETE ( FILE : in out FILE_TYPE );
     procedure RESET  ( FILE : in out FILE_TYPE; MODE : in FILE_MODE );
     procedure RESET  ( FILE : in out FILE_TYPE );

     function MODE    ( FILE : FILE_TYPE ) return FILE_MODE:
     function NAME    ( FILE : FILE_TYPE ) return STRING:
     function FORM    ( FILE : FILE_TYPE ) return STRING;

     function IS_OPEN ( FILE : FILE_TYPE ) return BOOLEAN;
```

```
--                  Control of default input and output files

   procedure SET_INPUT  ( FILE : in FILE_TYPE );
   procedure SET_OUTPUT ( FILE : in FILE_TYPE );

   function STANDARD_INPUT return FILE_TYPE;
   function STANDARD_OUTPUT return FILE_TYPE;

   function CURRENT_INPUT return FILE_TYPE;
   function CURRENT_OUTPUT return FILE_TYPE;

--                  Specification of line and page lengths

   procedure SET_LINE_LENGTH ( FILE : in FILE_TYPE; TO : in COUNT );
   procedure SET_LINE_LENGTH ( TO : in COUNT );

   procedure SET_PAGE_LENGTH ( FILE : in FILE_TYPE; TO : in COUNT );
   procedure SET_PAGE_LENGTH ( TO : in COUNT );

   function LINE_LENGTH ( FILE : in FILE_TYPE ) return COUNT;
   function LINE_LENGTH return COUNT;

   function PAGE_LENGTH ( FILE : in FILE_TYPE ) return COUNT;
   function PAGE_LENGTH return COUNT;

--                  Column, line, page control

   procedure NEW_LINE ( FILE : in FILE_TYPE;
                        SPACING : in POSITIVE_COUNT := 1 );
   procedure NEW_LINE ( SPACING : in POSITIVE_COUNT := 1 );

   procedure SKIP_LINE ( FILE : in FILE_TYPE;
                         SPACING : in POSITIVE_COUNT := 1 );
   procedure SKIP_LINE ( SPACING : in POSITIVE_COUNT := 1 );

   function END_OF_LINE ( FILE : in FILE_TYPE ) return BOOLEAN;
   function END_OF_LINE return BOOLEAN;

   procedure NEW_PAGE ( FILE : in FILE_TYPE );
   procedure NEW_PAGE;

   procedure SKIP_PAGE ( FILE : in FILE_TYPE );
   procedure SKIP_PAGE;

   function END_OF_PAGE ( FILE : in FILE_TYPE ) return BOOLEAN;
   function END_OF_PAGE return BOOLEAN;

   function END_OF_FILE ( FILE : in FILE_TYPE ) return BOOLEAN;
   function END_OF_FILE return BOOLEAN;

   procedure SET_COL ( FILE : in FILE_TYPE; TO : in POSITIVE_COUNT );
   procedure SET_COL ( TO : in POSITIVE_COUNT );

   procedure SET_LINE( FILE : in FILE_TYPE; TO : in POSITIVE_COUNT );
   procedure SET_LINE( TO : in POSITIVE_COUNT );

   function COL ( FILE : in FILE_TYPE ) return POSITIVE_COUNT;
   function COL return POSITIVE_COUNT;
```

```
    function LINE ( FILE : in FILE_TYPE ) return POSITIVE_COUNT;
    function LINE return POSITIVE_COUNT;

    function PAGE ( FILE : in FILE_TYPE ) return POSITIVE_COUNT;
    function PAGE return POSITIVE_COUNT;

--                  Character input-output

    procedure GET ( FILE : in FILE_TYPE; ITEM : out CHARACTER );
    procedure GET ( ITEM : out CHARACTER );
    procedure PUT ( FILE : in FILE_TYPE; ITEM : in CHARACTER );
    procedure PUT ( ITEM : in CHARACTER );

--                  String input-output

    procedure GET ( FILE : in FILE_TYPE; ITEM : out STRING );
    procedure GET ( ITEM : out STRING );
    procedure PUT ( FILE : in FILE_TYPE; ITEM : in STRING );
    procedure PUT ( ITEM : in STRING );

    procedure GET_LINE ( FILE : in FILE_TYPE;
                         ITEM : out STRING;
                         LAST : out NATURAL );
    procedure GET_LINE ( ITEM : out STRING; LAST : out NATURAL );
    procedure PUT_LINE ( FILE : in FILE_TYPE; ITEM : in STRING );
    procedure PUT_LINE ( ITEM : in STRING );

--                  Generic package for input-output of integer types

    generic
        type NUM is range <>;
    package INTEGER_IO is

        DEFAULT_WIDTH : FIELD := NUM'WIDTH;
        DEFAULT_BASE  : NUMBER_BASE := 10;

        procedure GET ( FILE  : in FILE_TYPE;
                        ITEM  : out NUM;
                        WIDTH : in FIELD := 0 );
        procedure GET ( ITEM  : out NUM; WIDTH : in FIELD := 0 );

        procedure PUT ( FILE  : in FILE_TYPE;
                        ITEM  : in NUM;
                        WIDTH : in FIELD := DEFAULT_WIDTH;
                        BASE  : in NUMBER_BASE := DEFAULT_BASE );

        procedure PUT ( ITEM  : in NUM;
                        WIDTH : in FIELD := DEFAULT_WIDTH;
                        BASE  : in NUMBER_BASE := DEFAULT_BASE );

        procedure GET ( FROM  : in STRING;
                        ITEM  : out NUM;
                        LAST  : out POSITIVE );
```

```
        procedure PUT ( TO   : out STRING;
                        ITEM : in NUM;
                        BASE : in NUMBER_BASE := DEFAULT_BASE );
    end INTEGER_IO;

--                 Generic package for input-output of real types

    generic
        type NUM is digits <>;
    package FLOAT_IO is

        DEFAULT_FORE : FIELD := 2;
        DEFAULT_AFT  : FIELD := NUM'DIGITS - 1;
        DEFAULT_EXP  : FIELD := 3;

        procedure GET ( FILE : in FILT_TYPE;
                        ITEM : out NUM;
                        WIDTH : in FIELD := 0 );
        procedure GET ( ITEM : out NUM; WIDTH : in FIELD := 0 );

        procedure PUT ( FILE : in FILE_TYPE;
                        ITEM : in NUM;
                        FORE : in FIELD := DEFAULT_FORE;
                        AFT  : in FIELD := DEFAULT_AFT;
                        EXP  : in FIELD := DEFAULT_EXP );

        procedure PUT ( ITEM : in NUM;
                        FORE : in FIELD := DEFAULT_FORE;
                        AFT  : in FIELD := DEFAULT_AFT;
                        EXP  : in FIELD := DEFAULT_EXP );

        procedure GET ( FROM : in STRING;
                        ITEM : out NUM;
                        LAST : out POSITIVE );
        procedure PUT ( TO   : out STRING;
                        ITEM : in NUM;
                        AFT  : in FIELD := DEFAULT_AFT;
                        EXP  : in FIELD := DEFAULT_EXP );
    end FLOAT_IO;
```

```
generic
    type NUM is delta <>;
package FIXED_IO is

    DEFAULT_FORE : FIELD := NUM'FORE;
    DEFAULT_AFT  : FIELD := NUM'AFT;
    DEFAULT_EXP  : FIELD := 0;

    procedure GET ( FILE : in FILT_TYPE;
                    ITEM : out NUM;
                    WIDTH : in FIELD := 0 );
    procedure GET ( ITEM : out NUM; WIDTH : in FIELD := 0 );

    procedure PUT ( FILE : in FILE_TYPE;
                    ITEM : in NUM;
                    FORE : in FIELD := DEFAULT_FORE;
                    AFT  : in FIELD := DEFAULT_AFT;
                    EXP  : in FIELD := DEFAULT_EXP );

    procedure PUT ( ITEM : in NUM;
                    FORE : in FIELD := DEFAULT_FORE;
                    AFT  : in FIELD := DEFAULT_AFT;
                    EXP  : in FIELD := DEFAULT_EXP );

    procedure GET ( FROM : in STRING;
                    ITEM : out NUM;
                    LAST : out POSITIVE );
    procedure PUT ( TO   : out STRING;
                    ITEM : in NUM;
                    AFT  : in FIELD := DEFAULT_AFT;
                    EXP  : in FIELD := DEFAULT_EXP );

end FIXED_IO;
```

```
--                  Generic package for input-output of enumeration types

    generic
        type ENUM is (<>);
    package ENUMERATION_IO is

        DEFAULT_WIDTH   : FIELD := 0;
        DEFAULT_SETTING : TYPE_SET := UPPER_CASE;

        procedure GET ( FILE  : in FILT_TYPE;
                        ITEM  : out ENUM );
        procedure GET ( ITEM  : out ENUM );

        procedure PUT ( FILE  : in FILE_TYPE;
                        ITEM  : in ENUM;
                        WIDTH : in FIELD := DEFAULT_WIDTH;
                        SET   : in TYPE_SET := DEFAULT_SETTING );

        procedure PUT ( ITEM  : in ENUM;
                        WIDTH : in FIELD := DEFAULT_WIDTH;
                        SET   : in TYPE_SET := DEFAULT_SETTING );

        procedure GET ( FROM  : in STRING;
                        ITEM  : out ENUM;
                        LAST  : out POSITIVE );

        procedure PUT ( TO    : out STRING;
                        ITEM  : in ENUM;
                        SET   : in TYPE_SET := DEFAULT_SETTING );

    end ENUMERATION_IO;

--                  Exceptions

    STATUS_ERROR : exception renames IO_EXCEPTIONS.STATUS_ERROR;
    MODE_ERROR   : exception renames IO_EXCEPTIONS.MODE_ERROR;
    NAME_ERROR   : exception renames IO_EXCEPTIONS.NAME_ERROR;
    USE_ERROR    : exception renames IO_EXCEPTIONS.USE_ERROR;
    DEVICE_ERROR : exception renames IO_EXCEPTIONS.DEVICE_ERROR;
    END_ERROR    : exception renames IO_EXCEPTIONS.END_ERROR;
    DATA_ERROR   : exception renames IO_EXCEPTIONS.DATA_ERROR;
    LAYOUT_ERROR : exception renames IO_EXCEPTIONS.LAYOUT_ERROR;

private
--                  implementation-dependent
end TEXT_IO;
```

APPENDIX F
PACKAGE SEQUENTIAL_IO

```
with IO_EXCEPTIONS;
generic
    type ELEMENT_TYPE is private;
package SEQUENTIAL_IO is
    type FILE_TYPE is limited private;
    type FILE_MODE is ( IN_FILE, OUT_FILE );

                    File management

    procedure CREATE ( FILE : in out FILE_TYPE;
                       MODE : in FILE_MODE := OUT_FILE;
                       NAME : in STRING := "";
                       FORM : in STRING := "");

    procedure OPEN   ( FILE : in out FILE_TYPE;
                       MODE : in FILE_MODE;
                       NAME : in STRING;
                       FORM : in STRING := "");

    procedure CLOSE  ( FILE : in out FILE_TYPE );
    procedure DELETE ( FILE : in out FILE_TYPE );
    procedure RESET  ( FILE : in out FILE_TYPE; MODE : in FILE_MODE );
    procedure RESET  ( FILE : in out FILE_TYPE );

    function MODE    ( FILE : in FILE_TYPE ) return FILE_MODE:
    function NAME    ( FILE : in FILE_TYPE ) return STRING:
    function FORM    ( FILE : in FILE_TYPE ) return STRING;

    function IS_OPEN ( FILE : in FILE_TYPE ) return BOOLEAN;

                    Input and output operations

    procedure READ   ( FILE : in FILE_TYPE; ITEM : out ELEMENT_TYPE );
    procedure WRITE  ( FILE : in FILE_TYPE; ITEM : in  ELEMENT_TYPE );

    function END_OF_FILE ( FILE : in FILE_TYPE ) return BOOLEAN;
```

```
--                    Exceptions

    STATUS_ERROR : exception renames IO_EXCEPTIONS.STATUS_ERROR;
    MODE_ERROR   : exception renames IO_EXCEPTIONS.MODE_ERROR;
    NAME_ERROR   : exception renames IO_EXCEPTIONS.NAME_ERROR;
    USE_ERROR    : exception renames IO_EXCEPTIONS.USE_ERROR;
    DEVICE_ERROR : exception renames IO_EXCEPTIONS.DEVICE_ERROR;
    END_ERROR    : exception renames IO_EXCEPTIONS.END_ERROR;
    DATA_ERROR   : exception renames IO_EXCEPTIONS.DATA_ERROR;

private

--                    implementation-dependent
end SEQUENTIAL_IO;
```

APPENDIX G
PACKAGE DIRECT_IO

```
with IO_EXCEPTIONS;
generic
    type ELEMENT_TYPE is private;
package DIRECT_IO is
    type FILE_TYPE is limited private;
    type FILE_MODE is ( IN_FILE, INOUT_FILE, OUT_FILE );
    type COUNT      is range 0 . . implementation__defined;
    subtype POSITIVE_COUNT is COUNT range 1 . . COUNT'LAST;

                  File management

    procedure CREATE ( FILE : in out FILE_TYPE;
                       MODE : in FILE_MODE := INOUT_FILE;
                       NAME : in STRING := "";
                       FORM : in STRING := "");

    procedure OPEN   ( FILE : in out FILE_TYPE;
                       MODE : in FILE_MODE;
                       NAME : in STRING;
                       FORM : in STRING := "");

    procedure CLOSE  ( FILE : in out FILE_TYPE );
    procedure DELETE ( FILE : in out FILE_TYPE );
    procedure RESET  ( FILE : in out FILE_TYPE; MODE : in FILE_MODE );
    procedure RESET  ( FILE : in out FILE_TYPE );

    function MODE    ( FILE : in FILE_TYPE ) return FILE_MODE:
    function NAME    ( FILE : in FILE_TYPE ) return STRING:
    function FORM    ( FILE : in FILE_TYPE ) return STRING;

    function IS_OPEN ( FILE : in FILE_TYPE ) return BOOLEAN;

                  Input and output operations

    procedure READ   ( FILE : in   FILE_TYPE;
                       ITEM : out ELEMENT_TYPE;
                       FROM : in   POSITIVE_COUNT );
    procedure READ   ( FILE : in   FILE_TYPE; ITEM : out ELEMENT_TYPE );
```

```
    procedure WRITE  ( FILE : in  FILE_TYPE;
                       ITEM : in  ELEMENT_TYPE;
                       TO   : in  POSITIVE_COUNT );
    procedure WRITE  ( FILE : in  FILE_TYPE; ITEM : in ELEMENT_TYPE );

    procedure SET_INDEX (FILE : in FILE_TYPE; TO : in POSITIVE_COUNT);

    function INDEX ( FILE : in FILE_TYPE ) return POSITIVE_COUNT;
    function SIZE  ( FILE : in FILE_TYPE ) return COUNT;

    function END_OF_FILE ( FILE : in FILE_TYPE ) return BOOLEAN;

                    Exceptions

    STATUS_ERROR : exception renames IO_EXCEPTIONS.STATUS_ERROR;
    MODE_ERROR   : exception renames IO_EXCEPTIONS.MODE_ERROR;
    NAME_ERROR   : exception renames IO_EXCEPTIONS.NAME_ERROR;
    USE_ERROR    : exception renames IO_EXCEPTIONS.USE_ERROR;
    DEVICE_ERROR : exception renames IO_EXCEPTIONS.DEVICE_ERROR;
    END_ERROR    : exception renames IO_EXCEPTIONS.END_ERROR;
    DATA_ERROR   : exception renames IO_EXCEPTIONS.DATA_ERROR;

private
--                  implementation-dependent
end DIRECT_IO;
```

ANSWERS TO SELF-TEST EXERCISES

Chapter 1

1. Algorithm to add two whole numbers:

begin

1. Write the two numbers down, one above the other, so they line up digit-by-digit with the rightmost digits one above the other; (If the two numbers are not the same length, add zeros to the front of the shorter number until they are of equal length.)
2. Add the two rightmost digits, obtaining a one- or two-digit number;
3. Write down the rightmost of these two digits as the rightmost digit of the answer, and remember the leftmost digit; call the digit that needs to be remembered by the name CARRY; (If the number has only one digit, the new value of CARRY is zero.)
4. Repeat 4a, 4b, and 4c again and again until you run out of digits. (If the two numbers are each only one digit long, then you ''run out'' before you start, so do 4a, 4b, and 4c zero times, that is, not at all.)
   4a. Move to the next pair of digits to the left;
   4b. Add these two digits and CARRY to obtain a new one- or two-digit number
   4c. Write the rightmost digit of the number so obtained as the next (reading right to left) digit of the answer, and use the leftmost digit of this number as the new (possibly changed) value of CARRY; (If the number has only one digit, then the new value of CARRY is zero.)
5. If CARRY is zero at this point (that is, at the left end of the two numbers), then you are done;
6. If CARRY is not zero, then write down the value of CARRY as the leftmost digit of the answer

end.

2. As with virtually all problems, there is more than one algorithm for this problem. The following is one algorithm:

begin

1. Write the word down on one line;
2. Write it down on the line below, but this time write it backwards; (Align the letters on the two lines.)
3. For each letter in the word, compare the letter to the one written just below it;
4. If all letters match, the word is a palindrome; if at least one mismatch is found, it is not palindrome

end.

3. This algorithm assumes that the input word is written on a sheet of paper.

begin

1. Write the letters of the alphabet down on a sheet of paper, one per line;
2. Write zero after each letter;
3. Place your finger on the first letter of the word;
4. Repeat the following until you run out of the letters (at the end of the word);
   - 4a. Read the letter pointed to by your finger;
   - 4b. Add one to the number written after the letter on the sheet of paper; (The old number is erased or crossed out.)
   - 4c. Move your finger to the next letter in the word (provided there is one);
5. The number of occurrences of each letter is written on the sheet of paper

end.

Chapter 2

1. `2 2`

2. `3`

3. `babc`

4. They are all *incorrect,* except the literal 4 (with no decimal point).

5. The following are all *incorrect*:

```
.89   -.89   3,987.85   4.   4
```

The rest are correct. 4 is a correctly formed literal of type INTEGER.

6. The following are all *incorrect*:

```
.57E12   57E3.7   57.9E3.7
```

The rest are correct.

7. `3.0*X   3.0*X+Y   (X+Y)/7.0   (3.0*X+Y)/(Z+2.0)`

8. (a) In a sense it is correct as is. The computer will accept it and process it properly. However, the style is very poor. The spacing and line breaks are not well designed for readability.
(b) Correct.
(c) Needs a semicolon after Float.
(d) Needs a semicolon at the end.

9. `INTEGER   INTEGER   CHARACTER   FLOAT   INTEGER`

10. Type it and compile it; the computer will tell you where the mistakes are. After correcting each mistake one at a time, recompile the program to find the next mistake.
(a) First line: The colon should be a semicolon.
(b) Fifth line: A quotation mark is missing.
(c) Sixth line: Both single quotes should be double quotes.
(d) Seventh line: The single quote should be a double quote.

11. −15 4 82 126 −2

14.
15 / 12 is 1	15 **rem** 12 is 3	15.0 / 12.0 is 1.25
24 / 12 is 2	24 **rem** 12 is 0	24.0 / 12.0 is 2.0
123 / 100 is 1	123 **rem** 100 is 23	123.0 / 100.0 is 1.23
200 / 100 is 2	200 **rem** 100 is 0	200.0 / 100.0 is 2.0
99 / 2 is 49	99 **rem** 2 is 1	99.0 / 2.0 is 49.5
2 / 3 is 0	2 **rem** 3 is 2	2.0 / 3.0 is 0.666666

Chapter 3

1. `START   -1234END`
   (There are 3 spaces between the T and the minus sign.)
2. `START  -12.34END`
   (There are 2 spaces between the T and the minus sign.)
6. ```
   Second Put
   Fourth Put
   ```
7. ```
   FALSE
   FALSE
   TRUE
   TRUE
   ```
8.
16.0	9.0
7	−7
7	−6
6.8	6.8
32767	−3.40232E+38

9. ```
   X ** 2 <= Y + 1
   ZULU > 0
   WATER /= 0
   EGGS rem 12 = 0
   ```
10. −3

Chapter 4

1. ```
   Begin Conversation
   Goodbye
   Hello
   One more time:
   Hello
   Goodbye
   End Conversation
   ```
2. ```
   3  6
   6  3
   ```
3. ```
   One
   OneTwo
   OneTwoThree
   ```
4. ```
   1  2
   2  2
   2  1
   ```
   ```

5.
```
procedure NO_NEGATIVE ( NUMBER : in out INTEGER ) is
begin
     if NUMBER < 0 then
          NUMBER := 0;
     end if;
end NO_NEGATIVE;
```

6.
```
procedure NO_CAPITAL_Y ( ANSWER : in out CHARACTER ) is
begin
     if ANSWER = 'Y' then
          ANSWER := 'y';
     end if;
end NO_CAPITAL_Y;
```

7. AXBXX

8. There are two problems:
(a) You cannot assign a value to a function name.
(b) Every function must have a return statement.

9.
```
function AREA ( LENGTH, WIDTH : INTEGER ) return INTEGER is
begin
     return LENGTH * WIDTH;
end AREA;
```

10.
```
function NP ( NUMBER : INTEGER ) return CHARACTER is
begin
     if NUMBER > 0 then
          return 'P';
     else
          return 'N';
     end if;
end NP;
```

11. (a) function
(b) function
(c) procedure
(d) procedure
(e) function

12.
```
hi
good-bye
```

13.
```
function DIVIDES ( FIRST, SECOND : INTEGER )
          return BOOLEAN is
begin
     return SECOND rem FIRST = 0;
end DIVIDES;
```

14.
```
function IN_ORDER ( FIRST, SECOND, THIRD : INTEGER )
          return BOOLEAN is
begin
     return FIRST <= SECOND
        and SECOND <= THIRD;
end IN_ORDER;
```

15. Yes

16. No

17. Yes

18. No

19. All of them can be used as actual **in** parameters.

20. Only X

21. Only X

22. Must be a variable.

23. Yes, but its value is unchanged by the subprogram.

24. No

25. Yes

Chapter 5

1.
```
7
11
```

2.
```
Hi Folks in procedure
21 outside of procedure
```

3.
```
1  2  3
4  5  6
4  5  3
```

4.
```
1  2  3
4  5  6
5  4  3
```

5.
```
1  2  3
5  5  6
5  2  3
```

6.
```
1  2  3
4  5  6
4  2  5
```

Chapter 6

1.
```
Start
First put
Next
Enough
```

2.
```
FALSE
TRUE
TRUE
FALSE
FALSE
```

3. • `2 + 2 = 4`
   • `( X + 7 > 100 ) or ( X + 7 < 50 )`
   • `( Z /= 'A' ) and ( Z /= 'B' ) and ( Z /= 'C' )`

   Also correct is

   ```
   not ( ( Z = 'A' ) or ( Z = 'B' ) or ( Z = 'C' ) )
   ```
   • `( X rem 3 ) /= 0`
   • `( X rem 3 /= 0 ) or ( Y rem 5 = 0 )`
   • `( X <= Y + 2 ) and ( Y + 2 <= Z )`

4. `A xor B`

   Also correct are

   ```
   ( A and not B ) or ( not A and B )
   ( A or B ) and ( not A or not B )
   ( A or B ) and not ( A and B )
   ```

5. ```
   First Put
   Fourth Put
   ```

6. ```
   with I_O; use I_O;
   procedure MAIN is
        ONE, TWO, THREE : INTEGER;
   begin
        PUT ( "Enter three integers:" ) NEW LINE;
        GET ( ONE ); GET ( TWO ); GET ( THREE ); SKIP LINE;
        if ONE <= TWO and TWO <= THREE then
             PUT ( "In order" );
        else
             PUT ( "Not in order" );
        end if;
        NEW LINE;
        PUT ( "End of program" ); NEW LINE;
   end MAIN;
   ```

7. ```
   PUT ( NUMBER );
   if NUMBER < 0 then
        PUT ( " is negative." );
   elsif NUMBER <= 100 then
        PUT ( " is between 0 and 100." );
   else
        PUT ( " is greater than 100." );
   end if;
   NEW LINE;
   ```

8. INTEGER, CHARACTER, and BOOLEAN, although BOOLEAN is best done with an **if-then-else**.

9. ```
   with I_O; use I_O;
   procedure MAIN is
        MONTH_NUMBER : INTEGER;
   begin
        PUT ( "Enter a month as a number between 1 and 12." );
        NEW_LINE;
        PUT ( "I'll tell you how many days it has in it." );
        NEW_LINE;
        GET ( MONTH_NUMBER ); SKIP_LINE;
   ```

```
    case MONTH_NUMBER is
        when 4 | 6 | 9 | 11 => PUT ( "30 days" );
        when 1 | 3 | 5 | 7 | 8 | 10 | 12 => PUT ( "31 days" );
        when 2 => PUT ( "28 days (29 if leap year)" );
        when others => PUT ( "value out of range" );
    end case;
    NEW_LINE;
    PUT ( "That's it!" ); NEW_LINE;
end MAIN;
```

10. **not** FOOT_LOOSE **and not** FANCY_FREE is equivalent to
not (FOOT_LOOSE **or** FANCY_FREE)
not (FOOT_LOOSE) **or not** (FANCY_FREE) is equivalent to
not (FOOT_LOOSE **and** FANCY_FREE)

Chapter 7

1. −2
2. 10 because the **exit when** condition is TRUE the first time, and the rest of the loop is never executed.
3. There is no output because TIME is never less than zero. The program stops because CONSTRAINT_ERROR is raised when TIME becomes larger than INTEGER'LAST.
4. There are two mistakes:
   (a) The value 1 is never output.
   (b) The value of ODD is never exactly 10, so there is an infinite loop. One way to correct the loop is as follows:

```
loop
    exit when ODD >= 10;
    PUT ( ODD );
    ODD := ODD + 2;
end loop;
```

5. -2
6. The body of a posttest loop is always executed at least once; the body of a pretest loop may be executed zero times.
7.

```
with I_O; use I_O;
procedure MAIN is
    LETTER : CHARACTER;
begin -- Main
    loop
        exit when END_OF_LINE;
        GET ( LETTER );
    end loop;
    PUT ( LETTER ); NEW_LINE;
end MAIN;
```

8. −6 −4 −2 0 2 4 6 8 10 12 14 16 18 20 22
9. 10 9 8 7 6 5 4 3 2 1

10.
```
for INDEX in 1 .. 12
loop
    PUT ( 2 * INDEX );
end loop;
```

11.
```
1  3
2  2
3  2
```

12. The output is too long to reproduce here. The pattern is indicated below:

1 times 10 equals 10
2 times 10 equals 20
. . .
10 times 10 equals 100
1 times 9 equals 9
2 times 9 equals 18
. . .
10 times 9 equals 90
1 times 8 equals 8
. . .

13. (a) A **for** loop
(b) and (c) Both require a pretest loop since the input lists may be empty.
(d) A posttest loop can be used since some nonzero number of tests will be performed.

Chapter 9

1. TEMPORARY_COUNT and GRADE_TALLY are illegal because the type FLOAT and subranges of FLOAT are not discrete types and thus cannot be used as array indexes.

2. (a)
```
subtype SCORE is INTEGER range 0 .. 10;
type SCORE_LIST is array( 1 .. 100 ) of SCORE;
```
(b)
```
type FLOAT_LIST is array( 'a' .. 'z' ) of FLOAT;
```
(c)
```
type LAST_TYPE is array( -5 .. 19 ) of CHARACTER;
```

3. (a)
```
subtype SCORE is INTEGER range 0 .. 10;
subtype EXTENDED_INDEX is INTEGER range 0 .. 100;
subtype INDEX is EXTENDED_INDEX range 1 .. 100;
type SCORE_LIST is array( INDEX ) of SCORE;
EXAM_1 : SCORE_LIST;
LAST : EXTENDED_INDEX := 0;
```
(b)
```
type TALLY_LIST is array( 'A' .. 'Z' ) of NATURAL;
COUNT : TALLY_LIST;
```
For example, COUNT('M') will hold the number of students whose last name start with 'M'.

(c)
```
subtype INDEX is INTEGER range 1 .. 100;
type CHECK_OFF is array( INDEX ) of BOOLEAN;
PASSED : CHECK_OFF;
```
For example, **if** PASSED(7) **then** student 7 can graduate.

4.
```
SUM := 0;
for ELEMENT in 1 . . 100
loop
     SUM := SUM + A( ELEMENT );
end loop;
```

5.
```
for INDEX in 0 . . 100
loop
     CENTIGRADE( INDEX ) := 0.0;
end loop;
```

A better way is shown as the solution to Exercise 6.

6. CENTIGRADE := 0 is not legal for two reasons:
(a) 0 is not a value of type FLOAT; 0.0 is correct.
(b) You must use an aggregate as follows:
```
CENTIGRADE := ( others => 0.0 );
```

7. The loop ends with INDEX equal to LAST. At that point INDEX + 1 evaluates to LAST + 1, so ELEMENT(INDEX + 1) has an illegal index and CONSTRAINT_ERROR is raised. To fix it, change the final expression of the **for** loop to LAST – 1.

8.
```
for INDEX in 1 . . 6
loop
     GET ( LETTER( INDEX ) );
end loop;
for INDEX in reverse 1 . . 6
loop
     PUT ( LETTER( INDEX ) );
end loop;
```

9.
```
LAST : NATURAL := 0;
NEXT : INTEGER;
. . .
loop
     GET ( NEXT );
     exit when NEXT < 0;
     LAST := LAST + 1;
     NUMBERS( LAST );
     exit when LAST = 10;
end loop;
PUT ( "The number of elements in the array is " );
PUT ( LAST ); NEW LINE;
for INDEX in 1 . . LAST
loop
     PUT ( NUMBER( INDEX ) );
end loop;
NEW LINE;
```

10. There is more than one right answer to these questions; these are just examples:
(a)
```
subtype GRADE is NATURAL range 0 . . 10;
type DISTRIBUTION is array( GRADE ) of NATURAL;
```
(b)
```
subtype AGE is POSITIVE range 5 . . 13;
type COUNT is array( AGE ) of NATURAL;
```

(c)
```
subtype STUDENT_NUMBER is POSITIVE range 661 .. 753;
type CHECK_AMOUNT is array( STUDENT_NUMBER ) of FLOAT;
```

11.
```
type WEEK_DAY is ( SUN, MON, TUE, WED, THU, FRI, SAT );
subtype WORK_DAY is WEEK_DAY range MON .. FRI;
type WORK_HOURS is array( WORK_DAY ) of NATURAL;
type PLAY_TIME is array( WEEK_ DAY ) of NATURAL;
```

12. `APPLE := BERRY;`

13. The function terminates after checking only the first value in the array.

14.
```
type LABEL is array( 0 .. 100 ) of CHARACTER;
...
procedure REVERSE ( LIST : in out LABEL ) is
    TEMPORARY : LABEL := LIST;
begin
    for INDEX in 0 .. 100
    loop
        LIST( INDEX ) := TEMPORARY( 100 - INDEX );
    end loop;
end REVERSE;
```

15. The relational operator in the **if** statement must be changed from **<** to **>**. The names of the function and two of the objects in the function do not make sense now, so they should be changed also.

16. Change the type declaration for the array, the type of the parameters in the EXCHANGE procedure, and the object SMALLEST_ELEMENT in function INDEX_OF_ SMALLEST all to FLOAT, as follows:

```
type INTEGER_ARRAY is array( INDEX_TYPE ) of FLOAT;
procedure EXCHANGE ( ITEM_1, ITEM_2 : in out FLOAT ) is
SMALLEST ELEMENT : FLOAT := LIST( START );
```

17. Make the following declaration and change all of the things in Exercise 16 to this type name:

```
subtype LOWER_CASE is CHARACTER range 'a' .. 'z';
```

Chapter 10

1. abbbb

2. Change the code for the procedure PUT_STRING from a PUT_LINE to a PUT.

3.
```
with STRINGS; use STRINGS;
    ...
LAST_CHILD : constant INTEGER := 17;
subtype ChILDREN is INTEGER range 1 .. LAST CHILD;
type NAME_LIST is array( CHILDREN ) of CHARACTER_STRING;
type BIRTH_LIST is array( CHILDREN ) of POSITIVE;
type VACCINATION_LIST is array( CHILDREN ) of BOOLEAN;
```

4. In the STRINGS package change

```
MAXIMUM_LENGTH : constant POSITIVE := 20;
```

to

```
MAXIMUM_ LENGTH : constant POSITIVE := 40;
```

and recompile the package.

5. The first four statements are allowed. The last one has less than five characters; it must be exactly five characters in length.

6. (a)
```
for INDEX in 1 . . 20
loop
    PUT ( SCREEN( INDEX, 1 ) );
    NEW_LINE;
end loop;
```
(b)
```
for INDEX in 1 . . 50
loop
    PUT ( SCREEN( 20, INDEX ) );
end loop;
NEW_LINE;
```
(c)
```
for LINE in 1 . . 20
loop
    for POSITION in 1 . . 50
    loop
        PUT ( SCREEN( ROW, POSITION ) );
    end loop;
    NEW_LINE;
end loop;
```

Chapter 11

1.
```
5A
6A
```

2.
```
type SAM is record
              COMPONENT_1 : INTEGER;
              COMPONENT_2 : FLOAT;
              COMPONENT_3 : CHARACTER;
          end record;
```

3.
```
with TEXT_IO; use TEXT_IO;
procedure SELF_TEST_11_3 is
type SAM is record
              COMPONENT_1 : INTEGER;
              COMPONENT_2 : FLOAT;
              COMPONENT_3 : CHARACTER;
          end record;
package INT_IO is new INTEGER_IO ( INTEGER );
use INT_IO;
package FLT_IO is new FLOAT_IO ( FLOAT );
use FLT_IO;
WALTON : SAM;
begin -- SELF_TEST_11_3
    PUT_LINE ( "Enter an integer." );
    GET ( WALTON.COMPONENT_1 ); SKIP_LINE;
    PUT_LINE ( "Enter a float value." );
    GET ( WALTON.COMPONENT_2 ); SKIP LINE;
    PUT_LINE ( "Enter a character." );
    GET ( WALTON.COMPONENT_3 ); SKIP LINE;
```

```
    PUT ( WALTON.COMPONENT_1 ); PUT ( ' ' );
    PUT ( WALTON.COMPONENT_2 ); PUT ( ' ' );
    PUT ( WALTON.COMPONENT_2 ); NEW LINE;
end SELF_TEST_11_3;
```

4.
```
subtype QUIZ_RANGE is INTEGER range 0 . . 10;
subtype EXAM_RANGE is INTEGER range 0 . . 100;
subtype NAME_TYPE is STRING( 1 . . 20 );
type QUIZ_LIST is array( 1 . . 10 ) of QUIZ_RANGE;
subtype GRADE_RANGE is CHARACTER range 'A' . . 'F';
type STUDENT is record
                    NAME : NAME_TYPE;
                    QUIZ_SCORE : QUIZ_LIST;
                    MIDTERM,
                    FINAL_EXAM,
                    FINAL_SCORE : EXAM_RANGE;
                    GRADE : GRADE_RANGE;
                end record;
```

5. (a) `WAREHOUSE( 3 )`
   (b) `WAREHOUSE( 3 ).PRICE`
   (c) `WAREHOUSE( 10 ).NAME.SYMBOL( 6 )`
   (d) `WAREHOUSE( 2 ).NAME.LENGTH`

6.
```
MAXIMUM : constant NATURAL := some_value;
subtype STOCK_NUMBER is NATURAL range 0 . . MAXIMUM;
subtype STYLE_NUMBER is NATURAL range 0 . . 50;
subtype SIZE_RANGE is NATURAL range 3 . . 14;
```

Parallel arrays:

```
type STYLE is array( STOCK NUMBER ) of STYLE_NUMBER;
type COUNT is array( STOCK_NUMBER ) of NATURAL;
type PRICE is array( STOCK_NUMBER ) of FLOAT;
```

Array of records:

```
type SHOE is record
                STYLE : STYLE_NUMBER;
                COUNT : NATURAL;
                PRICE : FLOAT;
            end record;
type SHOE_LIST is array( STOCK_NUMBER ) of SHOE;
```

7. (a) { 1 3 7 8 9 }
   { 8 }
   (b) { 7 8 9 }
   (c) { }
   (d) { 7 }
   (e) TRUE
   (f) FALSE
   (g) TRUE

Chapter 12

1. The problem is a "boundary" problem. When COUNT is equal to 100, the loop terminates without adding in the 100. The easiest way to fix it is to change the operator in the **exit when** condition from **>=** to **>** (making the condition COUNT > 100).

2. The values of ALPHA, BRAVO, and CHARLIE do not matter, but you need a collection of values for OMEGA. You need one value greater than or equal to 5 and one less than 5. You also need one value greater than zero and one less than or equal to zero. For example, the following two values for OMEGA will do: 5 and 0. In this case you do not need four different values to fully exercise the code.

3. There are four paths, but one is impossible. One of the many possible sets of values for OMEGA is 5, 4, 0. The values of ALPHA, BRAVO, and CHARLIE do not matter.

4. The program uses more storage than is necessary for a clear program. There is no need to use an array. All that is required is a single variable, as shown below:

```
NEXT : INTEGER;
         . . .
SUM := 0;
for INDEX in LIST_RANGE
loop
     GET ( NEXT );
     SUM := SUM + NEXT;
end loop;
AVERAGE := FLOAT ( SUM ) / 10.0;
```

Chapter 13

1.
```
      5      63
5 6
```

(Remember, blank spaces are characters.)

5.
```
Four score and seven years ago.
o
t
The End.
```

6.
```
ab
ghijkHi
```

7.
```
with TEXT_IO; use TEXT_IO;
procedure EX_7 is
     NEW_FILE : FILE_TYPE;
     package INT_IO is new INTEGER_IO ( POSITIVE );
     use INT_IO;
begin
     CREATE ( NEW_FILE, OUT_FILE, "EX_7_FILE" );
     for INDEX in 1 . . 10
     loop
          PUT ( NEW_FILE, INDEX ); NEW_LINE ( NEW_FILE );
     end loop;
     CLOSE ( NEW_FILE );
end EX_7;
```

8.
```
with TEXT_IO; use TEXT_IO;
procedure EX_8 is
     NEW_FILE : FILE_TYPE;
     NUMBER, SUM : INTEGER;
     package INT_IO is new INTEGER_IO ( POSITIVE );
     use INT_IO;
begin
     OPEN ( NEW_FILE, IN_FILE, "EX_7_FILE" );
     loop
          exit when END_OF_FILE ( NEW_FILE );
          PUT ( NEW_FILE, NUMBER ); NEW_LINE ( NEW_FILE );
          SUM := SUM + NUMBER;
     end loop;
     PUT ( "The sum is " ); PUT ( SUM ); NEW_LINE;
     CLOSE ( NEW_FILE );
end EX_8;
```

Chapter 14

1. 6
2. This is an example of infinite recursion. There will be no output. However, the program will terminate with an unhandled exception STORAGE_ERROR when the run-time stack overflows.
3. 24

   The function is the factorial function, usually written *n!* and defined as *n! = n*(n−1)* (n−2)* . . . *1.*
4. 3

   The function returns the value $log_2(N)$, that is, the logarithm to the base 2 of the number N, but you need not know that to see that the value returned is 3.
5. Hip Hip Hurray
6.
```
function MYSTERY ( N : POSITIVE ) return POSITIVE is
SUM : POSITIVE := 1;
begin
     for INDEX in 2 . . N
     loop
          SUM := SUM + INDEX;
     end loop;
     return SUM;
end MYSTERY;
```
7.
```
function ROSE ( N : POSITIVE ) return POSITIVE is
PRODUCT : POSITIVE := 1;
begin
     for INDEX in 2 . . N
     loop
          PRODUCT := PRODUCT * INDEX;
     end loop;
     return PRODUCT;
end ROSE;
```

8.
```
procedure STAR ( N : in POSITIVE ) is
begin
    PUT ( '*' ); NEW_LINE;
    if N > 1 then
        STAR ( N - 1 );
    end if;
end STAR;
```

Chapter 15

1.

+	0	1	2	3	4	5	6

–	0	1	2	3	4	5	6

+	1	2	3	5	+	0	3

–	1	2	3	5	+	0	3

+	1	2	3	1	–	0	2

–	1	2	3	1	–	0	2

+	3	1	4	2	+	0	1

2. The largest value in each case is as follows:
(a) +0.999E+999
(b) +0.99E+9999
(c) +0.99999E+9

3. 7, 5, 4, 27, 22, 0.5, 0.25, 0.125, 0.625, 1.125, 5.625

4. 32-bit machine: $2^{31} - 1 = 2{,}147{,}836$
64-bit machine: $2^{63} - 1 = 9{,}223{,}372{,}036{,}854{,}775{,}807$

5.
```
 0.30000000000 x 10^3
+0.00012345678 x 10^3
---------------------
 0.30001234567 x 10^3
```

After rounding, this is stored as 0.3001 × 10^3. Hence, the output is 0.3001E+03.

6. ABLE * BAKER * CHARLIE has the value
(0.1E-90 * 0.1E-25) * 0.1E+25
(0.1E-115) * 0.1E+25

but the first product produces floating point underflow and so is rounded to zero on our hypothetical computer. (In Ada it would cause NUMERIC_ERROR to be raised.) Hence, the final value is 0.0E+00 * 0.1E+25, which is equal to 0.0E+00. On the other hand, ABLE * CHARLIE * BAKER has the value

```
( 0.1E-90 * 0.1E+25 ) * 0.1E-25
( 0.1E-65 ) * 0.1E-25
0.1E-90
```

Therefore, the output is

```
0.0000E+00 0.1000E-90
```

(As this shows, rounding to zero can occasionally produce surprising results.)

Chapter 16

1.
```
with SEQUENTIAL_IO;
     ...
subtype EXAM_RANGE is NATURAL range 0 . . 100;
subtype NAME_TYPE is STRING( 1 . . 20 );
subtype GRADE_RANGE is CHARACTER range 'A' . . 'F';
type STUDENT is record
                        NAME : NAME_TYPE;
                        FINAL : EXAM_RANGE;
                        GRADE : GRADE_RANGE;
                   end record;
package STUDENT_IO is new SEQUENTIAL_IO ( STUDENT );
STUDENT_FILE : STUDENT_IO.FILE_TYPE;
```

2.
```
with SEQUENTIAL_IO;
procedure EXERCISE_16_2 is
package INTEGER_IO is new SEQUENTIAL_IO ( INTEGER );
use INTEGER_IO;
INTEGER_FILE : FILE_TYPE;
begin
    CREATE ( INTEGER_FILE, OUT_FILE, "EX_16_2.DAT" );
    for INDEX in 1 . . 10
    loop
        WRITE ( INTEGER_FILE, INDEX );
    end loop;
    CLOSE ( INTEGER_FILE );
end EXERCISE_16_2;
```

3.
```
with SEQUENTIAL_IO;
with TEXT_IO; use TEXT_IO;
procedure EXERCISE_16_3 is
package NUMBER_IO is new SEQUENTIAL_IO ( INTEGER );
use NUMBER_IO;
package INT_IO is new INTEGER_IO (INTEGER );
use INT_IO;
NUMBER : INTEGER;
NUMBER_FILE : FILE_TYPE;
begin
    OPEN ( INTEGER_FILE, IN_FILE, "EX_16_2.DAT" );
```

```
     loop
          exit when END_OF_FILE ( INTEGER_FILE );
          READ ( INTEGER_FILE, NUMBER );
          PUT ( NUMBER ); NEW_LINE;
     end loop;
     CLOSE ( INTEGER_FILE );
     end EXERCISE_16_3;
```

4.
```
with SEQUENTIAL_IO;
with TEXT_IO; use TEXT_IO;
procedure EXERCISE_16_4 is
package NUMBER_IO is new SEQUENTIAL_IO ( INTEGER );
use NUMBER_IO;
package INT_IO is new INTEGER_IO (INTEGER );
use INT_IO;
NUMBER : INTEGER;
NUMBER_FILE : FILE_TYPE;
KEY : INTEGER;
begin
     OPEN ( INTEGER_FILE, IN_FILE, "EX_16_2.DAT" );
     PUT_LINE ( "Enter integer to be searched for" );
     GET ( KEY ); SKIP_LINE;
     PUT ( KEY );
     loop
          if END_OF_FILE ( INTEGER_FILE ) then
               PUT_LINE ( " is not in the file." );
               exit;
          end if;
          READ ( INTEGER_FILE, NUMBER );
          if KEY = NUMBER then
               PUT_LINE ( " is in the file." );
               exit;
          end if;
     end loop;
     CLOSE ( INTEGER_FILE );
end EXERCISE_16_4;
```

5.
```
function SEARCH ( PAY_FILE : in PAY_IO.FILE_TYPE;
                  KEY : in POSITIVE ) return BOOLEAN is
     ONE_RECORD : EMPLOYEE;
begin
     loop
          if END_OF_FILE ( PAY_FILE ) then
               return FALSE;
          end if;
          READ ( PAY_FILE, ONE_RECORD );
          if KEY = ONE RECORD.NUMBER then
               return TRUE;
          end if;
     end loop;
end SEARCH;
```

Chapter 17

1.
```
10  20
20  20
30  30
40  40
```

2.
```
10  20
20  20
30  20
30  40
```

3. It would not change at all.

4.
```
P ──────────► | 1 | A | / | ◄──┐
                                │
HEAD ───────► | 2 | B | --| ───┘      | 3 | C | / |
```

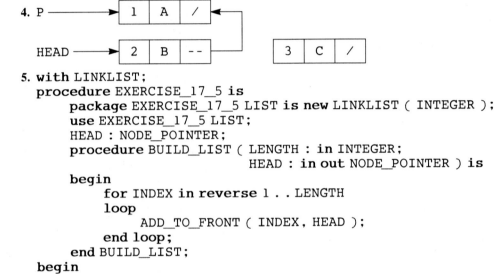

5.
```
with LINKLIST;
procedure EXERCISE_17_5 is
     package EXERCISE_17_5 LIST is new LINKLIST ( INTEGER );
     use EXERCISE_17_5 LIST;
     HEAD : NODE_POINTER;
     procedure BUILD_LIST ( LENGTH : in INTEGER;
                            HEAD : in out NODE_POINTER ) is
     begin
          for INDEX in reverse 1 . . LENGTH
          loop
               ADD_TO_FRONT ( INDEX, HEAD );
          end loop;
     end BUILD_LIST;
begin
     BUILD_LIST ( 10, HEAD );
end EXERCISE_17_5;
```

6.
```
procedure SHOW_LIST ( HEAD : in NODE_POINTER ) is
     WORK : NODE_POINTER := HEAD;
begin
     loop
          exit when WORK = NULL;
          PUT ( DATA_PART ( WORK ) ); NEW_LINE;
          WORK := SUCCESSOR ( WORK );
     end loop;
end SHOW_LIST;
```

7. There is no difference in the general form of the nodes. The difference is in the way they are used.

8.
```
type TREE_NODE;
type TREE_TYPE is access TREE_NODE;
type TREE_NODE is record
                       PARENT : TREE_TYPE;
                       LEFT   : TREE_TYPE;
                       DATA   : INTEGER;
                       RIGHT  : TREE_TYPE;
                  end record;
```

INDEX

W

X

Z

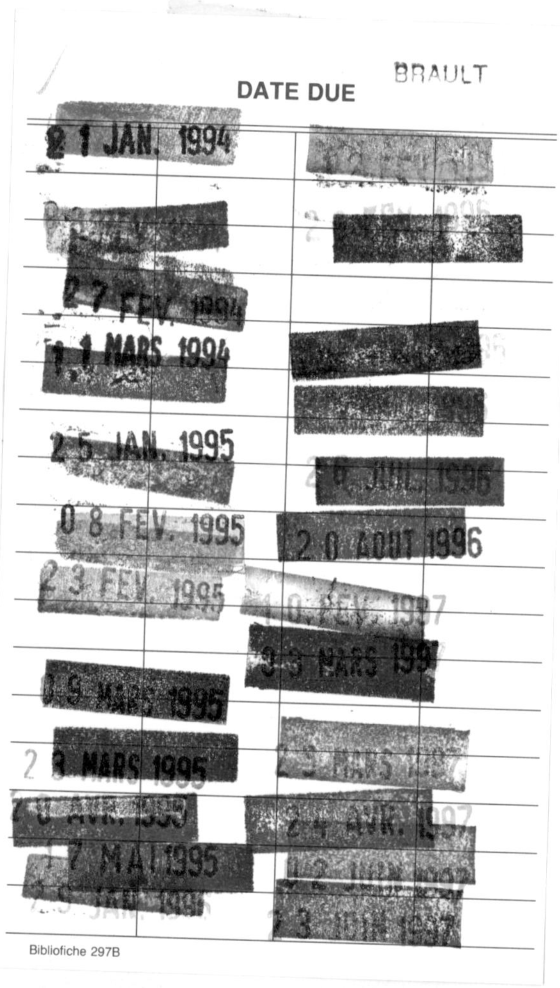
BRAULT
DATE DUE
21 JAN. 1994
27 FEV. 1994
11 MARS 1994
25 JAN. 1995
08 FEV. 1995
20 AOUT 1996
23 FEV. 1995
09 MARS 1995
17 MAI 1995
Bibliofiche 297B